Freedom of the Press

Library of Essays in Media Law
Series Editors: Eric Barendt and Thomas Gibbons

Titles in the series:

Freedom of the Press
Eric Barendt

Media Freedom and Contempt of Court
Eric Barendt

Free Speech in the New Media
Thomas Gibbons

Regulating Audiovisual Services
Thomas Gibbons

Freedom of the Press

Edited by

Eric Barendt

University College London, UK

ASHGATE

Published by
Ashgate Publishing Limited
Wey Court East
Union Road
Farnham
Surrey GU9 7PT
England

Ashgate Publishing Company
Suite 420
101 Cherry Street
Burlington, VT 05401-4405
USA

Ashgate website: http://www.ashgate.com

British Library Cataloguing in Publication Data
Freedom of the press. - (Library of essays in media law)
1. Freedom of the press
I. Barendt, E. M.
342'.0853

Library of Congress Control Number: 2008939267

ISBN: 978 0 7546 2782 1

Printed and bound in Great Britain by
TJ International Ltd, Padstow, Cornwall

Contents

PART IV FREEDOM OF THE PRESS AND PRIVACY

Acknowledgements

The editor and publishers wish to thank the following for permission to use copyright material.

Hastings Law Journal for the essay: Potter Stewart (1975), '"Or of the Press"', *Hastings Law Journal*, **26**, pp. 631–37.

Hofstra Law Review for the essay: C. Edwin Baker (2007), 'The Independent Significance of the Press Clause under Existing Law', *Hofstra Law Review*, **35**, pp. 955–1026.

Melbourne University Law Review for the essay: Andrew T. Kenyon (2004), '*Lange* and *Reynolds* Qualified Privilege: Australian and English Defamation Law and Practice', *Melbourne University Law Review*, **28**, pp. 406–37.

Monash University Law Review for the essay: Adrienne Stone and George Williams, (2000), 'Freedom of Speech and Defamation: Developments in the Common Law World', *Monash University Law Review*, **26**, pp. 362–78.

Oxford University Press for the essay: Eric Barendt (1995), 'Privacy and the Press', *Yearbook of Media and Entertainment Law*, **1**, pp. 23–41.

Sweet and Maxwell for the essays: Thomas Gibbons (1992), 'Freedom of the Press: Ownership and Editorial Values', *Public Law*, **92**, pp. 279–99. Copyright © 1992 Sweet and Maxwell Ltd.; Herdís Thorgeirsdóttir (2004), 'Self-censorship among Journalists: A (Moral) Wrong or a Violation of ECHR Law?', *European Human Rights Law Review*, **9**, pp. 383–99. Copyright © 2004 Sweet and Maxwell Ltd; M.A. Sanderson (2004), 'Is *Von Hannover v Germany* a Step Backward for the Substantive Analysis of Speech and Privacy Interests?', *European Human Rights Law Review*, **9**, pp. 631–44. Copyright © 2004 Sweet and Maxwell Ltd.

The University of California for the essay: Melville B. Nimmer (1968), 'The Right to Speak from *Times* to *Time*: First Amendment Theory Applied to Libel and Misapplied to Privacy', *California Law Review*, **56**, pp. 935–67. Copyright © 1968 California Law Review, Inc. Reprinted from California Law Review.

University of Chicago Press for the essay: Paul Gerwitz (2001), 'Privacy and Speech', *Supreme Court Review*, pp. 139–99. Copyright © 2002 The University of Chicago. All rights reserved.

University of Toronto Press Inc. for the essay: Elizabeth Paton-Simpson (2000), 'Privacy and the Reasonable Paranoid: The Protection of Privacy in Public Places', *University of Toronto Law Journal*, **50**, pp. 305–46. Reprinted by permission of University of Toronto Press Incorporated (www.utpjournals.com)

Vathek Publishing for the essay: Sir Louis Blom-Cooper, QC and Lisa R. Pruitt (1994), 'Privacy Jurisprudence of the Press Complaints Commission', *Anglo-American Law Review*, **23**, pp. 133–60.

Every effort has been made to trace all the copyright holders, but if any have been inadvertently overlooked the publishers will be pleased to make the necessary arrangement at the first opportunity.

Series Preface

Media law issues frequently dominate the news. A libel or privacy action by a politician or celebrity, an investigation into an alleged broadcasting scam, and the use of the Internet for downloading terrorist material or pornography are all stories which attract national, and increasingly international, publicity. Freedom of expression, whether on the traditional press and broadcasting media, or through the new electronic media, remains of fundamental importance to the workings of liberal democracies; indeed, it is impossible to see how a democracy could exist without a free, pluralist media for the dissemination of information and the discussion of political and social affairs. The media also provide us with celebrity gossip and popular entertainment.

But a free media does not entail the complete absence of law and regulation. Far from it. Laws are needed to balance the competing interests of the media, the public whom they inform and entertain and those individuals whose reputation, privacy, or even safety, might be endangered by newspapers, broadcasters and bloggers. All these branches of the media exercise considerable power and they can abuse it to distort the truth and harm individuals. Competition and other laws must be framed to prevent the emergence of media monopolies and oligopolies which are as incompatible with an effective democracy as is the domination of one political party. The Internet has been characterised by little or no regulation, beyond general criminal and civil laws, but it is legitimate to question whether this can remain the case given the ease with which, say, pornographic images can be circulated round the world in a moment. The globalisation of the media exacerbates legal problems, for a communication can be published more or less simultaneously in a number of different jurisdictions; some countries might, for example, protect privacy strongly, while others might not protect it at all because they consider privacy laws inimical to media freedom.

There is now a rich literature on many aspects of media law and regulation. The aim of these four volumes is to present a sample of this literature, grouped round particular themes. Some of them concern topics which have been explored in legal periodicals for decades: freedom of the press, the balance between this freedom and reputation and privacy rights, media publicity prejudicing fair trials. Others deal with more modern aspects of the law, in particular whether and how the broadcasting and electronic media should be regulated. Inevitably, many essays are drawn from United States periodicals, as that country, with its strong attachment to freedom of speech and its powerful media industries, has produced an immense literature on all areas of media law. But we have also included articles from many Commonwealth countries. We have selected those which discuss issues of media law from a theoretical or comparative perspective. Lawyers in all jurisdictions can learn something from the treatment of common problems in other countries. The globalisation of the media means that knowledge of comparative law in this area is now of importance to practising lawyers.

ERIC BARENDT, *University College London*
THOMAS GIBBONS, *University of Manchester*

Introduction

A free press is vital to the maintenance of a liberal democracy. It provides citizens with the information and variety of opinion necessary for them to debate political issues openly and intelligently, and to hold their government to account. Freedom of the press obviously precludes government licensing or the censorship of newspapers, books and other print media; it is also incompatible with punitive or discriminatory taxation which would make it in effect impossible for individuals and corporations to establish or maintain a newspaper. Further, in liberal democracies newspapers (though not the broadcasting media) have been free to support particular political parties and to take sides on social issues which divide their country. These principles lie at the core of press freedom.

But beyond these principles there is considerable controversy about the scope and meaning of press freedom. Almost everyone agrees that the freedom is not absolute; it is not incompatible with press freedom, for example, to prosecute a newspaper which has published information endangering national security for infringement of official secrets laws and, in extreme cases, it might even be right for a court order (a judicial 'prior restraint') to stop it from publishing this information. But there is less agreement on how far the law should limit the freedom of the press to publish defamatory allegations, particularly when they concern public officials and celebrities or when they are of real public interest. It is also unclear how far press freedom should give newspapers and other print media wide immunity from actions to protect the privacy of individuals who object to the disclosure of personal information. These difficult questions equally concern the broadcasting and new electronic media, which enjoy rights to freedom of speech or expression, though they are not strictly part of the 'press'. These questions are discussed in Parts III and IV of this volume.

However, there are other, more general problems concerning the concept of press freedom. One question is whether its scope is identical to that of the right to freedom of speech (or expression) which is enjoyed by all individuals under many constitutions, such as that of the United States and Canada, and which is guaranteed under international conventions and treaties, notably the International Covenant on Civil and Political Rights and the European Convention of Human Rights and Fundamental Freedoms (ECHR). Or is the press, which might include the broadcasting media in this context, entitled to wider legal rights and immunities, because it performs a distinctive role in investigating and reporting stories of public interest? Another question is whether, to use the well-known words of A.J. Liebling, '[F]reedom of the press is guaranteed only to those who own one' (1964, pp. 30–31).[1] In that case, press freedom might appear to have more in common with a press owner's property and commercial rights than it has with freedom of speech. These broad questions are canvassed by the essays in Part I of this volume.

---

1 The quotation is one of the epigraphs to Judith Lichtenberg's essay, 'Foundations and Limits of Freedom of the Press' (Lichtenberg, 1990, p.102).

The essays in Part II are concerned with another topic: self-regulation of the press, here understood to refer to the traditional print media of newspapers and magazines. As noted in the first paragraph of this introduction, government regulation obviously poses dangers to press freedom. Court orders and penalties may also pose this danger, even if the judiciary is genuinely independent of the government and applies, say, libel and privacy law fairly, without any prejudice against the press. The mere threat of a court fine or injunction may deter the press and other publishers from publishing material which legally they are entitled to issue – the so-called 'chilling effect' of the law. Self-regulation might, therefore, be regarded as a more acceptable means of control. Under it the press accepts a degree of regulation applied by a body, some of whose members may be newspaper editors and journalists themselves, able to understand the pressures under which newspapers operate; the press agrees to respect its decisions, although they do not carry with them any prospect of legal sanction. Some of the strengths and weaknesses of this method of control are canvassed in the essays in Part II, to some extent in relation to the informal systems of complaints against the press which have been adopted in the United Kingdom.

Press Freedom and Freedom of Expression

The First Amendment to the US Constitution provides: 'Congress shall make no law … abridging the freedom of speech, or of the press.' The first three essays in Part I address the question whether the Press Clause of the Amendment adds anything to the guarantee of freedom of speech afforded by its first limb. In what is now regarded as a classic essay (Chapter 1), Potter Stewart, an Associate Justice of the Supreme Court, contended that the Free Press guarantee is a structural provision, uniquely providing constitutional protection to a private business. Newspapers certainly enjoy the same rights to freedom of expression as individuals, but these are conferred by the Speech Clause. The Press Clause must mean more than that, for otherwise it would be redundant. In Stewart's view, the purpose of the provision was to establish an institution, 'the Fourth Estate', to act as a check on the activities of the three official branches of government: legislature, executive and the courts. The press therefore enjoys institutional autonomy. The implications of this argument are potentially considerable. Constitutional access rights for the press to attend and report, say, legislative and court proceedings, or to interview prisoners, might be recognized, and the claim by journalists to keep their sources confidential would be upheld as a matter of constitutional law (see the essays on journalists' privilege in Part IV of *Media Freedom and Contempt of Court*, another volume in the Essays in Media Law series).

Anthony Lewis, author of Chapter 2, was a distinguished columnist for the *New York Times* for more than thirty years. It is therefore particularly striking that he rejected Potter Stewart's argument. In his view, neither history nor the decisions of the Supreme Court provide much justification for the recognition of special constitutional rights for the press. More importantly, it would be wrong in principle to take this step. The recognition of such privileges would lead to calls for press accountability to counter newspaper hubris and irresponsibility. Moreover, it would be necessary to define the 'press' to determine which institutions should enjoy the special rights afforded by the Press Clause.

This last problem has also been raised by David Anderson (2002), in an essay regrettably too long to include in this volume. Anderson points out that news and comment are now distributed by a vast number of businesses and outlets – online news services, Internet Service Providers, electronic databases, client magazines and personal blogs – which might be able to claim the same rights as the institutional press (and broadcasting) media. Should they be entitled to the institutional autonomy and privileges advocated by Potter Stewart? Anderson concludes that, if the press is to enjoy some preferential treatment, it is better that it is allocated by statute or regulation than as a matter of constitutional right by court decisions. An administrative decision to allow some part of the press special access rights to attend, say, public briefings or meetings can be more easily modified in the light of changing circumstances than a court ruling allocating a newspaper this right under the First Amendment (Anderson, 2002, pp. 515–21).

A different perspective is offered by Edwin Baker in Chapter 3. His purpose is to challenge the general view that existing doctrine does not allow for special rights for the press under the Press Clause. He agrees with Potter Stewart that the Clause bears a different meaning to that of the Speech Clause. The former protects the instrumental role of the press, as a fundamental democratic institution, in providing citizens with information and ideas (see pp. 49–50), while the Speech Clause through its guarantee of individual speech rights reflects a concern for human liberty.[2] Baker, however, does not share Stewart's view that the Press Clause gives the media complete institutional autonomy. Arguably, regulation to compel cable operators to transmit programmes of educational or other merit, perhaps even a law to compel the press to print replies to hostile newspaper articles, might be compatible with freedom of the press.[3] (Right of reply laws have been held compatible with freedom of the press in Germany.) Unlike individual freedom of speech, press freedom does not entail a strong right to keep silent in the face of laws requiring the media to communicate ideas. But the Press Clause clearly gives the media wider communication rights than other private corporations; unlike the latter, newspapers are completely free, for example, to spend their resources on political campaigns. Baker's arguments are complex and subtle; though grounded in United States constitutional law, they raise important issues concerning the scope and meaning of press freedom of relevance to many other jurisdictions. Indeed, courts generally must consider whether the institutional press and broadcasting media are entitled in some contexts to rights which are not conferred by a free speech clause on all individuals.

In Chapter 4 Thomas Gibbons explores a different aspect of press freedom: its association with editorial autonomy. It is this association, in his view, which gives the freedom its special status. In contrast, press proprietors, or barons, rely essentially on property rights when they oppose any attempt at press regulation – for example, to prevent mergers and concentrations of ownership. After chronicling various attempts by press barons, almost invariably successful, to control the content of their newspapers, Gibbons examines ways in which editorial freedom could be more securely protected. He concludes that press freedom entails promotion of editorial values, and that the law has a role to play in this enterprise. Unfortunately, governments in the United Kingdom, and perhaps in other countries, are reluctant to challenge press proprietors on whose support they are dependent for success, particularly during election campaigns.

---

2 See Baker (1989), where the author develops this view of freedom of speech.

3 Baker (at pp. 61–2), however, appears to accept the Supreme Court decision in *Miami Herald* v. *Tornillo* 418 US 241 (1974), holding a state law providing a right to reply to press articles critical of election candidates incompatible with press freedom. Arguably, however, on his view of press freedom, and its rationale, the decision was wrong.

Self-regulation of the Press

Self-regulation of the press avoids many of the problems associated with legal control, in particular its 'chilling effect'. As John Ritter and Matthew Leibowitz point out in Chapter 5, press councils promote a fair and responsible press, while upholding the guarantee of press freedom (p. 141). Characteristically the councils consider and issue formal adjudications on complaints by members of the public about press misconduct, especially of the publication of inaccurate or misleading stories. Unlike courts, however, they cannot order coercive sanctions against a newspaper; at most they can request newspapers to publish their decisions. The only 'sanction' for a failure to comply with a request is political pressure to institute legal remedies, say, for infringement of privacy or press harassment; press councils are watchdogs that bark, but do not bite (see p. 146). Interestingly, Ritter and Leibowitz regard the British Press Council as some precedent for those established in the United States in the early 1970s. However, unlike the US Councils, the Press Council and its successor, the Press Complaints Commission (PCC) which replaced it in January 1991, have been very informal bodies, preferring to resolve complaints without an oral hearing; they have not allowed the parties to give evidence and cross-examine the other side.[4] The Press Complaints Commission almost always resolves a complaint within a few weeks of its receipt, if possible by an agreed settlement between complainant and newspaper, and that speed would almost certainly be lost if it held oral hearings and allowed legal representation. Another difficulty concerns the composition of the press council or commission. A system of self-regulation means that the press regulates itself, but a council composed entirely or largely of editors and journalists is unlikely to command the respect of the public. Equally, the decisions of a body dominated by lay, non-press members may be disregarded by newspaper editors. The British PCC now has a majority of lay members, with a lay chair, while its predecessor had a parity of press and lay members after 1977.[5]

The PCC has attracted very little scholarly commentary, though its merits have been extensively canvassed in reports of House of Commons Committees as well as in the press itself. Chapter 6, by Sir Louis Blom-Cooper (who was the last chairman of the old Press Council) and Lisa Pruitt, is unusual in its careful, but highly critical, analysis of early PCC decisions on complaints that newspapers had infringed privacy. In their view these were poorly reasoned and inconsistent; in particular, the Commission had failed to make clear its understanding of 'an individual's private life' (the term used in the first PCC Code) or the scope of the crucial 'public interest' defence which protected the freedom of the press to report matters of importance to the general public, even when the report infringed personal privacy. These particular problems may have lessened over the last fifteen years; the Code has frequently been redrafted to give more precision to its key terms, and there are now many more decisions to guide editors and journalists. But the authors' criticism raises the larger question of whether it is right to hold an informal complaints body to the same high standard

4 Cf. the account given by Ritter and Leibowitz of the procedures of the Minnesota Press Council and of the National News Council at pp. 146, 153 and 164.

5 At its inception in 1953 the British Press Council was composed entirely of press members, but lay members, including the chairman, were appointed from 1962, and parity of press and lay members was achieved in 1977: see Report of the Committee on Privacy and Related Matters (Calcutt *et al.*, 1990), ch. 14.

of intellectual rigour as one expects of the courts when they consider defamation or privacy actions. It is perhaps inherent in a system of self-regulation that, in its understandable concern to provide quick and informal rulings, it will fail, *pace* Blom-Cooper and Pruitt, clearly to 'delineate the boundary between freedom of expression and editorial responsibility' (p. 194).

In Chapter 7 Herdís Thorgeirdóttir draws attention to another type of control on press freedom, which has been almost entirely ignored in legal literature; journalists, like other professionals, are subject to economic and social pressures from their peers and more importantly from their superiors – editors and press proprietors. They are expected to produce stories which sell papers, and they know instinctively which topics to cover and what editorial line to take. A press journalist may not in practice, therefore, enjoy the same freedom as an independent writer or academic to publish what he conceives to be the truth of the matter. Thorgeirsdóttir explores these constraints in the context of media pluralism and the vital role of the press in informing the public; attention is drawn to a Council of Europe Resolution emphasizing the importance of journalists' independence from the ideology of press barons.[6] She contemplates a positive role for states to ensure that newspapers do present the truth as journalists see it. These are important issues, but it is unclear how far the law – however worthy its aims – could properly interfere with the management of newspapers and magazines without interfering with press freedom, at least as that freedom is usually understood.

Freedom of the Press and Libel Law

Libel law is widely regarded as the most important legal restriction on the exercise of press freedom, though of course it also impacts on the broadcasting and other media, including now use of the Internet. Defamation actions are not only brought to protect the reputations of politicians and other public figures, but may be used to defend the commercial standing of trading corporations, such as McDonald's or Tesco, when their business conduct is criticized by newspapers and other media. For a long time, it used to be thought, even in the United States, that defamatory allegations fell entirely outside the scope of press freedom, but in its landmark decision in *New York Times* v. *Sullivan*[7] the Supreme Court held that libel law was subject to limits imposed by the constitutional guarantees of freedom of speech and of the press. In the Court's view, the common law defences of truth and fair comment did not satisfy the requirements of the First Amendment, since a newspaper could not be sure that it would persuade a jury that the story was accurate. So it formulated the rule that a public official could not recover libel damages, unless he could show that the allegation had been published with 'actual malice' – that is, that the press knew that its story was false or was reckless whether it was true or false. The principle in *New York Times* (*NYT*) was subsequently extended to cover actions brought by public figures.[8] But as a result of the Court's decision in *Gertz* v. *Robert Welch* private individuals may recover damages if they prove that the newspaper published

6 Resolution 1003 (1993) of the Parliamentary Assembly of the Council of Europe on the ethics of journalism, Principle 13.

7 376 US 254 (1964).

8 By the decisions in *Curtis Publishing Cp* v. *Butts, Associated Press* v. *Walker* 388 US 130 (1967).

the allegations negligently, at least when they can show that they have suffered some loss as a result of their publication.[9]

These developments are discussed by David Anderson in Chapter 8. He points out that the *NYT* principle did not, as the Court had envisaged, prevent self-censorship by the press, or rather by its lawyers, as it did little to reduce the costs of defending libel proceedings. Defamation law in his view continued to exercise a 'chilling effect' on press freedom. He is also critical of *Gertz* for withdrawing the protection from libel actions conferred by an earlier Court decision,[10] under which defendants enjoyed immunity under the *NYT* principle whenever they published a story of public concern irrespective of whether it implicated a private individual or a public figure. The impact of *Gertz* was that the law gives more freedom to newspapers investigating, say, the probity of a politician or a major industrialist, who are characterized as public officials or figures, than it does to the press, typically popular magazines and the tabloid papers, when they publish material about ordinary people, characterized as private figures. The latter can recover damages if they can prove that the tabloid was careless or irresponsible in the way in which it investigated or wrote its story, while it is very difficult now for a public official or figure to win a libel action in the United States (see Anderson, 2007, pp. 865, 873).

In contrast to the position in the United States, courts in Commonwealth jurisdictions have been much less willing to extend press freedom in this context. Nevertheless, in the last fifteen years, decisions in most of these countries have significantly extended the freedom of the press and other media to publish defamatory allegations; that at least is the case when the stories concern politics and perhaps other matters of public concern, and when they have been published responsibly – that is, provided the newspaper or other media defendant has, say, asked the claimant to comment on the allegations and taken some steps to verify them before publication. Developments in India, Australia, South Africa, Canada, the United Kingdom and New Zealand are reviewed by Adrienne Stone and George Williams in Chapter 9. For the most part these jurisdictions have extended press freedom in this context, without embracing the principle in *NYT*; only in Canada has the leading court declined to give the media more protection than that afforded by the common law. The authors show how common law courts have carefully assessed the United States rules and have concluded that they do not place adequate weight on the important public interest in protecting the right to reputation.

Chapter 10, by Andrew Kenyon, another leading Australian scholar in this area of law, closely examines the reasoning of the appellate courts in two major recent free press and libel cases: that of the House of Lords in *Reynolds* v. *Times Newspapers*[11] and that of the High Court of Australia in *Lange* v. *Australian Broadcasting Corporation*.[12] In *Reynolds* the House of Lords held for the first time that the media in England could enjoy a qualified privilege defence in respect of inaccurate defamatory allegations communicated to the general public. The House rejected a generic defence which would immunize from libel proceedings the communication of any allegations concerning politics; that would not give politicians and other public officials any right to protect their reputation. Instead, it formulated a flexible

9 418 US 323 (1974).
10 *Rosenbloom* v. *Metromedia Inc.* 403 US 29 (1971).
11 [2001] 2 AC 127.
12 (1997) 189 CLR 520.

privilege for the communication of any matters of public interest, provided the press or other defendant satisfied the requirements of 'responsible journalism'. As Kenyon mentions (p. 298, n. 42), Lord Nicholls in the leading speech identified ten factors which courts should take into account in determining whether a newspaper has satisfied this standard. In *Lange* the High Court of Australia fashioned a narrower defence on the basis of the implied constitutional freedom of political communication. The privilege applies only to political communications, relatively narrowly defined, and only when the defendant has satisfied a 'reasonableness' test. Kenyon discusses some court decisions, subsequent to *Reynolds* and *Lange*, in which the implications of these rulings have been worked out.

Kenyon's essay is important in that, in addition to its doctrinal analysis, it summarizes his empirical research into the consequence of these decisions. Interviews with media lawyers established that *Reynolds* is regarded as a significant ruling, even though there is some uncertainty how the factors listed by Lord Nicholls are to be applied. Two of them were identified as particularly important: the need to contact the subject of the article for him to comment on it, and the overall tone of the article. The defence is more likely to succeed, it is felt, if defamatory allegations are presented cautiously and in a balanced manner, without the shrill headlines which characterize much tabloid journalism. Interestingly, therefore, Kenyon echoes the view, implicit in David Anderson's essay, that libel law, as developed by the courts, may discriminate against radical or innovative journalism. (Whether that discrimination is wrong is another matter; on one view, it is right to protect people from the publication of defamatory allegations that are not only untrue, but published in an intemperate or hostile manner.)

In contrast to the English defence, Kenyon finds that the privilege formulated by the Australian High Court in *Lange* has not proved very useful for the media, largely because it is confined to political communication – it does not apply, for example, to allegations implicating business or industry – and because of the 'reasonableness' requirement. But the privilege has apparently led to a reduction in the number of actions brought by politicians. Interviewees in Australia argued that *Lange* should be reconsidered, and they preferred the more flexible approach provided by the House of Lords in *Reynolds*. Kenyon's essay shows the importance of conducting empirical research to assess the significance of judicial rulings and the reaction of the media to them (see also Kenyon, 2006; Weaver *et al.*, 2006).

Freedom of the Press and Privacy

While the press has for long had to contend with the restrictions imposed by the law of libel, privacy law in most countries has only recently begun to pose problems for the exercise of press freedom. The reason is that the common law in England and in other Commonwealth jurisdictions has been reluctant to formulate an explicit right to privacy. However, in the context of infringement by the media, other torts, notably trespass to land and breach of confidence, have provided protection, when, say, journalists enter property to take photographs or a newspaper publishes a story obtained through a leak by the claimant's employees. It is only in the United States, and in continental Europe, that courts have for decades balanced the rights to freedom of speech and of the press against explicit privacy rights. To a large extent, the press, even in the United States, has exercised self-restraint in disclosing private matters, even when there was a good argument that they involved questions of legitimate public concern. For example, newspapers and other media in the United States were silent about John F. Kennedy's sexual affairs, both while he was a candidate for the Presidency and later while he occupied that office, and English newspapers said very little about the health of Winston Churchill when he suffered a stroke during the Second World War and when he was in effect unable to act effectively as Prime Minister in 1954.

The picture today is very different, particularly in England and other Commonwealth jurisdictions where privacy is now explicitly, or through the development of the breach of confidence action, quite strongly protected. Revelations about the private life of celebrities, particularly their sexual affairs, sell tabloids and magazines, so these publications find any restrictions imposed by privacy laws much more irksome than those imposed by libel law. One threshold question is whether the free press principles applied to defamation law by, for example, the US Supreme Court in *New York Times* v. *Sullivan* (discussed in the previous section) should be applied to privacy law. On one view, there is a good case for their application; indeed, it could be argued that the press should never be liable for the disclosure of accurate stories revealing details of a politician's or a celebrity's private life, because it should always be free to publish the truth.

The first two essays in Part IV point out the fallacies of these arguments. In a classic essay (Chapter 11), Melville Nimmer, who was a distinguished commentator on free speech and free press law in the United States, contends that it would be wrong to extend the strong free speech/press principle formulated in *New York Times* to privacy actions (or for that matter to libel actions brought by private individuals involved in public issues). The rationale for the *NYT* ruling was that it is crucial for the public to have information about the conduct of public affairs, even when it defames politicians or public officials. Later the principle was extended to cover public figures, about whose behaviour the public was also entitled to be informed. Moreover, people in those positions enjoy access to the media to put over their version of events in order to counter defamatory allegations. These arguments do not apply to the disclosure of private information about, say, an individual's sexual life or preferences, or his health. These are not generally matters of real public interest, so speech about them has little value. Moreover, a person complaining that his privacy has been infringed does not want media access to reply to the disclosure, which would only give the revelations wider currency; he wants the law to deter their publication in the first place.

In Chapter 12 Eric Barendt argues that the public is not always entitled to know the truth, just because it is the truth. As Fred Schauer (1991) has pointed out, it is important that the public has access to arguments about truth on matters about which it should form a view; but there are some matters on which it is not entitled to hold any belief at all. Ignorance about, say, the private life of a neighbour, or even a public figure or official, is good; there are some matters about which anyone is entitled to say to a journalist: 'Mind your own business!' Barendt also challenges the familiar argument that it would be wrong for Parliament or the judges to formulate an explicit right to privacy, because there are difficulties in defining 'privacy': does it cover, for instance, an individual's income or tax affairs? But definitional difficulties have not prevented the development of libel law, or for that matter the right to freedom of the press (see the arguments canvassed earlier in this Introduction). Moreover, the English Press Complaints Commission has developed some 'jurisprudence' about the scope of private life and the public interest defence, when it has applied the provisions in the PCC Code concerning complaints about the infringement of privacy, intrusion into grief and shock, and harassment (see Chapter 6 in this volume). The PCC cannot therefore oppose, as it has done, the introduction of privacy rights with spurious arguments about definitional problems. The courts can surmount these difficulties and draw a line between press freedom and privacy, just as well as the PCC has done itself.

Of course, there remain powerful free speech/press arguments against privacy laws. These are particularly strongly held in the United States, where the First Amendment guarantees press freedom, while the Constitution only protects privacy against infringement by government, not against press intrusion. Eugene Volokh (2000) has argued, for instance, against privacy laws that they entail a right to have the government intervene to stop a newspaper, or indeed anyone, speaking about individuals, though that also applies to defamation law, and in some circumstances to copyright law, which are allowed to limit press freedom. A more persuasive argument has been made by Fred Schauer (2000, p. 293), though it may only apply in the context of privacy suits by politicians. His argument is that some people may think that they are entitled to know everything about a candidate for public office – including details of his current or past intimate sexual life – before deciding how to vote. They argue that, if that candidate has cheated on a spouse or partner in his private life, he may be equally unreliable in public office. In Schauer's view, there may therefore be good free speech and press grounds for allowing newspapers to communicate information which some voters consider relevant to their democratic choices. The difficulty is that we would then have to accept that politicians have no privacy rights at all against the media.

In Chapter 14 Paul Gerwitz challenges that conclusion. His essay takes as its starting point the recent decision of the Supreme Court in *Bartnicki* v. *Vopper*,[13] in which it held that a radio broadcaster was free to play the tape of an illegally intercepted conversation between two union officials, because their conversation involved a matter of public concern – how the union should handle negotiations concerning school teachers' pay. In much of the essay Gewirtz points out that the case, properly understood, does not elevate media freedom over privacy. Of more general interest is his strong argument that press freedom should not in principle trump privacy whenever public interest is invoked. Too rigid an adherence to press freedom allows entertainment values to drive out serious news coverage. Paradoxically, stronger protection for privacy would enhance public debate by encouraging the media to focus on the official actions of politicians and their policies, rather than on their private lives. Most radically, he rejects the argument made by Schauer and others (see, in particular, Post, 1989, pp. 999–1002) that privacy should give way to democratic accountability: '[a]ccountability … should not trump all other values. … If public figures should have some zone of protected privacy, then some limits on the media's leeway to invade privacy will have to be accepted, even if this also means some limit on accountability' (p. 466). Unusually for the author of a United States law review article, Gewirtz draws on comparative law. He refers to cases in other jurisdictions, notably Germany and Canada, where privacy has been protected, even when it clashed with free press arguments. Courts in the United States should abandon, in his view, their unique, general preference for press freedom whenever it conflicts with privacy rights.

There remain hard questions about the proper scope of privacy protection when the media publish details, particularly in photographs, of what individuals consider their private activity – for instance, dining with a partner or with friends, shopping, or sun-bathing on a beach or in

13 532 US 514 (2001).

a garden. The media may argue that no individual has a right to privacy when he is in public, whether or not he is a celebrity. Their arguments are considered, but rejected, in an interesting comparative essay by Elizabeth Paton-Simpson (Chapter 13). She argues that people do not surrender their expectation of privacy when they enter public places such as the streets or parks. Further, the values which underlie privacy rights – individual dignity, the space and freedom to develop individual thoughts and to cultivate intimate relationships and friendships – are just as much at stake when people are out on the streets or using public transport as when they are at home. A privacy law which only protected people when they were on private property would wrongly discriminate in favour of the rich who are not dependent on public spaces for their recreation. Paton-Simpson also reviews how these issues have been resolved by courts in the United States, Canada and New Zealand. While American judges have tended to conclude that privacy is lost when the claimant is in public, Canadian and to some extent New Zealand courts have limited the freedom of the press in these circumstances. Particularly striking is the well-known decision of the Supreme Court of Canada upholding a Quebec judgement awarding damages to a young girl whose photograph was published in an arts magazine; the photograph had been taken without her consent, while she was sitting on the steps of a public building.[14] While admitting that the balance between press freedom (and artistic expression) and privacy was hard to strike in this case, the author concludes in favour of the decision (see pp. 421–2).

The subject of the final essay is the controversial ruling of the European Court of Human Rights in the Princess Caroline case.[15] The Court held there that Germany infringed the right to respect for private life, guaranteed by ECHR, art. 8, because its courts had failed to protect the privacy of Princess Caroline of Monaco when tabloid magazines had published photographs of her engaging in a variety of activities – for example, horse-riding, shopping, on holiday. The Court held that it had to balance her privacy rights against the magazines' freedom of expression, guaranteed by art. 10 of the ECHR; that freedom did not give the press carte blanche to publish photographs of a celebrity, who had not given her consent to their taking or publication, when they did not contribute to any discussion of real public importance. It would be different if the photographs had shown the Princess discharging some public duty. In Chapter 15 M.A. Sanderson explores some of the difficulties of this ruling. In his view the Court took too restrictive a view of the public interest in this sort of story, and it failed to explain why the German courts had been wrong to treat Princess Caroline as a public figure for the purpose of privacy law. The pictures taken of the Princess did not depict her engaging in any embarrassing conduct. Sanderson concludes that if the photographs had had a more revelatory content, then there might have been a stronger case for freedom of the press to publish them. The Court, in his view, reached its decision just because the information was too anodyne to contribute to any public debate. But equally the Princess would have had a stronger case for privacy protection, if the photographs had, say, shown her engaged in some aspect of her intimate, private life.

What is interesting about many of these essays is that the arguments over the correct balancing of freedom of the press (and of the other media) with privacy rights have not changed much since the publication of the seminal essay by Samuel Warren and Louis Brandeis in 1890. They

---

14 *Aubry* v. *Éditions Vice-Versa Inc.* [1998] 1 SCR 591.

15 *Von Hannover* v. *Germany* (2004) 16 BHRC 645. 77.

argued then that the introduction of privacy laws should impel the press to abandon celebrity gossip of little or no value and to concentrate on the investigation and reporting of real news of public importance. At the same time they pointed out that too strong an application of these laws would curtail press freedom; a privacy right should be balanced by due consideration for free speech and free press arguments. The question now, as then, is how the balance should be struck without sacrificing the core values of either freedom. The relationship of press freedom to privacy remains one of the most complex and intractable issues of media law. Moreover, it goes to the heart of what we understand by, and require of, press freedom.

Acknowledgement

The assistance of Nicholas Queree in making the selection of essays is acknowledged.

Select Bibliography

Press Freedom and Freedom of Expression

Anderson, D.A. (1983), 'The Origins of the Press Clause', *UCLA Law Review*, **30**, pp. 455–541.
Anderson, D.A. (2002), 'Freedom of the Press', *Texas Law Review*, **80**, pp. 429–530.
Baker, C.E. (1989) *Human Liberty and Freedom of Speech*, New York: Oxford University Press, ch. 10, 'Press Rights'.
Barendt, E.M. (2005), *Freedom of Speech*, Oxford: Oxford University Press, ch. XII, 'Freedom of Speech in the Media'.
Lange, D. (1975), 'The Speech and Press Clauses', *UCLA Law Review*, **23**, pp. 77–119.
Lichtenberg, J. (1990), 'Foundations and Limits of Freedom of the Press', in J. Lichtenberg (ed.), *Democracy and the Mass Media*, Cambridge: Cambridge University Press, pp. 102–35.
Liebling, A.J. (1964), *The Press*, New York, Ballantine Books.
Marshall, G. (1992), 'Press Freedom and Free Speech Theory', *Public Law*, pp. 40–60.
Nimmer, M.B. (1975), 'Speech and Press: A Brief Reply', *UCLA Law Review*, **23**, pp. 120–23.
Rowbottom, J. (2006), 'Media Freedom and Political Debate in the Digital Era', *Modern Law Review*, **69**, pp. 489–513.

Self-regulation of the Press

Calcutt, D. *et al.* (1990), *Report of the Committee on Privacy and Related Matters*, Cm. 1102, London: HMSO.
Campbell, A.J. (1999), 'Self-regulation and the Media', *Federal Communications Law Journal*, **51**, pp. 711–72.
Coad, J. (2003), 'The PCC – Some Myths about Self-regulation', *Entertainment Law Review*, **14**, pp. 211–14.
Munro, C. (1997), 'Self-regulation in the Media', *Public Law*, **6**, pp. 6–17.
Robertson, G. (1983), *People against the Press*, London: Quartet.

Freedom of the Press and Libel Law

Anderson, David A. (2007), 'Defamation and Privacy: An American Perspective', in S. Deakin, A. Johnston and B Markesinis (eds), *Tort Law* (6th edn), Oxford: Oxford University Press.

Barendt, E. (2005), *Freedom of Speech*, Oxford: Oxford University Press, ch. VI, 'Libel and Invasion of Privacy'.

Fischer, S.F. (2002), 'Rethinking *Sullivan*: New Approaches in Australia, New Zealand, and England', *George Washington International Law Review*, **34**, pp. 101–89.

Kenyon, A.T. (2006), *Defamation: Comparative Law and Practice*, London: UCL Press.

Post, R.C. (1986), 'Social Foundations of Defamation Law: Reputation and the Constitution', *California Law Review*, **74**, pp. 691–742.

Schauer, F. (1980), 'Social Foundations of the Law of Defamation: A Comparative Analysis', *Journal of Media Law and Practice*, **1**, pp. 3–23.

Weaver, R.L., Kenyon, A.T., Partlett, D.F. and Walker, C.P. (2006), *The Right to Speak Ill: Defamation, Reputation, and Free Speech*, Durham, NC: Carolina Academic Press.

Freedom of the Press and Privacy

Anderson, D.A. (1999), 'The Failure of American Privacy Law', in B.S. Markesinis (ed.), *Protecting Privacy*, Oxford: Oxford University Press, pp. 139–68.

Bezanson, R.P. (1992), '*The Right to Privacy* Revisited: Privacy, News, and Social Change, 1890–1990', *California Law Review*, **80**, pp. 1133–75.

Calcutt, D. *et al.* (1990), *Report of the Committee on Privacy and Related Matters*, Cm. 1102, London: HMSO.

Kenyon, A. and Richardson, M. (eds) (2006), *New Dimensions in Privacy Law: International and Comparative Perspectives*, Cambridge: Cambridge University Press.

Paton-Simpson, E. (2000), 'Private Circles and Public Squares: Invasion of Privacy by the Publication of "Private Facts"', *Modern Law Review*, **61**, pp. 318–40.

Post, R.C. (1989), 'The Social Foundations of Privacy: Community and Self in the Common Law Tort', *California Law Review*, **77**, pp. 957–1010.

Schauer, F. (1991), 'Reflections on the Value of Truth', *Case Western Law Review*, **41**, pp. 699–724.

Schauer, F. (2000), 'Can Public Figures have Private Lives?', in E.F. Paul, F.D. Miller, Jr and J. Paul (eds), *The Right to Privacy*, Cambridge: Cambridge University Press, pp. 293–309.

Volokh, Eugene (2000), 'Freedom of Speech and Information Privacy: The Troubling Implications of a Right to Stop People from Speaking About You', *Stanford Law Review*, **52**, pp. 1049–124.

Warren, S.D. and Brandeis, L.D. (1890), 'The Right to Privacy', *Harvard Law Review*, **4**, pp. 193–220.

Zimmerman, D.L. (1983), 'Requiem for a Heavyweight: A Farewell to Warren and Brandeis's Privacy Tort', *Cornell Law Review*, **68**, pp. 291–350.

Part I
Press Freedom and Freedom of Expression

[1]

"Or of the Press"†

By POTTER STEWART*

I turn this morning to an inquiry into an aspect of constitutional law that has only recently begun to engage the attention of the Supreme Court. Specifically, I shall discuss the role of the organized press—of the daily newspapers and other established news media—in the system of government created by our Constitution.

It was less than a decade ago—during the Vietnam years—that the people of our country began to become aware of the twin phenomena on a national scale of so-called investigative reporting and an adversary press—that is, a press adversary to the Executive Branch of the Federal Government. And only in the two short years that culminated last summer in the resignation of a President did we fully realize the enormous power that an investigative and adversary press can exert.

The public opinion polls that I have seen indicate that some Americans firmly believe that the former Vice President and former President of the United States were hounded out of office by an arrogant and irresponsible press that had outrageously usurped dictatorial power. And it seems clear that many more Americans, while appreciating and even applauding the service performed by the press in exposing official wrongdoing at the highest levels of our national government, are nonetheless deeply disturbed by what they consider to be the illegitimate power of the organized press in the political structure of our society. It is my thesis this morning that, on the contrary, the established American press in the past ten years, and particularly in the past two years, has performed precisely the function it was intended to perform by those who wrote the First Amendment of our Constitution. I further submit that this thesis is supported by the relevant decisions of the Supreme Court.

Surprisingly, despite the importance of newspapers in the political

† Excerpted from an address on November 2, 1974, at the Yale Law School Sesquicentennial Convocation, New Haven, Connecticut.

* Associate Justice, United States Supreme Court.

and social life of our country the Supreme Court has not until very recently been called upon to delineate their constitutional role in our structure of government.

Our history is filled with struggles over the rights and prerogatives of the press, but these disputes rarely found their way to the Supreme Court. The early years of the Republic witnessed controversy over the constitutional validity of the short-lived Alien and Sedition Act, but the controversy never reached the Court. In the next half century there was nationwide turmoil over the right of the organized press to advocate the then subversive view that slavery should be abolished. In Illinois a publisher was killed for publishing abolitionist views. But none of this history made First Amendment law because the Court had earlier held that the Bill of Rights applied only against the Federal Government, not against the individual states.

With the passage of the Fourteenth Amendment, the constitutional framework was modified, and by the 1920's the Court had established that the protections of the First Amendment extend against all government—federal, state, and local.

The next fifty years witnessed a great outpouring of First Amendment litigation, all of which inspired books and articles beyond number. But, with few exceptions, neither these First Amendment cases nor their commentators squarely considered the Constitution's guarantee of a Free Press. Instead, the focus was on its guarantee of free speech. The Court's decisions dealt with the rights of isolated individuals, or of unpopular minority groups, to stand up against governmental power representing an angry or frightened majority. The cases that came to the Court during those years involved the rights of the soapbox orator, the nonconformist pamphleteer, the religious evangelist. The Court was seldom asked to define the rights and privileges, or the responsibilities, of the organized press.

In very recent years cases involving the established press finally have begun to reach the Supreme Court, and they have presented a variety of problems, sometimes arising in complicated factual settings.

In a series of cases, the Court has been called upon to consider the limits imposed by the free press guarantee upon a state's common or statutory law of libel. As a result of those cases, a public figure cannot successfully sue a publisher for libel unless he can show that the publisher maliciously printed a damaging untruth.[1]

1. *See* Rosenbloom v. Metromedia, Inc., 403 U.S. 29 (1971); Curtis Publ. Co. v. Butts, 388 U.S. 130 (1967); New York Times Co. v. Sullivan, 376 U.S. 254 (1964).

The Court has also been called upon to decide whether a newspaper reporter has a First Amendment privilege to refuse to disclose his confidential sources to a grand jury. By a divided vote, the Court found no such privilege to exist in the circumstances of the cases before it.[2]

In another noteworthy case, the Court was asked by the Justice Department to restrain publication by the *New York Times* and other newspapers of the so-called Pentagon Papers. The Court declined to do so.[3]

In yet another case, the question to be decided was whether political groups have a First Amendment or statutory right of access to the federally regulated broadcast channels of radio and television. The Court held there was no such right of access.[4]

Last Term the Court confronted a Florida statute that required newspapers to grant a "right of reply" to political candidates they had criticized. The Court unanimously held this statute to be inconsistent with the guarantees of a free press.[5]

It seems to me that the Court's approach to all these cases has uniformly reflected its understanding that the Free Press guarantee is, in essence, a *structural* provision of the Constitution. Most of the other provisions in the Bill of Rights protect specific liberties or specific rights of individuals: freedom of speech, freedom of worship, the right to counsel, the privilege against compulsory self-incrimination, to name a few. In contrast, the Free Press Clause extends protection to an institution. The publishing business is, in short, the only organized private business that is given explicit constitutional protection.

This basic understanding is essential, I think, to avoid an elementary error of constitutional law. It is tempting to suggest that freedom of the press means only that newspaper publishers are guaranteed freedom of expression. They *are* guaranteed that freedom, to be sure, but so are we all, because of the Free Speech Clause. If the Free Press guarantee meant no more than freedom of expression, it would be a constitutional redundancy. Between 1776 and the drafting of our Constitution, many of the state constitutions contained clauses protecting freedom of the press while at the same time recognizing no general

2. Branzburg v. Hayes, 408 U.S. 665 (1972).
3. New York Times Co. v. United States, 403 U.S. 713 (1971).
4. Columbia Broadcasting Sys., Inc. v. Democratic Nat'l Comm., 412 U.S. 94 (1973).
5. Miami Herald Publ. Co. v. Tornillo, 94 S. Ct. 2831 (1974).

freedom of speech. By including both guarantees in the First Amendment, the Founders quite clearly recognized the distinction between the two.

It is also a mistake to suppose that the only purpose of the constitutional guarantee of a free press is to insure that a newspaper will serve as a neutral forum for debate, a "market place for ideas," a kind of Hyde Park corner for the community. A related theory sees the press as a neutral conduit of information between the people and their elected leaders. These theories, in my view, again give insufficient weight to the institutional autonomy of the press that it was the purpose of the Constitution to guarantee.

In setting up the three branches of the Federal Government, the Founders deliberately created an internally competitive system. As Mr. Justice Brandeis once wrote:[6]

> The [Founders'] purpose was, not to avoid friction, but, by means of the inevitable friction incident to the distribution of the governmental powers among three departments, to save the people from autocracy.

The primary purpose of the constitutional guarantee of a free press was a similar one: to create a fourth institution outside the Government as an additional check on the three official branches. Consider the opening words of the Free Press Clause of the Massachusetts Constitution, drafted by John Adams:

> The liberty of the press is essential to the security of the state.

The relevant metaphor, I think, is the metaphor of the Fourth Estate. What Thomas Carlyle wrote about the British Government a century ago has a curiously contemporary ring:

> Burke said there were Three Estates in Parliament; but, in the Reporters' Gallery yonder, there sat a Fourth Estate more important far than they all. It is not a figure of speech or witty saying; it is a literal fact—very momentus to us in these times.

For centuries before our Revolution, the press in England had been licensed, censored, and bedeviled by prosecutions for seditious libel. The British Crown knew that a free press was not just a neutral vehicle for the balanced discussion of diverse ideas. Instead, the free press meant organized, expert scrutiny of government. The press was a conspiracy of the intellect, with the courage of numbers. This formidable check on official power was what the British Crown had feared—and what the American Founders decided to risk.

6. Myers v. United States, 272 U.S. 52, 293 (1926) (dissenting opinion).

It is this constitutional understanding, I think, that provides the unifying principle underlying the Supreme Court's recent decisions dealing with the organized press.

Consider first the libel cases. Officials within the three governmental branches are, for all practical purposes, immune from libel and slander suits for statements that they make in the line of duty.[7] This immunity, which has both constitutional and common law origins, aims to insure bold and vigorous prosecution of the public's business. The same basic reasoning applies to the press. By contrast, the Court has never suggested that the constitutional right of free *speech* gives an *individual* any immunity from liability for either libel or slander.

In the cases involving the newspaper reporters' claims that they had a constitutional privilege not to disclose their confidential news sources to a grand jury, the Court rejected the claims by a vote of five to four, or, considering Mr. Justice Powell's concurring opinion, perhaps by a vote of four and a half to four and a half. But if freedom of the press means simply freedom of speech for reporters, this question of a reporter's asserted right to withhold information would have answered itself. None of us—as individuals—has a "free speech" right to refuse to tell a grand jury the identity of someone who has given us information relevant to the grand jury's legitimate inquiry. Only if a reporter is a representative of a protected *institution* does the question become a different one. The members of the Court disagreed in answering the question, but the question did not answer itself.

The cases involving the so-called "right of access" to the press raised the issue whether the First Amendment allows government, or indeed *requires* government, to regulate the press so as to make it a genuinely fair and open "market place for ideas." The Court's answer was "no" to both questions. If a newspaper wants to serve as a neutral market place for debate, that is an objective which it is free to choose. And, within limits, that choice is probably necessary to commercially successful journalism. But it is a choice that government cannot constitutionally impose.

Finally the Pentagon Papers case involved the line between secrecy and openness in the affairs of Government. The question, or at least one question, was whether that line is drawn by the Constitution itself. The Justice Department asked the Court to find in the Constitution a basis for prohibiting the publication of allegedly stolen govern-

7. *See* Barr v. Matteo, 360 U.S. 564 (1959).

ment documents. The Court could find no such prohibition. So far as the Constitution goes, the autonomous press may publish what it knows, and may seek to learn what it can.

But this autonomy cuts both ways. The press is free to do battle against secrecy and deception in government. But the press cannot expect from the Constitution any guarantee that it will succeed. There is no constitutional right to have access to particular government information, or to require openness from the bureaucracy.[8] The public's interest in knowing about its government is protected by the guarantee of a Free Press, but the protection is indirect. The Constitution itself is neither a Freedom of Information Act nor an Official Secrets Act.

The Constitution, in other words, establishes the contest, not its resolution. Congress may provide a resolution, at least in some instances, through carefully drawn legislation. For the rest, we must rely, as so often in our system we must, on the tug and pull of the political forces in American society.

Newspapers, television networks, and magazines have sometimes been outrageously abusive, untruthful, arrogant, and hypocritical. But it hardly follows that elimination of a strong and independent press is the way to eliminate abusiveness, untruth, arrogance, or hypocrisy from government itself.

It is quite possible to conceive of the survival of our Republic without an autonomous press. For openness and honesty in government, for an adequate flow of information between the people and their representatives, for a sufficient check on autocracy and despotism, the traditional competition between the three branches of government, supplemented by vigorous political activity, might be enough.

The press could be relegated to the status of a public utility. The guarantee of free speech would presumably put some limitation on the regulation to which the press could be subjected. But if there were no guarantee of a free press, government could convert the communications media into a neutral "market place of ideas." Newspapers and television networks could then be required to promote contemporary government policy or current notions of social justice.[9]

Such a constitution is possible; it might work reasonably well. But

8. *Cf.* Pell v. Procunier, 94 S. Ct. 2800 (1974); Saxbe v. Washington Post Co., 94 S. Ct. 2811 (1974).

9. *Cf.* Pittsburgh Press Co. v. Pittsburgh Comm'n on Human Relations, 413 U.S. 376 (1973).

it is not the Constitution the Founders wrote. It is not the Constitution that has carried us through nearly two centuries of national life. Perhaps our liberties might survive without an independent established press. But the Founders doubted it, and, in the year 1974, I think we can all be thankful for their doubts.

[2]

A PREFERRED POSITION FOR JOURNALISM?

*Anthony Lewis**

"Congress shall make no law . . . abridging the freedom of speech, or of the *news media*." That was the clarified version of the first amendment[1] proposed by Justice Stewart in his memorable 1974 address at the Yale Law School, *Or of the Press*.[2] Most parts of the Bill of Rights, he said, protect liberties whoever exercises them; but the press clause of the first amendment is "a *structural* provision"[3] protecting a particular institution: "the organized press,"[4] which Justice Stewart defined as "the daily newspapers and other established news media."[5] Journalism, in short, has a special constitutional status, with rights not available to others.[6]

The Yale speech broke important new ground. The Supreme Court had never really addressed the question posed by Justice Stewart—whether the press clause has an independent purpose and meaning—much less given his bold answer. The press clause, he said, did not merely join with the speech clause to guarantee freedom of expression to all; that would make it "a constitutional redundancy."[7] Rather, the "primary purpose" of those who framed it was "to create a fourth institution outside the Government as an additional check on the three official branches."[8] That purpose, Justice Stewart said, informed recent Supreme Court decisions on the rights of the press.[9]

---

* Columnist, the *New York Times*. Lecturer on Law, Harvard Law School. B.A., 1948, Harvard College.

1. The first amendment provides in relevant part: "Congress shall make no law . . . abridging the freedom of speech, or of the press . . . ." U.S. CONST. amend. I.

2. Address by Justice Stewart, Yale Law School (Nov. 2, 1974), *reprinted, except for opening courtesies, in* Stewart, *"Or of the Press,"* 26 HASTINGS L.J. 631 (1975).

3. *Id.* at 633 (emphasis in original).

4. *Id.* at 631, 632. Justice Stewart also speaks of "the established press." *Id.* at 632.

5. *Id.* at 631.

6. One who disagrees with the idea has described it, fairly enough, as a "preferred position for the press as an institution." Herbert v. Lando, 568 F.2d 974, 997 (2d Cir. 1977) (Meskill, J., dissenting), *rev'd*, 99 S. Ct. 1635 (1979). For the origin of the phrase "preferred position," see Kovacs v. Cooper, 336 U.S. 77, 88 (1949).

7. Stewart, *supra* note 2, at 633.

8. *Id.* at 634.

9. *Id.* at 635.

The media[10] welcomed the message. In recent years, news organizations, both print and broadcast, have become increasingly sensitive to perceived legal threats and increasingly determined to define their rights in the courts. The more aggressive mood no doubt stems in part from the experience of Vietnam and Watergate, which weakened the old premise of shared beliefs and mutual respect between press and government.[11] A growing sense of professionalism, fed by journalism schools and journalism reviews and press councils, also adds to journalism's pride of place. The news business in this country is now quick to use the law as both sword and shield. The last two terms of the Supreme Court alone have seen battles about access to news,[12] searches of news premises,[13] protection of confidential sources,[14] and the confidentiality of the editorial process.[15] I think Justice Stewart's speech contributed to the determination of news organizations to fight those cases, and to the legal doctrines advanced by their lawyers.

The speech is also finding its way into judicial opinions. It was cited in the Second Circuit's short-lived decision in *Herbert v. Lando*,[16] which gave aspects of the editorial process protection from discovery in a libel case; the dissenter, Judge Meskill, wryly responded that he would not take such a step "on the basis of a single speech, even one given by Mr. Justice Stewart."[17] Chief Justice Burger, in a case dealing with the free speech rights of corporations, wrote a concurring opinion to express a skeptical attitude toward "those who view the Press Clause as somehow

10. "Media" is a word ordinarily to be avoided in civilized discourse. Alas, there is no way to escape its use in discussing whether "the press" whose freedom is guaranteed by the first amendment favors journalism over other forms of publication.

11. A leading article in the wake of the *Pentagon Papers Case*, New York Times Co. v. United States, 403 U.S. 713 (1971), said publication of the papers "demonstrated that much of the press was no longer willing to be merely an occasionally critical associate [of the government] devoted to common aims." Edgar & Schmidt, *The Espionage Statutes and Publication of Defense Information*, 73 COLUM. L. REV. 929, 1077 (1973).

12. *See* Gannett Co. v. De Pasquale, 99 S. Ct. 2898 (1979) (access to pretrial suppression hearing); Houchins v. KQED, Inc., 438 U.S. 1 (1978) (access to prison).

13. *See* Zurcher v. Stanford Daily, 436 U.S. 547 (1978).

14. *See In re* Farber, 78 N.J. 259, 394 A.2d 330, *cert. denied*, 439 U.S. 997 (1978).

15. *See* Herbert v. Lando, 568 F.2d 974 (2d Cir. 1977), *rev'd*, 99 S. Ct. 1635 (1979).

16. *Id.* at 977 n.11 (citing Stewart, *supra* note 2, at 633).

17. *Id.* at 997 (Meskill, J., dissenting).

conferring special and extraordinary privileges or status on the 'institutional press.' "[18] If provoking judicial colleagues is one sign of effect, and it is, Justice Stewart can rest content with the impact of his Yale speech.

But in the end the Stewart thesis of press exceptionalism—of a preferred status for journalists—will succeed or fail in the marketplace of constitutional ideas. It should be tested there by three standards: its roots in history, its basis in the decided cases, and its wisdom in principle. By those tests I find it unconvincing.

History

"For centuries before our Revolution," Justice Stewart said in his Yale speech, "the press in England had been licensed, censored, and bedeviled by prosecutions for seditious libel. The . . . free press meant organized, expert scrutiny of government. The press was a conspiracy of the intellect, with the courage of numbers. This formidable check on official power was what the British Crown had feared—and what the American Founders decided to risk."[19]

Those words are an admirable tribute to the romance of journalism and to its high duty. But as history desigued to prove that the first amendment gave special status to the news media, the passage is less convincing. For "the press" that was licensed and bedeviled in England was not newspapers alone. Those who called for "freedom of the press" in the seventeenth and eighteenth centuries had in mind books and pamphlets and all kinds of occasional literature as much as newspapers. Indeed, some were not thinking of newspapers at all.

The most famous statement on behalf of press freedom in that period was John Milton's *Areopagitica*.[20] Published in 1644, it was an attack on the requirement that any printed work be read and licensed by official censors before publication—a requirement first established by the Crown in 1538[21] and reimposed by Parliament

---

18. First Nat'l Bank v. Bellotti, 435 U.S. 765, 797 (1978) (Burger, C.J., concurring). The Chief Justice did not actually cite Justice Stewart's speech, but it was plainly his target. He has cited it in support of the argument that the press has no constitutional right of access to government information. Houchins v. KQED, Inc., 438 U.S. 1, 14-15 (1978). *See* text accompanying notes 151-155 *infra*.

19. Stewart, *supra* note 2, at 634.

20. J. Milton, Areopagitica: A Speech for the Liberty of Unlicensed Printing to the Parliament of England (J. Dent ed. 1946).

21. F. Siebert, Freedom of the Press in England, 1476-1776, at 48-49 (1952).

in a statute of June 14, 1643, after the Puritan Revolution.[22] Milton argued that "regulating the Press"[23] could be accomplished by means less onerous than the licensing system. By "the Press" he meant any product of a printing press; at one point, for example, he ironically sympathized with the conscientious censor who must be "the perpetual reader of unchosen books and pamphlets, ofttimes huge volumes."[24]

To say that books and pamphlets were at issue in the long English debate about freedom of the press is to argue the obvious. The royal licensing system was first imposed by Henry VIII after the invention of printing had, as one leading commentator puts it, magnified the danger of "opinions deemed pernicious."[25] That was in 1538, before the development of newspapers. The classic history of the long struggle, Frederick Seaton Siebert's *Freedom of the Press in England, 1476-1776*, cites the Levellers' petition to Parliament of January 18, 1649, as an outstanding statement of the argument for press freedom; the petition made its case in terms of books and pamphlets.[26] Siebert also shows that well into the eighteenth century pamphlets as well as newspapers were the subject of prosecutions for seditious libel: A bookseller was tried in 1752 for publishing a pamphlet critical of the House of Commons.[27]

A scholarly brief filed in the 1978 Term of the Supreme Court by Floyd Abrams[28] and others relied on the Siebert book to demonstrate that many newspapers were published in England before 1776 and that they were a frequent object of repression.[29] The brief also showed that American newspapers played a significant role in arousing anti-British feelings before 1776.[30] Hence, it concluded, "the framers of the Constitution knew what the press was, knew how crucial a role it could play."[31] True enough. But no one

---

22. *Id* at 173.

23. J. MILTON, *supra* note 20, at 40.

24. *Id.* at 20.

25. L. LEVY, LEGACY OF SUPPRESSION 8 (1960).

26. F. SIEBERT, *supra* note 21, at 200-01.

27. *Id.* at 383. *See generally* THE OXFORD COMPANION TO ENGLISH LITERATURE 911-15 app. (4th ed. 1967) (*Censorship and the Law of the Press*).

28. *See generally* Abrams, *The Press* Is *Different: Reflections on Justice Stewart and the Autonomous Press*, 7 HOFSTRA L. REV. 563 (1979).

29. Brief for Respondents at 49-50, Herbert v. Lando, 99 S. Ct. 1635 (1979).

30. *Id.* at 50-51.

31. *Id.* at 51. But the very material cited in the brief, from A. SCHLESINGER, PRELUDE TO INDEPENDENCE (1958), shows compellingly that the American press in that period was far from the provider of "organized, expert scrutiny of government"

argues that the eighteenth-century concept of "freedom of the press" did not include newspapers. Justice Stewart's suggestion, rather, is that the concept was applied exclusively to newspapers. No historian of whom I am aware has produced any evidence to support that proposition.

The precise motives of those who drafted the speech and press clauses of the first amendment are unlikely to be discovered now, if indeed they were ever ascertainable. Madison sponsored in the House what became the first amendment, and another amendment that would have prohibited *state* abridgment of press and other freedoms; the latter was killed in the Senate.[32] Committee changes, unexplained in the materials left to us,[33] reduced the language to its final compelling simplicity: "Congress shall make no law . . . abridging the freedom of speech, or of the press."[34]

The most natural explanation seems the most probable: The framers wanted to protect expression whether in unprinted or printed form. Freedom of the press was more often mentioned in colonial and state bills of rights than freedom of speech; at the time of the first amendment ten state constitutions protected the former while only two the latter.[35] Very likely, as Chief Justice Burger has said, press freedom "merited special mention simply because it had been more often the object of official restraints."[36] But the two phrases were used interchangeably, then as now, to mean freedom of expression. And there is evidence suggesting that eighteenth-century Americans, when they thought about the rights of speech and press, regarded them as aspects of the same fundamental personal freedom. George Mason began drafting the Virginia Declara-

---

portrayed by Justice Stewart, Stewart, *supra* note 2, at 634. Professor Schlesinger said the press "trumpeted the doings of Whig committees, publicized rallies and mobbings, promoted partisan fast days and anniversaries, blazoned patriotic speeches and toasts, popularized anti-British slogans." Brief for Respondents at 50, Herbert v. Lando, 99 S. Ct. 1635 (1979) (quoting A. SCHLESINGER, *supra*, at 46). In short, the press in those days was highly partisan. And that character continued after independence and after the formation of the United States. While Jefferson was Secretary of State in the Washington administration, for example, he employed a journalist to attack Washington's Federalist Party. Lange, *The Speech and Press Clauses*, 23 U.C.L.A. L. REV. 77, 90 (1975).

32. E. HUDON, FREEDOM OF SPEECH AND PRESS IN AMERICA 5-6 (1963) (citing 1 ANNALS OF CONG. 432, 435, 778 (Gates & Seaton eds. 1789)).

33. *See* First Nat'l Bank v. Bellotti, 435 U.S. 765, 799 n.4 (1978) (Burger, C.J., concurring).

34. U.S. CONST. amend. I.

35. *See* L. LEVY, *supra* note 25, at 183-85.

36. First Nat'l Bank v. Bellotti, 435 U.S. at 800 (1978) (Burger, C.J., concurring).

tion of Rights, which included a striking assertion of the need for freedom of the press,[37] just two days after Dixon and Hunter's *Virginia Gazette* of May 18, 1776, carried the following on its front page:

> [T]he liberty of the press is inviolably connected with the liberty of the subject . . . [.] The *use* of *speech* is a *natural right*, which must have been reserved when men gave up their natural rights for the benefit of society. PRINTING is a more extensive and improved kind of speech.[38]

In sum, the Stewart thesis of a preferred position for the news media finds no support in history. Those who wrote the first amendment were familiar with newspapers. But there is no evidence that they meant to limit the freedom of "the press" to newspapers, excluding books and other publications, or that they intended to afford newspapers a higher standard of protection than other forms of expression.

THE DECIDED CASES

In his Yale speech, Justice Stewart said four groups of recent Supreme Court decisions reflected an understanding that the free press clause was "a *structural* provision of the Constitution," protecting "an institution."[39] His list was headed by the series of libel cases starting with *New York Times Co. v. Sullivan*,[40] in which the Court held libel actions by government officials subject to constitutional limitations. Officials are ordinarily immune from suit for what they say in the line of duty, Justice Stewart said, to encourage vigorous performance of their functions. He argued that the libel cases applied the same reasoning to the press. "By contrast," he said, "the Court has never suggested that the constitutional right of free *speech* gives an *individual* any immunity from liability for either libel or slander."[41]

This explanation of *Times v. Sullivan* is, well, breathtaking. Justice Brennan's great opinion for the Court in that case began as follows: "We are required in this case to determine for the first

37. Mason's first draft of the Virginia Declaration, a committee draft, and the final version are set out in H. MILLER, GEORGE MASON: GENTLEMAN REVOLUTIONARY 337-40 apps. (1975).

38. Va. Gazette, May 18, 1776, at 1, col. 2 (emphasis in original), *quoted in* H. MILLER, *supra* note 37, at 148 (1975).

39. Stewart, *supra* note 2, at 633 (emphasis in original).

40. 376 U.S. 254 (1964).

41. Stewart, *supra* note 2, at 635 (emphasis in original).

time the extent to which the constitutional protections for *speech and press* limit a State's power to award damages in a libel action brought by a public official against critics of his official conduct."[42] Not a word in the opinion intimated independent reliance on the press clause, or application of the new libel rule to media defendants only. Indeed, the decision reversed libel judgments against not only the *New York Times* but also four individual defendants, Alabama clergymen.[43]

Justice Brennan drew an analogy to the official immunity doctrine quite different from that suggested by Justice Stewart. Officials, he said, were immunized against damage suits that might dampen their ardor " 'in the unflinching discharge of their duties.' "[44] He continued: "Analogous considerations support the privilege for the citizen-critic of government. It is as much his duty to criticize as it is the official's duty to administer."[45] Not "the organized press" but "the citizen-critic"—which in philosophical terms is a pole apart. The vision that informs *Times v. Sullivan* is that of Alexander Meiklejohn, who saw free speech on public issues as the absolute right and duty of all citizens in a self-governing society.[46] It is a vision of democracy, Steven Shiffrin has said, not "mediaocracy."[47] Professor Shiffrin is surely right in saying that Justice Stewart's explanation "does violence to the language and underlying philosophy of *New York Times Co. v. Sullivan*."[48]

42. 376 U.S. at 256 (emphasis added).

43. *Id.* at 256, 286. A year later the Court summarily reversed a libel judgment won by a Mississippi police chief from a civil rights leader who, on being arrested, issued a public statement saying that his arrest was "a diabolical plot." *See* Henry v. Collins, 380 U.S. 356, 356 (1965). The facts are given in more detail in Petitioner's Brief for Certiorari at 4, Henry v. Collins, 380 U.S. 356 (1965).

44. 376 U.S. at 282 (quoting Barr v. Matteo, 360 U.S. 564, 571 (1959)).

45. *Id.* (citation omitted).

46. *See generally* A. MEIKLEJOHN, POLITICAL FREEDOM (1965). The belief that Meiklejohn's vision informed *Times v. Sullivan* led Professor Kalven to hope that it would prove to be the most important Supreme Court opinion "in the realm of freedom of speech." Kalven, *The New York Times Case: A Note on "The Central Meaning of the First Amendment,"* 1964 SUP. CT. REV. 191, 194.

47. Shiffrin, *Defamatory Non-Media Speech and First Amendment Methodology*, 25 U.C.L.A. L. REV. 915, 923 (1978).

48. *Id.* at 922. It should be added that there is some question now whether there is a constitutional difference between media and nonmedia publishers of defamatory statements about purely private persons. The Court dealt with libel of private persons in Gertz v. Robert Welch, Inc., 418 U.S. 323 (1974). The defendant in *Gertz* was a magazine publisher, and Justice Powell's opinion for the Court spoke of "the press and broadcast media," *id.* at 343. But the Court did not indicate whether the rule there established, that private libel plaintiffs must show at least negligent

Second, Justice Stewart found support for the idea of press exceptionalism in the Supreme Court's close division in *Branzburg v. Hayes*.[49] There, a five-to-four majority rejected claims for a journalist's privilege not to disclose confidential sources, holding that reporters were required to appear before grand juries to testify at least about crimes they had witnessed. If only a free speech claim had been at issue, Justice Stewart suggested, the question "would have answered itself. None of us—as individuals—has a 'free speech' right to refuse to tell a grand jury the identity of someone who has given us information relevant to the grand jury's legitimate inquiry. Only if a reporter is a representative of a protected *institution* does the question become a different one."[50]

But suppose a college lectnrer refused on first amendment grounds to answer a congressional committee's questions about his beliefs and associations. In that somewhat analogous situation the Supreme Court also divided five to four, rejecting the lecturer's claim.[51] Or suppose a professor visited Vietnam during the war, talked with American officials on the basis that he would not disclose their names, wrote a scholarly paper on the war—and was then called before a grand jury and asked the identity of his sources.[52] Would a claim of confidentiality on his part be utterly without weight because he is not a member of "the organized press"? I think many journalists would be uncomfortable with a doctrine of testimonial privilege that included them and excluded

publication of a damaging falsehood to recover, would apply to suits against nonmedia defendants. The American Law Institute has rejected any distinction, saying it would be "strange." *See* RESTATEMENT (SECOND) OF TORTS § 580B(e) (1977). A number of state courts have similarly rejected any distinction between media and nonmedia defendants in libel actions by private plaintiffs. *See, e.g.*, Jacron Sales Co. v. Sindorf, 276 Md. 580, 350 A.2d 688 (1976).

49. 408 U.S. 665 (1972).

50. Stewart, *supra* note 2, at 635 (emphasis in original).

51. *See* Barenblatt v. United States, 360 U.S. 109 (1959).

52. *See* United States v. Doe, 460 F.2d 328 (1st Cir. 1972), *cert. denied*, 411 U.S. 909 (1973). Popkin, an associate professor of government at Harvard, was imprisoned for contempt when he refused to answer certain questions before a grand jury investigating the distribution of the Pentagon Papers. *See* N.Y. Times, Nov. 22, 1972, at 1, col. 1. The president of Harvard appeared as his counsel, and one week later the grand jury's term was ended and Popkin was released. *See* N.Y. Times, Nov. 29, 1972, at 1, col. 1. For an instance of a judge protecting a scholar from forced disclosure in a civil case—on nonconstitutional grounds—see Richards of Rockford, Inc. v. Pacific Gas & Elec. Co., 71 F.R.D. 388 (N.D. Cal. 1976) (declining to enforce, on discovery, demand by plaintiff in civil damage action that third-party academic researcher identify sources of material in scholarly paper on defendant company).

others with similar reasons for silence. In any event I doubt that, for most judges, the question would "answer itself."

Third, Justice Stewart cited cases in which the Supreme Court had rejected claims of access to the press by outsiders.[53] In *Miami Herald Publishing Co. v. Tornillo*,[54] the Court unanimously held unconstitutional a Florida statute requiring newspapers to publish a reply submitted by any candidate for office whom they had criticized. Justice Stewart correctly described the decision as rejecting the idea that government may force a newspaper to be a "fair and open 'market place for ideas.' "[55] But that holding does not imply a distinction between the speech and press clauses of the first amendment. Government can no more require a speaker than a newspaper to be neutral. Justice Holmes' opinions on freedom of speech introduced the concept of the market in ideas,[56] and it was Holmes' point that the most extreme or hateful beliefs must be allowed to compete in that market.[57] His is now the accepted view.[58]

In Professor Nimmer's view, *Tornillo* in another sense did demonstrate that free speech and press can be distinct, even conflicting interests.[59] The Florida law enhanced the right of candidates to speak, he said, but infringed the freedom of the press by compelling publication; thus the two rights were directly in conflict in that case. But the vice of the law lay in the compulsion to publish; and I think the result would be no different if the case involved a compulsion to speak. If a state statute required any candidate who spoke falsely about another to make a corrective speech, would it survive challenge under the first amendment?

The last example given by Justice Stewart of cases assertedly reflecting the special character of the press clause was *New York*

53. Stewart, *supra* note 2, at 633, 635.

54. 418 U.S. 241 (1974).

55. Stewart, *supra* note 2, at 635.

56. *See* Abrams v. United States, 250 U.S. 616, 630 (1919) (Holmes, J., dissenting).

57. "[I]f there is any principle of the Constitution that more imperatively calls for attachment than any other it is the principle of free thought—not free thought for those who agree with us but freedom for the thought that we hate." United States v. Schwimmer, 279 U.S. 644, 654-55 (1929) (Holmes, J., dissenting).

58. "Under the First Amendment there is no such thing as a false idea." Gertz v. Robert Welch, Inc., 418 U.S. 323, 339 (1974). *See also* Collin v. Smith, 578 F.2d 1197 (7th Cir.) (ordinances enacted by village of Skokie, Illinois, to prevent march by American Nazis held unconstitutional), *cert. denied*, 439 U.S. 916 (1978).

59. *See* Nimmer, *Introduction—Is Freedom of the Press A Redundancy: What Does it Add To Freedom of Speech?*, 26 Hastings L.J. 639, 644-46 (1975).

Times Co. v. United States,[60] the *Pentagon Papers Case*, in which the Supreme Court refused to restrain newspaper publication of secret documents on the history of the Vietnam war. The per curiam opinion said that the Government had not met the heavy burden of justification for " '[a]ny system of prior restraints of expression.' "[61]

The doctrine disfavoring prior restraints was established by the opinion of Chief Justice Hughes in *Near v. Minnesota*,[62] a newspaper case. But cases rejecting restraints on publication are not limited to the news media; many have concerned books and pamphlets. The per curiam opinion in the *Pentagon Papers Case* itself relied on a recent decision setting aside an injunction that kept a community organization from distributing literature criticizing a real estate broker for "blockbusting."[63] One of the seminal first amendment decisions of the 1930's, *Lovell v. City of Griffin*,[64] set aside a conviction for distributing pamphlets without a city permit. Chief Justice Hughes, speaking for the Court, said the freedoms of speech and press were "fundamental personal rights."[65] Citing the history of the English struggle against press licensing, with a mention of Milton,[66] Hughes said: "The liberty of the press is not confined to newspapers and periodicals. It necessarily embraces pamphlets . . . ."[67] The city manager's unlimited power to allow or forbid the distribution of pamphlets, he said, "strikes at the very foundation of the freedom of the press."[68] The *Lovell* case was relied upon in *Talley v. California*,[69] which held unconstitutional a Los Angeles ordinance that forbade the distribution of handbills unless they included the names of their authors and distributors.

60. 403 U.S. 713 (1971). *See* Stewart, *supra* note 2, at 635.

61. *Id.* at 714 (quoting Bantam Books, Inc. v. Sullivan, 372 U.S. 58, 70 (1963)). The separate opinions of the six Justices in the majority actually gave two different bases for the judgment in favor of the newspapers. Five Justices relied in whole or part on the prior-restraint doctrine. Five relied in whole or part on the fact that Congress had not authorized the injunctive relief sought by the Government, or had indeed rejected legislation to authorize it: a separation-of-powers basis, as in Youngstown Sheet & Tube Co. v. Sawyer, 343 U.S. 579 (1952). For a view that the *Youngstown* point really decided the case, see Junger, *Down Memory Lane: The Case of the Pentagon Papers*, 23 CASE W. RES. L. REV. 3 (1971).

62. 283 U.S. 697 (1931).

63. 403 U.S. at 714 (citing Organization for a Better Austin v. Keefe, 402 U.S. 415, 419 (1971)).

64. 303 U.S. 444 (1938).

65. *Id.* at 450.

66. *Id.* at 451 (citing J. MILTON, APPEAL FOR THE LIBERTY OF UNLICENSED PRINTING).

67. *Id.* at 452.

68. *Id.* at 451.

69. 362 U.S. 60 (1960).

Justice Black's opinion for the Court, in which Justice Stewart joined, emphasized the value of anonymous books and pamphlets in English and American history.[70]

Nor is the prior-restraint doctrine limited to publications; it also protects freedom of speech and assembly. In *Shuttlesworth v. City of Birmingham*,[71] the Supreme Court reversed a conviction for parading without a permit. Justice Stewart wrote the opinion of the Court. The city permit ordinance was so vague, he said, that it gave officials virtually unbridled discretion. Thus it fell "squarely within the ambit of the many decisions of this Court over the last 30 years" against laws "subjecting the exercise of First Amendment freedoms to the prior restraint of a license."[72]

Case law, then, draws no line between "the organized press" and other publications—books, pamphlets, handbills—in their right to freedom of the press. Nor do the cases distinguish the quality of freedom assured to the press and to speech. Of course there are practical distinctions between speeches and publications, and between newspapers and books; and the law takes them into account. But as the decided cases show, they are distinctions without a difference in constitutional principle. No Supreme Court decision has held or intimated that journalism has a preferred constitutional position.

PRINCIPLE

The practical consequences of the Stewart thesis, if it became accepted constitutional doctrine, would not be as beneficial to journalists as many of them believe. And the thesis is against the real interest of the press, and of society, for deeper reasons of principle.

The whole idea of treating the press as an "institution" arouses uneasy feelings. In the American system, institutions are usually subject to external check. The press has operated as a freebooter, outside the system. The more formally it is treated as a fourth branch of government, the more pressing will be demands that it be made formally accountable.[73] Moreover, as Robert M. Kaus has

70. *Id.* at 64-65.

71. 394 U.S. 147 (1969); *accord*, Hague v. Committee for Indus. Org., 307 U.S. 496 (1939).

72. 394 U.S. at 150-51.

73. The following statement is illustrative: "The extraordinary protections afforded by the First Amendment carry with them somethiug in the nature of a fiduciary duty to exercise the protected rights responsibly—a duty widely acknowledged but not always observed by editors and publishers." Nebraska Press Ass'n v. Stuart,

suggested, the institutional view of the first amendment envisages a corporate organization of society, with groups assigned different roles and corresponding legal rights. The traditional American vision has been universal, positing a society of individuals with equal rights and responsibilities:[74] Justice Brennan's citizen-critics.[75]

Who Is the Press?

If a majority of the Supreme Court accepted the proposition that freedom of "the press" in the first amendment gives special status to the news media, the next question would be: Who is "the press"? Would the definition be limited to Justice Stewart's "established" newspapers, magazines, and broadcasters? Could it exclude underground papers? Journals of sexual exploitation? A sheet of viciously racist tone, like the new weekly at issue in *Near v. Minnesota*?[76] In the age of the electronic copier, what about the citizen moved by outrage at some local development to circulate his or her views among neighbors? Or what of a specialty publication such as a Wall Street tip sheet: Could the Securities and Exchange Commission regulate it without violating the freedom of "the press"?[77]

These questions are not fanciful. They would inevitably arise, and they would force the courts to go into the business of defining "the press," of deciding who qualified for the higher constitutional status. Justice White foresaw the problem in his opinion for the Court in *Branzburg*. Selecting those entitled to a journalist's constitutional privilege, he said, "would present practical and conceptual difficulties of a high order."[78] In making the selection, courts would be drawn into "discriminating on the basis of content."[79]

---

427 U.S. 539, 560 (1976). The opinion, by Chief Justice Burger, made that appeal for self-restraint in the context of a holding that the courts could not, except in the most extreme circumstances, enjoin publication of a story that might affect the opinions of jurors in a pending criminal case.

74. Kaus, *The Constitution, the Press and the Rest of Us*, WASH. MONTHLY, Nov. 1974, at 50, 52. As an example of the universalist outlook, Kaus refers to the rule of one man, one vote. *Id.*

75. *See* text accompanying notes 44-47 *supra.*

76. 283 U.S. 697 (1931). Only nine issues of the Saturday Press, the newspaper in *Near*, were published. *Id.* at 703. The paper's antisemitic character is made clear in Justice Butler's dissent. *Id.* at 724 n.1 (Butler, J., dissenting).

77. *See* SEC v. Wall St. Transcript Corp., 422 F.2d 1371 (2d Cir. 1970) (requiring investment advisory newspaper to register under Investment Advisers Act of 1940, 15 U.S.C. §§ 806-1 to -21 (1976), does not violate first amendment).

78. 408 U.S. at 703-04.

79. *Id.* at 705 n.40.

Would the media really welcome this new form of judicial licensing?

Some supporters of the Stewart thesis, perhaps recognizing the risks in its exclusivist character, have tried to make it more appealing by broadening its definition of "the press." In *Herbert v. Lando*, Judge Oakes, while relying explicitly on Justice Stewart's speech, said he would not draw any "distinction between the institutional press and the individual pamphleteer."[80] Floyd Abrams, in his Supreme Court brief for the media respondents in *Herbert*, embraced that position; the press clause of the first amendment, he said, fully covered "the lonely pamphleteer."[81] But if the definition is thus broadened, then any publication becomes "the press" and Justice Stewart's thesis loses its point. His argument was that the first amendment has special meaning for the news media.

The Danger of Exclusivity

The danger of exclusivity was demonstrated when Justice Stewart applied his thesis in literal terms to a case before the Court. The case was *Zurcher v. Stanford Daily*.[82] A majority held that authorities could search a newspaper office under warrant —that is, without notice or a prior adversary hearing—for documentary evidence of a crime committed by other parties. Justice Stevens dissented on the ground that notice should ordinarily be required before such a search of any third party: one not suspected of crime.[83] Justice Stewart, in an opinion joined by Justice Marshall, dissented on the ground that the search violated the freedom of the press. He wrote:

> Perhaps as a matter of abstract policy a newspaper office should receive no more protection from unannounced police searches than, say, the office of a doctor or the office of a bank. But we are here to uphold a Constitution. And our Constitution

80. 568 F.2d at 994 n.34 (Oakes, J., concurring).

81. Brief for Respondents at 55-56, Herbert v. Lando, 99 S. Ct. 1635 (1979) (citing Lovell v. City of Griffin, 303 U.S. 444 (1938)).

82. 436 U.S. 547 (1978).

83. *Id.* at 581 (Stevens, J., dissenting). Some immediate scholarly comment agreed with Justice Stevens' view of the case. *See* Harv. L. Rec., Sept. 29, 1978, at 5, col. 1 (comments of Professors Freund and Katz). The Stevens argument is the more compelling because the opinion of the Court failed to discuss a central fact noted by the dissent: that when the Court first allowed searches for "mere evidence," in Warden v. Hayden, 387 U.S. 294, 300 (1967), it was dealing with the evidence of a criminal suspect's clothes; it left open the more sensitive question of documentary evidence.

does not explicitly protect the practice of medicine or the business of banking from all abridgment by government. It does explicitly protect the freedom of the press.[84]

In Justice Stewart's view, then, the Constitution forbids the unannounced search of a newspaper office for photographs of a felony; but it allows the police, without notice, to search a psychiatrist's files,[85] or Ralph Nader's.[86] I think such a concept of the Constitution would be quite unacceptable to most Americans. The Constitution protects values, not particular classes of people. And the values are not limited to those listed by name in the Constitution; if the significance of that eighteenth-century document were limited by such literalism, it would long since have become a museum piece.[87]

If attention is focused on the rights of the organized press, damage to other vital first amendment interests may occur without adequate awareness or resistance. Relatively little outcry was heard when the Fourth Circuit developed the doctrine that in my judgment presents the most serious threat in American constitutional history to public knowledge of government: the secrecy-by-contract doctrine of *United States v. Marchetti*.[88] Because he had signed a secrecy agreement upon joining the agency, a former official of the Central Intelligence Agency was enjoined from publishing a book on CIA activities without the agency's prior censorship.[89] When

---

84. 436 U.S. at 576 (Stewart, J., dissenting).

85. The example is not hypothetical. *See A Justice Dept. Memo Says Liddy and Hunt Raided Office of Ellsberg's Psychiatrist*, N.Y. Times, Apr. 28, 1973, at 1, col. 4.

86. Nader would apparently be covered by legislation suggested by the Carter administration six months after the decision in *Zurcher*. The proposal was to prohibit searches by either state or federal officers for the work product of anyone preparing a publication or speech for dissemination in, or affecting, interstate commerce. The work product would include notes, drafts, outtakes, photographs, tapes, and files. The Justice Department said its intention was to cover not only the news media but scholars, freelance writers, and pamphleteers. *See* Lewis, *A Blow for Liberty*, N.Y. Times, Dec. 14, 1978, at A31, col. 1.

87. The word "reputation" is not found in the Constitution, but Justice Stewart once said that reputation has weight in the constitutional scale because it reflects "our basic concept of the essential dignity and worth of every human being." Rosenblatt v. Baer, 383 U.S. 75, 92 (1966) (Stewart, J., concurring).

88. 466 F.2d 1309 (4th Cir.), *cert. denied*, 409 U.S. 1063 (1972).

89. The court found the secrecy agreement to be a legally enforceable contract, which it said took the case out from under the prior-restraint rule that had just been reaffirmed by the Supreme Court in New York Times Co. v. United States, 403 U.S. 713 (1971). 466 F.2d at 1316-17. It did not discuss the need, suggested by Supreme Court cases, *see, e.g.*, Greene v. McElroy, 360 U.S. 474, 506-08 (1959), to find explicit authorization by Congress for executive action that raises serious constitutional doubts.

the agency made massive deletions and the author sought judicial review, the court gave the CIA virtually unreviewable discretion to delete any passage that it said contained information classified during the author's employment.[90] He was also enjoined for the rest of his life from disclosing such information "in any manner."[91] In a subsequent case[92] the United States sued another former CIA employee who had already published a book; the Government did not allege that he had disclosed any classified matter; but it claimed, and was awarded, damages because he had failed to submit the manuscript to the agency for clearance.

Those decisions have had much less attention in the news media than cases involving journalists, although they present direct and profound threats to the core purpose of the first amendment: keeping the public aware of what its government does. And the journalist-centered view of the first amendment may well reduce the legal prospects of a Victor Marchetti. The insistence that a particular class has special immunities under the first amendment is likely to suggest to judges that persons outside that class are of a lower order of constitutional concern.

The idea that the news media are constitutionally unique may also encourage hubris, the excessive pride that goes before a fall. Powerful newspapers and networks are not universally beloved as it is; there is talk about the arrogance of the media. Ordinary citizens may find it hard to understand why the press should have rights denied to them. And in the long run, rights depend on public understanding and support.[93] Professor Bork has put it succinctly: "To the degree that the press is alone in the enjoyment of freedom, to that degree is its freedom imperilled."[94]

---

90. *See* Alfred A. Knopf, Inc. v. Colby, 509 F.2d 1362 (4th Cir.), *cert. denied*, 421 U.S. 992 (1975). The book was published with blank spaces for the censored passages. V. MARCHETTI & J. MARKS, THE CIA AND THE CULT OF INTELLIGENCE (1974).

91. The text of the injunction appears in Petitioner's Petition for a Writ of Certiorari at 83a app., Alfred A. Knopf, Inc. v. Colby, 421 U.S. 992 (1975).

92. United States v. Snepp, 456 F. Supp. 176 (E.D. Va. 1978), *aff'd in part, rev'd in part*, No. 78-1651 (4th Cir. Mar. 20, 1979).

93. Vermont Royster of the *Wall Street Journal* has said:

> That first amendment we cherish is not some immutable right handed down to Moses on Mt. Sinai. It's a political right granted by the people in a political document, and what the people grant they can, if they choose, take away. There is no liberty that cannot be abused and none that cannot be lost.

Royster, *Reflections on the Fourth Estate*, Wash. Post, Dec. 25, 1978, at A19, col. 1.

94. R. Bork, Freedom, the Courts and the Media 13 (Dec. 8, 1978) (address to

The Right to Gather News

One legal issue has become the focus of the debate about a special constitutional position for journalists: the claim that the first amendment affords a right to gather news, and stemming from that a testimonial privilege to protect the confidentiality of news sources. It is this claim that journalists have lately been pressing with the greatest fervor, and that for some critics raises the sharpest questions about press exceptionalism.[95]

The issue was dramatized, for press and public, in *In re Farber*.[96] M.A. Farber, a reporter for the *New York Times*, was assigned in 1975 to follow up a tip about thirteen suspicious deaths in a New Jersey hospital a decade earlier.[97] On the basis of interviews with confidential sources, he wrote articles suggesting that "Dr. *X*" had poisoned the patients with curare. The local prosecutor reopened the case, and Dr. Mario Jascalevich was charged with five murders.

At his trial in 1978, Dr. Jascalevich's lawyer subpoenaed all the notes Farber had made in reporting the story in 1975 and 1976. He and the *Times* both declined to produce the notes, claiming a privilege under the first amendment and under a New Jersey shield law for journalists.[98] At a minimum, they argued, they should not have to respond to such an indiscriminate subpoena; the defendant should have to show that particular items were likely to be relevant, material, and unobtainable by other means.[99] The trial judge ordered the notes delivered to him for examination in camera, a process he said was necessary to pass on the legal arguments.[100] When the *Times* and Farber declined to

---

the William O. Douglas Inquiry into the State of Individual Freedom), *reprinted in* CENTER MAGAZINE, Mar./Apr. 1979, at 28, 34.

95. Royster has warned that

> [w]e should be especially wary of claiming for ourselves alone exemptions from the obligations of all citizens, including the obligation to bear witness once due process has been observed. There is nothing in the Bill of Rights, including the first amendment, that makes the press a privileged class apart. The risk is that the people may think us arrogant.

Royster, *supra* note 93, at A19, col. 1.

96. 78 N.J. 259, 394 A.2d 330, *cert. denied*, 439 U.S. 997 (1978).

97. For the history of Farber's involvement, see *An Almost Routine Assignment Led to Historic Case*, N.Y. Times, Nov. 28, 1978, at B8, col. 1.

98. *See* N.J. STAT. ANN. § 2A:84A-21 (West 1976 & Supp. 1979-1980).

99. Brief for Appellants at 31-35, *In re* Farber, 78 N.J. 259, 394 A.2d 330, *cert. denied*, 439 U.S. 997 (1978). *See In re* Farber, 78 N.J. 259, 276-77, 394 A.2d 330, 338, *cert. denied*, 439 U.S. 997 (1978).

100. State v. Jascalevich, No. S-495-76 (N.J. Super. Ct. June 30, 1978) (oral opinion of Arnold, J.).

obey that order, they were held in contempt. The *Times* was fined $100,000, plus $5,000 for each day it remained in contempt. Farber was fined $1,000, ordered to jail until he changed his mind, and, in addition, given a six-month sentence for criminal contempt to begin when he complied with the order or when the case was resolved.[101]

The New Jersey Supreme Court affirmed,[102] holding that the first amendment argument had been rejected in *Branzburg*[103] and that the state shield law, while in terms protecting Farber, had to yield to the New Jersey constitutional provision assuring defendants the right to compel evidence on their behalf.[104] In deference to the legislature's intent in enacting the shield law, the court agreed that a particularized showing of need was required to force production of a journalist's notes, even for purposes of in camera inspection;[105] but it said the facts were so obvious in this case that the judge did not have to bother with the requirement.[106] Farber had been in jail forty days, and the *Times* fined $285,000, by the time the trial ended in Jascalevich's acquittal. The further six-month prison sentence was then dropped.[107]

There is much to criticize in the performance of the courts in the Farber case. A rule requiring a particularized showing should apply in all cases, not every case except the one in which the rule is laid down. If a newly enacted statute squarely supports a claim of testimonial privilege, those who rely on it in good faith surely should not be imprisoned and subjected to huge fines unless and until an authoritative decision holds the statute void. Farber himself asserted no absolutes and sought no clash with the law; when he went to prison, on grounds of principle, he said: "I deeply appreciate how much our civilization, and civility, depend on order and the rule of law."[108] Yet he was treated in the state courts with a rigor seldom shown to thieves, and a federal judge verbally

101. *In re* Farber, No. S-495-76 (N.J. Super. Ct. July 24, 1978) (oral opinion of Trautwein, J.).

102. *In re* Farber, 78 N.J. 259, 394 A.2d 330, *cert. denied,* 439 U.S. 997 (1978).

103. *Id.* at 266-68, 394 A.2d at 333-34 (discussing Branzburg v. Hayes, 408 U.S. 665 (1972)).

104. *Id.* at 269-74, 394 A.2d at 335-37 (citing N.J. CONST. art. 1, ¶ 10).

105. *Id.* at 275-77, 394 A.2d at 338.

106. *Id.* at 277-81, 394 A.2d at 339-41.

107. *See* Wash. Post, Oct. 25, 1978, at A1, col. 2.

108. Farber, *Statements by Farber and the New York Times,* N.Y. Times, July 25, 1978, at B6, col. 4.

abused him without basis in fact or any effort to discover the facts.[109] Farber deserved respect.[110] But that is not the same as saying that his was the only side to the case.

During the proceedings the Executive Editor of the *Times*, A.M. Rosenthal, issued a statement saying:

> Mr. Farber and The Times have been fighting this case because they feel it goes to the heart of the constitutional guarantee of the first amendment. It has always been believed that the first amendment guarantees the right not only to print the news freely but to gather it freely. It is quite plain that without the right to gather information, the right to print it means little. We believe the right to gather information will eventually be destroyed if any branch of government, including the judiciary, has the right to seize and make public a reporter's notes, confidential information and raw material.[111]

Many in the news business share those views, but they are not the law—or the fact. Two professors of journalism, under a grant from a journalism-based foundation, recently made historical studies of the claim that the first amendment guarantees the right to

---

109. United States District Judge Frederick B. Lacey, after a brief hearing on a petition for habeas corpus, made findings that, among other things, " 'Farber has a stake in the conviction of Dr. Jascalevich . . . . This is a sorry spectacle of a reporter who purported to stand on his reporter's privilege when in fact he was standing on an alter [*sic*] of greed. . . . What he did here is . . . evil . . . .' " Application to Vacate Stay of Single Justice at 17, New York Times Co. v. New Jersey, 439 U.S. 886 (quoting United States District Court Judge Lacey), *cert. denied*, 439 U.S. 997 (1978). Judge Lacey's statements were based upon conclusions he erroneously drew from Farber's intention to write a book. The judge seemed to believe that the book contract, which was before him, made Farber's remuneration dependent upon the conviction of defendant Jascalevich; it did not. *See* Response of The New York Times Company and Myron Farber to Application to Vacate Stay at 1-7 app., New York Times Co. v. New Jersey, 439 U.S. 886, *cert. denied*, 439 U.S. 997 (1978), which demonstrates that the "findings" were made in the absence of any evidence or in contradiction of the record. In my opinion, the transcript presents a sorry spectacle of judicial abuse.

110. Professor Ronald Dworkin, in an article arguing that Farber, in seeking a privilege, asserted interests of public policy that had to yield to the rights of the defendant, nevertheless praised Farber and the *Times* for raising the issues. He added that the New Jersey courts were unreasonable in jailing Farber and making the *Times* "pay punitive daily fines while their legal arguments were pending before appellate courts." Dworkin, *The Rights of Myron Farber*, N.Y. REV. BOOKS, Oct. 26, 1978, at 34, 36. Dworkin challenged the relevance of Farber's book contract, criticized by Judge Lacey. *Id.* at 36 n.*. For a further decimation of the book-contract red herring, see Kwitny, *A Judicial War on the Press?*, Wall St. J., Aug. 23, 1978, at 12, col. 4.

111. N.Y. Times, Aug. 2, 1978, at A15, col. 6.

gather news.[112] One wrote that he was "sad to say there is no evidence" to support the claim.[113] The other concluded: "I can't think of a more dubious proposition for a journalist to try to support."[114]

No Supreme Court decision has ever enforced a constitutional right to gather news. Without such a right, the American press has performed more boldly and with greater freedom than any other press in the world. Judicial inspection of subpoenaed material in camera cannot accurately be described as seizing material and making it public; judges routinely examine trade secrets, national security records, and other sensitive matter to decide on its use, and they keep confidences. Nor is it accurate in this country to speak of courts as an arm of the state. They often stand against the state; they have stood up even to its highest officer. In *United States v. Nixon*,[115] the President asserted a privilege to withhold tapes of intimate White House conversations subpoenaed by the Special Prosecutor. The Supreme Court agreed that there was a qualified privilege based on the Constitution[116] but held that it was overridden

---

112. The studies, sponsored by the Gannett Foundation, were made by Professors Don R. Pember of the University of Washington and Harold L. Nelson of the University of Wisconsin. Articles by them were published, together with a comment by Professor Donald M. Gillmor of the School of Journalism, University of Minnesota, in BULL. AM. SOC'Y NEWSPAPER EDITORS, Dec./Jan. 1979, at 6-9. A leading newspaper writer on questions of journalism commented:

> The verdict of the professors will not end the claims of news people that the gathering of news must have special protection if the press is to serve effectively as the public's watchdog and informer. But it should put to rest any illusion that the position of the current Supreme Court is just an aberration—Nixon's Revenge, some journalists call it—and that all that is needed is a return to the thinking of the Founders.

Seib, *The Right to Publish (and Gather?) News*, Wash. Post, Dec. 22, 1978, at A13, col. 1.

113. Pember, *Founders (meeting in secret) protected our right to publish, but not to gather the news*, BULL. AM. SOC'Y NEWSPAPER EDITORS, Dec./Jan. 1979, at 6. Professor Pember wrote that a "right to gather news" was not discussed at the time of the first amendment's adoption, or for years after, for a simple reason:

> Consider the "newspapers" of that era. News-gathering was hardly a prime function. These were papers of opinion and ideas. . . . News-gathering, reporting, access to government information as we speak of it today was not really an important part of the American press of that era. It is not surprising then that that concept was not considered a part of the definition of freedom of the press. (Reporting, per se, really didn't begin to be important until the 1830's.)

Id.

114. Nelson, *Separating the inseparable? Linking news-gathering with publishing called 'dubious,'* BULL. AM. SOC'Y NEWSPAPER EDITORS, Dec./Jan. 1979, at 7.

115. 418 U.S. 683 (1974).

116. *Id.* at 705-06 (discussing U.S. CONST. art. II).

by the particularized needs of law enforcement.[117] Not even the argument that an adverse decision would cripple the Presidency[118] persuaded the Court to reject the claims of law. Most editors applauded the *Nixon* decision.[119] They should be slow to argue that the press will be crippled unless its claims of privilege always prevail.

Law and common sense both reject the notion that journalists alone in the society have an overriding constitutional claim to secrecy. Their interest is a serious one. But in the real world it must inevitably be balanced against other interests. That is plain if one considers how the courts would feel—how the public would feel, indeed—if various parties sought the same information that Farber had. The balance of interests would vary.

Suppose, for example, that a congressional committee subpoenaed Farber's notes and that he declined to produce them, relying on the first amendment. If the committee had only a general interest to justify its inquiry, Farber would surely have a good chance of persuading a court not to sustain a contempt citation. In *Sweezy v. New Hampshire*,[120] Justice Frankfurter, who did not treat state interests lightly, concluded that the state's asserted desire to investigate subversion had to yield to the claims of academic freedom—to the political privacy of a university lecturer.[121] In such a balance, I believe Farber's interest would be just as weighty.

Next, suppose a grand jury sought Farber's notes. *Branzburg* indicates that he would have to produce them unless he could show, in the words of Justice Powell's concurring opinion, that his information was "remote"[122] from the subject of the investigation or that he would be forced to disclose confidential sources "without a legitimate need of law enforcement."[123]

Finally, suppose a journalist's notes were sought by a defendant, as Farber's were—a defendant, moreover, who found himself

117. *Id.* at 706-07.

118. Counsel for President Nixon argued that an adverse decision would "impair markedly the ability of every President of the United States from this time forward to perform the constitutional duties vested in him," and would "alter the nature of the American Presidency profoundly and irreparably." Brief for Respondent at 135, 137, United States v. Nixon, 418 U.S. 683 (1974).

119. *See, e.g., The Court Speaks*, N.Y. Times, July 25, 1974, at 32, col. 1.

120. 354 U.S. 234 (1957).

121. *Id.* at 265-67 (Frankfurter, J., concurring in result).

122. 408 U.S. at 710 (Powell, J., concurring). Justice Powell's concurrence was crucial because he provided the fifth vote.

123. *Id.* (Powell, J., concurring).

in the dock largely because of articles by Farber. A defendant has an unusually explicit constitutional right to compel evidence on his behalf: "In all criminal prosecutions, the accused shall enjoy the right . . . to have compulsory process for obtaining witnesses in his favor . . . ."[124] And a reporter's notes could be useful. Witnesses sometimes change their stories, and a reporter's record of what a prosecution witness said years before about the defendant could be vital for impeachment purposes on cross-examination. That was the principle of *Jencks v. United States*,[125] holding that in federal prosecutions the defense must be allowed to see prior statements made by witnesses to the government. When a defendant seeks information from a journalist with genuine knowledge of the case, there are strong interests—constitutional interests—on the defendant's side. Those who assert a press privilege would win more respect for their position if they admitted as much.[126]

The outcome of the *Farber* case evoked some cries of doom in the press.[127] Theodore H. White, in an article headed "Why the

124. U.S. CONST. amend. VI.

125. 353 U.S. 657 (1957). The Jencks Act, 18 U.S.C. § 3500 (1976), was passed to codify and limit the *Jencks* decision. S. REP. NO. 981, 85th Cong., 1st Sess., *reprinted in* [1957] U.S. CODE CONG. & AD. NEWS 1861.

126. It is sometimes said that denial of a journalist's privilege is inconsistent with the granting of a privilege to lawyers and others. Kwitny wrote that journalists "are now being denied privileges commonly accorded to private lawyers, doctors, priests and so on." Kwitny, *supra* note 110, at 12, col. 4. In *Farber* the New Jersey Supreme Court did not explain, and should have, why it honors those privileges when created by statute, but held the shield law unconstitutional to the extent that it would deny a defendant relevant evidence; any privilege, after all, keeps out evidence. But I think there is an explanation. The older privileges are for the benefit not of the doctor or lawyer or priest, but of the patient or client or penitent, who alone can waive the privilege. Each of these persons is a defendant or prospective defendant, and the privilege in these situations is akin to the fifth amendment privilege against compelled self-incrimination: It protects a defendant from having a private confession used by the state, as if he had been tricked into incriminating himself. The journalist's privilege is designed not to protect an individual but to advance the general public interest in the flow of information.

But the differences between the claimed journalist's privilege and others do not justify judicial disrespect for a legislature's decision to extend a privilege to newsmen. A disturbing feature of the *Farber* decision was the abrupt way in which the New Jersey Supreme Court brushed aside a considered judgment of its legislature. The court might, for example, have accommodated the defendant's interest and the public interest found by the legislature by holding that the prosecution of Dr. Jascalevich must be dismissed unless Farber produced his notes for in camera inspection. At a minimum, the court might have discussed that and other possible accommodations of the statute and the Constitution. After all, in *Branzburg* the Supreme Court pointedly invited state legislatures and Congress to enact journalists' shield laws if they found that conditions so required. *See* 408 U.S. at 706.

127. *But see* Royster, *Minority View on Newsmen's Rights*, Wall St. J., Aug. 16, 1978, at 22, col. 4. Royster wrote: "What we in this craft must guard against is a knee-action reflex that anything we find inconvenient or annoying is somehow a vio-

Jailing of Farber 'Terrifies Me,' "[128] said the files that he had accumulated in forty years as a journalist would now be at the mercy of "any politician styled 'judge.' "[129] If the Supreme Court let the Farber decision stand, he said, "I should at once go back to my files and start burning up my old notes."[130] As an example of the danger, White wrote: "Had the jurisprudence that threw Farber into prison prevailed in 1974, the attorneys of Messrs. Mitchell, Haldeman and Ehrlichman could have demanded that [Bob] Woodward and [Carl] Bernstein give up their notes and so reveal the identity/identities of 'Deep Throat' or go to jail."[131] But the "jurisprndence" did exist in 1974. *Branzburg* had been decided in 1972,[132] and counsel for the Watergate coverup defendants were intelligent and determined enough to make use of it if it had promised to be helpful. Counsel did not subpoena the *Washington Post* reporters' notes because they obviously included no information significant to that trial, and a subpoena would not have been enforced.

Confidential sources are unquestionably crncial, these days, to a high function of the press: exposing abuse in our institutions. There is no real chance of discovering wrongdoing in the CIA[133] unless an insider decides to talk, and usually he does so only on condition that his name not be used. But it does not follow that the press will find no confidential sources unless it has an assured testimonial privilege not to name them in court. In Britain the press has no such privilege and operates in general under stringent legal inhibitions;[134] yet the serious newspaper with the largest circulation, the *Sunday Times*, produces outstanding investigative re-

---

lation of the first amendment. There are too many real battles to be fought for freedom of speech and of the press." *Id.*

128. White, *Why the Jailing of Farber "Terrifies Me,"* N.Y. Times, Nov. 26, 1978, § 6 (Magazine), at 27.

129. *Id.* at 84.

130. *Id.* The Court did. Has he burned his notes?

131. *Id.* at 76.

132. To be precise, *Branzburg* was decided on June 29, 1972. That was 12 days after the break-in at Democratic party headquarters in the Watergate. It has always seemed to me extraordinary prescience that Justice White included this observation in his opinion: "In *United States v. Burr*, 25 F. Cas. 30, 34 (No. 14,692d) (C.C. Va 1807), Chief Justice Marshall, sitting on Circuit, opined that in proper circumstances a subpoena could be issued to the President of the United States." 408 U.S. at 688 n.26.

133. *See, e.g., Huge CIA Operation Reported in U.S. Against Antiwar Forces, Other Dissidents in Nixon Years,* N.Y. Times, Dec. 22, 1974, § 1, at 1, col. 8 (by Seymour M. Hersh).

134. British restrictions on the press are canvassed in Evans, *The Half-Free Press*, in THE FREEDOM OF THE PRESS (Granada Guildhall Lectures 1974).

ports.[135] The idea of a testimonial privilege under the first amendment was not even raised in this country until 1958;[136] reporters managed to function without it. My guess is that most confidential sources talk to the press for their own compelling reasons of conscience or ideology or personal animus—and will continue to do so even if an occasional case demonstrates that reporters may come under legal pressure to name their sources.

A publicized case like Farber's will of course inspire some defense lawyers to try the gambit of press subpoenas.[137] But judges are capable of dealing with lawyers who abuse the process.[138] In this country, as in Britain, the number of reporters who have actually gone to jail to protect their sources for genuine pieces of investigative reporting is very small.[139] And one can hardly argue that the number of press reports based on confidential sources is decreasing. Theodore White said there "would have been no exposure of the My Lai massacre had it not been for the ability of a brave reporter to persuade a handful of men in the United States Army to tell the truth."[140] But that premier investigative reporter, Seymour M. Hersh of the *New York Times*, does not believe that the denial of a legal privilege to the press has made it harder to get confidential information.[141] It would be different, very different, if

135. *See, e.g.*, SUNDAY TIMES (LONDON), THE THALIDOMIDE CHILDREN AND THE LAW (1973).

136. *See* Branzburg v. Hayes, 408 U.S. 665, 698 (1972). The 1958 case in which the claim was first raised is Garland v. Torre, 259 F.2d 545 (2d Cir.), *cert. denied*, 358 U.S. 910 (1958). Justice Stewart, then a Sixth Circuit judge, but sitting by designation with the Second, wrote the opinion.

137. *Subpoenas of Notes of Reporters Grow*, N.Y. Times, Nov. 19, 1978, § 1, at 38, col. 1.

138. One judge has noted: " 'Lawyers are beginning to abuse the privilege of requiring newspaper reporters to come in with their notes and to testify. This is not the function of a newspaper reporter, not the function of the court.' " *3 Newspaper Reporters to Comply with Subpoenas to Testify on L.I.*, N.Y. Times, Mar. 5, 1979, at B2, col. 5 (quoting Judge Joseph Jaspin of New York Supreme Court).

139. According to the Reporters Committee for Freedom of the Press, since 1972 at least 12 reporters have gone to jail for refusing to disclose confidential sources and information. *See* Reporters Committee for Freedom of the Press, Reporters Taken into Custody (Apr. 18, 1979) (internal compilation on file in committee's Washington, D.C., office). But this compilation includes a number of reporters who were imprisoned for violating a court order against disclosure of grand jury minutes and refusing to tell the court where they had obtained the minutes—action that hardly rises to the level of genuine investigative reporting.

140. White, *supra* note 128, at 76.

141. I do not see any sign that reporters are finding it any more difficult to get secret information and documents now than before the Farber case. In fact, for the past ten years—when the issue of sources and concern about judicial decisions was developing—we have seen a steadily escalating volume of leaks.

Statement by Seymour M. Hersh to the Author (Dec. 1, 1978).

a government set out to expose the sources of embarrassing newspaper stories for political reasons, as has happened in South Africa.[142] But any such attempt in the United States would be fought in the courts and beaten. Nothing in *Branzburg* or *Farber* allows exposure for exposure's sake.[143]

The privilege cases have brought from some corners of the press strident attacks on the motives and character of judges. After the decision in *Zurcher v. Stanford Daily*, a columnist wrote that "one of the worst Supreme Courts in our history" had "delivered an atrociously un-American ruling."[144] During the *Farber* case a *Wall Street Journal* reporter commented: "The judiciary—certainly not all of it, but enough of it to lay down the law—has for all practical purposes declared war against the press."[145] Is such hysteria supposed to increase respect for the press' judgment? Only someone unfamiliar with the overwhelmingly conservative history of the Supreme Court[146] could describe the current Court as "worst" in first amendment terms. Only someone unwilling to look at the recent record of major press victories in the law[147] would be silly enough to talk of a judicial war on the press.

It seems especially ill advised to picture the courts as the enemy when judges have so often protected the press and the rest of society from the branch of government that most often tends to abuse its power, the executive. Yet journalists, perhaps currently intoxicated by the notion of press exceptionalism, do often see judges as enemies. At one conference of journalists, judges, and

142. *See* N.Y. Times, Dec. 12, 1978, at A3, col. 3. The story quotes Prime Minister P.W. Botha as promising legislation to curb "gossip mongering" by forcing "people or parties," including newspapers, to disclose their sources of information.

143. The Court said in *Branzburg* that it was not dealing with "a governmental institution that has abused its proper function, as a legislative committee does when it 'expose[s] for the sake of exposure.'" 408 U.S. at 699-700 (quoting Watkins v. United States, 354 U.S. 178, 200 (1957)).

144. Rowan, *This Supreme Court Doesn't Understand*, Wash. Star, June 7, 1978, at A19, col. 6.

145. Kwitny, *supra* note 110, at 12, col. 4.

146. "[N]ever in its entire history can the Supreme Court be said to have for a single hour been representative of anything except the relatively conservative forces of its day." R. JACKSON, THE STRUGGLE FOR JUDICIAL SUPREMACY 187 (1949).

147. The major press victories in the 1970's include: Nebraska Press Ass'n v. Stuart, 427 U.S. 539 (1976); Miami Herald Publishing Co. v. Tornillo, 418 U.S. 241 (1974); New York Times Co. v. United States, 403 U.S. 713 (1971). And for two cases holding that the press cannot be penalized for printing names that appear in court records but are officially designated as confidential, see Landmark Communications, Inc. v. Virginia, 435 U.S. 829 (1978) (name of judge under investigation for misconduct), and Cox Broadcasting Corp. v. Cohn, 420 U.S. 469 (1975) (name of rape victim).

lawyers—occasions that seem to bring out the machismo in journalists—a judge usually sympathetic to the press listened to the steady stream of abuse until he could remain silent no longer. He said:

> Where, ladies and gentlemen, do you think these great constitutional rights that you are so vehemently asserting, and in which you were so conspicuously wallowing yesterday, where do you think they came from? The stork didn't bring them. These came from the judges of this country, from these villains here sitting at the table.[148]

Justice Stewart is hardly to be held responsible if the press is sometimes strident in its own cause, sounding as if its own rights were central to freedom and all others peripheral. But on the question of confidential sources, which is more troubling to reporters and editors than any other legal issue, his opinions have embraced the press' cause. His dissent in *Zurcher* has been noted.[149] Dissenting in *Branzburg*, he sounded a major press theme when he said, "A corollary of the right to publish must be the right to gather news . . . . News must not be unnecessarily cut off at its source, for without freedom to acquire information the right to publish would be impermissibly compromised. Accordingly, a right to gather news, of some dimensions, must exist."[150]

But Justice Stewart's argument that a testimonial privilege arises from a first amendment "right to gather news" presents a paradox. For, two years after *Branzburg*, Justice Stewart wrote the opinion of the Court in *Pell v. Procunier*,[151] holding that the press has no greater right than the public at large to gather news in a prison. He relied on the majority's statement in *Branzburg* that " 'the First Amendment does not guarantee the press a constitutional right of special access to information not available to the public generally.' "[152] Toward the end of his Yale speech he made the point again, in words not so welcome to the press: "There is no constitutional right to have access to particular government information, or to require openness from the bureaucracy. . . . The

148. THE MEDIA AND THE LAW 36-37 (H. Simons & J. Califano eds. 1976). Under the rules of the conference, the book does not give the name of the judge it quotes.

149. *See* text accompanying note 84 *supra*.

150. 408 U.S. at 727-28 (Stewart, J., dissenting) (citations omitted).

151. 417 U.S. 817 (1974).

152 *Id.* at 833 (quoting Branzburg v. Hayes, 408 U.S. 665, 684 (1972)).

Constitution itself is neither a Freedom of Information Act nor an Official Secrets Act."[153] Then, in *Houchins v. KQED, Inc.*,[154] Justice Stewart indicated that government could completely exclude both press and public from jails and other public facilities: "The First and Fourteenth Amendments do not guarantee the public a right of access to information generated or controlled by government, nor do they guarantee the press any basic right of access superior to that of the public generally."[155]

How can a judge say in one case that the first amendment affords a "right to gather news," and in another that the amendment does not give anyone "a right of access to information generated or controlled by government"? How can he tell journalists in one breath that the Constitution treats them differently from everyone else, and in the next that they have no more rights than the public? The mystery has a solution, I think, but it requires some exploration.

Based on the precedents, Justice Stewart is plainly right that the Constitution does not give the press or anyone else a general right of access to information. Chief Justice Warren, writing for the Court when it rejected a claim that restrictions on travel to Cuba violated a right to acquire information, said: "The right to speak and publish does not carry with it the unrestrained right to gather information."[156] The most frequently cited judicial affirmation that such a right exists is Justice White's statement for the majority in *Branzburg* that "news gathering is not without its First Amendment protections,"[157] and only a Pangloss could take much comfort from that reluctant double negative. But it does leave open the possibility of judicial intervention to prevent the *total* denial of public access to public matters, if that extreme should occur—as, indeed, does the adjective "unrestrained" in Chief Justice Warren's statement. Imagine, for example, that large numbers of prisoners in a local prison died under unexplained circumstances and that the warden persistently refused to allow visits by any outside person: journalist, lawyer, relative, whomever. If an outsider sued for access, would Justice Stewart say that the Constitution has no application to those facts?

153. Stewart, *supra* note 2, at 636 (footnotes omitted).
154. 438 U.S. 1 (1978).
155. *Id.* at 16 (Stewart, J., concurring in judgment).
156. Zemel v. Rusk, 381 U.S. 1, 17 (1965).
157. 408 U.S. at 707.

The example of the sealed prison suggests that what is at stake in the prison-access cases is not really a right of journalists. It is, rather, the principle of our system of government that public institutions must in some way be publicly accountable. Justice Stevens made the point in his dissent in *Houchins*: "Without some protection for the acquisition of information about the operation of public institutions such as prisons by the public at large, the process of self-governance contemplated by the Framers would be stripped of its substance."[158]

Access to an institution is not the only way to assure its accountability. In *Branzburg* the Court noted, by way of showing the accepted limits on press access, that Supreme Court conferences have always been closed to press and public;[159] and it is true that the Justices could not exchange views candidly and effectively in a public forum. The exclusion is philosophically acceptable because the Court is held accountable in another way: in the persuasiveness of its opinions. But this alternative mode of accountability is not present in the example of the prison totally closed to public inspection, since conditions, decisions, and actions remain undisclosed. Nor is there good reason to keep the public ignorant of prison conditions, as there is to maintain the secrecy of court conferences. To the contrary, as Justice Stevens noted, imprisonment is part of the criminal-law process, and must be visible to the community if it is to attract the necessary public confidence. So long as public access is not allowed to interfere with prison management, Justice Stevens said, "there is no legitimate penological justification for concealing from citizens the conditions in which their fellow citizens are being confined."[160]

But if public accountability requires some access to a prison, why should a court grant access to a newspaper or television station rather than, say, a member of the prison reform league? Chief Justice Burger asked that question at the oral argument in *Houchins*. Justice Stevens answered in his dissenting opinion: because in this case the press is the only party seeking access.[161] And the press represents the public, as Justice Powell said in dissent in

158. 438 U.S. at 32 (Stevens, J., dissenting) (footnote omitted).

159. 408 U.S. at 684. *See also* Rehnquist, *Sunshine in the Third Branch*, 16 WASHBURN L.J. 559 (1977).

160. 438 U.S. at 36 (Stevens, J., dissenting) (footnote omitted). Justice Powell made the same argument four years earlier. Saxbe v. Washington Post Co., 417 U.S. 843, 861 (1974) (Powell, J., dissenting).

161. 438 U.S. at 39 (Stevens, J., dissenting).

the companion case to *Pell*, *Saxbe v. Washington Post Co.*[162] Individual citizens today, he said, cannot become personally familiar with the affairs of government;[163] nor is unrestrained public access often feasible.[164]

> In seeking out the news the press therefore acts as an agent of the public at large. It is the means by which the people receive that free flow of information and ideas essential to intelligent self-government.
>
> . . . The underlying right is the right of the public generally. The press is the necessary representative of the public's interest in this context and the instrumentality which effects the public's right.[165]

Justice Stewart in fact appears to have moved toward that position. In *Houchins*, three of the seven Justices who sat would have vacated in its entirety a district court injunction giving KQED access on special terms to the prison. Three others would have affirmed the district court order. Justice Stewart agreed with the first three that the station had no right of access to areas or sources of information in the prison from which the public was excluded.[166] But where the public was admitted, he said, the press' right of "equal access" had to reflect "the practical distinctions between the press and the general public";[167] the press had to have "*effective* access to the same areas."[168] Thus he agreed with the district court—and this became the law of the case[169]—that KQED had to be able to use cameras and sound equipment to show the viewers, effectively, what individual visitors could see with their own eyes. "When on assignment," he said, "a journalist does not tour a jail simply for his own edification. He is there to gather information to be passed on to others, and his mission is protected by the Constitution for very specific reasons. . . . Our society depends heavily

162. 417 U.S. 843 (1974).
163. *Id.* at 863 (Powell, J., dissenting).
164. *Id.* at 864 (Powell, J., dissenting).
165. *Id.* at 863-64 (Powell, J., dissenting).
166. 438 U.S. at 16 (Stewart, J., concurring in judgment).
167. *Id.* (Stewart, J., concurring in judgment).
168. *Id.* (Stewart, J., concurring in judgment) (emphasis in original).
169. On remand, defendant sheriff entered into a stipulation that representatives of the news media would be allowed frequent access to most areas of the prison with their cameras and recording equipment. Stipulation and Order Regarding Dismissal of Action, KQED, Inc. v. Houchins, No. C-75-1257 (N.D. Cal. Nov. 15, 1978).

on the press for . . . enlightenment."[170] In other words, as Justice Powell said in *Saxbe*, the press acts as the representative of the public.

Protection of the Editorial Process

The decided cases treat two phases of the press' work very differently. In acquiring information, it has little if any constitutional protection. In publishing, it has great protection: Once the press gets information, not even strong interests of national security[171] or privacy[172] or fair trial[173] justify interference with publishing. But there is something in between: the editorial process.[174] It is a legal battleground relevant to the search for Justice Stewart's position.

The Supreme Court has said in general terms that the editorial process is entitled to constitutional protection. In *Tornillo*, Chief Justice Burger wrote for the Court that "the exercise of editorial control and judgment" was "a crucial process" from which the first amendment had so far excluded goverument regulation.[175] In *CBS v. Democratic National Committee*,[176] rejecting the claim of would-be television advertisers that they had a constitutional right to buy advertising time, the Chief Justice said: "For better or worse, editing is what editors are for . . . ."[177]

But the specific reasons for protecting the editorial process were made clearer in an episode that arose not in the courts but in Congress. In 1971 CBS produced a television documentary, "The Selling of the Pentagon," on the Defense Department's public relations techniques. A subcommittee of the House Commerce Committee, responding to criticism that the producers had unfairly

---

170. 438 U.S. at 17 (Stewart, J., concurring in judgment) (citation omitted).

171. *See* New York Times Co. v. United States, 403 U.S. 713 (1971).

172. *See* Cox Broadcasting Corp. v. Cohn, 420 U.S. 469 (1975).

173. *See* Nebraska Press Ass'n v. Stuart, 427 U.S. 539 (1976).

174. *See* Herbert v. Lando, 568 F.2d 974, 976-78 (2d Cir. 1977), *rev'd*, 99 S. Ct. 1635 (1979). Chief Judge Kaufman divided the work of the media into acquiring, processing, and disseminating information.

175. 418 U.S. at 258. Justice White, concurring, said:

> We have learned, and continue to learn, from what we view as the unhappy experiences of other nations where government has been allowed to meddle in the internal editorial affairs of newspapers. Regardless of how beneficent-sounding the purposes of controlling the press might be, we . . . remain intensely skeptical about those measures that would allow government to insinuate itself into the editorial rooms of this Nation's press.

Id. at 259 (White, J., concurring).

176. 412 U.S. 94 (1973).

177. *Id.* at 124.

edited their film footage, subpoenaed the outtakes (the film not used in the final version); Dr. Frank Stanton, president of CBS, declined on first amendment grounds to comply with the subpoena.[178] The Commerce Committee cited him for contempt.[179] But the full House, by a vote of 226 to 181, killed the citation.[180] What that episode showed is that governmental intrusion into the editorial process may have a chilling effect. Editors are rightly concerned about any official effort to second-guess the editorial process. Inspection of the process by private litigants—the issue in *Herbert v. Lando*—seems to me less threatening; and it did not draw constitutional objection from Justice Stewart.[181]

Such considerations may explain the apparent inconsistency in Justice Stewart's words in *Branzburg*, on the one hand, and in *Pell* and his Yale speech on the other. When he spoke in *Branzburg* of "a right to gather news,"[182] he may not have meant a right to get government information against the government's wishes—a right he denied in later statements.[183] He may have meant, rather, a right to seek the news without official interference in the process.[184] If one analyzes *Branzburg* that way, then the grand jury

178. *See* N.Y. Times, June 25, 1971, at 71, col. 1.

179. *See* N.Y. Times, July 2, 1971, at 1, col. 5.

180. 117 CONG. REC. 24752-53 (1971); N.Y. Times, July 14, 1971, at 1, col. 8.

181. The Second Circuit in *Herbert* held that the first amendment protects media libel defendants from having to answer certain questions on discovery about their knowledge at the time of publishing the disputed material; that is, it limited inspection of the editorial process in a civil action. Herbert v. Lando, 568 F.2d 974 (2d Cir. 1977), *rev'd*, 99 S. Ct. 1635 (1979). The Supreme Court, reversing, observed that facts about libel defendants' state of knowledge are essential to recovery under the rule of *New York Times Co. v. Sullivan*, which requires proof that a defamatory falsehood was published with knowledge of its falsity or reckless disregard of the truth. Herbert v. Lando, 99 S. Ct. 1635, 1641 (1979) (discussing New York Times Co. v. Sullivan, 376 U.S. 254 (1964)), *rev'g* 568 F.2d 974 (2d Cir. 1977). Justice Stewart dissented on the ground that plaintiff had abused discovery in this case by asking questions irrelevant to the criteria of *Times v. Sullivan*; he would have remanded to the trial court with instructions to limit discovery. 99 S. Ct. at 1661-63 (Stewart, J., dissenting).

182. *See* text accompanying note 150 *supra*.

183. *See* text accompanying notes 152-155 *supra*.

184. But the principle of noninterference in newsgathering, if it does underlie Justice Stewart's dissent in *Branzburg*, is not an absolute for him. He urged only a qualified testimonial privilege in *Branzburg*. And in the *Farber* case, after temporarily staying the New Jersey Supreme Court's decision until the full Supreme Court could act, New York Times Co. v. New Jersey, 47 U.S.L.W. 3219 (U.S. Sept. 26, 1978) (No. A-284), he joined without comment in a vote to vacate the stay, New York Times Co. v. New Jersey, 439 U.S. 886 (1978). Before the New Jersey Supreme Court decision, stays had been denied by Justices White, New York Times Co. v. Jascalevich, 439 U.S. 1317 (1978), and Marshall, New York Times Co. v. Jascalevich, 439 U.S. 1331 (1978).

subpoena forcing disclosure of confidential sources is like the congressional subpoena for outtakes of "The Selling of the Pentagon." It is a chilling intrusion—one that, if sustained, could make editors trim their judgment in the future.

This explanation of Justice Stewart's "right to gather news" fits a suggestion, toward the end of his Yale speech, that relations between the press and the government should be seen as a contest. This image was used by the late Alexander M. Bickel, who after representing the *New York Times* in the *Pentagon Papers Case* wrote that the first amendment "ordains an unruly contest between the press, whose office is freedom of information . . . , and government, whose need is often the privacy of decison-making."[185] Justice Stewart spoke of the press' "autonomy." But autonomy, he said, "cuts both ways. The press is free to do battle against secrecy and deception in government. But the press cannot expect from the Constitution any guarantee that it will succeed. . . . The Constitution, in other words, establishes the contest, not its resolution."[186]

Justice Stewart's concept of press "autonomy" is a useful one—if not limited to journalism but embracing the pamphleteer and the publisher of Victor Marchetti's book.[187] But there is danger in the other side of the contest theory as Justice Stewart frames it: the government's right to deny access by press or public to information or institutions that it controls. How far Justice Stewart would carry that right was indicated when he wrote for the Court in *Gannett Co. v. De Pasquale* that "members of the public have no constitutional right under the Sixth and Fourteenth Amendments to attend criminal trials."[188]

CONCLUSION

Blackstone, recording the successful outcome of the long English struggle against press censorship, wrote: "Every freeman has an undoubted right to lay what sentiments he pleases before the public; to forbid this is to destroy the freedom of the press

185. A. BICKEL, THE MORALITY OF CONSENT 87 (1975).

186. Stewart, *supra* note 2, at 636.

187. The CIA learned of Marchetti's book, according to a CIA official's affidavit, from "a confidential source"—evidently someone in one of the six New York publishing houses to which Marchetti had submitted an outline. *See* Marks, *On Being Censored*, FOREIGN POL'Y, Summer 1974, at 93, 96.

188. Gannett Co. v. De Pasquale, 99 S. Ct. at 2911. *See* discussion in note 192 *infra*.

. . . ."[189] Every freeman, that is, not just those organized or institutionalized as "the press." Freedom of the press arose historically as an individual liberty. Eighteenth-century Americans saw it in those terms, and the same view is reflected in Supreme Court decisions; freedom of speech and of the press, Chief Justice Hughes said, are "fundamental personal rights."[190] To depart from that principle—to adopt a corporate view of the freedom of the press, applying the press clause of the first amendment on special terms to the "institution" of the news media—would be a drastic and unwelcome change in American constitutional premises. It would read the Constitution as protecting a particular class rather than a common set of values. And we have come to understand, after much struggle, that the Constitution "neither knows nor tolerates classes among citizens."[191]

The press is not a separate estate in the American system. Its great function is to act for the public in keeping government accountable to the public. And it would be a poor bargain, for the press and the country, if a special status for journalism were accompanied by greater latitude for government to avoid accountability by closing its proceedings.[192]

Justice Stewart's idea of a preferred constitutional position for the organized press was inevitably appealing to journalists, but it would hurt their real interests if it became accepted doctrine. It would separate the professional press from the public it represents, and increase the risk of arrogance. In our complex democracy, newspapers and magazines and broadcasters usually vindicate the

189. 4 W. BLACKSTONE, COMMENTARIES *152.

190. *See* text accompanying note 65 *supra*.

191. Plessy v. Ferguson, 163 U.S. 537, 559 (1896) (Harlan, J., dissenting).

192. That is the practical result of Gannett Co. v. De Pasquale, 99 S. Ct. 2898 (1979). The Court upheld against constitutional objection by a newspaper company the action of a New York judge in excluding press and public, at the joint request of prosecution and defense, from a pretrial hearing on a motion to suppress evidence. Justice Stewart, writing for a five-man majority, said the sixth amendment guarantee of the right to public trial was for the benefit of defendants and could be invoked only by them. As to the first amendment, Justice Stewart cited the prison-access cases, *see* notes 151, 154 & 162 *supra*, and said "[s]ome Members of the Court" believe that the press and public could not be completely excluded from prisons "in the absence of a significant governmental interest." *Id.* at 2911. (Interestingly, he put himself in that category by citing his concurrence in Houchins v. KQED, Inc., 438 U.S. 1, 16 (Stewart, J., concurring in judgment); *see* text accompanying notes 166-170 *supra*.) But even assuming arguendo such a qualified first amendment presumption of access to criminal trials, he found that in this case there were sufficient countervailing interests to overcome it. 99 S. Ct. at 2911-12. The effect of the *Gannett* deci-

" 'social interest in the attainment of truth.' "[193] They are at the cutting edge. But others play their part: scholars and conscience-stricken officials and citizen-critics. The first amendment was written for them, too, and freedom is indivisible. The safety of the American press does not lie in exclusivity.

---

sion was to immunize critical aspects of the criminal process in Seneca County, New York, where the case arose in 1976, from any realistic public accountability. Justice Blackmun noted in dissent, that in 1976 every felony prosecution in Seneca County was disposed of without a trial. *Id.* at 2934 (Blackmun, J., concurring in part and dissenting in part). In this case the suppression hearing "was the only proceeding at which the conduct of the police, prosecution, and the court itself were exposed to scrutiny." *Id.* at 2933-34 (Blackmun, J., concurring in part and dissenting in part).

193. Saxbe v. Washington Post Co., 417 U.S. 843, 862 (1974) (Powell, J., dissenting) (quoting Z. CHAFEE, FREE SPEECH IN THE UNITED STATES 33 (1954)).

[3]

THE INDEPENDENT SIGNIFICANCE OF THE PRESS CLAUSE UNDER EXISTING LAW

*C. Edwin Baker**

I. INTRODUCTION: THE SPEECH AND PRESS CLAUSES

In 1973, Jerome Barron asked the most important First Amendment question regarding the press: "freedom of the press for whom?"[1] Four years earlier, in 1969, relying very heavily on a newspaper precedent, *Associated Press v. United States*,[2] the Supreme Court gave an answer to Barron's question. In *Red Lion Broadcasting Co. v. FCC*,[3] probably its most famous broadcasting case, the Court asserted that "[i]t is the right of the viewers and listeners . . . which is paramount."[4] This claim—that the audience's interests are paramount—could not have been made when in a public school a child refused to salute the flag on the basis of conscience.[5] In *West Virginia Board of Education v. Barnette*,[6] the speaker's interests, or more precisely the would-be non-speaker's interests or, even better put, the individual's liberty, was paramount.[7] The difference between *Barnette* and *Red Lion*, as well as the Court's

---

* Nicholas Gallicchio Professor, University of Pennsylvania Law School. I thank Marvin Ammori, David Anderson, Ellen Goodman, and Michael Madow for very helpful comments on an earlier draft.

1. JEROME A. BARRON, FREEDOM OF THE PRESS FOR WHOM?: THE RIGHT OF ACCESS TO MASS MEDIA (1973). As the celebration of this conference recognizes, Barron effectively asked that question before the Court's decision in *Red Lion Broadcasting Co. v. FCC*, 395 U.S. 367 (1969). *See* Jerome A. Barron, *Access to the Press—A New First Amendment Right*, 80 HARV. L. REV. 1641, 1641-43 (1967).
2. 326 U.S. 1 (1945).
3. 395 U.S. 367 (1969). At three crucial places in its reasoning, the Court invoked *Associated Press*. *Id.* at 387, 390, 392.
4. *Id.* at 390.
5. Specifically, on the basis of religion, but the Court held that point not to be significant and, thus, did not rely on the religion clauses. West Virginia Bd. of Educ. v. Barnette, 319 U.S. 624, 629, 634-35 (1943).
6. 319 U.S. 624 (1943).
7. *See id.* at 633-34, 641-42.

reasoning in *Associated Press*, illustrates how the rationale for constitutional protection of the press differs from that of the protection of individuals. These different rationales lead, in turn, to somewhat different protection for the press and for individuals, with the press sometimes receiving special protections, but also with it sometimes being subject to regulations as structured enterprises that could not be applied to individuals. These different rationales even explain why regulation of the press sometimes actually serves the values embodied in the First Amendment—as Justice Black argued in *Associated Press*.[8] This Article aims to support each of these assertions.

A ubiquitous understanding of the constitutional guarantee of press freedom is that it aims to protect a Fourth Estate or, more expansively, to protect media entities because of their instrumental contribution to democracy and a free society. Nevertheless, despite the powerful presentation of this view by Justice Potter Stewart[9] (and also Justice William Brennan),[10] the Court has never explicitly recognized that the Press Clause involves any significant content different from that provided to all individuals by the prohibition on abridging freedom of speech.[11] The result is a common view that, at best, the Press Clause means that individuals have the right to disseminate their views as well as to voice them. According to this reading of Court decisions, the Press Clause is not meaningfully separate from the Speech Clause.

8.

> It would be strange indeed, however, if the grave concern for freedom of the press which prompted adoption of the First Amendment should be read as a command that the government was without power to protect that freedom. The First Amendment, far from providing an argument against application of the Sherman Act, here provides powerful reasons to the contrary. That Amendment rests on the assumption that the widest possible dissemination of information from diverse and antagonistic sources is essential to the welfare of the public, that a free press is a condition of a free society. Surely a command that the government itself shall not impede the free flow of ideas does not afford non-governmental combinations a refuge if they impose restraints upon that constitutionally guaranteed freedom.

Associated Press v. United States, 326 U.S. 1, 20 (1945).

9. Potter Stewart, *"Or of the Press"*, 26 HASTINGS L.J. 631, 634 (1975).

10. William J. Brennan, Jr., Address at the Dedication of the S. I. Newhouse Center for Law and Justice, Rutgers University (Oct. 17, 1979), *in* 32 RUTGERS L. REV 173, 174-75 (1979).

11. David Anderson points out that from the 1930s through the 1960s, the Court often invoked and appeared to rely on the Press Clause. David A. Anderson, *Freedom of the Press*, 80 TEX. L. REV. 429, 448 (2002). However, all those cases were ones that one suspects individual speakers would receive the same protection except, maybe, for special animosity to prior restraints as applied to the press. Near v. Minnesota, 283 U.S. 697, 716-19 (1931). Interestingly, *Near*, a press case, is the first case where the Court invalidated a state law on the basis of the First Amendment. *Id.* at 717-23.

In fact, the Court is sometimes portrayed as repudiating a separate role for the Press Clause. Most often cited for this proposition is *Dun & Bradstreet, Inc. v. Greenmoss Builders, Inc.*[12] The lower court, possibly relying on the pedigree of Justice Stewart's dubious proposition that the Court had never applied the *New York Times Co. v. Sullivan*[13] actual malice standard to non-media defendants,[14] held that these non-media speakers receive less protection. On this basis, it found Dun & Bradstreet liable. In contrast, by adding Justice White's concurrence to the opinion of the four dissenters, a majority in *Dun & Bradstreet* explicitly rejected giving the non-media defendants less First Amendment protection for their defamatory speech than is given to media defendants.[15] In addition to these five, the three member plurality opinion, while affirming the lower court result, explicitly withheld approval of the lower court's premise. Instead, Justice Powell found that the protection provided to the defendants in *Gertz v. Robert Welch, Inc.*[16] did not apply because here the negligently false defamatory speech (assertedly) did not involve an "issue of public concern."[17] No member of the Court recognized a difference in protection of individuals and the media, and a majority explicitly rejected the proposition in this context. Sometimes these opinions are taken to mean that the two clauses have no operationally different content.

That reading of the Court's decision does not follow. A principle of no greater protection for the press against defamation suits does not logically rule out the converse—that individuals receive greater rights in these contexts. More plausible though, *Dun & Bradstreet* could merely mean that any difference in protection provided by the two clauses does

12. 472 U.S. 749, 758-59 (1985).

13. 376 U.S. 254, 279-80, 283 (1964).

14. Stewart, *supra* note 9, at 635. Stewart's interpretation of *New York Times Co.* is curious. Although the *Times* did choose to accept the civil rights leaders' advertisement and, therefore, the ad could be seen as speech of a media defendant, it was also speech of the non-media defendants who signed and placed the ad. Their speech was not the speech of the media, although they did use the media. The Court applied the same actual malice standard to these individual defendants, apparently belying Stewart's subsequent interpretation. Thus, the only way to understand Stewart's position is not that the media have special rights but that whoever uses the media for their speech has these greater rights.

15. Justice White said he agreed with "Brennan that the First Amendment gives no more protection to the press in defamation suits than it does to others exercising their freedom of speech"—not, thereby, ruling out the converse, that the press receives less protection. *Dun & Bradstreet, Inc.*, 472 U.S. at 773 (White, J., concurring). Justice Brennan, however, also said that "in the *context of defamation law*, the rights of the institutional media are no greater and no less than those enjoyed by other[s]." *Id.* at 784 (Brennan, J., dissenting) (emphasis added).

16. 418 U.S. 323, 330-32 (1974).

17. *Dun & Bradstreet, Inc.*, 472 U.S. at 757.

not come into play in this context. In other contexts, however, their rights vary, with individuals some times and the press at other times having greater rights.[18] In fact, defamatory speech is a peculiar locus to test the thesis of independent meaning of the Press Clause. If individual liberty is the core of the speech freedom, individuals presumptively should have at least the rights to speak held by any mere instrumentally-valued "entity"—such as the press. If the press is, as Justice Stewart suggested, the only constitutionally-protected business, its speech rights should only be greater, if at all, than those of other businesses. Even if, as Justice Stewart argues, the normative rationale for the two constitutional provisions is different, it is still possible—as I mostly argue—that both the press and individuals have basically the same right not to be censored. Censorship interferes both with individuals' liberty and with the press's performance of its instrumental role. The press might even have less, not more, speech rights if there are circumstances where the instrumental justification for its protection is not at stake—for example, if the regulation does not involve censorship. In contrast, the context where there may be special rights for the press as compared to individuals (as well as compared to other businesses) is where its institutional integrity is at stake.

I and others have defended distinguishing the Speech and Press Clauses, usually understanding the Press Clause along the general lines of Justice Stewart's Fourth Estate approach.[19] Others reject this view, arguing that confusion and danger lie in giving the press any special

---

18. Later, I consider the possibility that individuals have greater rights to be free from mandatory speech requirements and greater rights to be unrestricted by copyright than the press. *See infra* notes 38-62 and accompanying text.

19. In addition to the articles by Justices Stewart and Brennan, many in the communications field assume that the press is different and legal articles giving reasons for the conclusion are not uncommon. *See, e.g.*, Floyd Abrams, *The Press Is Different: Reflections on Justice Stewart and the Autonomous Press*, 7 HOFSTRA L. REV. 563, 563-64 (1979); David A. Anderson, *Freedom of the Press in Wartime*, 77 U. COLO. L. REV. 49, 66-69 (2006). I have presented my views various places. *See* C. EDWIN BAKER, HUMAN LIBERTY AND FREEDOM OF SPEECH 225-71 (1989) [hereinafter BAKER, HUMAN LIBERTY AND FREEDOM OF SPEECH]; C. Edwin Baker, *Turner Broadcasting: Content-Based Regulation of Persons or Presses*, 1994 SUP. CT. REV. 57, 62 [hereinafter Baker, *Turner Broadcasting*]. I have also argued that Vincent Blasi's argument for the checking function as being a central First Amendment value relies on historical evidence and rationales related to the Press Clause, not the First Amendment generally. *Compare* Vincent Blasi, *The Checking Value in First Amendment Theory*, 1977 AM. B. FOUND. RES. J. 521, 523 (arguing that free expression has value because of the function it performs in checking the abuse of official power and examining how this "checking value" differs from other values that have dominated First Amendment analysis) *with* C. Edwin Baker, *Press Rights and Government Power to Structure the Press*, 34 U. MIAMI L. REV. 819, 830-31 (1980) [hereinafter Baker, *Press Rights and Government Power*].

rights.[20] The present Article is not intended to reenter this theoretical debate. Instead, this Article will challenge the common view that existing doctrine rejects the special rights or independent interpretation view. More specifically, the primary effort will be to: (i) consider the extent an independent interpretation of the Press Clause has been implicitly, though perhaps unwittingly, accepted by the courts. The argument will be that an independent interpretation either is implicit in decisions the Court has reached or provides a more appealing interpretation of good results that otherwise seem doctrinally anomalous. I will also consider: (ii) whether the independent interpretation would lead to the "better" and most likely resolution of issues that are currently doctrinally unresolved, that is, whether independent interpretation would be required. Finally, I will consider: (iii) whether it would provide correctives where good reasons exist for objecting to current doctrine. All the examples discussed below will fit into one of these three categories.

There are two doctrinal contexts in which this exploration takes place. Part II considers how constitutional treatment of the press differs from that of individuals and obviously, the differences could involve either greater, lesser, or merely different protection. Part III involves how treatment of the press differs from that given to non-media commercial enterprises. Here, the expected differences, if any, will always be in the direction of greater protection of the press. Part IV will conclude with brief remarks on how definitional problems related to special treatment of the press are more apparent than real.

II. DIFFERENT CONSTITUTIONAL RIGHTS OF INDIVIDUALS AND THE PRESS

Any differences between the Speech Clause and the Press Clause should depend on an understanding of the primary rationale behind each. This theoretical understanding could then provide a basis for predicting what differences should be found in an examination of doctrine if that doctrine corresponds to the proposed theory. Here, my hypothesis is that individual speech rights are based on respect for the individual's autonomy or liberty as an actor. In contrast, the press's rights are related to its instrumental role as a fundamental institution of a free and

20. Anthony Lewis, *A Preferred Position for Journalism?*, 7 HOFSTRA L. REV. 595, 609 (1979); William W. Van Alstyne, *The Hazards to the Press of Claiming a "Preferred Position"*, 28 HASTINGS L.J. 761, 768-69 (1977); David Lange, *The Speech and Press Clauses*, 23 UCLA L. REV. 77, 77 (1975).

democratic society. Most obviously this encompasses its Fourth Estate role, but more generally its role in developing and presenting information, opinion, and vision that is instrumentally valuable to its audience—the people in a free society.

This understanding of the basis of the rights predicts corresponding doctrinal positions. As to speech, an individual should be free to say, and, at least whenever her basic values are at stake, not to say whatever she chooses. In contrast, the press should be able to communicate whatever it, as an independent entity, believes serves its audience's need for facts, opinions, or vision. Thus, though for different reasons, the rationale for each clause requires freedom from censorship—that is, freedom from prohibitions or penalties for, in the case of the individual, expressive choices, and in the case of the press, its choices to communicate ideas or information. (This formulation does not exclude regulation of unprotected categories of speech, but the unprotected categories, whatever they are, should presumptively be the same for the individual and the press.) On the other hand, there may be differences. Most obviously, the individual should receive protection for her liberty and the press for its institutional integrity. Some regulations place one at issue but not the other.

The most obvious example of only individual liberty being at issue is where the individual claims the liberty right not to bear false witness to her values. This constitutionally required respect for individual autonomy provides no obvious reason that the press should have such a right not to speak—at least, unless a mandate to speak can be shown in the particular context to be inconsistent with its integrity as an institution. So, though as to affirmative speech, the two should have (virtually) the same right to speak, the individual may have greater rights not to speak. In contrast, special rights of the press should be expected, if at all, in the context of laws or government practices that would interfere with its integrity as an institution. Just as the autonomy value has little applicability to an instrumentally-valued institution, institutional integrity has little application to the individual. Thus, any special rights related to institutional integrity of the press can be expected to have no parallel in claims that individuals can raise on their own. These, then, are the theoretical expectations. The rest of Part II examines the relative case law—and, I claim, largely confirms the review of the separate role of the two clauses.

A. Protecting Institutional Integrity: Special Press Rights

1. Reporter's Privilege

The most discussed possibility, and one emphasized by Justice Stewart, is that journalists should have some privilege to refuse to identify confidential sources in judicial proceedings.[21] The argument is that since, without wrong-doing by the press, the press develops this information about sources solely within the constitutionally-protected activity of providing news, and since compelled breaches of this confidentiality will significantly interfere with the press's news-providing role, that compelled breaches undermine its integrity as an institution. Moreover, the government has no legitimate authority to appropriate for itself the products of the press's constitutionally-protected freedom (i.e., its institutional integrity).[22] Rather, the institutional integrity of the press can be seen to require that it be able to control its work product prior to publication.[23] The emphasis here is specifically on institutional integrity. Justice Stewart's complaint was that without this protection of journalists' capacity to promise confidentiality, the authorities could "undermine the historic independence of the press by attempting to annex the journalistic profession as an investigative arm of government" to the long run detriment even of the administration of justice.[24] The empirical claim is that the absence of this privilege will lead to the press being less able to provide quality news. The relevance of this instrumental point follows precisely from the basic claim that the Press Clause protects the institutional integrity of the press in order to benefit the public.

Nevertheless, in *Branzburg v. Hayes*, speaking for the five member majority, Justice White stated that "[t]he sole issue before us is the

---

21. *See, e.g.*, Branzburg v. Hayes, 408 U.S. 665, 725-52 (1972) (Stewart, J., dissenting).

22. *See* Zurcher v. Stanford Daily, 436 U.S. 547, 570-77 (1978) (Stewart, J., dissenting).

23. The 5-3 decision in *Zurcher* largely duplicated its split in the earlier *Branzburg* case. Justice White wrote for the five member majority including Justice Powell. Justice Powell, though, noted that in issuing a warrant a judge should interpret reasonableness in light of the value of the integrity of the press, *id.* at 570, a value which Justices Stewart and Marshall argued in dissent should prevent its issuance. *Id.* at 570-71. Even Justice White, though only arguing that judges should enforce the requirement of reasonableness for issuing warrants with special exactitude when the broader category of "First Amendment interests," not specifically press interests, were at stake, observed "that the struggle from which the Fourth Amendment emerged 'is largely a history of conflict between the Crown and the press." He then gave as a consideration against adopting a general rule restricting warrants for certain searches of the press the fact, as he saw it, that recent history "hardly suggests abuse." *Id.* at 564-66 (citation omitted).

24. *Branzburg*, 408 U.S. at 725 (1972) (Stewart, J., dissenting).

obligation of reporters to respond to grand jury subpoenas as other citizens do . . . ."[25] In response to the request to interpret the First Amendment as granting such a privilege, he said, "[t]his we decline to do."[26] Since this area of controversy is well known, I will only make a few brief comments. First, even taking Justice White's opinion for all it is worth, it is singularly narrow. It did not assert the broader proposition that the Press Clause does not provide for special rights. As Justice Powell was quick to emphasize, Justice White allowed that "news gathering is not without its First Amendment protections."[27] The majority's primary arguments were directed not at the commonly suggested view that freedom of the press does not provide for special rights.[28] Rather, the opinion offered reasons to conclude that denial of a journalist privilege does not undermine freedom of the press and, according to Justice White, this fact is the lesson that history teaches.[29] With a history providing different empirical evidence—or a different reading of the history that we do have—Justice White did not rule out a different result. More specifically, the opinion limited itself to the narrow issue of whether the First Amendment provided this privilege, and in saying no, Justice White's opinion said nothing about whether the Press Clause has independent significance in relation to other issues.

Second, if one Justice had moved from Justice White's majority to the dissenting view, the reigning doctrine would be that the Press Clause does provide different protection for the press than for individuals. Third, despite Justice White speaking for five Justices, many lower courts and commentators think that the case showed a different five Justices (a majority) supporting special constitutional claims of the press.[30] That is, many lower courts read Justice Powell's concurrence to require consideration of the needs of the press in a case-by-case determination of whether disclosure of a source is properly compelled, leading many lower federal courts—sometimes as a matter of federal common law but sometimes as a matter of the First Amendment—to

25. *Id.* at 682 (majority opinion).

26. *Id.* at 690.

27. *Id.* at 707.

28. The majority did note that recognition of a journalist privilege would create the difficulty of determining "those categories of newsmen who qualified" as well as other practical problems, but this hardly seemed determinative. *Id.* at 704. The contexts in which this problem of identifying a person as a journalist arises—specifically, after the journalist's investigation—may make this problem relatively easy to handle as compared to other contexts, such as a person wanting access to a facility on grounds that she may, as a freelancer, subsequently publish a story and thus should be considered part of the press.

29. *Id.* at 698-99.

30. *See, e.g.*, Commonwealth v. Bowden, 838 A.2d 740, 752 (Pa. 2003).

provide protection and to formulate a test very close to the one that Justice Stewart had proposed.[31] If these courts are right, this subsequent history can be read to show that *Branzburg* did in effect recognize an independent press right.

In sum, nothing in Justice White's opinion requires rejecting a view that the Press Clause has independent implications different from the Speech Clause and some elements suggest that it does. If Justice Powell's opinion is read as many lower courts have read it, the majority in this case does base special press rights on the Press Clause. Finally, anyone who believes that a constitutional journalist privilege should exist is committed to reading the Press Clause as having independent force. Of course, she could also believe in the independent force of the Press Clause even if she favored total rejection of any constitutionally-based reporter's privilege.

2. Required Speech: Mandatory Disclosure of Government Payment for Speech

This Section deviates from the Article's general approach by raising an important issue not yet litigated. Here I only claim that an independent interpretation of the Press Clause leads to the right result. Sometimes payment is made to get the payee to speak as the payor directs without the payee disclosing that she is not the originator, not the "author," of the speech. This practice, paying another person or entity to present a communication as if it were their own, is what Ellen Goodman has described (and condemned) as "stealth marketing."[32] Functionally, "stealth" refers to the failure to identify speech as having been paid for, for example, not identifying the communication as an advertisement.

---

31. MARK A. FRANKLIN ET AL., MASS MEDIA LAW 575 (7th ed. 2005) (citing Anthony L. Fargo, *The Journalist's Privilege for Nonconfidential Information in States Without Shield Laws*, 7 COMM. L. & POL'Y 241, 252-53 n.74 (2002)), reports that by 2002 "all but one of the federal circuit courts of appeal appeared to recognize some form of qualified constitutional privilege." The case book also noted opinions going the other way, *id.*, and, according to Bruce Sanford, the judicial attitude may be quickly changing "with a velocity that would make your head spin faster than Linda Blair in the Exorcist." *Id.* at 580. Of course, putting aside whether there is a First Amendment basis, many states rely on their own constitution, legislation, or state common law to find a privilege. For purposes of this essay, the main relevance of this fact may be that in the years after *Branzburg* a popular consensus (or sufficient lobbying power on the part of the press) seems to support a view that the press should be treated differently from individuals in this context, presumably because of the peculiar social role of the press.

32. Ellen P. Goodman, *Stealth Marketing and Editorial Integrity*, 85 TEX. L. REV. 83 (2006). *See also* Tamara R. Piety, *"Merchants of Discontent": An Exploration of the Psychology of Advertising, Addiction, and the Implications for Commercial Speech*, 25 SEATTLE U. L. REV. 377, 444 (2001).

Many media entities are legally required to disclose the fact of payment (or, equivalently, identify the communication as an advertisement)—though cynically it might be asked how often these requirements have been enforced and how easy they are to circumvent. Since the 1912 "Postal Act," newspapers and periodicals that receive second class mail privileges have been required to make this "mandated speech."[33] Congress has also imposed the same requirement on broadcasters and, in some cases, cable providers.[34] There seems to be little question of the constitutionality of these requirements.[35] Much less clear is whether disclosure can be required in cases where an individual, not a media entity or person working for a media entity, is paid to speak. The issue seldom arises, presumably because policy makers usually see no need for such a requirement in the case of individuals. Can, however, the government require political or charitable canvassers to identify themselves as either "paid" or "volunteer"? The Court has explicitly refused to decide the issue.[36] Assuming, as seems likely, that mandated disclosure can be expected to reduce the effectiveness of the payee's communication, the requirement would raise a difficult constitutional question.[37] If the disclosure requirement were impermissible here, the

33. 39 U.S.C. § 3685 (2000); Postal Service Appropriations Act of 1912, Pub. L. No. 62-336, 37 Stat. 539, 553-54 (1912).

34. *See* C. Edwin Baker, *The Media That Citizens Need*, 147 U. PA. L. REV. 317, 371 n.155 (1999).

35. For a good analysis, see Goodman, *supra* note 32, at 130-37. Although decided before any meaningful development of First Amendment doctrine, *Lewis Publ'g Co. v. Morgan*, 229 U.S. 288 (1913), upheld the 1912 Postal Act against a First Amendment challenge. 229 U.S. 288, 313 (1913).

36. The Court has held that requiring paid, but not volunteer, circulators of ballot measure petitions to identify themselves by name and to communicate the amount they are paid to circulate the petitions is unconstitutional. Buckley v. Am. Constitutional Law Found., Inc., 525 U.S. 182, 204 (1999). The Court repeatedly stated, however, that neither it nor the Court of Appeals expressed a view on whether the state could require that these canvassers identify their "paid or volunteer status, and if paid, by whom . . . ." *Id.* at 200; *see also id.* at 197.

37. Anonymity has been protected for varying instrumental reasons but primarily to aide vulnerable speakers. *See* Gia B. Lee, *Persuasion, Transparency, and Government Speech*, 56 HASTINGS L.J. 983, 1024-26 (2005). A speaker's right to use paid stand-ins is well established. *See, e.g.*, Meyer v. Grant, 486 U.S. 414, 422-24 (1988); Riley v. Nat'l Fed'n of the Blind of N.C., Inc., 487 U.S. 781, 803 (1988); Village of Schaumburg v. Citizens for a Better Environment, 444 U.S. 620, 633-34 (1980). Thus, a speaker can maintain anonymity and has a right to pay someone to stand in her place. The combination of these two rights could be seen to favor a right of non-identification. Moreover, a regulation is of doubtful constitutional validity if designed to reduce a speaker's effectiveness and only applies—only could constitutionally apply given the individual's right to anonymous speech—when the payee avails herself of her constitutional right to use the stand-in. The requirement then would be punishing the exercise of a constitutional right. Still, to merely force the party to disclose that she is a stand-in may not interfere with why anonymity is protected. Existing precedent is not very informative maybe because the primary non-media contexts where mandated identification in support of increasing audience's ability to assess

question then would be why the difference in the media and non-media contexts. I will not further speculate on how the Court would or should treat this open question. Rather, I turn to the issue of whether the First Amendment should ever be interpreted to *mandate* disclosure.

Unidentified payment for speech is especially troubling when the government is the ultimate speaker. Having met any state action requirement, the question can then be raised: Does the Constitution prohibit stealth advocacy by the government? This view has been forcefully advanced. The argument is, essentially, that "political accountability [is] a bedrock principle of our Constitution" that grounds a constitutionally-based transparency principle for government communications.[38] The government violates that principle when it speaks without identifying itself as the speaker. With this reasoning, Gia Lee finds a constitutional basis for mandating disclosure in the Constitution's structural democratic commitments to public accountability.[39] In the end, though, she concludes that this constitutionally-based transparency of government communications principle should play a role in constitutional litigation (for example, to bar the government from claiming that speech is its own if it had not disclosed that fact[40]) but, for practical reasons, violation of this constitutional principle should not itself create a cause of action.

Even watered down so as not to create a cause of action for those harmed by violations, recognizing this principle would be a radical step. A plausible analogy would be First Amendment claims for a right of access to government-held information or to government facilities. The democratic benefits from access are clear—but lack of information never stops a person from speaking, including accusing the government of

---

messages have mostly occurred either in commercial contexts (where commercial speech is protected only or primarily to serve listeners' interests) or in the campaign context, which, surprisingly to some, is probably the most regulated, and one of the most properly regulated, speech context. *See generally* C. Edwin Baker, *Campaign Expenditures and Free Speech*, 33 HARV. C.R.-C.L. L. REV. 1 (1998).

38. Lee, *supra* note 37, at 1016.

39. *Id.* at 1016-17.

40. Lee effectively criticized *Johanns*, and her views were roughly expressed by the dissent. "[I]f government relies on the government-speech doctrine . . . it must make itself politically accountable by indicating that the content actually is a government message. . . ." Johanns v. Livestock Mktg. Ass'n, 544 U.S. 550, 571 (2005) (Souter, J., dissenting). Still, *Johanns* may represent merely a sub-rosa rejection of *United States v. United Foods, Inc.*, 533 U.S. 405, 417 (2001), which has been subject to savage critique for inconsistency with the bulk of Supreme Court law on commercial speech, see Robert Post, *Compelled Subsidization of Speech:* Johanns v Livestock Marketing Association, 2005 SUP. CT. REV. 195, and a return to upholding this type of assessment as the Court did earlier in *Glickman v. Wileman Bros. & Elliott, Inc.*, 521 U.S. 457, 477 (1997).

"hiding" information that should be public, speculating about why it does so, and demanding that it come clean. Thus, how the denial of access violates speech freedom is unclear. Given the recognition that secrecy is sometimes desirable (whether to protect personal privacy or national security or many other legitimate interests), the better constitutional doctrine might be to treat the need for information not as giving rise to a constitutional right, but rather as providing a powerful argument for government (legislative or executive) action to make information available.[41] The claim should be that legislatures should enact strong freedom of information acts, as they often have.

Similarly, in the context of government speech, a host of *arguably* acceptable reasons explain why, and identify contexts in which, government might choose not to disclose that it is the ultimate source of a communication. Consider the use of undercover agents, promotion of views where the government only wants people to focus on the content, cases where, as is common in public relations-type promotions, an effort is made to identify the message with a personality popular among a targeted audience, and secretly authorized "leaks" of information. The propriety of these practices raise thorny policy issues, but it seems doubtful that constitutional analysis provides the right tools with which to resolve them. Thus, like in the relation between privacy and freedom of information acts, maybe the better approach is for the public to demand and for the legislature to enact general transparency rules, but to leave their extent up to legislative or other policy-making refinement.

Curiously, in Lee's argument for a constitutional basis for her "transparency of communications" principle, the main relevance of the First Amendment is as a potential obstacle.[42] Mandated transparency seems initially to conflict with the First Amendment right of anonymity. In response, Lee persuasively argues that requiring government self-identification does not conflict with any of the specific and limited reasons, all of which were only instrumental, for the First Amendment to

41. This conclusion is not unassailable. Though in concurrence, Justice Brennan, who viewed the individual's right to speak as virtually "inviolate," adopted a dual level First Amendment approach that treats some instrumentally grounded claims, such as a right of access to information, as having First Amendment status and as justifying various "balancing" or pragmatic structural doctrines that sometimes provide a constitutional basis for access. *See,*· *e.g.*, Richmond Newspapers, Inc. v. Virginia, 448 U.S. 555, 585-86 (1980) (Brennan, J., concurring). With this reasoning, Brennan went way beyond the majority's more limited argument for why the judicial process is uniquely a place where people have a First Amendment right to be present to gather information.

42. Lee, *supra* note 37, at 1023-24.

protect anonymity.[43] (She could have added the additional point that normally[44] the First Amendment does not protect government speech.)

Nevertheless, the First Amendment might bear more affirmatively on the issue Lee raised once media and individual speech are distinguished. The constitutional principle would then not be "transparency," no matter how desirable that would be in general, but "required respect for institutional integrity," which would be mandated as a core principle of the Press Clause. In the case of communications by individuals, it is difficult to see how the government violates that person's First Amendment rights by employing her to present the government's message even if the payment requires that she not identify herself as a government spokesperson. Are the First Amendment rights of a sports star violated when she is paid to say: "just say no!"? Sometimes terms of government employment that restrict her later speech may violate the First Amendment—but often not.[45] The government permissibly restricts speech of an employee on the job if (and probably only if) the restriction advances her proper performance of her job and not disclosing in her communication that the government is

43. *Id.* at 1020-21.

44. Whether the government, having created a particular government-owned institution, must recognize certain First Amendment rights of that institution is somewhat unsettled. For example, must the government respect First Amendment rights of public libraries? In *United States v. American Library Ass'n*, 539 U.S. 194 (2003), Justice Rehnquist's plurality opinion carefully avoided deciding this question, *id.* at 211-12, though Justice Stevens in dissent clearly found that it must. *Id.* at 226-27. Must the federal government respect First Amendment rights of local governmentally-created cable access channels? In *Denver Area Educational Telecommunications Consortium v. FCC*, 518 U.S. 727 (1996), the Court, in fractured opinions, found that the grant to cable operators of power to restrict certain offensive sexual programming on locally created public access channels violated the First Amendment, thereby implicitly finding that these public channels receive First Amendment protection. In concluding that a state-owned broadcast station did not violate candidate Forbes's First Amendment rights to participate in a campaign debate, the Court's reasoning assumed that, at least as then constituted, the state-owned broadcast stations had the same free speech rights that commercial stations had. Arkansas Educ. Television Comm'n v. Forbes, 523 U.S. 666, 669 (1998).

The general argument for these conclusions is that when the government sets up an institution or funds a person to play a particular role, regulation of its or her speech contrary to the social role of the institution violates the First Amendment. *See* Legal Servs. Corp. v. Velazquez, 531 U.S. 533, 536-37 (2001). In a recent case involving the *Stars and Stripes*, a newspaper that has over 280,000 readers and has considerable editorial independence, but is owned and published by the Department of Defense, the court, after accepting clear lower court precedent holding that a reporter's privilege is established by the First Amendment, held that the paper's journalists were entitled to the reporter's First Amendment privilege, finding no reason to deny the privilege simply because the government owned and published the paper. Tripp v. Dep't of Def., 284 F. Supp. 2d 50, 57 (D.D.C. 2003).

45. *See, e.g.*, Snepp v. United States, 444 U.S. 507, 509 n.3 (1980).

the communication's ultimate source can sometimes relate to that performance.

The media context is different. Assume, as argued here, that the press receives constitutional protection to be a voice independent of the government (or, at least, independent of the other three "estates") in order to perform the crucial democratic tasks of providing an independent source of vision and information, including performance of a watchdog role. Then the press's claim to special constitutional protection encompasses most importantly a demand that the government not purposefully undermine its institutional integrity in its performance of these roles. Payment to the press to present the government's message as the press's own message (as opposed to payment for carriage as an advertisement) undermines this independence and breaches the press's institutional integrity. The notion of a free press presumes that *its* speech represents *its* choices, not the government's choices. Though the individual media entity presumably enters voluntarily into the agreement with the government not to identify the government as a payee, *because* the protection of the integrity of the press is for the benefit of the public, the government's payment violates the public's rights relating to a free press.[46]

Even the media entity itself would object if the payment is to a media reporter or other employee who does not notify the media entity (i.e., its editor, publisher, or owner) that she has been paid by the government to have her story contain government-chosen content. In contrast, violation of institutional integrity does not occur if the communication is presented as that of the government, as it would if the content is explicitly identified as an advertisement. Likewise, the integrity of the press is not compromised, although its quality may be tested, when the government, through press releases or "leaks" or good public relations management or even lies, leads the press on the basis of the press's own reporting or journalistic routines to print stories that the government wants reported. As Justice Stewart puts it, "[t]he Constitution . . . establishes the contest" in which "[t]he press is free to do battle"—and that contest includes an "autonomous press" as a

46. In response to the practical question about "standing" to assert the violation, other non-compromised media entities can complain that the practice damages them since it both undermines the reputation of the press on which they rely and creates competitive pressure on them to accept such payments. The 1912 postal legislation, which prohibited publication of paid speech without identifying it as advertising, was strongly supported by members of the press that did not engage in the practice. LINDA LAWSON, TRUTH IN PUBLISHING: FEDERAL REGULATION OF THE PRESS'S BUSINESS PRACTICES, 1880-1920 111 (1993).

constitutionally-protected participant.[47] Essentially, this argument about a violation of institutional integrity takes the same form as did the argument for a reporter's privilege (to not expose the identity of confidential sources), but is logically even stronger though less familiar. The public knows that the press may err, but if there is a "free press" that constitutes a watchdog on government, the public has a right to know that the decisions as to what the press prints under its own name are those of the watchdog and not the watched government.

The objections to this use of the media lie most centrally in its destructive impact on democratic discourse.[48] The general legal prohibition of "stealth" in periodicals and in broadcasting embodies the popular perception that the practice is objectionable.[49] The law, however, has singled out governmental practices for special prohibitions. Typical appropriations legislation forbids government agencies from using government funds for "propaganda"[50]—a term of art given that many people reasonably view most of the government's huge budgets for public relations, advocacy, and "informative" communications as being spent essentially on propaganda. As interpreted to mean "*covert* propaganda," which involves "the concealment of [or failure to disclose] the agency's role in sponsoring the materials," these statutory requirements make the "stealth" interference with media integrity illegal.[51] The dual goal is to restrict the government and to protect the integrity of the press.[52]

Admittedly, the constitutional issue has not been decided and may not need to be decided given the (often ignored[53]) statutory prohibitions on governmental behavior. Still, the existing state of affairs represents a well-considered and quite explicit normative judgment about the nature of the press that a democracy should protect. Of course, the First

---

47. Stewart, *supra* note 9, at 636.

48. Goodman, *supra* note 38, at 112-17.

49. *Id.* at 84.

50. Typical language is: "No part of any appropriation [contained in this or any other Act] shall be used for publicity or propaganda purposes within the United States not heretofore authorized by the Congress." *See* U.S. Gov't Accountability Office, B-305368, Dep't of Educ.—Contract to Obtain Services of Armstrong Williams 6 (Sept. 30, 2005) [hereinafter GAO, B-305368].

51. *Id.* at 14-15 (citing U.S. Gov't Accountability Office, B-303495, Office of National Drug Control Policy—Video News Release (Jan 4, 2005)). Interpreting propaganda to mean covert propaganda, defined as communications "circulated as the ostensible position of parties outside the agency," has been consistent. *See id.* at 7 (quoting U.S. Gov't Accountability Office, B-229257, Appropriations/Financial Management (June 10, 1988)).

52. *See id.* at 6.

53. *Id.* at 14-15.

Amendment directly restricts only government, not private corruption of a free press. The destructive impact on the integrity of the media has led to legislative prohibitions on private forms of contracting.[54] The additional legislated limits on government agencies again represent a considered judgment about legitimate forms of public discourse. If presented with the issue, a court may, and I believe should, recognize the independent structural significance of the Press Clause, and find that government payments to the press to present the government's position as the press's own violates the public's right to a free press.

B. Protecting Individual Liberty

1. Right Not to Speak: Speaking as Others Direct

Possibly the doctrinal area in which an individual liberty theory of the First Amendment is most obviously in play is the right not to be coerced into making professions that one does not believe. In *Barnette*, the majority emphasized the foundation of the First Amendment in the liberty not to be coerced into pledging allegiance to the flag.[55] In contrast, in dissent, Justice Frankfurter in effect adopted a marketplace of ideas theory, which is concerned that everything worth saying can be said. Frankfurter emphasized that he would join the majority if any speech or any view was suppressed.[56] He observed, however, that both the children involved and their parents were entirely free to express their views, including their view about the horrendous nature of the compelled salute, both before and after the flag salute ceremony.[57] Of

---

54. *See, e.g.*, Consolidated Appropriations Act, 2004, Pub. L. No. 108-199, div F, tit. VI § 624, 118 Stat. 3, 356 (2004) (discussing the publicity and propaganda prohibition that prohibits the government from entering into certain contracts with private parties).

55. West Virgina Bd. of Educ. v. Barnette, 319 U.S. 624, 635-36 (1943). Though *Barnette* is used here to illustrate the claim, its holding has been repeated in subsequent cases. *See, e.g.*, Wooley v. Maynard, 430 U.S. 705, 713, 717 (1977). Closely related is the matter of freedom not to associate. Because it has complexities and, I believe, unresolved inconsistencies that are without any obvious parallels in the press context, I put it aside.

56. *See Barnette*, 319 U.S. at 664 (Frankfurter, J., dissenting).

57.

> It is not even remotely suggested that the requirement for saluting the flag involves the slightest restriction against the fullest opportunity on the part both of the children and of their parents to disavow as publicly as they choose to do so the meaning that others attach to the gesture of salute. All channels of affirmative free expression are open to both children and parents. Had we before us any act of the state putting the slightest curbs upon such free expression, I should not lag behind any member of this Court in striking down such an invasion of the right to freedom of thought and freedom of speech protected by the Constitution.

course, like the instrumentalist marketplace theory of speech, the instrumentalist Fourth Estate view of the Press Clause places value primarily on things being said and speech not being censored. Both, among other things, treat the value in the guaranteed freedom as lying in its instrumental contribution to a search for truth or, more generally, in providing for the listener's or audience's need for exposure to diverse content. If this view of the Press Clause is adopted, the liberty not to speak protected for individuals in *Barnette* would have little applicability to the press.[58] That turns out to be roughly the existing state of the law, a result inexplicable if the two clauses have a unified theoretical basis and scope.

Compelled speech in many media contexts is quite routine. Broadcasters have both general and specific affirmative speech obligations. They either now have, or previously had, speech duties involving fairness, public service, reasonable access for political candidates, children-oriented educational content, and more.[59] The primary current doctrinal question is whether these obligations can be cabined to the broadcast area on the basis of the view that broadcasting is a special case where First Amendment rights are less robust. *Miami Herald Publishing Co. v. Tornillo*[60] is regularly cited as representing the purportedly dominant print paradigm and as implying that compelled media speech would interfere with editorial autonomy.[61] But when it came to upholding "must carry" cable requirements in *Turner Broadcasting System, Inc. v. FCC*, the Court emphatically did not place cable in a category with broadcasting or any other purportedly less protected category. Rather, rejecting the cable systems claim of interference with editorial autonomy, the Court emphasized that *Miami Herald* was a case about the impermissibility of punishing editorial

---

Id. at 664.

58. Of course, there might be other justifications specially related to the Press Clause for objecting to compelled media speech, an issue I put aside for now.

59. As is well known, the FCC found that the Fairness Doctrine was unconstitutional but the Court of Appeals affirmed purely on statutory grounds. Syracuse Peace Council v. FCC, 867 F.2d 654, 656 (D.C. Cir. 1989). Particularly interesting, though speaking about the public interest not the constitutional issues, was Judge Wald's opinion, concurring in part and dissenting in part. She agreed with the result concerning the deterrent or penalty aspects of the balance prong—an analysis which has since become the dominant interpretation of what was wrong with the right of reply in *Miami Herald*, but saw no "reasoned decisionmaking" supporting the elimination of the requirement to air issues of great public importance. *Id.* at 669-73.

60. Miami Herald Publ'g Co. v. Tornillo, 418 U.S. 241 (1974).

61. *See, e.g.*, Denver Area Educ. Telecomms. Consortium v. FCC, 518 U.S. 727, 813 (1996); Marvin Ammori, *Another Worthy Tradition: How the Free Speech Curriculum Ignores Electronic Media and Distorts Free Speech Doctrine*, 70 MO. L. REV. 59 (2005).

content choices.[62] In other words, in the interpretation relied on in *Turner Broadcasting*, *Miami Herald* protected only against censorship, a result required by the press's Fourth Estate role; it did not recognize any institutional autonomy or liberty analogous to that with which *Barnette* was concerned.

2. Right Not to Speak: Anonymity

Since the 1912 Postal Act referred to earlier, Congress has required newspapers and other periodicals having second class or periodical publication privileges to furnish the government and, at least once a year, to include in the publication the name of the editor, managing editor, publishers and owners as well as certain other information about circulation.[63] That is, the statute purposely eliminates anonymity for much of the commercial press—in part out of a hope that the public will benefit from knowledge of the ownership, enabling them to resist manipulation.[64] On the other hand, drawing on a history going back to the publicists for the American Revolution, the Court interprets the First Amendment to protect anonymity of individuals in many contexts—especially in their distribution of pamphlets.[65] There is certainly no simple distinction that individuals have anonymity rights and the press does not. Often individuals also do not. For example, the Court has upheld disclosure requirements for contributors in political campaigns[66]—although it also required that an exception be made when the requirement would predictably deter contributions to an unpopular political group, thereby undermining their speech.[67]

The cases might be reconciled on the ground that there is no fundamental right of anonymity the way there may be for individual

---

62. Turner Broad. Sys., Inc. v. FCC, 512 U.S. 622, 653-56 (1994).

63. 39 U.S.C. § 3685 (2000); Postal Service Appropriations Act of 1912, Pub. L. No. 62-336, 37 Stat. 539, 553-54 (1912). The Court in *Lewis Publishing Co. v. Morgan* also upheld this requirement and it too is still on the books. 229 U.S. 288, 316 (1913).

64. *Lewis Publ'g Co.*, 229 U.S. at 316.

65. *See* McIntyre v. Ohio Elections Comm'n, 514 U.S. 334, 341-43 (1995); Talley v. California, 362 U.S. 60, 64-65 (1960).

66. Buckley v. Valeo, 424 U.S. 1, 143 (1976). *But cf.* Buckley v. Am. Constitutional Law Found., 525 U.S. 182, 200 (1999) (invalidating requirement that initiative petition circulators wear badge containing their name).

67. Brown v. Socialist Workers '74 Campaign Comm., 459 U.S. 87, 95, 98 (1982). *Cf.* Geoffrey R. Stone & William P. Marshall, Brown v. Socialist Workers, *Inequality as a Command of the First Amendment*, 1983 SUP. CT. REV. 583, 592 (describing the Court as mandating content discrimination). This result, however, follows easily from the perspective that the First Amendment primarily protects dissent. *See generally* STEVEN H. SHIFFRIN, DISSENT, INJUSTICE, AND THE MEANINGS OF AMERICA (1999).

speech—it is always a matter of pragmatic assessment. In many contexts, required disclosure can seriously deter speech. This deterrence of speech could then be seen as gratuitous, maybe even desired by the government, if the government could not give a convincing reason to require it.[68] Thus, invalidation would depend on the likelihood of deterrence and the credibility of and necessity for the government's rationale for requiring identification.

The area, however, remains in tension. Disclosure of identity sheds light that can reduce manipulation of audiences, a possibly good purpose, but often this same light can deter speech. As for now, the right of anonymity has been recognized only in the context of individual speakers, not the press, thereby representing the difference that this Article is seeking. Nevertheless, the hypothesis here is that greater rights of the individual relate to claims of formal autonomy or liberty. Though the instrumentalist argument for anonymity is not inconsistent with such claims, it does not seem like the right type of difference to demonstrate the thesis offered here. I suspect that there is no fundamental distinction between the press and individual speech rights here. The Court gave as one of its reasons for invalidating the ban on anonymous handbills in *Talley v. California*, not only the importance of anonymity to individual pamphleteers in the revolutionary era, but also noting that the "obnoxious press licensing law of England . . . was due in part to the knowledge that exposure . . . would lessen the circulation of literature critical of the government."[69]

3. Restricting the Right to Speak: Copyright

Like defamation law, copyright restricts speech absent permission from the protected party. Unlike defamation law, however, Fourth Estate press theory and individual liberty speech theory lead to different demands for limiting the copyright owners' claims of control.[70] Fourth Estate theory requires that the media be able to report all facts and ideas—which copyright's idea/expression distinction largely grants. Expansive right for non-owners to use copyrighted material in transformative uses likely contributes more than it "costs" in terms of

---

68. This would explain why the Court struck down mandated disclosure of membership lists in legislative investigations when the information was not germane to legitimate legislative purposes but upheld the disclosure requirement when it arguably seemed more relevant.

69. *Talley*, 362 U.S. at 64. In contrast, the dissent cited the press case, *Lewis Publishing*, as precedent for upholding the law. *Id.* at 70 (Clark J., dissenting).

70. *See* C. Edwin Baker, *First Amendment Limits on Copyright*, 55 VAND. L. REV. 891, 951 (2002) [hereinafter Baker, *First Amendment Limits*].

any reduced incentive to create originally. Giving *some* rights to copyright holders, however, arguably benefits the public by encouraging (commercial) creation. A media enterprise's duplication of the full content of an item offered by a copyright holding competitor clearly amounts to a copyright violation.[71] This restriction on publication, however, should hardly be troubling from a Fourth Estate perspective—publication occurs, the public gets access. That is, properly constrained, copyright can support the press in its central role. As a practical matter, the institutional press is able to perform its Fourth Estate role only due to its ability to sell its product (or sell its audience to advertisers). The incentive provided by ownership to produce saleable products turns copyright into a purported "engine of free expression,"[72] making it a plausible (though, of course, often controversial and not always persuasive) media policy aimed at expanding the quality (and, less importantly, maybe the quantity) of communications made available to the public.[73]

Individuals' *speech* freedom has no implications for freedom to profit from speech through market transactions. Market transactions involve exercises of power—each party to a transaction exercises power over the other by getting the other to do something she would not wish to do except for the fact of it leading to payment by the other.[74] In contrast, outside of market exchanges, gains to a speaker typically result either due to her speech affirming or assisting in her own goals irrespective of an audience or due to her speech convincing an audience to share her perspective—creating a form of solidarity between speaker and listener. That is, free speech provides liberty and solidarity rights, not market rights. Thus, any bar copyright imposes on commercial uses of "other people's expression" is not problematic from the perspective of individual speech freedom. It is otherwise, however, with limits on non-commercial uses of copyrighted speech. Here, speech freedom demands a largely unrestricted opportunity to use other people's words—a

71. Publication of unpublished work, however, would seem to serve the press's *Fourth Estate* role. A better ground for decision in *Harper & Row, Publishers, Inc. v. Nation Enters.*, 471 U.S. 539 (1985), may have been an unfair competition (a "scoop") theory, which is arguably consistent with a Fourth Estate or utilitarian perspective, than the theory offered by the Court, being unpublished, which in general might serve privacy interests but not public knowledge. *See, e.g.*, Int'l News Serv. v. Associated Press, 248 U.S. 215, 234 (1918).

72. *Harper & Row*, 471 U.S. at 558.

73. This is the democratic justification for copyright consistently emphasized by Neil Netanel. *See* NEIL W. NETANEL, COPYRIGHT'S PARADOX: PROPERTY IN EXPRESSION/FREEDOM OF EXPRESSION (2007).

74. *See* C. Edwin Baker, *Property and its Relation to Constitutionally Protected Liberty*, 134 U. PA. L. REV. 741, 769-71 (1986).

freedom implicit in early copyright legislation that only applied to commercial copying. The freedom to engage in non-commercial copying is still typically provided, as illustrated by individuals' fair use right to engage in recording of broadcasts for purposes of time-shifting.[75] Expressive freedom for an individual must include her right to copy word for word and distribute a complete political analysis or to copy and give or to quote to her lover a complete poem if she finds those words better express her sensibilities than anything she herself has composed.

As a matter of current copyright law, it seems clear that individuals have rights to non-commercial uses of copyrighted content not available to media entities.[76] Other statutory limits on copyright, especially the inability to copyright facts and ideas, clearly provide well-established opportunities needed by media entities in order to properly perform their constitutional role.[77] If the rights in both cases are constitutionally mandated, then this would be a case where different rationales for speech and for press freedom lead to different speech rights—with individual liberty providing more complete freedom than the limited usage rights required by media entities which are, themselves, often central beneficiaries of properly crafted copyright ownership rules.

This constitutional conclusion, however, is uncertain. The Court has said that "[t]o the extent [copyright's restrictions on a person making other people's speeches] raise First Amendment concerns, copyright's built-in free speech safeguards are generally adequate to address them"; it concludes that no more First Amendment scrutiny is required as long as "Congress has not altered the traditional contours of copyright protection. . . ."[78] A lot rides doctrinally, of course, on what "traditional contours" are taken to be. Here, however, my lament is somewhat different. Without identifying which of copyright's built in safeguards are required by the First Amendment and which are merely a matter of legislative grace, it cannot be concluded with certainty whether or not the rights of individuals to use copyrighted materials in their (non-commercial) expression and the usage rights also available to profit-oriented media firms represent First Amendment minimums or policy judgments. Still, existing differences between rights for commercial media and the greater rights for individual non-commercial uses can be taken to represent popular judgments about the scope of different values

---

75. Sony Corp. of Am. v. Universal City Studios, Inc., 464 U.S. 417, 432-34 (1984).

76. *Id.* at 442.

77. *See* Feist Publ'ns, Inc. v. Rural Tel. Serv. Co., 499 U.S. 340, 344-45 (1991).

78. Eldred v. Ashcroft, 537 U.S. 186, 221 (2003).

underlying commitments to both individual liberty and a Fourth Estate or, more broadly, a dynamic culture.

4. Doctrinal Basics: Content Discrimination

The presumptive impermissibility of content discrimination today constitutes a bedrock of First Amendment doctrine—or, maybe, of doctrinal confusion. This Section makes the following claim. The individual liberty concern of the Speech Clause and the democratic discourse concern that justifies special protection for the press suggest different objections to content discrimination. Given a presumption that when found it is bad, the different objections lead to different methods of identifying content discrimination. While this would not be problematic if the Court was clear about when to use one or the other conception of content discrimination, its failure to explain these different bases of objection has contributed to confusion in this area. Still, case law results (largely) correspond to what a dual Speech/Press Clause perspective suggests.

The modern doctrine condemning content discrimination is normally taken to have been initiated by the 1972 decision of *Police Department of Chicago v. Mosley*, where Chicago had prohibited picketing within 150 feet of a school while the school was in session except for "'peaceful [labor] picketing of any school involved in a labor dispute . . . .'"[79] In invalidating this ordinance, the Court made three arguments (as well as relying on two constitutional provisions—the First Amendment and the Equal Protection Clause, although later cases have made clear that the First Amendment itself encompasses all that is important in the equal protection argument and I will not attempt to separate the elements). First is a neutrality argument. The Court explained, "the ordinance itself describes impermissible picketing . . . in terms of subject matter. The regulation 'thus slip[s] from the neutrality of time, place, and circumstance into a concern about content.' This is never permitted."[80] Second is an objection to *restriction* of speech on the basis of content, which leaves open the possible permissibility of *promotion* on the basis of content. The Court said, "the First

79. Police Dep't of Chicago v. Mosley, 408 U.S. 92, 93 (1972). The application of the exemption only to labor picketing, as indicated by my brackets, was undisputed. *Id.* at 94 n.2.

80. *Id.* at 99 (citation omitted). Neutrality is also suggested by the Court's statement that the government "may not select which issues are worth discussing or debating in public facilities. There is an 'equality of status in the field of ideas,' and government must afford all points of view an equal opportunity to be heard." *Id.* at 96 (citation omitted). *Cf.* City of Madison Joint Sch. Dist. v. Wisconsin Pub. Emply. Relat. Comm'n, 429 U.S. 167 (1976) (allowing such selection).

Amendment means that government has no power to restrict expression because of its message, its ideas, its subject matter, or its content."[81] It further explained, the "government may not grant the use of a forum to people whose views it finds acceptable, but deny use to those wishing to express less favored or more controversial views."[82] Third is a defense of people's speech freedom on the grounds that permitting labor speech shows that a bar on a person's speech is not really required by the state's purpose in its use of this property. The theory is that gratuitous restrictions on speech are unconstitutional.[83] Thus, the Court says:

> Although preventing school disruption is a city's legitimate concern, Chicago itself has determined that peaceful labor picketing during school hours is not an undue interference with school. Therefore, . . . Chicago may not maintain that other picketing disrupts the school unless that picketing is clearly more disruptive than the picketing Chicago already permits. If peaceful labor picketing is permitted, there is no justification for prohibiting all nonlabor picketing, both peaceful and nonpeaceful. "Peaceful" nonlabor picketing, however the term "peaceful" is defined, is obviously no more disruptive than "peaceful" labor picketing. But Chicago's ordinance permits the latter and prohibits the former.[84]

Thus, the Court offered three different rationales for objecting to content discrimination involving, respectively, principles of neutrality, non-suppression, and speech freedom. Some observations can be made about each.

"Neutrality" has some intuitive appeal but, at least as normally understood, is entirely inconsistent with accepted practice. Periodically, the First Amendment is asserted to require government neutrality in the marketplace of ideas.[85] Such a view, however, would invalidate the accepted and hugely active role of government in engaging in speech,

---

81. *Id.* at 95. Along the same lines, the Court argued that "*[a]ny restriction* on expressive activity *because* of its content would completely undercut the 'profound national commitment to the principle that debate on public issues should be uninhibited, robust, and wide-open.'" *Id.* at 96 (quoting New York Times Co. v. Sullivan, 376 U.S. 254, 270 (1964)) (emphasis added).

82. *Id.* at 96.

83. *Id.* at 100.

84. *Id.* (citations omitted). This is the argument that the Court, in one of the deletions above, treats as an equal protection problem and later notes that such disruption can be handled by a more "narrowly tailored" or "narrowly drawn" statute. *Id.* at 101, 102. Interestingly, though citing equal protection cases for the narrowly tailored standard, all the other cases cited to illustrate why the law failed this constitutional standard were First Amendment cases. *See id.* at 101 n.8; Tinker v. Des Moines Indep. Cmty. Sch. Dist., 393 U.S. 503 (1969); United States v. O'Brien, 391 U.S. 367 (1968); Niemotko v. Maryland, 340 U.S. 268 (1951); Saia v. New York, 334 U.S. 558, 562 (1948).

85. Steven Shiffrin, *Government Speech*, 27 UCLA L. REV. 565, 566-67 (1980).

usually to promote the government's views.[86] Topics and views that the government expresses directly or promotes using others' speech have more than an equal status in the field of ideas and more than an equal opportunity to be heard. If "neutrality" refers to a constitutionally-required governmental stance toward the marketplace of ideas, the notion cannot be taken seriously as an aspect of constitutional doctrine. (There is also no available conception of a proper baseline of non-governmentally structured discourse from which to identify deviations from neutrality.)

A constitutional objection to government restrictions on, as opposed to objections to the promotion of, particular content or particular subject matters is more persuasive. Of course, any notion that suppression (treated as unacceptable) differs from promotion (treated as acceptable) also requires a baseline. This baseline, however, can be found through an examination of the purpose or interpretative meaning of the law—and the vitality of this "purpose" inquiry is well established.[87] Objection to suppression makes sense from a marketplace of ideas or a Fourth Estate perspective. Although there may be no standards for a neutral or properly working marketplace, and consequently no objection to any content that is added even when added and promoted by the government, preventing content from entering contradicts the fundamental notion of a free marketplace of ideas. Restrictions of particular content is, at least in many contexts, "censorship in its most odious form," according to Justice Black as quoted by the majority in *Mosley*.[88] In addition, suppression, at least as applied to individual speakers, is also objectionable as unjustified interferences with their liberty. Essentially, the claim here is that the key value of liberalism should be toleration, not neutrality—and suppression, restriction of speech out of objection to its content, is the opposite of toleration. Thus, restrictions as a means to suppress certain content, whether of particular subject matters or viewpoints, should be equally unconstitutional under either an individual liberty speech theory or a Fourth Estate press theory.

---

86. *See id.* at 568; MARK G. YUDOF, WHEN GOVERNMENT SPEAKS: POLITICS, LAW AND GOVERNMENT EXPRESSION IN AMERICA (1983); EDWARD S. HERMAN & NOAM CHOMSKY, MANUFACTURING CONSENT: THE POLITICAL ECONOMY OF THE MASS MEDIA 2 (1988).

87. *See* C. EDWIN BAKER, MEDIA CONCENTRATION AND DEMOCRACY: WHY OWNERSHIP MATTERS 138-41 (2007). Possibly the dominant reasons to ignore this feature of doctrine reflects, for conservatives, a tendency to adopt economic models and, for liberals, a tendency to be effects or outcome oriented.

88. *Mosley*, 408 U.S. at 98 (quoting Cox v. Louisiana, 379 U.S. 536, 581 (1965) (Black, J., concurring)).

The problem with this objection is that it does not fit the facts of *Mosley*. It is very difficult to believe that Chicago wished to suppress discussion of all issues except those involving labor disputes. The exemption of picketing about labor disputes is much better explained by the lobbying power of teachers' unions—they wanted to promote or enable their speech—than by any animosity to all other categories of speech. Surely, Chicago had no animosity to expression promoting the re-election of the mayor, even though the law restricted that expression. Thus, objections to suppression can hardly explain what is significant in the constantly cited case of *Mosley*.

The speech freedom principle provides the most interesting objection to content discrimination. As a matter of individual liberty, there should be a presumption that a person can engage in her chosen expressive activity whenever she chooses—certainly, should generally be able to do so at least in places that she otherwise has a right to be. The Court has held that the streets and parks are such places.[89] Still, despite a person's general right to be at some place, regulation is sometimes justified if her activities, *as activities*, would interfere with other uses to which the government wishes to dedicate the property, other uses that the government considers especially valuable. Given the potential legitimacy of such governmental choices to make use of public property to pursue public goals, the fear is that these reasons will constantly be available to override speech freedom.[90] A practical response is to develop evidentiary doctrines that identify when limits on liberty are best explained by lack of respect for expressive liberty rather than by real needs for the use of the property at issue. Permissible, then, would be regulations reasonably necessary given these government-dedicated uses.[91] Impermissible would be a regulation not necessary to serve the government interest—for example, a limit on leafleting, where the real evil is not leafleting but littering. There the government could (even if predictably less efficiently) simply prohibit littering—the real evil—rather than prohibit leafleting, that is, the speech.[92]

A parallel conclusion—that the government does not really believe its regulation is essential for serving the government needs in respect to the property—presumptively follows if the denial of freedom depends

89. *See, e.g.*, Hague v. Comm. for Indus. Org., 307 U.S. 496, 515-16 (1939). In modern language, these are traditional public forums.

90. *Mosley*, 408 U.S. at 98-99.

91. This approach interprets scrutiny tests as an aide to interpretation rather than a matter of instrumental rationality.

92. Schneider v. New Jersey, 308 U.S. 147, 162 (1939).

on the content of the expression. The evidentiary question, as the Court in *Mosley* noted, is whether the disallowed speech really interferes with the government's normal use of the property more than does the allowed speech.[93] The rationale of asking this question is not to identify a proper functioning of the marketplace of ideas or to prevent censorship. The specific point is to protect the individual liberty that the regulation would restrict. Thus, the central feature of the only coherent argument that fits the facts of *Mosley* is that content discrimination is often bad because it evidences an unnecessary restriction on individual expressive freedom. The objection exists even without a suppressive aim. No censorious purpose or danger need be shown.

Though the above is the only objection that fits the facts in *Mosley*, two points should be made about the second and third objections to content discrimination, the two that were found to be coherent. First, the speech freedom argument is most obviously relevant to individuals—that is, it is a Speech Clause claim. This is illustrated by its "official" origin in *Mosley* and the common interpretation of the prohibition on content discrimination as an offshoot of time, place, and manner doctrine.[94] Because the requirement relates to limits on people's use of government property, it has no obvious application to issues of media policy or regulation even if these policies are content-based. In contrast, the narrower concern with suppression is relevant in both contexts—that of press regulation and individual freedom. Media policies that suppress, as opposed to promote, speech on the basis of content, that is, policies that engage in censorship, should be invalidated.

This doctrinal distinction is fortunate. History provides a long line of socially desirable governmental attempts to promote quality media content.[95] Promotion of national news, local news, the arts, and educational content for children is constitutionally unobjectionable despite their content basis. In contrast, true attempts to suppress particular content, subjects, or viewpoints are objectionable as censorship. Purposeful suppression interferes both with the press's role in a democratic society and with individual autonomy. But by making

93. *Mosley*, 408 U.S. at 100.

94. Even if identified with *Mosley*, the objection to content discrimination has a longer history. It is implicit in the long recognized reasons to reject standardless permit systems—namely, that they allow "censorship in its baldest form." Lovell v. City of Griffin, 303 U.S. 444, 452 (1938). Again, though not clearly articulated as an objection to content discrimination, the point was generally well recognized before *Mosley*. *See* THOMAS I. EMERSON, THE SYSTEM OF FREEDOM OF EXPRESSION 303-04, 371-73 (1970) (public spaces must be made available to all on an equal basis; permit systems must be limited by standards sufficient to prevent uncontrollable authority).

95. *See* Baker, *Turner Broadcasting*, *supra* note 19, at 111.

the "evidence of lack of necessity" argument in *Mosley*, the Court implicitly adopted the liberty theory with respect to individual speakers and implicitly recognized special implications of the Speech Clause.[96]

Second, the two objections naturally suggest different criteria for identifying (presumptively objectionable) content discrimination. The concern with unnecessary restraints on individual expressive liberty is possibly best embodied in the test for content discrimination offered by Justice Brennan: "[A]ny restriction on speech, the application of which turns on the content of the speech, is a content-based restriction regardless of the motivation that lies behind it."[97] That is, any time a law applier must examine the content of the speech in order to determine the applicability of a regulation, content discrimination exists. On the other hand, the concern with suppression would suggest an alternative test: "The principal inquiry in determining content-neutrality . . . is whether the government has adopted a regulation of speech because of disagreement with the message it conveys."[98]

These two points add up to a third. The narrower test, "because of disagreement with the message," should always provide a basis to invalidate a law except where the government is in some sense the speaker. In particular, suppression—or regulation because of disagreement with the message—is equally objectionable under the Press Clause and Speech Clause analyses. Passing *this* test, however, should not end the inquiry when individual speech freedom is at stake. Then, the other test, "turns on the content of the speech," should also apply. Unfortunately, I cannot show that this is how the tests have been invoked. My sense is that the Court exhibits doctrinal confusion in its

96. *Mosley*, 408 U.S. at 97-98.

97. Boos v. Barry, 485 U.S. 312, 335-36 (1988) (Brennan, J., concurring). Similarly, in finding that a ban on editorializing by noncommercial broadcast stations was a content regulation, Justice Brennan explained that to determine "whether a particular statement by station management constitutes an 'editorial', . . . enforcement authorities must necessarily examine the content of the message." FCC v. League of Women Voters of Cal., 468 U.S. 364, 383 (1984).

98. This test has had a checkered life. It was originally formulated in *Ward v. Rock Against Racism*, 491 U.S. 781, 791 (1989), where the test was designed only to determine whether a facially content-neutral law should be found to be actually content-based. In that context, namely where the challenged law is not content-based on its face, the test makes perfect sense. The test has been used in about ten cases since, almost always in upholding a law after finding it not to be content-based. Interestingly, the Court in *Turner* quoted the *Ward* test but transformed it by adding in brackets around the words "agreement or" before the word "disagreement"—which makes the test seem to require neutrality, not merely suppression. Turner Broad. Sys., Inc. v. FCC, 512 U.S. 622, 642 (1994). Given that change, the dissent makes a persuasive argument that the must-carry law there was content-based. If, however, the proper test in the media context is, as I have argued, the suppression version of the test, the majority reached the right conclusion. *See* Baker, *Turner Broadcasting*, *supra* note 19, at 127-28.

oscillation between the two.[99] Nevertheless, Court results seem largely in line with what would be called for by an honest application of these tests in the manner recommended here. For example, the government's legitimate aim with its must-carry rules, upheld in *Turner Broadcasting*,[100] was not to suppress content, but to promote the availability of local content, especially local news and cultural or current affairs programming. Likewise, although violations of copyright obviously turn on examining the content of the infringing speech to see if it duplicates copyrighted expression, the legitimate goal of copyright as a media policy regulation is to promote, not suppress, production of quality speech. Often, maybe usually, this legitimate purpose should suffice to defeat challenges by commercial copiers. In contrast, the Speech Clause analysis mandates legal permission for most non-commercial copying. Here, the content regulation—the regulation requires examination and comparisons of content—unnecessarily interferes with individual liberty.[101]

C. *Summary*

Even if the Speech and the Press Clauses have different rationales and protect different types of agents, their rationales overlap in objecting to any government censorship. Hence, in respect to most core First Amendment issues, the same result follows whether the case involves an individual or the press. Bread and butter First Amendment cases, those involving run of the mill censorship, can be explained on either basis. Censorship equally infringes individual liberty and interferes with the constitutional role of the press—as well as violating any other First Amendment theory that has any judicial traction. Such cases do not test whether the Press Clause has an independent status.

---

99. In addition to this oscillation, members of the Court vary greatly in their attitude about the notion of content discrimination. Justice Kennedy, for example, argues that content discrimination should be per se unconstitutional, with no need to additionally flunk the traditional equal protection strict scrutiny test, while Justice Stevens frequently criticizes routine invocation of the doctrine. *See, e.g.*, Simon & Schuster, Inc. v. New York Crime Victims Bd., 502 U.S. 105, 124 (1991) (Kennedy, J., concurring); Young v. Am. Mini Theatres, 427 U.S. 50, 65-66 (1976). Moreover, all members of the Court agree that the doctrine applies differently in different contexts—e.g., depending on the type of forum at issue. In fact, all members agree that even the most extreme version of content discrimination, namely viewpoint discrimination, is sometimes justifiable without any scrutiny, for example, if the context is "not a forum at all" such as the day-to-day programming of a public broadcaster. Arkansas Educ. Television Comm'n v. Forbes, 523 U.S. 666, 678 (1998).

100. 512 U.S. 622 (1994).

101. For a further discussion of First Amendment implications on copyright laws, see Baker, *First Amendment Limits*, *supra* note 70, at 922-40.

Part II has shown that, where the hypothesis of a separate meaning of the two clauses would have relevance, actual case law either corresponds to the separate meaning hypothesis or is open, but in the later circumstance is most appealingly advanced by the separate meaning theory. Individual liberty is infringed if the government compels individuals to speak someone else's, for example, the government's chosen words, so the Court has protected these individuals. In contrast, requiring the media to carry information and sometimes even ideologically charged speech that the media entity would reject often interferes with neither a marketplace of ideas nor the capacity of the media to serve the public and its Fourth Estate role—in fact, it may promote these ends. These laws have always been upheld. Anonymity has also been instrumentally much more important to the communicative freedom of individuals than of media businesses, and that is where it has (sometimes) been protected. Individual liberty suggests a right to say anything one chooses even if one chooses to use expressions originally spoken or written by another person. In contrast, the instrumental justification of a free press is usually satisfied if the media is able to duplicate the facts or ideas that another person or entity has previously created.[102] Though not perfectly, copyright law largely corresponds to this distinction, explicitly leaving open whether the First Amendment compels these differing protections of the expression of, respectively, the individual and the press. Finally, clarity would be brought to the plastic and inconsistently formulated doctrinal objection to content discrimination if it were understood that one formulation primarily relates to protecting individual liberty and should be in play only when this liberty is the issue, while a more limited conception of content suppression should apply more broadly to protect audience as well as speaker interests, including audience interests related to the constitutional role of the media.

The key addition that a separate interpretation of the Press Clause offers the press involves its institutional integrity. A proposed interpretation of case law in relation to the validity of the thesis of protection of institutional integrity must face a potential indeterminacy. A failure to recognize a particular claim can be interpreted either as a conclusion that the First Amendment does not give special protection to the press's integrity or that its integrity is not threatened by rejecting the

102. Complications occur for the news media where the actual words (or pictures) constitute the news or for the creative media where the project requires the integration of former expression—issues potentially handled by fair use doctrines including the notion of news use and transformative uses.

claim.[103] Certainly, nowhere has the institutional integrity argument been clearly rejected,[104] with the law being apparently unsettled in the two contexts considered. Justice Powell's concurrence in *Branzburg* allowed many, probably most, lower courts faced with the issue to conclude that the First Amendment does justify at least some special attention to the press's claims not to be required to reveal confidential sources.[105] The view that this represents the proper understanding of the First Amendment has also clearly prevailed among journalists and arguably within popular opinion. The right to have the government not subvert the integrity of the press by the government paying the media to present the government's views as its own has not been presented to the courts. Legislative decisions to prohibit private parties from making such payments and media entities from accepting them, prohibitions on government that have been interpreted to bar primarily these "covert" payments, and popular outrage at such practices when exposed illustrate the popular view that this type of payment undermines a fundamental value of institutional integrity.

In sum, the independent interpretation of the two clauses is clearly evident in constitutional holdings respecting autonomy rights of individuals not granted to media entities and arguably in existing (and desirable) doctrine relating to special rights of media to protection of their institutional integrity.

103. Although Chief Justice Burger's later concurrence in *First National Bank v. Bellotti*, 435 U.S. 765, 797-802 (1978), was obviously hostile to any reading of *Branzburg* as recognizing a separate meaning for the Press Clause, Justice White's original opinion for the Court can be read as merely doubting that a reporter's privilege was needed to maintain institutional integrity and the press's ability to perform its role, leaving open what he would say in other cases. Thus, it is less clear what Justice White would say about payment to the press to present the government's views as the press's own or government power to license the press, compared to government's clear power to license other speaking occupations. *Cf.* Lowe v. SEC, 472 U.S. 181, 214-15 (1985) (White, J., concurring).

104. *Cf.* Zurcher v. Stanford Daily, 436 U.S. 547, 565 (1978) (rejecting newspapers special rights in relation to being subject to search warrants). *Zurcher* may well fall into the category of not being essential for institutional integrity. Certainly, the thrust of Justice White's opinion for the Court was to show that the press needed no such protection.

105. *See, e.g.*, United States v. Smith, 135 F.3d 963, 971 (5th Cir. 1998); Titan Sports, Inc. v. Turner Broad. Sys., Inc., 151 F.3d 125, 128 (3d Cir. 1998); Shoen v. Shoen, 5 F.3d 1289, 1292-93 (9th Cir. 1993); United States v. Long, 978 F.2d 850, 852-53 (4th Cir. 1992); United States v. LaRouche Campaign, 841 F.2d 1176, 1182 (1st Cir. 1988). *But see* McKevitt v. Pallasch, 339 F.3d 530, 532-33 (7th Cir. 2003).

III. DISTINCTION BETWEEN CONSTITUTIONAL STATUS OF THE PRESS AND OTHER BUSINESSES

Business entities are constituted by legal recognition of the significance of acts taken by individuals. Thus, ultimately, the moving parts are individuals. If there were no independent interpretation of the Press Clause, two possibilities would exist. The individuals, by being the actual authors of their business's speech, would be fully protected by the First Amendment, just like in respect to their other speech. Or, given that businesses are necessarily structured by law and subject to extensive and constitutionally unquestionable regulation, speech attributable to the business enterprise—itself a legal creation[106]—would be generally subject to regulation. On *either* view, without recognition of an independent interpretation of the Press Clause, the press would have no rights different from that of any other commercial or market-oriented endeavors. A business's speech (or its expenditures on speech) would be equally protected as ultimately that of an individual or equally subject to regulation as that of a business no matter what the business is.

Though either protecting or not protecting the speech of all business represents a coherent possibility, from the perspective of individual liberty, a corporation's potentially "immense aggregations of wealth . . . have little or no correlation to the public's support for the corporation's political ideas"—that is, its speech—while contributions of actual flesh and blood individuals to segregated funds do "accurately reflect[] contributors' support . . . ."[107] More generally, "the communications of profitmaking corporations . . . do not represent a manifestation of individual freedom or choice."[108] This conclusion presumably follows for both media and non-media business enterprises. In fact, in relation to typical examples of a corporation's speech, it may be more likely that more stockholders of General Motors will expect, maybe even desire, its speech, for example, about the merits of its cars, than the stockholders of a media conglomerate will desire its speech, for example, its Presidential endorsement. If there are instead greater speech

---

106. Tax law, corporate and partnership law, and a host of regulatory law distinguish people acting as business entities or entrepreneurs from people on their own.

107. Austin v. Michigan Chamber of Commerce, 494 U.S. 652, 660 (1990).

108. *Bellotti*, 435 U.S. at 805 (White, J., dissenting). Interestingly, Justice White then immediately distinguished some corporations organized for the express purpose of advancing ideological ideas and the press as cases where the corporation "may be viewed as merely a means of achieving effective self-expression." *Id.* This argument clearly applies to the ideological corporation, but the fact that the press is created, according to Justice White, to "disseminat[e] information and ideas" does not show why it should be viewed as a means of "self-expression." *Id.*

rights for the newspaper than the car company, it would seem that the right must lie not in protection of individual liberty (the Speech Clause), but in some independent status of the press (embodied in the Press Clause).

Thus, only if an independent status is given to the press by the Press Clause would the speech and other rights of the media be different from, in particular, greater than, those of other businesses—except maybe due to legislative grace.[109] Correspondingly, a test of the thesis that the Court has implicitly recognized an independent interpretation of the Press Clause is to see if it recognizes—or, maybe to consider if it almost certainly would recognize—different First Amendment rights of media and non-media enterprises.

This examination (conducted below) shows that there is no equivalence between the media and other business entities' legal rights. Most of the divergences are precisely those expected if the First Amendment protects the press as a provider of communicative content for an open democratic culture and all of the divergences are consistent with this thesis. Still, methodologically, there is a difficulty. Legislative decisions create most of these differences in rights. In all these cases, sound democratic policy reasons, independent of any constitutional mandate, may provide the basis for the differences. Whether the laws embodying the differences reflect merely policy or whether they also reflect legislators' implicit (and correct) judgments about their constitutional obligation to not violate press freedom cannot be determined analytically—and probably most legislators would not be conscious of the distinction. Still, sometimes this opaqueness is not present and, in other situations, reasonable conclusions can be made about constitutional mandates. Thus, in looking at various different treatments of the press and other businesses, Part III offers one or the other of three types of arguments depending on the example. In some cases, court decisions implicitly recognize the independent significance of the Press Clause by reaching constitutional holdings that, on grounds of consistency, cannot be understood other than as embodying an

109. Businesses are routinely subject to industry-specific regulation and sometimes industry-specific privileges. That this is true for the press might initially suggest equal protection challenges—but when made, these challenges should, and have, lost. For example, in *FCC v. National Citizens Committee for Broadcasting*, newspapers were distinguished from non-media corporations in being disabled from receiving broadcast licenses in their area of operation. Their equal protection challenge was noted, but rejected without discussion. 436 U.S. 775, 801-02 (1978). More generally, equal protection objections to industry specific regulation would suggest the potential unconstitutionality of the FCC as well as the Newspaper Preservation Act and much other legislation.

independent interpretation of the Press Clause. In other cases, reading the Constitution as embodying an independent meaning of the Press Clause provides a more satisfying basis for an intuitively right result that the Court reached in a confused way. Finally, often examples merely point to differences in legal rights that have been legislatively adopted but would only be constitutionally required if the Press Clause has independent significance. In many of these later cases, however, I suggest that most people would not want to accept and, in fact, the Court predictably would not accept a legislative failure to give the press the rights provided by existing law. Obviously, the first of these arguments provides the strongest evidence for the thesis of this Article that existing law embodies an independent interpretation of the Press Clause. The last two provide a strong incentive to adopt this view and a reasonable basis to predict that the Court would adopt it in the face of legislative failure. Although the categorization is crude, I try to organize the examples around different contexts or types of issues.

A. Media Speech Rights

1. Informational Privacy

Since Warren and Brandeis's classic article, *The Right to Privacy*, published in 1890,[110] the twentieth century has seen a huge growth in this area of law (a matter itself calling for sociological explanation), with protection of informational privacy being a fertile basis of statutory and judicial decision-making. Law school case books are written and conferences regularly held on how far this right should extend and what the best ways to protect it are. Many people simply do not want various facts about themselves exposed at all—or, if at all, only when they themselves make the exposure and maintain power to control subsequent uses of the information. The question here is whether the extent the law is constitutionally permitted to protect this interest varies depending on whether the protection is against press exposure or against other commercial, but still communicative,[111] uses. In every case decided so

---

110. Samuel D. Warren & Louis D. Brandeis, *The Right to Privacy*, 4 HARV. L. REV. 193 (1890).

111. Sometimes, rather than prevent the flow of information the law adopts the strategy of denying businesses the right to make use of the information in their decision-making. For example, some laws prohibit businesses from basing hiring, selling, or other commercial decisions on the race, gender, sexual orientation, religion or other categorical aspects of individuals even though it allows them to possess this information. This restriction does not directly relate to the flow of the

far by the Supreme Court, it has struck down attempts to protect individual privacy from truthful media exposure,[112] while (as far as I know) never finding unconstitutional legislative attempts to protect this privacy against intrusion by other businesses (or by the government). Thus, despite the huge and popular development of this "right," it remains possible to argue that the Supreme Court would not and should not uphold any restriction on media exposure. Pragmatically, this distinction may reflect that non-media businesses and government are the source of the more common intrusions that matter to most people. In any event, the law at present clearly embodies greater protection here of the speech rights of the media than of other businesses.

Doctrine in this area is still developing. Some, but decidedly not all, states presumably make it a tort to expose certain private information about a person.[113] Nevertheless, the category of private information protected by general tort law that applies to the media is usually very, maybe even vanishingly, narrow. For example, it usually covers only information that is both "not of legitimate concern to the public" and also is of a type whose disclosure "would be highly offensive to a reasonable person."[114] Cases where states have in fact recognized the tort, especially as applied to the media, have been rare and the tort has been subject to severe judicial and scholarly criticism.[115]

So far, the Supreme Court has only examined restrictions on communication of private information in media cases where statutes specifically restricted communication of discrete categories of information—for example, the name of rape victims, juvenile defendants, or information about confidential proceedings before a Judicial Inquiry and Review Commission investigating alleged improper behavior by a judge.[116] In every decision, the Court has upheld the

---

information, though gathering information about these qualities can sometimes be evidence of intent to make improper use of it.

112. Paul Gewirtz, *Privacy and Speech*, 2001 SUP. CT. REV. 139, 176.

113. Among the states, Oregon and New York have rejected the tort. *See* Anderson v. Fisher Broad. Cos., 712 P.2d 803, 814 (Or. 1986) (a carefully reasoned opinion by Hans Linde that paid great attention to free speech considerations); Roberson v. Rochester Folding Box Co., 64 N.E. 442, 447 (N.Y. 1902).

114. RESTATEMENT (SECOND) OF TORTS § 652D (1976); *see also* Haynes v. Alfred A. Knopf, Inc., 8 F.3d 1222, 1229 (7th Cir. 1993).

115. *See, e.g.*, *Anderson*, 712 P.2d at 808; Diane L. Zimmerman, *Requiem for a Heavyweight: A Farewell to Warren and Brandeis's Privacy Tort*, 68 CORNELL L. REV. 291, 296-99 (1983); *see also* C. Edwin Baker, *Autonomy and Informational Privacy, or Gossip: The Central Meaning of the First Amendment*, 21 SOC. PHIL. & POL'Y 215 (2004).

116. *See, e.g.*, Florida Star v. B.J.F., 491 U.S. 524, 530 (1989); Smith v. Daily Mail Publ'g Co., 443 U.S. 97, 98-100 (1979); Landmark Commc'ns v. Virginia, 435 U.S. 829, 837-38 (1978).

media's constitutional objections and protected their speech.[117] In every case, however, the Court cautiously wrote its opinion very narrowly—explicitly leaving open the possibility of upholding prohibitions on media exposure of private information in an appropriate case.[118] Still, the First Amendment clearly protects most, if not all, communication of "private" information by the media.

The situation changes when the legal regulation of the practices of other commercial entities is examined. They are subject to considerable regulation in their disclosure of personal information about individuals.[119] Probably the area of greatest societal concern has been information kept in databases, medical records, and credit reports. As a central example, consider credit reporting agencies—that is, private businesses engaged in providing personal consumer credit or related information to third parties.[120] Their communications are regulated in ways that clearly could not be imposed on newspapers or other mass media. For example, credit reporting agencies can only supply reports to certain persons—that is, the law limits the people to whom they can speak![121] They cannot include certain information, for example, about a bankruptcy that occurred over ten years before the report or about many other adverse events that occurred over seven years earlier.[122] In many cases—for example, if the report will be used in connection with an employment decision or in some cases when the information relates to medical records, the credit reporting agency can provide the information only with the consent of the person about whom it is speaking.[123]

117. *See, e.g.*, *Smith*, 443 U.S. at 106.

118. *See, e.g.*, *id.*

119. Joel R. Reidenberg, *Privacy in the Information Economy: A Fortress or Frontier for Individual Rights?*, 44 FED. COMM. L.J. 195 (1992).

120. 15 U.S.C. § 1681a(f) (2000) (defining consumer reporting agencies). Other commercial enterprises are similarly prohibited from disclosing information that the press or media could not be stopped from disclosing, at least, could not be in respect to their constitutional roles of communicating information to the public. For example, the Family Education Rights and Privacy Act of 1974, 20 U.S.C.A. § 1232g (b) (1) (2002), prohibits schools that receive federal money from releasing various information about a student—her confidential letters of recommendation, financial information, and educational records. If able to obtain the information, as it often has, a newspaper would undoubtedly be protected in including it within a news story. The same is true for the Video Privacy Protection Act of 1988, 18 U.S.C. § 2710 (2000), which regulates information that a videotape service provider can disclose about its customers, in particular the subject matter of the videos its customers rent—though surely, if the press had this information, it could publish it, for instance if were about a judicial nominee (the Act was passed in part in reaction to the exposure of such information during the nomination of Judge Robert Bork for a Supreme Court seat).

121. 15 U.S.C. § 1681b(a) (2000).

122. *Id.* § 1681c(a)(1).

123. *Id.* § 1681b(b)(2)(A)(ii), § 1681b(g).

Moreover, often the credit reporting agency's communications must include information that the consumer demands be included—for example, the fact that she disputes some of the information or that she is fearful that an identity theft is occurring.[124] If applied to newspapers, all of these requirements—that it only communicate with certain people, that it not communicate various factual information about the past, that it communicate information demanded by the person described in the story, that it not communicate information about the person without her consent—would clearly be unconstitutional. Both credit agencies and the press are in the speech business, but the First Amendment apparently protects the speech of only one, the newspaper.

2. Right of Publicity

As copyright and privacy law illustrate, all areas of legally granting property rights in information or expression—in the material subject to communication—have been subject to severe and powerful legal critique. This proposition is true, too, for the so-called right of publicity, the right of a person to control the use of her image or persona.[125] That general critique is not the present concern—rather the concern is the specific content of this modern, state-created, right of publicity.[126] The New York legislature created the most famous version soon after its highest court in 1902 rejected a claim of a common law right of privacy against an advertiser who had used a picture of the plaintiff, a very attractive young girl, in its advertising for Franklin Mills Flour.[127] The legislature created liability (and injunctive relief) for unauthorized "uses for advertising purposes, or the purposes of trade, [of] the name, portrait or picture of any living person . . . ."[128] But, the courts tell us, purposes of trade do not include uses by the media in their constitutionally-protected communicative roles.[129]

Various versions of this statutory protection of the right of publicity are common. California law, for example, provides liability for "[a]ny person who [without prior consent] knowingly uses another's name, voice, signature, photograph, or likeness, in any manner, on or in

124. *Id.* § 1681c-1.

125. *See, e.g.*, Michael Madow, *Private Ownership of Public Image: Popular Culture and Publicity Rights*, 81 CAL. L. REV. 125 (1993).

126. It is sometimes said that this right was first recognized in Haelan Labs., Inc. v. Topps Chewing Gum, Inc., 202 F.2d 866, 868 (2d Cir. 1953). *See* FRANKLIN ET AL., *supra* note 31, 403-08 (discussing the tort ensuing from the right of publicity).

127. Roberson v. Rochester Folding Box Co., 64 N.E. 442, 447 (N.Y. 1902).

128. N.Y. CIV. RIGHT L. §§ 50, 51 (McKinney 1992).

129. *See* Finger v. Omni Publ'n Int'l, Ltd., 77 N.Y.2d 138, 143 (1990).

products, merchandise, or goods, or for purposes of advertising or selling, or soliciting purchases . . . ."[130] The modern trend toward recognizing such rights is widespread.[131] Thus, the Restatement (Second) of Torts § 652C provides: "One who appropriates to his own use or benefit the name or likeness of another is subject to liability to the other . . . ."[132]

These limits on the "beneficial" or commercial uses of people's name or image, if the rights are as broad as the initial statement suggests (i.e., "use . . . in products") would destroy the press as we know it and especially undermine its Fourth Estate role. Unsurprisingly, exceptions to the various statutes and "comment d" to the Restatement make clear that the right does not cover legitimate media uses.[133] Undoubtedly, publications often include stories, pictures, and details about celebrities to attract audiences or, more generally, for profit making reasons. Still, "comment d" of the Restatement insists:

> The fact that the defendant is engaged in the business of publication, for example of a newspaper, out of which he makes or seeks to make a profit, is not enough to make the incidental publication a commercial use of the name or likeness. Thus a newspaper . . . does not become liable under the rule stated in this Section to every person whose name or likeness it publishes.[134]

Here, as the Restatement and many state statutes make clear, even though the press and other businesses both use people's persona and

---

130. CAL. CIV. CODE § 3344(a) (West 1999).

131. *See* Stacey L. Dogan & Mark A. Lemley, *What the Right of Publicity Can Learn from Trademark Law*, 58 STAN. L. REV. 1161, 1167-75 (2006).

132. RESTATEMENT (SECOND) OF TORTS § 652C (1976).

133. As used here, "legitimate" refers objectively to the type of use, not a subjective evaluation of the propriety of the editorial judgment. Given the constitutional role of the media, knowing falsehoods—e.g., falsehoods that are not mere negligent errors are not aspects of the press or of speech that is protected by the First Amendment. *See* New York Times Co. v. Sullivan, 376 U.S. 254, 279-80 (1964). Thus, knowing (or probably reckless) falsity would deny the media content the status of being a protected press product and turn its use of a person's image into a mere commercial use. *See, e.g.*, Cher v. Forum Int'l, Ltd., 692 F.2d 634, 639 (9th Cir. 1982). On the other hand, some uses within advertising may not equate to a regulated advertising use. One court found that the press's advertising for itself did not involve a commercial use of a person's image when the advertisement merely printed a copy of the advertised publication to illustrate the publication's content despite the copy containing a picture of a celebrity. *See* Booth v. Curtis Publ'g Co., 223 N.Y.S.2d 737, 743-46 (N.Y. App. Div. 1962), *aff'd without opinion*, 11 N.Y.2d 907 (1962).

134. RESTATEMENT (SECOND) OF TORTS § 652C, cmt. d (1976). The words "incidental" and "every" person suggest that sometimes a newspaper story could be the basis of liability but that has not been the case at least as to true accounts that would generally be protected by the First Amendment.

image to make money, when it is used for press purposes, the law does not grant the person used any "right to object."[135]

As described here, the difference between the treatment of the press and other businesses is a matter merely of statutory or common law grace. Surely, however, the notion that the law could require the press to gain consent before describing or picturing the day's newsmakers or society's corrupt officials is a constitutional non-starter. The currently accepted capacity of the state to give people rights against many commercial forms of exploitation of their image would be unconstitutional if the state attempted to restrict the press's freedom to report on people's role in the world or to print images of people participating in public life. Given the presumptively legitimate public interest in the full scope of people's lives as a matter of awareness of the norms and foibles of the people in their society, the prominence or lack thereof of the person or the nature of the story is not likely to change this conclusion. Except for the lack of need due to the statutory exemption of the press, the constitutional basis for protecting the press's use of people's names or images could easily be developed using constitutional analyses from defamation and privacy cases as doctrinal resources. Thus, the right of publicity illustrates a distinction that currently exists statutorily between media enterprises and other business enterprises, but that constitutionally could not plausibly be eliminated by treating the press the way other commercial users are now treated. Although legislation and common law restrict some businesses' profitable use of people's personae or images in their product or to promote their product, it would be unconstitutional to do so to press's use within its product—no pictures of the candidates or the home run sluggers in the paper! Of course, there are line-drawing issues that may or may not have constitutional dimensions.[136] Still, here, a constitutional difference surely exists between speech by the press and by other businesses.

---

135. *Id.*

136. *See* Montana v. San Jose Mercury News, Inc., 40 Cal. Rptr. 2d 639, 643 (Cal. Ct. App. 1995); Namath v. Sports Illustrated, 371 N.Y.S.2d 10, 11-12 (N.Y. App. Div. 1975); *Booth*, 223 N.Y.S.2d at 743-46. If the Press Clause is interpreted, as I have argued it should be, from the perspective of complex democracy to include cultural media that are important for people's self-definition and groups' internal debates about identity and values, most cases where a persona or image of a person is the product itself, as opposed to merely being used in an advertisement or promotion, the Press Clause ought to prevent the right of publicity from being used to restrict this commercial use. *Cf.* Madow, *supra* note 125, at 239 (reaching this conclusion largely on policy grounds).

3. Campaign Expenditures

A narrow five member majority initially granted First Amendment protection to corporate political expenditures in the context of referenda, reasoning that "[t]he inherent worth of the speech in terms of its capacity for informing the public does not depend upon the identity of its source, whether corporation, association, union, or individual."[137] Then in two subsequent cases, adopting reasoning closely paralleling a dissent in the earlier case, the Court reversed course.[138] It emphasized the centrality of individual self-expression and the importance for First Amendment purposes of the actual speakers' allegiance to the viewpoint expressed.[139] On this basis, the Court in *Austin v. Michigan Chamber of Commerce* and *McConnell v. Federal Election Commission* upheld strict limits on corporate use of money to support electoral candidates,[140] relegating the notion of "[t]he inherent worth of the speech . . . for informing the public" to the wishes of very irate dissents.[141]

Each restriction on corporate political speech either exempted the press or, in *Bellotti*, its applicability to the press was not before the Court.[142] In upholding the restrictions in *Austin*, the Court rejected the non-media corporations' argument that exempting the media violated equal protection.[143] The much more troubling question—and an issue brought up in each case by those objecting to limits on corporate campaign speech—is whether the press must be exempted, that is, whether the First Amendment requires that the press be allowed to use its resources to write stories and publish commentary about candidates.[144] (Portions of the Bipartisan Campaign Reform Act of 2002—"BCRA"—upheld by the Court barred non-media business corporations from using general treasury funds for broadcast ads that even "refer to" candidates in the period shortly before elections, which

137. First Nat'l Bank of Boston v. Bellotti, 435 U.S. 765, 777 (1978).

138. *See* McConnell v. Fed. Election Comm'n, 540 U.S. 93, 233 (2003); Austin v. Mich. Chamber of Commerce, 494 U.S. 652, 667-68 (1990).

139. *McConnell*, 540 U.S. at 205; *Austin*, 494 U.S. at 666.

140. Obviously, the cases are formally distinguishable on grounds that the first involved a referendum and, thus, there was no candidate subject to corruption, but the rationale of the first case easily encompasses the later cases and rationale of the later cases is essentially the rationale of the dissent in the first.

141. *Austin*, 494 U.S. at 700 (Kennedy, J., dissenting); *McConnell*, 540 U.S. at 257 (Scalia, J., dissenting); *id.* at 328 (Kennedy, J., dissenting as to this issue).

142. *Bellotti*, 435 U.S. at 781-82 n.17.

143. *Austin*, 494 U.S. at 667-68.

144. *Id.* at 667 ("We have consistently recognized the unique role that the press plays in 'informing and educating the public, offering criticism, and providing a forum for discussion and debate.'") (quoting *Bellotti*, 435 U.S. at 781); *see also McConnell*, 540 U.S. at 208.

raises the question of whether the press too could be barred from referring to candidates for political office during the period leading up to an election.)[145] Surely, the answer must be that the First Amendment requires that the press be permitted to refer to political candidates. But without an independent meaning for the Press Clause, it is unclear how to make an argument for mandatory exemption. In contrast, given independent constitutional protection for the press, the argument is easy. Unlike other businesses, evaluation of candidates by the press is part of its constitutional role. Since surely no one would think BCRA can be permissibly applied to the news media in their media roles,[146] if one also assumes (as I do)[147] that existing doctrine is correct, that is, that the Court was correct to uphold restrictions on general corporate political participation, it is hard to avoid the conclusion that First Amendment must provide the press special protection different from and greater than that of other enterprises.

The opposite view—that media cannot be distinguished from other businesses for First Amendment purposes—was, of course, a possibility advanced by the dissenting Justices. That conclusion would surely lead to striking down the restrictions on corporate expenditures. Thus, Justice Scalia, beginning with the assertion that the Court has "consistently rejected the proposition that the institutional press has any constitutional privilege beyond that of other speakers," concludes that one can only "hope . . . that Michigan will continue to provide this generous and voluntary exemption," a hope that he suggests should give the institutional press "little reason for comfort."[148] Justice Kennedy combines the conclusion, offered in reliance on a quote from Justice Brennan in *Dun & Bradstreet* that the institutional media has (at least in the context of that case) no special constitutional rights, with the point that "[i]t is beyond peradventure that the media could not be prohibited from speaking about candidate qualifications," to conclude that the bar on corporate campaign expenditures must be invalid.[149] In *McConnell*, Justice Thomas argues: "The chilling endpoint of the Court's reasoning

145. 2 U.S.C. § 434 (Supp. 2001-2004).

146. Like other corporations, presumably they can be restricted in the campaign contributions or campaign expenditures that are unrelated to their media business.

147. BAKER, HUMAN LIBERTY AND FREEDOM OF SPEECH, *supra* note 19, at 196-97; C. Edwin Baker, *Paternalism, Politics, and Citizen Freedom: The Commercial Speech Quandary in* Nike, 54 CASE W. RES. L. REV. 1161, 1170 (2004) [hereinafter Baker, *Paternalism, Politics, and Citizen Freedom*]; C. Edwin Baker, *Realizing Self-Realization: Corporate Political Expenditures and Redish's the Value of Free Speech*, 130 U. PA. L. REV. 646, 652 (1982).

148. *Austin*, 494 U.S. at 691-92.

149. *Id.* at 712 (Kennedy, J., dissenting).

is not difficult to foresee: outright regulation of the press. . . . [N]one of the reasoning employed by the Court exempts the press . . . . The press now operates at the whim of Congress."[150]

Analytically correct conclusions are clear. One can strike down laws restricting corporate political expenditures without taking a position in regards to an independent interpretation of the Press Clause. But to uphold these laws, as the Court has done in both *Austin* and *McConnell*, requires the Court to at least implicitly accept an independent interpretation of the Press Clause. As Justice Kennedy put it, "it is beyond peradventure" that the Court would leave the press vulnerable to these regulations. The press must be exempt from these laws not simply as a matter of legislative grace but of constitutional right. And there seems no basis for that exemption absent an interpretation of the Press Clause that gives the media special rights.

B. *The Press Compared to Other Speaking Professions*

1. Duty of Care: Press Versus Accountants, Lawyers, or Other Speaking Professions

Many businesses are liable for pecuniary losses caused by their supplying negligently "false information for the guidance of others in their business transactions."[151] The Ohio Supreme Court has held this duty applies to accountants in relation to their clients.[152] Then, in *Gutter v. Dow Jones, Inc.*, it distinguished accountants in explaining that this duty does not apply to newspapers in relation to its readers.[153] In addition to describing how its holding represented the "general view" among jurisdictions about reasons for not holding the media liable for harms resulting from people's reliance on its negligently false statements, the Court also emphasized that First Amendment principles likely preclude liability.[154]

150. McConnell v. Fed. Election Comm'n, 540 U.S. 93, 283, 286 (2003) (Scalia, J., dissenting).

151. RESTATEMENT (SECOND) OF TORTS § 552(1) (1977).

152. The court described its earlier holding involving accountants. Haddon View Inv. Co. v. Coopers & Lybrand, 436 N.E.2d 212, 215 (Ohio 1980) (citing Rusch Factors, Inc. v. Levin, 284 F. Supp. 85, 93 (D.R.I. 1968)).

153. Gutter v. Dow Jones, Inc., 490 N.E.2d 898, 900 (Ohio 1986).

154. *See id.* at 901. The court also noted factual differences between the communications of newspapers and accountants—the number of clients or customers who might rely on the communication and the reasonableness of the reliance—that arguably support, on policy grounds, the distinction. Whether the product of any business other than the press is "communications to the world" is unclear but, if so, an attempt to impose liability on that business might test the issue of

This merely represents one of many areas where professionals of various sorts are subject to liability for negligent speech while the press generally receives greater protection. "Speaking professions" commonly are subject to malpractice liability for negligently failing to base advice on facts or wisdom they are expected to possess; they can even be liable for failure to speak when required by professional standards.[155] That is true, for example, in the context of regulation of the medical profession[156] and lawyers.[157] Speech restrictions designed to maintain quality of performance of these speaking professions are and should be upheld. This standard applied for liability is, however, a far cry from standards typically applied to the press. There, criteria for liability are typically "reckless disregard of the truth" or "knowingly false," which apply to the press in tort law as illustrated most clearly by defamation law, or versions of the clear and present danger test, which applies in many other situations.[158]

For example, the First Amendment allows regulation of lawyers if the regulation is designed to assure their proper performance—though the notion of proper performance may have constitutional overtones itself given the constitutional establishment of their role in maintaining due process.[159] Thus, Chief Justice Rehnquist, speaking for a majority in *Gentile v. State Bar of Nevada*, held that a defense attorney, during the pendency of a case in which she is involved, can be punished for having a press conference in which she (truthfully) offers her view about the innocence of her client and the existence of police corruption even though this speech would clearly be protected if made either by a private

---

whether the First Amendment protection that the court discussed applied to all business because of the context. More likely, the protection applied especially to newspapers (or media), the entities of First Amendment concern that the court emphasized throughout its opinion and were emphasized in the cases it cited and in its quote from *American Jurisprudence 2d*. *See id.* at 900.

155. Daniel Halberstam, *Commercial Speech, Professional Speech, and the Constitutional Status of Social Institutions*, 147 U. PA. L. REV. 771, 834-50 (1999).

156. *See id.* at 834; *see generally* Robert Post, *Informed Consent to Abortion: A First Amendment Analysis of Compelled Physician Speech*, 2007 U. ILL. L. REV 939.

157. *See* Halberstam, *supra* note 155, at 834.

158. *Compare* Hustler Magazine, Inc. v. Falwell, 485 U.S. 46, 52 (1988) (noting the standard for liability that applies to the press in tort law and quoting New York Times Co. v. Sullivan, 376 U.S. 254, 279-80 (1964)) *and* Herceg v. Hustler Magazine, Inc., 814 F.2d 1017, 1022-23 (5th Cir. 1987) (applying the incitement test from *Brandenburg v. Ohio*, 395 U.S. 444 (1969), to deny media liability) *with* Gentile v. State Bar of Nev., 501 U.S. 1030, 1038-39 (1991) (discussing the standard that applies to lawyers).

159. The central difference between the opinions of the majority and dissent in *Gentile* can be read as a disagreement about the appropriate conception of the lawyer's role, and on that a very good case can be made that the dissent had the better of the argument.

individual or the press.[160] That is, Rehnquist rejected a "clear and present danger" of "actual prejudice or an imminent threat" standard and rejected other analogies to protection of speech by the press as appropriate standards to be met "before any discipline may be imposed on a lawyer who initiates a press conference such as [the one conducted in *Gentile*]."[161] More generally, the clear and present danger standard that the Court has applied to communications by individuals[162] and the press[163] for speech about pending legal proceedings is precisely the speech that the Court in *Nebraska Press Association v. Stuart* suggested restricting in the case of participating lawyers.[164] Lawyers, it seems, because of their occupation or "business" have less speech rights than the First Amendment provides the press (or private individuals).

2. Licensing Securities Advisors

In *Lowe v. SEC*, the Court avoided the question of whether the government can require a newspaper that provides the public with financial information to be licensed under rules that allow the government to deny or revoke the license for past unethical or illegal behavior.[165] Surely, however, such a regime would constitute a system of prior restraints.[166] The law at issue, however, provided such licensure requirements for securities advisors.[167] Although Lowe was now seemingly publishing a newsletter, the SEC characterized his practice as coming under the law and took action to prevent him from continuing to distribute his newsletter. The Court majority rejected this result by

---

160. *Gentile*, 501 U.S. at 1071.

161. *Id.* at 1069.

162. *See, e.g.*, Bridges v. California, 314 U.S. 252, 260-62 (1941).

163. Nebraska Press Ass'n v. Stuart, 427 U.S. 539, 570 (1976). By counting Justices, *Nebraska Press* can be read to leave open the possibility of even greater protection than offered by the clear and present danger test, namely for Justice Brennan's view that an injunction should never be issued to stop publication by the press of information about criminal proceedings. Likewise, in referring to *Bridges* context, Justice Brennan asserted in *New York Times Co. v. Sullivan* that the speech not only does not lose its protection because the utterances contain misinformation and half-truths but also that "repression [of the speech] can be justified, *if at all*, only by a clear and present danger of the obstruction of justice," which "Bridges' threat to cripple the economy of the entire West Coast" apparently did not create. 376 U.S. 254, 272-73 (1964) (emphasis added); LAURENCE H. TRIBE, AMERICAN CONSTITUTIONAL LAW 624 (1978).

164. *Nebraska Press Ass'n*, 427 U.S. at 552-54 (citing with approval such steps as recommended in Sheppard v. Maxwell, 384 U.S. 333, 362-63 (1966)).

165. Lowe v. SEC, 472 U.S. 181, 189-90, 211 (1985).

166. *Cf.* Near v. Minnesota, 283 U.S. 697 (1931) (prior objectionable behavior was found not to be basis for enjoining future publication).

167. *See Lowe*, 472 U.S. at 203-09 (discussing the licensure requirements and exceptions under 15 U.S.C. § 80b-2).

finding that Lowe came within the *statutory* exception for the publishers of a "bona fide newspaper, news magazine or business or financial publication of general and regular circulation."[168]

No one questioned that these licensure requirements could be imposed on the business of investment advising, but would the Constitution permit them to be imposed on the press? In many ways, the question resembles the issue of the accepted authority of the government to impose license requirements on speaking professions—say doctors or psychiatrists or lawyers—as a precondition for practicing their trade despite the recognized right of newspapers to have its journalists or columnists write medical reports or columns, personal self-help advice columns, or legal columns that provide information that many people rely on in lieu of going to a professional. In these examples, the law requires neither the newspaper nor its "reporters" or columnists to have a professional license, at least as long as neither the paper nor its reporter falsely claims to be a doctor or lawyer. Still, both the person for whom the law requires a license and the publication and its writers are in the business of providing information, opinion, and advice and the content of the information or advice may be identical in each case. What, then, is the relevant difference? Only the latter is the "press." This fact apparently bars imposing the license requirement.

In *Lowe*, Justice White, joined by two other Justices, found that the statute did cover Lowe.[169] This interpretation raised the question of government power noted above. Without questioning the power of the government to require a revocable license for security advisors, Justice White then concluded that the statute violated the First Amendment when applied to Lowe. He was not entirely clear about the basis of his conclusion—for example, he did not decide whether Lowe's speech was "fully protected" or was "commercial." And he did not specifically rest on the Press Clause as opposed to the protection the First Amendment provides for speaking and publishing.[170] However, his method of distinguishing this case from regulatable speech of professionals looked precisely at the factors that distinguish the professionals' business from the press—factors such as a "personal nexus between professional and client."[171] In other words, it seems that the premise required for the proper result—a result that one suspects the rest of the Court would reach except for their different statutory interpretation and would surely

168. *See id.* at 210; 15 U.S.C. § 80b-2(a)(11)(D) (2000).

169. *See Lowe*, 472 U.S. at 211 (White, J., concurring).

170. *See id.* at 234-35.

171. *See id.* at 232.

reach if the law were applied to the reporters for the business section of the *New York Times*—is that the press is a special constitutionally-protected business.

3. Speaking Professions and the Perversion of Defamation Law

As noted in the introduction and contrary to some interpretations, *Dun & Bradstreet, Inc. v. Greenmoss Builders, Inc.*[172] does not require rejection of an independent status of the Press Clause. The Court only refused to give the press greater protection than given an individual.[173] The Court's reasoning, however, is problematic. Though right not to distinguish the press from individuals,[174] by failing to distinguish the press from credit reporting agencies, the Court cast doubt on the logic of vast areas of law that treat the press differently than other businesses. Thus, here I offer three observations. First, the Court could have reached its final result much more easily than it did. Second, the method it chose greatly and unwisely deformed defamation law. Finally, if read as rejecting an independent role of the Press Clause, this decision would come at the cost of destroying the whole regime of regulation of credit reporting agencies in particular and regulation of medical records and other databases in general.

In *Dun & Bradstreet*, the majority of the Court stated that the media did not have greater protection in defamation suits than individuals do.[175] Any other holding would, I believe, be absurd. Given that defamation law normally (though the exceptions are considerable) treats repeaters of defamatory content as if they were original speakers,[176] giving lesser protection to individuals leads to the absurdist image of a person at the breakfast table reading a passage from a newspaper to her partner and then being held liable for her reading while the First Amendment protects the newspaper that originally published the story. But to say that the press receives no greater protection than an individual does not mean that it cannot receive greater protection than other businesses. Such a view would have allowed the Court to reach the outcome it reached. Instead, by failing to recognize this role for the Press Clause, the plurality found it could only reach its (correct, in my view) result of upholding liability for the credit agency by deforming defamation law in

172. 472 U.S. 749 (1985).

173. *See supra* notes 12-17 and accompanying text.

174. *Dun & Bradstreet*, 472 U.S. at 753.

175. *Id.* at 773 (White, J., concurring); *id.* at 784 (Brennan, J., dissenting).

176. *See, e.g.*, RESTATEMENT (SECOND) OF TORTS § 578 (1977).

two unfortunate ways.[177] The plurality, first, increased the general availability of punitive damages in defamation law—which also increased the practical significance of the difficult task of drawing lines between matters of public concern and purely private information; second, it gave the notion of "matters of public concern" an intolerably narrow interpretation.[178]

As to the first point, in *Gertz v. Robert Welch*, the Court announced that a "private defamation plaintiff who establishes liability under a less demanding standard than that stated by *New York Times* may recover only such damages as are sufficient to compensate him for actual injury."[179] This complete rejection of punitive damages absent a showing of *New York Times* actual malice was also noted in opinions of other Justices.[180] The important limitation the Court changed eleven years later in *Dun & Bradstreet*. In respect to speech that is not on "matters of public concern," that is, "speech on matters of purely private concern," the plurality in *Dun & Bradstreet* held "that the state interest adequately supports awards of presumed and punitive damages—even absent a showing of 'actual malice.'"[181] This holding troublingly expands the potential for punitive damages in defamation cases[182] unless the category of matters "not of public concern" is a null set.

The second move, criticized vigorously by Brennan's dissent as a radical and ill-advised departure, is the plurality's characterization of the speech at issue. Brennan's complaint is that speech reporting the bankruptcy of a local employer is "potentially of great concern to residents of the community" and comes well within the category of a matter of public concern as that term had previously been used.[183]

---

177. *Dun & Bradstreet*, 472 U.S. at 757-63.

178. *Id.* On the dangers of bowing to majoritarian norms implicit in this line-drawing, see Anderson v. Fisher Broad. Cos., 712 P.2d 803, 809 (Or. 1986).

179. Gertz v. Robert Welch, Inc., 418 U.S. 323, 350 (1974). The Court asserted essentially this proposition repeatedly. For example, it said: "We also find no justification for allowing awards of punitive damages against publishers and broadcasters held liable under state-defined standards of liability for defamation." *Id.* "It is necessary to restrict defamation plaintiffs who do not prove knowledge of falsity or reckless disregard for the truth to compensation for actual injury." *Id.* at 349.

180. *See id.* at 354 (Blackmun, J., concurring); *id.* at 368-69 n.3 (Brennan, J., dissenting)

181. *Dun & Bradstreet*, 472 U.S. at 759, 761.

182. Five of the Justices in *Dun & Bradstreet* observe that this amounts to a rejection of *Gertz* and an expansion of when liability can occur. *See id.* at 772 (White, J., concurring); *id.* at 785 n.11 (Brennan, J., dissenting).

183. *Id.* at 789. Interestingly, Justice Brennan argues that the bankruptcy report is a matter of public concern and, even if it were not, is "well within the range of valuable expression for which the First Amendment demands protection." *Id.* at 790 (Brennan, J., dissenting). Justice Brennan, implicitly accepting the relevance of *Gertz*'s rule structure in this context, quotes a law review

Justice Powell's explanation for a contrary conclusion is difficult to construct and appears to be entirely driven by his effort to achieve the right result—subjecting the credit reporting agency's speech to legal regulation.[184] Justice Powell cites a holding that concluded that, for purposes of the speech rights of government employees, the determination of whether their speech was a matter of public concern depended on its "content, form, and context."[185] Although Brennan suggested that Justice Powell "appear[s] to focus on primarily on subject matter" (that is, "content"), Justice Powell actually never says anything about subject matter but only about form and context.[186] Justice Powell does point to the relevance of contextual factors that characterize the credit report as speech offered by a business (the report was done for profit and had other qualities that the Court has identified with commercial speech) and other factors that also typify credit reporting but that distinguish it from media speech (the report had a limited, discrete audience who are contractually prohibited from further circulating the information).[187] On this basis, the result would have been easy if Justice Powell had merely asserted that First Amendment protection accorded individuals and the press did not encompass the speech of (at least some) non-media businesses. This step, the basis for which he had laid, would implicitly recognize the independent significance of the Press Clause. Failure to take it and instead to announce purportedly general principles led directly to the deformation of defamation law identified here.

The Court's refusal to rest liability on the difference between the press and credit reporting agencies initially caused fear in the press about potential liability under the *Dun & Bradstreet* standard. Nevertheless, reasons for worry apparently have not materialized. Courts, properly disinclined to second guess editors about what is of public concern, have in effect treated the press differently from other

---

article that shows that the Fair Credit Reporting Act would, as does *Gertz*, allow liability here for negligence but that the Act is best interpreted to rule out, as would *Gertz*, punitive damages. That is, despite the wide disparity between the speech regulations imposed by the Fair Credit Reporting Act and those that would be constitutional if applied to the press, Brennan appears not to object to the Fair Credit Reporting Act, thereby implicitly being committed, as the earlier discussion of privacy showed, to a separate interpretation of the Press Clause. *Id.* at 796 n.19 (Brennan, J., dissenting) (quoting Virginia G. Maurer, *Common Law Defamation and the Fair Credit Reporting Act*, 72 GEO. L.J. 95, 126 (1983)); *see also* Brennan, *supra* note 10 at 175-77.

184. *Dun & Bradstreet*, 472 U.S. at 761-63.

185. *Id.* at 761. Brennan complained that the Court had explicitly limited this test, taken from *Connick v. Myers*, 461 U.S. 138 (1983), to the public employee "context." *Id.* at 789-90 n.14 (Brennan, J., dissenting).

186. *Compare id.* at 786 (Brennan, J., dissenting) *with id.* at 761-62.

187. *Id.* at 762-63.

businesses by deferring to the press's judgments about what matters are of public concern.[188] Brennan had already observed that the speech in *Dun & Bradstreet* "would clearly receive the comprehensive protections of *Gertz* were the speech publicly disseminated."[189] In effect, lower courts, and maybe Justice Powell, have *sub rosa* embodied an independent reading of the Press Clause in their interpretation of "context" as a criterion of "public importance."[190] The fact that the press originates the speech seems in practice to represent a "context" that shows that it is of public importance and should receive protection.

Interestingly, existing regulations of the speaking professions and of credit reporting in behalf of protecting privacy illustrate that the route not taken in *Dun & Bradstreet* is firmly embedded in existing law. Nevertheless, *Dun & Bradstreet* leaves defamation as an area where I cannot claim that the Court has implicitly recognized the independent significance of the Press Clause. However, it represents an area where the failure to recognize this principle has led to doctrinal shambles and where the pressure for the correct principle, an independent status for the press, has led to its *sub rosa* acceptance that fortunately allows for appropriate protection of the press. Certainly, recognizing the Press Clause as distinguishing the press from other businesses is by far the easiest way to reach a result that the Court reached—upholding state defined standards of liability for inappropriate, here false, credit reporting. (This interpretation would also allow the dissent to use the significant—even though reduced—protection granted commercial speech to frame its objection to the majority's conclusion.)

C. Other Reduced Speech Rights of Non-Media Businesses

1. Compelled Identification of Non-Media Originated Speech

Part II observed that statutes often require the media to identify the source of communication content that it was paid to carry. Of course, as the Court of Appeals observed in *SEC v. Wall Street Publishing Institute, Inc.*, "forcing a magazine to label its contents as published in return for consideration received from the subject of its articles carries an inherently pejorative connotation."[191] Still, the court there upheld the general requirement to disclose the fact of consideration and the amount

188. FRANKLIN ET AL., *supra* note 31, at 312.

189. *Dun & Bradstreet*, 472 U.S. at 795 n.18 (Brennan, J., dissenting).

190. *See, e.g.*, *id.* at 762 n.8; *id.* at 786 n.12, 795 n.18.

191. SEC v. Wall Street Publ'g Inst. Inc., 851 F.2d 365, 376 (D.C. Cir. 1988).

paid for publishing a story promoting a particular financial security.[192] This compelled identification could either deter the media from carrying the "paid for" speech or deter the entity that paid from being willing to do so. In either event, the requirement "burdens" the speech. *Miami Herald* teaches that the government cannot punish or penalize the media for its choice to carry particular (protected) content, for example by requiring it to include additional unwanted content in response to its initial speech choices.[193] That "penalty" is precisely what is accomplished by requiring the media to identify material as paid content. The two holdings are in apparent conflict.

The special constitutional status of the press eliminates the conflict. If the media receives special protection only for speech it originates (and that is constitutionally valued precisely because the speech originated in an independent press), and if this protection is not given to other commercial entities for their speech, the mandatory disclosure should not be troublesome. The mandated disclosure will burden or deter speech, but only speech whose ultimate basis lies in another, non-media business.[194] Thus, for the Court to uphold the provision of the Securities Act that makes it unlawful to describe a security for consideration unlawful without disclosing the fact and the amount of consideration[195] makes sense only if the rights recognized in *Miami Herald* apply only to the press (and maybe private individuals), but not to businesses in general.[196] In fact, as discussed in Part II, requiring this disclosure enhances rather than violates the institutional integrity of the media.

---

192. The court held that mere receipt of free text would not amount to consideration, but the facts alleged could show the necessary quid pro quo. *Id.*

193. *See* Miami Herald Publ'g Co. v. Tornillo, 418 U.S. 241, 256-58 (1974); Turner Broad. Sys., Inc. v. FCC, 512 U.S. 622, 653-56 (1994).

194. Presumably, the other business that paid to have its message carried could itself be a media entity—certainly the media actively advertise their products. The type of speech for which a Fourth Estate interpretation of the Press Clause requires protection is, however, the speech that originates in the Fourth Estate entity identified with the speech. In having another media entity promote its media content by carrying its message, the media entity is in the same position of any other business—and presumably can be required to self-identify. *See infra* note 206.

More interesting is if the outside payment comes not from a business but an individual claiming a speech right to pay for politically salient speech and also asserting free speech rights of anonymity. Here, requiring the media to identify the source, thereby discouraging the individual's anonymous speech, must be understood as holding that individuals, although free to maintain anonymity on their own (e.g., in their leafleting), can be prohibited from activities that undermine the integrity of the media as legislatively understood, a holding for which *Associated Press v. United States*, 326 U.S. 1, 20 (1936), provides ample support.

195. 15 U.S.C. § 77q(b) (2000).

196. Another way to describe this conclusion is to find the "paid for content" constitutes commercial speech, a rather obvious conclusion in most cases. The court, however, rejected this characterization of the paid-for promotional speech in *Wall Street Publishing* but instead argued:

2. Commercial Speech

The last discussion may be merely an illustration of a more general distinction between the speech of media enterprises and other businesses. As is well known, in an earlier period the Court,[197] and even so-called First Amendment absolutists on and off the Court,[198] found commercial speech entirely outside First Amendment protection.[199] Since the early 1970s, however, the Court has accorded commercial speech some, but reduced, protection—with the extent of subsequent protection actually, though not "officially," waxing and waning.[200] Thus, even now, commercial speech is subject to many regulations that are clearly unconstitutional if applied to the press.[201] Prior restraints are allowed. The government can require that advertisers include communicative content—i.e., disclosures—which is a requirement that would constitute an unconstitutional penalty on the advertising speech under any interpretation of *Miami Herald*. Misleading commercial speech is subject to prohibition—but think of applying that restriction to either the speech of politicians or stories in newspapers! Falsity in

---

"Speech *relating* to the purchase and sale of securities, in our view, forms a distinct category of communications in which the government's power to regulate is *at least* as broad as with respect to the general rubric of commercial speech." *Wall Street Publ'g Inst. Inc.*, 851 F.2d at 373 (emphasis added, though the court proceeded to suggest these communications were even more subject to regulation than commercial speech). Since the speech itself did not propose the "purchase or sell of securities" or directly relate to such sales, the court might understand "relating to" as meaning "likely to" or maybe "intended to" *influence* sales or purchases of securities. Such an interpretation would seem to cover most newspaper financial advice columns and maybe even news stories about public companies. If this means that these newspaper columns and stories are subject to routine regulation, the result would be in huge tension with the First Amendment. The better reading of the opinion is probably to understand the court as limiting its point to regulating the "communication of the regulated parties." *Id.* at 372. This reading is even more appropriate given that the court, in its interpretation of "consideration," was careful to describe it narrowly enough to avoid interference with the normal practices of the media and cited approvingly *Miami Herald*'s protection of the editorial integrity of the press. *Id.* at 374. If this reading is correct, the court essentially adopts the view, argued for in the text, that businesses when engaged in the sale of securities have different and lesser protections for its corresponding speech activities than does the media when engaged in its Fourth Estate function.

197. Valentine v. Chrestensen, 316 U.S. 52, 54 (1942).

198. *See* Baker, *Paternalism, Politics, and Citizen Freedom*, *supra* note 147, at 1162 (noting that Justice Black, Meiklejohn, Emerson and others, including eminent free speech theorists such as John Stuart Mill, would exclude commercial speech from the scope of free speech principles).

199. *See id.*; *see also Valentine*, 316 U.S. at 54.

200. *See* Virginia State Bd. of Pharmacy v. Virgina Citizens Consumer Council, Inc., 425 U.S. 748, 772 (1976) ("In concluding that commercial speech enjoys First Amendment protection, we have not held that it is wholly undifferentiable from other forms."); Baker, *Paternalism, Politics, and Citizen Freedom*, *supra* note 147, at 1162-63.

201. The Court provided a list of permissible restrictions, noted in the text, which at this point are not, I believe, controversial. *Virginia State Board of Pharmacy*, 425 U.S. at 771-72 n.24.

commercial speech does not get even the limited protection of *Gertz*'s requirement of fault. These restrictions all apply even before coming to the *Central Hudson* test, which further allows regulation of content if the government can show it provides a properly narrow means to advance an important state purpose.[202] There the Court suggested that New York could bar advertising that undermined energy conservation—although it invalidated the restriction before it for being overbroad and not narrowly tailored to these energy conservation goals.[203]

Normally, the issue of commercial speech has not been considered from the perspective of the issue considered here—whether the Press Clause provides independent protection to the media business. Rather, the point has simply been that commercial speech is a protected—but not fully protected—category of speech. Here, however, the questions are first, whether the communications of the commercial, profit-oriented mass media are commercial speech—they are usually designed to make money for the publisher. Second, if not commercial speech, how does the Court distinguish commercial speech and media?

As early as *New York Times Co. v. Sullivan*, the Court distinguished the speech of newspapers sold for profit (as well as the advertisement placed by activists) from commercial speech, holding that neither the advertising format nor the general commercial rationale for newspaper publication justified treating the press as a commercial speaker.[204] More recently, as a necessary step in upholding a statute that appeared to bar broadcast of all lottery information, the Court strained to interpret it not to cover the press's own publication of the information but only advertising involving lotteries.[205] The Court quite clearly does not consider the content of commercial media to constitute commercial speech despite the profit motive that lies behind it and even when the media *content* is identical to regulatable commercial speech. As the list of ways in which commercial speech can be regulated makes clear, treating the media's product as commercial speech would drastically contradict existing doctrine protecting media speech.

Thus, the second question becomes the interesting one: how are the two different? On the factual level, the most obvious difference is that

---

202. Cent. Hudson Gas & Elec. Corp. v. Public Serv. Comm'n, 447 U.S. 557, 563-64, 576 (1980).

203. *Id.* at 570-71.

204. In distinguishing *Valentine v. Chrestensen*, 316 U.S. 52 (1942), the Court said: "That the Times was paid for publishing the [editorial] advertisement is as immaterial in this connection as is the fact that newspapers and books are sold." New York Times Co. v. Sullivan, 376 U.S. 254, 265 (1964).

205. United States v. Edge Broad. Co., 509 U.S. 418, 429-30 (1993).

the speech of the press is its product, while the speech of other businesses instrumentally aims to aid its sale of its non-speech products or its other endeavors to achieve profits.[206] In fact, this is the answer that in a moment I will assert is also constitutionally salient—but note that it has constitutional relevance *only* if the press is constitutionally a specially protected business such that its product, even if it has the same expressive content as something put out by another business, receives protection. But first consider whether there are any good alternatives. One possible alternative, the profit orientation of speakers, has already been shown not to work.[207] Both media and other businesses are typically profit oriented. Rather, possibly the most common attempt to offer an alternative is to focus on content. The expectation is that commercial speech is identified by its content and it receives reduced protection because of something about this content. Certainly, content has been a central feature of other areas of reduced or denied First Amendment protection. It is the primary factor that identifies obscenity; and false content, combined with fault, is central to defamation. Various Court statements in commercial speech cases focus on content.[208]

Nevertheless, content has never been a determinative factor.[209] In the foundational case, *Virginia State Board of Pharmacy v. Virginia Citizens Consumer Council, Inc.*, using examples such as ads for

206. Of course, the media also advertises and otherwise promotes its media, that is, speech, products. It is unlikely that the press's constitutionally protected Fourth Estate role would suggest a right to an exemption from a *general* regulation of advertising or solicitation any more than from a general regulation of its labor practices or wages. In contrast, a regulation specifically of the media's self-promotion would be hard to interpret other than as an attempt to burden the press in its protected role of communicating with the public. Roughly, this reasoning was sometimes invoked to explain *Bigelow v. Virginia*, 421 U.S. 809 (1975), decided the year before *Virginia State Board of Pharmacy*, made clear that commercial speech was protected. The argument was that *Bigelow* showed the impermissibility of specifically barring information, even when communicated by advertising, about a constitutionally protected activity—abortions. Similar is a possible interpretation of *Booth v. Curtis Publishing Co.*, 223 N.Y.S.2d 737, 745 (N.Y. App. Div. 1962), *aff'd without opinion*, 11 N.Y.2d 907 (1962) (denying application of New York's privacy—read, "right of publicity"—statute to a magazine's use of a picture of a person previously published in its magazine for an advertisement for the magazine). The argument is that applying the law here would prevent only publications, not other businesses, from using pictures of its product in its advertisements—and thus this application would be a media-specific limit on advertising. In any event, the issue is not crucial for the argument here, and I put it aside.

207. *See New York Times v. Sullivan*, 376 U.S. at 266; Pittsburg Press Co. v. Pittsburg Comm'n on Human Relations, 413 U.S. 376, 385 (1973).

208. Still, probably descriptively the most accurate of the Court's discussions involving commercial speech, which occurred in one of the few cases where identification was difficult, makes content only one factor. *See* Bolger v. Youngs Drug Prods. Corp., 463 U.S. 60, 65 (1983).

209. *See generally* Baker, *Paternalism, Politics, and Citizen Freedom*, *supra* note 147 (discussing the distinction between content and speaker identity as factors in the analysis of commercial speech cases).

artificial furs as an alternative to those that contribute to the extinction of fur-bearing mammals or for domestically produced products that are said to preserve American jobs, the Court noted that sometimes commercial speech will refer to public issues about which speech by the individuals or the media would undoubtedly be fully protected.[210] Content, in other words, is not what turned the ads into commercial speech. Rather, it was something about the identity of the speaker. Actually, in *all* cases of regulation of commercial speech, the law applied only to businesses promoting their commercial interests. The laws were never general bans on a category of speech defined by content—the laws did not restrict the *same* content published by others.[211] The occasionally offered argument that the regulations manifest a paternalistic governmental view, namely, that people should not be exposed to particular information or assertions,[212] has never been quite right. Those not involved in market transactions promoted by the restricted speech—that is, individuals, or consumer and other public interest groups, or newspapers—have always been left free to communicate. They are free to say smoking is great, turn up the air conditioner, or that drug prices are less at these stores than at those.[213] That is, if there is paternalism, the paternalism is about the parties who should participate in the discourse, not about what is said or what people should read or hear. Flesh and blood individuals, their non-commercial associations, and the media always have full discourse rights.

Possibly, the point about content not being the basis of regulation is best illustrated by a series of lower court cases. The same expressive content about the science, efficacy or other features of some product, process, or activity might be either published as a book sold for a profit or distributed without, or at a reduced, cost by a commercial enterprise with the aim to promote the profitable sale of the firm's products or business. The same content, the very same book, might even play both roles in separate contexts. When faced with this dichotomy, lower courts have been quite uniform in their results.[214] The communicative content is fully protected speech when sold as a media product and is commercial speech subject to regulation for being misleading when provided within

210. Virginia State Bd. of Pharmacy v. Virginia Citizens Consumer Council, Inc., 425 U.S. 748, 764 (1976).

211. An exception is the language of the statute in *Edge Broadcasting* noted earlier, but the Court interpreted it to apply only to advertising, thereby justifying the claim in the text above.

212. *See, e.g.*, *Virginia State Bd. of Pharmacy*, 425 U.S. at 769-70.

213. Justice Rehnquist emphasized this point in his dissent in *Virginia State Board*. *See id.* at 782 (Rehnquist, J., dissenting).

214. *See infra* note 215.

a promotional campaign for a firm or its products.[215] Thus, the distinction between commercial speech and media publications is neither the aim of profits nor the content. There seems little explanation for the constitutionally salient distinction other than the identity of the parties. That is, the business of the press, whose media content is its product, is constitutionally special and receives a degree of First Amendment protection that other businesses, whose speech content is not their product but is used instrumentally to advance profits, do not receive.

3. Discriminatory Taxation

Government authority to tax media businesses is unabashedly limited in ways that its authority to tax other businesses clearly is not. In general, governments can discriminate incredibly between businesses in imposing tax liability—imposing unique taxes that in addition to raising revenue clearly (and, one suspects, purposively) suppress demand for the products of the targeted businesses. Basically, at least since 1935, the Federal Constitution imposes almost no meaningful limits on discretion in the use of the federal taxing power to further virtually any policy goal.[216] State power too is largely constitutionally unconstrained—though state taxes cannot discriminate against out-of-state businesses in violation of the Commerce Clause. Only in extraordinary circumstances, for example, an application of a state tax that dramatically violates a state's declared legal policy about its taxes, has the Court found a state tax practice irrational enough to violate equal protection.[217]

In contrast, since the ill-fated stamp taxes of the eighteenth century, the taxing power has been seen as a threat to a free press.[218] Although it

---

215. The issue usually comes up in the context of the Lanham Act, 15 U.S.C. § 1125(a) or state unfair competition statutes. *See, e.g.*, Gordon & Breach Sci. Publishers v. Am. Inst. of Physics, 859 F. Supp. 1521, 1544 (S.D.N.Y. 1994) (stating that articles were fully protected when initially published but were commercial speech subject to regulation under Lanham Act, 15 U.S.C. § 1125 (2000), when distributed as promotional materials to encourage purchase of defendant's products). *Compare* Oxycal Lab., Inc. v. Jeffers, 909 F. Supp. 719, 726 (S.D. Cal. 1995) (finding book protected when, despite its relevance to commercial transactions, the book was not used as promotional material), *with* Semco, Inc. v. Amcast, Inc., 52 F.3d 108, 113-14 (6th Cir. 1995) (holding that article constituted commercial speech when publication may reflect the willingness of the company that employed the author to take out advertising in the publication and where article was used as promotional material in trade shows and communications to customers).

216. *See* JESSE H. CHOPER, RICHARD H. FALLON, JR., YALE KAMISAR & STEVEN H. SHIFFRIN, CONSTITUTIONAL LAW 111 (9th ed. 2001) ("since [United States v.] Constantine, [296 U.S. 287 (1935),] no federal tax has been held invalid because of a regulatory motive outside federal power").

217. *See* Allegheny Pittsburgh Coal Co. v. County Comm'n, 488 U.S. 336, 346 (1989).

218. Often opposition to these "taxes on knowledge" is given a rose-tinted account. Initial American opposition to the Stamp Act had more to do with colonial objections to taxation without representation than any concern with the press freedom. In England, a plausible historical account

is unquestioned that the media is subject to general taxes, special tax treatment is another story. I will not here try to summarize or reconcile this disputed area of doctrine,[219] but it is clear that significant First Amendment limits exist to the taxation of the press. For example, the government cannot justify a tax placed specifically on the press by the claim that it is merely seeking to raise revenue—the alternative view that the tax purposefully burdens press freedom seems obvious given the government's inability to reply to press's query: if only interested in revenue, why not apply the tax more generally, not just to us?[220] After a series of cases invalidating media taxes as discriminatory, many observers concluded that the First Amendment imposed "a nondiscrimination principle for like-situated members of the press."[221] Though it is now established that the government can differentially grant exemptions to different segments of the media, including different segments within a single general category,[222] any tax policy that seems oriented toward specially burdening the media or burdening particular out-of-favor media entities is clearly unconstitutional.[223]

Thus, the constitutional power to tax is more restricted for media businesses than others. Though these tax cases might be seen as free speech or general First Amendment cases, not free press cases, this logic does not entirely work. As this Section has emphasized, from merely a speech perspective, it is difficult to distinguish between businesses. A special tax on an oil company limits its capacity to speak just as a tax on the press limits its speech capacity. Maybe a special tax on the press can

---

given by James Curran and Jean Seaton is that the stamp taxes, initially intended to control the press serving the rabble, had backfired. JAMES CURRAN & JEAN SEATON, POWER WITHOUT RESPONSIBILITY, THE PRESS AND BROADCASTING IN BRITAIN 12, 26 (5th ed. 1997). Radical, working-class papers flourished by illegally not paying the tax that established middle and upper class competitors paid. *Id.* at 12. Their non-payment counterbalanced the advertising "subsidy" received by the established press, and on this comparatively equal playing field, these radical papers flourished. *Id.* As some members of Parliament realized, by eliminating the tax, the established papers could competitively undersell the radical papers, taking enough audience away to bankrupt them. Elimination of the tax was, thus, at least in part a means not to free knowledge but to suppress radical working-class papers. *Id.* at 26.

219. *See* C. EDWIN BAKER, ADVERTISING AND A DEMOCRATIC PRESS 130-32 (1994).

220. Minneapolis Star & Tribune Co. v. Minnesota Comm'r of Revenue, 460 U.S. 575, 586 (1983).

221. Leathers v. Medlock, 499 U.S. 439, 454 (1991) (Marshall, J., dissenting). Although I never viewed this as a correct description of the principles in this area, in discussion I heard it from many media scholars before *Medlock*, most of whom expected the challenge in that case to prevail.

222. *Id.* at 453.

223. *Id.* at 444-47.

be understood as having a bad purpose.[224] The bad purpose, however, would be to burden specifically the press, or some part of it, as compared to other businesses. To object to that purpose requires a notion of the special constitutional status of the press.

4. An Excursus: Structural Regulation

In other writings, I have argued that the Court interprets the First Amendment to allow great structural regulation of the media in virtually any manner, despite sometimes harming or disadvantaging particular media entities, as long as the structural regulation can reasonably be thought to represent a plausible legislative judgment about how to improve the democratic quality or societal value of the media. In fact, I have gone beyond that argument and claimed that the Supreme Court has never invalidated a true structural regulation of the media[225]—although this assertion cannot be applied to lower federal courts. Apparent exceptions always involve situations where the law is better characterized as involving a content-based suppression or penalty on particular types of communicative content.[226] Here, however, I want to offer an observation pointing in the opposite direction.

In the post-*Lochner* era, almost any structural regulation of business—regulation of who has power to make various decisions, what conditions must be met for the power to exist, the relations between different parts of the business (think of labor and corporate law), who owns the business, under what conditions, and with what powers—either

---

224. Though the difference between intent or motive on the one hand and purpose on the other is important, with the latter usually being constitutionally dispositive, *Leathers* questions whether this characterization is crucial, stating that "illicit legislative intent" is not required. *Id.* at 445.

225. Baker, *Turner Broadcasting*, *supra* note 19, at 93-94; BAKER, *supra* note 87, at 124-62; *Los Angeles v. Preferred Commications, Inc.* is a possible exception, though the Court did not invalidate the law but merely reinstated a cause of action, thus leaving my claim in the text formally true. Los Angeles v. Preferred Commc'ns, Inc., 476 U.S. 488, 494-96 (1986). Still, *Preferred Communications* is an exceptional case. A typical policy issue in structural regulation is whether the government should intervene to prevent concentration and disperse ownership. In *Preferred Communications*, the challenged law intervened to assure monopoly ownership. *Id.* at 492. Though in fact policy arguments can be made favoring that choice, especially if the cable company is operated more like a common carrier, the Court indicated that for the government to create a monopoly control of a particular form of communication would be unconstitutional unless the government could make an adequate showing that competition would undermine the media that people receive or otherwise create some significant problem. *Id.* at 494.

226. For example, *Miami Herald* gave both structural and content penalty arguments to justify invalidating the right-of-reply statute, which would indicate the Court's willingness to strike down the statute for its improper structural features, but subsequently in *Turner Broadcasting* the Court implicitly rejected the structural objection in favor of the content penalty analysis. *Compare* Miami Herald Publ'g Co. v. Tornillo, 418 U.S. 241, 254-58 (1974), *with* Turner Broad. Sys., Inc. v. FCC, 512 U.S. 622, 640-42 (1994).

in general or in relation to specific business types, is uncontroversially constitutional. In contrast, such structural regulation of a flesh and blood body that determines who has authority is virtually an incoherent notion, unthinkable in the post-slavery world.[227] This might be a slight overstatement—some acceptable regulations of individuals may be characterized as structural,[228] but for the most part legal regulation of people is probably better described as behavioral. So structural is a category of legal regulation that seems best understood as related to artificial, not natural entities. And, as to these artificial entities, government has generally unassailable freedom to make the rules as it likes and for purposes it chooses—until it comes to the media.

Even if I am right that the government can structurally regulate the media in any case where it can make a good faith claim that it does so for legitimate reasons, these structural regulations are inevitably challenged in the courts and are widely thought to raise real First Amendment issues. The point here is that the expanse of acceptable reasons available to justify regulation of most businesses is, as the tax cases surely indicate, narrower in the context of the media. Proper challenges, I believe, are ones that can show that the challenged regulation is best understood as aimed at interfering with or burdening the press's broad Fourth Estate role. Given what I consider the best theory of democracy, the media has multiple, somewhat conflicting Fourth Estate roles, and very different regulations can represent plausible judgments about legitimate regulation with which courts should not interfere. Still, the widely recognized greater vulnerability to constitutional challenge of structural regulations of the media, like the greater protection of the media from discriminatory tax burdens, can only be explained by a constitutionally special status of these businesses. The Press Clause provides the only obvious basis for this status. The proper analysis in evaluating these regulations involves two steps. First, it involves accepting that the Press Clause establishes that these regulations must meet particular constitutional standards, a conclusion implicit in these regulations being so commonly challenged. Second, it involves giving a proper interpretation of the Press Clause, which I argue the Court has concluded is one that defers generally to the government, a

227. Maybe not totally! A state tried to give husbands power to veto legal abortions by their wives, but the Court predictably invalidated the legislation. Planned Parenthood v. Danforth, 428 U.S. 52, 71 (1976).

228. Structural regulation might, for example, be a way to characterize legal regulation of the status of marriage, parenthood, parental authority, and guardianship—but the whole way of thinking about these differs greatly from the way of thinking about structural regulation of economic entities.

conclusion which I also argue follows from a proper theory of democracy.

D. *Summary*

The introduction to Part III argued that any differences in the constitutional status of media speech and other corporate speech can only be explained by the Press Clause. The investigation then found that legal differences abound. Most often they exist in non-constitutional legal policies that establish special privileges or exemptions for the media or particular portions of it. Few commentators argue that the Constitution requires most of these press privileges—ones that I have not discussed in Part III. Consider, for example, providing the press with special press facilities, press passes, and other access to government facilities, or waived charges for receipt of information under the Freedom of Information Act ("FOIA"). Few believe, however, that the press can constitutionally be denied other privileges or exemptions. That is true, I believe, in the case of being permitted to spend money on speech that identifies candidates for office or supports their candidacy during the period before elections, of using the name or persona of people to advance their profit interests when that usage involves inclusion in media content, or of a lesser duty of care owed to those who use or are affected by its product.

Because of legislative overreaching, some differences between the press and other businesses are already a matter of constitutional doctrine. Protection of personal privacy from disclosures by various businesses, such as credit agencies, exists and the Court held it cannot be applied to media speech. Law also subjects businesses to many other regulations aimed at preserving degrees of privacy that would be unconstitutional if applied to regulating media content. Courts give media speech greater constitutional protection than other businesses' profit-oriented speech (commercial speech) even when the two have the exact same content. In a different context, Justice White argued, and one suspects other Justices would agree if forced to face the issue, that the government can require that security advisors have a license that the government can deny or revoke for misbehavior, but that the First Amendment prevents imposing this requirement on journalists or the press. Compulsion to identify the fact that speech within the media was formulated and paid for by an outside party burdens or penalizes this outsider's speech, a burden of the sort that *Miami Herald* held is unconstitutional in relation to the media's own speech. Courts protect the media from discriminatory taxation, protection that it denies other businesses.[229] One area in which the Court failed to explicitly recognize this difference between types of businesses, namely defamation, resulted in an unfortunate perversion of doctrine. Even there, though, the propriety of recognizing this constitutional difference between the press and other businesses reasserted itself in practice through the way the standard, "matter of public concern," is applied. Overall, vast areas of law would be disrupted by any failure to recognize the special constitutional status of the media—presumably based on the Press Clause.

IV. PROBLEMS WITH SEPARATE CONSTITUTIONAL STATUS OF THE PRESS MORE APPARENT THAN REAL

Commentators have alleged various problems with reading the Press Clause to provide independent protection of the press. Some objections really only apply to particular asserted special rights. Often, the right response is that a sound interpretation of the Press Clause would not recognize that particular asserted right. In the context of objecting to any special rights for the press as compared to individual speakers in the defamation area, Steve Shiffrin provocatively argues that "[t]he idea that the [F]irst [A]mendment protections should be consciously divvied out in more generous doses to those with knowledge, wealth, and capacity to cause damage is indefensible."[230] Shiffrin is right. Note, however, that the only differences identified in Part II between the *speech* rights of individuals and the press were where the press had the lesser right. This reflects that both have the same right in relation to freedom from censorship but that the individual has additional rights related to personal liberty or autonomy. In the specific area that concerned Shiffrin, defamation, both the theory of separate speech and press rights and the Court's actual holdings properly suggest identical constitutional rights[231]—a result consistent with Shiffrin's argument. Moreover, in contrast to many constitutionally gratuitous privileges of the press, such as receiving press facilities, the particular constitutional rights that it arguably has that individuals do not have, especially a reporter's privilege to keep sources confidential, is more a benefit to the reporters and their capacity to perform their constitutional

229. *See supra* Part III.C.3.

230. Steven Shiffrin, *Defamatory Non-Media Speech and First Amendment Methodology*, 25 UCLA L. REV. 915, 934 (1978).

231. This aspect of *Dun & Bradstreet* is unimpeachable but did contradict Justice Stewart's own development of the Fourth Estate theory. Dun & Bradstreet, Inc. v. Greenmoss Builders, Inc., 472 U.S. 749, 773 (1985).

role of serving the people than to the media's wealthy owners.[232] A reporter's privilege, and probably other rights related to institutional integrity of the media, have a complex relation to the circumstances of the politically or economically weak and vulnerable. On the whole, however, to the extent these rights or privileges better enable the media to perform its watchdog role, they are often likely to especially benefit those less powerful and will often contribute to information that benefits the democratic process.

Other commentators fear that a Fourth Estate constitutional status for the press will lead to demands for accountability or regulation as a public fiduciary that are inconsistent with the press's, and especially the journalist's, historical and proper nature "as a freebooter outside the system."[233] Possibly! Still, there seem to me three persuasive responses to this fear. First, any proper interpretation of a special status should invalidate any attempt to impose formal (behavioral) accountability.[234] Reading the Press Clause as a structural provision should give the press protection precisely against such attempts. Of course, a proper interpretation of the special constitutional status of the press cannot be assured. Nevertheless, the possibility of an objectionable interpretation should not be used as an excuse to avoid an interpretation that otherwise makes sense and serves democracy[235]—any contrary view would likely wipe out all constitutional law. Second, though under a proper interpretation of the Press Clause accountability cannot be legally enforced, society would benefit from frequent popular and public demands that the press properly live up to its constitutional role. Democracy is served both by a free media and by media criticism.

Third, I admit the attraction of Anthony Lewis's romantic vision of freebooter outside the system.[236] I would go further. Not only does the communications order, as I have argued in three books, need legally-based structural reform to prevent profit-maximizing concerns of both

232. If Press Clause protection of the press's institutional integrity prevents the government from paying the press to present the government's message as the press's own, the rule protects journalism at the cost of reducing owners' flexibility in making profits.

233. Lewis, *supra* note 20, at 605; *see also* Van Alstyne, *supra* note 20, at 768-70.

234. *Cf.* Miami Herald Publ'g Co. v. Tornillo, 418 U.S. 241, 256 (1974) ("A responsible press is an undoubtedly desirable goal, but press responsibility is not mandated by the Constitution and like many other virtues it cannot be legislated.").

235. *See* Nebraska Press Ass'n v. Stuart, 427 U.S. 539, 559-60 (1976) (quoting Sheppard v. Maxwell, 384 U.S. 333, 350 (1966) ("A responsible press has always been regarded as the handmaiden of effective judicial administration, especially in the criminal field. Its function in this regard is documented by an impressive record of service over several centuries. The press does not simply publish information about trials but guards against the miscarriage of justice . . . .").

236. Lewis, *supra* note 20, at 605.

media corporations and their advertisers from undermining these "freebooters," which would also undermine the quality of journalism in the press and creativity in the cultural media. The communications order also depends on Lewis's strong-willed media professionals remaining committed to their journalistic ideals. Often legislative structural interventions and journalists' commitments are alike in one respect. Both often oppose the profit orientation of (many) owners. A key aim of both is to assure journalists more opportunities to perform their professional roles as they understand these roles. On the whole, this country has received great benefit from having such strong-willed, committed journalists and editors. The legal question is how the legal order can best nourish this spirit among journalists and editors. My guess is that culturally and legally recognizing the special *constitutional* importance of their role is more likely to contribute than an approach that views journalists and editors merely like any other workers employed by any other profit-oriented business.[237]

Commentators also raise questions concerning constitutional history. Chief Justice Burger, for example, raised this issue in his concurrence in *Bellotti*, arguing that there was no historical grounding for a special reading of the Press Clause.[238] Putting aside, I think, persuasive objections to how history should influence constitutional interpretation, Burger seems to be simply wrong about history. Much better supported is the view that "[h]istorically, there is little doubt that the Press Clause was viewed as having independent significance."[239]

Most critiques of independent content for the Press Clause emphasize a final problem: the difficulty of defining "the press."[240] Here, I do not propose any canonical solution but, instead suggest some partial responses. First, however, I wish to express some dismay at the claim. At the 2007 annual meeting of the American Association of Law Schools, on different two section panels, two distinguished scholars, one from Columbia and one from Chicago, despite finding important normative and practical reasons for giving the press special protection, rejected reading the Press Clause as providing this because of the difficulty of definition.[241] The same point is ubiquitous in scholarly

---

237. *See generally* Anderson, *supra* note 11 (providing some illustrations of this spirit among media professionals and the opposite among financial consultants).

238. First Nat'l Bank v. Bellotti, 436 U.S. 765, 796-802 (1978) (Burger, C.J., concurring).

239. FRANKLIN ET AL., *supra* note 31, at 56; *see also* Anderson, *supra* note 11, at 533-37.

240. This difficulty, continually expressed by both commentators and Justices, probably began for the Court with Branzburg v. Hayes, 408 U.S. 665, 703 (1972).

241. *See* AALS Annual Meeting, http://www.aals.org/am2007/program.html (last visited July 31, 2007).

writing. But line-drawing problems are ever present in constitutional law. Does speech include nude dancing?[242] The real difficulty of defining or identifying speech does not justify ignoring the Speech Clause. When history and normative theory both suggest the propriety of an independent interpretation of the Press Clause, courts should face up to the difficult task of line-drawing, recognizing that here, as everywhere else, the edges will require controversial judgments. Both grey areas and occasional lapses in judgment are inevitable. Still, the protection that the courts do provide will generally serve the purposes of a society that accepts judicial review. The difficulties here are little different from interpretative difficulties in constitutional interpretation more generally.

A. *Difficulties of Definition*[243]

The necessity of defining the press is no stranger to the law. David Anderson notes, in a very partial listing, that "the press gets preferential access to legislative chambers, executive news conferences, trials, war zones, disaster scenes, prisons, and executions. State and local statutes protect the press from otherwise legal police searches."[244] Anderson continues, noting state "shield laws" that create "reporters' privileges," exemptions "from some securities regulations and campaign-expenditure limitations," "special postal rates," fee waivers for information sought by FOIA requests, and, in California, the right to receive from the police the "addresses of arrestees and crime victims" when sought for "journalistic purposes."[245] In each case, the law either formally or in practice had to define the press—or, at least, had to offer some way to determine who are the beneficiaries of the governmentally-created right. Most observers, however, do not find these ubiquitous definitions much help for constitutional purposes. The rights Anderson identified are all at least arguably gratuitous. Given that it is well established that some media entities, even some within the same rough category, can be given privileges that the government denies to other media entities, the law can grant these privileges either to a narrower or broader category than the

---

242. Erie v. Pap's A.M., 529 U.S. 277, 289-90 (2000).

243. Though I mostly follow conventional practice and use the term "definition," that usage should not be taken to mean a precise linguistic formulation. Rather, it seems more likely that the notion of the press will involve an overlapping set of features no one of which is essential, but taken together can allow relatively clear application with some border line cases. These features or "family resemblances" might be better described as representing a conception than a definition.

244. Anderson, *supra* note 11, at 432.

245. *Id.* at 432, 445.

"press" in its constitutional sense.[246] It is this constitutional definition or conception of the press that must be specified. As to constitutionally claimed rights, since an entity gets the right if, but only if, it is the press, excluding an entity properly defined as the press would seem to violate its rights—thus, precise definition seems to be required.[247]

A first mechanical step toward definition is purely descriptive. The claim is that the media's product is speech—or more generally, communicative, whether verbal, visual, musical or some combination—while other businesses's products are non-communicative for which they then use (commercial) speech to aid in selling. (I will say more below about whether the First Amendment term "press" should be treated as referring to the mass media generally or only to some sub-category such as the "news media" or media engaged in the "journalistic function." David Anderson gives strong reasons to favor the narrower conception.)[248] This speech-product formulation does not quite work. As noted in Part III, speech is also the product of a number of businesses that few would consider the "press" or even "mass media"—consider

246. *See, e.g.*, Leathers v. Medlock, 499 U.S. 439, 453 (1991) (holding that a state can grant tax exemption to one entity but not another even though they are in the same media category, video delivery services); Committee for an Indep. P-I v. Hearst, 704 F.2d 467, 481 (9th Cir. 1983) (holding that law can grant newspapers an exemption from antitrust act even though only some newspapers qualify and their exemption can harm other papers that are not exempted); Sherrill v. Knight, 569 F.2d 124, 129 (D.C. Cir. 1977) (not challenging aspect of policy that makes only Washington-based journalists eligible for Justice White House press pass); Los Angeles Free Press, Inc. v. City of L.A., 88 Cal. Rptr. 605, 609 (Cal. Ct. App. 1971) (upholding policy of only granting daily papers providing certain daily police and fire stories receive press passes).

247. Anderson suggests, however, maybe not. Anderson, *supra* note 11, at 68-69, 91-98. Given the instrumental basis of the Press Clause as serving the public, it might be adequate to hold that the relevant right does not necessarily go to particular rights-bearing parties or to all members of the press as long as the right exists for elements of the press in a manner beneficial to the public. As a matter of constitutional law, courts would determine where the type of right in question exists, but would defer to the government's determination that a particular claimant should not receive it, at least should defer *as long as* the government's definition is neither arbitrary nor exercised for invalid reasons and extends to sufficient elements of the press that the press's constitutional role is served. This approach arguably embodies Justice Stewart's insight that press freedom is an institutional right. Essentially this approach is now used in practice in respect to many of the gratuitous press rights mentioned above.

The unusual nature of this approach reflects, and can be justified, on the ground that while most rights are for the benefit of individuals and hence it violates their right if they are improperly denied the right, press rights exist to benefit the amorphous public and as long as the rights are given adequate scope to provide this benefit, individual claimants have no grounds to object if excluded. Anderson applies this argument in the context of arguing that "the press," but not any particular person claiming to be a part of the press, must be given access to war zones. *Id.*

248. Anderson, *supra* note 11, at 436-47; *see also* Anderson, *supra* note 20, at 52 ("When I use the term media, I mean to cast a wider net, to include not only the press but also media entities that do not have plausible claims to Press Clause protection.").

accountants, financial advisors, lawyers, doctors, or psychiatrists.[249] In the defamation case discussed earlier, no Justice or judge in the lower courts thought Dun & Bradstreet was the press although its primary product was speech. The obvious distinction may be that the media or the press makes the same product *non-selectively available* to a broad public.[250] Denying Press Clause protection for individualized professional or commercial communications—lawyers' work or credit reports, for example—creates no problem for individuals' typical non-market oriented speech[251] since this speech is fully protected under the liberty or autonomy theory of the Speech Clause.

Justice Stewart, in his defense of an independent interpretation of the Press Clause argued that "[t]he publishing business is . . . the only organized private business that is given explicit constitutional protection."[252] Following Justice Stewart's lead, the criterion suggested above allows a distinction between the press and other businesses.

One red-herring should be mentioned. Sometimes those who assert a practical impossibility of identifying the press argue that conglomerate ownership and technological online convergence eliminate any historical capacity to identify the press. After purchasing a newspaper or network or setting up a web site, is General Electric the "press," and thus a beneficiary of the rights of the press? The question is more imposing when expressed this generally than when asked in relation to a particular right of the press—that is, when asked in places where it matters. When so narrowed, General Electric's web site or its expenditures on campaign "advertising" or other speech unassociated with its media "properties" is likely to constitute commercial speech. In contrast, its newspapers or broadcast network (including the newspapers' or network's web site) may be protected from various regulations in relation to their specific media activities. The law can and constantly does deal with corporate

---

249. *See infra* Part III.B.

250. This criterion hides a complexity that might be decided either way. Should a business that limits the people to whom it will disclose its reports still be considered the "press"? If the press is protected because of its Fourth Estate role or because of its being the most important institution of a democratic public sphere where speech is presumptively addressed to all, no one should be denied access to its communications. Then the idea of a press that refused to make its product available to some willing to pay the cover price would contradict its democratic role and the non-exclusive requirement would be appropriate. On the other hand, the significance of limited public spheres of subaltern publics, a feature of complex democracy, *infra* note 270 and accompanying text, might justify greater sympathy for at least some claims of being the press despite audience selectivity.

251. Givhan v. W. Line Consol. Sch. Dist., 439 U.S. 410, 413 (1979) (protecting teacher from dismissal for her private conversations with the school principal about allegedly racially discriminatory policies).

252. Stewart, *supra* note 9, at 633.

parts. Few rights related to the institutional integrity of the press would sensibly apply to General Electric as a whole—in fact, in structurally supporting press freedom, the law could prohibit General Electric from owning these media entities—while press rights can apply to the activities or practices of the specific media "properties" that General Electric owns.

Commentators also often note that the First Amendment should protect the lonely pamphleteer just as much as *The New York Times* or CBS even though the pamphleteer "sells" no product. Two not inconsistent routes to understanding protection for this pamphleteer are available: recognize her liberty rights as an individual speaker or treat her as the press by analogy to the characterizations of the so-called institutional press. As for the first route, the pamphleteer's speech—her pamphlet—is surely protected simply on the basis of the Speech Clause.[253] As noted in Part II, any occasional difference between the press and individual in relation to their "speech" rights favors the individual. Under existing law, the pamphleteer has speech rights apparently not available to the commercial media, for example, a right of anonymity that does not apply to the ownership of the commercial press.[254] Moreover, if the issue were raised, I suspect that these pamphleteers, in reliance on *Barnette*, would have rights not to be conduits for other speakers' messages.[255]

Doctrinally, this resolution is admittedly not very tidy. During the middle decades of the twentieth century, when the Supreme Court sometimes seemed to explicitly rest many decisions on the Press Clause,[256] the Court put pamphleteers into the press category.[257] Of course, this does not matter unless the press receives some special constitutional rights in comparison to individuals (Part III argues that they clearly receive special rights as compared to other businesses and

253. Talley v. California, 362 U.S. 60, 64 (1960) (describing law as interfering with "freedom of expression").

254. *Compare id.* at 64-65 (invalidating city ordinance which prohibited distribution of pamphlets unless it identified the names and addresses of persons who prepared, distributed, or sponsored it), *and* McIntyre v. Ohio Elections Comm'n, 514 U.S. 334 (1995) (invalidating statute that prohibited distribution of campaign literature unless it contained identifying information), *with* 39 U.S.C.A. § 3685 (2000) (requiring each owner of a publication having periodical publication mail privileges to provide the government and publish in the publication once a year information properly identifying the editor, managing editor, publishers, and owners as well as various other information specified by the statute or the Postal Service), *and* Post Office Appropriations Act of 1912, Pub. L. No. 62-336, 37 Stat. 539, 553-54 (1912) (same except required twice a year).

255. *See* West Virginia State Bd. of Educ. v. Barnette, 319 U.S. 624 (1943).

256. *See* Anderson, *supra* note 11, at 448.

257. *See* Lovell v. City of Griffin, 303 U.S. 444, 450-51 (1938).

also are discretionarily given rights as compared to individuals by legislation or policy). If it does, are pamphleteers also the beneficiary? The relevant area lies in the possibility that the press receives "defensive rights" that protect its institutional integrity.[258] The continuing controversy about the privilege to protect confidential sources presents the obvious test case. If the privilege exists, the most obvious argument is that when individuals, even on a non-commercial basis, seek out information not merely because of their own curiosity, but precisely in order to then communicate their "edited" or selected finding to a broad public, they are performing a central function of Justice Stewart's constitutional business and should receive the same protection. In the context of blogging, at least one court has reached this conclusion, giving the web site editors contesting a subpoena the same right as a journalist who works for the commercial mass media.[259] On the argument here and as the court decided, the right should not go automatically to all bloggers, but should depend on the purposes of the individual blogger when she gathered the information.[260]

The possibility of these alternative doctrinal approaches to the lonely pamphleteer (today, the blogger) suggests two points. First, though the commercial press should be evaluated solely under the rationale of the Press Clause and, thereby be distinguished both from the individual who has obvious liberty interests in her speech and from other businesses, arguably the lonely pamphleteer or part-time "volunteer"

---

258. The term "defensive rights" is taken from BAKER, HUMAN LIBERTY AND FREEDOM OF SPEECH, *supra* note 19, at 225; Baker, *Press Rights and Government Power to Structure the Press*, *supra* note 19, at 839. Following Justice Stewart's analysis, I suggested that the Press Clause should be understood to establish special right that are inherent in, that "defend," the institutional integrity of press entities but not "offensive rights," that is, rights, as an initial matter, to engage in behavior not permitted for other people—such as to violate the speed limit or break and enter an office in order to get a story or to have unique, constitutionally protected access to governmental files. Stewart consistently favored what I characterized as "defensive rights" but not "offensive rights." *Id.* at 837-48.

259. O'Grady v. Superior Court, 44 Cal. Rptr. 3d 72, 97 (Cal. Ct. App. 2006). After finding that the petitioners should receive the benefit of California's statutory reporter privilege, the Court also found that the petitioners should receive the constitutional privilege arising from the California and federal constitutional guarantees of a free press. In so holding, the court said of the petitioners: "It is established without contradiction that they gather, select, and prepare, for purposes of publication to a mass audience, information about current events of interest and concern to that audience . . . [i]f their activities and social function differ at all from those of traditional print and broadcast journalists, the distinctions are minute, subtle, and constitutionally immaterial." *Id.* at 106.

260. The Court in *Grady* distinguished "the open and deliberate publication on a news-oriented Web site of news gathered for that purpose by the site's operators—with the deposit of information, opinion, or fabrication by a casual visitor to an open forum such as a newsgroup, chatroom, bulletin board system, or discussion group" and indicated that it was recognizing a privilege only for the former. *Id.* at 99.

journalist should not only have full Speech Clause protection but also, in appropriate cases, Press Clause protection. For example, it is possible that she can have both rights of anonymity or exemption from carriage obligations and, in an appropriate case, a "reporter's privilege." As to any specific issue, she should be able to claim the characterization that provides the greater protection.

Second, earlier discussion suggested that the line-drawing problem for identifying the press may not present courts an insurmountable problem. Largely by using functional reasoning relating to the distinctions between the press and both individuals and other businesses, courts may be able to make practical decisions on a case-by-case basis. This approach, despite leaving grey areas, is not uncommon in constitutional law and in principle should not be any more troublesome here. The problem may, however, be reduced given the contexts in which identification is necessary. If the only evidence that a person is an embodiment of the press is her unadorned assertion, the difficulty of an accurate and principled evaluation of the claim is obvious. But the individual will not need to assert the status of the press for speech rights where the only (minimal) differences favor the individual. Offensive rights would apply in cases before outward evidence of being a journalist appear but, I have argued, the Press Clause does not justify this category of journalistic rights. Thus, the only context in which the issue must be resolved relates to "defensive rights." There, the question of identification occurs, however, only after the person has done her investigations, sought out the confidential source, and thus occurs in a factual context where evaluating her claim about the nature of her activities will be more concrete and subject to more objective resolution.

B. Journalism or Entertainment and Culture

The First Amendment protects movies, art, music, and fiction.[261] It would seem obvious that these can all be important forms of individual self-expression and, as such, receive full protection under the Speech Clause. Successful versions of these forms, however, are often the products of large-scale commercial development and exploitation. If businesses other than the press are subject to many restrictions and

---

261. The Court has opined that the First Amendment "unquestionably shield[s] painting of Jackson Pollock, the music of Arnold Schoenberg, or Jabberwocky verse of Lewis Carol." Hurley v. Irish-Am. Gay, Lesbian and Bisexual Group of Boston, Inc., 515 U.S. 557, 569 (1995); *see also* Joseph Burstyn, Inc. v. Wilson, 343 U.S. 495, 502 (1952) (holding that the First Amendment guarantees of the freedom of speech and of the press apply to motion pictures).

regulations of their speech that do not apply either to individuals or to the press, the obvious question is how to think of these forms of expression—often entertainment—when they are products of commercial entities.

Historically, some theorists, most famously Alexander Meiklejohn, but also others including Robert Bork, would deny these cultural forms of expression First Amendment protection.[262] After serious attack for drawing an unsustainable line of protecting only speech about public matters,[263] Meiklejohn reversed course and saw that these media nourished reflective thought on which democracy depends.[264] Though he did not engage in any discussion of possible distinctions between speech and the press, given his unwillingness to recognize any protection for commercial speech of business enterprises, he was necessarily committed to some type of distinction between the products of some cultural or media businesses from those of other businesses—and a role for the Press Clause logically follows.[265]

Nevertheless, many First Amendment commentators, probably most journalists and likely many professionals in the entertainment business, see the "press" as the portion of the media oriented toward current affairs and public policy—basically journalism[266] and related expression historically identified with newspapers.[267] Likewise, if either history or Justice Stewart's image of the Fourth Estate is the impetuous for understanding the special nature of the press, probably these cultural expressions would not be included. What defines the press is the provision of "news."

Still, the issue of scope merits more sustained consideration. Elsewhere I have argued that a democracy needs protection for production and distribution of information and vision independent of the governmental dictates and control.[268] Entertainment and cultural media

---

262. ALEXANDER MEIKLEJOHN, FREE SPEECH AND ITS RELATION TO SELF-GOVERNMENT 46 (1948); Robert H. Bork, *Neutral Principles and Some First Amendment Problems*, 47 IND. L.J. 1, 20 (1971).

263. Zechariah Chafee, Jr., 62 HARV. L. REV. 891, 899 (1949) (book review).

264. Alexander Meiklejohn, *The First Amendment is an Absolute*, 1961 SUP. CT. REV. 245, 256-57 (including other forms of expression, such as philosophy, literature, and art, in his definition of "political speech").

265. *Id.* at 258-59.

266. Anderson, *supra* note 11, at 445-47.

267. Interestingly, in the nineteenth century, newspapers regularly combined "news" with publication of often serialized fiction and poetry. Today, one need only think of *The New Yorker* to recognize that publications often combine these varying types of content.

268. C. Edwin Baker, *First Amendment Limits on Copyright*, 55 VAND. L. REV. 890, 898, 919 (2002).

play central roles in stimulating, exploring, critiquing, and ratifying ways that people think of themselves, their society, and the issues that confront them. Moreover, these media do so with a sensibility for human flaws and weaknesses, with a capacity for inspiring change, and with recognition of human variability that effectively debate and teach much that is relevant for public as well as private self-government.

If the First Amendment protects the press for its service to democracy, a proper conception of the press would depend on what mass communications a democracy requires. The answer to this question depends, in turn, on the appropriate conception of democracy. Elsewhere I outlined arguments for four models or ideal type conceptions of democracy—elite, liberal pluralist, republican, and complex.[269] There I argued that "complex democracy" was both normatively most appealing and descriptively most in line with existing Court doctrine. Complex democracy argues that a free society requires not only both republican or inclusive discourses aimed at forming conceptions of the public good and liberal discourses aimed at obtaining fair bargains between different groups, but also internal discourses within subgroups of society aimed at these subgroups' self-understanding and identity formation. Without this last category of discourse and, presumably, the media that serves it, the likelihood of marginalization and ultimately the oppression of subaltern groups[270] is huge. It seems that cultural media are crucial both for the broader society to understand itself, a crucial step in the republican search for a common good, and possibly even more so (and more endangered) for subgroups to be able to debate and form or understand their otherwise marginalized identity. If this conception of democracy is accepted, it provides an ample democratic reason to interpret the Press Clause expansively as protecting these broader forms of cultural media.

V. CONCLUSION: WHY IT MATTERS

The constitutional order has long done without any explicit recognition of an independent interpretation of the Press Clause.[271] So it

269. C. EDWIN BAKER, MEDIA, MARKETS, AND DEMOCRACY 129-53 (2002). The model I label complex democracy, which combines elements of liberal pluralist and republican democracy plus adding emphasis on internal self-definitional discourses of subgroups, duplicates closely Habermas's discourse theory of democracy. JURGEN HABERMAS, BETWEEN FACT AND NORM 118-31 (1996).

270. Nancy Fraser, *Rethinking the Public Sphere: A Contribution to the Critique of Actually Existing Democracy*, *in* HABERMAS AND THE PUBLIC SPHERE 109-142 (Craig Calhoun ed., 1992).

271. *But see supra* note 11 (discussing but doubting the significance of reliance on the press clause between the 1930s and the 1960s).

is natural to ask, does this issue really matter (much)? A plausible answer is: "no." First, not only has the legal order, the country, and the press gotten along until now without recognition of an independent (judicial) interpretation of the Press Clause, but radical commentators who claim to be more critical of the history of the country, of the legal order, and even of the operating press seldom attribute the problem to this corner of constitutional law. Even the legal areas I have discussed in this Article have done relatively well without explicit acceptance of this interpretation. Second, freedom from censorship—(purposeful) government penalties on the communicator's chosen content—is surely the most important guarantee provided by the First Amendment's constitutional protection of expression. As long as this stands, other concerns can mostly take care of themselves. In particular, the press is usually well positioned to convince the government of the utility of various privileges that will help it perform its constitutional role.

Still, this answer is unwelcome. The Court and the law should get it right! History and normative theory both support the independent interpretation. Although a relatively intellectualized point, as long as existing legal doctrine (and other results that are clearly appropriate if the issue arises constitutionally) requires the assumption of an independent status to the Press Clause, the absence of this interpretation denies the important virtues of clarity, coherence, and consistency to the law. More pragmatically, without this recognition, the tensions embedded in existing law can be a source of legal instability that could lead to wrong results and a failure to provide appropriate guidance as to new issues. Thus, these final remarks explore five pragmatic considerations that indicate the importance of formally recognizing the independent status of the Press Clause that the Article shows is already implicit in existing law.

First, only such recognition will prevent the obvious democratic importance of press freedom from giving general corporate interests a powerful but unjustified rhetorical edge in arguing that regulation of their speech is constitutionally indistinguishable from regulating the press and, hence, impermissible. This phenomenon has recently been most evident in the campaign finance debate. The refrain is either: "if the government can restrict our expenditures, the press should tremble because its speech freedom will also be at the mercy of the legislature;" or, "since the government cannot do this to the press, it similarly cannot do it to other corporations." Whatever the merits of various regulations of businesses' speech, the judgment about that policy issue should not be influenced by the fact that some of these regulations could not and should not be applied to the press. Only recognition of the independent status of the Press Clause prevents this distortion of proper policy debate—and, when relevant, only this recognition will lead to proper court holdings.

Second, though acting within legislative halls and with popular support, the press often is able to protect rights essential to its integrity, government administrations come and go; popular opinion is fickle. Many see popular support for the press recently to have been at a low ebb and see the Bush administration to be particularly indifferent to the integrity of the press. Only recognition of the independent status of the Press Clause provides legal security for this important democratic institution. Moreover, for those properly doubtful of the power of court decisions where the spirit of the people is not behind it, in the case of finding an independent meaning for the Press Clause the courts would be ratifying largely popular understandings of the constitutional status of the press. In doing so, the courts would be reinforcing and most likely contributing to the stability of this important value.

Third, recognition of the constitutional basis of protecting the institutional integrity of the press provides a foundation for properly addressing new or previously unrecognized threats to that integrity.[272] For example, my defense of the press's independence in Part II-A considered two issues, one well worn (reporter's privilege) and the other virtually unknown within the existing legal literature. The novel claim was that the integrity of the institution could be undermined equally by, to use Justice Stewart's words, the government "annex[ing] the journalistic profession as an investigative arm of government" or by the government using payments to "annex" the watchdog by making it a secret mouthpiece of the government.[273] Recognizing the independent status of the press provides a basis to understand, evaluate, and arguably invalidate both institutional threats as well as others not now evident and that may have not yet even arisen.

Fourth, only through recognition of the independent status of the press will courts not be placed in the position of distorting proper constitutional doctrine in trying to reach the right results as, at least so I argued, occurred in the case of defamation law in response to the issues posed by *Dun & Bradstreet*.[274]

---

272. *See supra* Part II.A.

273. Branzburg v. Hayes, 408 U.S. 665, 725 (1972) (Stewart, J., dissenting).

274. *See supra* notes 9-19 and accompanying text.

Finally, as a parallel to the first point above, failure to recognize the press's unique constitutional special status creates the danger that proper regulation of the press will be thwarted not on the merits but because of analogizing the press to individuals. Jerome Barron's advocacy of access rights, with which this Article began, raises complex issues concerning the proper understanding of the Press Clause. This analysis would be improperly truncated (in a manner inconsistent with existing Supreme Court precedent!) if the instrumental and institutional constitutional status of the press were not recognized. Without this recognition, provisions that compel media carriage of outsiders' speech (especially for communications contrary to the ideological views of the relevant decision-makers within a media entity) would seem to interfere with press autonomy the same way the compelled speech interfered with the liberty of the schoolchild in *Barnette*.[275]

Rejection of an independent meaning of the Press Clause blinds analysis. It leads both to the view that there is no First Amendment-based distinction between the press and individual speakers, a view that Part II shows is rejected by existing constitutional law (as well as statutory law) and to the view that there are no First Amendment based distinctions between the press and other businesses, a view that Part III shows existing constitutional law (as well as statutory law) rejects. The only conclusion can be that, though unacknowledged, existing law embodies an independent role for the Press Clause—essentially, some version of Justice Stewart's Fourth Estate theory.[276]

Both the press and a democratic country obviously can get by without an independently interpreted Press Clause in its Constitution. This absence leaves no vital human right subject to simple governmental abridgment, nor prevents the possibility of having a robust and free press. Largely because of its lobbying capacity, the press is likely to secure most of the privileges and exemptions that serve a society, as well as some that do not, from either the legislature, executive, or the administrative agencies. Nevertheless, this Article has claimed that failure to acknowledge an independent status of the Press Clause of the United States Constitution is not only a theoretical mistake, contrary to the historical meaning of the Press Clause and contrary to the best normative interpretation of the Constitution and, as this conclusion has argued, a potentially significant pragmatic mistake. It is also inconsistent with existing law.

---

275. *See* West Virginia State Bd. of Educ. v. Barnette, 319 U.S. 624 (1943).

276. *See* Stewart, *supra* note 9, at 634.

[4]

FREEDOM OF THE PRESS: OWNERSHIP AND EDITORIAL VALUES

THOMAS GIBBONS*

No sooner had the press revised its system of self-regulation, and established the Press Complaints Commission in response to the criticisms of the Calcutt report, than it was subjected to scrutiny by a different set of policy-makers. In 1991, the European Commission organised a conference to sound out the possibility of introducing a directive on the press, to follow the one issued in respect of broadcasting some years ago. Not surprisingly, newspaper publishers have opposed any additional restrictions on their industry, and they have tended to voice their opposition in terms of the undesirable effects that regulation would have upon freedom of the press.[1] Yet there is continued concern that one of the most potent sources of danger to press freedom comes from the proprietors themselves. Occasionally, newspapers will carry stories of the most blatant examples[2] but, amongst journalists generally, and amongst reformers,[3] there is a feeling that proprietorial interference continues to occur all too often and in ways that are inconsistent with the maintenance of good editorial practice.

This article examines the case for controlling ownership of the press. It will be argued that the special status of freedom of the press is based on its association with editorial autonomy and that, whatever grounds owners may have for resisting regulatory intervention, it will not be sufficient for them to assert their property rights. Indeed, it may be that the only way to protect freedom of the press is to limit those interests.

I. THE TRADITIONAL APPROACH

In the traditional, liberal approach, freedom of the press is regarded as an element of the broader political principle of freedom of speech.[4] It is recognised that the press may have an important role in facilitating the activities that are recognised as justifying special pro-

---

* Lecturer in Law, University of Manchester. An earlier draft of this article was presented at the *Public Law* seminar held at the Institute of Advanced Legal Studies, London, on June 27, 1991. I am grateful for the helpful comments that I received from the participants on that occasion. For other articles based on papers given at the same seminar, see pp. 40, 61 and 73 above.

[1] See "Publishers oppose Delors press laws," *The Guardian*, July 3, 1991, reporting the proceedings of the European Press Assizes in Luxembourg.

[2] See "African despot of influence brings the Observer to heel," *Sunday Times*, July 7, 1991.

[3] See J. Curran *et al.* (eds.), *Bending Reality* (1986) App. I (statement of aims of the Campaign for Press and Broadcasting Freedom).

[4] See F. Schauer, *Free Speech: A Philosophical Enquiry* (1982), pp. 106–109; E. Barendt, *Freedom of Speech* (1985), pp. 67–77.

tection for free speech. In particular, the political content of the press has a special affinity with participation in a democracy, but the press may also advance the search for knowledge and certain aspects of personal fulfilment. At the same time, it is accepted that the press will not have these pursuits as its main interest, which is more likely to be commercial success in the provision of information and entertainment. Freedom of speech does not imply freedom of the press, therefore, where that is taken to stand for some privileged status for the press as an institution which provides special protection for free speech.

Consequently, the idea of freedom of the press does not in British law add any extra dimension to the right of individuals to express their opinions freely. In itself, that right is no more than the negative liberty to speak without interference by the state. The significance of press ownership lies in the extent to which proprietors can provide that condition of independence. As Dicey put it, "the so-called liberty of the press is a mere application of the general principle, that no man is punishable except for a distinct breach of the law."[5] Freedom of the press is regarded as a manifestation of free speech but, in practice, it means little more than "the freedom to found a newspaper, free from licensing restrictions and discriminatory taxation."[6]

It follows that the law does not recognise any special claims made on behalf of the press, represented by editors and journalists, as distinct from the owners of their newspapers. The basic position is that the editor is an employee of the proprietor, who can be expected to select the person that he considers appropriate for the job as he defines it. A candidate's political persuasion is as likely to be one of the qualifications for the post as is journalistic and managerial ability. From a legal perspective, then, editorial autonomy is nothing more than the freedom that the proprietor allows to his editor. If there is a serious disagreement between them, the law will not treat that as worthy of special consideration. The editor will have to decide whether or not to continue in post or to resign, and the issues will be resolved in accordance with the usual principles of employment and contract law.

This general approach is reflected in those areas of substantive law that touch upon the editorial function. In the civil law, the nature of liability and the defences available all serve to implicate the owner, who has an obvious interest, therefore, in controlling his editor's activities. To take the law of defamation, for example, it is well established that everybody who takes part in publishing a libel, or in procuring its publication, is prima facie civilly liable.[7] That includes the

[5] A. V. Dicey, *The Law of the Constitution* (8th ed., 1923), p. 244.
[6] Barendt (*supra*, n. 4), pp. 71–72.
[7] See *Gatley on Libel and Slander* (8th ed., 1981), para. 236.

editor of a newspaper,[8] but it also applies to the proprietor whether or not he knows of the publication. The reason is that the editor is the proprietor's employee whose job entails the selection of material for publication, and the proprietor is required to be vicariously responsible for any libel that may result. In *R.* v. *Gutch*, it was said:

> "Surely a person who derives profit from, or who furnishes means for carrying on the concern, and entrusts the conduct of the publication to one whom he selects, and in whom he confides, may be said to cause to be published what actually appears, and ought to be answerable although you cannot show that he was individually concerned in the particular publication."[9]

Liability may be incurred, therefore, not only where the publication is simply within the scope of the employment but also where the agent or servant is expressly forbidden to publish any defamatory material.[10] The proprietor is also liable for the content of the material and, consequently, for the author's state of mind.[11] The obverse situation occurs when defamatory imputations are made against newspapers. Here, the law takes the consistent position that disparaging statements that a paper is prejudiced, dishonest or corrupt may be defamatory of the proprietor as the person responsible for it.[12] Generally, the effect of the law is to give proprietors the primary responsibility for liability and a clear interest in managing their company's product. As a result, where the proprietor is a defendant in an action, he may be expected to conduct his defence so as to minimise the amount of damages payable by him. That may mean that editors and journalists will be required to acquiesce in retractions and apologies (if they have not in any case surrendered control over litigation to their employer in return for an indemnity against liability), perhaps against their professional judgment, for the sake of securing advantageous settlements.[13]

In relation to criminal liability, the dominant principle of individual responsibility means that owners will not usually be liable for offences committed by their employees. But in the area that impinges most upon press activities, contempt of court,[14] there has been some modification of this approach. Normally, it is the person who publishes who is liable and that has been held to include the editor of a paper, as the one who has central responsibility for the publication.[15] The courts appear to have gone further, however, and imposed

[8] *R.* v. *Dover* (1663) 8 How.St.Tr. at p. 547.
[9] (1829) Moo. & Mal. 433, 437.
[10] *Gatley* (*supra*, n. 7), para. 941.
[11] *Ibid.*, para. 948.
[12] *Ibid.*, para. 73.
[13] *Cf. Tracey* v. *Kemsley Newspapers*, *The Times*, April 9, 1954, where a journalist succeeded in obtaining damages in respect of an apology that implied that she was an irresponsible journalist.
[14] See C. J. Miller, *Contempt of Court* (1989), pp. 292–297.
[15] *R.* v. *Evening Standard, ex p. D.P.P.* (1924) 40 T.L.R. 833.

vicarious liability on editors for a journalist's contempt, using reasoning which implies that editors are to be regarded as the same as proprietors for this purpose.[16] Whether or not vicarious liability for criminal contempt can be supported, and it has been doubted in terms of both general principle and authority,[17] it is clear that a proprietor who is incorporated may be held liable for contempt under the *alter ego* doctrine. This applies where a person is regarded as the embodiment of a company, so that his actions and his state of mind are taken to be those of the company.[18] As Miller suggests, an editor is likely to be in a sufficiently senior position for his or her actions to be attributed in this way.

In practice, in respect of most issues of media law, the proprietor will be the main target for litigants or prosecuting authorities, whether the matter concerns defamation, breach of confidence, contempt of court or official secrets. From a legal perspective, the possibility of liability is regarded as one of the incidents of ownership. Insofar as interests in society wish to limit certain types of publication by law, it can be assumed that the owner's control will restrain editorial action. In this regard, the newspaper owner's position is little different from any person who wishes to publish on a more modest scale.

In relation to broadcasting and other electronic media, similar principles apply, with appropriate modifications to take account of the way in which the bodies concerned are constituted. The BBC, for example, is a public corporation whose governors are responsible for the programmes that it broadcasts.[19] In the independent sector, it is the individual programme companies which are responsible for any liability arising out of production or broadcasting. But the electronic media differ from the press in the important respect that, unlike newspaper proprietors, their "owners" do not have unlimited editorial scope (subject to the general law). Instead, they are obliged to take account of a number of independent standards relating to matters such as taste, decency and quality.[20] The effect is to create a type of buffer that has the potential to separate proprietorial and editorial decision-making.

II. Press Freedom and Economic Power

The principal objection to the traditional approach to press freedom is that it ignores the extent of economic power in controlling com-

[16] *R.* v. *Evening Standard* [1954] 1 Q.B. 578.
[17] Miller (*supra*, n. 14), p. 296.
[18] *Tesco Supermarkets Ltd.* v. *Nattrass* [1972] A.C. 153.
[19] See the BBC's *Charter* (1981, Cmnd. 8313), Arts. 1, 5–7. The members of the former IBA bore a corresponding responsibility.
[20] *BBC Licence and Agreement* (1981, Cmnd. 8233); Broadcasting Act 1990, ss.6, 16, 90.

Freedom of the Press 283

munication.[21] In terms of speakers' interests, not everybody is in the position to found a newspaper and the possession of a negative liberty to speak may be of little use in actually reaching a readership. To adopt Rawls' phrase, the "worth of liberty"[22] is more significant than its mere existence. For him, the need to enhance the worth of liberty is an issue of distributional justice, one which falls to be decided according to principles that are independent of free speech itself. But free speech theorists have avoided the distributional issue on the ground that there is no clear reason why positive provision for communication should take priority over the distribution of other resources, for example, for education.[23] In practice, it is readership or audience interests that are likely to be decisive. In respect of them, the significance of economic power in the media is that access to certain knowledge may be restricted and a diversity of viewpoints may not be made available.

It is these grounds for concern about economic power in the media that manifest themselves in calls to regulate ownership of the press. In considering them, there are three main issues to be discussed. The first is an objection of principle to the control of ownership. The other two are separate, albeit closely related. One is the significance of proprietorial influence over editorial decisions. The other is the implications of concentrated ownership in the press, including cross-media ownership in the electronic media.

(A) *Control of ownership and freedom of speech*

Traditionally, freedom of speech has been viewed as a "negative" liberty, being concerned with the extent to which there is no state interference with the speaker's act to communication. But that is a rather narrow view of free speech.[24] For the state is not the only source of constraints upon speech and, as Barendt notes,[25] if there is no difference between official censorship and the private censorship exercised by the press, there may be arguments for giving the state a more positive role in protecting interests in communication.

Such arguments generally adopt the approach that the reasons why speech is considered sufficiently valuable to justify special protection from interference should be used also to judge whether the absence of interference is justified. It is a more constructive conception of free speech, emphasising the purposes for which speech might be used and its particular contribution to them. It has been most extensively discussed in relation to the question of access to the media, including

---

21 See, *e.g.* P. O'Higgins, *Censorship in Britain* (1972), Chap. 4.
22 J. Rawls, *A Theory of Justice* (1971), pp. 204 *et seq.*
23 See Schauer (*supra*, n. 4), pp. 125–128.
24 *Cf. ibid.*, pp. 128–129.
25 *Supra*, n. 4, p. 83.

the right to reply, with the function of the media as a public forum being seen as a ground for allowing greater readership and audience participation.[26] More recently, there has been some shift towards the wider issue of regulation in general, although the focus continues to be upon the potential of the press for actively promoting public discussion.

By way of example, Fiss has drawn a distinction between a free speech principle based upon autonomy and one based upon public debate.[27] Both, he suggests, may be seen as ways of furthering the democratic purposes of the First Amendment of the United States' Constitution. Historically, it has been autonomy that has been seen as the best method of bringing debate into operation: "the hope is that a rule denying the state the power to silence speech on the basis of its content will produce the broadest possible debate." But Fiss observes that the debate will inevitably be dominated by those who have the means of speech. He suggests, therefore, that their autonomy should only be protected when it "enriches public discourse" and that state interference to achieve that is justified. As he puts it, "the issue is not market failure but market reach."[28]

A similar approach has been adopted by Lichtenberg, who distinguishes between a "non-interference or no censorship principle" and a "multiplicity of voices principle."[29] The latter encapsulates the idea that the purposes of free speech are realised when expression, and especially a diversity of expression, flourish. She points out that the two principles may clash; in particular, a newspaper's proprietorial autonomy, protected by the non-interference principle, may serve to inhibit a multiplicity of voices. Furthermore, it is not sufficient to assert what are, in fact, the property rights of publishers against all claims to regulate the press.[30] As she puts it, the question is "whether a policy of nonregulation of the press is good for the values underlying free speech."[31] Her point is that where the press is serving a public function, the proprietor cannot define his role in wholly private terms.

More recently, Barendt has described freedom of the media as "an institutional right," "a constitutional value which should influence the whole of the law" because "the media foster free speech, in par-

[26] Access to the media is beyond the scope of this article but a recent review of the, mainly U.S., literature may be found in D. Caristi, "The Concept of a Right to Access to the Media: A Workable Alternative?" (1988) 22 Suffolk Univ. L.R. 103 at 105–118. See also Barendt (*supra*, n. 4), pp. 83–86.

[27] O. Fiss, "Why the State?" (1987) 100 Harv.L.R. 781.

[28] *Ibid.*, p. 788.

[29] J. Lichtenberg, "Foundations and Limits of Freedom of the Press" (1987) 16 *Philosophy and Public Affairs* 329.

[30] As Barendt observes, this was the basis of the U.S. Supreme Court decision in *Miami Herald* v. *Tornillo* 418 U.S. 241 (1974) in denying the constitutionality of a right of reply in the press: *supra*, n. 4, p. 100.

[31] Lichtenberg (*supra*, n. 29), p. 347.

ticular by providing fora for vigorous and uninhibited public debate."[32] His theme reflects a growing body of writing, from a quite different perspective, which draws upon Habermas' concept of a "public sphere" as the basis for an "ideal speech situation" in which there is free, equal and fully informed discussion without domination by particular groups or the state.[33] As these writers have recognised, however, these ideas have been accepted more readily as a basis for regulating broadcasting. In the United States, the so-called "scarcity rationale," the recognition that there is a practical limit on the number of frequencies that can be made available, was an important reason for accepting the constitutionality of the "fairness doctrine" which allowed politicians certain rights of reply.[34] In the United Kingdom, there has been an additional theme in public service broadcasting, an emphasis on its universality. This has been defined not in terms of the lowest common denominator, however, but the facility to allow a diversity of viewpoints to engage with each other through the medium of television and radio.[35] More especially, the fact that public service broadcasting has operated under a system of close regulation has not been seen as inimical to free speech interests. Rather, as Garnham suggests, the existence of institutions that focus public opinion, encouraging the provision of political debate and information, is very important to the national political process.[36]

These points are not intended to suggest that the press ought to take on some public service role. What they do suggest, however, is that any attempt to separate the editorial values from the interests of the owner should not be regarded as inconsistent with freedom of speech. Rather, editorial values may often be identical with the constructive conception of free speech that seeks to enhance those objectives, the gaining of knowledge and active citizenship,[37] that give free speech its importance.

(B) *Proprietorial influence*

In considering the question of proprietorial influence, two kinds of anxiety need to be distinguished. One relates to the content of the

---

[32] E. Barendt, "Press and broadcasting freedom: does anyone have any rights to free speech?" (1991) 44 C.L.P. 63, 66–67.

[33] See J. Curran, "Mass media and democracy: a reappraisal" in J. Curran and M. Gurevitch (ed.), *Mass Media and Society* (1991), p. 82. For earlier work, see N. Garnham, "The media and the public sphere" in P. Golding *et al.* (ed.) *Communicating Politics* (1986), p. 36; P. Scannell, "Public service broadcasting and modern public life" (1989) 11 *Media, Culture and Society* 135.

[34] *Red Lion Broadcasting* v. *Federal Communications Commission* 395 U.S. 367 (1969).

[35] See, *e.g.* (Annan) *Report of the Committee on the Future of Broadcasting* (1977, Cmnd. 6753), paras. 3.21 *et seq.*

[36] See Garnham (*supra*, n. 33). See also K. Kumar, "Public Service and the Public Interest" in C. McCabe and O. Stewart (ed.) *The BBC and Public Service Broadcasting* (1986), p. 46.

[37] See J. Keen, "Citizenship and Freedom of the Media" (1989) 60 *Political Quarterly* 285.

messages that the newspaper disseminates. It may be that the paper tends to one end of the political spectrum, for example, or that it sensationalises and trivialises in order to maximise sales. In this case, the basis of the objection is not that the proprietor's views are thereby reflected, for similar worries might be expressed if it were the editor who was responsible for the paper's policy. Rather, the concern is with an excess of power in the media, that one perspective on knowledge is unduly dominant. As such, this problem will be discussed in a subsequent section, on media concentration.

(i) *Ownership and the public interest*

A different matter is the issue of direct proprietorial interference with editorial decision-making. Why should this be thought to raise a problem? The very idea of such interference implies that editors normally do or should enjoy a degree of autonomy from newspaper owners. But this view does not reflect the current legal position, discussed above. Nor does it reflect the historical development of the press. In their earliest days, newspapers were promoted by political parties and were used overtly for political propaganda, and it was not assumed that that fact was, in itself, a ground for criticism. As the press became commercialised during the nineteenth and early twentieth centuries, the politics and perspectives of the owners were substituted for those of the politicians, but this did not make the editors any more independent.[38] Historically, the period of greatest proprietorial influence took place between the two world wars, the "era of the press barons."[39] These were men such as Beaverbrook and Northcliffe, and also Kemsley and Rothermere, who took a close interest in the details of their papers' editorial policy. As well as determining the general style and politics of their papers, they frequently decided which stories should be published and how, and the content of any comment and opinion about them. Although the transition was gradual, the nature of the press has altered noticeably since the second world war.

Today, newspaper ownership is characterised by its corporate structure and the process of conglomeration.[40] Media ownership is concentrated in the hand of a relatively few large companies, some specialising in media matters but others regarding the media as a further diversification of already widespread interests. Whilst pat-

---

[38] See L. Brown, *Victorian News and Newspapers* (1985).

[39] See J. Curran and J. Seaton, *Power Without Responsibility* (1990), Chap. 5; S. Koss, *The Rise and Fall of the Political Press in Britain* (1990), Chaps. 15–18.

[40] See G. Murdock, "Large corporations and the control of the communications industries" in M. Gurevitch *et al.* (ed.), *Culture, Society and the Media* (1982), p. 118.

terns of ownership are well documented,[41] the influence of owners' views on editorial choice today is less easy to quantify. The nature of corporate ownership often makes it difficult to locate the source of any influence and, as Murdock emphasises, there are different types of control, ranging from the general allocation of resources and development of financial policy to intervention in the operational decisions that are made in day-to-day production. In this context, some have seen a decline in the influence of proprietors as personalities who impose their own values on a paper.[42] Others have noted "a new generation of partisan, interventionist proprietors" who are not simply led by the need to make their companies profitable, but who wish to use their papers to advance particular political views.[43] Certainly, there is much anecdotal evidence of the active role of proprietors in editorial matters[44] although, for some,[45] the evidence does not give cause for concern. Recently, the Sadler Enquiry found what it might be reasonable to expect, that there is pressure within newspapers, both subtle and not so subtle, to slant stories in certain ways (in the particular context, to promote the organisation's commercial interests).[46] While it is difficult to generalise about the pervasiveness of interventions, it seems clear that they do occur and that they are resented by journalists.

The question remains, why should it matter that proprietorial interference takes place? For some, the existence of competition in the newspaper industry may be considered a sufficient response to any problems caused by the dominance of a few proprietorial voices. Readers may recognise a newspaper for what it is, including the proprietorial opinions that it canvasses, and will choose whether or not to buy it accordingly. Yet there is a persistent concern that, even if ownership were to be diversified, proprietorial interference is an unacceptable practice and should be minimised. Thus, if a newspaper appears to promote the proprietor's interests in satellite television,[47] or if a newspaper appears to be drawn into a campaign being waged by the proprietor against his commercial rivals,[48] or if a proprietor

---

[41] The most recent British survey is C. Veljanovski, *The Media in Britain* (1990). Formerly, the annual reports of the Press Council provided details of newspaper ownership. An interesting American study is B. Compaine, *Who Owns the Media* (2nd ed., 1982). For a preliminary report of a project of the European Institute for the Media, see A. Sanchez-Taberno and P.-Y. Lochon, "Media Concentration" (1991) 8(2) *Media Bulletin* 6.

[42] *E.g.* Koss (*supra*, n. 39).

[43] Curran and Seaton (*supra*, n. 39), Chap. 7.

[44] Examples are H. Evans, *Good Times, Bad Times* (1983) and F. Giles, *Sundry Times* (1986). See also Curran and Seaton (*supra*, n. 39), Chap. 7.

[45] See R. Morgan, *The Guardian*, July 15, 1991. Morgan was then the editor of the *Sunday Express* and he discusses a disease that he calls "Proprietorial Influence Syndrome."

[46] (Sadler) *Enquiry into Standards of Cross-Media Promotion* (1991, Cm. 1436).

[47] A well-known example is News International's association with British Sky Broadcasting.

[48] It is well known that *The Observer*, which is owned by Lonhro, provides extensive coverage of that company's affairs. For the uses to which the paper was put to serve the company's interests, see *Re Lonrho plc* [1990] 2 A.C. 154.

simply corrects the editor's proofs in the newsroom,[49] there are justifiable worries that the power of the media is being harnessed for inappropriate purposes.

In part, the objection is to a simple excess of power. But the basis of the concern lies in the nature of claims that are made on behalf of freedom of the press. As a political idea, it clearly implies more than entrepreneurial freedom, the proprietor's liberty to spend or invest his money as he likes. Rather, it suggests that the press is more than simply writing and publishing and connotes a set of values, admittedly ill-defined, that imply objectivity, detachment and independence of thought.[50] These values are typically identified with editorial or journalistic autonomy, although good journalism or editorship does not aim to satisfy only those values. But when editors make strong claims that their work should not be interfered with, they are appealing to some dimension of their work that sets it apart from ordinary commercial judgments. There is a public interest in the way that the media of mass communication are used.

It might be, of course, that the objection to proprietorial interference is no more than a self-serving claim made by journalists. Tunstall, for example, writes of the "sovereign editor myth" and suggests that where editors have been successful in exercising exclusive control over editorial content, it is likely to have been "through a mixture of luck, commercial success and support from above."[51] He maintains that the myth continues to have a hold because editors are seen to be in charge from day-to-day and, more importantly, because "one of the editor's main tasks is to be the paper's public face." Furthermore, he notes that journalism has become more professional and that journalists have become a more powerful group within the newspaper industry.[52] It remains the case, however, that editors seek to legitimise their position in terms of a public interest in communication and it is that interest, if any, which should inform arguments for imposing some form of control on proprietorial behaviour.

What are these arguments for the public interest? First, the operation of the media industry is qualitatively different from the exercise of speech by an individual. It is usually not the case that the owner is a person who is simply using his liberty to speak. Instead, the publication of a newspaper is an exercise in mass communication, intended to reach as wide an audience as possible. The fact that it is part of a

---

[49] Evans (*supra*, n. 44), Chaps. 6, 8.

[50] See (Ross) *Royal Commission on the Press, Report* (1949, Cmd. 7700), paras. 361 *et seq.*; (Finer/McGregor) *Royal Commission on the Press, Final Report* (1977, Cmnd. 6810), Chap. 2. More recently, the Sadler Enquiry endorsed the values of the *Sunday Times*' own code of editorial standards, endorsing the values of accuracy, providing opportunities to reply and distinguishing between conjecture and fact: *supra*, n. 46.

[51] J. Tunstall, *The Media in Britain* (1983), p. 186.

[52] *Ibid.*, pp. 188–190.

wider conglomerate, with strong pressure to sell the paper to maximise profits for the wider organisation, points away from treating the press as worthy of special treatment in terms of freedom of communication. But, from the readers' perspective, if not from that of the proprietor-as-speaker, the role of the press will be special where its impact, whatever its financial organisation, has a dominant role in public discussion.

Secondly, the presence of the editor, as a mediator between the owner and the readership, has the effect of altering the nature of the enterprise. The editor provides not only the public face of the newspaper, a person chosen for personal appeal and a gift for communication, but also fills a role which connotes the exercise of independent judgment that gives some public dimension to what would otherwise be personal opinion. Furthermore, editors do not simply say things on their own behalf or that of their owner. Rather, they select material for publication from the statements of journalists and others who want access to their paper. There is a plurality of information and they exercise control over the reach of others' speech. This applies, albeit to varying degrees, whether the paper is one "of record" or is a more popular tabloid.

If freedom of the press has any significance, other than the owner's economic right to start a newspaper or his liberty to speak, it is in its identity with editorial autonomy conceived in this sense of serving a public interest in communication. Preserving freedom of the press entails, then, the protection of the freedom to make editorial judgments on the basis of values that are independent of the partisan views of particular, powerful individuals. It does not imply the broader view that the media (as an institution) should be privileged, but it does suggest the value of finding some method of distancing the editor's function from the owner's interests.

It may be replied, however, that any increase in editorial autonomy would amount to an unwarranted interference with the proprietor's interests. To assess this claim, two types of interest need to be distinguished. One is the owner's individual right to free speech, which may be thought to be compromised by any attempt to separate it from the editor's right to speak. In terms of negative liberty, the owner continues to be free to issue whatever propaganda he wishes. Furthermore, it may be that determining the tone of a newspaper is itself a sufficient act of "speech" for his right to have been asserted. The real issue, however, is the extent to which constraints may be imposed upon the proprietor's commercial autonomy. For it may be said that the proprietor should be able to use his economic resources as he wishes, including the publication of a newspaper. The force of this claim rests upon two uncertainties, however. One is that the economic freedom is so closely associated with the political freedom (of speech) that any interference in one is an interference with the other. The other ambiguity concerns the aims of the newspaper, and the extent to which it is being held out as an organ with mass appeal or simply as a mouthpiece for the owner's views.

In a legal context, ownership is never granted on unconditional terms. As a business, there are no grounds for exempting the media from business regulation. As a business with interests in communication, there are no grounds for immunising owners from restrictions on their activities that affect the public interest in the wide dissemination of information and opinion. In particular, the use of mass media to publish partisan viewpoints may be seen as an unjustifiable use of economic power to secure political advantage. By way of response, it may be objected that any form of regulation will limit the organisation's profitability and that, in itself, is unacceptable.[53] It should be clear, however, that the argument is not directed against commercial success but at the way in which it may be achieved.

(ii) *Ways of limiting proprietorial interference*

One way of enabling an editor to take an independent view, based upon standards of professional journalism and free from proprietorial pressure, is to incorporate some protection into his contract of employment. The third Royal Commission on the Press identified a number of "basic rights" for editors, including the right to reject material provided by central management, the right to determine the contents of the paper (within the bounds of reasonable economic considerations and the established policy of the publisher) and the right to criticise the paper's own group or other parts of the same corporate structure.[54] It recommended that an agreed description of duties and powers should be drawn up for each editor and that editorial contracts should incorporate a clause requiring 12 months notice of termination.

It is not likely to be easy, however, to enforce special recognition for the editor's status within the context of a commercial enterprise like the newspaper industry, although the Royal Commission was told that its catalogue of rights did represent existing practice. Proprietors will want to maintain control of the ventures that they have financed. From a practical point of view, it would be difficult to separate owners' and editors' liabilities, as opposed to their rights, in con-

---

[53] Arguments of this type were advanced to justify the refusal to extend restrictions on cross-media ownership to take account of Sky Television's relationship, as a non-domestic satellite service, with newspaper holdings in the United Kingdom. See the discussion on Broadcasting Act 1990, Sched. 2, in H.C.Deb., Standing Committee F, cols. 294–394, January 25 and 30, 1990.

[54] Cmnd. 6810 (*supra*, n. 50), para. 16.3.

tracts of employment.[55] The separation might also have the effect of denying plaintiffs a defendant worthy of suing, but leave editors vulnerable to litigation that they could not afford to defend. Now editors may not want special status, or may appreciate that holding their posts may depend upon not asserting any claim to such status.[56] But, even if they were allowed relative independence, it would still need to be asked whether one unacceptable source of control over a powerful medium was being replaced with another. The point is that the interest in editorial autonomy is not solely that of the editor, so that a mechanism that concentrates upon individual editors' rights will not necessarily be the best way of protecting the public interest in maintaining autonomy for editorial values.

An alternative approach is to secure some form of institutional protection for the editor. The model provided by broadcasting in this country, albeit imperfect, shows that such protection is workable, although this does not mean that it could simply be transplanted into the press. In broadcasting, the legal position in relation to ownership and control is formally similar to that in the press, but a set of conventional understandings have developed to provide greater autonomy for editors.

In the case of the BBC, it is the governors who are responsible for the programmes which are released. Under the Charter, they are the broadcasters, and the Director-General and his staff are employees with the task of managing the Corporation from day to day.[57] In practice, the programmers have enjoyed greater autonomy than the constitutional position would suggest, partly as a result of an agreement that the first Director-General, John Reith, secured from the chairman of the governors in 1932, John Whitley. The "Whitley Document," as it is known, establishes that the governors' responsibility is "general and not particular" in relation to major issues of policy and finance.[58] Although this was a doubtful interpretation of the Charter, it has provided the basis for the relationship between the governors and professional broadcasters, and interference by the former in the details of programming policy is generally considered to be irregular. The practice was challenged by both the Beveridge[59] and the Pilk-

[55] For a case which appears to be an exception, see *Union of Construction Allied Trades and Technicians* v. *Brain* [1981] I.C.R. 542. It was held that a request to sign an undertaking not to publish further the same or similar libels in a union magazine was not one with which the employing union was entitled to ask its employee editor to conform. See P. F. Carter-Ruck and R. Walker, *Carter-Ruck on Libel and Slander* (1985), p. 189.

[56] In West Germany, from the late 1960s to the early 1980s, there was a debate about the "internal freedom of the media." It was largely fuelled by broader considerations of worker participation. A draft law, demarcating the competencies of publishers and editors, was published in 1974 but there was insufficient political will to bring it to fruition. See P. Humphreys, *Media and Media Policy in West Germany* (1990), pp. 104–111.

[57] Cmnd. 8313 (*supra*, n. 19), arts. 5, 12.

[58] See T. Burns, *The BBC: Public Institution and Private World* (1977), p. 22.

[59] *Report of the Broadcasting Committee* (1951, Cmd 8116), paras. 552–557.

ington[60] committees, who suggested that the governors' role was analogous to that of ministers; as public representatives, the governors were expected to mediate between their staff and the audience. Some chairmen of the governors did attempt to exert their authority, the most successful being Lord Hill. The BBC's internal bureaucracy has made it difficult for the governors to intervene greatly, however. The practice of referring difficult or controversial decisions up to superiors within the hierarchy of programmers means that, by the time a matter has been passed to the governors for decision, it is difficult to see how they can bring new light and wisdom to bear.[61] The governors can set the tone of the Corporation, however, by employing those who, in their judgment, will provide the best management of the Corporation. In turn, the government can set the tone of the Board through the governors that it appoints. Not unnaturally, the use of such powers attracts keen discussion and sometimes controversy, as the government's and the governors' choices will be seen as indicating the direction of broadcasting policy that is intended to be secured. Sometimes, change may be dramatic: in 1987, the appointment of a new chairman was soon followed by the enforced resignation of the then Director-General.[62]

Occasionally, the governors do become involved in the decision whether or not to allow a broadcast to proceed. Their role is illustrated by the notorious "Real Lives" affair which took place in 1985.[63] This concerned a programme which examined the attitudes of a nationalist and a loyalist to the situation in Northern Ireland. Following ministerial pressure, the governors decided to cancel the broadcast, and the programme was shown only later in modified form. Whatever the arguments about government interference and weakness by the governors, however, there is no doubt that they were technically correct in assuming responsibility for the programme. What made their role controversial was that they intervened in the face of editorial decisions by their staff to go ahead. This intervention was unusual, and considered improper, because the governors were regarded as allowing extraneous considerations to be brought to bear on a decision that would otherwise be determined only by reference to production values.

In the independent services, the relationship between members of the (former) IBA and programme contractors and, in turn, their relationship with their editors, was technically different from that in the

[60] *Report of the Committee on Broadcasting* (1962, Cmnd. 1753), paras. 404–409.

[61] As Burns observes (*supra*, n. 58), p. 33. By way of exception, in programming relating to Northern Ireland, and especially broadcasts within Northern Ireland, there is much stricter control and supervision, which means less autonomy for individual producers.

[62] For the circumstances of Alastair Milne's resignation, see *The Independent* and *The Guardian*, January 30, 1987 and *The Observer*, February 1, 1987.

[63] See L. Curtis, "British Broadcasting and Ireland" in *Bending Reality* (*supra*, n. 3.), p. 58.

BBC.[64] But it was similar in substance, since the independent sector's practice was based upon that of the BBC. While programme makers were not isolated from commercial pressures, as was the case with their counterparts at the BBC, there does not appear to have been direct interference in editorial decision-making by programme contractors. According to Lord Thompson, a former chairman of the IBA, the commercial lobby shared the IBA view on public service broadcasting.[65] In both sectors of broadcasting, there have been various instances of involvement by senior management in junior decisions. Usually, however, they have been justified by reference to editorial standards. Whilst producers may disagree with or resent such interference, it is usually regarded as part of the normal process of debate about the institution's aims and objectives. Where that becomes a form of censorship, albeit self-censorship, is when decisions to override producers' work is explained by reference to external influences (whether from government or commercial interests).

To what extent is it possible to introduce similar institutional constraints in the press? One way is to employ some form of external scrutiny of the relationship between an editor and his or her proprietor. One example is the arrangements for the ownership of *The Guardian*. The paper is owned by the Guardian and Manchester Evening News plc, which is owned, in turn, by the Scott Trust. Editors are employed on the basis that the paper "shall be carried on as nearly as may be upon the same principles as they have heretofore been conducted."[66] The Trust selects its own members, thereby perpetuating its own values, and it selects editors very carefully. But, once the editor is chosen, the trustees do not intervene in editorial policy, whether or not it will affect circulation figures. Indeed, the Trust is used to subsidise the newspaper in times of economic hardship.

The position of *The Guardian* is unusual and only continues because the Trust, as proprietor, wishes it to do so. An analogous situation is that of *The Independent*, where the editor is chief executive of, and an important shareholder in, the parent company. Another approach is to draft a company's articles of association in a manner that protects the editor's position. Harold Evans provides a fascinating account of the negotiations that took place between his editorial team at *The Sunday Times* and the new proprietor, Rupert Murdoch, to secure that protection. Yet Evans was well aware that the "tradition" of editorial independence that had been enjoyed by

---

[64] Broadcasting Act 1981, s.1.

[65] See Lord Thompson, "Thirty Years of Independent Broadcasting" (1985) 22 *Television* 212. This may not be surprising, since it was the IBA who selected the programme contractors that they felt they could work with. The statutory basis for regulation also made it more difficult to intervene.

[66] See P. Schlesinger, *The Scott Trust* (1986), p. 7.

himself and his predecessors was ephemeral and not easily reduced to rules.[67] Furthermore, since a proprietor who wholly owns the company can easily change its articles of association, there may be no guarantee that editorial autonomy will persist.[68]

In theory, the situation might be different where independent directors are appointed to safeguard editorial values. When the Thomson organisation (with extensive television interests and existing ownership of *The Sunday Times*) applied to buy *The Times* in 1966, it proposed that four independent directors should be appointed to the paper's board to ensure editorial independence. The Monopolies Commission was not impressed, however, and regarded the appointments as only symbolic. It considered that the national directors could not be expected to intervene in the highly technical process of producing a newspaper. "Moreover, in the event of a dispute about the authority of an editor or the appointment or dismissal of an editor, there would be no assurance that national figures would take any different view of the best interests of the company from that of their fellow directors."[69] Nevertheless, the approach was used again when *The Times* and *The Sunday Times* were taken over by News International. It was also adopted when *The Observer* was taken over by Lonhro.[70] In the latter case, the independent directors have been able to exercise some indirect influence, not by virtue of their power in the company, but by publicising the unacceptable behaviour of the proprietor. In 1984, the chairman and chief executive of Lonhro, Tiny Rowland, publicly criticised the editor for publishing allegations of atrocities in Zimbabwe, where Lonhro had commercial interests. The independent directors issued a rebuke, saying that there had been improper proprietorial interference in editorial freedom.[71] The proprietor's response was to reject the directors' interpretation of their role, to stress that the newspaper was a very expensive concern, and to continue negotiations for its sale to Robert Maxwell. The sale did not materialise, but relations between *The Observer*'s editor and proprietor have continued to be strained.[72]

The alternative to restricting proprietorial interference from within the institution, a method that has had very limited success, is to opt for some system of press regulation. The aim would be to provide minimum standards of editorial practice which could be enforced

---

[67] Evans (*supra*, n. 44), Chap. 6.

[68] In the event, Evans resigned after fundamental disagreements between himself and Murdoch: Koss (*supra*, n. 39), pp. 1110–1111.

[69] Monopolies Commission, *The Times and Sunday Times* (1966–67, H.C. 273).

[70] See Monopolies Commission, *The Observer and George Outram & Co.* (1981–82, H.C. 378).

[71] See *The Guardian*, April 25, 1984.

[72] A recent example concerned a report that criticised life in Malawi under its despotic ruler, Banda. See *Sunday Times*, July 7, 1991.

against newspapers. This would establish an environment in which similar expectations were made of all newspapers, thereby giving editors some leverage against the unreasonable demands of their owners. Usually, such standards are advocated as a response to readers' complaints about journalistic practice. But the code of practice suggested by the Calcutt committee, and currently being enforced by the Press Complaints Commission,[73] may also be seen as a positive way of minimising interference in editorial decision-making. As present, the success of the code and of the Commission depends upon the goodwill and commitment of the proprietors, but they may come to realise that some degree of editorial autonomy may not necessarily compromise their interests in securing the prosperity of their business.

Although it is a different industry, and the practice and traditions of the one cannot be transplanted into the other, the electronic media again provide a model of the way that standards can co-exist with commercial success. In particular, the provisions for separating advertising from programming content have worked well for many years[74] and there will be similar regulation of sponsorship. Thus, "No sponsor is permitted any influence on either the content or scheduling of a programme" and sponsorship must be clearly identified.[75] One object of this type of regulation is to provide, to use the current jargon, "a level playing field" so that no company is at a competitive disadvantage compared to its rivals, in terms of restrictions on the scope of the proprietor's role. Indeed, in relation to the press, it cannot be expected that editors will ignore the need to maximise circulation figures nor that they will be unaware of the subtle pressures that advertisers may bring to bear, either directly or through the proprietor. But editors who wish to make choices on the basis of editorial values would be in a stronger position if some regulatory buffer existed to justify their stance.

(C) *Concentrations of ownership*

I indicated earlier, in seeking to address the difficulties raised by the economic power of the press, that the issue of proprietorial interference is frequently merged with that of concentration of media ownership. They are in fact separate, for multiple ownership does not imply proprietorial interference or vice versa. But concentrations of ownership *may* mean that there are risks which are too great to be ignored.

---

[73] (Calcutt) *Report of the Committee into Privacy and Related Matters* (1990, Cm. 1102). See C. Munro, "Press Freedom—How the Beast was Tamed" (1991) 54 M.L.R. 104.

[74] See ITC, *The ITC Code of Advertising Standards and Practice* (1991), reflecting many provisions in the former IBA's Code.

[75] See ITC, *Code of Programme Sponsorship* (1991), p. 5. This draws upon the European Community's Directive on Broadcasting, O.J.E.C. No. L298/23, October 17, 1989.

Owners may decide to exert direct control over editorial policy or decide, simply, that corporate objectives will constrain the scope for editorial independence. In either case, the fear is that the content of a large portion of media output will be dominated by one or a few powerful voices. Should there be evidence of proprietorial interference, of course, the problem of concentration is exacerbated.

Determining what is an unacceptable concentration of ownership is a matter of judgment about these risks. In relation to a newspaper proprietor, relevant considerations will be the size of the paper's market share and the extent to which he or she is able to control other media interests. In addition, economists will stress the issue of market contestability: whether a monopoly may be said to exist depends upon the extent to which competition is restricted or facilitated. In Veljanovski's words,

> "Consider the newspaper industry . . . while some media companies have many interests and are relatively large, they are not dominant. Newcomers can and do challenge established newspapers, which must compete both with those new entrants and with other established titles."[76]

For many, however, this view may appear technical and unreal. While the potential for competition may exist, in practice a 25 per cent. share of national newspaper circulation may well be thought to constitute effective dominance.[77] As many commentators have observed,[78] it is rather expensive to start a newspaper.

To some extent, public policy in the United Kingdom does address these issues, although it has not been successful in preventing effective dominance by large media companies. One aim of reducing concentrations of ownership is to produce a wider range of opinion and expression in the media. But the main reason is simply to encourage a greater diversity of ownership as a matter of competition policy. In relation to the press, newspaper transfers and mergers are governed by the Fair Trading Act 1973. Under section 58, a newspaper may not be transferred to a proprietor whose newspapers would have an average circulation of 500,000 copies per day (including the paper to be acquired) unless the Secretary of State for Trade and Industry gives his consent. Unless a large-circulation paper is not intended to be continued as a going concern or a decision is required urgently, that consent can be given only after a report from the Monopolies and Mergers Commission. Under section 59, the Commission have to consider whether the transfer may be expected to operate against the

[76] Veljanovski (*supra*, n. 41), p. 18.

[77] In 1989, *The Sun's* share of the daily market was 28 per cent. and that of *The Daily Mirror* 21.5 per cent. Including *The Sun*, News International's total share of the daily market was 35 per cent. They also secured 36.6 per cent. of the Sunday market, of which Mirror Group Newspapers took another 31.4 per cent. See Veljanovski (*supra*, n. 41), p. 29.

[78] For a recent discussion, see Curran (*supra*, n. 33).

public interest, taking into account all relevant interests and, "in particular, the need for accurate presentation of news and free expression of opinion."

The main difficulty with this procedure is that it has not proved capable of resisting commercial responses to loss-making ventures such as quality newspapers. *The Times* was not financially viable when it was bought by the Thomson Organisation in 1966 and the then Monopolies Commission had little choice but to accept assurances that editorial autonomy would be respected. When the same paper was bought by News International, the matter was not referred to the Commission by the minister, presumably on the basis that the paper's survival was at stake, despite the fact that *The Sunday Times* was included in the deal and remained a going concern. When *The Observer* was bought by Lonhro, it also was in financial straits and the Monopolies Commission approved the change of ownership. In all these cases, as mentioned above, the appointment of independent directors was thought to provide some protection against any interference that the concentration of ownership might bring.

It should be stressed again that, apart from considerations of competition policy, placing restrictions on concentrations of ownership is an answer to fears that proprietorial interference will occur. Diversity of ownership is assumed to result in diversity of publication. Where proprietorial control or corporate influence cannot be proved or quantified, diversification may be seen as the minimum response consistent with a liberty to speak. A similar approach has been adopted for the electronic media,[79] the aim being "to keep the market open for newcomers and to prevent any tendency towards editorial uniformity or domination by a few groups."[80] In their case, however, restrictions on ownership are to be found in very detailed rules rather than being a matter of broad discretion for the regulatory bodies. Of particular interest are the restrictions on cross-holdings between the press and licensed services. Proprietors of national newspapers cannot have more than a 20 per cent. interest in a Channel 3 or 5 or national radio service and a 5 per cent. interest in any second holding. Local proprietors are not allowed more than a 20 per cent. holding in a local radio or delivery service. There are broadly reciprocal restrictions on licensees' holdings in newspapers.

One anomaly, however, is the relationship between newspapers and satellite services: restrictions have not been imposed on national proprietors' holdings in Astra services. Curiously, it is in this sector that restrictions might be thought to be most needed, for it enjoys only minimal regulation[81] and, as indicated above, the presence of

[79] Broadcasting Act 1990, s.5 and Sched. 2.

[80] *Broadcasting in the 90's: Competition, Choice and Quality* (1988, Cm. 517), para. 6.48.

[81] See Broadcasting Act 1990, s.45 (licensing of non-domestic satellite services).

regulatory standards can provide an important buffer between editorial autonomy and proprietorial control. Despite vigorous parliamentary discussion,[82] the government argued that restrictions would curtail investment and that Astra services were already sufficiently diversified. Whether or not cross-ownership between newspapers and electronic media will lead to more homogenised editorial positions, the more immediate problem has been that of cross-media promotion, for example, indirectly advertising a satellite service by reporting its activities in the news columns of a paper with shared ownership. The Sadler Enquiry, which was established to examine the issue, suggested that existing restrictions on concentration should be supplemented with an informal code to encourage transparency of ownership, to enable readers to make up their own minds about the weight to be given to editorial pronouncements and to guarantee independent editorial judgment. For example, papers would be expected to include regular statements, in a prominent position, about the commercial interests associated with them. They would also be expected to allow free access to advertising by rivals and to preserve professional standards of journalism.[83] Perhaps understandably, such a scheme has not been embraced enthusiastically by the newspaper industry. It would, however, make a positive way of controlling cross-media promotion and, more significantly, it would provide a basis for minimising proprietorial interference in general.

III. Conclusions

The need for further regulation of press ownership depends upon the value that is placed on freedom of the press. I have suggested that the freedom represents more than proprietors' liberty to publish and that editorial values are worth enhancing, but that they may be compromised by proprietorial influence. In dealing with the risks of such influence, we can adopt one of two strategies, which are not mutually exclusive. One is to focus on the reduction of media concentration in the hope that, regardless of proprietorial interference, there will be a sufficient diversity of viewpoints, including editorial opinion. If this is the favoured method, there is a need for stricter scrutiny of newspaper mergers and a more consistent approach to cross-ownership with the electronic media than the legislation currently provides. Given the vulnerability of newspapers to financial pressures, however, there are reasonable grounds for doubting whether further restrictions on concentrations of ownership could be effective. A second strategy would be to address directly the possibility of pro-

82 See H.C.Deb., Standing Committee F, Broadcasting Bill, cols. 294–392, January 25 to January 30, 1990.

83 (Sadler) *Enquiry into Standards of Cross-Media Promotion* (1991, Cm. 1436), paras. 5.21 *et seq.*

prietorial interference. Of the modes examined above, the imposition of common standards of practice is likely to be the most successful in balancing a feasible competitive base with the preservation of editorial values. This does not imply the requirements of quality and taste that are appropriate for broadcasting. But a code might include the matters endorsed by Sadler, such as the separation of financial from editorial decisions, the preservation of professional standards of accuracy, the opportunity to reply and comment, the separation of conjecture from fact, and the right of the editor to criticise the paper's parent company and its associates.

There are bound to be residual anxieties about imposing any restrictions on the press. A major worry is the possibility that regulation could become an excuse for further encroachment by the state on media activities.[84] While the likelihood of this occurring should not be underestimated, the experience of the electronic media suggests that the fear may be exaggerated. Furthermore, current threats to press freedom do not originate from attempts to preserve editorial standards but from efforts to restrict their scope through the law relating to contempt, confidentiality, official secrecy and libel.

Not every restraint on the press should be seen to curtail freedom of speech and it cannot be assumed that an EC Directive on the press would inevitably have that effect. Some forms of regulation could well have such an impact. But, if proprietors wish to demonstrate that, they will have to prove that more is at stake than their commercial interests. For freedom of the press entails the promotion of editorial values, and the onus is on the proprietors to show that they are capable of protecting them and willing to do so.

---

[84] See Munro, *supra*, n. 73.

Part II
Self-regulation of the Press

[5]

PRESS COUNCILS: THE ANSWER TO OUR FIRST AMENDMENT DILEMMA†

JOHN A. RITTER* AND MATTHEW LEIBOWITZ**

The first amendment guarantees a free press but not a fair press. The Supreme Court's most recent decisions on two first amendment issues, access to the press and libel, underscore the inability of legal institutions to resolve this dilemma. In *Miami Herald Publishing Co. v. Tornillo*[1] and *Gertz v. Robert Welch, Inc.*,[2] members of the Court suggested a press council, an independent arbitration board, as a means of resolving free press-fair press conflicts. Two major press councils are now functioning in the United States, the Minnesota Press Council and the National News Council. An examination of their procedures and decisions demonstrates that the press council mechanism can foster a fair and responsible press while upholding the first amendment's guarantee of a free press.

THE NEED FOR PRESS COUNCILS

Advocates of a free press traditionally point to the first amendment ideal of an unrestricted marketplace of ideas where the open dis-

---

† The authors are grateful to the Ford Foundation and the American Bar Association-Law Student Division for travel-study grants to investigate press councils.

* Associate Professor of Law, University of Miami School of Law; B.S. 1965, Northwestern University; J.D. 1968, Case Western Reserve University; LL.M. 1970, Yale University.

** B.S. 1972, Syracuse University; J.D. expected in 1975, University of Miami School of Law.

1. 94 S. Ct. 2831, 2838 n.19 (1974).

HEREAFTER THE FOLLOWING CITATIONS WILL BE USED IN THIS ARTICLE:

H.P. LEVY, THE PRESS COUNCIL (1967) [hereinafter cited as LEVY];

THE SOCIETY OF PROFESSIONAL JOURNALISTS, SIGMA DELTA CHI, CODE OF ETHICS (1973) [hereinafter cited as JOURNALISTS CODE OF ETHICS];

Balk, *Background Paper*, in THE TWENTIETH CENTURY FUND, A FREE AND RESPONSIBLE PRESS (1973) [hereinafter cited as Balk].

2. 94 S. Ct. 2997, 3019 n.2 (1974) (Brennan, J., dissenting).

cussion of public affairs can take place; they demand a hands-off approach.[3] Finding this traditional approach inadequate to meet the realities of modern mass media, fair press forces have advocated a legal right of access to the news media.[4] Advocates of enforced access argue that the first amendment is primarily meant to provide for full debate on issues of public import so that the citizenry can make informed decisions.[5] Since public affairs are no longer debated on soap boxes or in political pamphlets but in a limited number of newspapers and broadcasting stations, the ownership of which is concentrated in increasingly fewer hands,[6] enforced access for persons opposed to the views taken by the mass media is seen as harmonious with, if not mandated by, the first amendment.[7] Senator Sam Ervin, Chairman of the

---

3. This view was developed by Mr. Justice Holmes in his free speech decisions and is known as the theory of "the marketplace of ideas."

> [T]he ultimate good desired is better reached by free trade in ideas—that the best test of truth is the power of thought to get accepted in the competition of the market . . . . Abrams v. United States, 250 U.S. 616, 630 (1919) (Holmes, J., dissenting).

Therefore, it is argued that when ideas compete in the marketplace for acceptance, without any government control, the truth will emerge as the victor. *See* Red Lion Broadcasting Co. v. FCC, 395 U.S. 367, 390 (1969); Ginsberg v. New York, 390 U.S. 629, 649 (1968) (Stewart, J., concurring); Dennis v. United States, 341 U.S. 494, 584-85 (1951) (Douglas, J., dissenting); Whitney v. California, 274 U.S. 357, 375-77 (1927) (Brandeis & Holmes, JJ., concurring).

4. The leading work which advocates this right is Barron, *Access to the Press—A New First Amendment Right,* 80 HARV. L. REV. 1641 (1967). There have been a multitude of law review articles written on the subject of access to both the print and broadcast media, with a majority favoring a right of access to both. A complete list appears in Lange, *The Role of the Access Doctrine in the Regulation of the Mass Media: A Critical Review and Assessment,* 52 N.C.L. REV. 1, 2 n.5 (1973).

5. *See, e.g.,* Barron, *supra* note 4 *passim*; Donnelly, *The Right of Reply: An Alternative to an Action for Libel,* 34 VA. L. REV. 867 (1948); Comment, *Constitutional Law: The Right of Access to the Press,* 50 NEB. L. REV. 120 (1971).

6. *See generally* Johnson & Westen, *A Twentieth-Century Soapbox: The Right to Purchase Radio and Television Time,* 57 VA. L. REV. 574 (1971). For statistics on the concentration of ownership see Bennett, *Media Concentration and the FCC: Focusing with a Section Seven Lens,* 66 NW. U.L. REV. 159, 181-86 (1971); Flynn, *Anti-trust and the Newspaper: A Comment on S. 1312,* 22 VAND. L. REV. 103, 120 (1968); Johnson & Hoak, *Media Concentration: Some Observations on the United States Experience,* 56 IOWA L. REV. 267, 269-70 (1971).

7. Professor Barron has proposed two mechanisms through which a right of access would be initiated. The first involves creating a new judicial remedy.

> One alternative is a judicial remedy affording individuals and groups desiring to voice views on public issues a right of nondiscriminatory access to the community newspaper. This right could be rooted most naturally in the letter-to-the-editor column and the advertising section. Barron, *supra* note 4, at 1667.

The second mechanism consists of access through statutes.

> Another, and perhaps more appropriate, approach would be to secure the right of access by legislation. A statute might impose the modest requirement, for example, that denial of access not be arbitrary but rather be based on rational grounds. *Id.* at 1670.

United States Senate Committee on Constitutional Rights, has reasoned that the first amendment's purpose of stimulating public discussion imposes on publishers and broadcasters a duty to disseminate such information as will enable readers, viewers, and listeners to arrive at the truth and to make well-informed decisions on issues of public concern.[8] This reasoning suggests that enforced access statutes[9] have a constitutional imprimatur.

The arguments in favor of enforced access to the media were presented to the Supreme Court in *Miami Herald Publishing Co. v. Tornillo*.[10] The issue in *Tornillo* was the constitutionality of a Florida statute[11] which provided for a right of reply for political candidates assailed by newspapers. The Court recognized that strong arguments can be made in favor of enforced access[12] but held that, regardless of the validity of those arguments, upholding the statute would strain the meaning and history of the first amendment's prohibition against governmental regulation of the press.[13] The *Tornillo* decision is clearly consonant with the express language of the first amendment,[14] with

---

8. *Media and the First Amendment in a Free Society*, 60 GEO. L.J. 867, 872 (1972) (Introduction by Senator Ervin).

9. *See, e.g.*, FLA. STAT. ANN. § 104.38 (1973) (held unconstitutional in Miami Herald Publishing Co. v. Tornillo, 94 S. Ct. 2831 (1974)). The proposed Massachusetts enforced access statute was also construed as unconstitutional in Opinion of the Justices, 298 N.E.2d 829 (Mass. 1973). Statutes which allow a defendant in a defamation suit to limit the amount of damages recoverable against him by publishing a conspicuous and timely retraction (the so-called London Libel Law) can also be considered as a form of enforced access. Twenty-five states have such statutes. *E.g.*, CAL. CIVIL CODE § 48(a) (West 1954); FLA. STAT. ANN. §§ 770.01-.02 (1973); N.C. GEN. STAT. §§ 99-1 to -2 (1972). An excellent discussion of the right of retraction appears in Note, *Vindication of the Reputation of a Public Official*, 80 HARV. L. REV. 1730 (1967).

10. 94 S. Ct. 2831 (1974).

11. FLA. STAT. ANN. § 104.38 (1973).

12. The enforced access proponents first made the point that control of the news media is being concentrated in fewer and fewer hands. 94 S. Ct. at 2835-36. It was then argued that "the First Amendment acts as a sword as well as a shield, that it imposes obligations on the owners of the press in addition to protecting the press from government regulation." *Id.* at 2836.

13. *See id.* at 2838-40. Even in the broadcasting industry in which the first amendment's blanket protection has been modified by the FCC's fairness doctrine, *see* Red Lion Broadcasting Co. v. FCC, 395 U.S. 367 (1969), proponents of enforced access have suffered setbacks. For example, in National Broadcasting Co. v. FCC, 43 U.S.L.W. 2133 (D.C. Cir. Sept. 27, 1974), the Court of Appeals for the District of Columbia Circuit held that a television program which was critical of pension plans did not violate the fairness doctrine. The court indicated that the primary discretion as to whether the fairness doctrine required a balanced program was not vested in the government agency but in the licensee.

14. "Congress *shall make no law* . . . abridging the freedom of speech, or of the press . . . ." U.S. CONST. amend. I (emphasis added).

the judicial gloss on that language,[15] and probably with the intent of the founding fathers.[16]

In the *Tornillo* opinion, Chief Justice Burger noted that "the implementation of a remedy such as an enforceable right of access necessarily calls for some mechanism, either governmental or consensual."[17] Although legislative and judicial mechanisms were effectively foreclosed by *Tornillo*, consensual means of implementing such access were not. As an example of such a consensual mechanism concerned with press fairness, the Chief Justice pointed to the National News Council.[18] The National News Council is a press council—an independent board of journalists and laymen which undertakes a neutral examination of claims of press inaccuracy and unfairness.

The possibility of using press councils has been suggested in another area of first amendment law which has caused the Court great difficulty, the law of libel. When a member of the news media is sued for defamation, the Court has yet to formulate a clear legal solution to the free press-fair press conflict. In *New York Times Co. v. Sullivan*,[19] the Supreme Court reasoned that the first amendment requires a press uninhibited by the threat of huge judgments in libel cases.[20] Thus, the Court held that a public official must prove either knowing falsity or reckless disregard for the truth in order to recover from a newspaper in a libel suit.[21] The scope of the *New York Times* privilege

15. *See, e.g.*, Pittsburgh Press Co. v. Human Relations Comm'n, 413 U.S. 376, 381-82 (1973); Columbia Broadcasting Sys., Inc. v. Democratic Nat'l Comm., 412 U.S. 94, 117 (1973); Mills v. Alabama, 384 U.S. 214, 218-19 (1966); New York Times Co. v. Sullivan, 376 U.S. 254, 269-77 (1964); Associated Press v. United States, 326 U.S. 1, 20 (1945).

16. Thomas Jefferson once wrote in a letter to a friend, "I deplore . . . the putrid state into which our newspapers have passed, and the malignity, the vulgarity, and mendacious spirit of those who write them." Letter from Thomas Jefferson to Dr. Walter Jones, Jan. 2, 1814, *reprinted in* 14 T. JEFFERSON, THE WRITINGS OF THOMAS JEFFERSON 47 (A. Bergh ed. 1907). Yet Jefferson, who himself was much criticized by the press, contended that the situation presented "an evil for which there is no remedy . . . [since] liberty depends on the freedom of the press . . . ." Letter from Thomas Jefferson to Dr. James Currie, Jan. 28, 1786, *reprinted in* 9 T. JEFFERSON, THE PAPERS OF THOMAS JEFFERSON 238 (J. Boyd ed. 1954).

17. 94 S. Ct. at 2838.

18. *Id.* at 2838 n.19.

19. 376 U.S. 254 (1964).

20. *Id.* at 277-78. The possibility that the press could be inhibited by large libel judgments was quite real. For example, a $500,000 jury verdict was returned against the *New York Times* in a leading case, New York Times Co. v. Sullivan, 273 Ala. 656, 144 So. 2d 25 (1962), *rev'd*, 376 U.S. 254 (1964); likewise, in another notable libel action, a jury verdict of $800,000 (reduced to $500,000 by the trial judge) was returned against the Associated Press, Associated Press v. Walker, 393 S.W.2d 671 (Tex. Civ. App. 1965), *rev'd sub nom.* Curtis Publishing Co. v. Butts, 388 U.S. 130 (1967).

21. 376 U.S. at 279-80.

was steadily expanded,[22] culminating with the opinion joined in by three members of the five-man majority of the Supreme Court in *Rosenbloom v. Metromedia, Inc.*,[23] which extended that privilege to news media defamation of private persons involved in matters of general interest.[24] Although it was generally concluded after *Rosenbloom* that the news media, as a matter of constitutional right, were practically immune from libel and slander suits,[25] the five separate opinions in that case evidenced the great difficulty that the Justices were having in resolving the conflicting rights. Thus, it was not too surprising that *Rosenbloom* was redefined by *Gertz v. Robert Welch, Inc.*,[26] in which the Court held that a private person can recover actual damages in a defamation action against the news media without meeting the *New York Times* standard of knowing or reckless falsity.[27] Yet even in *Gertz*, six separate opinions were written, and Justice Blackmun joined the five-man majority only to eliminate "the unsureness engendered by *Rosenbloom's* diversity."[28]

The diversity of *Rosenbloom* and *Gertz* demonstrates the Supreme Court's inability to use existing legal mechanisms to define clearly and satisfactorily the boundary between defamation and the first amendment. Even after the "Court has struggled for nearly a decade to define the proper accommodation between the law of defamation and the freedoms of speech and press,"[29] the accommodation reached in *Gertz* was able to draw the wholehearted support of only four Justices. Justice Brennan intimated in his dissent in *Gertz* that a nonlegal mechanism may be necessary to deal with charges of

---

22. *See* Time, Inc. v. Pape, 401 U.S. 279 (1971); Greenbelt Publishing Ass'n v. Bresler, 398 U.S. 6 (1970); St. Amant v. Thompson, 390 U.S. 727 (1968); Time, Inc. v. Hill, 385 U.S. 374 (1967); Rosenblatt v. Baer, 383 U.S. 75 (1966); Garrison v. Louisiana, 379 U.S. 64 (1964). For a detailed discussion of the progeny of *New York Times*, see Comment, *The Expanding Constitutional Protection for the News Media from Liability for Defamation: Predictability and the New Synthesis*, 70 MICH. L. REV. 1547 (1972).

23. 403 U.S. 29 (1971). The judgment of the Court was announced in an opinion written by Justice Brennan, in which Chief Justice Burger and Justice Blackmun joined. *Id.* at 30. The other members of the plurality were Justices Black and White. Justice Black restated his view of absolute immunity for the press, *id.* at 57, while Justice White concurred on the narrower ground that the press had immunity in the case because the event reported involved action of governmental officials, *id.* at 62.

24. *Id.* at 43-44.

25. *See* Levine, Times *to* Rosenbloom: *A Press Free From Libel—The Editors Speak*, 27 U. MIAMI L. REV. 109 (1972); *cf.* Comment, *supra* note 22, at 1568.

26. 94 S. Ct. 2997 (1974).

27. *Id.* at 3010.

28. *Id.* at 3014.

29. *Id.* at 3000.

defamation by the news media; the example he noted was the National News Council.[30]

The establishment of a nonlegal mechanism is a possible solution to the dilemma raised by the failure of existing legal mechanisms to resolve press access and defamation disputes. In both the *Tornillo* and the *Gertz* decisions a press council was suggested as a possible nongovernmental means of accommodating the conflicting interests.[31] A press council is an independent board of journalists and laymen which acts as a nonbinding arbitration board. Consideration of a problem is initiated by the filing of a complaint against a member of the news media. The council will not hear a dispute until the parties have met to attempt reconciliation.[32] If a settlement cannot be reached, a hearing is called. All parties are given adequate notice and a full opportunity to present relevant evidence, to cross-examine witnesses, and to be represented by counsel.[33] However, formal rules of procedure and evidence are not strictly followed.[34] The press council renders a decision by a written opinion which includes a statement of the facts, a ruling for one of the parties, and a discussion of the considerations on which the ruling is based. All members of the news media within the council's geographical area are notified of the decision and are requested to publicize it.

The power to publicize its decisions is the only sanction of a press council. Thus, it has been said that a press council is like a toothless watchdog—it lacks bite, but has a loud bark.[35] It is from this "loud bark" of publicity that the press council derives its real power, that of

30. *Id.* at 3019 n.2.

31. See notes 18 & 30 *supra* and accompanying text.

32. *E.g.*, Minnesota Press Council, Grievance Comm. Procedural Rule I.A.: "No grievance should be processed unless the matter has first been presented to the newspaper by the complainant"; National News Council, Grievance Comm. Rules of Procedure Relating to Public Complaints, Rule 9: "The Grievance Committee will not hear a complaint unless the complainant has first sent written notification of the complaint to the news organization complained against and has received either an inadequate response or no response . . . ."

33. *E.g.*, Minnesota Press Council, Grievance Comm. Procedural Rule II.F.: "All parties will have the opportunity to appear in person and give oral testimony. . . . A right to cross examination and a right to counsel are available for both parties." National News Council, Grievance Comm. Rules of Procedure Relating to Public Complaints, Rule 20: "Each party shall have the right to engage counsel, to call and examine witnesses, and to cross-examine witnesses called by other parties or the Committee."

34. "At all times the desirability of informality and flexibility of the proceedings must be recognized." Minnesota Press Council, Grievance Comm. Procedure Rule II.F. For example, the Minnesota Press Council has refused to let technical mootness of the instant case prevent it from deciding an important question. Rachner v. Union Advocate, Minnesota Press Council Decision No. 3, at 4-5 (1973).

35. Balk 29.

developing public awareness of problems in the free press-fair press area.[36] A press council provides the means of simultaneously attaining the following four community benefits: (1) freeing of the news media from restraints imposed by the threat of economic or criminal sanctions, (2) determination of press disputes by both laymen and journalists, (3) correction of inaccurate or unfair reporting, and (4) growth of a set of journalistic standards for the news media.[37]

THE HISTORY OF PRESS COUNCILS

The concept of a press council is not new. It began in 1916 when the Swedish government formed the Press Fair Practices Commission to serve as an intermediary between the press and the public. Since then fifteen other European nations have established press councils, the twenty-year old British Press Council standing out as the most successful.[38]

The British Press Council was formed in 1953, but its origin lies in the recommendations of a Royal Commission established by the British Parliament after World War II as a result of public concern over newspaper mergers, closings, and charges of biased news reporting.[39] The major objectives of the Council are to preserve freedom of the press, to maintain high professional standards of journalism, to deal with complaints about conduct of the press, and to review developments which might tend to restrict the supply of information.[40] The Council itself feels that its most useful function has been that of maintaining professional standards of journalism.[41] The Council has jurisdiction over only the print media, although some feel that a similar body should exist for the broadcast media.[42]

The British Press Council is composed of twenty-five members, twenty of whom are publishers and working journalists, the other five of whom are lay members selected from the public by the professional

---

36. *See* LEVY 465-66. The power of publicity obviates the need for sanctions:

> The answer, therefore, to the question whether sanctions are necessary, is that they are not and the [British] Press Council has proved it. . . .
>
> The role of the Press Council is that of educator, not inquisitor; its method is persuasion not force; its weapon is publicity not punishment; its appeal is to conscience and fair play. In a free press sanctions would be an incongruity. *Id.* at 466.

37. See text accompanying notes 104-11 *infra.*

38. T. PETERSON, J. JENSEN & W. RIVERS, THE MASS MEDIA AND MODERN SOCIETY 98-99 (1971).

39. LEVY 3-10.

40. [BRITISH] PRESS COUNCIL: ARTICLES OF CONSTITUTION art. 2, *reprinted in* LEVY app. I, at 473-74; *see* LEVY 19-22.

41. LEVY 21.

42. Balk 30.

members.[43] The Council receives over 400 complaints per year concerning the contents of newspapers and the behavior of journalists,[44] and it renders approximately 300 decisions per year[45] dealing with all facets of newspaper performance, including reporting of confidential documents,[46] false and biased reporting,[47] and the right of privacy.[48] In the first fourteen years of the Council's existence, only five newspapers refused to print a decision.[49] The British Press Council has not solved all of the problems that face the press; however, it has reportedly been successful in establishing a body of professional journalistic standards for newspapers. One legal commentator has referred to these standards as a "common law" of journalism.[50]

Numerous groups have proposed press councils in the United States. The first formal recommendation came in 1947 from the Commission on Freedom of the Press, chaired by Robert Hutchins, chancellor of the University of Chicago and former dean of Yale Law School. Stressing that the only way for the press to remain free was to be responsible, the Commission called for creation of an independent agency to appraise and report annually on press performance.[51] In 1951, Senator William Benton of Connecticut proposed that a similar body for the electronic media be established by Congress with its members appointed by the President.[52] John Lofton of Stanford's Institute for Communication Research in 1961 called for the development of a body "to monitor and report on press performance."[53] In 1963, University of Minnesota Journalism Professor J. Edward Gerald asked that a national press council be formed and supported by the established professional and educational associations.[54] In 1967, it was suggested by journalist and media critic Ben H. Bagdikian that universities serve as centers in creating press councils for their respective

43. [British] Press Council: Articles of Constitution art. 3-4, *reprinted in* Levy app. I, at 474.

As originally established in 1953 the British Press Council was composed entirely of representatives of the press. Levy 19. The present composition is the result of a reorganization of the Council in 1963. *Id.* The addition of lay members increased the public's confidence in the Council without hindering its operation. *See id.* at 462-64.

44. Levy 26.

45. *Id.*

46. *See id.* at 39-51.

47. *See id.* at 83-144.

48. *See id.* at 240-69.

49. Balk 28.

50. Lord Devlin, *Preface* to Levy.

51. Balk 31.

52. *Id.*

53. *Id.*

54. *Id.* at 32.

areas.[55] The National Institute of Public Affairs in Washington in its 1968 meeting outlined a proposal for a national press council made up of distinguished laymen.[56] In 1970, a Task Force of the National Commission on the Causes and Prevention of Violence called for a "national media study center with . . ., 'clearly delineated powers of monitorship, evaluation, and publication, but without sanction.' "[57]

The first American councils were not what would be considered press councils today. They were citizen participation groups intended to bring newspapers closer to the people, and they served a need recently referred to by the Supreme Court: "[T]he public has lost any ability to respond or contribute in a meaningful way to the debate on issues."[58] The first prototype of this kind of council was established in 1950 by William Townes, a publisher of the Santa Rosa *Press Democrat*, and was called a "Citizens' Advisory Council."[59] Although Townes continued to determine the newspaper's policies alone, he welcomed criticisms and suggestions from the Council. Townes felt that the Council helped improve his paper and continued the Council until he left.[60] In reviewing this project, a respected journalism publication stated:

> This is an experiment in getting closer to the community which strikes us as valuable. The good points outweigh the bad and if conducted properly and regularly can only result to the benefit of the newspaper.[61]

There have been several other citizen advisory councils, many of which were financed by the Mellet Foundation.[62] Like the Santa Rosa experiment, these councils dealt only with one newspaper each and did not render any formal decisions. Acting as a link between newspapers and the public, they served as forums for citizens to discuss community problems. Although these councils served a useful function, they were not designed as a mechanism for achieving press fairness.

Modern American Press Councils

The Minnesota Press Council

The first major American experiment with a British-type press council, *i.e.*, one concerned with press fairness, is the Minnesota Press

55. *Id.*
56. *Id.*
57. *Id.*
58. Miami Herald Publishing Co. v. Tornillo, 94 S. Ct. 2831, 2836 (1974).
59. Balk 32.
60. B. Blankenburg & W. Rivers, Backtalk: Press Councils in America 13 (1972).
61. Editor and Publisher, July 28, 1951, at 36, *cited in* Balk 32-33.
62. *See* B. Blankenburg & W. Rivers, *supra* note 60.

Council.[63] That Council was established in 1971 by the Minnesota Newspaper Association, the membership of which is composed of the daily and weekly newspapers in the state. The chairman of the Council is a Minnesota Supreme Court Justice, the Honorable C. Donald Peterson, whose selection was influenced by the British Press Council's practice of selecting its chairman from the judiciary. The Council has eighteen members, half laymen and half journalists. The lay members were selected with the view of including representatives of influential subgroups such as women in public affairs, leaders of educational institutions, government leaders, and persons from minority groups. The journalist members must include at least two individuals who are not related to either ownership or management. To avoid any appearance of collusion with the press, the Council's first act was to declare itself independent from the Minnesota Newspaper Association. At an early stage of development it was decided not to include the electronic media, but this decision is now being reconsidered. Not all newspapers actively support the Press Council. However, one major Minnesota newspaper which does not support it, the St. Paul *Dispatch-Pioneer Press*, does cooperate by appearing at Council proceedings and by referring individuals with complaints to the Council.[64]

In its three year existence, only eleven cases have been fully adjudicated. Many other complaints have been dismissed as being insignificant, such as a newspaper's food column including recipes which require alcoholic ingredients or charges that a newspaper is "too liberal." Several complaints have also been withdrawn as a result of reconciliation between the parties themselves; such a meeting is a condition precedent to Press Council consideration of a complaint.[65] Through its decided cases, the Minnesota Press Council has begun to establish a body of standards for responsible press performance on issues of national importance to the news media and the public: libel, access to the press, newsman's privilege not to disclose sources, and biased news reporting. An examination of the cases decided by the Minnesota Press Council will demonstrate that the Council is providing a viable means of resolving free press-fair press conflicts.

The Minnesota Press Council's first case, *Lindstrom v. Union Advocate*,[66] illustrates how a press council can function as both an al-

63. On a smaller scale, a city-wide Community-Media Council has been established in Honolulu. *See* Balk 46-55.

64. Interview with John Finnegan, Editor of the St. Paul *Dispatch—Pioneer Press*, in St. Paul, Minnesota, Jan. 11, 1974.

65. *See* Minnesota Press Council, Grievance Comm. Procedural Rule I.A.

66. Minnesota Press Council Decision No. 1 (1972).

ternative to a court libel action and an effective means of access to the press. Mr. Lindstrom, a state legislator, alleged the inaccuracy of two news stories in which it was reported that he had voted for a liquor tax increase after being entertained by lobbyists in a restaurant. He agreed to drop his libel suit prior to filing a Press Council complaint in order to comply with the Council's requirement that a complainant waive his right to sue prior to submitting to a Press Council determination.[67] The evidence presented by the complainant established that the reported restaurant meeting between the lobbyists and the legislator did not take place. No evidence was produced by the newspaper to controvert the complainant's evidence, nor would the paper disclose the name of its confidential source.

The Council ruled that the news articles were inaccurate and that the newspaper had violated its journalistic obligation to check its information with the principals and others known to be present.[68] In an effort to uphold a newsman's right to withhold the names of his sources, the Council refused to request the disclosure of the story's source and asserted that the policy of not demanding disclosure would continue in the future.[69]

The result was that the defamed complainant received his desired vindication without the expense of a trial. The publicizing of the decision in every newspaper in the state, including the one which printed the inaccurate stories, gave the complainant a better right of access than any right of reply statute would allow, since such statutes only

67. *See* Minnesota Press Council, Grievance Comm. Procedural Rule I.C.:

> No grievance will be considered if legal action based on the same subject matter is pending against the newspaper or an individual journalist. A grievance will not be processed until the complainant waives any possible future civil action that he may have arising out of the grievance for matters occurring prior to the filing of the grievance.

See text accompanying notes 150-53 *infra* for a discussion of the validity of such a waiver.

68. *Accord*, THE AMERICAN SOCIETY OF NEWSPAPER EDITORS, CODE OF ETHICS: CANON IV, ¶ 1 ("By every consideration of good faith a newspaper is constrained to be truthful. It is not to be excused for lack of thoroughness or accuracy within its control, or failure to obtain command of these essential qualities."); JOURNALISTS CODE OF ETHICS: ACCURACY AND OBJECTIVITY ¶ 3 ("There is no excuse for inaccuracies or lack of thoroughness.").

69. Confidentiality of sources is not guaranteed in the Minnesota Press Council's Constitution or Grievance Committee Rules; however, it is specifically provided for by the National News Council's Rule 11 of the Grievance Committee Rules of Procedure Relating to Public Complaints. *See* NATIONAL NEWS COUNCIL, BY-LAWS AND RULES OF PROCEDURE 16 (1973); *accord*, JOURNALISTS CODE OF ETHICS: ETHICS ¶ 5 ("Journalists acknowledge the newsman's ethic of protecting confidential sources of information."). No parallel provision exists in the Code of Ethics of the American Society of Newspaper Editors.

apply to the newspaper carrying the story.[70] It should be noted that the decision is consonant with the *Gertz* decision, in which the Court stated that the "first remedy of any victim of defamation is self-help—using available opportunities to contradict the lie or correct the error . . . ."[71] The *Gertz* Court went on to say it was easier for a public official or public figure to accomplish this remedy than the private individual, since the public official and public figure "enjoy significantly greater access to the channels of effective communications."[72] However, through the use of a press council, even the private individual can enjoy significant access to the "channels of communication" by the publication of the press council's decisions. In addition, a press council decision is likely to be accorded greater weight than a self-serving reply.

The issue of inaccurate and biased reporting was again before the Council in *Long & Erickson v. Worthington Daily Globe*.[73] In that case, two legislators filed a complaint alleging that a newspaper headline and a related editorial were inaccurate and unfair. The headline read: "Rep. Erickson, Rep. Long Vote Continued Support for War." The story which accompanied the headline was an Associated Press release about their votes against a resolution in the state legislature to urge Congress to halt war appropriations. After hearing all the evidence produced by the parties, the Council concluded that the headline was in fact inaccurate and unfair. The decision went on to lay down the general guideline that "[n]ews headlines should be allowed a reasonable latitude," however, they should be "generally correct, objective, non-misleading and non-opinionated . . . [and] supported by facts within the news story."[74]

In regard to the related editorial, the Council held that it would not be stepping beyond its proper reach to discuss *factual* inaccuracies and misstatements, but that it must confine its consideration to only factual questions so as "not to trespass upon or discourage the maximum freedom for newspapers to express opinions in editorial columns."[75] As a result of this policy, the Council did not pass upon the

70. See statutes cited in note 9 *supra*.

71. 94 S. Ct. at 3009.

72. *Id.*

73. Minnesota Press Council Decision No. 5 (1973).

74. *Id.* at 3-4; *accord,* AMERICAN SOCIETY OF NEWSPAPER EDITORS CODE OF ETHICS: CANON IV, ¶ 2 ("Headlines should be fully warranted by the contents of the article which they surmount."); JOURNALISTS CODE OF ETHICS: ACCURACY AND OBJECTIVITY ¶ 4 ("Newspaper headlines should be fully warranted by the contents of the article they accompany.").

75. Minnesota Press Council Decision No. 5, at 8 (1973).

validity of the editorial's opinion, but it did suggest that specific factual errors in the editorial constituted a breach of professional responsibility.[76] The decision was careful to emphasize that the Council encourages newspapers to express their opinions in editorials and to welcome letters in reply as the newspaper in the instant case had done.

Another aspect of the *Long-Erickson* case involved the right-of-reply issue. Part of the procedure of the Minnesota Press Council is a requirement of a face-to-face discussion between the parties before a hearing is held.[77] In the meeting in this case the newspaper involved offered the complainants space to reply at length. The legislators refused the offer, demanding a retraction with the same front page publicity as the headline and refusing to be put in the position of appearing to feel compelled to justify their position. The Council's decision supported the complainants: "We find it the newspaper's responsibility to correct its own headline error. The offended citizen should not have to bear the burden of writing the correction . . . ."[78]

In two cases, *Rachner v. Union Advocate*[79] and *Blahauvietz v. Pipestone County Star*,[80] the Council considered the issue of access to a newspaper through paid advertisements. In *Rachner*, a school board candidate complained that her paid political advertisement had been refused by the newspaper because she was not endorsed by labor. The *Union Advocate*, the paper involved, is the official AFL-CIO newspaper in St. Paul and is mailed to union members as an incident of membership. The Press Council recognized that newspapers should have considerable latitude in establishing policies governing the acceptance of advertising and that there is no legal duty to accept all advertising offered to them.[81] The right of the *Union Advocate* to re-

76. *Id.* at 8-9; *accord*, AMERICAN SOCIETY OF NEWSPAPER EDITORS: CANON III, ¶ 2 ("Partisanship, in editorial comment, which knowingly departs from the truth does violence to the best spirit of American journalism . . . ."); JOURNALISTS CODE OF ETHICS: ACCURACY AND OBJECTIVITY ¶ 6 ("Partisanship in editorial comment which knowingly departs from the truth violates the spirit of American journalism.").

77. *See* Minnesota Press Council, Grievance Comm. Procedural Rule I.A.

78. Minnesota Press Council Decision No. 5, at 5 (1973); *accord*, AMERICAN SOCIETY OF NEWSPAPER EDITORS CODE OF ETHICS: CANON VI, ¶ 2 ("It is the privilege, as it is the duty, of a newspaper to make prompt and complete correction of its own serious mistakes of fact or opinion, whatever their origin."); JOURNALISTS CODE OF ETHICS: FAIR PLAY ¶ 4 ("It is the duty of news media to make prompt and complete correction of their errors.").

79. Minnesota Press Council Decision No. 3 (1973).

80. Minnesota Press Council Decision No. 6 (1973).

81. Minnesota Press Council Decision No. 3, at 5-6 (1973); *see* Chicago Joint Bd. v. Chicago Tribune Co., 435 F.2d 470 (7th Cir. 1970), *cert. denied*, 402 U.S. 973 (1971); Opinion of the Justices, 298 N.E.2d 829, 835 (Mass. 1973); *cf.* Pittsburgh Press Co. v. Human Relations Comm'n, 413 U.S. 376 (1973); Columbia Broadcasting Sys., Inc. v. Democratic Nat'l Comm., 412 U.S. 94, 130-31 (1973).

fuse paid political advertisements was upheld on the ground that it is a part of the "special interest" press and, therefore, does not accept "the obligation to function as a general newspaper or to be bound by the convention usually associated with general publications."[82] However, the Council went on to urge that non-"special interest" newspapers clarify and publish their advertising acceptance policies and stated that "[a] standard under which only the advertising of political candidates approved by the publisher is accepted would be patently offensive to fundamental principles of fairness and responsibility."[83]

The *Blahauvietz* case concerned access through political advertising on election day. The newspaper involved refused to run Mr. Blahauvietz's election day advertisement because of a Minnesota statute which had been interpreted to bar any political advertising on election day. The case was complicated by the fact that the same newspaper inadvertently ran the advertisement of Mr. Blahauvietz's opponent on election day. Since the discrimination was unintentional, the Council simply ordered the newspaper to make an apology. Although the decision appears to be a Pyrrhic victory for Mr. Blahauvietz, it is significant for establishing guidelines "governing the publication of political advertising to assure fair and equal treatment of all candidates."[84] In addition, the opinion suggested that the state statute forbidding political advertisements on election day might be unconstitutional and that it might be appropriate to set up a test case.[85] A dissenting member condemned the majority for recommending a system which he felt encouraged private blackouts of political advertisements.[86]

The issue of access to the media through letters to the editor was raised in *Shearin v. Rochester Post-Bulletin*.[87] That case dealt with a newspaper's rejection of a second letter after publication of a previous letter by the same author on the same subject. The Council held for the newspaper, recognizing that newspapers must deal with limitations of space and form. The editor was held entitled to establish rea-

82. Minnesota Press Council Decision No. 3, at 7 (1973).

83. *Id.* at 6.

84. Minnesota Press Council Decision No. 6, at 10-11 (1973).

85. *Id.* at 8-11. The Council felt that the case of Mills v. Alabama, 384 U.S. 216 (1966) (holding that editorials on election day cannot be constitutionally prohibited), was determinative of the issue of constitutionality.

86. Minnesota Press Council Decision No. 6, at D6-D11 (1973) (Gerald, dissenting). Mr. Gerald argued that the majority's statement that newspapers should "set forth the condition and final publication dates for [political] advertising," *id.* at 11, would encourage newspapers to impose political advertising blackouts on election days. *Id.* at D10.

87. Minnesota Press Council Decision No. 4 (1973).

sonable controls, such as the format of the letters (here the letter included footnotes and a bibliography), the frequency with which certain subjects are treated, and when to terminate publishing letters on a particular topic.[88] The Council pointed out that all of these controls should be based on the considerations of fairness and reasonable presentation of conflicting views.

In *Samuelson v. Thief River Falls Times*,[89] a second case concerned with letters to the editor, a newspaper had previously stated that all letters to the editor must be signed, but that names would be withheld upon request. Mr. Samuelson wrote a letter critical of the city council and requested that his name be withheld. Without notifying Mr. Samuelson, the newspaper released his name at the request of the chairman of the city council. In response to the complaint, the newspaper urged that it was following its usual practice of withholding names upon request, but releasing the name of the author to anyone who, in the newspaper's opinion, had a legitimate interest in finding out who the author was. The Council found for the complainant and called upon the newspaper to apologize to Mr. Samuelson and to publish all the conditions which attach to the withholding of the names of letter writers.[90]

The case of *Minnesota Education Association v. 32 Minnesota Newspapers*[91] gave the Council the opportunity to address the issue of attribution and identification of sources of news releases. The case arose out of a press release which was distributed to all Minnesota newspapers by the Minnesota School Board Association (MSBA). The Minnesota Education Association, which opposed the views expressed by the MSBA in its news release, charged that thirty-five newspapers had published the release either as an editorial or as a news story without naming the MSBA as the source of the story. The Council took note of the facts that the MSBA was a lobbying and pressure group and that the news release expressed the view of the MSBA on a controversial issue. The Council then decided that the publication of the news release as an editorial without attribution was a "breach of faith with the readers";[92] the use of the release as a news story without attribution was labeled a violation of a "long acknowledged and established principle of responsible journalism."[93] Setting out a general policy to-

88. *Id.* at 6.
89. Minnesota Press Council Decision No. 2 (1972).
90. *Id.* at 5.
91. Minnesota Press Council Decision No. 7 (1973).
92. *Id.* at 14.
93. *Id.*

ward attribution of sources, the Council stated:

> As a general guideline . . . the Minnesota Press Council urges that newspapers adopt a consistent policy that published editorials from outside sources, or written by persons other than newspaper staff members, should carry attribution as to their source or author. Such attribution may appear in the text of the editorial, or if verbatim publication is made, attribution may be in the form of a credit line at the beginning or the conclusion of the copy.
>
> . . . .
>
> With respect to news stories, attribution or identification of source is a vital facet of responsible reporting—a yardstick by which readers can better measure the veracity and reliability of the viewpoints expressed. Such attribution is particularly crucial to readers in evaluating stands taken in regard to political issues or pending legislation. News stories should be attributed to sources.[94]

It should be noted that the Council was addressing the issue of attribution of sources of an article written in the form of a news release and not the issue of undisclosed sources of information used in an article.[95]

In *Guthrie v. Minneapolis Tribune*,[96] the Council considered the conduct of investigative reporters in a criminal case. The case arose out of a kidnapping case in which newspaper reporters, by monitoring a police radio, were able physically to follow an FBI agent making the ransom drop. As a result of the presence of the news media members at the drop site, the FBI was unable to make the drop. Finding that "[a]ny experienced reporter or editor must know that the ransom drop involves a time of substantial tension and concern in a kidnapping case,"[97] the Council held that the newspapers involved had acted irresponsibly and urged that the press exercise "restraint in matters involving the personal safety of individuals."[98] In response to the defense that other media members were engaged in the same activity, the Council ruled that the fact that competitors fail to exercise restraint constitutes no excuse.[99] The Council went on to observe that

> the media would have been substantially assisted in evaluating its responsibilities in cases such as this if the police would inform the media of its concerns regarding the present reporting or non-reporting of specific events . . . .[100]

94. *Id.* at 13-14, 16.
95. See text accompanying notes 68-69 *supra.*
96. Minnesota Press Council Decision No. 11 (1974).
97. *Id.* at 4.
98. *Id.* at 6.
99. *Id.* at 4.
100. *Id.* at 5.

Three recent decisions are important because they show that the public is looking to the Council for correction of unfair or inaccurate reporting. In *Connors v. St. Paul Pioneer Press*,[101] the complainant alleged that he had been misquoted by a newspaper. The complaint was dismissed on the basis that the story which appeared in print was a fair interpretation of the complainant's remarks. In *Robb v. The Minneapolis Star*,[102] the complainant alleged that a newspaper editorial misinterpreted certain of his statements which appeared in a county board resolution. In rejecting the complaint, the Council reaffirmed the policy stated in the *Long-Erickson* case of not attempting to exercise any control over opinions which appear in editorials. A charge of inaccurate reporting was the basis of the complaint in *Fugina & Johnson v. Duluth News Tribune*.[103] The case was resolved prior to the Council hearing when the newspaper agreed to publish a clarifying article acceptable to both parties.

After three years of decision-making, it is safe to conclude that the Minnesota Press Council has gained acceptance on the part of both the press and the public. Newspapers which did not actively cooperate with the Council at its inception now find it a useful institution to which they can refer their complaints. Thus, it seems clear that press councils can achieve at least the first two of the four ends[104] for which they are established: (1) freeing the news media from restraints imposed by the threat of economic or criminal sanctions, and (2) determination of press disputes by a mixture of ordinary citizens and persons with experience and expertise in journalism. The Minnesota Press Council's decisions also show that press councils can fulfill the third role which they are expected to play, that of providing a forum for correction of inaccurate or unfair reporting. The *Lindstrom* and *Long-Erickson* decisions demonstrate that press councils can effectively serve such a corrective function, even in cases in which it is very doubtful that the complainant could secure relief from a court of law.[105] Most importantly, the Minnesota decisons establish that a press council can use its decisional process to promulgate a set of journalistic standards. For example, the *Lindstrom* decison made it clear that newspapers are expected to verify their stories whenever possible,[106] and the *Long-Erickson* decision set out the Council's guidelines for fair and accurate

101. Minnesota Press Council Decision No. 9 (1974).
102. Minnesota Press Council Decision No. 10 (1974).
103. Minnesota Press Council Decision No. 8 (1973).
104. See text accompanying note 37 *supra*.
105. See notes 65-78 *supra* and accompanying text.
106. See note 68 *supra* and accompanying text.

headlines and editorials.[107] The *Rachner* and *Blahauvietz* decisions suggested standards for the acceptance of political advertisements by both general and "special interest" newspapers.[108] Certain aspects of the Council's view regarding the proper handling of letters to the editor were described in the *Shearin* and *Samuelson* decisons.[109] The *Minnesota Education Association* decision promulgated the general policy toward attribution of news releases.[110] Finally, the *Guthrie* decision called for media restraint when covering news stories in which interference by the media could cause personal injury.[111] In sum, the short experience of the Minnesota Press Council bodes well for the use of press councils as a means of resolving free press-fair press conflicts.

The National News Council

The British Press Council and the Minnesota Press Council have been used as models for the first nationwide press council, the National News Council. Unlike the Minnesota Council, which was initiated by the press, the National Council was initiated by private foundations. In 1972, the Twentieth Century Fund released a report of a task force made up of nine journalists and five public members, calling for the establishment of a national press council which would entertain any complaints involving the principal national suppliers of news: nationwide wire services, supplemental wire services, national weekly news magazines, national newspaper syndicates, national daily newspapers, and nationwide commercial and noncommercial broadcast networks.[112] With an announced goal of preserving freedom of communication and advancing accurate and fair news reporting, the National News Council was formally established in August 1973.[113] It was funded by several national foundations, and former California Supreme Court Chief Justice Roger Traynor was named as the first chairman.[114]

In its first nine months the Council received 160 complaints.[115] Of these, 132 were disposed of by the staff without proceeding to the

107. See notes 73-76 *supra* and accompanying text.

108. See notes 79-86 *supra* and accompanying text.

109. See notes 87-90 *supra* and accompanying text.

110. See notes 91-95 *supra* and accompanying text.

111. See notes 96-100 *supra* and accompanying text.

112. The Twentieth Century Fund Task Force, *Report of the Task Force*, in THE TWENTIETH CENTURY FUND, A FREE AND RESPONSIVE PRESS 3-4 (1973).

113. *"Monitoring" National News Suppliers—A Unique Proposal*, COLUM. JOURNALISM REV. Mar.-Apr., 1973, at 43.

114. Stanley Fuld, former Chief Judge of the New York Court of Appeals, has recently succeeded Justice Traynor.

115. REPORT BY THE NATIONAL NEWS COUNCIL 3 (1974).

first stage of formal Council action, consideration by the Grievance Committee.[116] Many were settled when the staff referred the initial complaint to the media member complained against. For instance, the American Medical Association charge that an NBC documentary had made derogatory comments about the medical profession was resolved without further action when NBC agreed to the appearance of an AMA spokesman on its "Today" show to rebut the comments.[117]

The twenty-eight complaints considered by the Council's Grievance Committee have all involved charges of biased or inaccurate reporting. Since many have concerned naive and trivial matters,[118] the Council has been cautious in pronouncing judgment. However, it has defined some standards and announced two significant news media transgressions.

The most significant case thus far is the complaint of Mobil Oil Corporation against ABC-TV for inaccurate and biased reporting in a documentary on the oil crisis. In its introduction, the program was described as "a primer on oil and oil policy . . . designed to help understand the current crisis."[119] The Council's investigation resulted in a finding that ABC had selected facts that pointed in one direction and omitted others that pointed elsewhere: "[The] organization of the facts presented . . . created one specific editorial impression: namely that government policy on oil has been manipulated over the years by the oil industry . . . ."[120] Nonetheless, the Council found the program to be within the bounds of robust opinion journalism:

> ABC was not under any obligation to give a scrupulously balanced presentation.
>
> . . . .
>
> . . . [S]hort of outright factual misstatements, the interests of free expression are best served by allowing full scope to a variety of views, very definitely including those that are one-sided.[121]

However, the Council did hold that ABC had violated acceptable journalistic standards by giving the impression that a documentary on a controversial subject was striving for balance and fairness when in fact it was not.[122]

---

116. *Id.*
117. *Id.* at 10.
118. For example, a charge that a news report was inaccurate in reporting that a man died from drinking too much carrot juice, *id.* at 8, and a charge that pro-abortion forces were given larger coverage than anti-abortion groups, *id.* at 6, did not require action by the Council.
119. National News Council Decision in Mobil Oil Corp. v. ABC News 1 (1974).
120. *Id.* at 2.
121. *Id.* at 3.
122. *Id.* at 2.

It could be contended that this Solomon-like attempt to give something to both sides satisfied neither. The winner, however, was the journalistic community, because a standard of unbiased reporting has been set for the broadcast media: Thou shalt not label editorials as news reports. The Council could have relied upon the Code of Ethics of the Society of Professional Journalists, Sigma Delta Chi, which states that "[s]ound practice makes clear distinction between news reports and expressions of opinion."[123] Yet neither the National Council nor the Minnesota Council have referred to the Sigma Delta Chi or American Society of Newspaper Editors Codes of Ethics. This practice is probably an imitation of the British Press Council which has voted not to draft a code for the press.[124] The practice of an unwritten constitution, however, seems in keeping with British, but not American, custom.

In a second case, the Council upheld a conflict of interest complaint against Victor Lasky, a syndicated editorial page columnist who wrote signed political comment appearing in over 100 newspapers. In 1972, while he was writing the column, Mr. Lasky accepted a $20,000 fee from the Committee for the Re-election of the President to ghost-write speeches. This fact was learned from testimony in the Senate Watergate hearings, and a complaint was filed by the National Conference of Editorial Writers.

The Council stated that "[p]ublic trust in the press is diminished if an editorial page columnist engages in activities which produce a conflict of interest or even the appearance of one."[125] Thus, the standard was established that a syndicated editorial page columnist is under a responsibility to inform the syndicate for which he writes if he benefits financially from an organization active in an area on which he regularly comments. Secondly, the syndicate was given the responsibility, once it learns of such a relationship, to inform its subscribers.[126]

In two cases major news media members have refused to furnish information or cooperate with the Council. A complaint against the Public Broadcasting Corporation for being one-sided in a "Black Journal" program met with a reply that the Council had no jurisdiction to consider such matters. Even so, the Council proceeded to vindicate

---

123. JOURNALISTS CODE OF ETHICS: ACCURACY AND OBJECTIVITY ¶ 5.

124. *See* LEVY 464-65.

125. National News Council Decision in National Conference of Editorial Writers v. Lasky 1 (1974).

126. *Id.* The Council again could have relied on the Code of Ethics of the Society of Professional Journalists, Sigma Delta Chi: "Secondary employment, political involvement, holding public office, and service in community organizations should be avoided if it compromises the integrity of journalists and their employers." JOURNALISTS CODE OF ETHICS: ETHICS ¶ 2.

the Corporation by approving a wide range of editorial judgment by television program producers.[127]

The most adamant objector to the National News Council is the *New York Times.* A complaint against the *Times* was filed concerning a story about a study done by the National Academy of Science on the effect of herbicides in South Vietnam. The *Times* story[128] was printed before the official release of the Academy's report and was based mainly on the minority dissent from the report. The *Times* refused to respond to the National News Council's requests for information and refused to comment on the Council's decision[129] that the newspaper should have called to the attention of its readers the information in the full report. Nevertheless, the *Times* did print a report of the decision.[130]

Of the many early objectors to the Council, the *Times* is one of the few still refusing to cooperate. At the Council's commencement, the three major television networks and the *New York Times* announced they would not cooperate, while the *Washington Post* promised cooperation on only a limited basis.[131] After the Council's first year of operation, all three television networks are cooperating by furnishing program transcripts and position statements. The *Post* is also cooperating.

The reason for dwindling opposition is plain from the Council's one year record. It has acted cautiously in criticizing media performance and has approved wide open expression of opinion, so long as opinion is not labeled as fact. The press should find no fault with the Council from its first year's performance; the public should find cause to applaud a mechanism which is finally defining press responsibility in hard specifics rather than easy generalizations.

Objections to Press Councils

Lack of support from the journalistic community is the main reason that more experiments with press councils have not been attempted. Many journalists have serious objections to a press council and will not participate in one even on an experimental basis. Some feel that a press council would result in more government control, arguing that "voluntary acceptance of an outside agency to prevent misuse of pub-

127. National News Council Decision in Rowley v. Corporation for Pub. Broadcasting (1974).
128. N.Y. Times, Feb. 22, 1974, at 1, col. 6.
129. National News Council Decision in Accuracy in Media v. New York Times News Serv. (1974).
130. N.Y. Times, June 26, 1974, at 37, col. 2.
131. Time, Jan. 29, 1973, at 42.

lic trust" will lead to formal governmental regulations.[132] It should be noted that the basic purpose of a press council is to provide an independent forum, not connected with government, for debate about media responsibility and performance so that the debate will not take place in government hearing rooms, political campaigns, or court rooms.[133] The Minnesota Press Council and National News Council have demonstrated that this can be done successfully. Furthermore, it is interesting to observe that English newspaper publishers and editors voiced the same fear over the British Press Council's birth,[134] but in actual experience no repressive governmental regulation eventuated. In fact, many observers believe that the existence of a press council may neutralize attempts at regulation by the government.

A second contention of many publishers and editors is that press councils are unnecessary since readers are given adequate opportunity to criticize newspaper performance through letter-to-the-editor columns.

> We at the *Tribune* consider that we are monitored daily by 170,000 subscribers and on Sundays by 200,000. We cheerfully listen to complaints, correct errors and provide in our Letters columns free space for any reader to criticize our news reporting and editing or challenge our editorial positions. (Last year we published 2,128 letters).[135]

The significance of letters to the editor has been studied elsewhere, and it has been concluded that such mail does not accurately reflect the opinions of the reading public.[136] This same issue arose in the Bend, Oregon, Press Council, one of the Mellet Foundation experiments, when a public member aptly pointed out that many working class people were intimidated from writing because they feared that the newspaper would publicly scoff at their efforts through a reply.[137] Hence, for the reader who is in effect isolated from the rest of the community, it would seem that the newspapers are actually further away than a letter to the editor.

Another existing mechanism that journalists point to as an indication of the reader's ability to criticize performance is the newspaper's circulation, for they reason that if a reader is dissatisfied, he does not have to buy the newspaper.[138] Again, this is not an accurate reflection

132. Letter from James A. Clendinen, Editor of *The Tampa Tribune*, to John A. Ritter, Aug. 24, 1973, on file at the *Duke Law Journal*.

133. Balk 5.

134. LEVY 9.

135. Letter from James A. Clendinen, *supra* note 132.

136. Brown & Levy, *Letter to the Editor*, 1970 JOURNALISM Q. 454.

137. T. PETERSON, J. JENSEN & W. RIVERS, *supra* note 38, at 49.

138. Letter from Gloria N. Biggs, Editor and Publisher of the Melbourne *Evening*

of the reality of the situation, especially since there exists a growing concentration of ownership of an ever decreasing number of newspapers.[139] In most communities a reader does not have a second newspaper to choose, or if there is a second paper, it is often not a meaningful alternative for a dissatisfied reader.

Many journalists feel that a press council would inhibit editors.

> The effect of a Press Council would be inhibiting on editors and would open an editorial prerogative to busybodies, no matter how well intentioned. We believe the best judge of our newspaper to be the reading public.[140]

However, the absence of sanctions and the decisions to date should lead to the opposite conclusion. The fact that editors need not fear decisions limiting their prerogative is demonstrated by the *Long-Erickson* decison of the Minnesota Press Council. That decision encouraged editors to feel "free to express honest opinion of whatever sort" and stated that "it's for the reading public—not the Press Council—to distinguish between 'good' opinion and 'bad' opinion in newspaper editorials."[141]

It has also been suggested that press councils serve no purpose since responsible newspapers don't need a press council and irresponsible newspapers will ignore it.[142] The experience of one responsible newspaper in Minnesota which thought it did not need a council is to the contrary. The editor of the St. Paul *Dispatch—Pioneer Press* takes advantage of an existing council by referring to it complaints that the newspaper is unable to resolve.[143] The former dean of the Columbia School of Journalism, Edward Barrett, also took this position when he stated "these experiments indicate that managements of reasonable character have nothing to fear and definitely something to gain."[144]

Arthur Ochs Sulzberger, publisher of the *New York Times*, believes a press council lacks due process in its proceedings. When discussing the National News Council he wrote:

> Council hearings would call into question the *Time's* [*sic*] credibility

---

Times, to John A. Ritter, Aug. 2, 1973, on file at the *Duke Law Journal*.

139. See note 6 *supra*.

140. Letter from Don Shoemaker, Editor of *The Miami Herald*, to John A. Ritter, Aug. 1, 1973, on file at the *Duke Law Journal*.

141. Minnesota Press Council Decision No. 5, at 9 (1973). See notes 73-78 *supra* and accompanying text.

142. Letter from James A. Clendinen, *supra* note 132.

143. Interview with John Finnegan, *supra* note 64.

144. Barrett, Book Review, COLUM. JOURNALISM REV., Mar.-Apr., 1972, at 55.

under a procedure so lacking in due process that one organization would function as investigator, prosecutor and judge rolled into one.[145]

However, it is submitted that Mr. Sulzberger is mistaken in his analogy to the elements of a criminal prosecution; a press council proceeding is more closely analogous to a civil or administrative proceeding. There is no prosecutor, only an allegedly injured party seeking redress against another party. The essential requirements for due process in a civil proceeding[146] or an administrative hearing,[147] notice and an opportunity to be heard, are provided. An examination of both the National News Council and the Minnesota Press Council discloses provisions that all parties to a grievance shall have the opportunity to appear in person, to give evidence, and to present testimony.[148] Two further elements of due process are granted by both Councils, the rights to counsel and to cross-examination.[149]

One objection voiced by lawyers is the necessity of waiving all right to pending or future civil suits arising out of the subject matter of a press council complaint.[150] The requirement of a waiver of a cause of action is not completely foreign to American jurisprudence,[151] but the question exists whether such a waiver is necessary or valid in the press council context. In point of fact, a waiver by the complainant of his right to legal action is vital to the success of a press council. Members of the news media would not cooperate with a council, and would even resist its inquiries, if they were simply participating in pre-trial discovery for future lawsuits.

Generally, waiver of a legal right such as the right to sue is valid if made voluntarily and with full knowledge of the law and facts.[152]

---

145. TIME, *supra* note 131.

146. Mullane v. Central Hanover Bank, 339 U.S. 306 (1950).

147. Barsky v. Board of Regents, 347 U.S. 442 (1954); Anderson Nat'l Bank v. Luckett, 321 U.S. 233 (1944).

148. See note 33 *supra*.

149. See note 33 *supra*.

150. See note 67 *supra*.

151. For example most workmen's compensation statutes require the employee to waive his right to sue except as provided by the statute. *See e.g.*, CAL. LABOR CODE § 3601 (Cumulative Supp., 1974), *amending* CAL. LABOR CODE § 3601 (West 1971); FLA. STAT. ANN. § 440.11(1) (Cumulative Supp., 1974); N.C. GEN. STAT. § 97-10.1 (1972).

152. *See* Yates v. American Republics Corp., 163 F.2d 178 (10th Cir. 1947):

> Waiver is the voluntary relinquishment or surrender of some known right. Its constituent elements are an existing right; knowledge of such right; and an intention to relinquish or surrender it. *Id.* at 179.

Accord, Brown v. Cranston, 214 Cal. App. 2d 660, 668, 29 Cal. Rptr. 725, 729 (Dist. Ct. App. 1963); Fireman's Fund Ins. Co. v. Vogel, 195 So. 2d 20, 24 (Fla. Dist. Ct. App. 1967); Beneficial Fin. Co. v. Norton, 76 N.J. Super. 577, 581-82, 185 A.2d 218, 220-21 (1962).

Thus, before a press council accepts a party's waiver of his right to sue on the subject matter of his complaint, it should be sure that the party has consulted an attorney and is aware of his legal rights. A further requirement of some courts for a valid waiver is consideration or estoppel.[153] It is unlikely that consideration would exist in submission of a complaint to a press council unless the potential plaintiff can be said to receive consideration from the press council's examination of his complaint. However, an estoppel would undoubtedly be raised by the production of evidence by a respondent newspaper or broadcaster which has relied on the waiver.

A second objection raised by lawyers to press council procedure is the lack of a right of appeal. An examination of the Minnesota Press Council and the National News Council rules of procedure reveals that this objection has some basis. The Minnesota Press Council allows a party to submit responses to the recommendations of the Grievance Committee before consideration of recommendations by the full Press Council in order to correct errors of fact or law.[154] The rules of the Minnesota Press Council also provide for a discretionary appeal from a final decision in the limited cases of dismissal by the Grievance Committee, or from a report of the Council in a case where the party has not previously appeared before the Council concerning the case in question.[155] The National News Council provides only for a discretionary appeal within fifteen days from a final decision but does not limit this right as does the Minnesota Press Council.[156] In both Councils, a majority vote is necessary for a case to be reconsidered since the appeal is discretionary. Thus, the right-of-appeal objection has some merit since the appeal is limited in scope and must be considered by the same body which heard the case in the first instance.

---

153. *See, e.g.*, Chambers & Co. v. Equitable Life Assurance Soc'y of America, 224 F.2d 338, 345 (5th Cir. 1955); Peal v. Gulf Red Cedar Co., 15 Cal. App. 2d 196, 199, 59 P.2d 183, 184 (Dist. Ct. App. 1936); Summer v. Fabregas, 52 N.J. Super. 399, 409, 145 A.2d 659, 665 (1958); *In re* Dimon's Estate, 32 N.Y.S.2d 239, 243 (Sur. Ct. 1941).

154. Minnesota Press Council, Grievance Comm. Procedural Rule III.A.:

> Each party will be given a period of ten days to submit responses to the recommendations [of the Grievance Committee] in writing before the consideration of the recommendations by the Press Council.

155. *Id.* Rule IV.A.:

> Appeals from a dismissal by the Grievance Committee, or from a report of the Council in grievances where the parties have not previously appeared before the Council, will be permitted only at the discretion of the Press Council.

156. National News Council, Amended Rule 24:

> Within fifteen days of the day the Council mails notice of its decision to the parties, a party may ask the Council to reopen the case for further consideration. The Council shall consider the request at its next regular meeting. The request shall be granted if it is favored by a majority of the Council members voting on the question at a meeting at which a quorum is present at the time of the vote.

A review of the journalists' and lawyers' objections to press councils shows them to contain some validity; however, the experience of the Minnesota and National Councils shows that in practice the problems anticipated by these objections have not materialized. The good points of press councils outweigh the bad, suggesting that local, regional, and state councils should be tried, at the very least, on an experimental basis.

CONCLUSION

The law can guarantee a free press, but it is incapable of guaranteeing a fair press. The journalism profession must recognize that while its enterprise is and should remain a private business, free from government regulation, its efforts to define and realize standards of performance are also a community concern. A mechanism is needed through which individuals who understand the complexities of modern journalism and members of the community can meet and discuss press performance and press responsibility. Their discussions should not be restrained by strict interpretations of the first amendment; elementary fairness and high journalistic standards should serve as their guides. A press council satisfies this need.

[6]

PRIVACY JURISPRUDENCE OF THE PRESS COMPLAINTS COMMISSION

By SIR LOUIS BLOM-COOPER, QC and LISA R. PRUITT

> "[W]e commend to the [Press] Council the possibility of a codification of its adjudications on privacy, in a form which would give rather readier guidance to busy practising journalists, and to the interested public, and that it should be kept up to date."
>
> Report of the (Younger) Committee on Privacy 1972.[1]

Introduction

Two departmental committees, two decades apart, which focused on the persistent and unresolved problem of reconciling press freedom with press responsibility, particularly as regards invasion of privacy, look like bearing fruit.[2] Responding to the Fourth Report of the National Heritage Committee, *Privacy and Media Intrusion*[3], the Lord Chancellor's Department and the Scottish Office have recently issued a consultation paper, *Infringement of Privacy*[4] proposing the creation of a civil remedy against whomever infringes an individual's privacy. The consultation paper envisaged a Press Ombudsman established by the press (and hence non-statutory) to deal with complaints from the public about press conduct as a quicker and less formal remedy than court proceedings in privacy cases involving the press. An Ombudsman scheme, which "would probably not be obliged to follow the procedures built up under a new law"[5] would exist alongside the statutory remedy, as a complement to it. How

---

1. Cmnd.5012, para.193 at 55.
2. Report of the Committee on Privacy and Related Matters, 1990, Cmnd.1102, [hereinafter Calcutt Mark I]. The committee was reviewed subsequently by its chairman, Sir David Calcutt, QC, Review of Self-Regulation of the Press, 1993, Cm.2135 [hereinafter Calcutt Mark II].
3. HC 294-1, March 24, 1993.
4. July 30, 1993.
5. *Op. cit.*, para.6.3, p.41.

should the non-statutory remedy develop, having regard to the past experience of the Press Council and its successor body, the Press Complaints Commission?

The call by the Younger Report in 1972 for codification and a developed body of case law fell on deaf ears, until the scare of legislative intervention in 1989[6] and the report in June 1990 of Calcutt Mark I propelled the newspaper industry to set up the Press Complaints Commission, equipped with an industry-drafted code - including an article on privacy - which the Commission was charged to interpret and apply. In spite of long-standing concerns about invasion of privacy, neither the Press Council's uncodified corpus of decisions over the 37 years of its existence (1953-1990), nor the early attempts of the Press Complaints Commission have adequately addressed the problem. Comprehensive and coherent guidelines about the boundaries of the private arena of individual lives which the press must not invade, by journalistic investigation or editorial publication, have yet to be established. Since a law of privacy, if enacted by Parliament, must be some way off, and any ensuing jurisprudence of the courts are unlikely to emerge before the end of the century, any non-statutory development of the principles applicable to protection of private lives from press intrusion must be welcome.

It was not until 1976 that the Press Council bowed to pressure and issued a declaration of principle regarding privacy.[7] Even then, the standard articulated was a vague one, and subsequent adjudications did little or nothing to clarify the line over which the press should not step. The perceived failings of the Press Council generally, and in the invasion of privacy context specifically, were undoubtedly a factor that discredited it in the eyes of the public and led to its disbandment and replacement by a new body charged with adjudicating on complaints under

6. The Protection of Privacy Bill was introduced by Mr John Browne, MP for Winchester, in 1988. It passed committee stage but was withdrawn before Report, on the announcement of the setting up of the Calcutt Mark I in April 1989.

7. See *The Press and the People*, 24th Annual Report of the Press Council (1977) pp.109-11 (quoting the Declaration of Principle in its entirety).

a Code of Practice framed exclusively by the industry. The early decisions of the Press Complaints Commission on privacy deserve close attention and evaluation, as a pointer to future development.

It may help the reader of this article to see the relevant article of the Press Industry's Code of Practice on privacy as set alongside the suggested article in both Calcutt Mark I and the proposed code of practice in the report of the National Heritage Committee:

THE PRESS INDUSTRY'S CODE OF PRACTICE	CALCUTT COMMITTEE'S PROPOSED CODE OF PRACTICE	THE NATIONAL HERITAGE COMMITTEE'S PROPOSED CODE OF PRACTICE
4. Privacy	**4. Privacy**	**4. Privacy**
Intrusions and inquiries into an individual's private life without his or her consent are not generally acceptable. Publication can only be justified when in the public interest.	(i) Making inquiries about the personal lives of individuals without their consent is not generally acceptable.	(i) Making inquiries about the personal lives of individuals without their consent is not generally acceptable.
This would include:	(ii) Publishing material about the personal life of individuals without their consent is not generally acceptable.	(ii) Publishing material about the personal life of individuals without their consent is not generally acceptable.
(i) Detecting or exposing crime or serious misdemeanour. (ii) Detecting or exposing seriously anti-social behaviour. (iii) Protecting public health and safety.	(iii) An intrusion into an individual's personal life can be justified only for the purpose of detecting or exposing crime, or seriously anti-social conduct, protecting public health or safety, or preventingthe public being misled by some public statement or action of that individual.	(iii) An intrusion into an individual's personal life can be justified only for the purpose of detecting or exposing crime, protecting health or safety, or preventing a harmful deception of the public.
(iv) Preventing the public from being misled by some statement or action of that individual.	(iv) An individual's	(iv) An individual's personal life includes matters of health, home personal relationships, correspondence and

personal life includes matters of health, home, personal relationships, correspondence and documents but does not include his trade or business.	documents but does not include his trade or business.

While relatively few complaints have been brought under clause 4 of the PCC's code, several of the privacy adjudications have been among the highest profile matters yet to be considered by the Commission.[8] The relative rarity of invasion of privacy adjudications - only a handful of adjudications citing clause 4 were issued in the PCC's first year - makes it difficult to analyse the Commission's privacy jurisprudence in a systematic way. Difficulty in discerning privacy principles from the adjudications is exacerbated by the Commission's failure to draft them with any sense of juridical purpose - that is, to identify essential issues arising from a complaint and then to apply the rule of the relevant Code article to determine the proper result. The difficulty was further compounded by the fact that adjudications were not issued separately but were included in a monthly bulletin, whilst the shortness of the reasoning for decisions was further trouble. A number of other adjudications, some of which are discussed below, could properly be considered as privacy cases, although clause 4 was not cited.

Consider the Clare Short matter. Because the complaint dealt with a number of issues that have arisen in subsequent complaints, it *might* have set precedents to influence or determine the outcomes of those matters.

Ms Short's allegations of invasion of privacy arose from an investigation by a *News of the World* reporter and story

8. The Princess Eugenie and Clare Short adjudications provoked extensive press commentary. See, eg, "Discipline of the Press," (1991) *The Times* (London), August 10, (discussing *The People's* flouting of the PCC ruling in the Princess Eugenie case); "Up and Down the City Road," (1991) *The Independent Magazine*, August 17, p.9 (discussing the Clare Short case); Kate Muir, "Short Story Long on Headlines," (1991) *The Times* (London), February 1, (interviewing Clare Short about her complaint).

subsequently published by that newspaper. Her complaint, enumerating a number of incidents arising from the reporter's activity and the subsequent publication, raised both clause 1 (inaccuracy)[9] and clause 4 (privacy) issues. In brief, the chronology of events leading to Ms Short's complaint was that, in 1986, she had introduced a bill in Parliament which would have curtailed publication of "page 3 girl" photos, which she considers pornographic.[10] She alleged she was subsequently the object of a "campaign of vilification" by *The Sun* and its sister paper, *The News of the World*. Ms Short complained about two specific incidents where the latter had linked her, in quite a misleading fashion, to pornography. The Commission upheld her complaint in this regard, albeit on unspecified grounds, noting the "inescapable suspicion" that the paper engaged in these objectionable activities with a purpose to embarrass Ms Short in retaliation for her anti-pornography stance.[11] It is unclear whether this reprehensible motive carried over, and was relevant to other activities about which Ms Short complained.

In late 1990, Ms Short had received several reports indicating that she was being investigated by a *News of the World* reporter. The reporter had first contacted her former husband, asking him for a photo showing Ms Short topless or in a nightgown. The reporter's knowledge that the former husband was mentally unstable and that he had previously threatened Ms Short was undisputed. Secondly, the reporter had investigated Ms Short's friendship, during the early 1970s, with John Daniel, a man who had been convicted of various criminal offences prior to that friendship. Several years after the end of his relationship with

---

9. Accuracy: (i) Newspapers and periodicals should take care not to publish inaccurate, misleading or distorted material; (ii) whenever it is recognized that a significant inaccuracy, misleading statement or distorted report has been published, it should be corrected promptly and with due prominence; (iii) an apology should be published whenever appropriate; (iv) a newspaper or periodical should always report fairly and accurately the outcome of an action for defamation to which it has been a party.
10. Press release No.91-121/No.11, Press Complaints Commission, May 31, 1991 [hereinafter Short adjudication].
11. *Id.*, p.3.

Ms Short, Daniel had been the victim of a murder for which no one had ever been charged. Early in 1991, convinced that the *News of the World* was about to publish a story related to these investigations, Ms Short gave a speech in the House of Commons outlining these investigations into her private life and attacking the publication and its staff. The material about which she had spoken was published by the *News of the World* a few days later.

Ms Short's complaint was considered under clauses 1 and 4 of the Code of Practice.[12] The invasion of privacy claims may have related only to the investigation, and the inaccuracy claims may have related only to the publication.[13] This is logical, given the manner in which Ms Short presented her case. After all, any information that was "private" was first published by her House of Commons speech which attacked the investigative tactics used by the *News of the World* reporter. Accordingly, she would have waived any right to complain of invasion of privacy over its subsequent publication in the newspaper. A complaint that the newspaper report contained inaccuracies and misrepresentations was, however, appropriate.

---

12. Whether she expressly identified the inaccuracy and privacy issues, along with the corresponding code sections, is uncertain. It is more likely that the PCC categorized the complaint in this manner. Although in its early adjudications the PCC frequently failed to cite any clause of the code, in later adjudications the Commission has more often referred to a specific clause. The Commission declines to decide complaints in which a *prima facie* breach of the code does not arise. This rule implicitly requires that a code clause be identified for each complaint adjudicated. In practice, however, the Commission often issues adjudications, referring to a vagary it calls the "spirit of the code." The introduction to the code specifically states: "The code applies in the spirit as well as in the letter." While the National Heritage Committee Report echoes this, Calcutt Mark I significantly omits such a vacuous phrase. Is there any reason to treat self-regulation in this respect differently from a quasi-judicial tribunal?
13. The adjudication expressly states that "Ms Short's complaint is that the article misrepresented her criticism of the [*News of the World*] in Parliament. *Id.*, p.10. However, only a few sentences later it states that, in publishing the story about Ms Short, the newspaper should have "taken special care that it did not use the article as cover for publication of irrelevant facts about Ms Short's private life, which it could not otherwise justify under clause 4." *Id.*, p.11.

One issue on which the Commission correctly focused, as a determinative element of the adjudication, was Ms Short's status as a public figure - at least inasmuch as that brought the matter within the purview of "public interest." As both Ms Short and the *News of the World* accepted, the paper was justified in inquiring into aspects of a public figure's private life on the assumption that information discovered might be in the public interest. Still, the Commission held that such inquiries could not justify publication of the information unless the facts discovered in the course of the investigation satisfied the "public interest" test of clause 4. Commenting on the meaning of "public interest," the Commission stated that it is not merely "whatever happens to interest the public."[14] The adjudication expressly recognized that "circumstances in the private life of [an MP] may bear on her conduct of that office or fitness for it," but it never concluded whether the test was satisfied on the known facts. The Commission simply noted that the *News* had not sought to "suggest that information it possessed ... would have justified an article about her which was in the public interest,"[15] implying that both parties agreed there was none on the facts revealed by the investigation. At no point was any specific part of clause 4's four-prong public interest test discussed, leading us to wonder whether the Commission considered the codified test at all.

Rather than concluding its inquiry with this finding, that "public interest" could not justify publication of the offending statements, the Commission in its adjudication considered several other matters, stating some informative dicta, but also making several comments that served only to obscure the issues on which the decision turned - or at least should have turned. Among its more positive contributions, the Commission noted that passage of time does not necessarily diminish the relevance of justification for publishing material that otherwise meets the "public interest" test.[16] As with many American courts' handling of suits for

14. *Id.*, p.6.
15. *Id.*, p.11.
16. *Id.*, p.6. This is consistent with the dominant rule in the privacy jurisprudence of most American states. Restatement (2d) of Torts, 652D, comment k (1977) [hereinafter Restatement (2d)]. This would also be

publication of private facts, the Commission was also sensitive to the investigative, newsgathering techniques employed by the *News of the World* journalist. The Commission considered the report's knowledge of the former husband's psychiatric condition particularly damning, calling the journalist's behaviour "indefensible."[17] It upheld Ms Short's complaint "in this respect," a statement which is somewhat confusing by its implication that an independent basis for complaint arises from the investigative technique of the journalist. If the Commission considered this activity independently to give rise to a privacy complaint, it should have been explicit about that finding. Generally, under the common law of most American states for example, deceptive or otherwise offensive newsgathering techniques do not independently give rise to a cause of action, unless they rise to the level of "intrusion upon seclusion" - as literally into one's home.[18] The method of obtaining information is relevant as a potentially aggravating factor, but it is not generally the subject of ultimate inquiry.

The Commission appeared to attribute more import to investigative process. This is consistent in some ways with the Calcutt Mark I's recommendation that certain forms of physical intrusion should be criminal offences in England and Wales.[19] Ms Short's physical privacy, however, was not invaded in any of the ways enumerated in Calcutt Mark I's recommendation so it is surprising that the adjudication did not specifically refer to the Calcutt proposal. What the Commission ought to have recognized - and probably sought to in the Clare Short

---

supported by a May 1992 adjudication of a complaint by Mr David Sullivan in which the Commission upheld the *News of the World's* mention of the complainant's 12-year-old spent conviction for living off immoral earnings by running a massage parlour. See David Sullivan II, *infra*, note 40.

17. Short adjudication, *supra*, note 7, at 18.

18. This "intrusion upon seclusion" refers to both physical intrusion and to other types of intrusion upon one's "solitude." See generally Restatement (2d) *supra*, note 13, at 652B.

19. See *infra* note 37 and accompanying text (discussing the details of the recommendation). The recommendation was repeated in Calcutt mark II, ch.7, p.51-2.

adjudication - is that one's privacy may be invaded in the investigative phase leading to an anticipated publication, not only by the publication itself. This can mean psychic or emotional privacy, not only physical privacy. Thus, Ms Short's privacy was invaded by the "[i]ntrusions and inquiries into [her] private life" - to quote the code language. The Commission considered *inquiries* into her relationship with John Daniel to be justified in the public interest,[20] while inquiries made to her former husband seeking a salacious photo of the MP were not.[21] None of the information disclosed as a result of either inquiry, however, rose to the level of public interest that would have justified its publication.

Under the laws of most American state jurisdictions, this is certainly the case. The motive of the publisher/defendant is simply not discussed. The only instance in which it arguably is relevant is when a public official or public figure is the plaintiff. In those cases, the rules of *New York Times* and its progeny, which establish different standards of intent for those allegedly defaming different types of defamation plaintiffs, also apply to public official and public figure plaintiffs bringing invasion of privacy actions. The level of culpability which public figure/official defamation plaintiffs must prove is "actual malice," further defined as "knowledge of falsity" or publication "with reckless disregard as to truth or falsity" of the statement.[22]

In the 1967 case of *Time, Inc. v. Hill*, the US Supreme Court held that the First Amendment precluded application of a New York privacy statute to redress reports of matters of public interest, even if they depicted the plaintiffs in a "false light," absent proof that the defendant had published the report with "knowledge of its falsity or in reckless disregard of the truth."[23] However, the actual malice standard defined in *New York Times* does not transfer comfortably or sensibly into any privacy context except the false light one. This is because "knowledge of falsity" or "reckless disregard" as to truth or falsity is irrelevant to

20. Short adjudication, *supra*, note 7, at 6-7.
21. *Id.*, p.8.
22. *New York Times v. Sullivan*, (1964) 376 US 254; see generally Restatement (2d) *supra*, note 13, at 580A.
23. (1967) 385 US 374, 378.

"private facts" cases, in which "privacy," not "falsity" is the key inquiry. American courts have exhibited some confusion as to how this standard should be applied in privacy cases. Some have roughly translated actual malice as knowledge that a publication would constitute an invasion of privacy or reckless disregard as to whether it would or not.[24] Most courts have determined that the standard applies only to false light cases.[25]

Thus, a US legal analysis of the Short complaint might find the publisher's bad motive relevant, but it is unlikely because her allegations would be considered publication of private facts rather than a false light type of invasion of privacy, the latter being generally necessary to trigger an "actual malice" analysis.

The adjudication discussed at length the motives of both Ms Short and the *News of the World*. This may be because each party sought to focus on the reprehensible motive of the other. As previously noted, Ms Short alleged that the *News of the World* was pursuing a long-standing vendetta against her over her political crusade to ban "page 3 girls," and the Commission gave credence to the relevance of this motive by acknowledging the "inescapable suspicion" that the newspaper sought to embarrass Ms Short in retaliation for her political stance on pornography. Motive, we suggest, should not necessarily be an issue with regard to invasion of privacy. Either an invasion has occurred, or it has not. The motive of the publishers is of no moment. Generally, a complainant's behaviour is relevant only insofar as he or she may have waived any right to action, because of previous publication of the sensitive information, or because he or she may otherwise have consented to the disclosure.[26] With the Short complaint, the Commission apparently considered her behaviour relevant because the *News of the World* claimed that Ms Short's speech in the House of Commons in January, 1991, had provoked it to

24. See, eg, *Lerman v. Flynt Distributing Co., Inc.* (2d Cir. 1984) 745 F.2d 123, *cert. denied,* (1985) 471 US 1054 (implicitly applying "actual malice" - though not defining it - to a commercial appropriation type of privacy case).

25. See, eg, *Machleder v. Diaz,* (1987) 801 F.2d 46, *cert. denied,* 107 S.Ct. 1294; *Lorentz v. Westinghouse Elec. Corp.* (W.D.Pa. 1979) 472 F.Supp. 946.

26. See generally Restatement (2d), *supra,* note 13, at 652D, comment b; see *infra,* text accompanying notes 42-48.

publish the objectionable story. During her parliamentary speech, Ms Short strongly condemned the behaviour of the paper and its staff, including that of editor Ms Patricia Chapman, who coincidentally was the chairperson of the committee that drafted the industry's Code of Practice and who, from its inception, was a member of the Press Complaints Commission. Ms Short said she made the speech in the expectation that publication of a *News of the World* article was imminent. The *News of the World* editor resisted Ms Short's complaint, in part by claiming that it had not decided to publish a story based on its investigations until Ms Short made her speech in the House of Commons, after which the editor claimed that an article and editorial were the "only effective way" to answer Ms Short's accusations and to correct her alleged inaccuracies.[27] The Commission was sympathetic to this justification, but on the whole accorded far too much attention, and therefore implicitly assigned far too much importance to the motive issues.

The Press Complaints Commission appears never to have been quite able to sort through the complexity of Clare Short's complaint, and it stumbled several times because of its lack of understanding about how a privacy analysis might best proceed. For example, the initial inquiry might logically have been whether any invasion of privacy had occurred. Clause 4 asserts the basic unacceptability of "intrusions and inquiries into an individual's private life." But what does "private life" mean? Does it include a person's home or private business address? Information about a person's sexual practices? About a family member's drug problem? The Commission did not, in the Short adjudication, and has not in handling any subsequent complaint, dealt with the meaning of "privacy" or "private life" as a term of art representing a concept on which a complaint may be based. Beyond this threshold issue, the Commission should next determine whether there has been an "intrusion" or "inquiry" into, or "publication" relating to, this private sphere. If the answer is "yes" the defences of "consent" and "public interest" become relevant.

27. *Id.*, p.9.

The Short adjudication may represent the least satisfactory adjudication of the Press Complaints Commission. This is not necessarily because it got the result wrong. Rather, it is because it did not proceed with such step-by-step analysis. Accordingly, very few free-standing principles about privacy can be garnered from it. The adjudication, in its construction and language, lacked a sense of juridical purpose. The Commission seemed to focus only on making a decision about a matter at hand; it was seemingly oblivious to any implications it might have for subsequent cases. It was similarly oblivious to its obligations to interpret in a meaningful way the Code of Practice, and to provide guidelines of acceptable press behaviour for both the media and the public.

The following discussion is organized according to various distinct issues that may arise in the course of a methodical analysis of privacy complaints. Although the Commission has not frequently issued adjudications that refer to these matters expressly, various principles may be discerned from a close reading of the relevant adjudications.

The Meaning of "Privacy"

Not every matter that a complainant considers an invasion of privacy actually constitutes an invasion into the private sphere of life. The Calcutt Committee discussed the meaning of "privacy" at great length, considering the parameters set by the laws of various other countries. The Committee tentatively concluded that it is the "right of an individual to be protected against intrusion into his personal life or affairs, or those of his family, by direct physical means or by publication of information".[28]

The report went on to note that the right to privacy "could include" protection against: (a) "physical intrusion;" (b) "publication of hurtful or embarrassing personal material (whether true or false);" (c) "publication of inaccurate or misleading personal material;" and (d) "publication of

---

28. Calcutt Report, *supra*, note 2, II, 3.7, at 7. The Younger Report discussed the meaning and import of privacy even more extensively than did Calcutt. See generally Younger Report, *supra*, note 1, at ch.4.

photographs or recordings of the individual taken without consent."[29] Although the Committee did not expressly acknowledge such, three of these four categories roughly correspond to those recognized by American privacy tort jurisprudence: intrusion, publication of private facts, and false light.[30] As regards the first "photography" element of the fourth Calcutt category, it is similar in some instances to the American "appropriation" type of privacy invasion which redresses the grievance of a person whose image has been exploited for commercial purposes.[31] Despite the Calcutt Committee's apparent dalliance with American privacy concepts, these rather distinct types of privacy invasions are not reflected in the Code of Practice which is enforced by the Press Complaints Commission. As reflected in its quotation above, clause 4 of the Code speaks more generally of "intrusions and inquiries" into an individual's private life being unacceptable. It goes on to enumerate instances when such intrusions may be justified as in the public interest, but it does not provide further guidance as to what manner or sorts of intrusions or inquiries are objectionable.

Both the National Heritage Committee[32] and the Government's consultation paper[33] discuss the meaning and importance of privacy as an aspect of human personality. The Code of Practice does not reflect these categories. As noted in relation to the Clare Short case, privacy may refer to either or both psychic privacy and physical privacy. These may be invaded either by *inquiries* into a personal matter, as in the Short case, or by *publication* of personal information.

The sort of information that the Commission considers sufficiently private to be the basis of litigation is difficult to discern from its frequently cursory adjudications. Not a single 1991 adjudication of a clause 4 complaint engages in any

29. *Id.*, II, 3.8.
30. Restatement (2d), *supra*, note 13, at 652A; Prosser, "Privacy," (1960) 48 Calif.L.Rev. 383.
31. Restatement (2d), *supra*, note 13, at 652C.
32. Paragraphs 47-59, pp.xii-xv.
33. Chapter 3, pp.8-12.

substantive discussion of what is sufficiently "private" to support a complaint on this basis. One could deduce that the Commission deems certain matters sufficiently private simply because complaints based on disclosure of these matters have been upheld under clause 4. Of course, if the Commission has not actually considered the privacy implications of such disclosure, this may be presumptuous and inappropriate. Still, without more explicit guidance from the Commission, it is all that either the media or the public have on which to base their decisions.

Consider the Princess Eugenie adjudication in which the Commission held that *The People's* publication of nude photos of the infant princess breached clause 4.[34] In response to the newspaper's defence that the photos were "charming" and "natural", published "good naturedly and affectionately", the Commission responded that such claims were irrelevant, as was the offensiveness of the photos, because they were simply an invasion of privacy.

What the Commission failed to recognize is that issues of offensiveness and naturalness may be evidence of the ultimate issue of privacy invasion. Under the "publication of private facts" prong of American privacy law, for example, a matter disclosed must be sufficiently private to "violate ordinary decencies" or "offend", in order to give rise to a cause of action. Thus, an offensiveness inquiry should not have been so summarily dismissed by the Commission. It assumed, probably correctly, that nude photos of a child, taken surreptitiously and published in a national newspaper, were sufficiently invasive of privacy to justify complaint. Even though the adjudication discounted an "offensiveness" analysis, it perhaps implicitly engaged in one by noting the circumstances of both acquisition and publication of the photos, rather than focusing merely on their content, which, as the Commission noted, would be quite unexceptionable if only displayed in a family album. The Commission missed other

34. Press release No.91-868/No.28, Press Complaints Commission, August 8, 1991 [hereinafter Princess Eugenie adjudication]. The decision to uphold the complaint was also based upon clause 11, which states that journalists should not normally photograph children under the age of 16 without their parents' consent. *Id.*, p.1.

opportunities to distinguish between disclosures which are of a sufficiently *personal* nature to constitute an invasion of privacy and matters which do not violate ordinary decency, even though the subject of them might prefer that they not be made public.

In adjudicating a complaint by the then-leader of the Labour Party, Mr Neil Kinnock, and his daughter, who complained about an article in *Today* reporting a "dust-up" between Mr Kinnock and four youths who were taunting him as he was "ticking off" his daughter, the Commission held that the story did not breach the Code of Practice.[35] No particular clause of the Code was ever cited; however, several references were made to the lack of "intrusion into privacy," so it is fair to infer that it was decided on clause 4 principles. Though the Commission did not expressly find such, it might well have concluded simply that the matters published was not sufficiently "private" or "personal" to constitute an invasion of privacy. Instead, it obscured this threshold issue by also noting that politicians seek and must expect regular exposure to the press, implying that "public interest" had more to do with the decision than perhaps it should have.[36]

An early 1992 adjudication of a complaint by one of us (L.B-C) similarly failed to grasp this crucial issue upon which the decision might have turned. A group of publicly-known figures wrote a letter to the editor of *The Times*, attacking aspects of the Government's Asylum Bill. When the *Evening Standard* responded with an editorial implying the hypocrisy of the authors and noting that Welsh Nationalists might like to know the address of L.B-C's home in Wales (which was given in full in the

35. Press release 91-405/No.14, the Press Complaints Commission, June 5, 1991 [hereinafter Kinnock adjudication].

36. The Press Complaints Commission failed to distinguish between Mr Kinnock and his daughter. The same failure to distinguish between a public official and someone associated with that official may be observed in the incident involving Mr Paddy Ashdown and Mrs Patricia Sullivan, the woman with whom he had an affair. While no complaint was lodged with the Press Complaints Commission in that matter, the injunction granted by the Queen's Bench Division included no explicit consideration of "public interest" and did not differentiate between Mr Ashdown as a public figure and Mrs Sullivan, with whom he was associated. Queen's Bench Division, Minutes of Order, 1992 A. No.485.

editorial) should they desire to burn it, a complaint was lodged with the Press Complaints Commission. The Commission categorized the complaint under clause 4, as an alleged invasion of privacy. To this the *Evening Standard* responded that L.B.-C had waived any right to any such complaint, by allowing his address to be published as part of his entry in *Who's Who*. Ignoring the consent question, the Commission upheld the complaint, perhaps never considering that mere publication of an address might be insufficiently private or personal to give rise to a complaint for invasion of privacy. The gravamen of the complaint was that the editorial served potentially to incite Welsh Nationalists to commit arson, and the adjudication stated that the paper's publication of the address was "reckless."[37] Yet because the Code contains no provision proscribing a publication likely to encourage a criminal offence, and because the Commission considers only complaints of acts stating a *prima facie* breach of the Code, the Commission handled the complaint strictly as a privacy one, neglecting its more objectionable character as potentially inciting a crime. It also resorted to the device of holding that the editorial breached the "spirit" of the Code, thus foregoing any substantive analysis of privacy issues.

Various adjudications indicate, some without expressly stating so, that disclosures related to one's sexuality and sexual practices are sufficiently private to merit redress when they are publicly disclosed.[38] The Commission upheld one such complaint expressly on the basis of clause 4. The complaint was brought by a woman who had been identified as one of a man's three

---

37. Blom-Cooper adjudication, Report No.7, the Press Complaints Commission, March 1992, at 6. On the day of the release of the adjudication the *Evening Standard* published the adjudication and an editorial justifying its earlier editorial. One member of the Press Complaints Commission, Mr Max Hastings (editor of the *Daily Telegraph*) subsequently announced that he was not present at the Commission's meeting to adjudicate, and disagreed with the verdict.

38. The Code of Practice contains a separate provision regarding irrelevant disclosures relating to "sex or sexual orientation." Code of Practice, *supra*, note 4, at clause 14. The Rachael Webb complaint, discussed below, construed this section.

lovers.[39] Correctly discerning that truth or falsity was not the issue, the Commission declined to make a finding of fact on conflicting allegations of truth and falsity stating simply that this violation of the complainant's privacy was "impossible to justify."[40]

Consider also two adjudications in which sufficient information about a sex crime was published, so that in one case the victim was identifiable and in the other she was "likely to be identified." In both cases the Commission upheld the complaints, though these decisions were likely based on separate Code sections, specifically clauses 12 and 13. These clauses provide that the press should not identify child victims of sexual offences nor other victims of sexual assault, unless, by law, such identification is permissible. In neither adjudication was any specific clause cited - not 4, 12, nor 13 - nor were privacy concerns mentioned. In one matter the Commission noted the editorial duty to "protect the identities of young persons who are believed to have been the victims of sex crimes,[41] reflecting the language of clause 12. In the other, it expressed "profound sympathy with the victim," focusing upon the additional agony she would suffer because of the offending publication.[42]

Although these adjudications fail to cite any specific clause of the Code, one may reasonably infer that the interest at issue in these cases was the victim's privacy interest. Suits that have arisen in the US from public disclosure of a victim's name have been brought under state privacy laws because the matter made public is such an intensely private one - and one for which a stigma still attaches to the victim, albeit through no fault of her own.[43]

---

39. Press release 91-204/No.16, Press Complaints Commission, June 10, 1991.
40. *Id.*, p.2.
41. Press release 91-469/No.42, Press Complaints Commission, October 11, 1991.
42. Press release 91/1154/No.69, Press Complaints Commission, December 13, 1991.
43. These privacy suits have not been successful because of the overriding free speech interests protected by the First Amendment to the US Constitution. See, *Florida Star v. BJF*, (1989) 491 US 524; *Cox Broadcasting Corporation v. Cohn*, (1975) 420 US. However, the privacy interest of the

Without more attention to the very essence of an invasion of privacy claims, the Press Complaints Commission effectively encourages a variety of even moderately offensive publications to be analysed as such.[44] If the Commission is to rise to Calcutt's challenge to state meaningful press guidelines on privacy, it must give more consideration to this threshold issue.

Intrusion upon Seclusion

As noted previously, under American law, intrusion upon one's seclusion may give rise to a privacy action, even if no publication results from information gathered.[45] Indeed, as noted previously, the Calcutt Committee recognized the seriousness of such invasion, and recommended that certain types of physical intrusion should be criminal offences in England and Wales. These included: (1) entering private property, without consent of the lawful occupant, with intent to obtain personal information with a view to its publication; (2) placing a surveillance device on private property, without consent of the lawful occupant, with the same intent; and (3) taking a photograph, or recording the voice, of an individual who is on private property, without his consent, with a view to its publication and with intent that the individual should be identifiable.[46]

Physical privacy invasions arguably occurred in several scenarios that gave rise to complaints adjudicated by the Commission in its first 18 months of operation. Only two of these, both brought by *Sunday Sport* publisher Mr David Sullivan, were, however, analysed under clause 4.[47] In one adjudication

---

victim in preventing disclosure of the information is undisputed.

44. Calcutt Committee Report, *supra*, note 2, II 10.13, at 39.

45. See, *supra*, note 15 and accompanying text.

46. Calcutt Report, *supra*, note 2, II 6.33, at 23. The recommendations were repeated in Sir David Calcutt's "Review of Press Self-Regulation" in March 1993 Ch.2135. Chapter 7, pp.51-55, in particular paras.7.25 and 7.26 at p.55.

47. Two others might have been analysed as privacy complaints, although the Commission decided them on different grounds. *The News*, Portsmouth, took and published a photo of the mother of a missing boy, along with her companion. Although the couple had repeatedly refused

the Commission declined to uphold Mr Sullivan's intrusion complaint[48] and in the other the intrusion issue was settled by an apology from the offending paper.[49] The first was against the *News of the World* which published a photo of Mr Sullivan's new house, taken from within the property's outer perimeter wall. Although the editor saw fit to offer an apology for publication of the photo, conceding the invasion of privacy, in a very similar matter the Press Complaints Commission ruled in favour of the *Daily Mail*, which had also published a photo of Mr Sullivan's home. In the second matter, the *Daily Mail* photographer took the offending photos from a helicopter hovering above the property. The height of the helicopter and the length of time for which it hovered over the property were in dispute, though the newspaper conceded that the minimum time was five minutes and the minimum height was 500 feet. The *Daily Mail* took the stance that the photographs were of public interest, because the

---

to be interviewed or photographed during the course of the search for her son, a *News* reporter, while trespassing on private property, took the objectionable photo. The couple were, however, in a public place when the photo was taken. The PCC upheld the complaint on this basis of clause 9 which calls for sympathy and discretion in cases of personal grief. Press release 91-463/No.30, Press Complaints Commission, August 19, 1991. The complaint might well have been analysed under clause 4 as an invasion of privacy issue. Indeed, the invasion complained of is similar to that in para.(3) of the Calcutt recommendations on criminalizing certain invasions.

One other complaint might have been classified as a physical intrusion case. A press agency employee asked an 11-year-old boy to snatch a photo of a relative about whom the agency was writing a story. A complaint against the agency was upheld, though neither privacy nor any specific clause of the code was mentioned in the adjudication. Press release 91-409/No.19, Press Complaints Commission, July 15, 1991.

48. David Sullivan adjudication, Report No. 8, the Press Complaints Commission, at 6 [hereinafter David Sullivan I].

49. David Sullivan adjudication, Report No. 8, the Press Complaints Commission, at 8 [hereinafter David Sullivan II]. A second issue in the complaint, arising from the *News of the World's* publication about Mr Sullivan's previous conviction for living off immoral earnings by running a massage parlour, was not upheld. The Commission considered the information relevant to a matter of public interest. See, *infra*, notes 55-56 and accompanying text.

house was one of the largest built in Britain in recent years, and the Commission agreed, without further explanation or analysis under the specifics established in clause 4.

The Commission did state that the existence of a public interest did not deny Mr Sullivan a "fair measure of privacy,"[50] whatever that may mean. Given the dispute about the extent of the disturbance, however, the Commission said only that it was unable to conclude that either the taking or publishing of the photograph breached clause 4. We think the Commission was remiss in failing to address the intrusion issues, particularly in light of the Calcutt Committee's particular concern - to the extent of advocating criminal sanctions - about precisely this type of privacy intrusion. Perhaps the Commission was reticent to act in reliance upon the Calcutt recommendation and to uphold the complaint because the "trespass" was not a typical one in that the property of the complainant was not physically touched. Relying on such a technicality, however, ignores the virtually unlimited manoeuvrability and operational capabilities of the helicopter, which makes this form of aerial surveillance more susceptible to misuse than ground surveillance as an instrument of unreasonable intrusion upon private activities.

Consent or Waiver as a Defence

A few of the Commission's privacy adjudications have expressly acknowledged the relevance of a consent defence. The theory is that if a matter is already public knowledge, particularly by consent of the potential complainant, the party has no right to claim redress under a privacy theory when a matter is, in essence, re-published.

A complaint brought by Chris Quentin, former star of "Coronation Street," headlined "Quentin Sister's £200 for kinky sex" and linking him with his sister's promiscuous lifestyle, was not upheld because the Commission determined that he "had already placed his own private life so firmly in the public domain by encouraging ... stories about it." Accordingly, he had "no

50. *Id.*

privacy left to invade" and clause 4 had not been violated.[51]

For similar reasons a complaint brought by Rachael Webb, a Lambeth councillor, was not upheld. Ms Webb complained to the Commission when several newspapers mentioned her 1983 sex-change operation in otherwise general articles about the London borough's Labour politicians.[52] Although her claim was brought under clause 14, which encourages the press to avoid pejorative reference to a person's sex or sexual orientation, privacy concerns were implicated, and it could well have been brought as a clause 4 complaint. Indeed, the Commission expressly recognized that "sexual conditions and orientations are generally private matters on which newspapers are not justified in reporting."[53] However, because Ms Webb had previously spoken openly to the press about being a transsexual, the Commission found the newspaper's reference to her sex change a permissible comment. In effect, it determined that she had waived any right she might previously have had to complain.

In the Kinnock complaint, already discussed above in relation to the meaning of privacy, one of the disclosures about which he complained was the publication of his home address. In what might be labelled a finding of waiver or consent, the Commission noted that the location of the home was sufficiently well-known, so that further publicity of it in the offending article did not constitute a breach of the Code.[54] Contrary to that opinion, the complaint by L.B.-C, also discussed above, did not turn on the complainant's previous waiver with regard to the information at issue. Indeed, in spite of the fact that the consent issue might have been dispositive, the adjudication mentioned the issue only in noting that the *Evening Standard* had raised it as a defence.

---

51. Press release 91-160/No.22, Press Complaints Commission, July 21, 1991. While few would quarrel with the decision reached, the PCC did not address in its adjudication whether he had previously disclosed this particular bit of private information. Rather, the focus was upon his openness generally and on other instances when he had sought publicity.
52. Press release 91-304/305/329/No.23, Press Complaints Commission, July 26, 1991.
53. *Id.*, p.2.
54. Kinnock adjudication, *supra*, note 25, at 3.

One highly-publicized Commission decision[55] turned on the issue of consent. Ruling that two newspapers did not invade family privacy when they published the name of Jennifer Bennet as the child featured in Labour's election broadcast on the National Health Service, the Commission noted that the parents' actions in agreeing to allow their daughter's case to be used in the broadcast had propelled the matter of her treatment into the public domain. Even though the child's parents had given information of her case study to the Labour party, with the proviso that her identity would not be revealed, their action made the child's treatment "an appropriate subject of investigation by newspapers."[56] Accordingly, the newspapers were deemed not to have breached the Code of Practice. Interestingly, although the adjudication mentioned invasion of privacy, it did not cite clause 4 of the Code. Nor did it engage in a public interest analysis, apparently considering "consent" to be the threshold issue.[57] As with so many other issues, the Commission's approach appears to be a scattershot one - attuned to threshold issues at one turn, oblivious to them at the next.

Public Interest Test

The Calcutt Committee expressed unease with a "public interest" concept,[58] suggesting instead the concept of "seriously anti-social conduct." The Government's consultation paper suggested that

---

55. The decision was not considered by the Press Complaints Commission to be an adjudication and, indeed, has not been included in its regular reports summarizing adjudications. However, the Commission clearly offered an opinion on the matter. See "Papers Cleared of Privacy Breach in Naming Election Broadcast Girl," (1992) *The Guardian*, April 29.

56. *Id.*

57. Oddly, in dealing with yet another privacy complaint, the Commission apparently deemed the consent "defence" sufficient to cause it to conclude that no *prima facie* breach of the Code was committed. Accordingly, the complaint was not adjudicated. See "No *Prima Facie* Breach of the Code," Report No.7, the Press Complaints Commission, No.53, p.18.

58. Calcutt Committee Report, *supra*, note 2, 19-3.23, at 8-9, see also David Calcutt, "Cowboys Cool it in the Last Chance Saloon," (1991) *The Guardian*, June 17, p.23.

the Calcutt Committee was right to draw attention to the vagueness of the term "public interest," and stated that it would be preferable to indicate those matters that are of public interest, such as "crime or seriously anti-social conduct; public health or safety; the discharge of a public function; the correction of a misleading statement."[59] The paper invited comments as to how the public interest definition should be formulated, and in particular whether it is preferable to define it in special terms or to be most specific. The comparable concept in US privacy jurisprudence has until recently been "newsworthiness," a term of art so broadly construed that it is now considered to be essentially whatever the press considers it to be. The preferred option in the US is now, anything which is of "legitimate concern to the public."

The Code of Practice, that the Press Complaints Commission is charged with enforcing, embraces the concept of "public interest" and employs it as a justification or defence for an invasion of privacy. In the amended Code of Practice, ratified by the Press Complaints Commission on June 30, 1993, a public interest exception can now be relied on in relation to new provisions barring bugging devices and the use of long-lens cameras to photograph people on private property. Exceptions are allowed only in the public interest, which is newly defined as "detecting or exposing crime or a serious misdemeanour; protecting public health and safety; protecting the public from being misled by the statement or action of an individual or organization." The amended Code goes on to state that in any cases raising issues beyond those definitions, the Press Complaints Commission will require a full explanation by the editor, seeking to demonstrate how the public interest was served.[60] It is not clear whether the defined exceptions are

---

59. *Id.*, para.5.66, p.39.

60. There is also a much expanded provision on dealing with any case involving a sexual offence against a child. This is designed to ensure that the identity of the child cannot be deduced from the disclosure of related information. This makes clear that the adult should be identified but the child should not; that terms such as "incest" should be avoided; and that care should be taken that nothing in the report should imply the relationships between the accused and the child. Finally, in addition

applicable to justification for a defence to an alleged breach of the privacy provisions in the Code. It is also difficult to understand the reference to "misdemeanour," a criminal law concept abandoned by the legislature in 1967.

Even among the few adjudications that have assessed the "public interest" rationale, it is difficult to discern any consistent application of the term. None has referred explicitly to the guidelines set forth in clause 4. Consider again the Clare Short adjudication, in which the Commission stated that "public interest" is not synonymous with whatever interests the public. It emphasized that maintenance of the distinction between those two concepts is crucial, especially with respect to those people who are in public life.[61] Contrast these comments with those responding to Neil Kinnock's complaint. Stating that "[l]eading politicians seek, experience and must expect regular exposure in the press," and that the article "dealt largely in trivia about Mr Kinnock and his family in which *readers might be interested*," the Commission declined to uphold the complaint.[62] Although both decisions were probably decided correctly, their language regarding what does and does not constitute "public interest" is internally inconsistent. The adjudications send mixed messages about the sorts of justifications to which the Commission is sympathetic, one scoffing at public curiosity, the other legitimizing it.

No doubt any adjudicator in this difficult area of regulation will be influenced by the way the courts have interpreted the public interest defence in actions for breach of confidence and in defamation cases. In a case in the former class of action, Ungoed-Thomas, J, in *Beloff v. Pressdram*[63] said that justification

---

to their general responsibility for the actions of their journalists, editors are specifically required to ensure that the code's provisions on harassment are observed. In particular, unless justified on public interest grounds, journalists may not photograph individuals on private property without their consent; should not persist in telephoning or questioning individuals after having been asked to desist; and should not remain on the property when asked to leave.

61. Short adjudication, *supra*, 10.

62. Kinnock adjudication, *supra*, 29.

63. [1973] 1 All ER 241, 260P.

for breach of confidentiality could be founded on "matters carried out or contemplated in breach of the nation's security, or in breach of law, including statutory duty, fraud, or otherwise destructive of the country or its people including matters basically dangerous to the public, and doubtless other misdeeds of similar gravity."

In *Francome v. Mirror Group Newspaper* Sir John Donaldson, MR referred to the public interest in exposing conduct which involves a breach of the law or is anti-social, that is to say, seriously contrary to the public interest.[64]

Another adjudication, subsequent to both the Short and Kinnock decisions, and dealing with a lower echelon public official, a leader of a county council, might also have "public interest" implications. The articles of which the councillor complained, published in a local paper, stated that he had refused - despite persistent attempts by the press - to disclose his occupation.[65] The councillor complained that the reports were misleading and unfair. No express ruling was made on any clause 4 privacy claim. The Commission, in what might be considered an *obiter dictum,* stated that the newspaper did not "unjustifiably invade his privacy" by seeking to learn his occupation: "When a politician holding important office regionally or nationally refuses to respond to a newspaper's request for information which should be in the public domain ... the paper may pursue [an] attempt to encourage or provoke disclosure."[66] This view seems to assume that such information about the politician - although not a local one - is in the public interest.

In a statement in June 1992 responding to media hype, speculation and furore about the marital difficulties of the Prince and Princess of Wales, the Commission shed some further light on the public interest concept. In the most strongly-worded pronouncement of its brief history, the Commission conceded the existence of a "legitimate public interest in the situation of the heir to the throne." Noting that the state of the marriage was

64. [1984] 1 WLR 892, 898A.
65. Press release 91-1122/No.68 Press Complaints Commission, December 11, 1991.
66. *Id.*, p.3.

already in the public domain by virtue of the "outward behaviour of the spouses," the Commission nevertheless opined that the manner and tone of reporting on the private lives of the couple was beyond doubt in breach of the Code of Practice.[67] The implication of the statement was that even a finding of "public interest" cannot necessarily justify intrusive and speculative treatment, and what the Commission called "dabbling [journalistic] fingers in the stuff of other people's souls" in a manner which adds nothing to the discussion of that matter of public interest.[68] No Code section was cited in the Commission's statement, perhaps because it was not strictly an adjudication, but only pontificating precipitately about a widely-publicized event.

Perhaps the most unhelpful "public interest" decision was that made in the David Sullivan adjudication, noted above in relation to the intrusion issue. Without even mentioning the complainant's occupation and notoriety as a "sex publisher" or "pornographer," the Commission summarily concluded that publication of aerial view photos of his new house was in the public interest, apparently merely because it was among the largest built in the country.[69] The Commission may have been deducing from this that the luxury mansion was financed with the profits of pornography, a matter that might indeed have been in the public interest.[70] Because the Commission never expressly

---

67. "Odious" example of Royal reporting, *The Guardian*, June 9, 1992, p.2, col.4 (providing a full text of the Press Complaints Commission statement about media coverage of the Prince and Princess of Wales). Incidentally, the statement was not issued in response to a specific complaint. Rather, the Commission was apparently unprompted in taking upon itself the task of commenting on the situation. Indeed, it was motivated by self-interest, noting in its statement that media behaviour in this regard was jeopardizing the future of the Commission and the self-regulatory system.
68. *Id.*
69. David Sullivan I, *supra*, note 42.
70. Indeed, in adjudicating the other complaint by Mr David Sullivan, the Commission, in speaking to the "public interest" test, acknowledged the relevance of Mr Sullivan's role as "publisher of sex magazines and national daily and Sunday publications, both of which advertised chat lines." In that instance, the objectionable article claimed that construction

states this, however, the public and the media are left guessing as to the real basis of the decision and can discern no certain guidance from the adjudication. Such adjudications make a mockery of the public interest test, a defence which ideally should spawn a comprehensive jurisprudence, striking the appropriate balance between respect for an individual's privacy and the need to encourage the media to investigate and report on matters of importance to the health, safety and education of a decision-making populace.

Conclusion

An essential function of any regulatory system - particularly a self-regulatory system - is to provide to the industry being regulated, as well as to the public, adjudications clarifying the precise scope and meaning of the provisions of the relevant code of conduct. That is precisely what the Younger Report asked for 20 years ago. Although the Code of Practice adopted by the Press Complaints Commission includes a clause on privacy, adjudications interpreting and applying it have proved internally inconsistent and have provided little guidance as to precisely what standards are expected of journalists and editors. The decisions frequently include only summary analysis, thus failing to provide insight into the bases for them. Furthermore, that analysis, which the adjudications do feature, often misses the most obvious points and hence obscures the issues that should be dispositive.

The quality of output of Commission adjudications cannot encourage anyone to conclude that the industry's "last opportunity" to make self-regulation work has been grasped with that degree of effectiveness which would allay disquiet about the lack of press responsibility. Indeed, Calcutt Mark II stated that "the press has demonstrated that it is itself unwilling to put in

---

of Mr Sullivan's new home had been financed by profits of his business, which was based on pornography and sex shops. David Sullivan II, *supra*, note 43. The Commission's adjudication does not indicate whether this same link was explicitly stated in the *Daily Mail* story and, if so, whether the information influenced its decision on the "public interest" issue.

place a regulatory system which commands [respect], not only of the press ... but also of the public, and which fairly holds the balance between them." Sir David Calcutt, QC, made no analysis of the Press Complaints Commission's case law (as we have sought to do in respect of clause 4 on privacy) yet he saw "no realistic possibility of that [unwillingness] being changed by voluntary action."[71]

Whatever government may decide to do about the regulatory system for the future conduct of the press, it is tolerably clear that there will soon be some private law remedy for the infringement of privacy. While the proposal is being translated into legislative action, and some statutory guidelines given to the crucial issue of the public interest defence, the industry and the public will look to the Press Complaints Commission for assistance in a delicate area of social policy - the more so if Government withdraws from its move towards a law on privacy. The Press Complaints Commission must in the future deal more thoughtfully with the "public interest" concept. Second only to the basic notion of what is "private," the breadth of public interest defence will have more impact on the Commission's privacy jurisprudence than any other sub-issue. Editors and journalists, as well as the public, must be provided with meaningful guidelines about precisely what is in the public interest, lest it be concluded that any determination of what is permissibly publishable on grounds of newsworthiness is left to the self-serving interests of the press. It is a prime function of a regulatory body (even more so a self-regulatory one) that it should delineate the boundary between freedom of expression and editorial responsibility.

71. Paragraph 5.29, p.42.

[7]

Self-Censorship among Journalists: A (Moral) Wrong or a Violation of ECHR Law?

Herdís Thorgeirsdóttir

Dr Jur. Associate Professor of Law at Bifrost School of Business, substitute member to the Council of Europe Commission for Democracy through Law

The article explores the constitutional value of press freedom and the problem of self-censorship occurring through official and unofficial privileging of powerful group viewpoints and influences on editorial independence. The author analyses legal regulation, market regulation and self-regulation and how journalism is torn between legal regulation and market regulation. She explores the pressures on the freedom of expression in various states including the Member States of the Council of Europe, before looking at the answers offered by the European Convention on Human Rights (ECHR) and the impact on its case law of the American first amendment jurisprudence. She ends by answering the question she poses of whether media self-censorship is itself a breach of Art.10 ECHR.

I. Self-censorship within the media

Self-censorship has long been one of journalism's most ineffable hazards. A Council of Europe report submits that freedom of expression throughout Europe is facing new challenges resulting from the ongoing process of globalisation of the media market along with the convergence between different media, leading to new alliances and further concentration, which may restrict diversity of opinions and views in the media.[1] The domination of entertainment conglomerates exerts a consistently corrosive effect on journalism. Due to a high degree of concentration in the media market in most of the more economically advanced Member States of the Council of Europe, the options available to journalists are severely diminished.[2] Print media across Europe are facing growing economic difficulties. Four out of five daily newspapers in Western Europe have disappeared in the last 80 years.[3] According to a Council of Europe report, there has been an overall "social dumping" in the status of the journalistic profession.[4] The media fighting for independence from external pressures is, in many of the Council of Europe Member States, the victim of precarious economic conditions, which make it

[1] Parliamentary Assembly Doc.9000, March 19, 2001, Freedom of Expression and Information in the Media in Europe.

[2] See *e.g.* Austria, Belgium, Greece, the Netherlands and Norway to name a few, according to a Council of Europe, Steering Committee on the Mass Media (CDMM) Restricted MM-S-JF 13 DEF (Strasbourg, February 10, 1995). Group of Specialists on Journalistic freedoms report.

[3] R. Negrine, *The Communication of Politics* (Sage Publications, 1996), p.178.

[4] Council of Europe report, n.2 above, p.36.

easy prey for mighty political and economic interests.[5] Publishers turn to local business interests or influential people for a financial lifeline. In the process, they lose their journalistic independence and are "transformed into mercenaries acting upon orders".[6] Self-censorship is when journalists purposely avoid newsworthy stories as they anticipate negative reactions from their superiors, based on built-in penalties and rewards for doing what is expected. The main lever is the internalisation of values.

The constitutional value of press freedom goes far beyond the financial and political interests of individuals and companies. Journalism, however, relies on a medium that is a part of a corporate structure and is partly if not wholly conditioned thereon. The impact of business pressures on editorial decisions is a widely recognised problem. Catherine MacKinnon emphasises that censorship in our time occurs less through explicit state policy than through official and unofficial privileging of powerful groups and viewpoints.[7] Aidan White, the general secretary of the International Federation of Journalists, describes the situation: "Living and working in conditions of fear, poverty or employment insecurity, journalists often submit to self-censorship, the most corrosive and insidious form of censorship of all".[8] According to a recent OSCE report there is rampant self-censorship in newsrooms.[9] Many staff writers are kept in constant fear of being dismissed. The report mentions examples of how the advertising industry is holding the media on a very short leash and full-time journalists are replaced by cheaper and (because of their economic predicament) more accommodating freelance writers.[10] Journalists do not dare to bite the hand that feeds them. Why should they risk their livelihood? Italian political analyst Norberto Bobbio spoke in the 1980s of the impact of the "survival of the invisible power as one of the broken promises of democracy along with the persistence of oligarchies and the suppression of mediating bodies".[11] The traditional division of public and private abuse no longer holds, so the absolutist claim that public authorities are the main threat to journalism is far too simplistic. Journalists today are confronted with the secrecy of private and public power, intertwined interests that make up an insurmountable obstacle in news-gathering and research.[12] Journalists are faced not only with the threat of state interference but also with the "double state",[13] the invisible state alongside the visible state.[14] Important intelligence is subsequently kept away from the public, so the tenuous control that the public should have on governance is further weakened.

[5] Parliamentary Assembly Doc.9000, n.1 above.

[6] *ibid.*

[7] C. MacKinnon, *Only Words* (Harvard University Press, 1993), p.77.

[8] *cf.* P. Cronau, "Self Censorship", *Media Bulletin No.7*, Summer 1996/97, Australian Centre for Independent Journalism at the University of Technology, Sydney.

[9] J. von Dohnanyi and C. Möller, *The Impact of Media Concentration on Journalism* (OSCE, 2003).

[10] *ibid.* pp.58–59.

[11] N. Bobbio, *The Future of Democracy* (University of Minnesota Press, 1987), p.33.

[12] H. Thorgeirsdottir, *Journalism Worthy of the Name: A Human Rights Perspective on Freedom within the Press* (Lund University, 2003).

[13] A concept used by A. Wolfe, "The Limits of Legitimacy", quoted in Bobbio, n.11 above, p.33.

[14] When John Milton was fighting for freedom of the press in the seventeenth century—his growing concern over church-state relations may be seen as analogous to the corporate-state alliance today.

This in a way is what Mill in the nineteenth century called "mental slavery"; great intellectual thinkers can thrive in such an environment[15] but "there never has been, nor ever will be, in that atmosphere, an intellectually active people".[16]

Whatever the amount of financial pressure on journalism, the mere presence of the power of the business community and the unclear division between it and the political sphere is a reminder of the much more complex ways of "interference" not prescribed by law that are present at the dawn of the twenty-first century than were at the conception of the Convention in 1950. This is why Jürgen Habermas[17] and others emphasise that the public sphere works most effectively when it is institutionally independent of the state and society's dominant forces.[18]

Journalists operating in an environment of interlocked financial and political interests are under pressure that they as a profession may never have encountered before. Although this problem has been recognised for quite some time, supra-national bodies at the Council of Europe level have emphasised self-regulation to promote responsible journalism and human rights, albeit recognising that public authorities should be aware of the "relationship with third parties who have influence on the editorial independence of the media".[19]

Legal regulation, market regulation and self-regulation

The operation of the media in society is conditioned by legal regulation, market regulation and self-regulation.[20] Legal regulation does not adequately presuppose the impact of market regulation and self-regulation within the media. It is based on the assumption that press freedom is mainly a negative liberty to be free from interference by public authorities unless the press oversteps the bounds set forth to protect other legal interests. It does not presume that market regulation and self-regulation may actively be impeding the press in carrying out its positive duties. To focus merely on legal regulation disregards several factors that have a significant impact on the operation of the media in modern societies. Despite the growing and real concern over the media's failure to perform, the most widely suggested solution to the problem of lack of journalistic integrity and editorial independence is "the voluntary enforcement of the social responsibility by the media itself".[21]

[15] Aleksandr Solzhenitsyn and Vaclav Havel are outstanding examples of such dissidents in the former Soviet Union and communist Eastern Europe in the latter half of the twentieth century.

[16] J.S. Mill, *On Liberty* (Bantam, 1993), p.40.

[17] J. Habermas, *Between Facts and Norms: Contributions to a Discourse Theory of Law and Democracy*, translated by W. Regh (The MIT Press, 1996), p.299.

[18] *cf.* E.S. Herman and R.W. Machesney, *The Global Media, The New Missionaries of Corporate Capitalism* (Cassell, London, 1997).

[19] Resolution No.2: Journalistic Freedoms and Human Rights of the 4th European Ministerial Conferences on Mass Media Policy (Prague, December 7–8, 1994).

[20] *cf.* D. Voorhoof, "From Governmental Regulation to Market Regulation? Press and the Meaning of Article 10 of the European Human Rights Convention" in K. Nordenstreng and W. Kleinwächter, eds, *CSCE and Information, Proceedings of a seminar of experts*, Tampere, April 24–27, 1992, University of Tampere, p.19.

[21] C.S. Stepp, "Access in post-social-responsibility age" in J. Lichtenberg, ed., *Democracy and the Mass Media* (Cambridge University Press, 1995), p.189.

According to Jürgen Habermas, the media ought to understand themselves as mandatory for an enlightened public whose willingness to learn and capacity for criticism they at once presuppose, demand, and reinforce; like the judiciary, they ought to preserve their independence from political and social pressures.[22] In mass communication theory, the media are widely expected to promote at least four main goals[23]:

- maintaining a constant surveillance of events, ideas and persons active in public life, leading both to a flow of information to the public and exposing violations of the moral and social order;
- providing an independent and radical critique of the society and its institutions;
- encouraging and providing the means for access, expression and participation by as many different actors and voices as is necessary and appropriate;
- contributing to shared consciousness and identity and real coherence of the community as a whole as well as its component groups.

Michael Gurevitch and Jay G. Blumer have summarised the tasks the media *ought* to fulfil in democratic societies and, amongst the ones they mention, in addition to others that accord with the above, is:

- a principled resistance to the efforts of forces outside the media to subvert their independence, integrity, and ability to serve the audience.[24]

The means by which journalists appear to assert the integrity of their conduct and the independence from external pressures are their codes of conduct. Such ethical guidelines have been adopted by most journalists' unions and are neither stipulated in law nor legally enforceable. The most wide-ranging of such codes cover areas of publicity rules, integrity of journalists with regard to outside pressures, rejection of interference by public authorities, protection from employers and advertisers, the right to refuse assignments, and separation of advertisements and editorial material.

Self-regulation is intended to achieve the impossible since it takes place in an environment where positive objectives struggle against economic aims. The European Commission on Human Rights, the present Court's predecessor, held in the case of *Lingens* against Austria that it was not only the right of journalists to criticise those in power but their duty.[25] Such jurisprudence emerges from cases where journalists have been convicted of overstepping the negative obligations of the press in not hurting the reputation of others. The press's failure in tackling issues of immense public interest when journalists censor themselves does not evolve into legal disputes since negligence in carrying out the political debate is not a wrong in the strict legal sense. The permanent conflict between the publishers' entrepreneurial right to react opportunistically to external financial and political conditions and the demands on journalists to

[22] Habermas, n.17 above, pp.378–379.

[23] D. McQuail, *McQuail's Mass Communication Theory* (4th ed., Sage Publications, 2000), p.161.

[24] M. Gurevitch and J.G. Blumer, "Political communication and democratic values" in Lichtenberg, n.21 above, p.270.

[25] *Lingens v Austria* (B/28): Commission's report, October 11, 1984, at [74].

adhere to their acclaimed responsibilities is a constant dilemma which in the end confirms the maxim that freedom of the press is limited to those who own one.[26]

Journalism is torn between the alleged legal regulation and market regulation. The European Court of Human Rights has acknowledged the fact that the media rely on the market and that it is essential for a medium to keep its audience which requires it to maintain its financing from advertising revenue; for the employees, it is a matter of their job security as journalists.[27] It is not the economic enterprise *per se*, which is protected under Art.10, but the media as a legal person attending to the vital role of the Public Watchdog. Its operation must take into account the economic logic necessary to survive and hence protect the essential means of publication.

Hightened level of seriousness in era of globalisation and relevance of international law

It is widely recognised that certain states have continued to exert and allow impermissible pressure on the media in their respective countries. The levels of harrassment may be different but the general aim is the same: to suppress pluralism and open debate on issues of concern to citizens. In many countries laws are in place, such as criminal defamation laws, which unduly restrict the right to freedom of expression. Imprisonment of journalists and the closing down of newspapers and television stations are gross violations of human rights. Journalists are killed while carrying out their jobs, even in the Member States of the Council of Europe, as evident in cases against Turkey. The European Court of Human Rights has concluded that even though journalists may be acting as propaganda tools, this does not provide justification for authorities in failing to take steps effectively to investigate and, where necessary, provide protection against unlawful acts involving violence.[28] Unfortunately the cases against Turkey are a horrendous testimonial of how little respect is shown to freedom of expression[29] and the vital role of the media when people are faced with torture and murder for airing their views publicly; this is above and beyond the usual severe penalties, long imprisonments and fines which can result in job loss.[30] In the more "civilised" Member States of the Council of Europe, the fear of expressing anti-establishment opinions does not usually carry the fear of losing one's life.[31] Most journalists are, however, aware of the fact that opinions not favoured by the "establishment" may cost them their

[26] Famous quote of journalist A.J. Liebling (1904–63). See J.A. Barron, *Freedom of the Press for Whom? The right of access to mass media* (Indiana University Press, 1973).

[27] *Groppera Radio AG v Switzerland* (A/173): (1990) 12 E.H.R.R. 321 at [49].

[28] In *Özgur Gündem v Turkey* (2000) 31 E.H.R.R. 49, the applicants claimed that the government of Turkey, directly or indirectly, sought to hinder, prevent and render impossible the production of the newspaper *Özgur Gündem* by the encouragement of or acquiescence in unlawful killings of journalists, and by failure to provide any or adequate protection of journalists when their lives were clearly in danger and despite requests for such protection. *Cf. Kilic v Turkey* (2000) 33 E.H.R.R. 58 at [85].

[29] *cf.* Committee of Ministers Interim Resolution Res DH (2001) 106: "The Court or the Committee of Ministers have notably found that the criminal convictions of the applicants [in several cases against Turkey], on account of statements contained in articles, books, leaflets or messages addressed to, or prepared for, a public audience, had violated their freedom of expression guaranteed by Article 10 of the Convention".

[30] *cf. Ceylan v Turkey* GC (1999) 30 E.H.R.R. 73; *Karatas v Turkey* [GC] (App. No.23168/94), judgment of July 8, 1999.

[31] Evidently journalists have been killed in other Member States of the Council of Europe.

388 Self-Censorship among Journalists

livelihood.[32] A common form of punishment of journalists within the media may be frequent staff changes or refusal to assign meaningful work.[33] Severe political pressure on journalists has been reported from several countries according to an OSCE survey.[34] According to the same source temptations to gag the media are not limited to the transitional societies.[35] In Germany politicians allegedly choose the journalists by whom they accept to be interviewed not on the basis of professional quality but on the level of docility.[36] It is becoming more apparent that professional journalism is facing new and disturbing challenges not only from the outside: "Direct and indirect pressure is put on journalists not to report negatively or even critically on events, institutions or people who might be important to publishers or editors and their friends from politics and industry. Such pressure often leads to 'politically correct' reporting by journalists—a euphemistic description of self-censorship."[37]

Berlusconi's immense media power and his position as Prime Minister of Italy has evoked much concern internationally as evident from a joint declaration adopted by three international mandate-holders on freedom of expression, stipulating that "elected political officials and members of government who are media owners must separate their political activities from their media interests".[38]

A recent report adopted by the EU Parliament,[39] not least with regard to concerns over the situation in Italy, stresses that a free and pluralist media is essential to freedom of expression and information. It goes on to consider that where EU Member States fail to take adequate measures the European Union has a political, moral and legal obligation to ensure within its competence that media pluralism is respected. The EU

[32] The term "establishment" is used here to emphasise the connected interests of politics and dominant economic forces in society forming an establishment, which not only determines access to public positions but often also individual opportunities in the private domain. Complying with the expectations of the establishment may be so repressive as to amount to an intrusion in a parallel manner as when public authorities in authoritarian regimes try to regulate the minds of their subjects. (The *Oxford Advanced Learner's Dictionary* defines "establishment" as "those persons in positions of power and authority, exercising influence in background of public life or other field of activity".)

[33] *cf.* J. Curran and J. Seaton, *Power without responsibility: The Press and Broadcasting in Britain* (5th ed., Routledge, 1997), pp.8290.

[34] Dohnanyi and Möller, n.9 above, p.48.

[35] *ibid.* p.50. Australian-American media tycoon Rupert Murdoch decided to end the transmission of the BBC's World Wide Service via his Hong Kong based Star Satellite TV in order to maintain good political and industrial relations with the political leadership in Bejing.

[36] *ibid.* quoting Michael Rutz, editor in chief of the German weekly newspaper *Rheinischer Merkur* in a speech on "Freedom and Pluralism of the Media", Berlin, May 30, 2003, p.51.

[37] *ibid.* p.55.

[38] Joint Statements of the International Mechanisms for Promoting Freedom of Expression, November 2001, Internet and Broadcasting; Security and Countering Terrorism. International Mechanisms for Promoting Freedom of Expression, the UN Special Rapporteur on Freedom of Opinion and Expression, the OSCE Representative on Freedom of the Media and the OAS Special Rapporteur on Freedom of Expression (Having met with representatives of NGOs, UNESCO, journalists' associations and human rights experts in London on November 19–20, 2001, under the auspices of Article 19, Global Campaign for Free Expression, assisted by Canadian Journalists for Free Expression).

[39] Report on the risks of violation, in the EU and especially in Italy, of freedom of expression and information (Art.11(2) of the Charter of Fundamental Rights) (2003/2237(INI)) Doc.A5–0230/2004 Procedure: Own-initiative Debate: April 20, Vote: April 22, 2004.

report noted that the situtation within many of the Member States is characterised by a high level of concentration in the media market in both television and press sectors, as in the Netherlands. In Sweden the media is characterised by a fairly high degree of cross-media ownership and interlocking ownership structures between major players in the audiovisual field. As regards Italy, the EU Parliament said "there could be a risk of breaches of the right to freedom of expression and information". The Parliament noted that "the level of concentration of the television market is currently the highest within Europe". It noted "therefore, that the Italian system presents an anomaly owing to a unique combination of economic, political and media power in the hands of one man—the current President of the Italian Council of Ministers". The report emphasised that the EU Constitution should contain a provision on the need to ensure pluralism in the media and encouraged Member States to incorporate into their constitutions an active duty to promote respect for freedom and diversity in the media.

Although it is questionable to speak of a coherent European media policy it is safe to assert that pluralism of voices and opinions is an absolute European standard. The Council of Europe's Committee of Ministers has stressed that states should promote political and cultural pluralism by developing their media policy in line with Art.10 ECHR, which guarantees freedom of expression and information, and due respect for the principle of independence of the media.[40]

Article 11(2) of the EU Charter of Human Rights provides that the freedom and pluralism of the media shall be respected. Major mergers and business failures in the press sector were already the focus of attention by the Council of Europe in the 1970s.[41] The Council of Europe's Committee of Ministers in a 1999 recommendation on measures to promote media pluralism recalled that the existence of a multiplicity of autonomous and independent media outlets at various levels enhanced pluralism and democracy. The potential shortcoming of existing media pluralism is attributed to the existing regulatory frameworks focusing on traditional media. It is noted that dominant positions and increased media concentration are furthered by convergence between differing sectors. Increased transparency as regards the control of media enterprises is viewed as a contribution to the existence of a pluralistic media landscape. Editorial independence of newsrooms is to be achieved mainly through external regulation of ownership of broadcasting and the press in the same way as licences given to private broadcasters are meant to condition them to promote diversity of views in the discharge of "their mission".[42] When it comes to freedom within the media, the recommendation encourages media organisations to strengthen editorial and journalistic independence *voluntarily* through editorial statutes or *other self-regulatory means*. With a view to enhancing media pluralism and diversity, Member

[40] Recommendation No.R (99) 1 of the Committee of Ministers to Member States on Measures to Promote Media Pluralism (Adopted by the Committee of Ministers on January 19, 1999, at the 656th meeting of the Ministers' Deputies).

[41] 6th European Ministerial Conference on Mass Media Policy, Cracow (Poland), June 15–16, 2000, "A media policy for tomorrow", MCM (2000)3.

[42] *cf. Informationsverein Lentia v Austria* (A/276): (1993) 17 E.H.R.R. 93 at [38]. The Court reiterated that the third sentence of Art.10(1) gives scope to authorities to grant licences on conditions other than technological.

390 Self-Censorship among Journalists

States are encouraged to consider financial support schemes for both the print and broadcast media.[43]

The most radical contribution to this discussion clearly favouring action within the media came from the Parliamentary Assembly of the Council of Europe in Resolution 1003 (1993), emphasising that journalism is a part of a corporate structure and that legitimate respect for publisher's and owner's ideological orientations is limited by the absolute requirements on truthful news reporting and ethical opinions to respect the citizen's fundamental right to information.[44] Resolution 1003 recommended that rules governing editorial staff should regulate relations between the journalists and the publishers and proprietors within the media separately from the normal requirements of labour relations.[45] It furthermore made clear that "entrepreneurial objectives have to be limited by the conditions for providing access to a fundamental right".[46] Subsequently the resolution emphasised the relationship between ethics and self-regulation where self-regulatory bodies or mechanisms must be set up for issuing resolutions on respect for ethical precepts in journalism, with prior commitment on the part of the media to publish the relevant resolutions.

The European Federation of Journalists called for common minimum standards of editorial independence in 1993, which should apply in all media throughout Europe.[47] In the aftermath of September 11, 2001, three international mandate holders on freedom of expression adopted a joint declaration encouraging media owners and media professionals to conclude agreements to guarantee editorial independence.[48] It was emphasised that commercial considerations should not unduly influence media content.

It is a common assumption that a well-functioning economic market is sufficient to secure an independent, free and pluralistic press. At most we need competition law to break up monopolies.[49] Constitutional scholars have pointed to the fact that despite quite strict, long standing anti-trust rules in the United States; programmes in the media are very homogenous.[50] The need to enhance business opportunities and maintain the establishment's goodwill does not disappear with an increased number of media outlets, rendering the requirement legally to guarantee responsible journalism within the media even more urgent.

A distinction must be drawn between what Fiss calls "market determined" or "democratically determined" speech on the one hand and the First Amendment goal of "uninhibited, robust and wide-open" public debate. He rightly emphasises that neither

[43] See n.40 above.

[44] Parliamentary Assembly of the Council of Europe, Resolution 1003 (1993) on the ethics of journalism, Doc.6854, para.10.

[45] *ibid.* para.32.

[46] *ibid.* para.11.

[47] The journalists' unions from 15 European countries do not distinguish between the printed press and broadcasting when requesting a guarantee for editorial independence within the media. The EFJ/IFJ Milan Declaration on Editorial Democracy in European Media (*www.ifj.org/regions/europe/milan*).

[48] See n.38 above.

[49] *cf.* C.R. Sunstein, *Democracy and the Problem of Free Speech* (Free Press paperback edition, 1995), p.3.

[50] *cf.* E. Barendt, "Access to the Media in Western Europe" in A. Sajó and M. Price, eds, *Rights of Access to the Media* (Kluwer Law International, 1996), p.109.

the market nor the majority choice may guarantee the above. Democracy ascribes the ultimate responsibility to the public on the presumption that people have adequate information. If the press plays its vital role the public is aware of the contending or conflicting points at issue. Suppose people are not interested in the political debate and choose mind-dulling entertainment, or newspapers or television programmes that give expressions to their sexual fantasies? According to Fiss, democracy is not to respect such a choice any more than a commitment to contractual freedom requires one to respect a contract in which someone sells himself into slavery.[51] He contends that the "robust public debate" should be seen as the standard against which the output of the market should be measured. A democratically determined speech may not result in a pluralistic political agenda since to survive in the market the media must please those who really run the show.

In recent years, governments and supra-national bodies have encouraged national and multi-national media corporations to promote self-regulation. Voluntary regulation through codes of ethics can take place in a single medium, mainly newspapers, or at the level of the entire profession, in some cases through press councils. The prevailing assumption is that journalists and editors submit their decisions under critical examination in an intellectual manner and that the blinkers that prejudice, self-interest and ignorance impose on the motives of rational people are distant. The self-regulatory bodies are to function as *a posteriori* supervision or barometer in individual news-related cases, guaranteeing recognition of content as a part of public accountability. This voluntary conduct is typically applicable in cases where editorial discretion is crucial in evaluating the thin red line that should not be crossed to protect other important rights rather than guaranteeing that the press is making an effort to provide far-reaching criticism of the establishment. It is however questionable how voluntary regulation can protect journalists in resistance to the efforts of forces outside the media to subvert their independence, integrity, and ability to serve the audience.[52] Public authorities are delegating the matter to private bodies, hoping thus to solve the issue. In so doing, governments are privatising censorship without assuming responsibility and accountability for it themselves, and without offering legal redress either for those who censor themselves or for the public robbed of its right to receive information and ideas of legitimate concern.

II. Does the Convention provide an answer to the problems within the media?

Although freedom of the press is not mentioned in Art.10(1), a great deal of the case law of the European Court of Human Rights concerns journalists and the proper functioning of the media. Press freedom is certainly part of the overall protection offered by Art.10 and rests on the same foundation as the individual freedom of expression. The imparting process itself, however, requires a separate theory and justification.[53] Whether one looks at the protection afforded by Art.10 as just protecting freedoms and not rights, media freedom is of little value unless viewed in a societal context where everyone can benefit from it. It is quite clear from jurisprudence concerning Art.10 that the Convention aims at a far broader protection of the media

[51] O.M. Fiss, "Building a Free Press" in Sajó and Price, *ibid.* p.92.
[52] Thorgeirsdottir, n.12 above.
[53] *cf.* G. Marshall, "Press freedom and free speech theory" [1992] P.L. 40.

than the traditional conception of this freedom proposed. Even those holding extreme liberal views of media freedom as a purely negative liberty accept some form of state interference to protect individuals against being harmed by others. The principle of freedom of expression is thus far from absolute. The guarantee afforded by Art.10 ECHR is reflected in the jurisprudence that has emerged from the case law of the Court and the former Commission of Human Rights. The principle itself, applying both to natural as well as legal persons, opens the ground for conflicting interests between practising journalists, the receivers among the public, the individual subjects of journalism and the owners and the publishers of the media who may have their own agenda to pursue. The character of Art.10 is mysterious, protecting both the natural instinct of individual expression in every conceivable form at the same time as it is loaded with the weight of civil and political obligations in society, giving it a character of a collective right rather than just an individual freedom. It protects the civil right of the individual not to be interfered with by the state. At the same time it protects the right of the citizen to be enlightened, calling into question the positive obligation of authorities to ensure that process. It hands out a promise of citizen access to the governing process through democratic procedures, where the media serves a major role, shedding light on the indivisibility of all human rights whether of economic, social or cultural origin. The freedoms protected in Art.10 are useful only in the context of a social and economic structure where there is a sufficient range of choices. Accordingly, the freedoms of opinion, expression, imparting and receiving information and ideas are a collective rather than merely an individual good.

When the case law is scrutinized with regard to Art.10 it becomes clear that freedom of the press is not merely the freedom to found a newspaper free of licensing, or to be free from discriminatory taxation or public interference. The press is more than a marketable commodity. There is much tension between the conception of the press as a private enterprise subject to the logic of the market and the press as an instrument of democracy. The instrumental value of press freedom is, to begin with, defined in terms of the paramount protection that the Court has afforded to political speech.[54] The press may not overstep certain bounds at the same time, as it must adhere to its duty of informing the public. The press has the task of informing the public properly[55] and to that extent setting things in analytical context.[56] In order to do so journalism must be daring and not hesitate to go against accepted views,[57] as the importance of political opposition is crucial in democracy.[58] Journalistic conduct involves shocking and disturbing sections of the population to shed light on various sides of reality. Concerning the importance in processing information or putting it into perspective, the Court has expressly rejected the contention that "the task of the press [is] to impart information, the interpretation of which ha[s] to be left primarily to the reader".[59] This is a notable description of the role of the press, assigning an active role of interpretation of facts to the journalists. It is accordingly not enough to submit the information in the

[54] *Lingens v Austria (No.2)* (1986) 8 E.H.R.R. 407; *Observer and Guardian v United Kingdom* (1991) 14 E.H.R.R. 553.

[55] *Sunday Times v United Kingdom (No.1)* (1979) 2 E.H.R.R. 245.

[56] *Lingens v Austria*, n.54 above, at [30].

[57] *Handyside v United Kingdom* (1976) 1 E.H.R.R. 737 at [49].

[58] *Castells v Spain* (1992) 14 E.H.R.R. 445.

[59] *Lingens v Austria*, n.54 above, at [30].

form of news as spare parts on a conveyor belt. The media is responsible for putting facts into context within an analytical framework, grasping a complex situation in a nutshell. This requires not only a voluntary press, but is also a requirement of journalists and their capability, skilfulness and competence. The Court attaches the highest importance to the freedom of expression in the context of political debate and considers that very strong reasons are required to justify restrictions on political speech.[60] The media cannot achieve its democratic goals without representing conflicting views in society.[61] The Commission has submitted that the very function of the press in a democratic society is to "participate in the political processes".[62] The Committee of Ministers in a declaration in February 2004 emphasised the need to protect political debate, reaffirming the pre-eminent importance of freedom of expression and information, in particular through free and independent media, for guaranteeing the right of the public to be informed on matters of public concern.[63] The text reaffirms the right of the media to disseminate negative information and critical opinions concerning political figures and institutions. It states that the humorous and satirical genre allows an even wider degree of exaggeration and provocation, as long as the public is not misled about the facts. The declaration echoed the general principles set forth in the European Court of Human Rights case law concerning journalism, emphasising the special duties and responsibilites of journalists.

The Court speaks of the "vital role"[64] of the Public Watchdog and its rightful role.[65] The concept of the Public Watchdog has, however, evaded a clear legal definition, despite its recurrent usage in Convention jurisprudence. The media in a democratic society *is* "a purveyor of information and Public Watchdog".[66] By demarcating the role of the media with such a distinctive term the Court is accordingly assigning a role to journalism which is to be taken seriously, in particular where, through the press, it serves to impart information and ideas of general interest.[67] A fundamental principle in interpreting Art.10 is that the press has a duty to impart—in a manner consistent with its obligations and responsibilities—matters of public concern, hence freedom within the press "affords the public one of the best means of discovering indispensable part of the democratic system, given its task of enlightening the public".[68]

The meaning of the fiduciary duty in American First Amendment jurisprudence

It is undeniable that the wealth of American Supreme Court case law concerning freedom of speech and freedom of the press as protected under the First Amendment to the US Constitution has had significant impact on jurisprudence elsewhere,

[60] *Feldek v Slovakia* (2000) 30 E.H.R.R. 291 at [83].

[61] *Handyside v United Kingdom*, n.57 above.

[62] *Z v Switzerland* (1984) 6 E.H.R.R. 367.

[63] Council of Europe, Committee of Ministers, Declaration on Freedom of political debate in the media, adopted by the Committee of Ministers on February 12, 2004 at the 872nd meeting of the Ministers' Deputies.

[64] *Observer and Guardian v United Kingdom*, n.54 above, at [59(b)].

[65] *cf. Dalban v Romania* (1999) 31 E.H.R.R. 39 at [49]; *Bladet Troms{Swedish o} and Stensaas v Norway* (1999) 29 E.H.R.R. 125 at [59].

[66] *Lingens v Austria*, n.54 above, at [44].

[67] *Informationsverein Lentia v Austria*, n.42 above, at [38].

[68] *Sunday Times v the United Kingdom*, n.55 above, at [65].

including that of the European Court of Human Rights. In 1975 Justice Potter Stewart of the US Supreme Court pointed out that the press clause in the First Amendment was in essence a structural provision, extending protection to an institution, adding: "The publishing business is, in short, the only organized business that is given constitutional protection".[69] The Constitutional guarantee was not merely to guarantee newspaper publishers freedom of expression. If the free press guarantee meant no more than freedom of expression or the same as individual freedom of speech it would be a constitutional redundancy. The primary purpose of the press clause, according to Justice Stewart, was "to create a fourth institution outside the government as an additional check on the three official branches", the relevant metaphor being the Fourth Estate.[70] Chief Justice Burger of the US Supreme Court described the fiduciary duty of the press in 1976:

> "That the extraordinary protections afforded by the First Amendment carry with them something in the nature of a *fiduciary duty* to exercise the protected rights responsibly—a duty widely acknowledged but not always observed by editors and publishers."[71]

Due to the changed nature of the modern media, the claim that newspapers must be surrogates of the public interest carries with it a concomitant fiduciary obligation to account for that stewardship. The political peril of the phenomenon of self-censorship has been highlighted in US First Amendment jurisprudence from the early twentieth century. Justice Brennan wrote, in what has been termed "the most far reaching, extraordinary and beautiful decisions in American history"[72]:

> "[T]he pall of fear and timidity imposed upon those who would give voice to public criticism is an atmosphere in which the First Amendment freedoms cannot survive."[73]

The famous *New York Times v Sullivan* decision has left the impression that adversary journalists and the media should be considered an official "fourth branch" of the American government. Freedom of the press, on this understanding, protects not a private right but rather a public function.[74] Journalists are the professionals who carry out the fiduciary role—"holding citizenship in trust for us".[75] The *Sullivan* decision with its now classic phrase of the "uninhibited, robust and wide-open" debate has become the guiding purpose of the First Amendment—and even of Art.10 ECHR —making one contemplate whether the state might have more of a role to play in regulating the press than had been previously allowed.[76]

[69] P. Stewart, "Or of the Press" [1975] 26 *Hastings Law Journal* 631, reprinted in K. Middleton and R. Mersky, eds, *Freedom of Expression, A collection of best writings* (Buffalo, New York, 1981), p.425.

[70] *ibid*. The quoted excerpt is in F.S. Haiman, *Speech and Law in a Free Society* (The University of Chicago Press, 1981), p.11.

[71] *Nebraska Association v Stuart*, 427 U.S. 539 (1976). Emphasis added.

[72] Famous attorney Floyd Abrams, 10 *Media Law Report*, para.17, April 24, 1984, News Notes, quoted in D.L. Teeter, D.R. Le Duc and B. Loving, *Law of Mass Communications: Freedom and Control of Print and Broadcast Media* (9th ed., Foundation Press, 1998), p.214.

[73] *New York Times Co v Sullivan*, 376 U.S. 254 (1964).

[74] *ibid*.

[75] Schudson, quoted in McQuail, n.23 above, p.159.

[76] *cf*. O.M. Fiss, *The Irony of Free Speech* (Harvard University Press, 1996), p.52.

There have been two major concerns related to this discussion. One concern is that the media, due to its role in conducting investigative journalism, needs added protection. The other concern is that "a higher constitutional status" for the established press "would present practical and conceptual difficulties" and go against the constitutional guarantee of freedom of expression for all.[77]

At the dawn of the twenty-first century the conception of the Public Watchdog resembles US Supreme Court Justice Stewart's theory of the Fourth Estate, set forth in 1975. At the time there was no established case law on the press in the Convention's jurisprudence.[78] The landmark case of the *Sunday Times* against the United Kingdom marked the beginning of the European Court of Human Rights' instrumental view of the press in democratic society where it was explicitly stated that the press has a duty to guard the public interest. The growing case law since has incrementally developed the substantial guarantee that Art.10 ECHR affords the press in attending to its obligations and the state's role in guaranteeing the public's right to receive.

In *Informationsverein Lentia v Austria*, the Court minimised the threat of private monopolies, when it stated: "In many States of a comparable size to Austria, in which the coexistence of private and public stations, according to rules which vary from country to country and accompanied by measures preventing the development of private monopolies, shows the fears expressed [by the Austrian government] to be groundless".[79] All the same it stressed the fundamental role of freedom of expression in a democratic society, adding:

> "[I]n particular where, through the press, it serves to impart information and ideas of general interest, which the public is moreover entitled to receive. Such an undertaking cannot be successfully accomplished unless it is grounded in the principle of pluralism, of which the State is the ultimate guarantor. This observation is especially valid in relation to audio-visual media, whose programmes are often broadcast very widely."[80]

The decisive stand of the Court is illustrative of its dynamic interpretation of Art.10 and the criterion that pluralism is indispensable for press freedom. This finding, however, seems at the same time to be based on the presumption that journalists or editors have "regulative control" to ensure what is written and what is not[81] and that the outcome is responsive to the editorial staff only, *i.e.* journalists and editors have control over what is published/reported independent of corporate contexts. Given the pre-eminent role of the press in democratic society the Court acknowledges its right to battle against the powerful, yet without sufficient guarantee that the press will, or stands a chance to, succeed.

[77] Justice White in *Branzburg v Hayes*, 408 U.S. 665 (1972), at 726.

[78] Only the case of *De Becker v Belgium* (1962) 1 E.H.R.R. 43 (struck off the list) concerning a lifelong prohibition on the applicant in Belgium from exercising the professions of journalist and author.

[79] *Informationsverein Lentia v Austria*, n.42 above, at [42].

[80] *ibid.* at [38]. Citations omitted. Emphasis added.

[81] P.A. French, *Corporate Ethics* (Harcourt, Brace & Company, 1995), p.43.

396 Self-Censorship among Journalists

Is the act of self-censorship within the media a breach of Art.10?

The Court expects journalists to exercise voluntary regulation. If journalists, on the basis of their specific function, do not regulate their conduct in congruity with the codes of ethics, they are not worthy of Art.10 protection.[82] In a recent case the Court reiterated the "great importance" it attaches to the fact that journalists "act in accordance with the rules governing the journalist profession".[83] Evidently it goes against the grain of the media as a business enterprise to disseminate information that may harm its interests. The media enterprise as a legal person enjoys protection under Art.10, even in its profit motive, but the owners and publishers are also vicariously subject to the "duties and responsibilities" which authors take on when they disseminate their opinions to the public.[84] If media owners or the journalists' superiors impede their staff in telling the truth when of legitimate public concern, then the media as a legal person forfeits its Art.10 protection.[85]

Self-regulation, according to some, should lighten the burden of the government's executive and legislative work.[86] There have been attempts to give self-regulation an analogous status to some external control. Sublime rhetoric is used to describe the alleged regulation as "a regulatory activity carried out by specific organizational units in order to eliminate incorrect behaviour within their internal structures from which they operate".[87] It is reasoned that the key factor is the involvement of journalists in the regulatory process, relying on their codes of ethics, which are not subject to public power of enforcement, and on the fact that journalists scrutinise each other's behaviour to ascertain whether it complies with standards and norms.[88] This view of self-regulation is based on the presumption that individual responsibility can fill the legal void. It accentuates the "necessary" self-restraint by the state as part of protecting the negative freedom within the media. It is also based on the presumption that journalists or editors have "regulative control" to ensure what is written and what is not and that the outcome is responsive to the editorial staff only. Hence, "if the [journalistic] profession regulates its own affairs, the state has no reason or excuse to intervene".[89]

In a study on self-regulation within the EU Member States, Ukrow assesses its relevance under Art.10 ECHR, accentuating the positive dimension of the Convention in obliging its contracting parties to create legal conditions in compliance with the "constitutive/institutional function" of the media.[90] The use of this term is in all likelihood analogous to the adjectival phrase "instrumental value of the media", as it presupposes the democratic mission of the press as the Public Watchdog. He points to

[82] *Perna v Italy* (App. No.48898/99), judgment of July 25, 2001 at [40].

[83] *Lopez Gomes da Silva v Portugal* (2002) 34 E.H.R.R. 56.

[84] *Öztürk v Turkey* [GC] (App. No.22479/93), judgment of September 28, 1999.

[85] *Goodwin v United Kingdom* (1996) 22 E.H.R.R. 123 at [39]; *Bergens Tidende v Norway* (2001) 31 E.H.R.R. 16 at [53].

[86] Conclusions of the Experts' Seminar on media self-regulation held in Saarbrücken, April 19–21, 1999.

[87] J. Ukrow, *Self-regulation in the Media Sector and European Community Law: an independent study of European Law*, prepared at the request of the Federal Commissioner for Cultural Affairs and the Media at the Institute of European Media Law, 1999, p.15.

[88] *ibid.* p.14.

[89] *ibid.* p.5.

[90] *ibid.* p.88.

the positive obligations that arise from Art.10 and the obligation of Member States to shape their legal systems in a way that conforms to the Convention and states that its scope also applies to relationships between individuals. This positive dimension of Art.10 is therefore important for self-regulation within the media. For if self-regulation is inadequate in ensuring the public interest then the Member State in question is in breach of its guarantee for "openness" in the communication process. He goes on to ask if only laws in the formal sense are capable of restricting the rights described in Art.10(1), which he says cannot be answered beyond doubt on the basis of the wording of Art.10(2). He points to the Court's case law where professional codes have been regarded as laws[91] as well as unwritten law.[92] With the same reasoning, Ukrow provides, restrictions on media freedom through self-regulation might be classified as legal reservations under Art.10(2). Journalists may abuse their scope under self-regulation to restrict the imparting process protected under Art.10(1). They may impose excessive restrictions on themselves, filtering and withholding information, which may call democracy as a whole into question. "Admittedly", he continues, "it is questionable where the legal system draws the line in this regard."[93] Since a comprehensive approach of "the duty of information has not yet managed to win acceptance", he leaves the argument there, referring to the Court's case law in *Leander* and *Gaskin*.[94] In these cases the Court held that the right to receive information basically prohibits authorities from restricting a person from receiving information that others may be willing to impart to him. Furthermore, the Court held that Art.10 does not embody an obligation on the government to impart such information to the individual.[95] These cases concerned an individual's right of access to a register containing information on his personal position. The points at issue were thus far from debating the instrumental value of press freedom in democratic society. In cases touching directly upon the role of the press the Court has stressed the importance of journalistic duties, stating that "the public has a right to receive information as a corollary of the specific function of journalists, which is to impart information and ideas on matters of public interest".[96]

As the Court does not subscribe to the view that Art.10 imposes on states a duty to make available information to the public[97] it is in fact conferring upon private parties, individual journalists and media enterprises a role with which it does not want to burden the state. The Court has held that a state cannot absolve itself from responsibility by delegating its obligations to private bodies or individuals.[98] More recent case law emphasises that authorities may entrust the responsibility of carrying out fundamental rights to private parties. The state must, however, achieve the result called for by the

[91] *Barthold v Federal Republic of Germany* (1985) 7 E.H.R.R. 383.

[92] *Sunday Times v United Kingdom*, n.55 above.

[93] Ukrow, n.87 above, p.99.

[94] *Leander v Sweden* (1987) 9 E.H.R.R. 433; *Gaskin v United Kingdom* (1990) 12 E.H.R.R. 36.

[95] *Leander v Sweden*, *ibid.* at [74].

[96] *Guerra v Italy* (1998) 26 E.H.R.R. 357 at [53]; *Observer and Guardian v United Kingdom*, n.54 above, at [59]; *Thorgeirson v Iceland* (1992) 4 E.H.R.R. 843 at [63].

[97] *Guerra v Italy*, *ibid.* at [53].

[98] *Costello-Roberts v United Kingdom* (1995) 19 E.H.R.R. 112.

Convention.[99] Under Art.1 ECHR, states shall secure to everyone within their jurisdiction the rights and freedoms defined in the Convention. If self-regulation within the media is inadequate the state must ensure its effectiveness by intervening in a process that is not rendering the desired result.

The requirement of a democratic necessity to interfere with the Art.10(1) rights corresponds to the principle of proportionality and indicates the existence of a pressing social need where the model of democratic society is to be the guide. The press must be able to 'play its vital role of the Public Watchdog' and the rights of others constitute a legitimate aim of restriction of the media's activities.[1]

The government may be accused of restricting the rights of others by not affording adequate protection to the willing imparter, the journalist in his effort to do his duty. If self-regulation works to the effect of silencing the press and its journalists, reference may be made to the Court's criteria of restrictions "prescribed by law" where the professional codes are violated. The case law has provided the codes with a legal basis although they do not have the status of a legal standard within the legal systems of the Member States. The Court has made adherence to the codes a condition for Art.10 protection. Breach of the codes is hence an infringement of activity "prescribed by law". The codes of conduct adopted by journalists' unions within the Member States of the Council of Europe might serve as an appropriate legal basis for action against those preventing the codes' effectiveness.

Conclusion

Self-censorship within the media is a serious threat to the democratic objective ascribed to the press of imparting matters of legitimate public interest. The voluntary enforcement of journalistic codes of ethics is acknowledged in the Court's jurisprudence as a legitimate way of regulating affairs within the media. It does not, however, exclude other forms of regulation. To solve the predicament of the media's "iron cage" the remedies need to be confined to journalistic activities within the media, in agreement with the prescribed obligations required of the Public Watchdog in Convention jurisprudence. If the Member States of the Council of Europe entrust private companies with the responsibility of guaranteeing the respect of basic rights, the Court does not object, as long as the contracting states achieve the results called for by the Convention.[2]

The duty to seek the truth in matters of public interest, involves the difficult task of exposing corruption in high places. The duty in that context is a burden due to the press's economic logic. Self-regulation is hence not succeeding in the task of conducting constant surveillance of public life with significant analysis providing an independent and radical critique of society and its institutions. Editors and journalists are concerned about being perceived by the public as professionals with a code of ethics and a sense of public responsibility. Journalists are, however, not able to defend their imparting rights and the corollary right of the public to an adequately responsible press. The ethical rules made by the profession itself do not provide the shield journalists need to carry out their positive duties. Restrictions on the information flow due to self-

[99] *Vgt Verein gegen Tierfabriken v Switzerland* (2001) 34 E.H.R.R. 4 at [78].
[1] *Observer and Guardian v United Kingdom*, n.54 above, at [59].
[2] *Vgt Verein gegen Tierfabriken v Switzerland*, n.99 above, at [78].

regulation may, however, qualify as legal restrictions under Art.10(2), hence rendering the state liable for not guaranteeing the fundamental right of journalists and the public's right to receive information and ideas on matters of crucial importance. "Insufficient legal and political safeguards for the practice of the right which is the absolute prerequisite for a functioning democracy"[3] is a breach of the Convention by the state itself as is the negligence of allowing third parties to crush the fundamental rights of others. It may require a creative understanding of the Convention to accept the view that it is necessary to legislate on activities within the media to afford press safeguards that are practical and effective.

[3] In the words of the former Parliamentary Assembly of the Council of Europe President, Lord Russel-Johnston, Strasbourg, May 3, 2001.

Part III
Freedom of the Press and Libel Law

[8]

Libel and Press Self-Censorship

David A. Anderson*

I. Introduction

The Supreme Court in the past decade has created an entirely new system of liability for defamation. Until 1964, when *New York Times Co. v. Sullivan*[1] was decided, the victim of a defamatory statement was entitled to recover unless the defendant could prove the truth of his statement—and sometimes his good motives as well[2]—or establish that he had a privilege to publish the statement in question and had not abused that privilege.[3] Malice was presumed,[4] as, in many cases, was damage to the victim's reputation.[5] The publisher's care was im-

* Assistant Professor of Law, The University of Texas. A.B. 1962, Harvard College; J.D. 1971, The University of Texas. The author wishes to express his appreciation to Dean John W. Wade of Vanderbilt University, whose analysis has been most helpful, particularly in dealing with the adaptation of negligence concepts to defamation and the actionability of statements of opinion.

1. 376 U.S. 254 (1964).

2. *E.g.*, Perry v. Hearst Corp., 334 F.2d 800 (1st Cir. 1964); Standke v. B.E. Darby & Sons, Inc., 291 Minn. 468, 193 N.W.2d 139 (1971); Zeck v. Spiro, 52 Misc. 2d 629, 276 N.Y.S.2d 395 (Sup. Ct. 1966). In most states, statutes make truth a defense, sometimes with the qualification that publication must have been for justifiable purposes or good motives. C. Angoff, The Book of Libel (rev. ed. 1966), contains a state-by-state compilation of state constitutional and statutory provisions relevant to defamation, including statutes providing that truth shall be a defense.

3. *E.g.*, Phoenix Newspapers, Inc., v. Choisser, 82 Ariz. 271, 312 P.2d 150 (1957) (privilege to report on public meeting); Slocinski v. Radwan, 83 N.H. 501, 144 A. 787 (1929) (privilege to protect common interest of group); Campbell v. New York Evening Post, 245 N.Y. 320, 157 N.E. 153 (1927) (privilege to report official proceedings); Shenkman v. O'Malley, 2 App. Div. 2d 567, 157 N.Y.S.2d 290 (1956) (privilege to defend own interests). All of these privileges were qualified; the plaintiff could defeat such a privilege by showing that the defendant had abused it, *e.g.*, by circulating the defamatory statement more widely than necessary to accomplish the purposes of the privilege, or by publishing for an improper motive. Some privileges, however, were absolute; *i.e.*, if the occasion was privileged, the defendant's state of mind and conduct were irrelevant. *See, e.g.*, Barr v. Matteo, 360 U.S. 564 (1959) (statements of executive agency head absolutely privileged); Scott v. Stansfield, L.R. 3 Ex. 220 (1868) (defamatory statements of judge absolutely privileged).

4. *E.g.*, Times Publishing Co. v. Carlisle, 94 F. 762 (8th Cir. 1899); Bromage v. Prosser, 107 Eng. Rep. 1051 (1825).

5. *E.g.*, First Nat'l Bank v. N.R. McFall & Co., 144 Ark 149, 222 S.W. 40 (1920); Hinkle v. Alexander, 244 Ore. 267, 417 P.2d 586 (1966). This presumption was abandoned, and the plaintiff was required to show "special damages" in the case of statements not considered libelous per se. *See, e.g*, Hoeck v. Tiedebohl, 74 N.M. 146, 391 P.2d 651 (1964); Jordan v. Lewis, 20 App. Div. 2d 773, 247 N.Y.S.2d 650 (1964). This distinction produced the famous, bitter, and unproductive argument over "libel per quod." *Compare* Prosser, *Libel Per Quod*, 46 Va. L. Rev. 839 (1960), *with* Eldredge, *The Spurious Rule of Libel Per Quod*, 79 Harv. L. Rev. 733 (1966); Prosser, *More Libel Per Quod*, 79 Harv. L. Rev. 1629 (1966), *with* Eldredge, *Variations on Libel Per Quod*, 25 Vand. L. Rev. 79 (1972).

Libel and Self-Censorship

material; he could be liable even though he had exercised every conceivable precaution.[6] This was assumed to be of no first amendment concern, because the Court had said repeatedly in dicta that libelous words were not protected by the Constitution.[7]

In 1975, after *Gertz v. Robert Welch, Inc.*,[8] the victim of defamation finds himself in a quite different world. He may recover[9] only if he can prove (1) that the statement is false; (2) that the defendant is chargeable with some quantum of fault in publishing it; and (3) that the statement actually injured the plaintiff's reputation.[10] If the victim is a public person (a public official or a "public figure"), he has an even heavier burden of proof: he must meet the *Times* requirement of demonstrating with "convincing clarity" that the defendant published knowing the statement to be false, or with reckless disregard of its truth or falsity.[11]

Until *Gertz*, all of the Court's incursions into the defamation field had the effect of protecting the press from libel judgments.[12] *Gertz*,

6. The leading case is Jones v. E. Hulton & Co., [1909] 2 K.B. 444, *aff'd*, [1910] A.C. 20. A newspaper that published a story about a fictitious "Artemus Jones" was held liable for 1750 pounds in damages to a real "Artemus Jones," whose existence was unknown to the newspaper. Prosser commented, "The effect of this strict liability is to place the printed, written or spoken word in the same class with the use of explosives or the keeping of dangerous animals." W. PROSSER, HANDBOOK OF THE LAW OF TORTS § 113, at 773 (4th ed. 1971).

7. *See* cases cited in New York Times Co. v. Sullivan, 376 U.S. 254, 268 n.6 (1964).

8. 418 U.S. 323 (1974).

9. The term "recover" here refers to an award of monetary damages. It is conceivable that a plaintiff might be permitted to obtain a declaratory judgment or nominal damages without meeting the minimal requirements of *Gertz*. *See* text accompanying notes 244-49 *infra*.

10. The *Gertz* Court required that actual injury be shown "at least when liability is not based on a showing of knowledge of falsity or reckless disregard for the truth," 418 U.S. at 349, *i.e.*, at least when the *Times* test, 376 U.S. at 279-80, is not met. Thus, the question of whether presumed or punitive damages will be allowed if the plaintiff can carry the *Times* burden of proof is left open. *See* text accompanying notes 230-43 *infra*.

The Court has not expressly held that the burden of proving falsity rests with the plaintiff, but it would seem that in order to meet his burden of showing negligence or recklessness with respect to falsity, the plaintiff necessarily must also prove falsity. But see Cox Broadcasting Co. v. Cohn, 43 U.S.L.W. 4343, 4350 (U.S. Mar. 3, 1975), which asserts that the Court has left open the question whether the Constitution requires the states to recognize a defense of truth in defamation actions brought by private individuals. If the Court has not even decided that truth must be allowed as a defense, then a fortiori it has not decided that plaintiff must prove falsity. A sounder view is expressed by Justice Powell, concurring in *Cohn*: ". . . in cases in which the interests sought to be protected are similar to those considered in *Gertz*, I view that opinion as requiring that the truth be recognized as a complete defense." *Id.* at 4353.

11. 376 U.S. at 278-80.

12. *See* notes 143-48 *infra* & accompanying text.

however, represents a retrenchment. The Court took two modest steps forward and one large step backward. It enhanced press protection by holding that first amendment interests preclude the states from imposing liability without fault and from awarding presumed or punitive damages, at least absent a showing of reckless or knowing falsity. But the Court severely constricted press protection by refusing to apply the *Times* privilege to persons who, although not public officials or public figures, are involved in matters of public or general concern.[13]

The *Times* Court's conclusion that a constitutional privilege is necessary to protect uninhibited public debate[14] has been widely approved.[15] Attention has focused on the desirability of extending the privilege to other kinds of plaintiffs, such as private persons and those claiming invasion of privacy,[16] and on the need to retain some protection for reputation.[17] It has been assumed that, since *Times* has made recovery more difficult for potential plaintiffs, it must have been equally successful in alleviating the self-censorship pressures on potential defendants. That assumption may not be justified; the system of constitutional privileges may have diminished the protection afforded to reputation without adequately protecting the public from the danger of press[18] self-censorship.

The *Times* privilege has failed to prevent self-censorship primarily because it does little to reduce the cost of defending against libel claims. Instead, it perpetuates a system of censorship by libel law-

13. 418 U.S. at 342-50.

14. 376 U.S. at 270.

15. *See, e.g.*, T. EMERSON, THE SYSTEM OF FREEDOM OF EXPRESSION 529 (1970); Kalven, *The* New York Times *Case: A Note on "The Central Meaning of the First Amendment,"* 1964 SUP. CT. REV. 191; Pedrick, *Freedom of the Press and the Law of Libel: The Modern Revised Translation*, 49 CORNELL L.Q. 581, 608 (1964). The view of Justices Black and Douglas that the *Times* privilege did not go far enough has gained little additional support, at least in the judiciary.

16. *E.g.*, Nimmer, *The Right to Speak from* Times *to* Time, 56 CALIF. L. REV. 935 (1968); Wright, *Defamation, Privacy, and the Public's Right to Know: A National Problem and a New Approach*, 46 TEXAS L. REV. 630 (1968).

17. *See, e.g.*, Keeton, *Some Implications of the Constitutional Privilege to Defame*, 25 VAND. L. REV. 59 (1972); Merin, *Libel and the Supreme Court*, 11 WM. & MARY L. REV. 371, 418 (1969); Shapo, *Media Injuries to Personality: An Essay on Legal Regulation of Public Communication*, 46 TEXAS L. REV. 650 (1968).

18. The term "press" as used in this article includes all media of communication that are engaged in journalism. This term, rather than "media," is used because some of the latter are not engaged in journalism at all, and many are involved only secondarily. Although the entertainment and journalistic functions of the media are to a considerable extent inseparable, and although some entertainment may be as important and as worthy of protection, the central concern here is with matters normally considered journalism: gathering, reporting, and commenting on "news."

Libel and Self-Censorship

yers—a system in which the relevant question is not whether a story is libelous, but whether the subject is likely to sue, and if so, how much it will cost to defend. The *Gertz* decision perpetuates the deficiencies of the *Times* privilege and creates some new ones of its own. By importing the vocabulary of negligence into defamation, *Gertz* threatens to confuse further what already is one of the most complex areas of the law. Most importantly, it reflects a restrictive view of first amendment goals, a view that discriminates against certain segments of the press and certain types of discussion. The decision does, however, leave open several important questions that, if answered correctly, can help to reduce press self-censorship.

This article is concerned only with the effectiveness of the *Times-Gertz* privilege in preventing self-censorship; it does not attempt to assess its impact on reputation. The nature of reputational interests, the desirability of protecting them, the feasibility of monetary compensation for injury to them, and the availability and effectiveness of alternative methods of protecting these interests, are all important questions that deserve thoughtful study, extensive empirical research, and careful analysis. Such investigation might indicate that reputational interests require more protection, whatever the cost in terms of a diminished flow of information. The Supreme Court has created a privilege that attempts, on the one hand, to prevent self-censorship, and on the other, to preserve some protection for reputation. This article deals only with its effectiveness in accomplishing the former.

II. SELF-CENSORSHIP AND THE *Times* PRIVILEGE

A. *How Much Self-Censorship Is Too Much?*

The purpose of the *Times* privilege was to diminish the threat of libel judgments to reduce the incentive for the press and other critics of official conduct to censor themselves, thereby to preserve the "national commitment to the principle that debate on public issues should be uninhibited, robust, and wide-open."[19] To achieve this goal, the Court established a constitutional privilege adapted from a qualified privilege that a minority of the states had recognized as a matter of common law: the privilege to discuss the character and qualifications of public officials and candidates for public office, a subspecies of the more widely recognized "common interest" privilege.[20] The common

19. 376 U.S. at 270.
20. The leading case was Coleman v. MacLennan, 78 Kan. 711, 98 P. 281 (1908).

law qualified privileges are defeasible upon a showing that the defendant published with an unjustifiable motive.[21] This state of mind is described as "actual malice" to distinguish it from the implied, or "legal," malice ostensibly required to establish a cause of action.[22] Calculated falsehoods apparently were never within the common law privileges, perhaps because of a belief that "there is no social advantage in the publication of a deliberate lie,"[23] or perhaps because of an inherent inconsistency between a calculated falsehood and the notion of justifiable motives.

Reckless falsehoods usually were not privileged. Most courts added to the basic "actual malice" test a requirement that the defendant have probable cause to believe the truth of his statements.[24] This is sometimes described as a "reasonable grounds" requirement and may be attributable to the influence of negligence law on defamation.[25] Not all courts inquired into the reasonableness of the defendant's belief, however; some held that if he actually, even though unreasonably, believed his statements truthful, they were privileged.[26]

There was little agreement among the states concerning the proper scope of this privilege. All states apparently recognized some qualified privilege to discuss the conduct and qualifications of public officials, but the majority held that this privilege extended only to statements of opinion, rather than fact. *See* Noel, *Defamation of Public Officers and Candidates*, 49 COLUM. L. REV. 875 (1949). Because it did not cover misstatements of fact, it was usually called the "fair comment" privilege. *See, e.g.*, Owens v. Scott Publishing Co., 46 Wash. 2d 666, 284 P.2d 296, *cert. denied*, 350 U.S. 968 (1956). Under the majority rule, the publisher was not protected unless he could qualify for the fair comment privilege with respect to his statements of opinion and also maintain a defense of truth with respect to his factual statements. This combination of privilege and defense became known as a "rolled-up plea." *See* L. GREEN, W. PEDRICK, J. RAHL, E. THODE, C. HAWKINS & A. SMITH, INJURIES TO RELATIONS 345 (1968). The minority rule, recognizing a qualified privilege for misstatements of fact as well as comment, apparently was accepted in only about nine states. *See* Noel, *supra* at 896-97.

21. *See* note 3 *supra*.

22. *See, e.g.*, Jolly v. Valley Publishing Co., 62 Wash. 2d 537, 388 P.2d 139 (1964), holding that the "fictitious 'legal malice' which is 'implied' as a disguise for strict liability in any case of unprivileged defamation" is not enough to provide the "actual malice" necessary to defeat a qualified privilege. *Id.* at 543, 388 P.2d at 143.

23. W. PROSSER, *supra* note 6, § 115, at 795. *But see* Hallen, *Character of Belief Necessary for the Conditional Privilege in Defamation*, 25 ILL. L. REV. 865, 875-76 (1931), suggesting instances in which one might be justified in reporting what he has heard even though he does not believe it to be true; *e.g.*, "Must a mother have reasonable grounds before repeating some rumor to her daugher about the latter's fiance?" *Id.* at 875.

24. *E.g.*, O'Rourke v. Lewiston Daily Sun Publishing Co., 89 Me. 310, 36 A. 398 (1896); Stevenson v. Morris, 288 Pa. 405, 136 A. 234 (1927); Ranous v. Hughes, 30 Wis. 2d 452, 141 N.W.2d 251 (1966).

25. *See* Hallen, *supra* note 23, at 867-68.

26. *E.g.*, H.E. Crawford Co. v. Dun & Bradstreet, Inc., 241 F.2d 387 (4th Cir. 1957); Hemmens v. Nelson, 138 N.Y. 517, 34 N.E. 342 (1893); International & Great N. Ry. v. Edmundson, 222 S.W. 181 (Tex. Comm'n App. 1920, jdgmt adopted).

Libel and Self-Censorship

While the *Times* Court labeled as "actual malice" the type of conduct that would defeat its constitutional privilege, it departed from the common law understanding of that phrase[27] by defining it in terms of a "reckless disregard" standard.[28] The term "reckless disregard" did not appear in the *Coleman v. MacLennan* opinion,[29] the leading case that formed the basis of the *Times* privilege, or in any other case that the Court cited[30] in support of the "actual malice" rule.[31] The Court did not indicate the source of its new definition, but the language apparently derived from a line of Connecticut cases holding that qualified privileges might be lost by reckless disregard of the truth.[32]

An evaluation of the effectiveness of the *Times* privilege in reducing self-censorship and thereby protecting open debate is complicated by the fact that the Court did not seek to prevent all self-censorship; only an absolute privilege would achieve that result. In drawing its privilege to protect all but calculated or reckless falsehoods, the Court impliedly determined that exclusion of such statements from the flow of information was acceptable. The *Times* case itself, however, con-

27. *See* 376 U.S. at 279-80; Coleman v. MacLennan, 78 Kan. 711, 98 P. 281 (1908). One authority has noted that "actual malice defined by the Supreme Court in the *New York Times* case is essentially a new and technical concept, and bears little relation to the malice which defeated the privilege under the old 'public official' rule." Hanson, *Developments in the Law of Libel: Impact of the* New York Times *Rule*, 7 WM. & MARY L. REV. 215, 216 (1966).

28. For brevity's sake, the *Times* definition of the quantum of fault required to defeat the constitutional privilege will be referred to as the "reckless disregard" standard. This seems less likely to cause confusion than the shorthand phrase used by the Court, "actual malice," because that term has meanings other than the one given it in *Times*. The full statement of the standard is: "with knowledge that [the statement] was false or with reckless disregard of whether it was false or not." 376 U.S. at 280. This formulation can be shortened, without significant loss of content, to: "with reckless disregard of the falsity of the statement." Reckless disregard surely encompasses publication of a known falsehood.

29. 78 Kan. 711, 98 P. 281 (1908).

30. *See* 376 U.S. at 280 n.20.

31. The phrase did appear in a case involving the New York Times Co. decided the year before *Times*. The Second Circuit, applying Connecticut law, affirmed a judgment based on a jury finding that the Times had abused its common law privilege to report on police activities by recklessly disregarding the truth or falsity of the publication. Hogan v. New York Times Co., 313 F.2d 354, 355-56 (2d Cir. 1963). The Supreme Court briefs in *Times* did not cite *Hogan*.

32. Charles Parker Co. v. Silver City Crystal Co., 142 Conn. 605, 116 A.2d 440 (1955); *cf.* Ely v. Mason, 97 Conn. 38, 115 A. 479 (1921); Barry v. McCollom, 81 Conn. 293, 70 A. 1035 (1908). The *Charles Parker Co.* case also appears to have been the basis for the majority's holding, 376 U.S. at 287-88, that the Times' failure to investigate, even if negligent, would not establish actual malice. Charles Parker Co. v. Silver City Crystal Co., *supra* at 618, 116 A.2d at 446. The Court also cited Phoenix Newspapers, Inc. v. Choisser, 82 Ariz. 271, 277-78, 312 P.2d 150, 154-55 (1957), but that case did not involve a question of failure to investigate; it merely held that "actual malice" could not be inferred from other articles that also were privileged.

tains no analysis of the circumstances under which self-censorship is desirable or tolerable.

The Court rejected the argument that the defense of truth provides sufficient protection against self-censorship because "[u]nder such a rule, would-be critics of official conduct may be deterred from voicing their criticism, even though it is believed to be true and even though it is in fact true, because of doubt whether it can be proved in court or fear of the expense of having to do so."[33] But the difficulty and expense of proving the truth obviously were not the Court's only concerns; that problem could have been solved by requiring the plaintiff to prove falsity. The primary concern was protection of public debate, and the Court recognized the potential contribution of even a false statement, "since it brings about 'the clearer perception and livelier impression of truth, produced by its collision with error.' "[34] The Court declined to limit the constitutional privilege to innocent falsehoods, presumably in the belief that publishers would continue to censor themselves because of the possibility that a jury might find fault in their conduct.[35] Calculated falsehoods, however, were afforded no protection, perhaps because, as Justice Brennan explained in a later case, such statements "[fall] into that class of utterances which 'are no essential part of any exposition of ideas, and are of such slight social value as a step to truth that any benefit that may be derived from them is clearly outweighed by the social interest in order and morality.' "[36]

33. 376 U.S. at 279. The reliability of juries in separating truth from falsity has often been doubted: "Any nation which counts the *Scopes* trial as part of its heritage cannot . . . readily expose ideas to sanctions on a jury finding of falsity." Time, Inc. v. Hill, 385 U.S. 374, 406 (1967) (Harlan, J., concurring in part and dissenting in part).

34. 376 U.S. at 279 n.19, *quoting* J. MILL, ON LIBERTY 15 (R.B. McCallum ed. 1948). The value, if any, of falsehoods has been hotly debated throughout our history. It was a subject of disagreement during the debates in Congress over the Bill of Rights, *see* Merin, *supra* note 17, at 377, and again in the context of the Sedition Act, *see* L. LEVY, LEGACY OF SUPPRESSION 258-62 (Torchback ed. 1963). Professor Emerson has observed:

> Discussion must be kept open no matter how certainly true an accepted opinion may seem to be; many of the most widely acknowledged truths have turned out to be erroneous. Conversely, the same principle applies no matter how false or pernicious the new opinion appears to be; for the unaccepted opinion may be true or partially true and, even if wholly false, its presentation and open discussion compel a rethinkiug and retesting of the accepted opinion.

T. EMERSON, *supra* note 15, at 7.

35. *Cf.* Time, Inc. v. Hill, 385 U.S. 374 (1967), in which the Court noted: "A negligence test would place on the press the intolerable burden of guessing how a jury might assess the reasonableness of steps taken by it to verify the accuracy of every reference to a name, picture, or portrait." *Id.* at 389.

36. Garrison v. Louisiana, 379 U.S. 64, 75 (1964), *quoting* Chaplinsky v. New Hampshire, 315 U.S. 568, 572 (1942).

Libel and Self-Censorship

In drawing the boundary for protected statements somewhere between negligent and reckless falsehoods, the Court did not decide that the social value of negligent falsehoods outweighs the conflicting social interest in redressing injury to reputation, while the value of reckless falsehoods does not. The notion of determining the relative social utility of various kinds of falsehoods is contrary to the spirit of the *Times* rule. As Emerson has pointed out, the privilege was not designed to classify the types of statements that do or do not deserve constitutional protection. The real focus of *Times* is not on truth versus falsity, but on the practical effect that restraints on false statements have on truthful speech.[37]

The pragmatic reason for defining actual malice in terms of knowing or reckless falsehood was that any less rigorous definition probably would not have protected the Times from Sullivan's claim. There is little doubt that the newspaper was negligent in several respects; indeed the *Times* jury found malice in the more common sense of "ill will."[38] Thus, the Court's choice of a "reckless disregard" standard was primarily an attempt to adapt an existing common law privilege to the exigencies of the *Times* case.

Although it is impossible to state precisely how much self-censorship the Court intended *Times* to prevent, it is clear that the majority contemplated a privilege that would provide greater protection against self-censorship than any state provided. The Court established a privilege not even recognized by most states and adopted a more stringent definition of "actual malice" than that recognized at common law. By omitting the "proper motives" qualification that makes common law privileges defeasible upon a showing that the defendant was motivated by ill will, spite, or other improper state of mind,[39] the Court constructed a privilege far more durable than the common law privilege recognized by a minority of the states. Finally, by the gloss subsequently given to the "reckless disregard" standard, the Court demonstrated its intention to free the press from self-censorship of even unsubstantiated statements.[40]

37. T. EMERSON, *supra* note 15, at 536.
38. 376 U.S. at 262, 283 & n.24.
39. *See* Garrison v. Louisiana, 379 U.S. 64, 72-74 (1964).
40. For example, the Court held that failure to investigate is not recklessness for purposes of the *Times* test. St. Amant v. Thompson, 390 U.S. 727, 731 (1968). The Court suggested the possibility of exceptions "when the publisher's allegations are so inhereutly improbable that only a reckless man would have put them in circulation," and when "there are obvious reasons to doubt the veracity of the informant or the accuracy

Texas Law Review Vol. 53:422, 1975

B. The Threat Remains

Even though the *Times* privilege was not intended to free the press entirely from the libel threat, it obviously was expected greatly to reduce that threat. In fact, some assumed that the libel action would wither, if not disappear altogether.[41] Dean Prosser called *Times* "unquestionably the greatest victory won by the defendants in the modern history of the law of torts."[42]

Although no accurate measure of the volume of litigation is available, it is clear that the libel action is far from dead. More libel decisions were reported in the United States in 1973 than in 1963, the last full year before the upheaval began.[43] Of course, this does not prove that there has been an overall increase in litigation; the figures may indicate only that a higher proportion of libel judgments are now being appealed. Also, more appeals do not necessarily indicate more recoveries. The figures do demonstrate, however, that libel actions continue to pose a threat to the press.

1. Self-Censorship After Times.—That the *Times* principle has had an impact is unquestionable. Few journalists whose experience includes both the pre- and post-*Times* periods would deny that the fear of libel is a much less pervasive influence in the newsroom since that decision. Lawyers who represent news media suggest that material is now being published that would not have been before *Times*.[44] Nevertheless, self-censorship remains. Its full extent is impossible to determine. Much of it is inherently unmeasurable; it occurs whenever a reporter or editor omits a word, a passage, or an entire story, not for

of his reports." *Id.* at 732 (footnote omitted). The result, in theory, is to require a publisher to censor himself only when he in fact entertains serious doubts about the truth of his publication. *Id.* at 731.

41. *See, e.g.*, Coonradt, *The Courts Have All But Repealed the Libel Laws*, 4 CENTER REP., Dec. 1971, at 26.

42. W. PROSSER, *supra* note 6, § 118, at 819. Alexander Meiklejohn is reported to have said of the *Times* decision, "It is . . . an occasion for dancing in the streets." Kalven, *supra* note 15, at 221 n.125.

43. The *American Digest* shows 117 reported decisions in libel cases at the appellate level in 1973, compared with eighty-seven in 1963. The general counsel of the American Newspaper Publishers Association estimates that 1100 libel suits have been filed against newspapers alone in the past eleven years. 4 [MORE], Sept. 1974, at 6. He also estimates that the number of libel suits has expanded by several hundred perceut since the late 1950's. 1 A. HANSON, LIBEL AND RELATED TORTS vii (1969). *See also* LeMaistre, *Who Needs Egg on His Face?*, 4 JURIS DOCTOR, May 1974, at 33, quoting lawyers for several uewspapers to the effect that the *Times* decision "has not yet made libel suits a thing of the past." *Id.*

44. *See* LeMaistre, *supra* note 43, at 33-34.

Libel and Self-Censorship

journalistic reasons but because of the possible legal implications.[45] The self-censors may become so accustomed to making these deletions that they no longer realize they are responding to the danger of potential lawsuits. Some self-censorship decisions, including some at the institutional level, are made deliberately, but these generally are not publicized because no journalist is proud of a decision to suppress for nonjournalistic reasons.[46]

Occasionally, however, an instance of calculated self-censorship, directly attributable to the threat of libel litigation, comes to light. [*More*], a journalism review, recently informed its readers in an editor's note that it had deleted certain passages from an article for fear that publication of them would result in legal action. The review had consulted its lawyers, who advised that it would probably win a libel suit, "but that the cost of defending it might easily bankrupt the magazine. After a good deal of agonizing, . . . we decided the risk was not worth it."[47] The article in question charged that the New York Times had refused to publish a manuscript by one of its investigative reporters, even though that newspaper's lawyers also had reviewed the charges and concluded that a libel suit would probably be filed, but could be defended successfully.[48] The passages censored by [*More*] were excerpts from that manuscript; thus neither publication printed the material, even though lawyers for both independently had concluded that it probably was not libelous. Another recent report concerns withdrawal of a book from the market by a major publishing

45. Some expansion of the forbidden zone—and therefore some undesirable self-censorship—is inevitable in the process of translating rules of law into working rules for news personnel. For example, a pamphlet described as "'must' reading for every Associated Press staff member," THE ASSOCIATED PRESS, THE DANGERS OF LIBEL 1 (1964), gives this advice:

> There are three steps to be taken in the evaluation of a story.
>
> The first question is whether it is libelous, that is, whether it is actionable on its face. If it is, then the test is whether the facts stated are provably true. If the answer to the first question is in the affirmative, and you are not certain as to the second, then you must decide whether the story is qualifiedly privileged.
>
> *If the story is libelous or potentially libelous and it fails to survive the two tests mentioned, then there is only one course of action to be followed:* KILL IT AT ONCE.

Id. at 4 (emphasis in original).

46. The prevailing jornalistic ethic is reflected in this passage: "It's easy for a lawyer (it's probably his duty to do so) to tell a client not to print something. But it's nobler for an editor to print it nevertheless, if he feels that he is in possession of enough of the truth about a situation and that he owes it to his public to let them know about it." C. ANGOFF, THE BOOK OF LIBEL vii (2d ed. 1966).

47. Hume, *The Mayor, The Times, and the Lawyers*, 4 [MORE], Aug. 1974, at 17.

48. *Id.* at 1, 17.

house because a person named in the book filed a libel suit; the publisher apparently feared that the book's continued distribution would increase the amount of any eventual judgment.[49] The investigator who described this incident named six other recent nonfiction books that are the subjects of thirteen libel suits.[50]

There are some publications and individuals for whom the libel laws apparently provide little deterrence because they are confident of their ability to defend successfully, of their capacity to absorb libel judgments as a cost of business,[51] or of their de facto immunity from the libel law by virtue of insolvency; a few mistakenly believe they are invulnerable. Much of the press is financially capable of compensating for the harms it causes to reputation.[52] Publishing and broadcasting are profitable industries,[53] and one reason for their financial success is that the law has relieved them of liability for most of the reputational injuries they cause. They should be willing in return to give us fearless journalism, even if that means taking risks that may consume a part of those profits.

The issue, however, is not whether the press should be less timid

49. Rubin, *The Perils of Muckraking*, 4 [MORE], Sept. 1974, at 5.

50. *Id.* at 8.

51. The most notable modern example of a journalist who considered libel litigation a cost of doing business was the late columnist Drew Pearson. His attorney estimated that Pearson and the journals that carried his column were sued for libel approximately 275 times for amounts totaling over $200 million. O. PILAT, DREW PEARSON: AN UNAUTHORIZED BIOGRAPHY 10 (1973). Pearson lost only one suit, which he settled for $40,000, *id.* at 255, but he spent "hundreds of thousands of dollars in legal fees" to defend against libel claims, *id.* at 15.

Among the major contemporary publishers, Time, Inc. appears to be the most active libel litigant; it has been defendant in at least fifteen reported cases since 1969.

52. The Second Circuit has noted that

> [n]ewspapers, magazines, and broadcasting companies are businesses conducted for profit and often make very large ones. Like other enterprises that inflict damage in the course of performing a service highly useful to the public, such as providers of food or shelter or manufacturers of drugs designed to ease or prolong life, they must pay the freight . . . .

Buckley v. New York Post Corp., 373 F.2d 175, 182 (2d Cir. 1967); *see* 418 U.S. at 390-91 (White, J., dissenting). The flaw in this analogy is that the other enterprises mentioned have no choice but to accept the additional risk of liability if they are to continue their profit-making activities, while most broadcasters and publishers can avoid liability, without discontinuing their activities or reducing their profits, by ceasing to carry material that creates the risk of liability—*i.e.*, by increasing their self-censorship.

53. Among the nation's 500 largest corporations in 1973, those engaged in broadcasting are reported to have produced a median return on stockholder's equity of 15.3%, and those in publishing and printing 13.4%; the median for all industries was 12.4%. The broadcasting and publishing industries both produced a median return on sales of 6.0%, compared with a median of 4.5% for all industries. FORTUNE, May 1974, at 253-54. These figures may understate the profitability of publishing and broadcasting because the most profitable of these operations is not necessarily the largest.

or whether publishers and broadcasters can afford the risks that current libel law creates, because ultimately it is impossible to require fearless journalism, and economic considerations militate against risk-taking. The press has virtually no economic incentive to publish anything that might lead to a libel suit. In the case of daily newspapers, whatever incentive was once provided by the danger that a competitor would publish the suppressed material has largely disappeared along with competition.[54] More importantly, even where competition exists, little can be gained by taking chances. Publishers and broadcasters gain or lose their audiences for reasons that are unrelated to the boldness or timidity of their journalism. A newspaper competing for circulation is more likely to fight the battle with comics, color photos, stock tables, or contests than with more daring treatment of potentially defamatory material.[55] When a broadcaster's ratings slip, he is likely to respond by hiring a more congenial anchorman, or by replacing news and public affairs programming with entertainment, instead of opting for more aggressive journalism.[56]

In book publishing, and to a lesser extent in magazine publishing, the economic pressures for self-censorship are exacerbated by the practice employed by many companies of requiring authors to agree to indemnify their publishers for some or all of the losses resulting from libel suits.[57] In some cases the writer promises only to indemnify ultimate judgments. Other agreements require him to pay the judgment and a specified portion of the costs of defending all suits, whether successful or unsuccessful. Still others require him to bear all costs of litigation as well as pay any settlement or judgment. At least one major underwriter of libel insurance insists that its policyholders obtain indemnification agreements from writers.[58] Some publishers and insurers maintain that the losses caused by libelous statements should be borne by those writing them and that indemnification provides insurers

54. Sixty years ago the country had 2442 daily newspapers, and 689 cities had competing dailies. A 1972 study found that the number of dailies nationwide had dwindled to 1748 and, perhaps more significantly, only forty-two cities with competing dailies remained. *Media and the First Amendment in a Free Society*, 60 GEO. L.J. 867, 892 (1972).

55. *See, e.g.*, A. LEE, THE DAILY NEWSPAPER IN AMERICA 282-85 (1937); J. LYLE, THE NEWS IN MEGALOPOLIS 25-26 (1967).

56. *See* Fuller, *News Doctors: Taking Over TV Journalism?*, BROADCASTING, Sept. 9, 1974, at 21 (describing the methods prescribed by professional news consultants to improve ratings of broadcast news programs); *cf.* THE POLITICS OF BROADCASTING 1971-1972, at 9-11 (M. Barrett ed. 1973).

57. Rubin, *supra* note 49, at 5.

58. *Id.* at 6.

with their only means of protection against irresponsible writers.[59] This argument, however, is untenable when indemnification is not limited to ultimate judgments. To require the author to bear the costs of successfully defending a suit deters him not only from writing libelous statements, but also from writing statements that, although not libelous, may nevertheless be the subject of a suit. For the authors these defense costs are overwhelming. In the instance of the six books mentioned above,[60] the authors reported defense costs ranging from $10,000 to $19,000, figures that represented twenty-five to 100 percent of their royalties.[61]

Although these economic incentives create a strong pressure for self-censorship, noneconomic incentives to take chances do exist. Reporters and editors share a professional ethic that encourages them to seek to inform the public, even at the risk of libel litigation. This may even be institutionalized, so that it represents the prevailing ethic of a publishing or broadcasting organization;[62] "all the news that's fit to print" presumably includes some news that creates a danger of legal action. Although impossible to measure, this professional pressure to publish is probably the strongest force against self-censorship. Journalism reviews and other media critics are becoming increasingly active in exposing press timidity.[63] Editors, publishers, and broadcasters value the esteem of their professional peers, and the honors frequently go to those who have been willing to take chances.

Strong as this incentive may be, however, the professional ethic is not a dependable safeguard against real economic pressure. A system of free expression is not secure if it must rely on the press to subordinate economic self-interest to the abstract principle of free speech. The only reliable method of maximizing discussion is to reduce the economic pressures that constrict it, even though that may increase the wealth and power of some elements of the press.

59. *Id.*

60. *See* text accompanying note 50 *supra.*

61. Rubin, *supra* note 49, at 8-9. At the date of the cited report, of the suits that had proceeded to judgment the defendants were successful in six, while the lone judgment for a plaintiff was being appealed. The remainder of the cases were still in pretrial stages.

62. A former general news editor of the Associated Press relates an incident in which the AP carried potentially defamatory material, even though it could obtain no legal assurance that the material would not be actionable because "it seemed to us it was in the public interest to report it fully." Blackman, *Be Careful How You Say It*, SATURDAY REV., Apr. 10, 1971, at 48, 49.

63. *See, e.g., The New Press Critics*, 11 COLUM. JOURNALISM REV., Nov./Dec. 1972, at 29-40.

2. *Why* Times *Failed to End Self-Censorship.*—Libel litigation not only has survived, it appears to be thriving. The *Times* decision did not succeed in easing sufficiently the threat posed by libel and, with it, the incentives for self-censorship. Dean Green has aptly described post-*Times* libel law as "a gun behind the door";[64] it offers little real protection to reputation, but still serves to intimidate the press.

The reasons for the *Times* rule's failure to fulfill the hopes of its enthusiasts—and the fears of its critics—are complex. One may be that potential libel plaintiffs are motivated by something more than a rational calculus of their chances of recovery; believing they have been wronged, they seek to clear their names and perhaps to retaliate, and they may be able to accomplish those objectives even if they fail to collect damages.[65] Second, if a plaintiff does win a libel suit, the recovery may be large. A jury awarded former University of Georgia athletic director Wally Butts $3.06 million (reduced by the trial court to $460,000);[66] Senator Barry Goldwater won $75,000 in punitive damages from Ralph Ginzburg and his magazine even though the jury found that Goldwater had suffered only nominal harm.[67] Thus, even though chances for recovery may be remote, the prospect of a windfall payoff probably lures some plaintiffs into court. Third, the *Times* rule did little to reduce the plaintiff's chances of negotiating a modest settlement. A libel suit, no matter how groundless, is damaging to the public image of a publisher or broadcaster; the media therefore have some incentive to pay a small amount to prevent a suit from being filed. If the plaintiff's claim is at all credible, he can obtain a more-than-modest settlement, simply because it is cheaper to settle than to defend.[68] The cost of defending a full-fledged libel suit

64. Green, *Continuing the Privacy Discussion: A Response to Judge Wright and President Bloustein*, 46 TEXAS L. REV. 750, 756 (1968). Dean Green, it should be noted, believes that the gun "should be kept loaded." *Id.*

65. One plaintiff described his motives as follows: "It would be childish of me to deny that I am delighted to have won a monetary victory. Of course I am. But I did not enter into combat with the defeudants as a monetary investment. The six-year fight against their destructive conspiracy has been crowned with victory." J. FAULK, FEAR ON TRIAL 397 (1964).

66. Curtis Publishing Co. v. Butts, 388 U.S. 130, 138 (1967).

67. Goldwater v. Ginzburg, 414 F.2d 324 (2d Cir. 1969), *cert. denied*, 396 U.S. 1049 (1970) ($1.00 actual damages, $75,000 punitive damages). *See also* Reynolds v. Pegler, 223 F.2d 429 (2d Cir.), *cert. denied*, 350 U.S. 846 (1955) ($1.00 actual damages, $175,000 puuitive damages); Field Research Corp. v. Patrick, 30 Cal. App. 3d 603, 106 Cal. Rptr. 473, *cert. denied*, 414 U.S. 922 (1973) ($150,000 actual damages, $150,000 punitive damages).

68. *See, e.g.*, Buckley v. Esquire, Inc., 344 F. Supp. 1133 (S.D.N.Y. 1972). After the court denied the publisher's motion for summary judgment, Esquire reportedly settled

probably begins at about $20,000[69] and can run much higher; the successful defense of *Rosenbloom v. Metromedia, Inc.*[70] is reported to have cost nearly $100,000.[71] The ineffectiveness of the *Times* rule in reducing defense costs is the most important reason for the continuing pressure to censor. It is the magnitude of this financial burden, more than any other factor, that makes libel a threat to the press today.[72]

The *Times* case failed to alleviate this problem primarily because it usually has no effect until a case reaches the trial stage. The basic *Times* rule merely changes the instructions under which the case is submitted to the jury; by the time the litigation reaches that point, a major portion of the defense costs have been incurred. If the "reckless disregard" standard had been the only rule to emerge from *Times,* the decision would not have succeeded in protecting the press. Plaintiffs' lawyers have had little difficulty in persuading juries to find "actual malice."[73] Anticipating this, the court constitutionalized the question

with columnist William F. Buckley for $115,000. Stevens, *Defamation of Political Figures: Another Look at the* Times-Sullivan *Rule,* 27 FED. COM. B.J. 99, 104 n.27 (1974). The same source reports a settlement of $15,000 in Miller v. Argus Publishing Co., 79 Wash. 2d 816, 490 P.2d 101 (1971), a case in which the publisher won a reversal because it was not clear that the trial court had applied the *Times* standard.

69. *Cf.* LeMaistre, *supra* note 43, at 34. The publisher of a small Texas journal recently sued for libel has advised his readers that the estimated cost of defending the suit is $30,000. Dugger, *A Report to Our Friends,* The Texas Observer, Feb. 14, 1975, at 17.

70. 403 U.S. 29 (1971).

71. Ek, *Libel Insurance,* in H. NELSON & D. TEETER, LAW OF MASS COMMUNICATIONS 678 App. D (2d ed. 1973).

72. The editor of the *Nation* has described how libel law affects his magazine:

> Another limitation is the libel laws, which, although they have been somewhat relaxed, still warn publications—particularly small circulation publications—away from important subject matter. It has been my experience that individuals and corporations will threaten—and actually sue—small journals of opinion when they would hesitate to threaten or sue the New York *Times* for the same material. On occasion I have arranged for authors to testify before Congressional committees to get stories before the public simply because a publication such as the *Nation* cannot afford the luxury of winning a libel action. About a year ago we were sued for libel and the case was thrown out—but it cost us $7,500 to win.

McWilliams, *Is Muckraking Coming Back?,* 9 COLUM. JOURNALISM REV., Fall 1970, at 8, 15.

73. *See, e.g.,* Curtis Publishing Co. v. Butts, 388 U.S. 130 (1967), in which Justice Harlan, discussing the companion case of *Associated Press v. Walker,* said:

> The Associated Press received the information from a correspondent who was present at the scene of the events and gave every indication of being trustworthy and competent. His dispatches in this instance, with one minor exception, were internally consistent and would not have seemed unreasonable to one familiar with General Walker's prior publicized statements on the underlying controversy. Considering the necessity for rapid dissemination, nothing in this series of events gives the slightest hint of a severe departure from accepted publishing standards.

Libel and Self-Censorship

of recklessness.[74] This strengthened the *Times* privilege considerably by requiring the appellate courts to make a de novo review of the evidence of recklessness. An additional consequence, however, is that the *Times* rule frequently is ineffective even at the trial stage; the defendant may have to endure not only a costly jury trial, but also an expensive series of appeals, before the privilege provides any benefit.[75]

In short, the trouble with the *Times* privilege is that it operates at the wrong end of the litigation. In order to effectively prevent self-censorship, it would have to operate at the beginning, protecting the press not only from the threat of eventual liability, but also from expensive litigation.[76] Additionally, such a rule would better serve the financial interests of potential plaintiffs; it would save them the cost and inconvenience of litigating through the trial stage, only to learn at

Id. at 158-59 (footnote omitted). Yet a Texas jury, in awarding punitive damages, impliedly found that the AP was motivated by "ill will, a bad or evil motive, or that entire want of care which would raise the belief that the act or omission complained of was the result of a conscious indifference to the right or welfare of the person to be affected by it." *Id.* at 141.

74. The Court stated that its "duty is not limited to the elaboration of constitutional principles; we must also in proper cases review the evidence to make certain that those principles have been constitutionally applied," 376 U.S. at 285, and concluded that the courts must " 'make an independent examination of the whole record,' " *id., quoting* Edwards v. South Carolina, 372 U.S. 229, 235 (1963).

75. The history of Pape v. Time, Inc., 401 U.S. 279 (1971), vividly illustrates this problem. Pape instituted a libel action against Time in federal court prior to the *Times* decision. The district court granted Time's motion to dismiss on the basis of common law privilege. The court of appeals reversed. 318 F.2d 652 (7th Cir. 1963). Subsequent to remand, the *Times* decision was announced. The district court, on the basis of that case, granted Time's motion for summary judgment, but the court of appeals again reversed, holding Pape's allegations to be sufficient to raise an issue of fact concerning whether Time had acted with "actual malice." 354 F.2d 558 (7th Cir. 1965). The case then went to jury trial, but at the close of the evidence the district court granted Time's motion for a directed verdict, finding no evidence of "actual malice." 294 F. Supp. 1087 (N.D. Ill. 1969). The Seventh Circuit reversed for a third time, holding that the determination of "actual malice" was a jury question. 419 F.2d 980 (7th Cir. 1969). At this point the Supreme Court granted certiorari, 397 U.S. 1062 (1970), and, making its own review of the evidence, held that: "[I]t can hardly be said that Time acted in reckless disregard of the truth. . . . Time's conduct reflected at most an error of judgment," 401 U.S. at 292. Justice Harlan, dissenting, would have affirmed the court of appeals and remanded the case for another jury trial on the issue of reckless disregard. *Id.* at 293.

76. Another method of attacking the problems of defense costs in libel suits might be to require unsuccessful plaintiffs to pay defendants' attorneys' fees. This is not an attractive solution because it could impose a severe—possibly disastrous—penalty on the plaintiff who miscalculates the merit of his claim. If the law is to retain a remedy for defamation, it should not put a plaintiff in such great peril for seeking to avail himself of that remedy. Restricting the award of attorneys' fees to suits deemed "frivolous" is no solution because it does not address the real problem—the cost of defending suits in which the plaintiff has a colorable claim of injury, but the claim may be barred by a privilege. The only satisfactory answer is to reduce the cost of determining whether the privilege will prevail.

the appellate level that the defendant's conduct was constitutionally privileged. Some federal courts and a few state courts have attempted to approximate this through summary judgment procedure,[77] but in most state courts the *Times* privilege provides little protection until at least the trial stage.

3. The Libel Lawyer's Role.—Post-*Times* censorship is not exactly self-censorship; it is more accurately censorship by libel lawyer because the pivotal factors in deciding whether to publish are ones that the press itself cannot fully evaluate. This is not because the decisive issues are legal ones that nonlawyer editors are incapable of resolving. The lawyer's role would be less significant if the decision turned solely on such questions as whether the potential plaintiff is a public figure or official, whether the statement is false and defamatory, and whether the circumstances would support a finding of recklessness; these are questions that journalists can and do evaluate for themselves. But under the present state of libel law, the central issue is not necessarily whether the material is libelous. Rather, the question often is whether its publication will result in a lawsuit, and if so, what the cost of successfully defending a suit will be. Proper evaluation of these questions requires knowledge of both the practical and legal intricacies of the litigation process, and the lawyer's advice may be decisive. As the [*More*] incident[78] indicates, his answer is likely to be that the publication is defensible, but that it will be expensive to do so.

Libel lawyers' awareness of their censorship power and their sensitivity to the public interest in their decisions no doubt vary widely. The ideal libel lawyer, at least from the public's point of view, would be one who feels an obligation to maximize the flow of information to readers and viewers and who can utilize all the opportunities the law provides for accomplishing that goal. The reality is that the lawyers who handle the libel problems of publishers and broadcasters usually are the same ones who handle their tax work, collections, contracts, labor relations, and other corporate legal work. These lawyers are unlikely to be accustomed to pushing the law to its outer limits. In addition, they rarely handle more than one or two libel suits a year; since few of those ever go to trial and even fewer are appealed, they may

77. *See, e.g.*, Time, Inc. v. Johnston, 448 F.2d 378 (4th Cir. 1971); Time, Inc. v. McLaney, 406 F.2d 565 (5th Cir.), *cert. denied*, 395 U.S. 922 (1969); McCunn v. California Teachers Ass'n, 3 Cal. App. 3d 956, 83 Cal. Rptr. 846 (1970); Tagawa v. Maui Publishing Co., 50 Hawaii 648, 448 P.2d 337 (1969).

78. *See* text accompanying notes 47-48 *supra*.

have no experience in actual libel litigation. One may doubt whether the nature of these lawyers' practice will give them either the time or the inclination to contemplate seriously the subtle constitutional and societal interests at stake in libel litigation.[79]

Even if the lawyer is sensitive to the broader implications of his decisions, and even if he handles enough libel matters to develop some expertise in the field, another problem still inhibits his effectiveness: he has a serious role conflict, and the more capable he is, the more serious the conflict. The libel lawyer must have some relationship, direct or indirect, with his client's news personnel. If he is to be fully effective he must have their respect and confidence so they will be willing to alert him to problems and consult him in the early stages of potentially troublesome stories. But the lawyer's ultimate responsibility—and therefore his loyalty in the event of conflict—must be to the owner who employs him. Theoretically, the owner and the news personnel share the goal of maximizing the flow of information while minimizing the danger of loss through libel. In practice, however, their goals are likely to diverge. News personnel have professional and psychological incentives to take risks, and the possibility of losing the gamble is a weak deterrent because normally it is the publisher who pays. A reporter who has invested his time and talent in a story and risked his credibility by presenting it for publication has a strong interest in seeing it published or broadcast. The owner, on the other hand, usually has no psychological stake in the story, feels less professional pressure to publish it, and has a stronger financial incentive to avoid the risk. Thus, no matter how keenly the libel lawyer may appreciate the interest of the public (and the newsroom) in running the story, when a conflict develops he must protect the interest of his client, the publisher, or station owner.[80]

In addition to the personal and professional factors that tend to make the lawyer a poor censor, there are practical limits on his effectiveness. Although some magazine and book publishers submit all

79. There are, of course, some notable exceptions. Harold R. Medina, Jr., representing Time, Inc., is an imaginative libel lawyer who, perhaps more than any other, has influenced the post-*Times* development of libel law. James Goodale, vice-president and general counsel of the New York Times, has often demonstrated a keen sensitivity to the public's interests, not only in libel law matters but in other areas of press law as well. *See* Goodale, *Subpoenas of News Reporters to Compel Disclosure of Confidential Information*, 49 L.A. BAR BULL. 133 (1974).

80. For some interesting glimpses of the relationships between lawyers and their press clients in another context, see S. UNGAR, THE PAPERS AND THE PAPERS (1972).

copy to their lawyer before publication,[81] that is impossible for a daily newspaper or a broadcaster. Usually the lawyer is not consulted unless someone in the newsroom spots a potential problem and brings it to his attention.[82] That frequently does not happen, either through oversight or because news personnel hesitate to give the lawyer an opportunity to kill a story. Even if he does see all the copy, the lawyer cannot spot all possibly defamatory material because it is not always apparent on its face.[83]

Even when the lawyer is consulted and the problem is evident, it is often impossible for him to evaluate the risk with any certainty. Every newscast and every edition of a newspaper or magazine contain scores of potentially defamatory statements. Since it would be impractical to indicate all of these, the lawyer tries to identify those that pose a significant risk and then estimate the magnitude of the risk. The number of variables involved in the evaluation process is enormous. The legal questions are numerous enough: Does the statement refer to an identifiable plaintiff? Are the words defamatory? Would any of the many common law privileges apply? Would the potential plaintiff be considered a public figure or official? Could a jury find the recklessness necessary to defeat the constitutional privilege or the malice to defeat a common law privilege? Could the plaintiff show special damages? Would he be required to do so? Are punitive damages a possibility? What court would have jurisdiction? Where would venue lie? The nonlegal variables are even more numerous: Does the potential plaintiff have access to lawyers? Is he accustomed to litigating? Is he already hostile toward the client? Does he have hidden skeletons that he could ill afford to expose in a libel suit? Is republication, which may increase the damages,[84] likely? Because of all these uncertainties,

81. *Cf.* Rubin, *supra* note 49, at 5.

82. "[T]he reporter constitutes the first line of defense for his newspaper against legal liability for the printing of news. . . . There is little enough time before deadlines to make a conscientious check of the accuracy of the facts of a story, and no time at all to seek competent legal counsel." W. SWINDLER, PROBLEMS OF LAW IN JOURNALISM vii (1955).

83. *See, e.g.*, Karrigan v. Valentine, 184 Kan. 783, 339 P.2d 52 (1959) (bachelor falsely identified as father in birth announcement); Natchez Times Publishing Co. v. Dunigan, 221 Miss. 320, 72 So. 2d 681 (1954) (white woman mistakenly identified as Negro); Hoeck v. Tiedebohl, 74 N.M. 146, 391 P.2d 651 (1964) (woman reported to be "knitting little things" was divorced and not pregnant).

84. The first publisher generally is held liable for damages resulting from republications that he might reasonably have anticipated. *See* Painter, *Republication Problems in the Law of Defamation*, 47 VA. L. REV. 1131 (1961); *cf.* RESTATEMENT OF TORTS § 576(c) (1938).

Libel and Self-Censorship

the lawyer's advice may be little more than a guess.

Finally, censorship by lawyers is objectionable because it contains a built-in bias against the poor, the powerless, and the unsophisticated. In evaluating the risk of publishing a potentially defamatory statement, a major consideration is the likelihood that the victim will sue. A person who has access to lawyers and is accustomed to using the legal system to achieve his goals is more likely to sue than one who has no experience with the legal system; a businessman, professional, or mobster poses a more serious risk than a housewife, student, or worker. Therefore, the lawyer is more hesitant to approve publication of a damaging statement about one of the former than one of the latter. As a result, other things being equal, the weak are more likely to be defamed than those with power and wealth.

In summary, while the *Times* privilege undoubtedly has reduced press self-censorship, it has not eliminated it. Libel law still induces censorship, not only of reckless falsehoods, but also of statements that ultimately would be held constitutionally privileged if fully litigated. Moreover, because the privilege is usually ineffective until late in the expensive litigation process, it does little to reduce the danger of self-censorship prompted by high defense costs. This has led to a system of censorship by the press' lawyers, who are not demonstrably well qualified as censors.

C. Effect of the Gertz *Decision*

The *Gertz* decision exacerbates the deficiencies of the *Times* privilege in at least three ways: (1) it makes recoveries more likely in some libel cases, thereby increasing the incentive to self-censor; (2) it creates a constitutional bias in favor of journalistic orthodoxy; and (3) it threatens to abort the recent and promising development of summary judgment in the field of defamation.

1. Restricting the Privilege to "Public" Plaintiffs.—The events that culminated in Gertz's libel action began with the much publicized killing of a youth named Nelson by a Chicago policeman. The boy's family retained Elmer Gertz, a prominent Chicago civil liberties lawyer, to bring a civil suit against the policeman, who subsequently was convicted of second degree murder. In 1969 *American Opinion* magazine published an article, entitled "Frame-Up," asserting that the prosecution was part of a nationwide communist "war on police." The author described Gertz as a member of various organizations said to be involved in a campaign to discredit the police.[85] The article repeatedly referred to Gertz as a "Communist" or "Communist-fronter," falsely identified him as a former member of the Marxist League for Industrial Democracy, and stated that "[t]he file on Elmer Gertz in Chicago Police Intelligence takes a big Irish cop to lift."[86]

Gertz filed a libel action in federal court. The court ruled that the publication was libelous as a matter of law and withdrew from the jury all issues except the measure of damages.[87] The jury awarded Gertz $50,000, without indicating whether that represented actual, presumed, or punitive damages.[88] Subsequently the trial judge determined that the *Times* privilege was applicable and entered judgment for defendant notwithstanding the verdict.[89] The court of appeals affirmed[90] on the basis of *Rosenbloom v. Metromedia, Inc.*,[91] decided after the district court's *Gertz* decision.

The Supreme Court reversed, a one-vote majority holding that "so long as they do not impose liability without fault, the States may define for themselves the appropriate standard of liability for a publisher or broadcaster of a defamatory falsehood injurious to a private individual."[92] Justice White, in dissent,[93] and much of the press characterized this as an expansion of first amendment protection,[94] an assessment that will be valid in some cases. All plaintiffs, regardless of their public-private status, now must prove some species of fault in order to recover, at least in suits against news media.[95] Previously,

85. The article is reproduced in full in Appendix at 19-36, Gertz v. Robert Welch, Inc., 418 U.S. 323 (1974).

86. *Id.* at 23. Justice Powell apparently considered this an implication that Gertz had a criminal record. *Id.* at 326.

87. Gertz v. Robert Welch, Inc., 322 F. Supp. 997, 998 (N.D. Ill. 1972).

88. *Id.* In his complaint Gertz sought only $10,001 in actual damages but $500,000 in punitive damages. Appendix at 16, Gertz v. Robert Welch, Inc., 418 U.S. 323 (1974). The judge instructed the jury that the plaintiff need not prove any actual damage in order to recover, *id.* at 63, and that punitive damages were permissible, *id.* at 62.

89. 322 F. Supp. at 1000.

90. 471 F.2d 801 (7th Cir. 1972).

91. 403 U.S. 29 (1971).

92. 418 U.S. at 347. Four justices dissented, but the vote to reverse actually was six to three. Chief Justice Burger dissented, objecting to the majority's revision of the common law of defamation but agreeing that Gertz should recover. He would have remanded for reinstatement of the verdict, however, while the majority remanded for a new trial.

93. *Id.* at 390-92.

94. *See, e.g.*, TIME, July 8, 1974, at 58: "[T]he net effect of the decision is to cut back on the chance that any newspaper, magazine, book publisher, TV or radio station acting in good faith will ever have to pay any substantial libel claims."

95. *Gertz* does not compel any distinction between press and nonpress defendants.

Libel and Self-Censorship

plaintiffs not subject to the *Times* test might recover without any showing of fault.[96]

The additional protection is more apparent than real, however. First, it is doubtful that there have ever been many recoveries—at least substantial ones—when there was no fault. Strict liability has been more theoretical than actual; because of the many privileges recognized at common law,[97] most plaintiffs are required to prove something akin to fault, usually called "malice," to defeat the defendant's claim of privilege.[98] The gap between the theory of strict liability

Throughout the opinion, however, Justice Powell uses the phrase "publishers and broadcasters." In holding that the states may define the requisite degree of fault, for example, the Court refers to "the appropriate standard of liability for a *publisher or broadcaster* . . . ." 418 U.S. at 347 (emphasis added). Moreover, the Court's discussion of the dangers of self-censorship refers to press self-censorship and does not address the problem in the case of other types of defendants.

The *Times* privilege also initially was envisioned as a privilege for the press and was justified by the threat of self-censorship, but there is little doubt now that it applies to nonmedia defendants as well. *See* Pickering v. Board of Educ., 391 U.S. 563 (1968); Garrison v. Louisiana, 379 U.S. 64 (1964). In most instances there is little apparent reason to distinguish between press and nonpress defendants. It is not inconceivable, however, that the Court would decide that there are certain types of defendants for whom, in comparison with the press, the danger of self-censorship is less. For example, the Court might conclude that self-censorship is not a real threat in the case of credit reporting agencies or that a business entity attacking the products or services of a competitor has a greater incentive to take risks than would a press critic of the competing business. Any proposal to give less favorable treatment to certain types of nonpress defendants, however, would raise difficult questions concerning the roles of the press and other speakers in our society.

96. *See, e.g.*, Szalay v. New York American, Inc., 254 App. Div. 249, 4 N.Y.S. 620 (1938). *See generally* W. PROSSER, *supra* note 6, § 113.

97. The *Restatement of Torts* recognized thirteen common law privileges, five conditional and eight absolute. RESTATEMENT OF TORTS §§ 585-605 (1938). *Gertz* could make all the conditional common law privileges obsolete; the negligence required to maintain a cause of action under *Gertz* arguably is enough to defeat any conditional privilege. But cases decided since *Gertz* continue to recognize common law privileges. In a number of cases statements alleged to be defamatory were held to be absolutely privileged at common law. *See, e.g.*, Brubaker v. Board of Educ., 502 F.2d 973 (7th Cir. 1974); Macy v. TWA, Inc., 381 F. Supp. 142 (D. Md. 1974); Abercrombie v. McClung, — Hawaii —, 525 P.2d 594 (1974); Bergman v. Hupy, 64 Wis. 2d 747, 221 N.W.2d 898 (1974). Common law conditional privileges were recognized in more than ten post-*Gertz* decisions. *See, e.g.*, Conley v. Southern Import Sales Inc., 382 F. Supp. 121 (M.D. Ala. 1974); City of Tempe v. Pilot Properties, Inc., — Ariz. —, 527 P.2d 515 (1974); Frisk v. Merrihew, 42 Cal. 3d 319, 116 Cal. Rptr. 781 (1974) Tomblin v. S.S. Kresge Co., 132 Ga. App. 212, 207 S.E.2d 693 (1974). It makes no sense to retain the conditional common law privileges, however, unless the quantum of fault required to defeat them is higher than the *Gertz* minimum of negligence.

98. More precisely, a qualified privilege to defame is lost if the defamer abuses it. Abuse may be found if the defendant publishes more information, or imparts it to more persons, than necessary to fulfill the purposes of the privilege. Even if the defendant communicates no more than the proper amount of information and only to appropriate persons, however, he still can lose the privilege if the court concludes that he published for the wrong reasons. It is this inappropriate state of mind that the common law de-

and the reality of privilege has led Dean Green to observe, "No other formula of the law promises so much and delivers so little."[99]

More significantly, in one important category of cases—those in which the plaintiff, although not a public figure or official, is involved in a matter of public concern—the *Gertz* decision reduces rather than expands the level of constitutional protection. In *Rosenbloom v. Metromedia, Inc.*[100] the Court affirmed the Third Circuit's reversal of a $275,000 judgment (reduced on remittitur from $750,000) in favor of a magazine distributor falsely described as a seller of obscene material. With eight justices participating,[101] the case produced five separate opinions. Justice Brennan, speaking for a plurality of three, concluded that the *Times* privilege should encompass "all discussion and communication involving matters of public or general concern, without regard to whether the persons involved are famous or anonymous."[102] Therefore the plurality determined that, even though Rosenbloom was not a public official or public figure, his arrest for possession of obscene literature and his subsequent lawsuit against officials and local news media involved a matter of public concern, and any recovery must be based on proof of reckless disregard. Justice White concurred in the applicability of the *Times* standard on the more limited ground that the press has "a privilege to report and comment upon the official actions of public servants in full detail, with no requirement that the reputation or privacy of an individual involved in or affected by the official action be spared from public view."[103] Justice Black provided the fifth vote, concurring in the result because of his belief that the first amendment requires absolute immunity of the press from libel judgments.[104] Three justices dissented; although they differed on other matters, the three agreed that states should be free to permit private individuals to recover on any basis except strict liability.[105]

The majority opinion in *Gertz* did not explicitly overrule *Rosenbloom*, but Justice Powell emphasized the fact that it was a plurality holding, noting that "no majority could agree on a controlling ration-

scribes as "actual malice." *See* W. PROSSER, *supra* note 6, § 115. *See also* 1 F. HARPER & F. JAMES, THE LAW OF TORTS § 5.27 (1956).

99. Green, *The Right to Communicate*, 35 N.Y.U.L. REV. 903, 907 (1960).

100. 403 U.S. 29 (1971).

101. Justice Douglas did not participate in the decision.

102. 403 U.S. at 44 (plurality opinion).

103. *Id.* at 62.

104. *Id.* at 57.

105. *Id.* at 64 (Harlan, J., dissenting); *id.* at 86-87 (Marshall & Stewart, JJ., dissenting).

ale."[106] Want of a controlling rationale, however, presumably does not mean that the result may be ignored, and five justices did agree that the *Times* privilege should apply to George Rosenbloom, even though he was neither a public figure nor a public official.[107] Since the *Gertz* decision rejects the rationale of *Rosenbloom* without offering any alternative explanation for the result in that case, it is probably safe to say that *Rosenbloom* has been effectively overruled.

In discarding *Rosenbloom*'s "public or general concern" test, *Gertz* restricts the *Times* doctrine's influence, confining its operation to "public plaintiff" cases. It thus undermines what had emerged as the dominant rationale for the constitutional privilege to defame—the conviction that the privilege is necessary to protect and encourage uninhibited debate on matters of public concern[108]—and signals a return to a more restricted view of the purposes of the first amendment, one in which only matters close to Meiklejohn's core of self-government[109] receive maximum protection.

Prior to the *Rosenbloom* decision, arguments advanced in support of the *Times* doctrine often reflected the then-prevailing limitation of the privilege to public officials and, subsequently, public figures. The *Times* opinion, which articulated the underlying rationale of encouraging public debate, also concluded that the privilege was "appropriately analogous" to the doctrine of official immunity, which protects public officials from liability for their defamatory statements about private citizens.[110] Later, other arguments in favor of the privilege were advanced, including the following: public officials and public figures are more likely than private citizens to have access to the press, and therefore better able to counter defamatory statements by means other than litigation;[111] and public figures and officials can be said to have waived some of their protection of reputation or assumed the risk of defama-

106. 418 U.S. at 333.

107. 403 U.S. at 43-45, 57, 62. The inclusion of Justice Douglas, who could be expected to adhere to his position that the first amendment bars any defamation recovery, would raise the total to six justices, five of whom would favor a rule at least as protective of the press as that of the *Rosenbloom* plurality. *See id.* at 58-59 (White, J., concurring).

108. *See* 403 U.S. at 40-44.

109. *See* Meiklejohn, *The First Amendment Is an Absolute,* 1961 SUP. CT. REV. 245, 255-57 (1961). *See also* A. MEIKLEJOHN, POLITICAL FREEDOM (1965).

110. 376 U.S. at 282. As Justice Goldberg indicated in his concurring opinion in *Times,* however, the constitutional privilege to defame is not analogous to the doctrine of official immunity; the latter is absolute, while the former is qualified. *Id.* at 304.

111. Time, Inc. v. Hill, 385 U.S. 374, 391 (1967). *See also* Curtis Publishing Co. v. Butts, 388 U.S. 130, 164 (1967) (Warren, C.J., concurring).

tory statements.[112] It soon became apparent, however, that the goal of maximizing protection for public discussion was the real basis of the privilege, and numerous lower courts anticipated *Rosenbloom* by concluding that the *Times* case could not be limited to public figures and public officials.[113]

Rosenbloom was thus a logical step in the evolution of defamation law, which until *Gertz* had been an "orderly development with a consistent basic rationale."[114] Justice Brennan, writing for the plurality, found no convincing justification for limiting the constitutional protection to discussion of matters related to responsible government and grounded the *Rosenbloom* decision squarely on this basic rationale.[115] The theory that public figures will be better able than private persons to respond to defamatory attacks he characterized as an "unproved, and highly improbable, generalization . . . [that] seems too insubstantial a reed on which to rest a constitutional distinction."[116] He dismissed the argument that public figures have assumed the risk of defamation, calling it a "legal fiction"[117] that "bears little relationship either to the values protected by the First Amendment or to the nature of our society."[118] He recognized that, in terms of the public interest, a public-private distinction in defamation law is artificial.[119]

> If a matter is a subject of public or general interest, it cannot suddenly become less so merely because a private individual is involved . . . . The public's primary interest is in the event; the public focus is on the conduct of the participant and the content, effect, and significance of the conduct, not the participant's prior anonymity or notoriety.[120]

112. Curtis Publishing Co. v. Butts, 388 U.S. 130, 164 (1967) (Warren, C.J., concurring).

113. *See, e.g.*, Wasserman v. Time, Inc., 424 F.2d 920 (D.C. Cir.), *cert. denied*, 398 U.S. 940 (1970); Times, Inc. v. McLaney, 406 F.2d 565 (5th Cir.), *cert. denied*, 395 U.S. 922 (1969); United Medical Labs., Inc. v. CBS, Inc., 404 F.2d 706 (9th Cir. 1968), *cert. denied*, 394 U.S. 921 (1969); Konigsberg v. Times, Inc., 312 F. Supp. 848 (S.D.N.Y. 1970). Probably the first case to apply the *Times* standard to a private plaintiff involved in matters of public concern was H.O. Merren & Co. v. A.H. Belo Corp., 228 F. Supp. 515 (N.D. Tex. 1964), which held that an article protected by the Texas statutory privilege of fair comment on a matter of public concern was also constitutionally protected under *Times*. *Id.* at 519.

114. Gertz v. Robert Welch, Inc., 418 U.S. 303, 354 (Burger, C.J., dissenting).

115. *See* 403 U.S. at 40-44 (plurality opinion).

116. *Id.* at 46-47.

117. *Id.* at 48.

118. *Id.* at 47. Justice Powell resurrected both of these theories in *Gertz*, concluding that they remain relevant even though they may not be valid in every instance. 418 U.S. at 344-45.

119. 403 U.S. at 41.

120. *Id.* at 43.

In the three years between *Rosenbloom* and *Gertz*, the extension of the constitutional privilege to private plaintiffs involved in matters of public concern proceeded apace.[121] The courts appeared to be evolving toward a system in which the great bulk of material contained in the press—far more than merely matters relevant to self-government—was subject to the *Times* privilege.[122] *Gertz* abruptly aborted that evolution.

The restrictive potential impact of the decision also is increased by the Court's definitions of "public figure" and "public issue." The

121. *See, e.g.*, Firestone v. Time, Inc., 460 F.2d 712 (5th Cir.), *cert. denied*, 409 U.S. 875 (1972); Cerrito v. Time, Inc., 449 F.2d 306 (9th Cir. 1971); Briscoe v. Reader's Digest Ass'n, 4 Cal. 3d 529, 483 P.2d 34, 93 Cal. Rptr. 866 (1971).

Although Justice Powell doubted the authoritativeness of the *Rosenbloom* plurality opinion, *see* 418 U.S. at 333, 346, few of the lower courts expressed any reservations. *See, e.g.*, Goldman v. Time, Inc., 336 F. Supp. 133, 137 (N.D. Cal. 1971) (applicability of *Times* rule to private plaintiffs involved in matters of public interest "is now unquestioned"); Miller v. Argus Publishing Co., 79 Wash. 2d 816, 825, 490 P.2d 101, 107 (1971) ("we may look to the expressions in the lead opinion as constituting the principles to which we should adhere."). In his dissenting opinion in *Gertz*, Justice White cited cases from seventeen states and four courts of appeals that he says "have felt obliged to consider the . . . *Times* constitutional privilege for liability as extending to . . . 'all discussion and communication involving matters of public or general concern.' " 418 U.S. at 377-80 n.10. In many of the cases cited, however, the *Times* privilege would have been available even without *Rosenbloom* because the plaintiff was a public figure or public official. Nevertheless, they do support the proposition that the lower courts considered the *Rosenbloom* plurality opinion to be a correct statement of the law.

The few courts that refused to apply *Rosenbloom* generally did so not because they doubted its authoritativeness, but on the grounds that the plaintiffs were not involved in matters of public concern. *See, e.g.*, Taggart v. Wadleigh-Maurice, Ltd., 489 F.2d 434 (3d Cir. 1973), *cert. denied*, 417 U.S. 937 (1974); Hood v. Dun & Bradstreet, Inc., 486 F.2d 25 (5th Cir. 1973), *cert. denied*, 415 U.S. 985 (1974); Matus v. Triangle Publications, Inc., 445 Pa. 384, 286 A.2d 357 (1971), *cert. denied*, 408 U.S. 930 (1972). *But see* Gordon v. Random House, Inc., 486 F.2d 1356 (3d Cir. 1973), *vacated*, 95 S. Ct. 27 (1974), in which Judge Aldisert expressed "some discomfort in accepting the *Rosenbloom* plurality opinion as a definitive statement," *id.* at 1359, and predicted that its authority "will depend upon the yet unarticulated First Amendment philosophies of Justices Powell and Rehnquist," *id.* at 1360. *See also* Dietmann v. Time, Inc., 449 F.2d 245 (9th Cir. 1971), holding that the *Times-Rosenbloom* privilege does not protect tortious newsgathering methods. Several student writers called attention to the lack of a majority for Justice Brennan's opinion and questioned the lower courts' acceptance of it. *See The Supreme Court, 1970 Term*, 85 HARV. L. REV. 3, 228 (1971); Note, *Misinterpreting the Supreme Court: An Analysis of How the Constitutional Privilege to Defame Has Been Incorrectly Expanded*, 10 IDAHO L. REV. 213, 216-18 (1974); Note, 6 SUFFOLK L. REV. 712, 717-18 (1972).

122. It was this trend that may have troubled at least two members of the *Gertz* majority. In his dissent in *Rosenbloom*, Justice Marshall, joined by Justice Stewart, observed that "all human events are arguably within the area of 'public or general concern.' " 403 U.S. at 79. This presented him with an unwelcome choice between allowing the media (and/or the public) to define the scope of privileged discussion or involving the courts in the business of deciding what kinds of discussion are relevant to self-government. *Id.*

defense argued that the *Times* privilege applied because Gertz was a public official or public figure.[123] The evidence showed that Gertz was a prolific writer, having authored four books and "thousands" of articles appearing in "historical, legal, literary, . . . and other publications;"[124] that he had made numerous radio and television appearances in Chicago and around the country[125] and had been the subject of over forty articles in Chicago newspapers;[126] and that he had served as an officer of various civic and professional organizations.[127] Some of these activities occurred many years earlier, however, and at the trial all of the jurors apparently stated that they had not heard of Gertz.[128]

The trial court never squarely decided the "public person" issue. By determining that the article was libelous under Illinois law and withdrawing all but the damage issue from the jury, the court implicitly held that Gertz was neither a public official nor a public figure.[129] On defendant's motion for judgment notwithstanding the verdict, however, the judge concluded that the *Times* privilege was available because the article clearly concerned a matter of public interest protected by the Constitution. The court emphasized the attention focused on the killing and subsequent indictment in the then-current climate of widespread criticism of the police and noted that, "[b]y representing the victim's family in litigation brought against the policeman, Gertz thrust himself into the vortex of this important public controversy."[130] The court of appeals questioned the assumption that Gertz was not a public figure,[131] but did not decide that issue because it was able to affirm on the *Rosenbloom* theory.

In the Supreme Court defendant again contended that Gertz should be considered a public figure or public official. Justice Powell quickly disposed of the public official argument,[132] but wrote at some length on the possibility that Gertz might be considered a public figure:

> That designation may rest on either of two alternative bases. In some instances an individual may achieve such pervasive

123. 322 F. Supp. at 998.
124. Appendix at 152-53, Gertz v. Robert Welch, Inc., 418 U.S. 323 (1974).
125. *Id.* at 153.
126. *Id.* at 107; *see, e.g., id.* at 158-59.
127. 418 U.S. at 351.
128. *Id.* at 352.
129. 322 F. Supp. at 998.
130. *Id.* at 1000.
131. 471 F.2d at 805 ("Plaintiff's considerable stature as a lawyer, author, lecturer, and participant in matters of public import undermine the validity of the assumption that he is not a 'public figure' as that term has been used by the progeny of . . . *Times.*").
132. 418 U.S. at 351.

> fame or notoriety that he becomes a public figure for all purposes and in all contexts. More commonly, an individual voluntarily injects himself or is drawn into a particular public controversy and thereby becomes a public figure for a limited range of issues.[133]

The Court concluded that Gertz had not attained such general fame or notoriety as to be a public figure for all purposes. Looking to the nature and extent of his participation in the particular controversy, the Court determined that he "plainly did not thrust himself into the vortex of this public issue, nor did he engage the public's attention in an attempt to influence its outcome."[134]

Gertz may be distinguishable from the leading public figure cases[135] on the ground that those plaintiffs—General Edwin Walker and athletic director Wally Butts—had achieved widespread notoriety in their communities, while Gertz was well known only within certain circles.[136] The conclusion that Gertz had not voluntarily become a public figure for limited purposes is less persuasive. The shooting and the subsequent murder indictment were the subject of widespread public debate, and there was no reason to believe that the civil action by the youth's family would not attract similar attention. By agreeing to represent the family in its suit, it could be said that Gertz voluntarily injected himself into the controversy.[137] But the Court found Gertz's involvement insignificant, noting that he did not participate in the policeman's prosecution and never discussed any aspect of either the civil or crimi-

133. *Id.* at 351. *See also* Buckley v. Esquire, Inc., 344 F. Supp. 1133 (S.D.N.Y. 1972).

134. 418 U.S. at 352.

135. Curtis Publishing Co. v. Butts, 388 U.S. 130 (1967) (with companion case, *Associated Press v. Walker*).

136. *But see* Pember & Teeter, *Privacy and the Press Since* Time, Inc. v. Hill, 50 Wash. L. Rev. 57 (1974). The authors conclude that the Court's refusal to treat Gertz as a public figure was unjustified:

> Gertz was a member of numerous boards and commissions in Illinois, had published several books on civil rights matters, had frequently been honored by civil rights groups and had represented some rather famous clients. . . . His publishing record belies the notion that he was a poor, helpless, private individual who could not gain access to the press. Gertz was a public figure in every sense of the term as defined by the Supreme Court in *Curtis v. Butts.* The *Rosenbloom* rule should not have been at issue in the case.

Id. at 75.

137. One may sympathize with Chief Justice Burger's view that the right to counsel would be jeopardized if lawyers representing unpopular causes "automatically became fair game for irresponsible reporters and editors . . . ." 418 U.S. at 355 (Burger, C.J., dissenting). Nevertheless, it is a well-known and unavoidable fact that an attorney who represents the disfavored risks public criticism and perhaps defamation. It is improbable that a lawyer, in deciding whether to accept such a client, will be influenced measurably by a calculation of his chances of winning a libel action in the event he is defamed.

nal case with the press. Thus, the Court apparently determined that the pertinent public issue was confined to the murder and subsequent litigation. The subject of the defamatory article, however, was much broader, alleging a nationwide communist-directed campaign to discredit and harass the police and charging Gertz, who was an outspoken critic of police brutality,[138] with complicity in that campaign through various activities and associations.[139] Rightly or wrongly, some persons would argue that activities such as those in which Gertz engaged interfere with law enforcement and discredit the police. Unless the Court considered this argument so untenable that it raised no issue, the relevant controversy should have been defined in these broader terms.

Justice Powell's statement that a private person may become a public figure by being "drawn in to a particular public controversy"[140] suggests a category of involuntary public figures.[141] Even if Gertz did

138. *See* Appendix at 158-59, Gertz v. Robert Welch, Inc., 418 U.S. 323 (1974). In a newspaper article about Gertz he is quoted as saying:

> The place to start getting law and order is with the police . . . .
>
> This phony cry of law and order has blinded too many people to the fact that one of the greatest dangers today is the police failure to understand freedom of expression, the right to dissent, the rights of minority groups, the separation of church and state, the fact that a young man's long hair is none of their business.
>
> The sad thing is you have to be vigilant day and night, or you have abuses.

Id. at 159.

139. *See* 418 U.S. at 325-26; Appendix at 17-36, Gertz v. Robert Welch, Inc., 418 U.S. 323 (1974).

140. 418 U.S. at 351. Elsewhere in the opinion, however, Justice Powell stated that "the instances of truly involnntary public figures must be exceedingly rare." *Id.* at 345.

141. Thus far, those held to be public figures have been persons who voluntarily injected themselves into public matters or held positions of public prominence. *See* Curtis Publishing Co. v. Butts, 388 U.S. 130 (1967); Pauling v. Globe-Democrat Publishing Co., 362 F.2d 188 (8th Cir. 1966). The plaintiff in Rosenblatt v. Baer, 383 U.S. 75 (1966), might have been viewed as an involuntary public figure, but the Court instead treated him as a "public official" because of his status as a former government employee. *Id.* at 86-87. The plaintiff in Time, Inc. v. Hill, 385 U.S. 374 (1967), also could be characterized as an involuntary public figure; his only exposure to publicity resulted from his being held hostage by escaped convicts. The Court applied the *Times* privilege, not because it considered Hill an involuntary public figure, but because the publication in question concerned a matter of public interest. *Id.* at 387-88.

Since *Gertz,* the Court has considered two cases brought by plaintiffs who arguably were involuntary public figures, but in neither did the Court reach that question. In Cantrell v. Forest City Publishing Co., 43 U.S.L.W. 4079 (U.S., Dec. 18, 1974), plaintiffs were the widow and son of a man killed in a widely publicized bridge disaster. A jury, instructed to apply the *Times* test, awarded compensatory damages on a false light theory of invasion of privacy. The court of appeals, interpreting the trial court's denial of punitive damages as a finding of no "actual malice," reversed. 484 F.2d 150 (6th Cir. 1973). The Supreme Court, however, held that absence of the common-law malice required for an award of punitive damages did not preclude a finding of "actual malice" for *Times* purposes. The Court consequently ordered affirmance of the trial court judgment without deciding whether the *Times* standard was applicable. *See also* Random

not become a voluntary public figure, then, the Court could have held that he had been involuntarily drawn into the larger controversy over police conduct. The Court apparently did not even consider that possibility, however, and its failure to do so probably indicates that the newly described category is not much broader than the one suggested by Justice White in his concurring opinion in *Rosenbloom*: "individual[s] involved in or affected by . . . official action."[142]

Finally, *Gertz* is significant in terms of momentum. From the *Times* case until *Gertz*, the Supreme Court's libel decisions all moved toward greater press protection. The privilege first recognized in *Times* quickly expanded to include criminal libel.[143] The term "public official" as used in *Times* received an expansive reading,[144] and the privilege was extended to public figures,[145] applied by analogy in the privacy area,[146] and injected into several nonmedia contexts.[147] The Court defined reckless disregard to preclude liability unless the defendant actually had serious doubts about the veracity of his statements.[148] Finally, in *Rosenbloom* the privilege was extended to one who was neither a public official nor a public figure.

This momentum encouraged less fearful journalism. The press believed, perhaps erroneously, that the Supreme Court would protect it from most libel awards. Potential plaintiffs—or at least their lawyers—perhaps shared that belief.[149] Simply because the Supreme

House, Inc. v. Gordon, 349 F. Supp. 919 (E.D. Pa. 1972), *vacated*, 486 F.2d 1356 (3d Cir. 1973), *vacated*, 95 S. Ct. 27 (1974).

In Meeropol v. Nizer, 381 F. Supp. 29 (S.D.N.Y. 1974), the court considered the effect of *Gertz* in both privacy and defamation contexts. Plaintiffs, sons of Julius and Ethel Rosenberg, sued Louis Nizer and his publisher for libel and invasion of privacy in connection with Nizer's book about the Rosenbergs' trial and execution. Although plaintiffs had changed their names and managed to conceal their parentage from all but a few persons for twenty years, the court held them to be public figures subject to the *Times* test, at least with respect to defamatory statements dealing with their past lives as Rosenberg children. On the invasion of privacy theory, the court held the statements to be constitutionally privileged because they concerned matters "properly within the orbit of public interest and scrutiny." *Id.* at 37.

142. 403 U.S. at 62.

143. Garrison v. Louisiana, 379 U.S. 64, 67 (1964).

144. Rosenblatt v. Baer, 383 U.S. 75, 84 (1966).

145. Curtis Publishing Co. v. Butts, 388 U.S. 130 (1967).

146. Time, Inc. v. Hill, 385 U.S. 374 (1967).

147. Pickering v. Board of Educ., 391 U.S. 563 (1968) (dismissal of public school teacher); Linn v. Plant Guard Workers Local 114, 383 U.S. 53 (1966) (labor dispute). For additional cases extending the *Times* privilege to nonmedia defendants, see Stevens, *Defamation of Political Figures; Another Look at the* Times-Sullivan *Rule*, 27 FED. COM. B.J. 99, 100-101 nn.5-15 (1974).

148. St. Amant v. Thompson, 390 U.S. 727, 731 (1968); Beckley Newspaper Corp. v. Hanks, 389 U.S. 81, 84-85 (1967).

149. *Cf.* Coonradt, *supra* note 41, at 26.

Court stood by it so unswervingly and extended it so readily, the *Times* privilege was more effective in preventing self-censorship than its actual operation warranted.

Whatever *Gertz*'s net effect, the decision clearly does not reflect the enthusiastic extension of first amendment protection that characterized other post-*Times* Supreme Court defamation cases. It represents a retrenchment and threatens to increase libel litigation for two reasons. First, it improves the chances for recovery by private persons involved in a matter of public concern; those plaintiffs, previously required to prove reckless disregard, now need show only negligence. Second, and more important, *Gertz* may change potential litigants' perceptions of their chances, even where the decision itself has not objectively altered them. Potential plaintiffs probably will feel that the Court is more sensitive to their interests, and the press is likely to sense that the Court is a less reliable protector than was previously believed.[150]

150. One other possible effect of *Gertz* should be mentioned. Justice Powell suggests that expressions of opinion cannot be actionable: "Under the First Amendment there is no such thing as a false idea. However pernicious an opinion may seem, we depend for its correction not on the conscience of judges and juries but on the competition of other ideas." 418 U.S. at 339-40 (footnote omitted). Another libel case decided the same day lends some support to this possibility. In Old Dominion Branch 496, Nat'l Ass'n of Letter Carriers v. Austin, 418 U.S. 264 (1974), the Court held that a publication calling plaintiffs "scabs" was not actionable, even though that epithet was embellished with Jack London's famous and virulent definition of the word, *id.* at 268, because there was no false statement of fact. *Id.* at 283-84. The *Times* standard was applied as a matter of federal labor law.

But it is still uncertain whether liability for the expression of opinion is constitutionally prohibited. *Austin* was decided based on labor law, not first amendment principles. Also, it is not clear whether the Court denied recovery because it considered the publication merely defamatory opinion or because it did not consider it defamatory at all; the opinion can be read as holding only that plaintiffs' description was hyperbole. *See id.* at 284; *id.* at 296 (Powell, J., dissenting). Moreover, Justice Powell, whose dictum in *Gertz* suggested the possible ban, would have held the union liable in *Austin*. Finally, the *Austin* holding would not necessarily apply to cases under *Gertz*, because *Austin* applied the knowing or reckless disregard test.

It would be futile to base a distinction of constitutional magnitude on the difference between "fact" and "opinion." If such a thing as a statement of pure opinion exists, it is unlikely to be defamatory. Most statements of opinion are also capable of conveying an implication of fact. This is clear in the case of a term like "scab." The word obviously conveys the speaker's opinion about the subject, but it also conveys—or at least is capable of conveying—a factual statement.

Instead of drawing a fact-opinion distinction, courts should focus on the basic issue that applies to statements of any kind: does the statement, read fairly and in context, tend to damage the plaintiff's reputation? The key words are "read fairly." They require courts to take a more active role in interpreting the language claimed to be defamatory. The Supreme Court's review of the word "blackmail" in Greenbolt Cooperative Publishing Ass'n v. Bresler, 398 U.S. 6 (1970), illustrates the proper approach. Even though the relevant state law made blackmail a felony, and a jury apparently believed the statement should be read as charging defendant with a crime, the Court reviewed

Libel and Self-Censorship

2. *Bias in Favor of Orthodox Media.*—From its inception, the *Times* privilege has best served those elements of the press that adhere to the most traditional and narrow journalistic role. The rule best protects those who concentrate on the workings of officialdom. The publisher or broadcaster whose sense of news does not extend beyond the activities of city hall, the courthouse, the statehouse, and Washington usually operates in protected territory. Extension of the privilege's protection to public figures allows for a slightly expanded sense of news: the publisher or broadcaster may go beyond officialdom, but he should not venture past matters relating to "public figures," that is, persons who already have attracted press attention.[151] Thus, the press can be confident of receiving maximum constitutional protection only so long as it concentrates on government and those persons upon whom the rest of the media focus.

A privilege to report on public officials and public figures offers little protection to segments of the press attempting to illuminate previously unexposed aspects of society. The sources and uses of private power—in business, the professions, the arts, the media—represent matters of increasing concern, yet the *Times* privilege encourages the press to confine its coverage to more traditional kinds of power. In the past few years the press has become increasingly aware of the need to report not only "events," but also trends, practices, mores, and conditions in the society.[152] *Rosenbloom* encouraged this development; discussions of the life styles of disaffected American youth,[153] the quality

the context of the statement and concluded that under the circumstances the word was not defamatory. With realistic review of jury findings on the defamation issue, the problem of liability for "opinion" can be solved without creating another constitutional rule.

151. The influence of the press in creating "public figures" is evident in Justice Powell's own definition of that term. He describes a "public figure" as one who has achieved "pervasive fame or notoriety" or has become involved in "a particular public controversy." 418 U.S. at 351. Perhaps fame, notoriety, or controversy can exist without press assistance, but usually media attention is the key ingredient.

152. *See, e.g.*, Foisie, *A DEW Line on the News*, in OF THE PRESS, BY THE PRESS, FOR THE PRESS (AND OTHERS, TOO) 233 (Babb ed. 1974); Barrett, *Sex, Death and Other Trends in Magazines*, 13 COLUM. JOURNALISM REV., July/Aug. 1974, at 24; Mintz, *Auditing the Media: A Modest Proposal*, 11 COLUM. JOURNALISM REV., Nov./Dec. 1972, at 20. Frequently the press fails to perceive the need for this type of journalism until someone else points it out. For example, there was little coverage of ghetto problems until the National Advisory Commission on Civil Disorders chastised the press for failing "to report adequately on the causes and consequences of civil disorders and the underlying problems of race relations." REPORT OF THE NATIONAL ADVISORY COMMISSION ON CIVIL DISORDERS 201 (1968).

153. Goldman v. Time, Inc., 336 F. Supp. 133 (N.D. Cal. 1971).

of private business services,[154] private investigative techniques,[155] racial tensions,[156] and competence of professionals[157] received the same protection under the *Rosenbloom* rationale as press coverage of officialdom.

Gertz reflects a more orthodox view of both the purposes of the first amendment and the proper scope of journalism. Full constitutional protection extends only to speech related to self-government, discussions of official conduct, fitness for public office, and activities of public figures. This gives conventional newspapers and broadcasters the most protection, while more innovative media—primarily magazines[158] and books—receive the least. From the viewpoint of readers and viewers, it means the private sectors of American life will be less fully explored than the public sectors.

This built-in bias favoring more conventional elements of the press will be exacerbated if courts define "negligence" under *Gertz* by reference to the standards of "responsible publishers." The *Gertz* majority offered no definition of negligence; indeed it spoke primarily of prohibiting liability without fault, and mentioned negligence only in passing. Yet the decision clearly requires some species of fault, and negligence probably is the minimum that will suffice.[159] Since the negligence at issue in suits against the press is negligence by a professional disseminator of news, presumably the defendant's conduct is to be measured against a professional standard, and customs and practices of the profession undoubtedly are relevant.[160] This creates a possibility that the negligence required by *Gertz* might be defined by something similar to the standard proposed by Justice Harlan in *Curtis Publishing*

154. *E.g.*, Bon Air Hotel, Inc. v. Time, Inc., 426 F.2d 858 (5th Cir. 1970); United Medical Labs., Inc. v. CBS, Inc., 404 F.2d 706 (9th Cir. 1968), *cert. denied*, 394 U.S. 921 (1969). *But see* Matus v. Triangle Publications, Inc., 445 Pa. 384, 286 A.2d 357 (1971), *cert. denied*, 408 U.S. 930 (1972).

155. Firestone v. Time, Inc., 460 F.2d 712 (5th Cir.), *cert. denied*, 409 U.S. 875 (1972).

156. *See* Gordon v. Random House, Inc., 349 F. Supp. 919 (E.D. Pa. 1972), *vacated*, 486 F.2d 1356 (3d Cir. 1973), *cert. granted, judgment vacated, and cause remanded*, 95 S. Ct. 27 (1974).

157. Dacey v. Florida Bar, Inc., 427 F.2d 1292 (5th Cir. 1970); Farnsworth v. Tribune Co., 43 Ill. 2d 286, 253 N.E.2d 408 (Ill. 1969).

158. In the words of one commentator: "Magazines, more than the daily press, mirror the mood, the mores, and the faddish tastes of society. In recent years, for example, they dealt heavily with ghettos and poverty, with bold treatment of sexual subjects, with the youth 'revolution,' and with inadequacies in the education system." Barrett, *supra* note 152, at 25.

159. *See* text accompanying notes 177-85 *infra*.

160. *See* Restatement (Second) of Torts § 299a (1965).

Libel and Self-Censorship

Co. v. Butts:[161] "the standards of investigation and reporting ordinarily adhered to by responsible publishers."[162]

A "responsible publishers" standard would discriminate unjustifiably against media or outlets whose philosophies and methods deviate from those of the mainstream. Fundamental disagreements exist within the profession concerning what constitutes responsible journalism.[163] The conventional view is that a "responsible" journalist must strive to separate fact from opinion, and to report the former "objectively"; a significant segment of the profession now maintains that to avoid taking a position is irresponsible.[164] There is disagreement over the extent of the profession's responsibility to inform the public; some believe good journalism must attempt to arrest the attention of the disinterested and therefore must try to entertain, shock, or outrage, while others see their function as simply making information available to those sufficiently motivated to seek it.[165] Although some deplore extensive editorial second-guessing and advocate maximum freedom for individual writers, others view the best journalism as a team effort by reporters, writers, and editors. Furthermore, there is little agreement within the profession on the acceptability of various journalistic practices, including the use of unnamed sources,[166] the unauthorized dissemination of classified government information,[167] and the technique employed by some of obtaining information without revealing one's identity as a reporter.[168] Some press outlets feel a responsibility

161. 388 U.S. 130 (1967).
162. *Id.* at 155.
163. *See, e.g.*, Booth, *Loathing and Ignorance on the Campaign Trail: 1972*, COLUM. JOURNALISM REV., Nov./Dec. 1973, at 7 (describing the divergent views and methods of two journalists in their books on the 1972 presidential campaign: T. WHITE, THE MAKING OF THE PRESIDENT 1972 (1973), and H. THOMPSON, FEAR AND LOATHING: ON THE CAMPAIGN TRAIL '72 (1973)).
164. *See generally* Hvistendahl, *The Reporter as Activist: Fourth Revolution in Journalism*, in READINGS IN MASS COMMUNICATION 116 (M. Emery & T. Smythe eds. 1972).
165. *See generally* E. DENNIS & W. RIVERS, OTHER VOICES: THE NEW JOURNALISM IN AMERICA (1974); T. WOLFE, THE NEW JOURNALISM (1973).
166. *See* Blasi, *The Newsman's Privilege: An Empirical Study*, 70 MICH. L. REV. 229 (1971), a survey in which the average journalist is estimated to rely on confidential sources in 22.2 percent of his stories. *See also* C. BERNSTEIN & B. WOODWARD, ALL THE PRESIDENT'S MEN (1974); Royster, *Shield Laws Have Boobytraps*, SEMINAR Q., June 1973, at 13.
167. The New York Times won a Pulitzer Prize for its publication of the Pentagon Papers; the Chicago Tribune did not print the papers and carried a front-page editorial criticizing the journalistic ethics of those who did. S. UNGAR, *supra* note 80, at 17; *cf.* Pearson v. Dodd, 410 F.2d 701 (D.C. Cir.), *cert. denied*, 395 U.S. 947 (1969), discussing the propriety and legality of publishing materials known to have been copied without authorization from private files.
168. *See* Dietemann v. Time, Inc., 449 F.2d 245 (9th Cir. 1971).

to suppress items whose veracity they are unable to ascertain, but others assert that the press has no more right than the government to deny information to the public unless it is demonstrably false.

The *Gertz* negligence standard should not require juries to resolve these disagreements about journalistic philosophies and practices. The standard of care should be sufficiently particularized so that a publisher with an unpopular philosophy, an unorthodox journalistic style, or limited resources will have its conduct measured against the standards of similar publishers, rather than those of the established, conventional press. But it seems inevitable that in practice those who stay closest to the mainstream will be more likely to escape a jury's disapproval.

3. *Impact on the Use of the Summary Judgment Procedure.*— The most serious deficiency of the *Times* privilege is that it operates too late in the litigation process.[169] But the constitutionalization of the reckless disregard standard, giving the appellate courts broad power to review findings of actual malice, opened the way for widespread use of summary judgment procedure, particularly in the federal courts. If the publication is one to which the constitutional privilege applies, the defendant is entitled to summary judgment[170] unless the plaintiff can produce evidence of reckless disregard. The specificity of the Supreme Court's definition of "actual malice" made this development possible. Actual malice may not be inferred from the language of the publication in question[171] or from the publisher's hostility toward the plaintiff,[172] and evidence of failure to verify usually will not establish recklessness.[173] Consequently, the defendant may be granted summary judgment unless the plaintiff can produce independent evidence

169. *See* text accompanying notes 72-77 *supra.*

170. A defendant may file a motion for summary judgment any time after the commencement of the suit. FED. R. CIV. P. 56(b).

171. *See* Greenbelt Cooperative Publishing Ass'n v. Bresler, 398 U.S. 6 (1970); Washington Post Co. v. Keogh, 365 F.2d 965 (D.C. Cir. 1965), *cert. denied,* 385 U.S. 1011 (1967).

172. Henry v. Collins, 380 U.S. 356 (1965); Tagawa v. Maui Publishing Co., 50 Hawaii 648, 448 P.2d 337 (1968), *cert. denied,* 396 U.S. 822 (1969).

173. *See* Time, Inc. v. McLaney, 406 F.2d 565 (5th Cir.), *cert. denied,* 395 U.S. 922 (1969); Washington Post Co. v. Keogh, 365 F.2d 965 (D.C. Cir. 1965), *cert. denied,* 385 U.S. 1011 (1967); McCunn v. California Teachers Ass'n, 3 Cal. App. 3d 965, 83 Cal. Rptr. 846 (1970). Justice White's opinion in St. Amant v. Thompson, 390 U.S. 727 (1968), left open the possibility that a defendant who fails to verify might be found reckless if his information is based on an anonymous telephone call, if his statements are "so inherently improbable that only a reckless man would have put them in circulation," or if he has "obvious reasons to doubt the veracity of the informant or the accuracy of his reports." *Id.* at 732.

that the defendant knew the material was false or entertained serious doubts concerning its veracity.[174]

This represents an important and useful step in the evolution of the *Times* principle, making the privilege effective close to the outset of the litigation. If the plaintiff cannot show recklessness, the litigation ends without the expense of a jury trial. If he can make a preliminary showing, his negotiating position improves considerably, and he has a preliminary indication that any verdict he wins may survive an appeal based on *Times*. *Rosenbloom* made summary judgment procedure even more promising by bringing the vast majority of libel suits against the press under the *Times* privilege.

Presumably *Gertz* will neither affect the procedure's utility in public plaintiff cases nor preclude its extension to private plaintiff cases. Nevertheless, courts probably will not grant summary judgments as readily under *Gertz* as under *Rosenbloom*. Some courts will deny summary judgment on the ground that a negligence standard requires the kind of factual determination that has always been regarded as peculiarly within the competence of juries.[175] But uncertainty concerning the definition of negligence represents the most important obstacle to summary procedure under *Gertz*. Whether it will be defined with the particularity that characterizes recklessness under *Times* remains to be seen, but unless the courts describe the negligence standard with some precision, the purposes of the *Gertz* privilege will be defeated just as surely as those of the *Times* privilege would have been if the Court had left the determination of reckless disregard to the unquestioned judgment of juries. Until a clear delineation emerges through the lengthy process of litigation, however, it will be difficult to determine whether genuine issues of material fact exist.

Another unanswered question potentially affecting the availability of summary judgment concerns whether negligence under *Gertz* is a "constitutional fact" requiring de novo appellate review of the evidence. If not, then presumably a court should be more reluctant to substitute its evaluation of the evidence for that of the jury. Also un-

174. *See* Time, Inc. v. Johnston, 448 F.2d 378, 384 (4th Cir. 1971); Bon Air Hotel, Inc. v. Time, Inc., 426 F.2d 858, 863 (5th Cir. 1970); Thompson v. Evening Star Newspaper Co., 394 F.2d 774, 776 (D.C. Cir.), *cert. denied*, 393 U.S. 884 (1968).

175. *See* cases cited in 10 C. Wright & A. Miller, Federal Practice and Procedure § 2729, at 560-61 n.75 (1973). Wright and Miller conclude, however, that "it would be wrong to assume that summary judgment is never appropriate in negligence actions." *Id.* at 561. For a more complete discussion of this question, see text accompanying notes 212-17 *infra*.

clear is whether negligence may be shown by the usual "preponderance of the evidence" standard or must be established with "convincing clarity," as *Times* requires.[176] The preponderance standard would make more difficult a finding that no genuine issue exists.

Eventually perhaps, courts will evolve a meaning for the *Gertz* negligence standard that will lend itself to the summary judgment procedure. But at least until such an understanding develops, growth of the summary procedure in private plaintiff cases will probably be greatly restricted.

III. DEFAMATION AND THE PRESS AFTER *Gertz*

Gertz does not diminish the press' protection from libel suits brought by public officials and public figures. In actions by private plaintiffs it provides more protection than the press had at common law, but less than the press had come to expect since *Rosenbloom*. A complete assessment of the decision's impact will be impossible until the courts address the questions that the Supreme Court left unanswered. The most important of these concern the nature and proof of the fault required to establish liability, the definition of "actual injury," and the recoverability of presumed and punitive damages when reckless disregard is proved. Depending on the courts' response, *Gertz*'s potentially detrimental impact on the press can be reduced. Answers to a few of these questions are suggested in the Court's opinion; others can only be surmised.

A. Negligence in the Defamation Context

1. Defining Fault.—Gertz ouly established a constitutional minimum: it permits any standard except strict liability.[177] Most states probably will adopt a negligence standard,[178] although they could require a greater degree of fault, such as gross negligence or reckless disregard. It is unlikely that any state will opt for a gross negligence standard. That term has proved troublesome enough in physical

176. Justice Brennan assumed that negligence under *Gertz* will be determiued by a preponderance of the evidence. 418 U.S. at 366 (dissenting opinion). *But see* text accompauying uotes 209-11 *infra*.

177. *Id.* at 347.

178. The Court seems to have assumed this result. Although Justice Powell stated the Court's holding in terms of a "caveat against strict liability," *id.* at 347 n.10, his opinion at one point indicated that the new standard for private defamation actions is to be a "negligence standard," *id.* at 350.

torts;[179] in defamation it would represent an entirely new concept whose parameters would be at least as difficult to develop as those of *Gertz*'s negligence standard. If some states choose a standard higher than ordinary negligence, they probably will apply the *Times* test.[180] They might do so in all defamation actions, only in those against media, or only in those involving matters of public or general concern.[181] States might prefer the *Times* privilege for several reasons. First, Justice Brennan's argument may persuade them that a distinction based on speech involving public issues is more consistent with first amendment purposes than one based on a belief that private plaintiffs as a class are more vulnerable and more deserving than public plaintiffs.[182] Second, they may seek to avoid the problems inherent in implementing an entirely new system of liability for defamation. By extending the *Times* test, most of the uncertainties involved in the *Gertz* scheme can be avoided. The *Times* system provides an accepted, workable, and understandable method for dealing with defamation actions, while a new standard inevitably creates some confusion. Third, states may hesitate to build an entirely new system of liability on the basis of a one-vote margin that could dissolve in the Court's next defamation decision.[183] While the four dissenters do not agree on an alternative, none has any enthusiasm for a negligence standard. A state that doubts the permanence of the *Gertz* majority probably can minimize the risk of reversal by adhering to the *Times* test. Finally, although state courts and legislatures will be reluctant to modify their common law or statutory defamation doctrines more drastically than the Supreme Court requires, all state constitutions have their own freedom

179. *See* W. PROSSER, *supra* note 6, § 34, at 181-86; Elliott, *Degrees of Negligence*, 6 S. CAL. L. REV. 91, 114-22 (1932).

180. *Cf.* Aafco Heating & Air Conditioning Co. v. Northwest Publications, Inc., 321 N.E.2d 580 (Ind. Ct. App., 1974) (rejecting the *Gertz* standard and interpreting the Indiana constitution's freedom of expression clause to require application of the *Times* standard when the plaintiff is a private individual involved in an event of general public interest).

181. *Cf.* TEX. REV. CIV. STAT. ANN. art. 5432(4) (1958), creating a privilege for "reasonable and fair comment or criticism of the official acts of public officials *and of other matters of public concern published for general information*" (emphasis added).

182. Gertz v. Robert Welch, Inc., 418 U.S. 323, 361 (1974) (dissenting opinion); Rosenbloom v. Metromedia, Inc., 403 U.S. 29, 41-54 (1971) (plurality opinion).

183. Even absent any change in Court membership, the *Gertz* majority may not be unshakeable; Justice Blackmun, a member of the *Rosenbloom* plurality, stated in *Gertz* that he would have adhered to his prior position except for his belief that a definitive ruling was more important. 418 U.S. at 354 (concurring opinion). As Justice White charged, "the Court discards history and precedent in its rush to refashion defamation law in accordance with the inclinations of a perhaps evanescent majority of the Justices." *Id.* at 380 (dissenting opinion).

of expression clauses,[184] and a state court occasionally interprets its own constitution more expansively than the Supreme Court does the federal constitution.[185] Nevertheless, many states probably will opt for a negligence standard, and these will face the task of providing substance to the standard outlined in Gertz.

States adopting a negligence standard will find that they cannot simply apply to defamation actions the existing body of negligence law developed in physical torts. Negligence as a constitutional prerequisite serves a function quite different from that of negligence as a common law basis of liability. As Dean Green has pointed out,

> [T]he law in a negligence case is made ex post facto and ad hoc; it is constructed on the spot for the particular case. Except as to process, precedent has little part to play other than to mark the outer bounds of liability as determined by broad policies. Even in process there is slight similarity from case to case except within a general pattern. Uniformity and certainty of result are not only impossible but undesirable.[186]

While some might quarrel with portions of this description, few would deny that negligence in the physical torts represents a very flexible mechanism for obtaining the judgment of both judge and jury on a specific fact situation.[187] But negligence under *Gertz* serves an entirely different purpose—the preservation of a minimum area of "breathing space" for the press—which it attempts to accomplish by freeing publishers and broadcasters from liability for innocent misstatements. *Gertz* envisions a regime in which publishers who exercise reasonable care need not fear libel judgments, but the hope that this will prevent unnecessary self-censorship is illusory. No one with the slightest appreciation for the myriad uncertainties of common law negligence would rely on the belief that reasonable care will preclude an adverse verdict. If the common law concept of negligence is applied

184. *See* LEGISLATIVE DRAFTING RESEARCH FUND, INDEX DIGEST OF STATE CONSTITUTIONS 484-86 (2d ed. 1959).

185. *See* Aafco Heating & Air Conditioning Co. v. Northwest Publications, Inc., 321 N.E.2d 580 (Ind. Ct. App., 1974). *Compare* Serrano v. Priest, 5 Cal. 3d 584, 487 P.2d 1241, 96 Cal. Rptr. 601 (1971), *and* Robinson v. Cahill, 118 N.J. Super. 223, 287 A.2d 187 (1972), *with* San Antonio Independent School Dist. v. Rodriguez, 411 U.S. 1 (1973).

186. Green, *The Duty to Give Accurate Information*, 12 U.C.L.A.L. REV. 464, 470-71 (1965).

187. This flexibility is evident from the *Restatement*'s definition of negligence as "conduct which falls below the standard established by law for the protection of others against unreasonable risk of harm," RESTATEMENT (SECOND) OF TORTS § 282 (1965), and its conclusion that standard of conduct may be established by statute, regulation, or judicial decision, or by the judge or jury in a particular case, *id.* § 285.

to defamation, the extent of a publisher's constitutional protection will depend on a jury's relatively unfettered, ex post facto appraisal of his conduct, and since the publisher has no way of knowing how large the jury will make the prohibited zone, he has no choice but to steer wide of it. To prevent this erosion of first amendment protection, *Gertz* negligence must be defined more specifically than the common law concept applied to physical torts.

The question of negligence in the publication of a defamatory falsehood involves far more complex issues than the question of negligence in causing a traffic accident. Potentially at least two types of negligent conduct exist in the defamation context. First, the defendant may be negligent regarding danger to reputation—for example, by negligently failing to recognize a statement's defamatory potential, either because he did not realize that the words could have a defamatory meaning,[188] or because he failed to recognize that the plaintiff might be identified as the person to whom the words referred.[189] Second, the defendant may be negligent with respect to the truth or falsity of a statement—for example, by not attempting to verify it or by failing to publish the statement accurately (such as by negligently transposing photo captions). It is unclear whether *Gertz* requires proof of negligence regarding both danger to reputation and veracity or only one of these.

Courts thus far have applied the *Times* test only to veracity; apparently no case has arisen in which the defendant did not act with reckless disregard for the truth or falsity of the statement, but was reckless concerning the danger to reputation.[190] If the *Gertz* standard is

188. For example, the defendant could fail to realize that the French word "cocotte," meaning poached egg, also is used to describe "a woman who leads a fast life, one who gives herself up for money." Rovira v. Boget, 240 N.Y. 314, 316, 148 N.E. 534, 535 (1925).

189. *See, e.g.*, American Broadcasting-Paramount Theatres, Inc. v. Simpson, 106 Ga. App. 230, 126 S.E.2d 873 (1962) (plaintiff, although not named in dramatization of real life episode, was identifiable to those familiar with facts); Thorson v. Albert Lea Publishing Co., 190 Minn. 200, 251 N.W. 177 (1933) (defendant correctly named man arrested, but failed to provide further identification to show that the subject of the arrest was not plaintiff, who bore the same name).

190. Prosser suggested that the *Times* privilege is applicable to the "disclosure" category of invasion of privacy suits as well as "false light" cases. W. PROSSER, *supra* note 6, § 118, at 827. If he is correct, the *Times* definition of actual malice obviously must be modified. Since the veracity of the publication is irrelevant when the tort is public disclosure of private facts, it would be absurd to inquire whether the defendant published with reckless disregard for the truth or falsity of the statements. Presumably, the inquiry would be whether the defendant published with reckless disregard for the plaintiff's privacy. The Supreme Court has not applied such a standard, however. The only "right

functionally analogous to the *Times* standard, differing only in the quantum of fault required, then presumably *Gertz* demands at least a finding of negligent falsity. Persuasive reasons exist for concluding that the two standards are analogous. Both create a constitutional privilege designed to give speakers more latitude than the common law allows. Both build on the premise that truth, no matter how negligently or recklessly used, cannot be actionable in defamation, and both concede that falsehoods also must have some protection if first amendment goals are to be realized. Justice Powell objected to strict liability because it permits the press to be "held liable in damages even if it took every reasonable precaution to ensure the accuracy of its assertions."[191] The two cases focus squarely on the issue of truth or falsity. Therefore, it seems probable that *Gertz* negligence is intended to differ only quantitatively from *Times* recklessness and that *Gertz* requires a finding of negligence with respect to veracity.

This is not to say that *Gertz* requires a showing of negligence only in the matter of a statement's truth or falsity or that *Times* requires only recklessness concerning veracity. It seems inconceivable that the Court would permit the imposition of liability under *Times* where the defendant, although reckless with respect to falsity, was innocent with respect to the danger to reputation. For example, suppose a magazine published a work of fiction that used a name believed and intended to be fictitious, but in fact the name was that of a public official, some readers believed that the publication referred to that official, and it defamed him. The plaintiff would have no difficulty meeting the *Times* standard with respect to falsity; the magazine knew its statements were false. Yet to permit recovery would be to permit a form of strict liability. Unless the magazine was negligent in failing to discover that

of privacy" cases to which the Court has applied the *Times* privilege are Time, Inc. v. Hill, 385 U.S. 374 (1967), and Cantrell v. Forest City Publishing Co., 95 S. Ct. 465 (1974), which are both "false light" cases, *i.e.*, cases in which plaintiff claimed that defendant had portrayed him in a false light. The Court applied the orthodox *Times* formulation, asking whether defendant knew of or was reckless with regard to the falsity of its portrayal of plaintiff. None of the cases on which Prosser relies are "disclosure" cases, and there is apparently no case in which the *Times* standard has been modified for application to such a privacy suit.

The Court so far has decided only one invasion of privacy case involving disclosure of true but embarrassing private facts, Cox Broadcasting Co. v. Cohn, 43 U.S.L.W. 4343 (U.S. Mar. 3, 1975). The Court held that "the States may not impose sanctions for the publication of truthful information contained in official court records open to public inspection." *Id.* at 4351. Nothing in the opinion suggests that the result would be different if the plaintiff could show reckless disregard for his privacy.

191. 418 U.S. at 346.

the fictional character might be confused with a real person, it is without fault, because it had no way of knowing that its fiction might damage reputation. Imposition of liability in this situation would make the *Times* privilege meaningless.

Justice Powell alluded to one aspect of this problem in *Gertz*. After holding that the states may define their own standards, short of strict liability, he explained:

> At least this conclusion obtains where, as here, the substance of the defamatory statement "makes substantial danger to reputation apparent." This phrase places in perspective the conclusion we announce today. Our inquiry would involve considerations somewhat different from those discussed above if a State purported to condition civil liability on a factual misstatement whose content did not warn a reasonably prudent editor or broadcaster of its defamatory potential.[192]

This passage leaves little doubt that a showing of fault with respect to veracity might not suffice where the statement is not defamatory on its face, but it is not clear what the Constitution does require.[193] At least three possibilities exist. One is to extend the *Times* test to such cases; statements that appear innocent would require a showing of knowing or reckless falsity, while statements defamatory on their face would be actionable on a showing of negligent falsity.[194] A second is a requirement that plaintiffs prove negligence regarding danger to reputation—for example, negligently failing to discover extrinsic facts that would make a seemingly innocent statement defamatory. The third possibility is that the Constitution precludes any liability for statements that pose no apparent danger to reputation.

The second of these provides the soundest solution. To import the *Times* test into this situation would be inappropriate. Presumably, what prompted Justice Powell's caveat was the inconsistency between the reasonable care regime that he envisioned and the possibility that a publisher might be held liable for a statement that he could not have

192. *Id.* at 348 (footnote omitted).

193. The Court had not suggested previously that apparently innocent statements might require different treatment. In Time, Inc. v. Hill, 385 U.S. 374 (1967), involving a statement innocent on its face, the Court remarked that "negligence would be a most elusive standard, especially when the content of the speech itself affords no warning of prospective harm to another through falsity." *Id.* at 389. But *Hill* applied the *Times* standard not because the statement was innocent on its face, but because it concerned a matter of public interest. *Id.* at 387-88.

194. Justice White believed that the majority clearly implied this result. 418 U.S. at 389 n.27 (dissenting opinion).

known was defamatory. To attack this problem by raising the ante on a quite different problem, the issue of truth, makes little sense. If the defendant could not have known that the publication posed a threat to reputation, he cannot, consistent with the principle of no liability without fault, be held accountable irrespective of any negligence or recklessness with respect to veracity. On the other hand, if the defendant knew or should have known of the threat, even though it was not apparent from the words alone, he should not obtain the benefit of a higher standard of culpability on the issue of truth or falsity. For the same reason, absolute constitutional protection from liability for statements not defamatory on their face would go further than necessary. As long as the danger to reputation is or should be apparent, the result should be identical whether the danger appears from the statement itself or from other circumstances.

The problem should be handled not by varying the level of constitutional privilege, but within a more familiar tort framework. The publisher has no general duty to avoid damage to reputation; on the contrary, he has an absolute privilege to defame so long as he does not do so falsely. Likewise, he has no general duty to avoid falsehoods; he may lie freely so long as his lies do not damage reputation.[195] His duty is only to use reasonable care to avoid injury to reputation through the publication of falsehood. The question is whether a duty exists when the danger of injury to reputation is not apparent. In most physical torts, the defendant may have a duty to use reasonable care to avoid consequences of which he is unaware and that he has no way of anticipating.[196] This is sometimes expressed in terms of foreseeability, but it bears little relation to what the defendant actually foresaw or should have foreseen. Rather, it represents the law's conclusion that as a matter of policy the defendant should be responsible for unforeseeable consequences of his negligent act.[197] But liability for unforeseeable injuries is inconsistent with the *Gertz* goal of protecting the press so long as it exercises reasonable care.[198] In practice, a system permit-

195. He also has a duty, of course, to avoid invading privacy, to avoid obscenity, and to avoid certain kinds of breaches of the peace, but these duties apply to truth as fully as to falsehood. The threat of suits for invasion of privacy can also lead to self-censorship. For an account of obstacles preventing distribution of a documentary film, see Strouse, *The Battle Over "Hearts and Minds,"* 4 [MORE], Dec. 1974, at 5.

196. *See* RESTATEMENT (SECOND) OF TORTS § 435 (1965).

197. *See* W. PROSSER, *supra* note 6, § 43, at 250; Green, *Foreseeability in Negligence Law*, 61 COLUM. L. REV. 1401 (1961).

198. *See* W. PROSSER, *supra* note 6, § 43, at 250 ("In so far as he is held liable for consequences which do not lie within the original risk which he has created, a strict

ting liability even when the publisher had no way of knowing the defamatory nature of his statement would operate similarly to the system of strict liability condemned by *Gertz*; it would place on the publisher the burden of using reasonable care to ascertain the truth of all his statements, not merely those that contain an apparent threat to reputation.[199]

The problem of liability for statements not defamatory on their face should be handled by a two-step inquiry: (1) Did the defendant know, or should he have known, that the statement was likely to cause injury to reputation? (2) If so, was the defendant negligent with respect to the truth or falsity of the publication? The second question does not arise unless the first is answered affirmatively because the defendant has no duty to use reasonable care to avoid injury to reputation unless he has reason to know that there is a danger of injury. This analysis should be applied to other situations in which the danger to reputation may not be evident. For example, even if the defendant was negligent with respect to the falsity of a statement defamatory on its face, he should not be liable if he was innocent in failing to recognize that the statement might be understood to refer to the plaintiff. Thus, *Gertz* should be read as requiring proof of negligence with respect to both veracity of the statement and the danger to reputation.

2. *Proof of Negligence.*—Another important question that *Gertz* leaves unanswered concerns the kind of evidence required to support a finding of negligence. One possibility would be to allow the jury to decide whether, under the circumstances, the defendant acted as a reasonable person would have.[200] But such a vague formulation would undermine the fault principle *Gertz* sought to establish. Lawyers will be tempted to argue—and jurors to believe—that publishers and broadcasters do not innocently disseminate defamatory falsehoods. To permit an inference of negligence from the mere fact of publication would make the press the guarantor of the truth of its statements, a role *Gertz* rejects. Instances will occur when, because of a statement's apparent improbability or highly damaging nature, its publication without verification will support a finding of negligence.[201] But failure to verify, in itself, generally should not suffice to support a negligence ver-

liability without fault is superimposed upon the liability that is logically to be attributed to his negligence itself.").

199. *Cf.* Time, Inc. v. Hill, 385 U.S. 374, 389 (1967).

200. *See, e.g.*, Restatement (Second) of Torts § 283 (1965).

201. *See* St. Amant v. Thompson, 390 U.S. 727, 732 (1968).

dict. Circumstances may exist in which the publisher has used reasonable care even though he made no effort to verify his statements—for example, the publication of reports based on official records, such as police reports and court documents. Absent any indication that the material is questionable, publication without further verification would be entirely reasonable.[202]

In defamation actions against the press, as in other cases requiring an evaluation of professional conduct, the customs and practices of the profession should provide the norm against which the reasonableness of the defendant's conduct is measured.[203] The exact formulation of the standard will be significant. In *Butts* Justice Harlan suggested the following: "the standards of investigation and reporting ordinarily adhered to by responsible publishers."[204] Such a standard, focusing on "responsible" publishers, incorporates a bias against unorthodox, impecunious, and unpopular media and invites jurors to measure journalistic conduct by their own values and prejudices. Furthermore, this formulation invites imposition of a uniform standard for all types of publishers and broadcasters. This is inconsistent with the recognition elsewhere in tort law that professional standards vary[205] and is unrealistic in view of the enormous diversity within the profession in terms of journalistic philosophy, resources, power, and technology.[206]

A more fruitful approach involves adapting existing tort principles. The basic rule would require publishers and broadcasters to exercise the skill and knowledge normally exercised by members of their profession[207] and would allow defendants to be judged by the standards

202. *Cf.* Drotzmanns, Inc. v. McGraw-Hill, Inc., 500 F.2d 830, 834 (8th Cir. 1974).

203. *See, e.g.*, Restatement (Second) of Torts §§ 295A, 299A (1965).

204. 388 U.S. at 158 (plurality opinion).

205. *See, e.g.*, Sinz v. Owens, 33 Cal. 2d 749, 205 P.2d 3 (1949) (standards of medical care may vary geographically); Nelson v. Dahl, 174 Minn. 574, 219 N.W. 921 (1928) (medical practitioner is entitled to be judged by standards of his particular school of medicine).

206. Dean Green has criticized the "responsible publisher" standard as follows:

> Such a formula seems beyond the reach of both the experience and knowledge of laymen, and it is doubtful that experts in the field could make the standards comprehensible to a jury. More doubtful would be a plaintiff's success in finding experts to support his cause. And another question remains: Are there in fact such standards?

Green, *supra* note 64, at 750, 754.

207. The *Restatement* provides: "Unless he represents that he has greater or less skill or knowledge, one who undertakes to render services in the practice of a profession or trade is required to exercise the skill and knowledge normally possessed by members of that profession or trade in good standing in similar communities." Restatement (Second) of Torts § 299A (1965).

of their own medium and school of journalism, at least if the school constitutes a respectable minority.[208] Thus, magazines would be evaluated according to the standards of the magazine publishing industry, not those of the broadcasting industry, and the "alternative" press would be measured by its own standards rather than those of the established media. Although rigid geographical limitations are unnecessary, community size and location should be considered; journalistic practices that Keokuk would find unreasonable might be fully accepted in New York. Finally, and most importantly, the defendant should be judged by the standards of publishers with comparable resources, deadline pressures, space limitations, and technological capabilities. To do otherwise would create an unwelcome pressure for uniformity.

The *Gertz* decision does not indicate whether plaintiffs must establish defendants' negligence with "convincing clarity," as *Times* requires for its reckless disregard standard,[209] or by a "preponderance of the evidence," the test generally applied to negligence issues. In his dissent Justice Brennan expressed the opinion that the preponderance standard would "doubtless" control,[210] but this conclusion hardly seems inescapable. The *Times* opinion did not articulate a rationale for the "convincing clarity" requirement. The *Rosenbloom* plurality, however, criticizing the preponderance standard for defamation actions, noted that in ordinary civil litigation, an erroneous verdict in favor of one party is considered no more serious than an erroneous verdict in favor of the other, but in libel cases, the plurality viewed "an erroneous verdict for the plaintiff as most serious. Not only does it mulct the defendant for an innocent misstatement, . . . but the possibility of such error . . . would create a strong impetus toward self-censorship."[211] This reasoning retains its validity and provides a ground for imposing a heavier burden of proof under the *Gertz* constitutional negligence standard than is required in other civil litigation.

The *Times* convincing clarity requirement complements the Court's constitutionalization of the reckless disregard standard, permitting de novo appellate review of the evidence. If the *Gertz* standard differs from that of *Times* only quantitatively, it would follow that negligence verdicts are reviewable on the same basis. The chief objection is that juries traditionally have been considered peculiarly competent

208. *See id.* comment (f), at 75.
209. 376 U.S. at 285-86.
210. 418 U.S. at 366.
211. 403 U.S. at 50.

Texas Law Review Vol. 53:422, 1975

to perform the kind of factfinding negligence requires and therefore should not be second-guessed by the courts. But *Gertz*' negligence is not the common law's community judgment concept. It is a constitutional standard no less than *Times*' recklessness. The *Times* Court provided for appellate review of the evidence to insure that the reckless disregard standard would be applied constitutionally. The potential for unconstitutional application of the *Gertz* standard—and therefore the need for appellate review—is surely no less. Presumably negligence is less easily distinguishable from innocent conduct than recklessness, and thus there appears to be an even greater need for review. If application of the standard is left to the largely uncontrolled discretion of juries, the courts will have effectively abdicated the responsibility of determining the scope of constitutional protection.

As the courts begin to supply answers to many of the foregoing questions and the *Gertz* standard takes on a more distinct form, many of the apparent obstacles to use of summary judgment procedure in private plaintiff defamation actions may disappear.[212] The objection to summary procedures in negligence cases, like the objection to appellate review of the evidence, centers on the jury's traditional function in tort litigation: "[E]ven when there is no dispute as to the facts, it usually is for the jury to decide whether the conduct in question meets the reasonable man standard . . . ."[213] In defamation cases, however, there is little reason for this reluctance. If *Gertz* does not permit an inference of negligence from the statement itself, then unless the plaintiff produces independent evidence of unreasonable conduct, he fails to raise a genuine issue of fact as to negligence. This is no more difficult to determine than whether a plaintiff has produced evidence of recklessness under *Times*.[214]

But even if the general objections to summary judgment are deemed as valid for defamation cases as for physical torts, the procedure nevertheless should be more easily available in defamation. In

212. For a discussion of summary jndgment under the *Times* case and the probable impact, at least for the immediate future, of the *Gertz* decision, see text accompanying notes 169-76 *supra*.

213. 10 C. Wright & A. Miller, *supra* note 175, § 2729, at 572-73. *See also* note 175 *supra*.

214. Answering the argument that summary judgment should not be used in cases where the *Times* rule applies, Judge Wright pointed out: "That state of mind should generally be a jury issue does not mean it should always be so in all contexts, *especially where the issue is recklessness, which is ordinarily inferred from objective facts*." Washington Post Co. v. Keogh, 365 F.2d 965, 967-68 (D.C. Cir. 1966) (emphasis added). There is no reason why the same should not be true when the issue is negligence.

an ordinary negligence case the considerations favoring summary judgment are essentially convenience factors.[215] Denial of summary disposition results only in the loss of those potential conveniences and threatens no more highly valued interest. Courts therefore may justifiably preserve the jury trial in cases where the appropriateness of summary judgment is in doubt.

In defamation cases, however, more is at stake than mere convenience. In the area of first amendment rights, summary procedures are "essential"[216] because "the very pendency of a libel action may cut across the public interest in free and untrammeled speech on public issues . . . ."[217] Here courts cannot justifiably resolve all doubts against use of summary procedures because the important interests are not all on the side of preserving jury trial. There exists an additional interest in protecting freedom of expression by reducing the expense of defending against constitutionally impermissible claims.

Summary judgment should be available under both *Times* and *Gertz*. It should be granted in *Times* cases when the plaintiff fails to show facts from which reckless disregard may be inferred and in *Gertz* cases if the plaintiff fails to show facts from which negligence may be inferred. Failure to produce evidence on any other essential element of the case—for example, actual injury to reputation—[218] also should result in summary disposition.

215. *See* 10 C. WRIGHT & A. MILLER, *supra* note 175, § 2712, at 370-72. Among these factors are prevention of undue harassment and delay, and conservation of court resources.

216. Washington Post Co. v. Keogh, 365 F.2d 965, 968 (D.C. Cir. 1966).

217. Thompson v. Evening Star Newspaper Co., 394 F.2d 774, 776 (D.C. Cir.), *cert. denied*, 393 U.S. 884 (1968).

218. If *Gertz* precludes all remedies unless actual injury to reputation is shown, *see* text accompanying notes 219-29, 244-49 *infra*, then the defendant is entitled to judgment as a matter of law unless the plaintiff produces evidence of actual injury. This will provide another means of weeding out constitutionally barred claims in advance of costly litigation and may enhance the effectiveness of the *Gertz* "actual loss" rule just as use of summary judgment strengthened the *Times* reckless disregard rule.

Obtaining summary judgment for want of evidence of actual injury, however, may prove difficult. The initial burden falls on the defendant, as movant, to show that no genuine issue of material fact exists, *i.e.*, that the plaintiff has suffered no actual injury. That carries all the difficulties of any attempt to prove a negative. Nevertheless, if the defendant can produce such evidence, *e.g.*, affidavits from persons who know the plaintiff, refuting his alleged reputational injury, the burden shifts; plaintiff then must bring in counter-affidavits or some other evidence of actual injury. If he fails to do so, summary judgment should follow. *See* FED. R. CIV. P. 56(c), (e). The plaintiff may be able to avoid that result simply by filing his own affidavit stating that his relations with others were damaged. But if there can be no recovery for emotional injuries without actual injury to reputation, then the plaintiff should not be able to preclude summary judgment merely by stating that he suffered humiliation or mental anguish.

Texas Law Review Vol. 53:422, 1975

B. Injuries and Remedies

1. Actual Injury.—The Court left to the trial courts the problem of defining "actual injury," expressing confidence in their "wide experience in framing appropriate jury instructions in tort actions."[219] In defamation, however, courts have been unable to define with any precision the losses that are properly compensable.[220] In large part this difficulty stems from the lack of understanding—or at least articulation—of the nature of the injury sought to be redressed. Defamation is described as an injury to a relational interest, an interference with one's relations with other persons.[221] This injury is most apparent when a defamatory statement disrupts the victim's relations with his employer or customers. This is the type of relational interest most highly protected by the law of defamation; statements damaging to such relations are actionable without proof of damages.[222] A relational injury also is almost certain to occur, though more difficult to quantify, when the relations disrupted are noncommercial but involve persons who know (or at least know of) the victim, such as his family, business associates, professional peers, friends, neighbors, fans, or constituents. With these persons the victim has existing relationships and a reputation. Injuries to these relationships are actionable, but sometimes the victim is required to prove pecuniary loss.[223]

219. 418 U.S. at 350.

220. More precisely, courts have not found a way to make juries restrict their awards to properly compensable losses. In Linn v. United Plant Guard Workers, 383 U.S. 53 (1966), the Court noted the "propensity of juries to award excessive damages for defamation." *Id.* at 64. Justice Black, concurring in *Times,* perceived an even more serious jury malfunction:

> The scarcity of testimony to show that [the plaintiff] suffered any actual damages at all suggests that these feelings of hostility [toward those who favor desegregation] had at least as much to do with rendition of this half-million-dollar verdict as did an appraisal of damages Viewed realistically, this record lends support to an inference that instead of being damaged [plaintiff's] political, social, and financial prestige has likely been enhanced by the Times' publication.

376 U.S. at 294.

221. *See, e.g.,* Pollard v. Lyon, 91 U.S. 225, 226 (1875); Albert Miller and Co. v. Corte, 107 F.2d 432, 435 (5th Cir. 1939), *cert. denied,* 309 U.S. 688 (1940); Green, *Relational Interests,* 31 ILL. L. REV. 35, 37-44 (1936). *See generally* Green, *The Right to Communicate,* 35 N.Y.U.L. REV. 903 (1960).

222. *See, e.g.,* Jones v. Jones & Another, [1916] 2 A.C. 481; RESTATEMENT OF TORTS § 573 (1938); *cf.* W. PROSSER, *supra* note 6, § 112, at 757-58.

223. If a statement is not actionable "per se," plaintiff is permitted to recover only if he can show "special damage," *i.e.,* that injuries to these relations resulted in a pecuniary loss. Because of the nonpecuniary nature of these relationships, that showing is often difficult. *See, e.g.,* Diplomat Elec., Inc. v. Westinghouse Elec. Supply Co., 378 F.2d 377, 382 (5th Cir. 1967); Chase v. New Mexico Publishing Co., 53 N.M. 145, 203 P.2d 594 (1949).

The injury becomes less self-evident and far more difficult to measure when the relations affected are those between the victim and the community at large—that is, persons with whom he presently has no relations and no reputation. The defamatory statement may prevent the formation of future relationships between the victim and such persons, and to the extent that potential relationships are aborted, the victim has suffered a relational injury that merits compensation. But the defamatory statement also causes another injury to the victim *vis a vis* the community at large: it creates a negative relationship where no relationship previously existed. This resembles a relational injury, but the harm is primarily subjective, internal, and emotional—the victim's own reaction to the realization that persons who previously did not think of him at all now may think of him unfavorably. These emotional injuries may accompany any type of relational injury, but they do not constitute relational injuries and do not necessarily flow from all such injuries.

If a newspaper falsely identifies a person as a criminal, for example, he probably will suffer two quite different kinds of loss: (1) disruption of existing and potential relationships; and (2) subjective injury caused by the humiliation, sorrow, anger, and frustration he feels from knowing there are persons who now regard him less favorably (or more unfavorably).[224]

The second of these injuries is inherently incapable of proof. It does not exist at all unless the victim's psyche is adversely affected by the belief that others' attitudes toward him have been unfavorably altered. That effect is normal and generally expected, but by no means inevitable. Conceivably, some persons are not psychologically vulnerable to the disapproval of strangers. More importantly, the extent of the subjective injury will vary enormously, depending on the strength of the victim's psychological dependence on the approval of others.

The *Gertz* concept of "actual loss" is hardly self-defining in this context, yet these injuries clearly are still compensable under *Gertz*. Damages in defamation cases traditionally have included redress for internal injuries. Even when the plaintiff must show special damages, once he does so he may normally recover not only for pecuniary losses flowing from the injury to his reputation, but also for his wounded feelings.[225] Moreover, Justice Powell's opinion states:

224. In theory, at least, a person with a bad reputation can be injured by a defamatory statement that makes his reputation even worse.

225. RESTATEMENT OF TORTS § 575, comment (a), at 185 (1938); W. PROSSER, *supra* note 6, § 112, at 761.

> Suffice it to say that actual injury is not limited to out-of-pocket loss. Indeed, the more customary types of actual harm inflicted by defamatory falsehood include impairment of reputation and standing in the community, personal humiliation, and mental anguish and suffering . . . . [A]ll awards must be supported by competent evidence concerning the injury, although there need be no evidence which assigns an actual dollar value to the injury.[226]

It is difficult to see how injuries such as "personal humiliation" and "mental anguish" can be established except by a process that in practice will be little different from presuming them. The plaintiff will have to produce some proof of his emotional injury—such as his own testimony that he felt humiliation and mental anguish—but beyond that the jury surely will infer the existence, nature, and extent of those injuries from the nature of the defamatory statement. Thus, emotional injuries, though not presumed, will be inferred. Such an insignificant change in practice seems unlikely to reduce substantially the amount of awards for emotional injuries.

The new rule must be given further effect. In the absence of a demonstration of *Times* recklessness, *Gertz* should preclude recovery for emotional injuries unaccompanied by injury to relational interests. This reading follows from the Court's insistence that the states not transcend their legitimate interest in compensating for actual injury to reputation.[227] Once plaintiff proves an injury to reputation, then the state may compensate him for ancillary emotional injuries; but absent such a showing, emotional injuries are not compensable. To permit recovery for emotional injuries when no actual injury to reputation exists would subvert the "actual loss" requirement. On the other hand, allowing recovery for emotional injuries only after actual injury to reputation is shown suggests a rule similar to the "special damage" requirement at common law.

But the Court clearly intended its actual injury requirement to provide more than a prerequisite to recovery of damages for emotional injuries. Justice Powell attacked the doctrine of presumed damages because it gives plaintiffs "gratuitous awards of money damages far in excess of any actual injury" and "invites juries to punish unpopnlar opinion rather than to compensate individuals for injury sustained by the publication of a false fact."[228] Neither of those dangers would be

226. 418 U.S. at 350.
227. *Id.* at 349.
228. *Id.*

reduced if the prohibition against presumed damages were removed once an actual injury to reputation was shown. If the rule is to prevent these evils, it must preclude presumption of damages to either reputation or psyche. *Gertz* requires that "all awards . . . . be supported by competent evidence,"[229] and courts must guard against presumptions of humiliation and mental anguish from the mere existence of an injury to reputation. It may be impossible, however, to prevent juries from drawing such inferences from the nature of the injury to reputation.

2. *Presumed and Punitive Damages.—Gertz* prohibits the award of presumed and punitive damages when liability rests on negligence, but leaves open the possibility that they may be permissible when the *Times* test is met.[230] If so, they are still recoverable by all public plaintiffs, who must meet the *Times* standard in any event, and by any private plaintiff who can prove not only the negligence required to recover actual damages, but also reckless disregard. Therefore, it is necessary to consider whether anything in the distinction between public and private plaintiffs, or in the difference between negligent misstatement and reckless or knowing falsehood, justifies different treatment of presumed or punitive damages.

The Court's objections to presumed and punitive damages were essentially that they permit the jury a breadth of discretion that poses dangers to freedom of expression and that they are unrelated to the state's legitimate interest in compensating private individuals for actual injury to reputation.[231] Clearly the former applies with equal force whether a public or a private plaintiff is involved. Therefore, if such damages are to be allowed to public, but not to private, individuals on the basis of some inherent difference between the two, the justification must be found in a legitimate state interest in awarding public plaintiffs damages in excess of "actual" injury.

The traditional justification for presumed damages rests on the belief that defamation produces injuries that, though real, cannot be proved,[232] either because the damage is too subtle to demonstrate or

229. *Id.* at 350 (emphasis added).
230. *Id.* at 348-49.
231. *Id.* at 348-49. *See generally* Murnaghan, *From Figment to Fiction to Philosophy—The Requirement of Proof of Damages in Libel Action*, 22 CATHOLIC U.L. REV. 1, 27-28 (1974), suggesting that the doctrine of presumed damages is incompatible with the compensatory philosophy of the common law.
232. *See* W. PROSSER, *supra* note 6, § 112, at 765: "[I]t is clear that proof of actual damage will be impossible in a great many cases where, from the character of the defam-

because potential witnesses are reluctant to admit that the defamatory statement has lowered their esteem for the plaintiff.[233] In the private plaintiff context, the Court concluded that the speech-inhibiting dangers of presumed damages outweigh any difficulty in proving actual loss, but the balance may differ in public plaintiff cases. One might argue that public plaintiffs will have more difficulty proving the full extent of actual injury because of their more extensive reputations. A private individual may be able to produce as witnesses most of the acquaintances (or at least representatives of most categories of acquaintances) whose esteem for him has diminished, but the public plaintiff may not even be able to identify all of those categories.

On the other hand, the public plaintiff with an extensive reputation has certain advantages. Because he has a larger pool of potential witnesses from which to draw, the task of obtaining willing witnesses may be easier. Additionally, the kinds of damages that public plaintiffs suffer may be more amenable to proof than those of private plaintiffs. When a private person is defamed, the injured relationships normally are ones providing largely intangible benefits—relationships with family, friends, neighbors, and potential future acquaintances. When the victim is a public person, on the other hand, the damaged relationships usually represent more concrete benefit to the plaintiff, and therefore harm is easier to establish under the Court's "actual injury" language.[234]

Thus, while the public plaintiff may have difficulty showing the full extent of damage to his reputation, he may find it easier than the private plaintiff to demonstrate some actual loss. In any event, the possibility that proving actual injury to reputation would present a greater burden to public plaintiffs as a class than to private plaintiffs is

atory words and the circumstances of publication, it is all but certain that serious harm has resulted in fact."

233. *See Developments in the Law—Defamation*, 69 HARV. L. REV. 875, 891-92 (1956). One may question whether the law should ever attempt to compensate for injuries too subtle to demonstrate. Moreover, the alleged reluctance of witnesses to testify seems speculative; the presumption of damage is not limited to cases in which there is reason to believe this reluctance exists.

234. Defamation of an entertainer, for example, generally injures relations with his present and prospective audiences and employers; these injuries normally are demonstrable and are clearly compensable as "actual loss." Defamation of a public official interferes with his relations with former, present, and future colleagues and constituents. While these relationships are not necessarily beneficial in a pecuniary sense, they nevertheless represent tangible benefit to the plaintiff, and ordinary methods of proof normally suffice to demonstrate their impairment. The damage resulting from loss of a friendship, on the other hand, defies quantification.

speculative at best. If presumed damages represent so great a threat to speech interests that they are constitutionally impermissible in private plaintiff cases, whatever marginal differences public plaintiffs may experience in difficulty of proof hardly seem significant enough to support a distinction of constitutional magnitude.

While nothing in the differences between public and private plaintiffs appears to justify allowing recovery of presumed damages by the former but not the latter, it could be argued that when a plaintiff, public or private, proves reckless or knowing falsity, the balance shifts in favor of permitting recovery. The contention that presumed damages in fact represent "actual" damages that are not demonstrable[235] might retain its validity in recklessness cases if proof of actual loss is more difficult in those cases. But the plaintiff's difficulty in proving damage to reputation bears no relation to the quantum of the defendant's fault; it is no greater or smaller when the statement is made recklessly than when it is made negligently.[236]

The Court's objection to presumed damages because of the dangers of uncontrolled jury discretion may be weaker if the plaintiff proves reckless disregard, on the theory that inhibition of defendants who are reckless, but not those who are merely negligent, is desirable. But inhibiting disfavored speech is not a proper role for presumed damages. If they have any justification at all, it must be based on the difficulty of proving damage—a difficulty that is not increased by the existence of recklessness or the requirement that reckless disregard be proved. The proper device for inhibiting speech—if any such device can be proper—is punitive damages.

Punitive damages have been justified[237] on the grounds that they are necessary to (1) compensate plaintiffs for the costs of litigation; (2) encourage citizens to initiate suits that otherwise would not be worth maintaining; (3) punish the wrongdoer, or more precisely, satisfy society's wish for revenge;[238] and (4) deter the wrongdoer and

235. As Justice White stated, "[The Court] ignores what . . . experience teaches, *viz.*, that damage to reputation is recurringly difficult to prove and that requiring actual proof would repeatedly destroy any chance for adequate compensation." 418 U.S. at 394 (dissenting opinion).

236. Justice White makes this point, concluding: "Why a defamatory statement is more apt to cause injury if the lie is intentional than when it is only negligent, I fail to understand." *Id.* at 395.

237. *See* W. PROSSER, *supra* note 6, § 2, at 9. *See generally* Walther & Plein, *Punitive Damages: A Critical Analysis*, 49 MARQ. L. REV. 369 (1965).

238. The vengeance ingredient is apparent from the name often given au award of punitive damages—"smart money." "The tort of defamation does in fact provide a nec-

other potential wrongdoers from committing similar acts in the future. None of these is persuasive in the context of defamation. If courts desire to compensate plaintiffs for attorneys' fees and other costs, they should do so directly, not by permitting punitive damages that may be wholly unrelated to those expenses. Even if there are meritorious claims that will not be brought unless punitive damages are recoverable, the courts should weigh the desirability of encouraging litigation in the defamation area against the danger that availability of punitive damages may encourage the filing of unmeritorious claims to harass the defendant or extort a settlement. Recognizing revenge as a legitimate objective of the law seems dubious enough even in the context of criminal activity without possible social value; revenge for speech is even more inconsistent with notions of civilized justice.

The least indefensible justification for punitive damages is deterrence. Punitive damages serve as private fines designed to discourage antisocial conduct. It is not at all clear that potential defamers of public plaintiffs need to be deterred more than potential defamers of private persons. Indeed, one might assume deterrence of speech would be even more suspect in discussions of public persons since those discussions have been allowed more "breathing space" than discussions of private persons.

Perhaps recklessness justifies a result that mere negligence would not, because the former is far more culpable. But what the *Gertz* Court rejected was not the imposition of punitive damages on a showing of negligence, since negligence was insufficient to support such an award at common law.[239] Instead, the Court repudiated the common law rule allowing recovery of punitive damages on a showing of malice. Malice in this sense, of course, is not the "actual malice" of *Times*. An award of punitive damages at common law generally requires no showing of recklessness, but may be based on "ill will," or "improper motive."[240]

essary outlet for the desire of the person defamed to make the defendant pay for what he did, in the same way as the criminal law provides for an ordered community revenge on the criminal who, by his actions, has affronted society." Hayes, *Newspaper Libel—The Deterrent and Vindicatory Effect of General Damages Awards*, 5 QUEENSLAND L.J. 370, 372 (1967).

239. At common law those claims deemed deserving of punitive damages have derived from acts labeled "wanton," "oppressive," "reckless," or "malicious," but not "negligent." *See, e.g.*, Sperry Rand Corp. v. A-T-O, Inc., 459 F.2d 19, 20-21 (4th Cir. 1972); Wright v. Everett, 197 Va. 608, 614, 90 S.E.2d 855, 859 (1956); RESTATEMENT (SECOND) OF TORTS § 908, comment b, at 80 (Tent. Draft No. 19, 1973).

240. The trial judge's instruction on punitive damages in *Times* is fairly typical:

[P]unitive damages may be awarded only in the event that you, the jury, are

Libel and Self-Censorship

Thus, the holding in *Gertz* does not preclude the possibility that punitive damages, though constitutionally impermissible on a showing of common law "malice," may be recovered where plaintiff can prove "actual malice" as defined by *Times*. A difference in result that has such staggering financial potential should not be based on so small a distinction, however. The enormity of many libel awards derives mainly from punitive damages.[241] Although frequently reduced on remittitur, the possibility of such huge judgments represents a significant threat of press self-censorship, which is exacerbated by the exclusion of punitive damages under many libel insurance policies.[242] If punitive damages represent such a pernicious factor in the balance of reputational interests against freedom of expression that they cannot constitutionally be awarded upon a showing of common law malice, it is difficult to understand how a showing of "actual malice" can make them constitutionally acceptable. More fundamentally, however, punitive damages simply have no place in a speech context, no matter what the requisite quantum of fault or the classification of the potential plaintiff may be. The only possible legitimate function of punitive damages is deterrence, and deterrence of speech because of its content—no matter how offensive, useless, false, or destructive that speech may be—is inconsistent with the whole thrust of the commitment to freedom of expression. The *Gertz* Court's conclusion that presumed and punitive damages are unconstitutional when liability is based on negligence is equally persuasive when it is based on reckless disregard, whether the plaintiff is characterized as "public" or "private." All defamation recoveries therefore should be limited to compensation for actual injury.[243]

> convinced by a fair preponderance of the evidence that the defendant . . . was motivated by personal ill will, that is actual intent to do the plaintiff harm, or that the defendant . . . was guilty of gross negligence and recklessness and not of just ordinary negligence or carelessness in publishing the matter complained of so as to indicate a wanton disregard of plaintiff's rights.

376 U.S. at 284 n.24.

241. *See* text accompanying notes 66-67 *supra*.

242. *See* Ek, *supra* note 71, at 678 (stating that two of the three major libel insurance underwriters "exclude punitive damages on the grounds that covering them would be contrary to the public interest"). *See also* 1 A. Hanson, *supra* note 43, at 141-43; *Developments in the Law—Defamation, supra* note 233, at 916.

243. Since *Gertz*, one lower court has held punitive damages constitutionally impermissible even when the *Times* test is met, Maheu v. Hughes Tool Co., 384 F. Supp. 166 (C.D. Cal. 1974), and there are indications that several members of the Supreme Court would also make that extension. Two justices have stated their belief that punitive and presumed damages are unconstitutional, at least in suits against the press. Justice Marshall, dissenting in *Rosenbloom*, concluded that "the appropriate resolution of the clash of societal values here is to restrict damages to actual losses." 403 U.S. at 86. He was speaking, of course, in the context of a private plaintiff involved in a matter of public

3. *Actions for Nonmonetary Relief.*—The actual loss requirement may bar nonmonetary remedies such as nominal damages or declaratory judgment, although *Gertz* did not decide this question. The argument for retaining those remedies would be that (1) the state has some legitimate interest in protecting reputation even in the absence of actual loss,[244] and (2) even if that interest is not as strong as the interest in compensating for actual injuries, neither is the countervailing first amendment interest as strong, because the press faces no threat of monetary judgments.[245] This argument, however, is unpersuasive. First, it is not clear that the state has any legitimate interest in the absence of actual harm. Those who perceive such an interest may base it on the theory of real, though unprovable, damages;[246] but since *Gertz*

concern, but there is no indication he would limit his proposed resolution to that kind of case; on the contrary, he rejects the attempt to distinguish cases involving matters of public concern. *Id.* at 79. Nor is there any indication that he finds presumed and punitive damages less objectionable in public plaintiff cases. Justice Douglas, who objects to the award of even actual damages, could be expected to cast a second vote against presumed and punitive damages even when the *Times* test is met. *See* Garrison v. Louisiana, 379 U.S. 64, 80 (1964) (concurring opinion); Gertz v. Robert Welch, Inc., 418 U.S. 323 (1974) (dissenting opinion). Justice Stewart joined Justice Marshall's *Rosenbloom* dissent, indicating that he too believes recoveries should be limited to actual losses, at least in suits against the press. Justice Stewart, however, also joined in the plurality opinion in *Butts*, which expressly approved the award of punitive damages. Curtis Publishing Co. v. Butts, 388 U.S. 130, 161 (1967).

The only present member of the Court who has indicated that he believes punitive and presumed damages to be permissible is Justice White. *See* Gertz v. Robert Welch, Inc., 418 U.S. 323, 392-98 (1974) (dissenting opinion). While Justice Brennan supports extension of the *Times* principle to all cases involving matters of public or general concern, *id.* at 361 (dissenting opinion); Rosenbloom v. Metromedia, Inc., 403 U.S. 29 (1971) (plurality opinion), he has not stated a position on the permissibility of punitive and presumed damages and has never voted to affirm a libel judgment that included such damages. Justice Brennan did, however, vote to deny certiorari in Ginzburg v. Goldwater, 414 F.2d 324 (2d Cir. 1969), *cert. denied*, 396 U.S. 1049 (1970), a case in which the judgment affirmed included $1 compensatory damages and $75,000 punitive damages.

Chief Justice Burger's dissent in *Gertz* suggests a reluctance to interfere with established rules in defamation, which may indicate that he would not find presumed and punitive damages constitutionally impermissible. *See* 418 U.S. at 354-55. Justices Rehnquist and Blackmun, by joining the majority in *Gertz*, have indicated they are at least concerned about presumed and punitive damage awards, but their views with respect to such awards in public plaintiff cases are not known. The key vote may well be that of Justice Powell, and at least the rhetoric in his *Gertz* opinion gives some reason to believe he would vote to prohibit presumed and punitive damages in all cases.

244. Justice White apparently read the majority opinion as precluding any relief in the absence of a showing of actual injury and found that deplorable: "[E]ven if the plaintiff should recover no monetary damages, he should be able to prevail and have a judgment that the publication is false." *Id.* at 393 (dissenting opinion).

245. Arguments for nonmonetary relief are set out in Leflar, *Legal Remedies for Defamation*, 6 ARK. L. REV. 423 (1952).

246. *See* text accompanying notes 232-33 *supra*. The argument in favor of both presumed and punitive damages is stated well in Green, *supra* note 64, at 756.

still permits considerable flexibility in proving actual loss, it is difficult to envision any significant number of cases in which "real" injuries would be unprovable. Others may argue that even if there is no injury to reputation, the state has an interest in establishing the truth, vindicating the plaintiff, and exposing falsehood.[247] The legitimacy of this interest is questionable.[248] The notion of designating the courts to certify truth rather than compensate for loss is offensive to our unproven but time-honored belief that truth is best discovered through the give-and-take of free discussion, rather than by state certification.

Second, the threat to first amendment interests does not disappear along with the threat of a monetary judgment. A suit for nominal damages or declaratory judgment would create significant defense costs. Such litigation would raise the full panoply of defamation issues, except those relating to amount of damages. Some savings might result from less frequent use of juries, but even if defense costs were only half as great, they would still be substantial enough to induce publishers to "steer far wider of the unlawful zone" than the first amendment requires.[249]

Award of nominal damages or a declaratory judgment in the absence of actual loss is subject to the same basic objection given to the award of damages in excess of actual loss: it creates a danger of self-censorship that is not outweighed by the countervailing state interest in compensating actual losses. In suits for nonmonetary relief, the danger of self-censorship is still real, while the state interest in compensating becomes highly speculative, if not illegitimate.

IV. Conclusion

Gertz, like *Times*, attempts to advance, enhance, and preserve maximum public discussion by reducing incentives for press self-censorship. Both seek these ends by creating a conditional constitutional privilege to defame. The *Times* privilege, however, has proved to be an inefficient and often ineffective method of preventing self-censorship, primarily because it usually provides no protection until both parties have incurred the full expense of trial, and often of appeal as well. Because it also adopts a conditional privilege mechanism, *Gertz* perpetuates and increases those deficiencies. It assures that the

247. *See* Leflar, *supra* note 245, at 425-28.
248. *But cf.* Rosenblatt v. Baer, 383 U.S. 75, 92 (1966) (Stewart, J., concurring).
249. Speiser v. Randall, 357 U.S. 513, 526 (1958).

high cost of defense will continue to be an important cause of self-censorship.

The *Gertz* decision to make the privilege more easily defeasible in private plaintiff cases, on a showing of negligence rather than reckless disregard, exacerbates some of the *Times* problems and creates some new ones. It introduces into defamation, a field whose own vocabulary is complicated enough, the vocabulary of negligence law as developed in the physical torts. Much of that vocabulary is inappropriate, confusing, or incomprehensible when applied to communications torts. Its use will require the courts to recognize that negligence as a constitutional prerequisite differs from negligence as a basis for common law liability. Adoption of a negligence standard threatens to retard the development of summary procedures in the defamation context, a trend that is beginning to make the *Times* privilege more effective. The decision to distinguish between public and private plaintiffs, more fully protecting speech concerning the former, discourages a welcome journalistic trend toward more investigation and exposure of the private sectors of society. This creates a constitutional bias in favor of media that focus their attention on persons who are already "public." Rejection of the *Rosenbloom* plurality's conclusion that the Constitution protects equally all discussions of matters of public concern reverses a decade of steady movement toward that more expansive first amendment rationale.

Fortunately, *Gertz* creates a few opportunities for gains—or at least for trimming losses—in the effort to eliminate self-censorship. By not defining its negligence standard, it leaves the lower courts free to create and adapt from the physical torts a system of negligence liability that will be workable in the defamation context. The most important first step in developing this system is to recognize that the *Times* recklessness standard and the *Gertz* negligence standard are first cousins. They are functionally similar, though quantitatively different, methods of defeating the same basic constitutional privilege. They should operate in the same way, except that the quantum of fault required to defeat the *Times* privilege is greater. This will make available in private-plaintiff cases the important ancillary *Times* doctrines of "clear and convincing proof" and full appellate review of the finding of negligence. It will also aid the extension of summary procedures to those cases.

Finally, by partially repudiating presumed and punitive damages, *Gertz* attacks what has been one of the major sources of dissatisfaction with the law of defamation: the obvious excessiveness of many jury verdicts. By making that repudiation complete, the Court could eliminate an important cause of intimidation and self-censorship of the press, which already is all too timorous in the face of financial loss from defamation.

[9]

Freedom of Speech And Defamation: Developments in The Common Law World

ADRIENNE STONE* AND GEORGE WILLIAMS**

This comment traces the relationship between freedom of speech and the common law of defamation in India, Australia, South Africa, Canada, the United Kingdom and New Zealand. A central theme is the treatment of the iconic decision of the United States Supreme Court in New York Times v Sullivan. This comment shows that while the use of foreign precedent by judges in common law countries is widespread, the use of such precedent is, in the main, not uncritical. The reaction of common law courts to New York Times *signals that these courts will usually reassess and exercise their own judgment in relation to even the most revered aspects of the American constitutional tradition.*

I INTRODUCTION

Over the last decade, the relationship between freedom of speech and the common law of defamation has preoccupied common law courts around the world; most recently the House of Lords in *Reynolds v Times Newspapers Ltd*[1] and the New Zealand Court of Appeal in *Lange v Atkinson*.[2] In the United States, this issue was dealt with long ago in the Supreme Court's landmark decision in *New York Times v Sullivan*.[3] In this comment, we examine the influence of *New York Times* in India, Australia, South Africa, Canada, the United Kingdom and New Zealand.

In *New York Times*, the United States Supreme Court held that the First Amendment's protection of freedom of speech required a 'federal rule that prohibits a public official from recovering damages for a defamatory falsehood relating to his official conduct unless he proves that the statement was made

* BA, LLB (UNSW), LLM (Colum). Senior Lecturer, Faculty of Law, The Australian National University.

** BEc, LLB (Hons) (Macq), LLM (UNSW), PhD (ANU). Barrister, NSW Bar. Anthony Mason Professor and Director, Gilbert & Tobin Centre of Public Law, Faculty of Law, University of New South Wales. We thank Graeme Hill, Simon Evans, Amelia Simpson, Rosemary Tobin and Leslie Zines for their comments on earlier drafts and other assistance and Jelita Gardner-Rush, Parissa Notaras and Theo Varvaressos for their excellent research assistance. This project has been assisted by a grant from the Faculties Research Grant Scheme at the Australian National University.

1 [1999] 4 All ER 609 ('*Reynolds*').

2 Unreported, Court of Appeal of New Zealand, Richardson P, Henry, Keith, Blanchard and Tipping JJ, 21 June 2000.

3 376 US 254 (1964) ('*New York Times*'). *New York Times* arose from a libel action brought against the New York Times by an Alabama official. The complaint related to an advertisement carried by the newspaper that was critical of the actions of Alabama authorities during civil rights protests. After a record verdict against the New York Times was upheld in the Alabama courts, the case was heard by the United States Supreme Court. For an historical account of the case, see Anthony Lewis, *Make No Law* (1991).

with "actual malice" ... or with reckless disregard of whether it was false or not'.[4] The Supreme Court considered that a requirement that a defendant prove the truth of otherwise defamatory statements would sometimes deter speakers (most importantly journalists and publishers) from publishing statements that they thought were true, but which they were not sure they could prove to be true.

The court therefore formulated a rule that protected the publication of *false* defamatory statements, even though it acknowledged that the rule would cause some harm by allowing reputations to be damaged by such statements. In the court's view, it was necessary to tolerate these evils in order to avoid the 'chilling effect'[5] of a requirement to prove truth and thus to protect freedom of speech.

Given the iconic status of *New York Times* within American free speech law and American constitutional law generally,[6] it is perhaps not surprising that it has been an important reference point in the deliberations in other countries of the relationship between free speech and defamation. What is notable, however, is the degree to which courts in the common law world have forged their own paths. Of the cases we examine here, it is striking that, with the possible exception of a decision of the Supreme Court of India, all have modified or entirely rejected the *New York Times* rule.

We examine these decisions in three groups. In Part II, we turn to India, Australia and South Africa; countries where courts have been at least somewhat receptive to the *New York Times* rule. We then turn, in Part III to Canada and the United Kingdom, where courts have been rather more sceptical about the rule before concluding, in Part IV, with a discussion of a recent decision of the New Zealand Court of Appeal. Two themes emerge from these decisions. First, the courts in these countries have been mindful of criticisms of *New York Times* by American scholars. In brief, these critics of *New York Times* argue that the shift in focus from the truth of the allegation to the propriety of the defendant's conduct, and the consequent complexity and expense of litigation under the rule, creates its own 'chilling effect' on political speech.[7] Some foreign modifications of the *New York Times* rule can be seen as technical alterations designed to address these concerns. In the case of New Zealand and the United Kingdom, moreover, this has been accompanied by a concern to adapt the local law to local circumstances, especially to the nature of local media.

4 376 US 254 (1964), 279–80.

5 Ibid 279: 'A rule compelling the critic of official conduct to guarantee the truth of all his factual assertions — and to do so on pain of libel judgments virtually unlimited in amount — leads to a comparable "self-censorship" ... Under such a rule, would-be critics of official conduct may be deterred from voicing their criticism, even though it is believed to be true and even though it is in fact true, because of doubt whether it can be proved in court or fear of the expense of having to do so ... The rule thus dampens the vigor and limits the variety of public debate.'

6 See Harry Kalven, Jr, 'The New York Times Case: A Note on "The Central Meaning of the First Amendment"' [1964] *Supreme Court Review* 191; Anthony Lewis, '*New York Times v Sullivan* Reconsidered: Time to Return to "The Central Meaning of the First Amendment"' (1983) 83 *Columbia Law Review* 603: 'The decision had from the first the ring of a great occasion in the law, sensed not only in the result but in the bold sweep of the court's opinion'. That is not to deny that the decision has also been much criticised. See, Lewis, ibid 603; Nadine Strossen, 'A Defence of the Aspirations * But not the Achievements * of the US Rules Limiting Defamation Actions By Public Officials or Public Figures' (1986) 15 *Melbourne University Law Review* 419.

7 See Lewis, above n 6; Strossen, above n 7.

More fundamentally, however, the failure in other countries to embrace fully the *New York Times* rule reflects scepticism of the philosophy underlying that decision. The central conclusion in *New York Times* is that some damage to reputation is necessary in order to protect freedom of speech. By contrast, in almost all cases studied here, we see rather more emphasis given to the protection of reputation (and in some cases privacy), and also some concern that too much tolerance of false information might undermine the quality of public debate.

II INDIA, AUSTRALIA AND SOUTH AFRICA: A (COMPARATIVELY) WARM RECEPTION

We begin our study in India, Australia and South Africa where courts have, to varying degrees, been sympathetic to *New York Times*.

India

India is perhaps an exceptional case in this study because there the *New York Times* rule has received a particularly enthusiastic reception. The rule was considered in the 1995 case of *Rajagopal v State of Tamil Nadu*,[8] not as a possible defence to defamation, but in the course of determining exceptions to the right to privacy conferred by the Indian Constitution.[9] Nonetheless, *New York Times* was clearly influential. A two member bench of the Indian Supreme Court carved out a number of exceptions to privacy that have regard to the need for open public discussion. The Indian Supreme Court's judgment shares much of the free speech philosophy that motivated *New York Times*, holding that:

> Our system of government demands — as do the systems of Government of the United States of America and United Kingdom — constant vigilance over exercise of governmental power by the press and the media among others. It is essential for a good Government.[10]

For this reason, although the Indian Supreme Court acknowledged that the protection of freedom of speech under its Constitution is not identical to 'the sweep of the First Amendment to the United States Constitution',[11] it

8 1995 AIR (SC) 264 ('*Rajagopal*').

9 Ibid 276–7. This case arose out of a petition by the publishers of a weekly magazine, who proposed to publish the autobiography of a convicted murderer, to prevent authorities in the Indian state of Tamil Nadu from taking any action with respect to the publication. The Supreme Court found that the constitutional right to privacy (implicit in the right to life and liberty guaranteed by Article 21 of the Indian Constitution) protected personal information from publication without consent of the person concerned, unless that person has thrust himself into controversy or the information is available in public records. The Court held that, although the authorities could not prevent the publication on this basis, the right to author's right to privacy may expose the publishers to subsequent action.

10 Ibid 275.

11 Ibid.

nonetheless adopted an exception to the right to privacy that is remarkably similar to the *New York Times* rule.[12] The Court concluded that the right to privacy did not allow for a defamation action in respect of statements made with respect to the discharge of public duties by public officials, even if the statements are false, unless the official could show that the publication was made 'with reckless disregard for the truth'.[13]

Australia

The response to *New York Times* in the other countries considered here has been more complex. In Australia, the High Court has been relatively enthusiastic about the rule, but has also adopted significant modifications.

Attention to *New York Times* arose in Australia shortly after the implied constitutional freedom of political communication was recognised by the High Court in 1992.[14] The case, *Theophanous v Herald & Weekly Times Ltd*,[15] was an obvious vehicle for consideration of *New York Times* as it concerned a member of the Federal Parliament who took action against a newspaper in response to published criticism regarding the performance of his public duties. Given the fame of the *New York Times* decision, it is not surprising that the defendant publisher argued for the adoption of a similar rule.

The High Court in its 1994 decision in *Theophanous* substantially accepted the defendant's argument,[16] fashioning a new constitutional defence to override the common law of defamation. In doing so, the court owes a clear intellectual debt to *New York Times*. In particular, the Court accepted that defamation law can have a 'chilling effect' on political communication, and also that the existing defences to defamation were inadequate to overcome this effect.[17] However, the constitutional defence adopted by the High Court made three important changes to the *New York Times* rule: it limited the defence so that it was available only to public officials and candidates for public office; it modified the actual malice standard to require that the publication be 'reasonable in the circumstances'; and it reversed the onus of proof.[18]

12 For the application in the United States of the *New York Times* rule as a defence to a tortious action for breach of privacy, see *Time Inc v Hill*, 385 US 374 (1967).

13 *Rajagopal* 1995 AIR (SC) 264, 277.

14 *Australian Capital Television Pty Ltd v Commonwealth* (1992) 177 CLR 106; *Nationwide News Pty Ltd v Wills* (1992) 177 CLR 1. See generally George Williams, *Human Rights under the Australian Constitution* (1999) 165–93. After these foundational decisions, the High Court heard only one freedom of political communication case (*Cunliffe v Commonwealth* (1994) 182 CLR 272) before hearing *Theophanous v Herald & Weekly Times Ltd* (1994) 182 CLR 104 ('*Theophanous*'), and its companion case, *Stephens v West Australian Newspapers Ltd* (1994) 182 CLR 211. Judgment in *Cunliffe* was delivered at the same time as *Theophanous* and *Stephens*.

15 (1994) 182 CLR 104.

16 Mason CJ, Toohey and Gaudron JJ, Deane J concurring; Brennan, Dawson and McHugh JJ dissenting.

17 *Theophanous* (1994) 182 CLR 104, 131 (Mason CJ, Toohey and Gaudron JJ), 182 (Deane J).

18 Ibid 137. So, under the new rule, the defence was available in respect of comment about a public official or candidate for public office where the *defendant* could establish that: (a) it was unaware of the falsity of the material published; (b) it did not publish the material recklessly, that is, not caring whether the material was true or false; and
(c) the publication was reasonable in the circumstances.

These alterations show the two kinds of divergence from the *New York Times* rule mentioned above. First, the High Court limited the operation of the rule to the political context.[19] This limitation might be expected given that the Australian freedom protects only political communication rather than speech or expression generally, but it is also a response to wide criticism in the United States of the extension of the 'public figure' test beyond the political context. Further, despite some affinity with the philosophy underlying *New York Times*,[20] the High Court showed some discomfort with the transcendent value placed on freedom of speech under the First Amendment. The reversal of the onus of proof and the addition of the reasonableness requirement reflect an assessment that the *New York Times* rule 'sets too little store by the reputation of the person defamed'.[21] It appeared from *Theophanous*, therefore, that reputation is more highly valued in comparison to freedom of expression in Australia than in the United States.

The story of *New York Times'* influence in Australia has since become complicated by the reformulation of the *Theophanous* doctrine in 1997 in *Lange v Australian Broadcasting Corporation*.[22] In Lange, the High Court held that the Constitution did not render rules of the common law invalid as such,[23] but rather that the common law should conform with constitutional requirements such as the implied freedom of political communication.[24] For this reason, the court rejected the idea that there was a *constitutional* defence to a defamation action (as was held in *Theophanous*), and instead extended the common law of qualified privilege to accord with constitutional values

19 Ibid 134 (Mason CJ, Toohey and Gaudron JJ): 'We should indicate our preliminary view that these extensions [of the public figure test under *New York Times*] other than the extension to cover candidates for public office, should not form part of our law.' Although he indicated his support for the conclusion reached by these judges, Deane J's preferred approach, at 185–8, was to abandon any limitation on the availability of the defence to a publisher for statements about 'the official conduct or suitability of a member of the Parliament or other holder of high Commonwealth office', thus responding to the arguments that rule's focus on the defendant's conduct itself created a chilling effect.

20 See Adrienne Stone, 'Freedom of Political Communication, the Constitution and the Common Law' (1998) 26 *Federal Law Review* 219.

21 *Theophanous* (1994) 182 CLR 104, 134.

22 (1997) 189 CLR 520 ('*Lange*'). See also *McGinty v Western Australia* (1996) 186 CLR 140; George Williams, 'Sounding the Core of Representative Democracy: Implied Rights and Electoral Reform' (1996) 20 *Melbourne University Law Review* 848.

23 *Lange* (1997) 189 CLR 520, 560. See Stone above n 20; Leslie Zines, T*he Common Law in Australia: Its Nature and Constitutional Significance* (1999).

24 *Lange* (1997) 189 CLR 520, 566: 'Of necessity, the common law must conform with the Constitution. The development of the common law in Australia cannot run counter to constitutional imperatives ... The common law and the requirements of the Constitution cannot be at odds. The common law of libel and slander could not be developed inconsistently with the Constitution, for the common law's protection of personal reputation must admit as an exception that qualified freedom to discuss government and politics which is required by the Constitution.'

represented by the freedom of political communication.[25] The court stated that the extended defence could not be relied upon:

> unless the defendant had reasonable grounds for believing that the imputation was true, took proper steps, so far as they were reasonably open, to verify the accuracy of the material and did not believe the imputation to be untrue. Furthermore, the defendant's conduct will not be reasonable unless the defendant has sought a response from the person defamed and published the response made (if any) except in cases where the seeking or publication of a response was not practicable or it was unnecessary to give the plaintiff an opportunity to respond.[26]

Despite the differences between the interpretive approaches of *Theophanous* and *Lange*, both decisions respond to *New York Times* in similar ways. The new common law rule laid down in *Lange* clearly shows the influence of *New York Times*, by giving greater protection to the discussion of public affairs than had previously been given by the common law of defamation. Similarly, like the *Theophanous* defence it replaced, it is somewhat more protective of reputation than the *New York Times* rule, preferring a requirement of proof of the reasonableness of the defendant's conduct to an actual malice standard.

South Africa

In South Africa, the Australian rule, as well as *New York Times*, has been influential in the interpretation of South African constitutional guarantees of freedom of expression.[27]

After some conflicting early decisions by single judges in lower courts,[28] an

25 Ibid 571. In its traditional form, the defence of qualified privilege had not protected publications in newspapers and broadcasts. Under the new approach, however, the Court recognised that 'each member of the Australian community has an interest in disseminating and receiving information, opinions and arguments concerning government and political matters that affect the people of Australia' and extended the defence of qualified privilege to publications and broadcasts of such material. This extension of the common law defence is clearly inspired by the freedom of political communication. 'Because the Constitution requires "the people" to be able to communicate with each other with respect to matters that could affect their choice in federal elections or constitutional referenda or that could throw light on the performance of ministers of State and the conduct of the executive branch of government, the common law rules concerning privileged communications, as understood before the decision in *Theophanous* ... failed to meet that requirement.'

26 Ibid 574.

27 This is now reflected in s 16 of the 1997 Constitution. Attention to *New York Times* and subsequent developments in other countries is not at all surprising in the South African context. Section 39(1) of the 1997 Constitution states that: 'When interpreting the Bill of Rights, a court, tribunal or forum ... (b) must consider international law; and (c) may consider foreign law'. See generally Hoyt Webb, 'The Constitutional Court of South Africa: Rights Interpretation and Comparative Constitutional Law' (1998) 1 *University of Pennsylvania Journal of Constitutional Law* 205.

28 *Gardener v Whitaker* 1995 (2) SA 672, 687 (Froneman J) (the common law of defamation 'may be at odds with the Constitution'); *Bogoshi v National Media Ltd* 1996 (3) SA 78 (finding that the guarantee of freedom of expression did not require any modification of the law of defamation because the common law had already struck an appropriate balance between freedom of speech and reputation.); *Holomisa v Argus Newspapers Ltd* 1996 (2) SA 588, 613, 617 (rejecting the *New York Times* 'actual malice' test as 'inappropriate and undesirable for our law' and adopting the *Theophanous* test but not the shift in the onus of proof to the defendant); *Buthelezi v South African Broadcasting Commission* 1997 (12) BCLR 1733 (rejecting the placement of the onus of proof on the plaintiff).

authoritative consideration of the relationship between the constitutionally guaranteed freedom of expression and the common law of defamation was provided in 1999 by the South African Supreme Court of Appeal in *National Media Ltd v Bogoshi*.[29] The Supreme Court of Appeal examined the Australian High Court's judgment in *Lange* and the English Court of Appeal's 1998 judgment in *Reynolds* (discussed below) in concluding that appropriate protection of freedom of expression required modification of the common law of defamation.[30]

In *Bogoshi*, the Supreme Court of Appeal modified the common law of defamation in the light of the constitutionally guaranteed freedom of expression, but was not prepared to accept the full *New York Times* test. Closely following the Australian solution, the court held that 'the publication in the press of false defamatory allegations of fact will not be regarded as unlawful if, upon a consideration of all the circumstances of the case, it is found to have been reasonable to publish the particular facts in the particular way and at the particular time'.[31] Moreover, the Court accepted the placement of the onus of proof on the defendant.[32]

This modification of the *New York Times* rule reflects discomfort with the American philosophy. In particular, rather than celebrating the encouragement of robust debate even to the point of sanctioning the publication of falsehoods, the Supreme Court of Appeal was sceptical of the value of such a debate, stating: 'Ultimately there can be no justification for the publication of untruths, and members of the press should not be left with the impression that they have a licence to lower the standards of care which must be observed before defamatory matter is published in a newspaper.'[33]

Thus, *New York Times* has been influential in India, Australia and South Africa, albeit that the rule has been modified in some significant respects in Australia and South Africa.

29 1999 (1) BCLR 1 (*Bogoshi*). The plaintiff in this case brought an action in defamation against the publisher, editor, distributor and printer of the *City Press* newspaper. The defendants sought to amend their plea to include a defence of good faith publication in part based the constitutional guarantee of freedom of expression. The Supreme Court of Appeal allowed the application for amendment and in, the course of judgement, gave considerable attention to the *New York Times* issue. (The South African Supreme Court of Appeal is the highest court of appeal in all but constitutional matters. The South Africa Constitutional Court has yet to give authoritative guidance on this issue, although it has alluded to the need to do so: *Gardener v Whitaker* 1996 (4) SA 337, 343–4 (Kentridge AJ); *Du Plessis v De Klerk* 1996 (3) SA 850, 883–5 (Kentridge AJ)).

30 *Bogoshi* 1999 (1) BCLR 1, 38–42. The Supreme Court of Appeal examined the revised common law in light of the guarantee of freedom of expression in the South African Bill of Rights. It held, at 57, that the common law 'achieves a proper balance between the right to protect one's reputation and the freedom of the press, viewing these interests as constitutional values'.

31 Ibid 42. Although its finding was not limited to the political context, the court, at 42–3, gave special emphasis to free expression in that context: 'In considering the reasonableness of the publication account must obviously be taken of the nature, extent and tone of the allegations. We know, for instance, that greater latitude is usually allowed in respect of political discussion ... and that the tone in which a newspaper article is written, or the way in which it is presented, sometimes provides additional, and perhaps unnecessary, sting. What will also figure prominently, is the nature of the information on which the allegations were based and the reliability of their source, as well as the steps taken to verify the information.'

32 Ibid 58–60.

33 Ibid 43.

III CANADA AND THE UNITED KINGDOM: A MORE SCEPTICAL APPROACH

We now turn our attention to Canada and the United Kingdom, where the reaction to the *New York Times* rule has been more sceptical.

Canada

Reluctance to embrace the *New York Times* principle is particularly striking in Canada. Given its cultural and geographical closeness to the United States, and the express protection of 'freedom of expression' found in s 2(b) of the *Canadian Charter of Rights and Freedoms*, it might be thought that Canada is the country most likely to adopt the *New York Times* rule. However, the much-observed difference between Canada and the United States in matters of free speech is evident again in the Canadian reaction to *New York Times*.[34]

The issue came before the Canadian Supreme Court in the 1995 case of *Hill v Church of Scientology*.[35] Like the Indian decision of Rajagopal, Hill presented an atypical context for the consideration of *New York Times*. Rather than an elected official suing a media organisation for statements about his or her public role, the case before the Canadian Supreme Court concerned two lawyers — a prosecutor suing an opposing counsel and his client (the Church of Scientology) for allegations, subsequently proved to be groundless, relating to the plaintiff's conduct during an investigation of the Church of Scientology.

It was not open to the defendants to argue that their allegations were directly protected by s 2(b) of the Canadian Charter because (like the Australian freedom of political communication) the Charter does not, as a general rule, apply to the common law.[36] Instead, they argued that, in light of the freedom of expression provided for by the Charter, the common law should be developed to reach a result similar to that reached on constitutional grounds in *New York Times*.[37] In particular, the defendants here argued that the Charter required either the adoption of the *New York Times* 'actual malice' standard as a rule of common law, or the extension of the law of qualified privilege to afford a defence in the particular circumstances at issue in the case.[38]

34 See Kent Greenawalt, *Fighting Words: Individuals, Communities, and Liberties of Speech* (1994).

35 [1995] 2 SCR 1130 (La Forest, Gonthier, Cory, McLachlin, Iacobucci and Major JJ; L'Heureux-Dube J concurring) ('*Hill*').

36 *Canadian Charter of Rights and Freedoms* 1982, s 32. The court in *Hill* [1995] 2 SCR 1130, 1159 provides an exception 'in so far as the common law is the basis of some governmental action which . . . infringes a guaranteed right or freedom'. No such government action was present in this case. The court rejected the argument that the plaintiff's action, as the action of an officer of the Crown, constituted government action. He brought the action, the court held, in his own capacity in response to the impugning of his, rather than the government's, reputation.

37 The Supreme Court's view is that the common law ought to be interpreted consistently with Charter values. See *RWDSU v Dolphin Delivery Ltd* [1986] 2 SCR 573, 603.

38 *Hill* [1995] 2 SCR 1130, 1158–9.

The Canadian Supreme Court declined to adopt the *New York Times* actual malice standard as a rule of the Canadian common law of defamation and, indeed, declined to undertake much revision of the Canadian common law. However, although the Canadian Supreme Court is even more resistant to the *New York Times* and its underlying philosophy than the courts discussed above, it scepticism stems from the same source. First, the Canadian Supreme Court was influenced by the arguments that the *New York Times* rule tended to defeat its own purpose by exacerbating the chilling effect of defamation law.[39] Further, like the South African Supreme Court of Appeal, the Supreme Court of Canada challenged the rationale underlying *New York Times*. For this reason, the Supreme Court did not merely reject aspects of the *New York Times* rule which have proved self-defeating, while accepting its rationale that political discussion needs to be protected from the chilling effect of a truth requirement (as in Australia).[40] Rather, the Supreme Court focussed on the resulting social cost of the deprecation of truth in public discourse to which it is said the rule gives rise,[41] and consequently seemed not to be troubled by any 'chilling effect' that defamation law may have on public debate. Writing for the court, Cory J stated :

> [D]efamatory statements are very tenuously related to the core values which underlie s 2 (b). They are inimical to the search for truth. False and injurious statements cannot enhance self-development. *Nor can it ever be said that they lead to healthy participation in the affairs of the community.* Indeed, they are detrimental to the advancement of these values and harmful to the interests of a free and democratic society.[42]

Thus, rather than expressing confidence in the capacity of a *New York Times* rule to improve discussion of public affairs, the Court was concerned with the adverse effects on participation in public affairs produced by a strong political expression defence deterring 'sensitive and honourable men from seeking public pos-itions of trust and responsibility'.[43] The Canadian Supreme Court concluded from this that the current truth requirement of the law of defamation gave appropriate protection to both reputation and speech.[44] Justice Cory stated:

39 Ibid 1182–3.

40 Jamie Cameron, 'The Past, Present, and Future of Expressive Freedom under the Charter' (1997) 35 *Osgoode Hall Law Journal* 1, 39.

41 *Hill*, above n 38, 1182–5. See *Dun & Bradstreet, Inc v Greenmoss Builders, Inc*, 472 US 749, 767–9 (1985) (White J; Burger CJ concurring): 'The *New York Times* rule thus countenances two evils: first, the stream of information about public officials and public affairs is polluted and often remains polluted by false information; and second, the reputation and professional life of the defeated plaintiff may be destroyed by falsehoods that might have been avoided with a reasonable effort to investigate the facts.'

42 *Hill* [1995] 2 SCR 1130, 1174 (emphasis added).

43 C Gately, *Gatley on Libel and Slander in a Civil Action* (4th ed, 1953) quoted in *Hill* [1995] 2 SCR 1130, 1174.

44 In the end then, the Canadian Supreme Court took only very limited steps, extending the common law defence to the report of the content of court documents not filed until shortly after the report of their contents: *Hill* [1995] 2 SCR 1130, 1192–3.

> I simply cannot see that the law of defamation is unduly restrictive or inhibiting. Surely it is not requiring too much of individuals that they ascertain the truth of the allegations they publish.[45]

Finally, the Canadian Court also shared the concern seen in the Australian and South African courts for the protection of reputation. Thus, at the same time as it rejected the American understanding of the value of robust debate, the court placed a correspondingly higher value on the protection of reputation. Indeed, it considered the protection of reputation to be closely linked to Charter values such as the 'innate worthiness and dignity of the individual'[46] and the right to privacy.[47]

United Kingdom

The first important British case to consider the *New York Times* rule was *Derbyshire County Council v Times Newspapers Ltd*,[48] in which the English Court of Appeal (in 1992),[49] and subsequently the House of Lords (in 1993), held that free speech considerations precluded a local government authority suing at common law for libel in respect of its governmental and administrative functions. The House of Lords' judgment shows that the connection between freedom of speech and democracy, so central to *New York Times*, is also recognised by the English common law. Their Lordships stated:

> It is of the highest public importance that a democratically elected governmental body, or indeed any governmental body, should be open to uninhibited public criticism. The threat of a civil action for defamation must inevitably have an inhibiting effect on freedom of speech.[50]

The *New York Times* rule then came before the House of Lords in 1998 in *Reynolds*, when a defamation action was brought by a former Irish Prime Minister against the *Sunday Times* newspaper. Despite the sensitivity to free speech concerns evident in cases such as *Derbyshire*, English courts previously had not adopted a public figure defence in the common law of libel.[51] Although it was not argued that the House of Lords should adopt a *New York Times*-like defence, it was put that the common law should recognise a new

45 Ibid 1187.

46 Ibid 1175: '[T]he good reputation of the individual represents and reflects the innate dignity of the individual, a concept which underlies all the *Charter* rights.'

47 This was accorded constitutional protection in *R v Dyment* [1988] 2 SCR 417, 427. See *Hill* [1995] 2 SCR 1130, 1179

48 [1992] 1 QB 770 (Court of Appeal); [1993] AC 534 (House of Lords) ('*Derbyshire*'). See Eric Barendt, 'Libel and Freedom of Speech in English Law' [1993] *Public Law* 449.

49 Although the Court of Appeal's decision was principally influenced by the European Convention on Human Rights, *New York Times* was regarded as a persuasive statement of basic free speech principle that accorded with the approach of the European Court of Human Rights: *Derbyshire* [1992] 1 QB 770, 831 (Butler-Sloss LJ), 826 (Ralph Gibson LJ).

50 *Derbyshire* [1993] AC 534, 547.

51 Barendt, above n 48, 455. See also Lord Lester of Herne Hill QC, 'Defaming Politicians and Public Officials' [1995] *Public Law* 1, 5–6; Kevin Williams, '"Only Flattery is Safe": *Political Speech and the Defamation Act* 1996' (1997) 60 *Modern Law Review* 388, 392–3.

'generic privilege' that would protect political discussion.[52] Under the suggested new rule, a libellous statement of fact made in the course of political discussion would not attract liability if published in good faith; a submission clearly influenced by the *New York Times* rule.[53]

However, the 'generic privilege' was rejected by the House of Lords, which also resisted the more limited concessions to free speech made by the Court of Appeal.[54] Instead, the House of Lords preserved the classical test of duty and interest[55] but emphasised that this test could be sensitive to free speech concerns by taking into account matters such as the nature of the publication, including its importance for public discussion.[56]

Once again, the conservative approach to the protection of political speech reflects the kind of concerns seen in other courts discussed above. Like the South African Supreme Court of Appeal and the Supreme Court of Canada, some members of the House of Lords were sceptical of the value of protecting false statements of fact.[57] Indeed, although there was some recognition of the chilling effect of libel action,[58] Lord Hope of Craighead regarded the requirements of the existing law of defamation as an important disciplining factor that appropriately constrained the media.[59] In addition, at other points there is much emphasis on the competing value in the protection of reputation.[60]

52 By 'generic privilege' it was meant a rule that would apply to a pre-determined category of cases. *Reynolds* [1994] 4 All ER 609, 621 (Lord Nicholls), 630 (Lord Steyn). This is opposed to the Court of Appeal's approach of preserving the existing common law rule but recognising that the requirements of qualified privilege should be 'rather more readily held to be satisfied' where the media has published criticism of political figures. This 'circumstantial test' would be applied in determining a claim for qualified privilege, under which a court would consider, among other matters, the nature, status and source of the material published and the circumstances of the publication. *Reynolds v Times Newspapers Ltd* [1998] 3 All ER 961. 'Political discussion', it seems, was meant to refer to discussion of matters relating to the public conduct of those elected to positions of responsibility in government. See *Reynolds* [1999] 4 All ER 609, 621, 630.

53 See *Reynolds* [1999] 4 All ER 609, 621 (Lord Nicholls).

54 The Court of Appeal had formulated a new 'circumstantial test'. See above n 52. In the House of Lords, this test was explicitly rejected by Lords Nicholls, Steyn, Hope and Hobhouse, the latter two expressing agreement with Lord Nicholls: ibid 625–6, 639, 654–5, 658–9. Their Lordships' concern was that the circumstances nominated by the Court of Appeal as relevant to the availability of the defence of qualified privilege might take on a greater status as elements of a rule that must be satisfied in each case. By contrast, Lord Cooke, who also expressed general agreement with Lord Nicholls, accepted the circumstantial test, but with the proviso that 'the circumstantial test should not be treated as something apart from the [traditional common law] duty-interest test.' Ibid 647.

55 See *Toogood v Spyring* (1834) 1 CM & R 181, 189; 149 ER 1044, 1049–50.

56 *Reynolds* [1999] 4 All ER 609, 625–6 (Lord Nicholls), 633 (Lord Steyn).

57 'There is no human right to disseminate information that is not true. No public interest is served by publishing or communicating misinformation.' Ibid 657 (Lord Hobhouse).

58 Ibid 654.

59 The protection of the media 'carries with it certain penalties . . . One of these is the discipline of having to justify each claim to the benefit of qualified privilege should the statements of fact which are made by the media turn out to be defamatory. The description of this discipline as having a "chilling" effect on free speech, as if this in itself shows that something is wrong with it, is too simple. Of course, it does "chill" or inhibit the freedom of the communicator. But there are situations in which this is a necessary protection for the individual.' Ibid.

60 Ibid 622 (Lord Nicholls): 'Reputation is an integral and important part of the dignity of the individual . . . [but] it should not be supposed that protection of reputation is a matter of importance only to the affected individual and his family. Protection of reputation is conducive to the public good. It is in the public interest that the reputation of public figures should not be debased falsely.'

There are two further distinctive features of this case. First, their Lordships were particularly sensitive to the need to adapt the law to suit distinctive conditions prevailing in the United Kingdom. In the words of Lord Steyn, balancing the competing interests in reputation and freedom of speech was a difficult task which could admit of more than one plausible answer:

> This is a branch of law in which common law courts have arrived at sharply divergent solutions . . . There are at stake powerful competing arguments of policy. They pull in different directions. It is a hard case in which it is unrealistic to say that there is only one right answer. *And in considering the decisions in other jurisdictions it is right to take into account that cultural differences have played an important role.*[61]

This caution as to the adoption of foreign solutions manifested itself in several ways. One way was the judicial distrust of the media evident in *Reynolds*, a distrust that was not evident in *New York Times*.[62] Lord Nicholls of Birkenhead suggested that 'reliance upon the ethics of professional journalism ... would not generally be thought to provide a sufficient safeguard . . . [T]he sad reality is that the overall handling of these matters by the national press, with its own commercial interests to serve, does not always command general con-fidence.'[63] Further, Lords Steyn and Cook rejected more extensive protection for political discussion out of concern to preserve the strong protection English law accords the media from pressure to reveal sources.[64] Finally, this sensitivity to cultural differences even led Lord Cooke of Thorndon to suggest that a different result might be appropriate in New Zealand, even though the Privy Council is that country's ultimate court of appeal. In Lord Cooke's words, 'the possibility of a difference between English and New Zealand common law on the issue has to be accepted, albeit not advocated'.[65]

Secondly, the court's resistance to a generic privilege reflects a strong preference for a test that would allow for 'a balancing exercise in the light of the concrete facts of each case'.[66] Thus it was recognised that a generic privilege, a rule that applied to a nominated category of cases, would by its very nature, limit the capacity of judges in individual cases to respond to the exigencies of that case.[67] This preference for more flexibility was partly based upon a desire

61 Ibid 630 (emphasis added).

62 Lewis, above n 3.

63 *Reynolds* [1999] 4 All ER 609, 623.

64 Ibid 631 (Lord Steyn), 640 (Lord Cooke). Lord Steyn compared the protection accorded by s 10 of the *Contempt of Court Act* 1981 (UK) and *Goodwin v United Kingdom* (1996) 22 EHRR 123, 143 with a plaintiff's entitlement in the United States to a pre-trial inquiry into sources and editorial decision making as held in *Herbert v Lando*, (1977) 441 US 153.

65 *Reynolds* [1999] 4 All ER 609, 643.

66 Ibid 631 (Lord Steyn). Lord Nicholls makes a similar point, at 625–6.

67 The choice between relatively defined rules that constrain the choice of judges and more flexible approaches has long been at the centre of debate over the shape of free speech law in the United States. In the United States the argument has been that defined rules are an important aspect of free speech protection. See generally Frederick Schauer, 'Categories and the First Amendment: A Play in Three Acts' (1981) 34 *Vanderbilt Law Review* 265. See also Adrienne Stone, 'The Limits of Constitutional Text and Structure: Standards of Review and the Freedom of Political Communication' (1999) 23 *Melbourne University Law Review* 668.

for consistency with the approach of the European Court of Human Rights exhibited in cases such as *Lingens v Austria*.[68] However, at other points, it is the flexibility itself that was attractive. Lord Hope of Craighead took the view that, in these circumstances, flexibility was valuable because the balancing of reputation against freedom of speech 'is particularly sensitive to changing circumstances, whether they be social or political, and to changes in the way in which information is presented or disseminated'.[69] It was said that a generic privilege would bring with it the danger that the privilege would not respond to these changing circumstances, and thus risk 'losing touch with the underlying justification for the creation of the category'.[70]

IV NEW ZEALAND: A SWING TO MORE PROTECTION?

The treatment of *New York Times* in *Reynolds* brings us finally to New Zealand. Although the position in that country was settled in June 2000 by the New Zealand Court of Appeal in *Lange v Atkinson*,[71] a complicated series of appeals had preceded that decision.

The case first came before the Court of Appeal on appeal from the 1997 decision of Elias J at first instance.[72] In that decision, although her Honour declined to recognise a free standing 'public figure' or 'political figure' rule derived from the *New Zealand Bill of Rights Act* 1990 (NZ) (partly in response to the well known criticisms of *New York Times*),[73] she reformulated the common law of defamation in response to free speech concerns.[74]

When the matter went to the New Zealand Court of Appeal, the defendants did not seek to reassert *New York Times* as the basis for a separate rule, and challenged only Lange's reliance on the reformulated doctrine of qualified privilege. However, in the Court of Appeal's 1998 decision,[75] the court's

68 (1986) 8 EHRR 407. See *Reynolds* [1999] 4 All ER 609, 635 (Steyn L).

69 *Reynolds* [1999] 4 All ER 609, 650. Lord Nicholls, at 623, also advocated a flexible approach even though he recognised that it would bring with it 'an element of unpredictability and uncertainty'. At 624, he was confident that this degree of uncertainty could be adequately resolved by a court which has 'the advantage of being impartial, independent of government, and accustomed to deciding disputed issues of fact and whether an occasion is privileged.'

70 Ibid 650. See also Schauer, above n 67.

71 Unreported, Court of Appeal of New Zealand, Richardson P, Henry, Keith, Blanchard and Tipping JJ, 21 June 2000. The case was brought by David Lange, the former Prime Minister of New Zealand, the same plaintiff who featured in the Australian case *Lange* (1997) 189 CLR 520. The action was brought against the author of articles critical of Mr Lange's performance as Prime Minister and against the publisher of the magazine in which they appeared.

72 *Lange v Atkinson* [1997] 2 NZLR 22. Her Honour is now Chief Justice of New Zealand.

73 Ibid 37, 47–8. In part Elias J also appears to have been influenced by certain cases in which New Zealand Courts had declined to recognise a special privilege available to the media. She held, at 44, that these cases bound her not to recognise a special rule that 'would deny the protection of the law of defamation to a section of the community.' In a final passage, at 48, Elias J also appears to place reliance on New Zealand's 'unitary system of law', although the precise relevance of this matter is not made clear.

74 Ibid 46: 'Qualified privilege … attaches to statements made to the general public about matters of government.'

75 *Lange v Atkinson* [1998] 3 NZLR 424.

general approach to the discussion of the common law extension of the privilege suggested that its underlying philosophy was closer to the vision of freedom of speech seen in other common law countries than the more speech protective United States vision.

Significantly, the New Zealand Court of Appeal moderated its enthusiasm for freedom of speech in a manner similar to other courts. It placed special emphasis on the limitation in s 5 of the *New Zealand Bill of Rights Act* in favour of regulation 'demonstrably justified in a free and democratic society'. Thus, although the New Zealand Court of Appeal in its 1998 decision did not reach precisely the same balancing of interests as other courts studied here, the New Zealand Court seemed to be open to the prospect that competing interests should prevail over freedom of speech.[76] In particular, like other courts, it was especially concerned with the competing interest of reputation which it regarded as related to the human dignity and privacy.[77]

The New Zealand Court of Appeal did, however, take a distinctive position. Unlike the Canadian Supreme Court in *Hill*, the Court of Appeal in its 1998 decision did not accept that existing common law rules provide adequate speech protection, nor did it anticipate the subsequent modest reformulation of the common law by the House of Lords in *Reynolds*. Rather, essentially in agreement with the court below, the Court of Appeal extended the common law of qualified privilege to cases of general publication of 'statements made about the actions and qualities of those currently or formerly elected to Parliament and those with immediate aspirations to such office, so far as those actions and qualities directly affect or affected their capacity ... to meet their public responsibilities'.[78]

In formulating a special rule, the New Zealand approach resembles the Australian and South African approaches but the New Zealand Court went a little further towards speech protection than even those courts. The court rejected the 'reasonableness' requirement by which the Australian High Court increased the protection of reputation, relying instead upon a statutory exception[79] that applies when the defendant's decision to publish was predominantly motivated by ill will towards the plaintiff or otherwise by the possibility of improper advantage.[80]

76 Ibid 466–7. This view is confirmed by the New Zealand courts' attitude in contempt of court cases when considering the conflict between freedom of expression and a fair jury trial. Although they rejected the Canadian rule directed specifically to the contempt of court issue, New Zealand courts have adopted the relatively deferential standard of review that the Canadian courts generally use to accommodate freedom of expression and other conflicting interests. See *Solicitor-General v Radio New Zealand Ltd* [1994] 1 NZLR 48, 61; *Gisborne v Solicitor-General* [1995] 3 NZLR 563, 573–4 (rejecting the holding in *Dagenais v Canadian Broadcasting Corporation* (1994) 94 CCC (3d) 289).

77 Though not mentioned in the *New Zealand Bill of Rights Act*, the right to reputation is recognised in the International Covenant on Civil and Political Rights to which the Bill of Rights purports to give effect. The preamble to the *New Zealand Bill of Rights Act* provides that a purpose of the act is '[t]o affirm New Zealand's commitment to the International Covenant on Civil and Political Rights'. See *Lange v Atkinson* [1998] 3 NZLR 424, 465–6.

78 Ibid 468.

79 *Defamation Act* 1992 (NZ), s 19(2).

80 *Lange v Atkinson* [1998] 3 NZLR 424, 469.

The Court of Appeal's 1998 decision was subsequently appealed to the Privy Council. However, having heard argument, the Privy Council remitted the case for reconsideration by the Court of Appeal in the light of the House of Lords' 1999 decision in *Reynolds*. Showing the concern, discussed above, that local law be adapted to local circumstances, the Privy Council emphasised that the New Zealand Court of Appeal was free to depart from *Reynolds* if it considered that local circumstances required it.[81]

On reconsideration, the Court of Appeal chose to maintain its previous position, despite developments in England. However it clarified a number of matters in its 2000 decision. First, it emphasised that the extended form of qualified privilege, recognised in its earlier decision, is context-dependant. That is, the court held that the determination of whether a publication is privileged depends upon a traditional common law analysis of whether there is a duty to disclose the information, and a concomitant interest in its receipt. Accordingly, not *every* statement made about the suitability of a candidate for public office is necessarily privileged. Although the Court of Appeal rejected the non-exhaustive list of matters that the House of Lords had indicated in *Reynolds* were relevant to the application of the English rule,[82] the Court nonetheless confirmed that the application of the New Zealand rule will depend upon the totality of the circumstances, including 'the identity of the publisher, the context in which the publication occurs, and the likely audience as well as the actual content of the information'.[83] Significantly, the Court of Appeal stressed that it is important to take context into account to ensure appropriate protection of reputation, even though it acknowledged that the consequent difficulty in predicting whether speech would be protected might contribute to a chilling effect.[84]

This qualification went some way to dealing with the Privy Council's suggestion that that the New Zealand rule might be unnecessarily wide.[85]

81 *Lange v Atkinson* [2000] 1 NZLR 257, 263: 'If satisfied that the privilege favoured in the [first New Zealand *Lange* case] is right for New Zealand . . . the New Zealand Court of Appeal is entitled to maintain that position.' See generally Rosemary Tobin 'Public Interest and the Defamation of Political Figures: The English Approach' (2000) 8 *Torts Law Journal* 152.

82 It did so in response to two concerns. First, the Court was concerned that this list created unnecessary uncertainty and thus added to the chilling effect of defamation laws. Further, the Court criticised the English rule for blurring the distinction between an occasion of privilege and the misuse of the privilege. In the Court of Appeal's view, the English test imported matters relevant to the determination of misuse (traditionally a matter for the jury) into the determination of whether a privileged occasion existed (traditionally a matter for the judge) and thus undesirably reduced the role of the jury in free speech cases. *Lange v Atkinson* (Unreported, Court of Appeal of New Zealand, Richardson P, Henry, Keith, Blanchard and Tipping JJ, 21 June 2000), paras [24]–[25].

83 Ibid para [13].

84 Although the Court expressed the opinion, at ibid para [22], that very little uncertainty would result from the rule, it held that 'the small level of uncertainty it may cause is a necessary price to pay to guard reputations against false imputations made on occasion which are outside the purpose of the privilege'. The Court thus sets itself well apart from the American free speech tradition which greatly values certainty as a means of protecting speech. See above n 67.

85 *Lange v Atkinson* [2000] 1 NZLR 257, 263.

However, importantly, in its 2000 decision, the Court of Appeal maintained its refusal to adopt the Australian 'reasonableness' requirement. The Court of Appeal pointed to several features of New Zealand society that it claimed justify somewhat more vigorous protection of public discussion. First, despite some emphasis on privacy in its earlier decision,[86] the court now seemed to down-play this value, noting that, unlike the *Human Rights Act* 1998 (UK) (which is still to come into force), the *New Zealand Bill of Rights Act*[87] contains no express mention of a right to privacy, nor does it contain an injunction (as does the UK Act) for courts to have regard to whether a journalistic publication is in the public interest or to relevant privacy codes. Additionally, the Court of Appeal held that 'History and circumstances give New Zealanders special reason for wanting to know what their Government is doing and why',[89] and found that New Zealand media is more trustworthy that its British counterparts.[90]

By marking itself out from the English position, the New Zealand Court seems, then, to have swung the pendulum back towards greater free speech protection. However, any such swing is slight. The Court of Appeal has certainly rejected the conservative approach of the House of Lords (thus also setting itself apart from the Supreme Court of Canada) and has adopted a rule that seems slightly more protective of certain types of speech than the Australian and South African rules. The New Zealand position remains, however, a long way from *New York Times*. Elias J's critique and subsequent rejection of the *New York Times* rule has never been questioned, and the New Zealand Court of Appeal, like most other courts studied here, employs a relatively flexible, contextual common law rule that gives more emphasis to the competing value of reputation than the American rule.

V CONCLUSION

This study of the interaction of the law of defamation and principles of freedom of speech demonstrates that most courts in the common law world are not committed to the particular vision of freedom of speech that characterises the First Amendment to the United States Constitution. With the possible

86 See above n 77 and accompanying text.

87 Section 14 provides: 'Everyone has the right to freedom of expression, including the freedom to seek, receive, and impart information and opinions of any kind in any form.' Although an Act of Parliament rather than an entrenched constitutional document, the *New Zealand Bill of Rights Act* has special status through s 6, which empowers the judiciary to interpret an enactment of the New Zealand Parliament so as to prefer 'a meaning that is consistent with the rights and freedoms contained in this Bill of Rights'.

88 *Human Rights Act* 1998 (UK) s 12(4).

89 *Lange v Atkinson*, (Unreported, Court of Appeal of New Zealand, Richardson P, Henry, Keith, Blanchard and Tipping JJ, 21 June 2000), para [32] citing a Parliamentary Committee Report *Towards More Open Government* (1980). That report refers to the small size of New Zealand (which requires that the government play a special role as a major developer of large scale projects as an alternative to overseas control) and the dependence of social support systems on central government.

90 Ibid paras [34]–[35].

exception of the Indian Supreme Court, courts have tempered their commitment to freedom of speech out of deference to other interests such as privacy and the protection of reputation. This suggests, then, that despite increased rights protection in common law countries, the fiercely protective free speech regime that dominates the United States is likely to remain unique to that country.

These decisions also point to two important features of modern judicial practice. First, the extensive discussion of *New York Times* shows that, despite some academic reservations,[91] comparative law is much practiced by judges in common law countries.[92] These cases provide an example of the widespread use of foreign precedent in high appellate courts of the common law world (a phenomenon fuelled perhaps by the ready accessibility of foreign judgments on electronic retrieval services and the Internet).[93] Moreover, they show that the use of foreign precedent is, in the main, not uncritical. This is especially significant given that, following constitutional change in many countries that has brought issues of individual rights to the fore, the United States Constitution[94] has become a particularly pertinent source of comparative analysis.[95] Notably, the courts considered here signalled that they would reassess, and exercise their own judgment in relation to, even this revered aspect of the American constitutional tradition.

91 These reservations date back at least to Montesquieu, *The Spirit of the Laws* (1748): 'the political and civil laws of each nation ... should be so appropriate to the people for whom they are made that it is very unlikely that the laws of one nation can suit another'. But see also Otto Kahn-Freund, 'On Uses and Misuses of Comparative Law' (1974) 37 *Modern Law Review* 1.

92 For a comprehensive analysis of the more general phenomenon by which legal systems 'borrow' or adopt features of other legal systems, see Alan Watson, *Legal Transplants: An Approach to Comparative Law* (1974).

93 American precedent has been a popular source of reference particularly in the rights context. See, for example, Gerard V La Forest 'The Use of American Precedents in Canadian Courts' (1994) 44 *Maine Law Review* 211; Anthony Lester QC 'The Overseas Trade in the American Bill of Rights' (1988) 88 *Columbia Law Review* 537; Paul E Von Nessen, 'The Use of American Precedent by the High Court of Australia, 1901–1987' (1992) 14 *Adelaide Law Review* 18.

94 For a comprehensive analysis of the influence of the United States Constitution in other countries, see Louis Henkin and Albert J Rosenthal (eds), *Constitutionalism and Rights: The Influence of the United States Constitution Abroad* (1990).

95 By contrast, the United States Supreme Court is far more reticent about comparative law than its counterparts in the English speaking world. See, for example, *Stanford v Kentucky*, 492 US 361, 369 n 1 (1989), rejecting an argument that the Eighth Amendment's bar on 'cruel and unusual punishments' should be interpreted by reference to penal practices in other 'advanced industrial societies'. See generally Mark Tushnet, 'The Possibilities of Comparative Constitutional Law' (1999) 108 *Yale Law Journal* 1225.

[10]

LANGE AND *REYNOLDS* QUALIFIED PRIVILEGE: AUSTRALIAN AND ENGLISH DEFAMATION LAW AND PRACTICE

ANDREW T KENYON*

[Australian and English case law has developed qualified privilege defences that are available to the media and appear to protect more political or public interest speech than traditional defamation law. This article draws on judicial decisions and qualitative research into defamation litigation to examine the defences' scope, strength and practicality in litigation. England's Reynolds privilege emerges as a well-supported, relatively strong, flexible and innovative defence, especially compared with Australia's narrower and weaker privileges under Lange and New South Wales legislation. The research strongly supports the further development of Australian privilege defences, as well as more careful consideration of judge and jury roles in each country. A closer understanding of Reynolds offers important benefits for protecting the publication of public interest news and commentary, and it is particularly useful in light of recent, and proposed, Australian law reforms.]

CONTENTS

I INTRODUCTION

Defamation law is often said to deter speech. The existence of such a 'chilling effect'[1] has some research support. For example, the leading United Kingdom study, *Libel and the Media: The Chilling Effect*,[2] extensively investigated the practices of journalists, editors and their legal advisers. It argues that both direct

* LLB (Hons) (Melb), LLM (Dist) (London), PhD (Melb); Senior Lecturer and Director, Centre for Media and Communications Law ('CMCL'), Law School, The University of Melbourne; Editor, *Media & Arts Law Review*. This paper draws on research supported by the University of Melbourne and its Faculty of Law (ECR Grant 2003) and research supported by the Australian Research Council (Andrew T Kenyon and Tim Marjoribanks, *Defamation Law in Context: Australian and US News Production Practices and Public Debate* (Discovery Project DP0343258, 2003–05)). Many thanks to Chris Dent (Research Fellow, CMCL) and Jason Bosland for their research assistance, and to all those who participated in the fieldwork: see below n 117.

1 For a review of the term's United States history, see Frederick Schauer, 'Fear, Risk and the First Amendment: Unravelling the "Chilling Effect"' (1978) 58 *Boston University Law Review* 685.

2 Eric Barendt et al, *Libel and the Media: The Chilling Effect* (1997).

and structural chilling effects exist under traditional defamation law. Media speech is chilled directly when lawyers recommend editing the content of publications, and is chilled structurally when journalists internalise the law's restrictive principles.[3] A separate Australian study, 'Defamation Law's Chilling Effect', involved a comparative content analysis of more than 1400 Australian and United States newspaper articles.[4] The study suggests that in the US — where defamation plaintiffs face much heavier burdens than under the Anglo-Australian law[5] — defamatory allegations against political and corporate actors are published more frequently than in Australia.[6] In the study's sample, the US articles contained defamatory allegations at nearly three times the rate of the Australian articles. In particular, the Australian media appeared to be less comfortable making allegations about corporate affairs than its US counterpart. Admittedly, the concept of a 'chilling effect' has obvious rhetorical appeal for participants in defamation practice or academic commentary. The concept, however, is also supported by existing empirical research which suggests that traditional Anglo-Australian defamation law may well chill media content.[7]

One important aspect of the apparent chilling effect is that defendants must generally prove the truth of the factual allegations they publish.[8] This follows in part from defamation law's unusual burden of proof for civil actions. Defamation plaintiffs need not prove that the publisher was at fault, nor that the publication was false. In addition, once published material about the plaintiff is shown to be defamatory, general damages are presumed.[9] Truth is central for defendant publishers because the primary defences of justification and fair comment require a publication's factual basis to be proven true. While truth need not be shown for the other major defences of absolute and qualified privilege, these defences have traditionally applied to few media publications, beyond fair reports of court proceedings or parliaments. Thus, defamation law has imposed liability on many media defendants who cannot prove their publications to be true. In this way, the law appears to focus more on protecting reputation than promoting wide debate about public interest issues.

The frequent need to prove truth is something that Australian and English developments in qualified privilege have sought to address. Since the mid-

3 Ibid 191–4.

4 Chris Dent and Andrew T Kenyon, 'Defamation Law's Chilling Effect: A Comparative Content Analysis of Australian and US Newspapers' (2004) 9 *Media & Arts Law Review* 89.

5 For detail about the US position, see Practising Law Institute, *Sack on Defamation: Libel, Slander, and Related Problems* (3rd ed, at April 2002); Libel Defense Resource Center, *LDRC 50-State Survey 2002–03: Media Libel Law* (2002).

6 Dent and Kenyon, above n 4, 106.

7 Further content analysis and news production research is being undertaken as part of ongoing research at the CMCL: see author's note. Among other issues, it should allow more detailed understanding of the wide variety of factors influencing media content and the particular contexts in which different defamation laws operate.

8 Barendt et al, above n 2, 77.

9 The presumption of general damages, which is another key aspect in the idea of a chilling effect, has received wide criticism: see, eg, Eric Barendt, 'What Is the Point of Libel Law?' (1999) 52 *Current Legal Problems* 110; John Fleming, 'Retraction and Reply: Alternative Remedies for Defamation' (1978) 12 *University of British Columbia Law Review* 15.

1990s, extended forms of qualified privilege have developed through *Lange v Australian Broadcasting Corporation*[10] and *Reynolds v Times Newspapers Ltd*.[11] The defences appear to protect more political or public interest speech than traditional law. *Reynolds* can be seen as 'conceptually, a different species of qualified privilege' from the general duty-interest defence,[12] or at least as a substantial expansion of the circumstances in which the defence can be satisfied.[13] *Reynolds* privilege seeks to protect defamatory material of public importance where defendants have published responsibly, irrespective of the material's truth or falsity.[14] *Lange* has also been described as making 'fundamental changes' to privilege's 'conceptual foundations'.[15] Under *Lange*, privilege has become a 'relatively egalitarian' defence that promotes '"free" discussion ... in which all citizens, so long as they act "reasonably", may participate on equal terms, rather than with some enjoying the status of "privileged publishers"'.[16]

This article considers whether the developments, in practice, do offer accessible defences for media publications. It combines case law analysis with qualitative investigation of defamation litigation in each country.[17] The research suggests that *Reynolds* is far more likely to reduce any chilling effect than *Lange*, but difficult issues of litigation practice remain for both defences. Part II briefly outlines the traditionally limited protection for media publications, before examining recent case law. It explains how the two new defences differ doctrinally, both in scope and in strength. *Reynolds* privilege is broad and flexible, and the judges who apply it appear sensitive to the free speech concerns underlying its development. It seems to offer the media meaningful benefits, at least for non-tabloid investigative reporting, and it may also develop to support wider commentary and public debate. *Lange* privilege is comparatively narrow, with its focus on political communication. More significantly, however, *Lange* privilege

10 (1997) 189 CLR 520 ('*Lange*').

11 [2001] 2 AC 127 ('*Reynolds*'). Similar changes have occurred in New Zealand, India and South Africa: see Adrienne Stone and George Williams, 'Freedom of Speech and Defamation: Developments in the Common Law World' (2000) 26 *Monash University Law Review* 362.

12 David Price and Korieh Duodu, *Defamation: Law, Procedure and Practice* (3rd ed, 2004) 107.

13 *Jameel v Wall Street Journal Europe SPRL [No 2]* [2004] EMLR 196, 202–7 (Eady J) ('*Jameel*'). The terms '*Reynolds* privilege' and '*Lange* privilege' are used in this article for clarity and brevity, rather than to suggest the defences have any necessary or complete separation from traditional qualified privilege.

14 See *Loutchansky v Times Newspapers Ltd [Nos 2–5]* [2002] QB 783. *Reynolds* privilege attaches to *publications* to the world at large, rather than to *occasions* in the traditional sense: *Kearns v General Council of the Bar* [2003] 1 WLR 1357, 1358 (Simon Brown LJ).

15 Michael Chesterman, *Freedom of Speech in Australian Law: A Delicate Plant* (2000) 106.

16 Ibid 109.

17 Left aside for separate analysis is the defence of qualified protection under the Queensland and Tasmanian defamation Codes, which appears wider and stronger than *Lange* in protecting publications made in good faith 'for the public good': see Des Butler and Sharon Rodrick, *Australian Media Law* (2nd ed, 2004) 86–92. Similarly not examined is the Australian Capital Territory defence of 'non-negligent publication' under s 66 of the *Civil Law (Wrongs) Act 2002* (ACT), which has not yet received judicial interpretation: see Matt Collins, 'New Defamation Law for the ACT' (2001) 6 *Media & Arts Law Review* 335. Also worth noting is the parallel New Zealand development of qualified privilege in *Lange v Atkinson* [2000] 3 NZLR 385: see Stone and Williams, above n 11, 374–7; Michael Gillooly, *The Third Man: Reform of the Australasian Defamation Defences* (2004) 129–39; Rosemary Tobin, 'Political Discussion in New Zealand: Cause for Concern?' [2003] *New Zealand Law Review* 215.

is weak. As with the longstanding statutory privilege under s 22 of the *Defamation Act 1974* (NSW), publishers appear likely to have trouble demonstrating to courts' satisfaction that they acted reasonably. Doctrinal analysis also suggests that judge and jury roles are problematic under the English and Australian defences.[18]

Part III examines defamation lawyers' perspectives on the defences, obtained in interviews with 50 leading practitioners in London, Melbourne and Sydney. The interviews suggest that *Reynolds* privilege is quite supported in England, despite some uncertainties about its future development and litigation practicality. *Reynolds* also appears to be affecting the media's pre-publication conduct and encouraging what may be seen as more balanced reporting. In Australia, *Lange* privilege appears to be a barely useable defence, primarily due to the reasonableness requirement. Practitioners suggest revising the defence, with preferable models offered by *Reynolds* or an expanded duty-interest privilege in the style of the earlier Australian approach under *Theophanous v Herald & Weekly Times Ltd*.[19] The fieldwork also suggests that privilege defences need to allocate judge and jury roles carefully. Otherwise, the greater protection of at least some types of speech, which appears to have been sought by developments in qualified privilege, will be substantially undercut.

As a final introductory matter, it is worth noting that this article's interview-based research takes a traditional sociolegal approach that is focused on legal practice. A longstanding interest of legal fieldwork has been legal actors, whether lawyers in courts,[20] or regulators outside courts.[21] Empirical research did display early concern with non-legal actors,[22] which has resurfaced since the late 1980s in qualitative investigations of the experiences and attitudes of laypeople who interact with the law.[23] The present research, however, may differ slightly in focus from some lawyer-centred sociolegal work. It starts from the expectation that *doctrinal* analysis can benefit from empirical research into litigation practice, at least for analysing laws that are commonly litigated. As a

18 Some material in Part II is examined in greater detail in Andrew T Kenyon, 'Developments in Qualified Privilege: England, Australia and Ireland?' in Eoin O'Dell (ed), *Freedom of Expression* (forthcoming).

19 (1994) 182 CLR 104 ('*Theophanous*'). See below nn 66–71 and accompanying text.

20 See, eg, Doreen McBarnet, 'Magistrates' Courts and the Ideology of Justice' (1981) 8 *British Journal of Law & Society* 181; Richard Ingleby, *Solicitors and Divorce* (1992).

21 See, eg, Richard Johnstone, *The Court and the Factory: The Legal Construction of Occupational Health and Safety Offences in Victoria* (PhD Thesis, The University of Melbourne, 1994).

22 Stewart Macaulay, 'Non-Contractual Relations in Business: A Preliminary Study' (1963) 28 *American Sociological Review* 55.

23 Significant northern hemisphere examples include: Belinda Fehlberg, *Sexually Transmitted Debt: Surety Experience and English Law* (1997); Patricia Ewick and Susan Silbey, *The Common Place of Law: Stories from Everyday Life* (1998); Austin Sarat and Thomas Kearns (eds), *Law in Everyday Life* (1993); William O'Barr and John Conley, 'Lay Expectations of the Civil Justice System' (1988) 22 *Law & Society Review* 137. Some Australian use of similar methods exists, for example, in sex discrimination: Rosemary Hunter and Alice Leonard, *The Outcomes of Conciliation in Sex Discrimination Cases* (1995).

result, the social in this research is quite confined: it is defamation law and practice.[24]

II Developing Qualified Privilege

A *The Traditional Defence*

Defamation law has long recognised various categories of qualified privilege, said to exist for the 'common convenience and welfare of society'.[25] Qualified privilege was available where publishers were under a legal, social or moral duty, or acted to protect an interest, *and* recipients had a corresponding duty or interest.[26] Shared duties or interests could exist for material published to small audiences,[27] but widespread publications were likely to see the defence fail.[28] Thus, while qualified privilege is longstanding for fair reports of parliamentary and court proceedings,[29] the defence has not generally protected media publications of political or public interest.[30] Established occasions of privilege can be criticised in many ways, not least for their historical class bases.[31] Qualified privilege did not protect media publications about suspected corruption. Instead, alleged malfeasance had to be reported to what courts regarded as proper authorities. Nor did privilege protect publications reasonably believed to be true. While the defence was narrow, it was strong because only malice would defeat publications made on, and relevant to, a privileged occasion. In both England and Australia, however, qualified privilege developed during the 1990s.

B *England — Reynolds v Times Newspapers Ltd*

Reynolds arose after *The Sunday Times* published a story in its London edition criticising Albert Reynolds, who had recently resigned as Ireland's Taoiseach (or Prime Minister).[32] Reynolds had played a major role in the Northern Ireland peace process, and his resignation was significant throughout the United

24 Issues of social power and access to law remain largely distinct from this doctrinal focus, although they appear acute for defamation: see, eg, Michael Newcity, 'The Sociology of Defamation in Australia and the United States' (1991) 26 *Texas International Law Journal* 1; Chesterman, above n 15, 173–4.

25 *Toogood v Spyring* (1834) 1 Cr M & R 181, 193; 149 ER 1044, 1050 (Parke B).

26 *Adam v Ward* [1917] AC 309, 334 (Lord Atkinson).

27 *Chapman v Ellesmere* [1932] 2 KB 431.

28 *Braddock v Bevins* [1948] 1 KB 580. The media might be able to rely on an ancillary or derivative protection, for example, if it published one person's reply to an attack by another.

29 Some jurisdictions have significant statutory fair report defences: see, eg, *Defamation Act 1996* (UK) c 31, s 15, sch 1; *Defamation Act 1974* (NSW) ss 24, 25, sch 2.

30 See, eg, *Wason v Walter* (1868) LR 4 QB 73; *Curry v Walter* (1796) 1 Bos & P 525; 126 ER 1046. For a re-examination of the history of qualified privilege and widespread publications, see Chris Dent, '"The Privileged Few" and Public Discourse: Practices of Classification in a History of Comment and Qualified Privilege' (Paper presented at the Australian and New Zealand Law and History Society, 23rd Annual Conference, Perth, 3 July 2004).

31 See, eg, Geoffrey Robertson and Andrew Nicol, *Media Law* (4th ed, 2002) 73–5; Chesterman, above n 15, 81–91.

32 Alan Ruddock and John Burns, 'Goodbye Gombeen Man', *The Sunday Times* (London), 20 November 1994, 19.

Kingdom. In its 1999 decision, the House of Lords held that the duty-interest requirement for privilege could be satisfied by media publications which the public had a right to know in all the circumstances.[33] This was a major development, making *Reynolds* the 'most important' recent privilege decision,[34] 'an important and potentially far-reaching reform'[35] and 'a marked liberalisation'.[36]

The House of Lords rejected a generic privilege for political material in order to maintain what it saw as adequate protection for reputation.[37] A qualified privilege for all political material was thought to protect too strongly the wrong type of speech. Protection would be too strong because, influenced by the European *Convention for the Protection of Human Rights and Fundamental Freedoms*,[38] journalists' confidential sources are very strongly protected. This makes it 'virtually impossible' to prove malice and defeat privilege.[39] In addition, the wrong speech would be protected in that a political defence would be too narrow. Instead, the defence should focus on the public interest qualities of a publication. While political speech is an important example of protected material,[40] *Reynolds* privilege is defined by a test of *public* interest.[41]

The House of Lords in *Reynolds* required multiple factors to be considered when deciding whether defendants have established privilege, with Lord Nicholls listing 10 illustrative factors.[42] A court will need to consider matters

33 *Reynolds* [2001] 2 AC 127, 195 (Lord Nicholls).

34 Richard Shillito and Eric Barendt, 'Libel Law' in Eric Barendt and Alison Firth (eds), *The Yearbook of Copyright and Media Law 2000* (2000) 391, 407.

35 Ian Loveland, 'Freedom of Political Expression: Who Needs the *Human Rights Act*?' [2001] *Public Law* 233, 233.

36 Kevin Williams, 'Defaming Politicians: The Not So Common Law' (2000) 63 *Modern Law Review* 748, 754. However, it has also been suggested that English judges were merely 'tiptoeing towards free speech': Geoffrey Robertson, 'Tiptoeing towards Free Speech', *The Guardian* (London), 29 October 1999, 22, cited in Ian Loveland, 'Political Libels — Whose Right Is It Anyway?' (2000) 53 *Current Legal Problems* 333, 356–7.

37 *Reynolds* [2001] 2 AC 127, 200, 204 (Lord Nicholls), 217 (Lord Cooke agreeing), 237 (Lord Hobhouse agreeing), 210–11 (Lord Steyn), 234–5 (Lord Hope). This followed the rejection by earlier law reform reports of a defence for public interest statements believed to be true and published with reasonable care, notably the Faulks Committee report: United Kingdom, *Report of the Committee on Defamation*, Cmnd 5909 (1975) 53–5.

38 Opened for signature 4 November 1950, 213 UNTS 221 (entered into force 3 September 1953).

39 Shillito and Barendt, above n 34, 408. See also Loveland, 'Political Libels', above n 36, 351; Paul Mitchell, 'Political Qualified Privilege' (2000) 11 *King's College Law Journal* 114, 115; *Gaddafi v Telegraph Group Ltd* [2000] EMLR 431.

40 See Loveland, 'Freedom of Political Expression', above n 35, 233: 'While the *Reynolds* principle does not extend to political information as a generic category, the judgment will undoubtedly provide a substantial degree of legal protection to diligent press coverage of political stories.'

41 See, eg, *Jameel* [2004] EMLR 196, 205 (Eady J).

42 [2001] 2 AC 127, 205:

> 1. The seriousness of the allegation. The more serious the charge, the more the public is misinformed and the individual harmed, if the allegation is not true. 2. The nature of the information, and the extent to which the subject matter is a matter of public concern. 3. The source of the information. Some informants have no direct knowledge of the events. Some have their own axes to grind, or are being paid … 4. The steps taken to verify the information. 5. The status of the information. The allegation may have already been the subject of an investigation which commands respect. 6. The urgency of the matter. News is often a perishable commodity. 7. Whether comment was sought from the plaintiff … An approach to the plaintiff will not always be necessary. 8. Whether the article contained the gist of the plaintiff's side of the story. 9. The tone of the article. A newspaper can raise queries or call for an investigation. It need not

about the publication — including its public importance, urgency and overall tone, and whether it included the claimant's position[43] — as well as matters about the information's source, such as steps taken by the publisher or another relevant body in verification.[44]

Commentators quickly suggested that courts would treat the *Reynolds* factors as a 'checklist'[45] or 'the standard template'.[46] Courts have done this, focusing on the idea of 'responsible' journalism. Subsequent cases suggest that the defence may fail where publications are sensational and repeated,[47] sources are unreliable, claimants are not contacted prior to publication (at least where publication has no urgency),[48] or suspicion is presented as fact.[49] But the defence's scope extends to matters of public importance such as bribery in professional soccer,[50] the use of child labour[51] and the detection of terrorism.[52] It is not limited to political communication. *Reynolds* privilege has flexibility, with the Privy Council emphasising the need to apply the responsible journalism standard practically.[53] Privilege need not be judged according to the meanings found to be conveyed by a jury. The standard looks more to conduct than to a publication's meaning: 'a journalist should not be penalised for making a wrong decision on a question of meaning on which different people might reasonably take different views.'[54]

Cases also show the defence's potentially far-reaching effects. *Reynolds* privilege can protect media reports of allegations being made by others, at times

adopt allegations as statements of fact. 10. The circumstances of the publication, including the timing.

43 The *Civil Procedure Rules 1998* (UK), which commenced on 26 April 1999, have substantially changed civil litigation in England, including altering some terminology: plaintiffs have become claimants, writs are called claim forms, and pleadings have been renamed statements of case. In relation to the Rules' influence on defamation, see Price and Duodu, above n 12, 271–5.

44 Although the House of Lords confirmed that a wider qualified privilege defence existed in law, a majority held that the defence was unavailable to *The Sunday Times* at retrial because the publisher had failed to put Reynolds' side of the story when making such serious allegations of political misconduct: *Reynolds* [2001] 2 AC 127, 206 (Lord Nicholls), 217 (Lord Cooke agreeing), 237 (Lord Hobhouse agreeing); cf 216–17 (Lord Steyn), 237 (Lord Hope).

45 Shillito and Barendt, above n 34, 410.

46 Williams, above n 36, 753. See also Roy Baker, 'Extending Common Law Qualified Privilege to the Media: A Comparison of the English and Australian Approaches' (2002) 7 *Media & Arts Law Review* 87; and the detailed consideration of each factor in Robertson and Nicol, above n 31, 130–3.

47 *Grobbelaar v News Group Newspapers Ltd* [2001] 2 All ER 437 (Court of Appeal). Note that this aspect of the decision was not challenged on appeal: *Grobbelaar v News Group Newspapers Ltd* [2002] 1 WLR 3024 (House of Lords).

48 *Jameel* [2004] EMLR 196, 209–10 (Eady J). There is a danger, however, that urgency will be evaluated with hindsight, rather than from the perspective of publishers who must decide, based on their own skill and experience, whether delaying a story is likely to produce more information about a claimant's version of events: Ian Cram, 'Reducing Uncertainty in Libel Law after *Reynolds v Times Newspapers*? *Jameel* and the Unfolding Defence of Qualified Privilege' (2004) 15 *Entertainment Law Review* 147, 149.

49 *James Gilbert Ltd v MGN Ltd* [2000] EMLR 680; see also *Khan v Euro Bangla Newspaper* (Unreported, Queen's Bench Division, Eady J, 13 January 2004).

50 *Grobbelaar v News Group Newspapers Ltd* [2001] 2 All ER 437 (Court of Appeal).

51 *James Gilbert Ltd v MGN Ltd* [2000] EMLR 680, 700 (Eady J).

52 *Jameel* [2004] EMLR 196.

53 *Bonnick v Morris* [2003] 1 AC 300, 309 (Lord Nicholls).

54 Ibid.

without publishers even attempting to verify the allegations. For example, *Al-Fagih v HH Saudi Research & Marketing (UK) Ltd*[55] concerned a political dispute within the Saudi Arabian community. In a series of articles, allegations by each disputing party against the other were published without any attempt at verification. The Court of Appeal held that the fact that allegations existed was important and could properly be reported. The repetition rule, which applies to the defence of justification,[56] does not limit qualified privilege. The rule does not 'require that an unadopted allegation ... be treated in the same way as an allegation asserted to be true' for the purposes of qualified privilege.[57] *Al-Fagih*'s support for neutral reportage shows the significance of a publication's tone under *Reynolds* — for example, are allegations presented as suspicions or facts, and are they merely reported or adopted by the publisher? Subsequently, the Court of Appeal has noted that reportage may have a wider application, with Simon Brown LJ stating:

> I am certainly prepared to recognise that the approach adopted in *Al-Fagih* may need to be taken further still — rather than perhaps confined merely to the reporting of statements (attributed and unadopted) by both sides to a political dispute ...[58]

Litigating claims of *Reynolds* privilege, however, may be difficult, particularly in relation to judge and jury roles.[59] Defamation law traditionally seeks a simple division under which judges determine whether occasions of publication are privileged, while juries decide if publications were affected by malice. Although there can be complications in judges deciding if a publication's content is *relevant* to privileged occasions,[60] these complications do not arise as a matter of course, nor do they depend on disputed facts. However, the *Reynolds* factors encompass matters traditionally dealt with under malice.[61] Many disputed facts could be relevant to the *Reynolds* factors, with juries needing to determine each of these facts before judges decide whether occasions are privileged. This could lead to very complex jury questionnaires, as in *Loutchansky v Times Newspapers Ltd [No 4]* where the jury sat an 'examination paper'.[62] Eady J has commented that in cases in which *Reynolds* is argued:

55 [2002] EMLR 215 ('*Al-Fagih*').

56 See *Shah v Standard Chartered Bank* [1999] QB 241.

57 *Al-Fagih* [2002] EMLR 215, 231 (Simon Brown LJ).

58 *Mark v Associated Newspapers Ltd* [2002] EMLR 839, 856 (Simon Brown LJ), 859 (Mummery and Dyson LJJ agreeing). A differently constituted Court of Appeal has referred to *Al-Fagih* without disapproval: *Loutchansky v Times Newspapers Ltd [Nos 2–5]* [2002] QB 783, 806–8 (Lord Phillips MR, Simon Brown and Tuckey LJJ). The decision has also been applied at first instance: *Al Misnad v Azzaman Ltd* [2003] EWHC 1783 (Unreported, Queen's Bench Division, Gray J, 21 July 2003).

59 Shillito and Barendt, above n 34, 411.

60 See, eg, *Bashford v Information Australia (Newsletters) Pty Ltd* (2004) 204 ALR 193, 201 (Gleeson CJ, Hayne and Heydon JJ), 247 (Kirby J), cf 203 (McHugh J).

61 See Loveland, 'Political Libels', above n 36, 357.

62 [2001] EMLR 898, 912 (Gray J). The questions should be framed to seek 'yes' or 'no' answers: *Jameel* [2004] EMLR 196, 200 (Eady J).

> It is now almost inevitable that ... the jury will be asked to answer a series of questions in order for the court to arrive at the necessary factual substratum upon which to base the ruling. The questions will be directed no doubt largely to establishing the raw data for answering those of the ten non-exhaustive tests identified by Lord Nicholls in *Reynolds* ... as may be relevant to the case in hand.[63]

Under this approach, judges retain significant powers to interpret and apply those jury answers, with '[a]ny value judgments, and to a large extent also any inferences to be drawn from the raw data' reserved for judges.[64]

Overall, *Reynolds* privilege is broad, not being limited to political publications. With strong protection for journalists' sources, a flexible approach to meaning and the recognition of some neutral reportage, *Reynolds* privilege appears to offer journalists meaningful benefits, while also requiring professional journalistic conduct. English protection for matters of political and public interest appears to have strengthened, at least for the classic investigative reporting that courts envisage.

C *Australia — Lange v Australian Broadcasting Corporation*

Australian privilege developed in two stages, each influenced by Australia's constitutional protection for political communication. The *Constitution* does not expressly protect speech, but creates what is called an implied freedom of political communication.[65] This limits legislative power to restrict speech about government or political matters. Any restriction must be appropriate to a legitimate end of the legislation. In addition, the common law — including its traditional approach to qualified privilege — is shaped by the implied protection.

The first stage in development was the 1994 *Theophanous* decision.[66] It created a *constitutional* defence for publications concerning political and government matters. The defence could apply where defendants were unaware that publications were false, had not published recklessly without caring about truth or falsity, and publication was reasonable in the circumstances.[67] *Theophanous* also expanded *common law* qualified privilege to cover media publications about political or government matters.[68] For such publications, defendants need not have met the constitutional defence's reasonableness requirement. The expanded

63 *Jameel* [2004] EMLR 196, 199–200 (Eady J).

64 Ibid.

65 See especially *Australian Capital Television Pty Ltd v Commonwealth* (1992) 177 CLR 106 ('*ACTV*'); *Nationwide News Pty Ltd v Wills* (1992) 177 CLR 1; *Theophanous* (1994) 182 CLR 104; *Stephens v West Australian Newspapers Ltd* (1994) 182 CLR 211 ('*Stephens*'); *Kruger v Commonwealth* (1997) 190 CLR 1; *Lange* (1997) 189 CLR 520; *Levy v Victoria* (1997) 189 CLR 579; *Roberts v Bass* (2002) 212 CLR 1.

66 *Theophanous* (1994) 182 CLR 104. See also *Stephens* (1994) 182 CLR 211. For an examination of the *Theophanous* defence and subsequent developments, see Butler and Rodrick, above n 17, 77–82; Sally Walker, *Media Law: Commentary and Materials* (2000) 207–28; Michael Gillooly, *The Law of Defamation in Australia and New Zealand* (1998) 188–96.

67 *Theophanous* (1994) 182 CLR 104, 140 (Mason CJ, Toohey and Gaudron JJ).

68 Ibid.

common law privilege was defeated only by malice, making it the most significant development for publishers in *Theophanous*.

The majority judgments in *Theophanous* also suggested that political communication was wide, and close to being communication about 'public affairs'.[69] Political communication included speech about governments, politicians, candidates, public officers, political and public bodies, and people whose activities were matters of political debate, such as trade union leaders and political commentators.[70] The majority cited Eric Barendt to describe 'political speech' as 'all speech relevant to the development of public opinion on the whole range of issues which an intelligent citizen should think about.'[71] With a privilege defence that could only be defeated by malice, *Theophanous* suggested that many public interest matters would be protected far more than previously: it appeared to be a wide and strong defence.

But the defence did not survive. The High Court's divisions in *Theophanous* and related cases led it to reconsider matters. The 1997 *Lange* decision forms the second and current stage of Australian developments. It concerned the leading current affairs program, *Four Corners*, which criticised the conduct of New Zealand's then Prime Minister, David Lange. The plaintiff pleaded that the program meant he was unfit to hold public office.[72] The High Court heard a pre-trial challenge to the availability of the *Theophanous* defences. In a unanimous judgment, the High Court confirmed the constitutional protection for political communication, but refashioned its effect on defamation law. The judgment combined elements of the constitutional and common law *Theophanous* defences into a new form of qualified privilege.

The High Court held that political communication could give rise to a privileged occasion, as 'each member of the Australian community has an interest in disseminating and receiving information, opinions and arguments concerning government and political matters that affect the people of Australia.'[73]

This means that *Lange* privilege could protect widespread publications, as did common law privilege under *Theophanous*. Protecting wide publications, in turn, requires defendants to establish that publication was *reasonable*, as under the *Theophanous* constitutional defence. To establish reasonableness, defendants must generally establish that they had reasonable grounds to believe publications were true, that they did not believe publications were false, and that they had made proper inquiries to verify them. In addition, defendants must have sought and published responses from potential plaintiffs, except where this was not practical or necessary.[74] Although malice defeats *Lange* privilege, it will

69 The *Theophanous* joint judgment referred approvingly to the use by Mason CJ of the term 'public affairs' in *ACTV* (1992) 177 CLR 106, 138–40: *Theophanous* (1994) 182 CLR 104, 122–3 (Mason CJ, Toohey and Gaudron JJ).

70 *Theophanous* (1994) 182 CLR 104, 124 (Mason CJ, Toohey and Gaudron JJ).

71 Ibid, citing Eric Barendt, *Freedom of Speech* (1985) 152.

72 *Lange* (1997) 189 CLR 520, 521.

73 Ibid 571.

74 Ibid 574.

generally have little room to operate.[75] The focus will be on whether defendants can establish reasonableness.

Lange privilege is weaker than *Theophanous* privilege because all political publications face the reasonableness test. In contrast, the *Theophanous* common law privilege was only defeated by malice. In addition, *Lange* is narrower because political communication appears to have been confined since *Theophanous*. *Lange* privilege appears to encompass only matters about politics and government 'in an electoral and parliamentary sense.'[76] Political communication may be limited to information for decisions about voting. For example, most criticism of judicial officers may fall outside the protection.[77] Criticism calling for a judge's dismissal may come within the protection,[78] but perhaps not criticism related merely to an individual case.[79] In terms of its formal doctrine, *Lange* privilege may protect far fewer media publications than *Theophanous*.

The defence's narrow scope helps explain the relative lack of subsequent decisions on *Lange* privilege. The cases, however, illustrate three related points about the defence's scope. First, the defence clearly does not extend to all matters of public interest.[80] Material about the corporate sector, whether profit-seeking or non-profit, can be expected to be excluded. For example, in *Rowan v Cornwall [No 5]*, criticisms from a public review panel about the administration of a women's refuge that was run by a non-government organisation were outside the defence.[81]

Second, discussion of public administration may come within the defence. For example, *Conservation Council of SA Inc v Chapman*[82] concerned a bitterly fought bridge development which had become an issue of national public concern. *Lange* privilege did not apply to allegations that property developers threatened litigation to silence residents opposing development, even for

75 Desiring to harm political opponents does not constitute malice: ibid. See also *Brander v Ryan* (2000) 78 SASR 234, 250 (Lander J), 235 (Prior J agreeing), 250 (Bleby J agreeing); *Roberts v Bass* (2002) 212 CLR 1, 14 (Gleeson CJ), 31–3 (Gaudron, McHugh and Gummow JJ), 70 (Kirby J).

76 *Herald & Weekly Times Ltd v Popovic* [2003] VSCA 161 (Unreported, Winneke ACJ, Gillard and Warren AJJA, 21 November 2003) [504] (Warren AJA) ('*Popovic*'). Some examples, however, do exist of wider approaches being taken to political communication, which may support arguments for a wider defence; for example, in a context outside defamation, see *Australian Broadcasting Corporation v Lenah Games Meats Pty Ltd* (2001) 208 CLR 199, 281–2 (Kirby J) ('*Lenah*').

77 Ibid [6], [9]–[10] (Winneke ACJ), [498]–[500], [504] (Warren AJA), cf [247]–[251] (Gillard AJA). See also *O'Shane v John Fairfax Publications Pty Ltd* [2004] NSWSC 140 (Unreported, Smart AJ, 16 March 2004) [187]–[196].

78 *Popovic* [2003] VSCA 161 (Unreported, Winneke ACJ, Gillard and Warren AJJA, 21 November 2003) [6], [9]–[10] (Winneke ACJ), [247]–[251] (Gillard AJA), cf [498]–[500], [504] (Warren AJA).

79 Ibid [6], [9]–[10] (Winneke ACJ).

80 See, eg, *Amalgamated Television Services Pty Ltd v Marsden* [2002] NSWCA 419 (Unreported, Beazley, Giles and Santow JJA, 24 December 2002) [1160] ('*Marsden*').

81 (2002) 82 SASR 152 (Debelle J). Similarly, in *NRMA v John Fairfax Publications Pty Ltd* [2002] NSWSC 563 (Unreported, Master Macready, 26 June 2002), material about aspiring candidates for a corporate board was beyond *Lange*'s scope.

82 (2003) 87 SASR 62 ('*Chapman*'). For general background to the development, see Margaret Simons, *The Meeting of the Waters: The Hindmarsh Island Affair* (2003), or the brief background provided by Besanko J in the Full Court: *Chapman* (2003) 87 SASR 62, 102–12.

publications couched in terms of free speech and misuse of the legal process.[83] Potentially within the defence's scope, however, were publications suggesting developers had engaged in 'token' consultation with indigenous groups, which was less than the statutory planning process required.[84]

Third, discussion of commercially significant matters can exceed the scope of *Lange* privilege, even when occurring within apparently political contexts. In *West v Nationwide News Pty Ltd*,[85] discussion by councillors at a council meeting and its subsequent media reporting were outside the defence. The discussion concerned development approval that had been obtained by a plaintiff, the degree to which development conditions had been complied with and the effects on local residents.[86] Although courts have repeatedly held that no narrow approach should be taken to the defence's scope,[87] success in *Lange* privilege may exist primarily for discussion about political candidates.[88]

Under *Lange* privilege, publishers' conduct must be reasonable. The history of statutory privilege under s 22 of the *Defamation Act 1974* (NSW) suggests that reasonableness will be hard to meet. The High Court considered *Lange* on the basis of New South Wales law, and held that it would unreasonably burden political discussion if not for s 22.[89] This meant that the common law required the expanded privilege set out by the High Court in order to meet the constitutional protection for political communication. *Lange*, however, left unresolved a doctrinal issue of possible importance. Under s 22, most defendants must establish their honest belief in the publication.[90] Defendants must also establish

83 *Chapman* (2003) 87 SASR 62, 71 (Doyle CJ), 127–8 (Besanko J), cf 98 (Gray J). This publication also exceeded the defence's scope at trial, even when the concept of 'Strategic Lawsuits Against Public Participation' ('SLAPPs') was raised in the publications: *Chapman v Conservation Council of South Australia* (2002) 82 SASR 449, 522–4 (Williams J). For a brief background to the development of SLAPPs, see Andrew T Kenyon, 'Defamation and Critique: Political Speech and *New York Times v Sullivan* in England and Australia' (2001) 25 *Melbourne University Law Review* 522, 524, 530–2.

84 *Chapman* (2003) 87 SASR 62, 72 (Doyle CJ), 97 (Gray J), 142 (Besanko J). This publication also came within the defence's scope at trial: (2002) 82 SASR 449, 528 (Williams J). Interlocutory decisions supporting the idea that *Lange* applies to discussion about public administration include: *Bristile Ltd v Buddhist Society of Western Australia Inc* [2000] Aust Torts Reports ¶81-548; *Cock v Hughes* [2002] WASC 108 (Unreported, Hasluck J, 14 May 2002); *Archer v Channel Seven Perth Pty Ltd* [2002] WASC 160 (Unreported, Hasluck J, 21 June 2002); *Marsden* [2002] NSWCA 419 (Unreported, Beazley, Giles and Santow JJA, 24 December 2002) [1149]; *Shave v West Australian Newspapers Ltd* [2003] WASC 83 (Unreported, Hasluck J, 5 May 2003). In *Marsden*, however, the New South Wales Court of Appeal expressed in obiter doubts that *Lange* did have this breadth: [2002] NSWCA 419 (Unreported, Beazley, Giles and Santow JJA, 24 December 2002) [1162].

85 [2003] NSWSC 505 (Unreported, Simpson J, 15 August 2003).

86 Ibid [135]. Simpson J held that

> the councillors were expressing their concerns, not about matters of policy or government, but about what they perceived to be the flouting by the plaintiff of the terms of the development consent, and their opposition to the development consent ... granted by the Land and Environment Court.

87 See, eg, *Popovic* [2003] VSCA 161 (Unreported, Winneke ACJ, Gillard and Warren AJJA, 21 November 2003) [8] (Winneke ACJ), [244] (Gillard AJA).

88 See *Featherston v Tully [No 2]* (2002) 83 SASR 347 (Court of Disputed Returns); *Brander v Ryan* (2000) 78 SASR 234.

89 (1997) 189 CLR 520, 573–5.

90 See *Morgan v John Fairfax & Sons Ltd [No 2]* (1991) 23 NSWLR 374 (Court of Appeal).

that the publication's manner and extent 'did not exceed what was reasonably required', that they exercised reasonable care in terms of making inquiries, and that their conclusions of fact or opinion 'followed logically, fairly and reasonably' from the information revealed by those inquiries.[91] In practice, these appear to be onerous requirements in the way they are applied. The approach 'effectively negates the availability' of the defence.[92] The requirements far exceed those for common law fair comment, for example, where opinion can be exaggerated, prejudiced or obstinate.[93] It is very difficult to establish the s 22 defence for publications based on facts not proven true, or where defendants did not make 'proper' inquiries.[94] The defence appears to be commonly pleaded, but has succeeded in only a handful of cases since 1974.[95] The issue *Lange* left unresolved is whether defendants need to establish their belief in a publication's truth, or merely reasonable grounds to believe in its truth. Academic commentary favours the latter approach, which differs from s 22 and is said to make *Lange* privilege more widely available.[96]

Case law has not yet dealt explicitly with this possible difference between the *Lange* and s 22 defences. But recent cases have noted that reasonableness under *Lange*, as well as under s 22, should not be inflexible.[97] The *Lange* factors[98] are neither 'principles of law' nor 'essential elements' in the defence.[99] For example, it can be reasonable to publish without seeking a response,[100] although failing to meet a *Lange* factor would 'in most cases prove fatal.'[101] Overall, however, courts' interpretation of reasonableness closely tracks s 22, notwithstanding the

91 Ibid 388 (Hunt AJA).

92 Steven Rares, 'Can I Say That?' (2004) 25 *Australian Bar Review* 45, 47.

93 See, eg, *Merivale v Carson* (1887) 20 QBD 275, 281 (Lord Esher MR), 283–4 (Bowen LJ). See also *Branson v Bower* [2002] QB 737, 741 (Eady J).

94 Sally Walker, '*Lange v ABC*: The High Court Rethinks the "Constitutionalisation" of Defamation Law' (1998) 6 *Torts Law Journal* 9, 21.

95 *Pinniger v John Fairfax & Sons Ltd* (1979) 26 ALR 55; *Barbaro v Amalgamated Television Services Pty Ltd* (1989) 20 NSWLR 493; *Bowin Designs Pty Ltd v Australian Consumers Association* [1996] 1070 FCA 1 (Unreported, Lindgren J, 6 December 1996); *Lear v Malter* (Unreported, Supreme Court of New South Wales, Donovan AJ, 14 March 1997). In addition, the defence was set aside on appeal in *Evatt v Nationwide News Pty Ltd* [1999] NSWCA 99 (Unreported, Sheller, Powell and Giles JJA, 19 April 1999).

96 See, eg, Walker, '*Lange v ABC*', above n 94, 28.

97 See, eg, *Rogers v Nationwide News Pty Ltd* (2003) 201 ALR 184, 191 (Gleeson CJ and Gummow J).

98 See above n 74 and accompanying text.

99 *Popovic* [2003] VSCA 161 (Unreported, Winneke ACJ, Gillard and Warren AJJA, 21 November 2003) [92], [197] (Gillard AJA).

100 In *Chapman*, no response needed to be sought where the subjects of a publication were 'making ample use of the media' to convey their points of view: (2003) 87 SASR 62, 143 (Besanko J), 73 (Doyle CJ agreeing), 98 (Gray J). See also *Brander v Ryan* (2000) 78 SASR 234, 249, 250 (Lander J), 235 (Prior J agreeing), 250 (Bleby J agreeing); *Popovic* [2003] VSCA 161 (Unreported, Winneke ACJ, Gillard and Warren AJJA, 21 November 2003) [213]–[218] (Gillard AJA), [453] (Warren AJA agreeing); *O'Shane v John Fairfax Publications Pty Ltd* [2004] NSWSC 140 (Unreported, Smart AJ, 16 March 2004) [204]; *Cock v Hughes* [2002] WASC 263 (Unreported, McLure J, 11 November 2002) [42]; *Mickelberg v 6PR Southern Cross Radio Pty Ltd* [2003] WASC 209 (Unreported, Master Newnes, 31 October 2003) [52]–[62].

101 *Popovic* [2003] VSCA 161 (Unreported, Winneke ACJ, Gillard and Warren AJJA, 21 November 2003) [92] (Gillard AJA).

peculiar New South Wales action where each pleaded imputation is a separate cause of action.[102]

A final issue about *Lange* privilege is the division of roles in a jury trial. It appears that the jury, where there is one, rules on questions of primary fact relevant to the defence — for example, it may need to answer multiple questions about whether certain inquiries were made by the defendant before publication. In light of the jury answers, the judge then rules whether the defence is made out. Although trial practices have varied, the Victorian Court of Appeal has unanimously endorsed this approach.[103] Thus, *Lange* privilege seems likely to follow the traditional approach in Australia, which is also reflected in the English developments discussed above. Equivalent questions arise about the complexity of this approach. Another possibility would be for the jury to determine whether the publication was reasonable, rather than any disputed facts relevant to reasonableness. Evidence from practice may suggest which approach is likely to be preferable in litigation.

D *Doctrinally Comparing the English and Australian Defences*

The new English and Australian privilege defences have been analysed above in terms of their scope, strength and trial practicality. These points are summarised here before examining litigation practice. English cases suggest the value of a broad defence, not limited to narrow, institutional conceptions of politics.[104] In addition, English cases apply a reasonably wide variety of factors in assessing publishers' conduct, and appear to apply them quite flexibly.[105] The English approach to publications' tone is a notable example,[106] though it is one that favours non-tabloid publications.[107] In comparison, the Australian approach under *Lange* privilege is narrow — it is not a public interest defence and rarely encompasses speech about commercial issues. It also appears to be weak because of the requirement for publication to be proven reasonable. Reasonableness under *Lange*, however, may be a more achievable standard than under s 22, depending on whether defendants will be required to establish their belief in the truth of the publication. In any event, neither *Lange* nor s 22 offer the strength of

[102] Courts do at times recognise that this means decisions under s 22 may have limited influence for the common law defence: see, eg, ibid [201] (Gillard AJA). On the strong, apparent benefits of the common law cause of action, see Andrew T Kenyon, 'Imputation of Publication: The Cause of Action in Defamation Law' (2004) 27 *University of New South Wales Law Journal* 100.

[103] *Popovic* [2003] VSCA 161 (Unreported, Winneke ACJ, Gillard and Warren AJJA, 21 November 2003) [13] (Winneke ACJ), [104], [116]–[117] (Gillard AJA), [509] (Warren AJA).

[104] See New South Wales Attorney-General's Task Force on Defamation Law Reform, *Defamation Law: Proposals for Reform in NSW* (2002) 20, citing Kenyon, 'Defamation and Critique', above n 83, 544.

[105] In particular, *Bonnick v Morris* [2003] 1 AC 300 illustrates the value of a non-technical approach to a publication's meaning for the privilege defence. Cf the history of s 22 in New South Wales: see above nn 89–96 and accompanying text. As to the very influential role of meaning in defamation law and litigation more generally, see Andrew T Kenyon, *Word Games: Meaning in Defamation Law and Practice in England, New South Wales and Victoria* (PhD Thesis, The University of Melbourne, 2002).

[106] *Al-Fagih* [2002] EMLR 215.

[107] *Grobbelaar v News Group Newspapers Ltd* [2001] 2 All ER 437 (Court of Appeal).

protection offered by *Theophanous* common law privilege. In terms of litigation practicality, *Theophanous* common law privilege and traditional qualified privilege offer a reasonably clear division between judge and jury roles. The jury addresses malice without needing to answer an 'examination paper' of questions about disputed events. It appears that such examination papers may arise under both *Reynolds* and *Lange* privileges, which may undercut the benefits aimed for in developing the defences.

Next, qualitative material about litigation practice is examined in relation to these issues about the defences' scope, strength and practicality in litigation.

III English and Australian Practice

A *Fieldwork*

To investigate privilege in action, interviews were conducted with 50 defamation practitioners in England, New South Wales and Victoria.[108] The 23 London interviewees comprised specialist defamation judges, barristers from two leading defamation chambers,[109] solicitors with substantial defamation practices and in-house lawyers for media companies.[110] In Australia, 27 defamation practitioners were interviewed from the two largest defamation jurisdictions, New South Wales and Victoria.[111] They included a specialist judge and leading defamation barristers, solicitors and in-house lawyers.[112] Defamation formed the major part of most interviewees' practices, often being a sizeable majority. Given the concentrated media law practices in each country, the interviewees represented a good cross-section of lawyers with significant defamation involvement.[113]

108 The interviews were associated with the two projects mentioned in the author's note, which examined many aspects of defamation law and practice.

109 The two chambers at 1 Brick Court and 5 Raymond Buildings account for a substantial majority of all London defamation work.

110 All English interviews were conducted in May 2003. They are identified here as 1 to 23. Five interviewees were women, and all interviews were conducted separately except for two pairs: 16 and 17, and 18 and 19.

111 There were 16 interviewees from New South Wales and 11 from Victoria.

112 Two Australian interviews were conducted in December 2002 (40 and 41), with all the others occurring in June and July 2003. The interviewees are identified here as 24 to 39 from New South Wales, and 40 to 50 from Victoria. Five interviewees were women, and all interviews were conducted separately, except for 45 and 46.

113 Obtaining a sample of experienced defamation lawyers means a sizeable minority of interviewees acted predominantly for the media — for example, in solicitors' firms retained by media companies to give pre-publication and litigation-related legal advice. However, a diverse group of experienced lawyers was sought, and the most common background for interviewees was to do significant amounts of work for both defamation plaintiffs (and claimants) and for defamation defendants (whether they were media or non-media defendants). A small minority of interviewees did more work for defamation plaintiffs (and claimants). In any event, no direct relationship was apparent between interviewees' professional backgrounds and their views about defamation law and litigation. For example, one strong comment within the Australian interviews was that *Lange* had not improved the position of publishers (see below n 204), while in England many interviewees suggested *Reynolds* had improved the media's position (see below nn 130–3 and accompanying text). In Australia, the 13 responses came from five lawyers who predominantly did media defence work, one lawyer who conducted more plaintiff work, and seven lawyers with roughly even practices. In England, the 16 responses came from six lawyers with predominantly

Each interview lasted approximately one hour, with all except two being audio recorded and transcribed.[114] Transcriptions were analysed according to the legal issues discussed, with major areas being the scope, strength and litigation effects of qualified privilege. Quotations are direct transcriptions from interviews, with only minimal changes made to interviewees' words for clarity and readability.[115] To protect interviewees' confidentiality, no quotation is identified with a named interviewee. Instead, interviewees are referred to by number, along with their professional role: solicitor ('S'), barrister ('B'), Queen's Counsel ('QC') or Senior Counsel ('SC').[116] All those who assisted in relation to the interviews are sincerely thanked.[117]

The 50 interviews generated a very large amount of material,[118] but offered the most viable source of empirical information. Alternatives to interviews such as observing litigation were not pursued. Litigation activities take place over many months in multiple locations and observation only reaches the small portion of the litigation process visible in court. Interviews can encompass activities across a wide range of times and locations.[119] Their flexible structure compared with other methods, such as questionnaires, was also more likely to reveal differences in the use of terminology in each jurisdiction, which is an important issue for comparative research.[120]

In what way can extrapolations be drawn from the material?[121] Does the research have what is often called reliability and validity?[122] Using recognised

media practices, three lawyers with mainly claimant practices, and seven lawyers with roughly equal practices.

114 Handwritten notes were made at two interviews: once due to background noise preventing audio-recording, and once to accord with the interviewee's wishes.

115 Such editing of interview transcripts is common; for a discussion of the general approach, see, eg, Ewick and Silbey, above n 23, 259.

116 QC is the title used in England, while both QC and SC are used in Australia. In this article, QC is used for senior English barristers and SC for Australian ones. Judges are referred to as QC or SC to mirror their major prior experience.

117 These individuals assisted with the interviews used here (each is identified with any title then held): Adrian Anderson, Ian Angus, Peter Bartlett, Alastair Brett, Desmond Browne QC, Godwin Busuttil, Bruce Burke, Siobhain Butterworth, David Caspersonn, Iain Christie, Richard Coleman, Dr Matthew Collins, Stephen Collins, Jacob Dean, the Hon Justice David Eady, Anne Flahvin, the Hon Justice Charles Gray, Tim Hale SC, Alister Henskens, Will Houghton QC, Jan Johannes, the Hon Justice David Levine RFD, Jennifer McDermott, Michael Martin, Tom Molomby SC, Patrick Moloney QC, Justine Munsie, Leanne Norman, Peter O'Donahoo, Laurence Maher, Matthew Nicklin, Stephen O'Meara, Adrian Page QC, Marcus Partington, Susan Poffley, Richard Potter, David Price, Nicholas Pullen, Richard Rampton QC, Steven Rares SC, Rhory Robertson, Georgina Schoff, Richard Shillito, Michael Skrein, Michael Smyth, Adam Speker, Belinda Thompson, Robert Todd, Mark Warby QC and Simon Wilson QC. Many other practitioners assisted with the two larger research projects: see author's note. Their contributions will be reported elsewhere.

118 The interview transcriptions drawn on here, which dealt with many aspects of defamation law and practice, totalled 400 000 words.

119 See Clive Seale, *The Quality of Qualitative Research* (1999) 59.

120 For a brief discussion of questions about meaning-equivalence in comparative research, see Tim May, *Social Research: Issues, Methods and Process* (1993) 161–2. Clive Seale provides an overview of similar concerns about survey research: ibid 133–5.

121 This may be a more useful concept than 'generalizability': Pertti Alasuutari, *Researching Culture: Qualitative Method and Cultural Studies* (1995) 156–7, cited in David Silverman, *Doing Qualitative Research: A Practical Handbook* (2000) 110–11.

legal categories goes some way towards addressing reliability concerns. One could expect broadly similar material would be found by another researcher or presented by these interviewees at another time. At the same time, the transcription and coding method aimed to maintain good access to the material — to what people said and the way they described the legal categories. As well as concerns about reliability, researchers often consider their material's validity. In this context, validity can be understood as referring to realistic representation of social phenomena. In the limited context of this legal research, that description can be accepted. That is not to suggest that validity is an unproblematic concept,[123] but the representations drawn from this material should be meaningful in terms of how legal practitioners operate with certain categories in defamation law. In addition to remembering the limited legal scope of this project, aiming at a comprehensive treatment of the interview material and including atypical cases improves validity. It addresses a weakness in some qualitative research — namely, its anecdotalism. For example, a researcher can quote a few comments from interviews, without it being apparent how representative the responses are and without contrary examples being considered.[124] Here, the extensive footnoting allows readers to assess both issues, at least to some degree — that is, a simple counting of responses within the material is made relatively transparent to the reader.[125]

B *English Interviews*

Three broad, related issues are drawn from interviews with London practitioners and discussed here. First, despite uncertainties about its future development, *Reynolds* privilege is strongly supported and is affecting pre-publication legal advice and media conduct. Second, particular concerns exist about each party's position under *Reynolds* privilege and the focus on media conduct. Third, the division between judge and jury roles is also problematic at trial, but may be difficult for trial judges to improve.

First, *Reynolds* is overwhelmingly seen as significant. It offers a comparatively strong defence for media publications. There is uncertainty about how it will develop and how its multiple factors will apply in any litigated case. Two factors, however, are seen as central: attempting to contact the subjects of

[122] See Silverman, *Doing Qualitative Research*, above n 121, 175. For an overview of current qualitative approaches to reliability, see Seale, above n 119, ch 10.

[123] See Silverman, *Doing Qualitative Research*, above n 121, 177.

[124] Ibid 10–11.

[125] The approach follows that of David Silverman, *Interpreting Qualitative Data: Methods for Analysing Talk, Text and Interaction* (1993) 163. See generally Seale, above n 119, ch 9. Note, however, that not every interviewee commented on each issue. Interviews were semi-structured, allowing respondents a degree of latitude to focus on what they believed to be the most significant matters about defamation law and litigation. The footnoting of interviewee numbers is not intended to suggest percentage responses to particular issues. Rather — and similarly to the way in which it would be misleading to treat interviewees primarily as advocates for, or against, the media (see above n 113) — the material reported here should be assessed with the understanding that: where an issue receives many comments, practitioners see the issue as important; where many interviewees hold a particular view, that view is likely to be common among experienced practitioners; and divergences of views are noted in the reporting.

potential publications, and publications' tone or balance. These factors mean *Reynolds* privilege appears to alter pre-publication conduct. Not surprisingly, London interviewees described *Reynolds* as important.[126] It offers a 'whole new defence', arguable in almost all media cases,[127] which is 'revolutionary'[128] and a 'massive change'.[129] It is a 'significant improvement' for the media,[130] as it provides a useable, or even strong, defence.[131] For some, initial doubts or disappointments have given way: 'I remember the first time I read *Reynolds* thinking that this is all rather a disappointment ... [B]ut gradually re-reading it, one began to see its potential and the actual results have been really very considerable.'[132] More cautious responses still saw the potential in *Reynolds* for a 'very useful defence'.[133]

While some interviewees suggested that *Reynolds*' flexibility had value,[134] a major area of criticism was its uncertainty and unpredictability.[135] An experienced barrister commented: 'I think the problem with *Reynolds* in practice is that it is a "sniff test". Does it have a bad smell about it or does the judge feel warm about it?'[136] How will courts balance publications' public interest qualities, the potential harm to subjects' reputations, and defendants' conduct before publication? It is difficult to predict how any particular situation will be interpreted in light of relevant factors:

> Things like how urgent was it? Was it really necessary to publish this? How far do you have to check it in the heat of the moment? ... [It is] very difficult to say [and] newspapers rather take a punt.[137]

It is difficult to predict whether some publications will be found to have 'the right calibre of public interest',[138] or how the degree of public interest relates to the required level of investigation.[139] Yet the checklist should not be 'rigid'[140] —

126 Almost all interviews emphasised the decision's importance: 1S, 2S, 3S, 4QC, 5QC, 8B, 9B, 11S, 12B, 14S, 16S, 17S, 18S, 19S, 21QC, 22S. Along with some of these respondents, other interviewees suggested that *Reynolds* will develop significance over time (7QC, 10B) while 20QC suggested that it was too early to tell whether it would achieve the desirable strengthening of qualified privilege. 6B emphasised the defence's unpredictability, with which 15QC agreed (while noting it has led to innovative subsequent decisions). 13QC supported a qualified privilege defence for media publications but believed that the traditional duty-interest style of qualified privilege, expanded to include at least some media publications, would be far preferable.

127 11S; similar 2S, 6B, 10B, 19S, 21QC. However, many respondents noted the differing positions of broadsheet and tabloid newspapers: eg, 16S, 17S, 22S. Others also noted the importance of deciding whether to plead *Reynolds* in any particular case because of the way it alters a trial's focus: 12B, 16S, 20QC, 23S.

128 1S.

129 8B.

130 3S, 5QC; similar 2S, 8B, 14S, 16S, 19S, 22S.

131 1S, 4QC, 17S, 21QC, 22S.

132 4QC; similar 1S.

133 9B; similar 7QC, 10B, 20QC.

134 1S, 3S, 9B.

135 2S, 4QC, 5QC, 6B, 7QC, 10B, 11S, 13QC, 15QC, 16S, 20QC, 21QC, 22S.

136 5QC. Others commented on the power the approach gives judges: 8B, 14S, 18S, 23S.

137 11S.

138 20QC.

139 7QC.

140 9B; similar 17S.

'fluidity' is wanted, rather than having the 10 factors 'set in stone'.[141] While subsequent decisions have clarified somewhat *Reynolds*' scope and strength,[142] the defence's uncertainty — its 'inherently case-by-case' analysis — seems likely to continue.[143]

Of the 10 *Reynolds* factors, however, two were more influential for interviewees: contacting a publication's subject,[144] and carefully considering its tone or balance.[145] Notwithstanding comments about the defence's uncertainty in litigation, these two factors were seen as particularly important and were also reported as being central to changing pre-publication conduct. Speaking to the subject and publishing a response is seen as 'the litmus test',[146] although it is 'not clear how much time you should give them to respond'.[147] At the least, the defence is very likely to fail if there has been no attempt to contact the subject.[148] In theory, perhaps *Reynolds* should not affect what is published, 'because a newspaper ... ought not ever have published unless it had taken reasonable care and honestly believed that what it was saying was true'.[149] However, the way in which tone is 'critically important' changes this position.[150] Interviewees suggested that *Reynolds* assists the media to raise more allegations or suspicions,[151] and to publish more public interest or whistle-blowing stories.[152] At the same time, it encourages what may be seen as more balanced reporting — publications are more likely to include subjects' points of view.[153] Before *Reynolds*, 'if you had a story which was clearly defamatory, but you had a pretty good source there would be little point in publishing it in a balanced way. So you'd simply go for it'.[154] But now publishers are likely to consider *Reynolds* and moderate the tone of publications. Television journalism in particular 'will be well served by *Reynolds*' because its longer lead times mean that everyone involved can work to 'the *Reynolds* programme'.[155] These comments suggest

141 11S.
142 2S, 11S.
143 21QC; similar 11S.
144 1S, 3S, 4QC, 5QC, 7QC, 8B, 12B, 16S, 17S, 19S, 22S.
145 2S, 7QC, 8B, 12B, 14S, 16S, 17S, 19S, 22S.
146 5QC.
147 16S. The courts' attitude to urgency was also raised as a matter needing clarification: 10B, 12B, 14S, 17S.
148 Attempting contact is necessary if not sufficient: 7QC. Not attempting to make contact 'is such a moronic failure, you're almost holed below the water line': 12B.
149 21QC.
150 22S; similar 7QC, 16S, 19S.
151 2S (due to the tone factor), 8B, 16S. 7QC also noted the reportage line of cases. 'Reportage' refers to *Al-Fagih* and related decisions: see above nn 55–8 and accompanying text. Other interviewees saw the decision in *Al-Fagih* as 'altogether odd' (1S; similar 9B), or at least a distinct development beyond what would have been expected with *Reynolds* (7QC, 8B); cf 21QC, who strongly endorsed the development.
152 3S, 16S, 17S, 19S, 22S.
153 1S, 3S, 4QC, 5QC, 7QC, 8B, 12B, 16S, 17S, 19S, 22S.
154 8B.
155 12B; similar 16S.

Reynolds is affecting publishing practices more widely and publishers are exercising greater care when they research and write stories.[156]

Second, concerns were expressed about each party's position under *Reynolds*. Claimants face particular difficulties because they lack knowledge of many *Reynolds* factors.[157] Most often, claimants will know only whether they were approached for comment before publication. They will not know what research journalists have undertaken. This differs from other defences that involve truth or a clear occasion of privilege, such as reporting parliamentary debates. Correspondence between the parties, often referring explicitly to *Reynolds*' factors, may help to clarify the position for claimants.[158] But *Reynolds*, which 'spotlights the newspaper', can make claimants feel that their interests have been overlooked.[159] One interviewee stated that '[c]lients do not really care whether the journalists were ethical or not; they care that a falsehood has been stated about them',[160] and several interviewees suggested claimants would like to seek declarations of falsity under *Reynolds*.[161] For claimants, the uncertain 'shadow of *Reynolds*'[162] deters claims and encourages settlements.[163] *Reynolds* is 'very expensive to defeat'[164] with 'almost no claimant [being] confident of victory, and therefore reasonable settlements for reasonable awards, or indeed for apologies and costs, are becoming [more] common'.[165]

The position of defendants also drew concerns. As for claimants, the costs of trying the defence were raised: 'even in the case of a newspaper article, and a relatively short one at that, you can have a four week trial involving a lot of detailed factual issues and a number of legal issues and vast expense and an enormous amount of time.'[166] Other respondents, however, noted that publications could involve comparatively small amounts of background material. The information sources and documentary evidence held prior to publication were 'finite',[167] though the amount varied between 'very little' and 'massive'.[168] Justification, by way of contrast, can draw on a far wider range of material, and was described as potentially a more unwieldy defence.[169] Concerns were also

156 1S, 2S, 3S, 4QC, 8B, 11S, 14S, 22S. While solicitors and in-house media lawyers reported that pre-publication practices were changing, and that uncertainty was not a problem at that stage, an experienced barrister thought difficulties in predicting how a judge might apply the *Reynolds* factors would also exist at the pre-publication stage.

157 4QC, 6B, 7QC, 21QC.

158 19S. Similarly, 2S noted claimants are able to judge the content of publications, if not any underlying investigation, which is important in assessing their position.

159 11S; similar 1S, 4QC, 10B, 20QC, 21QC.

160 21QC.

161 1S, 2S, 4QC.

162 21QC.

163 2S (there is a 'chilling effect' on claimants), 7QC, 12B, 15QC, 21QC.

164 6B.

165 21QC; similar 7QC.

166 7QC; similar 6B, 8B, 10B.

167 11S; similar 2S, 19S, 22S.

168 6B; similar 11S.

169 10B, 11S.

raised about focusing on publishers' conduct:[170] 'for defendants, the *Reynolds* defence is a bit of a Trojan horse because it changes the dynamics of the trial. If you run a *Reynolds* defence alone the trial will turn into a trial of your journalists.'[171]

Journalists' motives and actions will be more closely scrutinised than has been routine, notwithstanding the issues that historically have arisen on malice.[172] There is a 'much less benign atmosphere for media defendants than was expected',[173] and the evaluation of journalists' conduct by courts 'can be very painful'.[174] Interviewees were unsure whether courts could fully understand the pressures associated with daily news production:[175] '[i]f you're a newspaper on a 24 hour turnaround ... you're not going to be able to do all the things that they want you to do'.[176] Judges and journalists appear to hold markedly different views about standards: 'the highest level of journalistic endeavour' achieved in the media is seen as being 'miles short of where the court sets the lowest standard for journalistic endeavour'.[177]

Third, interviewees strongly criticised the division between judge and jury,[178] emphasising the complexity of the defence in practice.[179] Its 'odd dichotomy'[180] of roles creates a 'bad system'.[181] An experienced barrister stated: 'I can't imagine a more clumsy and unsatisfactory way of determining an issue'.[182] Practitioners thought courts had been 'blind to the practical consequences of simply saying the jury can find the primary facts'.[183] The key difficulty appears to be the number of factual determinations juries may need to make under *Reynolds*.[184] A trial can end with 'twenty questions for the jury, all on tiny bits of fact about who said what, what was the journalist told, and did the journalist phone twice to check or only once?'[185] Asking the jury to address many detailed questions is 'completely different from how juries have always been regarded' in English defamation and subverts their traditional role of delivering general verdicts.[186] At a trial's outset, it is unclear what questions the jury will need to answer. Specific questions emerge from evidence — 'if anyone ... tried to forecast in advance what questions they would have to have decided, it would

170 3S, 5QC, 6B, 7QC, 12B, 17S, 20QC, 21QC, 23S.
171 12B; similar 17S, 23S.
172 3S, 5QC, 6B.
173 20QC; similar 5QC, 7QC, 21QC.
174 20QC.
175 14S, 17S.
176 16S.
177 12B.
178 4QC, 6B, 8B, 9B, 11S, 12B, 13QC, 16S, 20QC, 21QC, 22S.
179 4QC, 6B, 8B, 9B, 11S, 13QC, 22S.
180 11S.
181 22S.
182 13QC.
183 4QC; similar 6B 12B, 15QC, 21QC.
184 4QC, 6B, 8B, 9B, 21QC.
185 8B; similar 12B who had planned to ask a particular jury 40 questions.
186 8B; similar 13QC.

[be] folly'.[187] These complexities mean that 'if you asked the jury afterwards to explain what was going on [with] qualified privilege, [jury members] wouldn't have a bloody clue'.[188] To the 'bemused' jury,[189] the questions must appear 'slightly irrelevant and thoroughly trivial'.[190] Through such specific questions, juries will seek to deal with whether publishers deserve to succeed. As one interviewee suggested: 'I'm not sure that's very satisfactory at all, because embedded in the long list of factual questions which the jury [is] going to answer is always the ultimate question: was this behaviour responsible?'[191] In its allocation of judge and jury roles, *Reynolds* is 'totally unsatisfactory'.[192] It makes the jury's role far more difficult, if not 'almost impossible'.[193]

These views led to suggestions either to increase the jury's role on qualified privilege or sideline it. Some respondents suggested that the jury 'should be asked general questions. Do you find for the claimant or the defendant? ... I think this intermediate idea of asking them a huge taxonomy of different questions is just unsatisfactory and counterproductive'.[194] Other interviewees suggested that early judicial rulings on privilege would be valuable.[195] But such rulings require that no factual issues be in dispute. This is difficult to achieve given the range of factors that can be relevant to *Reynolds* privilege. Defendants may decide 'to concede facts' to seek a summary ruling.[196] Some interviewees suggested removing juries entirely, or removing them in relation to qualified privilege: 'I think the simple answer to all this is that we should get rid of the juries'.[197] Other respondents made a related point that *Reynolds* privilege makes more sense in judge-only trials[198] and that this change may be happening, to a degree, through judicial rulings that cases can be tried conveniently without juries.[199] Interviewees also suggested that the jury is being sidelined in that judges have room to decide whether *Reynolds* privilege succeeds by interpreting jury answers,[200] sometimes because of the inconsistency of the jury's answers.[201]

Overall, although the *Reynolds* defence is seen as having difficulties at trial, London practitioners describe the developments as 'sensible'[202] and 'evidently justifiable'.[203]

187 4QC.
188 14S.
189 22S.
190 13QC; similar 11S, 14S, 21QC.
191 20QC.
192 13QC.
193 12B; similar 9B, 10B.
194 9B; similar 4QC, 20QC.
195 5QC, 6B, 9B, 21QC.
196 5QC.
197 9B; similar 12B, 16S, 22S.
198 20QC, 21QC.
199 4QC, 20QC, 21QC. See *Supreme Court Act 1981* (UK) c 54, s 69 as to jury trial being usual in defamation.
200 1S, 8B, 18S, 22S.
201 13QC.
202 2S, 3S, 22S; similar 1S, 5QC, 9B, 14S.
203 21QC; similar 17S, 20QC.

C *Australian Interviews*

Four issues from Australian interviews are considered here. First, *Lange* privilege is not seen as a useable defence. Its reasonableness requirement, which almost all practitioners equate with the defence under s 22 of the *Defamation Act 1974* (NSW), is the primary reason for this failing. Second, notwithstanding its legal weaknesses, *Lange* appears to have reduced suits by politicians. Third, the roles of judge and jury under *Lange* are seen as problematic, echoing concerns from England. Fourth, most interviewees suggested that *Lange* needs review, with *Reynolds* being seen as one preferable approach and the *Theophanous* form of common law privilege also receiving substantial support.

First, in marked contrast to the English situation under *Reynolds*, Australian interviewees suggested that *Lange* has not improved the position of publishers.[204] While *Lange* privilege allows defendants to raise more issues, it 'was quite clearly constructed to be … in results, pro-plaintiff'.[205] Judges have suggested that political discussion requires greater protection, but *Lange* has not achieved this 'at all'.[206] The media has attempted to 'stretch the boundaries'[207] of the defence. Where stories have a political 'slant'[208] or a 'hint'[209] of politics, *Lange* will be pleaded.[210] Judges, however, retain 'the discretion to knock things out on what seem to be fairly technical grounds'.[211] For example, the interpretation of political and government matters in *Popovic v Herald & Weekly Times Ltd*[212] to exclude much criticism of judges was not supported,[213] with a wider scope being preferred.[214]

204 24SC, 25SC, 31S, 33SC, 34S, 35S, 36S, 38S, 39S, 42B, 44S, 47SC, 50B. There were only two more supportive views: 'I see the *Lange* defence as a very important defence for publishers, a very practical defence in terms of what it allows to be published': 40S; and *Lange* 'has been very positive for the media': 41S.

205 33SC; similar 47SC, 50B.

206 50B.

207 34S; similar 28SC, 50B.

208 50B.

209 47SC.

210 37S, 47SC. It is pleaded 'more often than not' by the media: 43B. One barrister went further to suggest that 'in almost all media cases involving public figures … *Lange* generally has a run': 33SC.

211 43B; similar 29S.

212 [2002] VSC 174 (Unreported, Bongiorno J, 21 May 2002). See also *Popovic* [2003] VSCA 161 (Unreported, Winneke ACJ, Gillard and Warren AJJA, 21 November 2003). See above nn 74–7 and accompanying text.

213 40S, 41S, 44S, 47SC (*Popovic* is 'bizarre'), 48B, 50B.

214 34S, 40S, 41S, 44S, 47SC, 48B, 50B.

While *Lange* privilege's scope raised some concerns, interviewees more strongly criticised the reasonableness requirement. Its restrictive interpretation was seen as a key failing in the defence.[215] Under *Lange* 'you walk straight into reasonableness'.[216] Reasonableness 'is the stumbling block and will always be the stumbling block'.[217] It is the 'killer'[218] that one 'always come[s] back to':[219]

> Why should a defendant have the added burden of reasonableness when the High Court [judges] are trying to espouse a principle that in political speech there should be more freedom. In fact, there's less freedom because defendant publishers can never or hardly ever get up to that standard of reasonableness.[220]

A related point was raised about s 22 of the *Defamation Act 1974* (NSW). *Lange* privilege is seen to have done little in New South Wales because it is merely a subset of the s 22 defence.[221] *Lange* is believed to operate, within the area of political communication, in *effectively* the same restrictive manner as s 22. As noted in Part II, academic commentary and law reform documents suggest differences between the *Lange* and s 22 defences.[222] Under s 22, publishers must virtually always believe publications to be true, while under *Lange*, it appears that they only need reasonable grounds to believe publications to be true. Notably, however, many interviewees did not see this distinction as having any practical importance.[223] It is 'too fine' to change arguments at trial,[224] except in very rare cases. A small minority of respondents suggested or hoped a different approach would emerge for *Lange* reasonableness,[225] or even that reasonableness under s 22 would be interpreted less strictly to meet constitutional requirements for political communication.[226] But the overwhelming impression was that reasonableness, under *Lange* or s 22, remains a *very* difficult hurdle.

Although comparatively narrow in scope and weak in strength, *Lange* privilege appears to have one effect like *Reynolds*: it encourages the media to seek comment.[227] *Lange* privilege 'brings into sharp focus what was done before the publication, and ... the need to provide the opportunity for comment'.[228] The attention paid to investigation is good,[229] and not seeking comment would most

[215] 25SC, 28SC, 29S, 30S, 31S, 33SC, 35S, 36S, 37S, 38S, 39S, 43B, 44S, 45S, 46S, 47SC, 50B.
[216] 38S.
[217] 28SC; similar 30S: 'People regard the reasonableness test as too high to be jumped over and frankly judges pretty much make it too high to be jumped over'.
[218] 47SC.
[219] 37S; similar 47SC.
[220] 47SC.
[221] 24SC, 25SC, 26B, 27B, 28SC, 33SC, 34S, 35S, 36S, 37S, 38S, 39S, 48B.
[222] See, eg, Walker, '*Lange v ABC*', above n 94; New South Wales Attorney-General's Task Force on Defamation Law Reform, above n 104, 219.
[223] 25SC, 26B, 34S, 35S, 36S, 38S, 43B.
[224] 43B; similar 34S.
[225] 29S, 32S. Others expressed far less confident hopes for such a change: 31S, 39S.
[226] 45S.
[227] 32S, 35S, 40S, 44S.
[228] 46S; similar 31S, 32S, 41S, 45S, 47SC.
[229] 28SC, 34S, 40S, 45S.

probably cause the defence to fail.[230] To a degree this has clarified journalists' responsibilities,[231] but interviewees were concerned about uncertainty in the concept of reasonableness.[232] Journalists need some clear benchmarks,[233] applied with flexibility in the context of each publication.[234] The law, however, sets out 'a suggested way that things are to happen, in relation to publications … generally … [W]hat is reasonable in the circumstances is never looked at … There is no differentiation for the circumstances.'[235]

Second, notwithstanding their limited impact on doctrine, *Lange* and the preceding High Court decisions have reduced suits by politicians and related figures,[236] and lowered the costs of settlement.[237] The 'spectre' of *Lange* privilege dissuades lawsuits.[238] *Lange* has given politicians 'pause to stop';[239] politicians now appear to have a 'generic belief' that they cannot sue.[240] This reported shift in litigation patterns may explain why 'almost every barrister and judge in the country' believes *Lange* has not changed anything in substance, but 'almost every journalist in the country thinks it has'.[241]

Third, Australian interviewees echoed concerns from England about judge and jury roles. Doctrinal orthodoxy might suggest that the roles under *Lange* should resemble those under *Reynolds* — namely, where there is a jury, the jury would resolve disputed facts while judges would determine whether occasions of publication are privileged. When interviews were conducted, Australian case law had not yet examined the division of roles in any detail.[242] Some juries had been asked the general question: Was this publication reasonable?[243] Interviewees supported this approach, generally strongly.[244] It was seen as a jury question in principle,[245] and one of great importance:[246] 'whether something is reasonable or not is quintessentially a jury question. Juries have grappled with that question always'.[247] If the jury deals with reasonableness, it need not address a potentially complex series of questions on specific factual matters.[248] As in England,

230 42B, 49SC.
231 32S.
232 35S, 43B, 44S, 49SC, 50B.
233 35S.
234 42B.
235 38S.
236 31S, 35S, 37S, 41S, 42B, 43B, 44S, 47SC, 49SC.
237 41S, 42B, 45S.
238 37S.
239 49SC.
240 35S; similar 42B, 43B, 44S.
241 30S. Further, 'the media loves *Lange* [and is] obsessed with it': 42B.
242 See now *Popovic* [2003] VSCA 161 (Unreported, Winneke ACJ, Gillard and Warren AJJA, 21 November 2003).
243 See, eg, *Popovic v Herald & Weekly Times Ltd* [2002] VSC 174 (Unreported, Bongiorno J, 21 May 2002).
244 40S, 43B, 44S, 47SC, 49SC, 50B. It was contrasted by some interviewees with New South Wales' s 22 defence where reasonableness is an issue for the judge: eg, 47SC.
245 44S, 47SC, 48B, 50B.
246 49SC, 50B.
247 50B.
248 49SC.

practitioners supported juries having a *general* role in addressing reasonableness.

Fourth, *Lange* privilege had little support overall, apart from dissuading some political plaintiffs: 'when you actually get to trial ... *Lange*'s hopeless, completely hopeless, about as hopeless as you can possibly get and still be a defence'.[249] It is 'a bit of a disaster'.[250] Some interviewees did suggest that *Lange* may have more effect in time,[251] with reasonableness being interpreted less restrictively.[252] Most interviewees, however, suggested that *Lange* should be reviewed.[253] 'We have all been waiting for the High Court to really take *Lange* to the next stage in saying "well clearly it's been set too high, the benchmark" and we should have known that in the first place'.[254] Australian interviewees gave far more support to *Reynolds*.[255] The 'very different',[256] 'strong'[257] and 'sensible'[258] defence 'has provided a better basis for evolution of doctrine than *Lange*':[259]

> We really need to look at this in the context of *Reynolds* and whether there should be a broad based public interest privilege defence ... Is there a role for it in Australia in terms of lowering the benchmark for reasonableness [and] widening the ambit outside politics?[260]

In any event, the application of *Lange* privilege could be developed. Although the current High Court may not be 'minded to expand' the defence,[261] reasonableness need not be narrow: *Lange* privilege could be applied far more like *Reynolds* while remaining unchanged in terms of law.[262]

An alternative development that interviewees raised would be a duty-interest style of privilege for media publications.[263] This existed for political publications under *Theophanous*. These lawyers saw the reasonableness requirement of *Lange* privilege as 'wrong in principle',[264] compared with the traditional defence that would only be defeated by malice. Such a defence would give the jury a

249 42B.
250 39S.
251 30S.
252 29S, 32S, 42B, 45S (who could see the arguments extending to s 22).
253 Eg, 25SC, 28SC, 29S, 30S, 31S, 34S, 35S, 36S, 39S, 40S, 41S, 42B, 43B, 44S, 45S, 47SC, 48B, 50B. Only four interviewees offered any notable support for the current law on privilege: 24SC, 26B and 27B approved of s 22, while 49SC suggested that *Lange* struck a happier balance between parties than the common law qualified privilege defence under *Theophanous*.
254 35S.
255 28SC, 30S, 35S, 36S, 41S, 42B, 50B. One solicitor suggested that 'the outcome is pretty much the same' under both defences: 45S.
256 42B.
257 36S.
258 50B.
259 28SC; similar 30S.
260 35S.
261 35S; similar 45S. Another participant suggested that 'the High Court [is] champing at the bit to have another go at it': 36S.
262 42B.
263 29S, 35S, 36S, 39S, 44S, 45S, 47SC, 50B. Some interviewees, however, did not support such a 'massive change': 24SC; similar 49SC.
264 47SC.

clearer role and place defendant publishers in a much stronger position. Without such changes, truth will remain the vital defence,[265] and the aim of *Lange* privilege to reduce the chill of defamation law appears unlikely to be achieved.

Overall, *Lange* privilege was seen to offer only the smallest improvement on the traditional common law defence, and none on New South Wales' restrictive s 22. *Lange* was not described with anything like the support that English practitioners offered for *Reynolds*, even allowing for the qualifications they had about *Reynolds*' predictability and trial practicality. There was much support for reforming Australian *Lange* and s 22 privileges, or at least substantially developing their application.

IV CONCLUSION

Roy Baker has suggested, in a detailed comparison of *Reynolds* and *Lange*, that both Australian and English courts had given the media what it 'had sought for decades' by 'significantly' extending privilege's application 'to stories of public importance appearing in the mass media'.[266] The empirical research underlying this article suggests that this is true for the English developments under *Reynolds*, but unfortunately Baker may have been too optimistic about the Australian changes: reasonableness under *Lange* is 'more onerous' for defendants than responsibility under *Reynolds*.[267] *Lange* appears not to have improved the position of publishers to any significant degree. It has not reduced the apparent chill of defamation law, apart perhaps from reducing suits by politicians. *Lange* is 'completely hopeless'[268] as a defence and, if anything, is 'constructed to be … in results, pro-plaintiff'.[269] There is no evidence to support the suggestion made by Callinan J in *Australian Broadcasting Corporation v Lenah Games Meats Pty Ltd* that *Lange* 'had the impact of the detonation of a hydrogen bomb' on defamation practitioners.[270] But *Lange* does appear to have encouraged more diverse reporting, in the limited sense of encouraging publications to include subjects' points of view.

Reynolds privilege has done more to affect media conduct through the wide range of factors that are clearly relevant to the defence and the more achievable standard that appears to be required of publishers. Importantly, English practitioners suggested that the media can publish more allegations and stories of public interest under *Reynolds*.[271] This follows from the approach of English courts to a publication's tone. Nevertheless, tone remains a problematic factor for tabloid

265 25SC, 31S, 42B, 43B, 49SC.

266 Baker, 'Extending Common Law Qualified Privilege to the Media', above n 46, 88.

267 See Chesterman, above n 15, 104.

268 See above n 249 and accompanying text.

269 See above n 205 and accompanying text.

270 (2001) 208 CLR 199, 333 (Callinan J), cf 287 (Kirby J). Callinan J made this comment in relation to both *Theophanous* and *Lange*. While research does not support this characterisation in relation to *Lange*, it offers some support for the possibility that the *Theophanous* duty-interest defence had a meaningful impact on defamation law. That impact, however, would appear to be more a matter of 'measured reform' than the detonation of any bomb.

271 See above nn 149–52 and accompanying text.

newspapers,[272] which do not produce 'the sort of journalism ... judges want to read'.[273] *Grobbelaar v News Group Newspapers Ltd*,[274] for example, may suggest that a publisher will be 'penalised by the court for being a tabloid newspaper.'[275] Overall, however, the English courts' approach to tone, particularly in relation to reportage and the degree to which publications distinguish suspicions and allegations of fact,[276] is innovative. It may grow to support a far more diverse range of public debate. These matters about tone and reportage do not arise explicitly under *Lange* and have been little considered in Australia.[277] The research suggests that Australian courts should make clear that a wide range of factors can be relevant to *Lange* reasonableness, and those factors should be applied flexibly.

The empirical research also underlined difficulties in litigation practice that may follow from judge and jury roles. The problems in seeking jury responses to multiple, detailed questions may thwart many of the benefits sought through the doctrinal changes. In England, the division in roles was very strongly criticised,[278] while in Australia there was strong support for asking juries a general question about whether publication was reasonable.[279] Subsequent Australian case law is against that approach,[280] but the research reported here suggests that both reasonableness under *Lange* and responsibility under *Reynolds* should be determined by the jury. To do otherwise will make trials difficult to run and could severely undermine protection for discussion of matters of political or public importance. While another response to the interview material could be to advocate judge-only trials for defamation,[281] existing research suggests the benefits in simplifying defamation litigation that are offered by jury trial.[282] Most Australian courts, in jurisdictions where defamation juries are available, have some flexibility to use the jury in a *general* role of assessing reasonable-

272 3S, 8B, 14S, 16S, 17S, 22S, 23S. 5QC commented that *Reynolds* itself suggested a 'transformed' judicial attitude to tabloids, although later cases have seen a 'slipping back' against tabloid styles of presentation.

273 14S.

274 [2001] 2 All ER 437 (Court of Appeal). See above n 47 and accompanying text.

275 Sarah Thomas, 'Red Devils', *The Guardian* (London), 4 November 2002, Media Guardian 10. Others, however, supported the decision: see, eg, Paul Robertshaw, 'The Review Roles of the Court of Appeal: *Grobbelaar v News International*' (2001) 64 *Modern Law Review* 923, 927: 'This detailed cogitation by the Court of Appeal of the publication and its context ... demonstrate[s] not only judicious balance, but a sound grasp of the way in which contemporary tabloid journalism is produced and published.'

276 See above nn 55–8, 150–6 and accompanying text.

277 Tone, however, was expressly considered in *Rowan v Cornwall [No 5]* (2002) 82 SASR 152. In addition, the way in which *Lange* qualified privilege may protect comment is an underdeveloped area in Australia: see Roy Baker, 'Defamatory Comment on the Judiciary: *Lange* Qualified Privilege in *Popovic v Herald & Weekly Times*' (2002) 7 *Media & Arts Law Review* 213.

278 See above nn 178–93 and accompanying text.

279 See above nn 244–8 and accompanying text.

280 *Popovic* [2003] VSCA 161 (Unreported, Winneke ACJ, Gillard and Warren AJJA, 21 November 2003).

281 Attorney-General's Department, Commonwealth of Australia, *Outline of Possible National Defamation Law* (2004) 5.

282 See Kenyon, *Word Games*, above n 105.

ness.[283] This article's research strongly suggests that Australian courts should take that opportunity. English trial courts may have more difficulty, after statements about judge and jury roles in *Reynolds*,[284] but the preferable approach is equally clear. If English law cannot move directly to having the jury determine the responsibility or otherwise of publication, English courts will need to contain the complexities posed by a large number of jury questions,[285] without unnecessarily limiting the defence. Appellate courts should not be 'blind to the practical consequences' of judge and jury roles in moving to simplify those roles.[286]

Lange and *Reynolds* are worth examining comparatively not just because they are significant legal developments with potentially important influences on speech. *Reynolds* also appears to have been under-appreciated in some Australian material. A 2002 New South Wales report certainly did not overlook the *Reynolds* decision.[287] It examined the factors set out in *Reynolds*, noting that no factor required publishers to establish that they believe in their publications' truth. It recommended amending s 22 of the *Defamation Act 1974* (NSW) to similar effect:

> the 'reasonableness requirement' in s 22 should have attached to it a statutory set of factors to be considered by a court in determining whether the publication is protected by qualified privilege. Such a list ought to make clear to decision makers that it is not necessary for a publisher who wishes to invoke qualified privilege to prove that they had objective grounds for believing in the truth of the matter published.[288]

New South Wales legislation now includes a wider set of factors to consider in relation to reasonableness.[289] Interviewees, however, suggested these changes

283 Victorian trial courts remain bound by *Popovic* [2003] VSCA 161 (Unreported, Winneke ACJ, Gillard and Warren AJJA, 21 November 2003).

284 See above nn 59–62 and accompanying text.

285 See, eg, *Jameel* [2004] EMLR 196, 199. See also above nn 63–4 and accompanying text.

286 See above n 190 and accompanying text.

287 New South Wales Attorney-General's Task Force on Defamation Law Reform, above n 104, 28.

288 Ibid 29.

289 *Defamation Act 1974* (NSW) s 22(2A) provides that:

> In determining … whether the conduct of the publisher … is reasonable in the circumstances, a court may take into account the following matters and such other matters as the court considers relevant:
>
> (a) the extent to which the matter published is of public concern,
>
> (b) the extent to which the matter published concerns the performance of the public functions or activities of the person,
>
> (c) the seriousness of any defamatory imputation carried by the matter published,
>
> (d) the extent to which the matter published distinguishes between suspicions, allegations and proven facts,
>
> (e) whether it was necessary in the circumstances for the matter published to be published expeditiously,
>
> (f) the sources of the information in the matter published and the integrity of those sources,
>
> (g) whether the matter published contained the substance of the person's side of the story and, if not, whether a reasonable attempt was made by the publisher to obtain and publish a response from the person,
>
> (h) any other steps taken to verify the information in the matter published.

added little or nothing to the law.[290] The list of factors is 'insulting'[291] and 'an absolute waste of time'.[292] It merely re-expresses what courts have always been able to do.[293] However, the new statutory factors reflect the *Reynolds* approach. Given widespread support for *Reynolds* by Australian interviewees, s 22(2A) of the *Defamation Act 1974* (NSW) may offer a very useful basis for innovative arguments to revise reasonableness under the New South Wales statutory defence. For example, the legislation now explicitly refers to 'the extent to which the matter published distinguishes between suspicions, allegations and proven facts'.[294] This could support arguments drawing on the English reportage cases.[295] Since s 22 is wide — it is not limited to *Lange* privilege's political communication — the arguments should be open in many cases. This article's examination of *Reynolds* in action suggests that such a reinterpretation of s 22 is warranted and that decisions on *Reynolds* privilege offer much to New South Wales courts.

While the recent New South Wales report did not overlook *Reynolds*, other Australian proposals have sidestepped its possibilities. A 2003 report from Western Australia, for example, notes that the State has power to broaden or strengthen the constitutionally-based *Lange* defence. But the report simply suggests: 'The [proposed new Western Australian defamation] Act should do no more than refer to the existence of this defence [related to discussion on political or government matters] — it should not attempt to define it or prescribe its limits.'[296] Similarly, a brief discussion paper issued by the Commonwealth Attorney-General in March 2004 does not refer to *Reynolds* at all.[297] It suggests that a statutory defence for reasonable publication should *replace* all qualified privilege. The defence would be modelled on s 22 of the *Defamation Act 1974* (NSW), notwithstanding its very restrictive history.[298] The research reported in this article suggests that the Attorney-General's initial proposal for qualified privilege would do nothing to encourage diverse speech on matters of public concern. Rather, such a form of statutory qualified privilege would restrict speech and maintain the chill that appears to exist under Australian defamation law.

This article's doctrinal and empirical research points towards a broader and stronger Australian defence — one that is neither limited to a narrow version of political communication, nor requires an onerous standard of reasonableness.

290 25SC, 28SC, 33SC, 35S, 37S, 39S ('unless judges decide to interpret [reasonableness differently]').

291 35S.

292 33SC.

293 37S.

294 *Defamation Act 1974* (NSW) s 22(2A)(d).

295 See above nn 55–8 and accompanying text.

296 Defamation Law Reform Committee, *Western Australian Defamation Law: Committee Report on Reform to the Law of Defamation in Western Australia* (2003) 18.

297 Attorney-General's Department, above n 281.

298 The Attorney-General's discussion paper takes this approach primarily from the Australian Law Reform Commission, *Unfair Publication: Defamation and Privacy*, Report No 11 (1979), which predated the widespread recognition of failings in New South Wales' s 22 defence: ibid 74–5.

First, *Lange* should be broader. The diverse range of publications that can seek protection on *Reynolds* privilege,[299] the criticism of *Lange*'s narrow scope in interviews[300] and existing academic literature[301] all support a broader Australian defence. As Lord Cooke noted in *Reynolds* itself:

> It is doubtful whether the … new defence could sensibly be confined to political discussion. There are other public figures who exercise great practical power over the lives of people or great influence in the formation of public opinion or as role models. [Their] power or influence may indeed exceed that of most politicians. The rights and interests of citizens in democracies are not restricted to the casting of votes. Matters other than those pertaining to government and politics may be just as important in the community; and they may have as strong a claim to be free of restraints on freedom of speech.[302]

The High Court has noted that it is possible for the common law defence under *Lange* to be broader than the constitutional protection for political communication.[303] Thus the development appears to be open in Australian law, and it should be made. Existing hesitancy by appellate courts should not dispose of the issue,[304] and *Reynolds* should be drawn on to develop *Lange* privilege. Second, *Lange* should be stronger. The difficult task of meeting the reasonableness requirement was one of the clearest problems seen through the interview research.[305] Again, as already discussed for s 22 in the New South Wales legislation, *Reynolds* offers very useful material.

In terms of how developments in *Lange* or s 22 may be promoted, recent comments by two members of the High Court are noteworthy. In *Rogers v Nationwide News Pty Ltd*,[306] Gleeson CJ and Gummow J discussed the need for greater consideration of the circumstances of news production:

> In the respondent's written submissions, reference was made, without elaboration, to 'the circumstances in which daily newspapers are published'. It may be enlightening if … courts were given more evidence as to those circumstances. … Where, as here, serious errors are made, and attributed to 'the circumstances in which daily newspapers are published', a court would be in a better position to judge the reasonableness of the publisher's conduct if it were told exactly what those circumstances were, why they prevailed, and how they contributed to the error.[307]

299 See above nn 50–8 and accompanying text.

300 See, eg, above nn 213–14 and accompanying text.

301 See, eg, Chesterman, above n 15, 99; Baker, 'Extending Common Law Qualified Privilege to the Media', above n 46; Kenyon, 'Defamation and Critique', above n 83.

302 [2001] 2 AC 127, 220. This quotation has some currency in New Zealand at least: Geoff McLay, '*Lange v Atkinson*: Not a Case for Dancing in the Streets' [2000] *New Zealand Law Review* 427, 435–6; John Burrows, '*Lange v Atkinson* 2000: Analysis' [2000] *New Zealand Law Review* 389, 392.

303 *Lange* (1997) 189 CLR 520, 571.

304 See, eg, *Marsden* [2002] NSWCA 419 (Unreported, Beazley, Giles and Santow JJA, 24 December 2002) [1168]–[1170].

305 See above n 215 and accompanying text.

306 (2003) 201 ALR 184.

307 Ibid 191–2.

Their Honours' invitation for more detailed material on news production accords with ongoing academic research into defamation law and news production.[308] It suggests that *if* the media can provide more substantial material about what is reasonable, then the courts' strict approach could be revised as they adopted more appropriate approaches to imposing '"quality control" standards within journalism'.[309] The English experiences outlined in this article underline how poorly Australian law has responded to defamation law's traditional limits.

English and Australian law is attempting to overcome the traditional limitations on speech that follow from requiring many defendants to prove truth. As Barendt and his co-researchers noted of the situation before *Reynolds*:

> in order to have a defence against every possible defamation ... [newspapers] would require certainty that in every case there were witnesses willing and able to appear in court ... or that conclusive and legally admissible documentary evidence be in the editor's hands. If such certainty were required for everything controversial, there would be no newspapers worth reading.[310]

Reynolds offers much to address such concerns, and it may inform Australian developments more easily than moving to the stronger protection offered by a *Theophanous*-style privilege that applied to matters of public interest.[311] That, however, may be where the law must move if it is to meet the aims of *Lange* and *Reynolds* to reduce defamation law's burden of proving truth.[312] Whichever developments are pursued, if privilege defences are to assist diverse speech and reduce any chill from defamation law, courts would do well to remain 'slow to conclude that a publication [is] not in the public interest' and resolve doubts 'in favour of publication'.[313]

308 See, eg, Timothy Marjoribanks and Andrew T Kenyon, 'Negotiating News: Journalistic Practice and Defamation Law in Australia and the US' (2003) 25 *Australian Journalism Review* 31.

309 Roger Magnusson, 'Freedom of Speech in Australian Defamation Law: Ridicule, Satire and Other Challenges' (2001) 9 *Torts Law Journal* 269, 297.

310 Barendt et al, above n 2, 77.

311 The New South Wales Attorney-General's Task Force on Defamation Law Reform, above n 104, 31–2 offers one illustration that such changes removing the reasonableness requirement may be difficult to achieve. Two of the Task Force's four members recommended introducing a statutory privilege, subject only to malice, for broadly 'political' material, but the recommendation did not appear in the subsequent Bill.

312 See, eg, Sallie Spilsbury, 'Bloodhounds and Watchdogs — Qualified Privilege, Malice and the Publication of Material in the Public Interest' (2000) 11 *Entertainment Law Review* 43, 46–7, who suggests that judges should determine privileged occasions according to whether publications have public interest content, and that juries should deal with the circumstances of publication in terms of malice.

313 *Reynolds* [2001] 2 AC 127, 205 (Lord Nicholls).

Part IV
Freedom of the Press and Privacy

[11]

THE RIGHT TO SPEAK FROM *TIMES* TO *TIME*: FIRST AMENDMENT THEORY APPLIED TO LIBEL AND MISAPPLIED TO PRIVACY

*Melville B. Nimmer**

I

THE SEARCH FOR A VIABLE THEORY

The extent to which men are free to speak without restraint from government is the principal measure of the degree of reality which lies beneath the rhetoric that tells us we are a free people living under a free government. But the very phrase "free government" contains a paradox, since a government which is not prepared in some circumstances to apply restraints and thus lessen freedom is no government at all. Democratic theory supposedly resolves this seeming contradiction by legitimizing state power in its restraint on conduct while immunizing from the reach of the state speech and other forms of expression. Every civics student knows that by virtue of the first amendment "Congress shall make no law. . . abridging the freedom of speech, or of the press," and that by reason of the fourteenth amendment the same restraints are imposed upon state governments. The only thing wrong with this conventional view of the role of the first amendment in our society is that it is untrue. To be sure, it contains an important element of truth, but it neither is nor can be wholly and literally true.

Some have thought that the first amendment must be interpreted and applied with absolute literalness. Justice Black, who is usually

*A.B. 1947, University of California, Berkeley; LL.B. 1950, Harvard University. Professor of Law, University of California, Los Angeles.

regarded as the foremost exponent of such a position, has said that the first amendment command that Congress shall make "no law" abridging freedom of speech literally "means no law,"[1] and that this is true "without any ifs, buts, or whereases."[2] To one sympathetic to the values of free expression this at first glance states an attractive view, supported as it is by the clear, unequivocal language of the Constitution. Nevertheless, it will not wash. Everyone, including Justice Black, will concede that there are circumstances when the act of speaking or otherwise expressing oneself may be subject to governmental restraint.

Even the holders of an absolutist view read the first amendment guarantee of free speech as subject to the qualification that speech may be abridged if the time, place, or manner of its expression makes an abridgement reasonable. It was Justice Black who wrote the recent opinion for the Court in *Adderley v. Florida*[3] which upheld the arrest of university students for staging a nonviolent civil rights demonstration outside a Florida county jail. In that opinion he expressly rejected "the assumption that people who want to propagandize protests or views have a constitutional right to do so whenever and however and wherever they please."[4] And the dissenting opinion of Justice Douglas, which argued that the right of free speech should have been upheld on the particular facts presented in *Adderley*, conceded the same qualification:

> "There may be some instances in which assemblies and petitions for redress of grievances are not consistent with other necessary purposes of public property. A noisy meeting may be out of keeping with the serenity of the statehouse or the quiet of the courthouse. No one, for example, would suggest that the Senate gallery is the proper place for a vociferous protest rally. And in other cases it may be necessary to adjust the right to petition for redress of grievances to the other interests inhering in the uses to which the public property is normally put."[5]

Lest the reference to "noisy" and "vociferous" be thought to beg the question, can anyone doubt that if during a session of the Supreme Court a spectator were to rise and proceed to make a speech, loud enough to be heard by those present, but in no way raucous or noisy, he might properly be restrained?

Time, place, and manner considerations are not the only qualifications of the first amendment which most people, probably including

[1]Cahn, *Justice Black and First Amendment "Absolutes":A Public Interview*, 37 N.Y.U.L. Rev. 549, 553 (1962).

[2]*Id.* at 559. The same phrase is to be found in Beauharnais v. Illinois, 343 U.S. 250, 275 (1952) (Black, J., dissenting).

[3]385 U.S. 39 (1966).

[4]*Id.* at 47-48. *Accord,* Cahn, *supra* note 1, at 558.

[5]385 U.S. at 54.

those who hold an absolutist position, would accept as inherently necessary and impliedly contained in the freedom of speech guarantee. Agreements in restraint of trade are a form of expression, but does anyone believe that the first amendment invalidates our antitrust laws? Would anyone argue that perjury in a judicial proceeding could not be made a crime because it is a form of speech? Can it be maintained that one who passes "top secret" material to unauthorized persons is immunized from prosecution because he is engaging in a form of expression? Are our copyright laws unconstitutional because they abridge an infringer's freedom of expression? Many other examples might be added,[6] but these perhaps will suffice to indicate that no one can responsibly hold the position that the first amendment is an absolute in the sense that it literally protects all speech.

Justice Black and others have sometimes sought to find absolute boundaries for the scope of the first amendment by invoking the distinction between "speech" and "action."[7] But this is no more than a metaphorical device for rationalizing a line already drawn. If I cry "Fire!" in a crowded theater, I am speaking no less than when I engage in a political debate. The consequences of the former may differ markedly from

[6]"Federal securities regulation, mail fraud statues, and common-law actions for deceit and misrepresentation are only some examples of our understanding that the right to communicate information of public interest is not 'unconditional.' " Opinion of Mr. Justice Harlan, joined by Justices Clark, Stewart, and Fortas, in Curtis Pub. Co. v. Butts, 388 U.S. 130, 150 (1967).

[7]For example, Justice Black in his dissenting opinion in Communist Party v. Subversive Activities Control Bd., 367 U.S. 1, 168 (1961), stated: "The Founders drew a distinction in our Constitution which we would be wise to follow. They gave the Government the fullest power to prosecute overt actions in violation of valid laws but withheld any power to punish people for nothing more than advocacy of their views." Likewise, Mr. Justice Douglas in a concurring opinion in Garrison v. Louisiana, 379 U.S. 64, 82 (1964) stated categorically: "I think it is time to face the fact that the only line drawn by the Constitution is between 'speech' on the one side and conduct or overt acts on the other."

Justice Douglas goes on to acknowledge, however, that "freedom of expression can be suppressed if, and to the extent that, it is so closely brigaded with illegal action as to be an inseparable part of it." (Justice Douglas originally expressed this view in Roth v. United States, 354 U.S. 476, 514 (1957)). This concession surely obliterates the usefulness of an absolutist distinction between speech and conduct. It requires balancing, see text at note 9 *infra*, to determine whether the speech is "so closely brigaded with illegal action" as to warrant its suppression. Justice Black (with Justice Douglas and Chief Justice Warren concurring) conceded in Barenblatt v. United States, 360 U.S. 109, 141-42 (1959), that balancing is required in determining the validity of a law "which primarily regulates conduct but which might also indirectly affect speech." Consider also Justice Black's dissent in Konigsberg v. State Bar, 366 U.S. 36, 68-70 (1961), where he expressly acknowledged the need for such balancing only in those cases involving the right of a city to control the use of its streets, but mentioned such cases by way of example and not as an exhaustive category.

The distinction between speech and conduct has also been invoked by those members of the Court who are unsympathetic to an absolutist interpretation of the first amendment. For example, Mr. Justice Harlan, in Curtis Pub. Co. v. Butts, 388 U.S. 130, 152-53 (1967), stated that ". . . neither the interests of the publisher nor those of socicty neeessarily preclude a damage award based on

that of the latter, but it is a fiction which beclouds rather than clarifies to say that the former is not speech. Whether a cry of "Fire!" is the type of speech which should find protection under the first amendment may validly be questioned, but the answer must be sought elsewhere than in the speech-action dichotomy.[8]

But if the first amendment does not protect all speech, how is the Court to determine which speech is subject to abridgment, and which immunized by the first amendment? Here those concerned with the preservation of the values which underlie the first amendment become properly alarmed. If we may not cling to the anchor of an absolute, unqualified rule, is not the alternative no rule at all? If the judges are not required to protect all speech, doesn't this mean that the only speech which will be protected is that which, on an ad hoc basis, the judges may from time to time approve? That this fear is not fanciful is all too clearly illustrated by a line of cases in which the Court engaged in what has been called ad hoc balancing.[9]

The first of these was *American Communications Association v. Douds*,[10] where Mr. Chief Justice Vinson, on behalf of the Court, rejected an "absolutist test" of first amendment rights, and concluded that as between the claims of free speech and the claims of public order "the duty of the courts is to determine which of these two conflicting interests demands the greater protection under the particular circumstances presented."[11] Similarly, Mr. Justice Frankfurter, concurring in *Dennis v. United States*,[12] stated that: "The demands of free speech in a democratic society as well as the interests in national security are better served by

improper conduct which creates a false publication. It is the conduct element, therefore, on which we must principally focus if we are successfully to resolve the antithesis between civil libel actions and the freedom of speech and press." If the reference to a principal "focus" is intended to suggest that only conduct and not speech is being suppressed, it is surely misleading. Conduct may be a necessary element in a libel action, but there can be no libel without libelous speech.

[8]This distinction breaks down not only because some verbal expressions do not and should not command first amendment protection, see text at note 6 *supra*, but also because some action which does not consist of verbal expression properly belongs within the sphere of first amendment protection. As Mr. Justice Harlan, concurring in the sit-in case Garner v. Louisiana, 368 U.S. 157, 201-02 (1961) observed: "Such a demonstration in the circumstances . . . is as much a part of the 'free trade in ideas' . . . as is verbal expression, more commonly thought of as 'speech.' It, like speech, appeals to good sense and to the 'power of reason as applied through public discussion' . . . just as much as, if not more than, a public oration delivered from a soapbox at a street corner. This Court has never limited the right to speak, a protected 'liberty' under the Fourteenth Amendment . . . to mere verbal expression."

[9]*See* Emerson, *Toward a General Theory of the First Amendment*, 72 YALE L.J. 877, 912-14 (1963); Frantz, *The First Amendment in the Balance*, 71 YALE L.J. 1424 (1962).

[10]339 U.S. 382 (1950).

[11]*Id.* at 399.

[12]341 U.S. 494, 524-25 (1951).

candid and informed weighing of the competing interests, within the confines of the judicial process, than by announcing dogmas too inflexible for the non-Euclidean problems to be solved." And Mr. Justice Harlan for the Court in *Barenblatt v. United States*[13] asserted that: "Where First Amendment rights are asserted to bar governmental interrogation resolution of the issue always involves a balancing by the courts of the competing private and public interests at stake in the particular circumstances shown."[14]

But what is wrong with the rational weighting of competing interests that occurs under the ad hoc balancing approach? Such an approach may well be desirable with respect to nonconstitutional issues—in fact, it appears to be basic to the common law system. It may even be the most sensible technique in some constitutional areas.[15] But those who subscribe to ad hoc balancing would be untrue to their philosophy if they were unprepared to balance the merits and faults of the very system of balancing against those of a different system in particular contexts. I would assert that in the sensitive and vital area of freedom of expression, constitutional protection must not be predicated on ad hoc balancing.

There are at least three serious objections to the use of ad hoc balancing in resolving free speech issues. First, ad hoc balancing by hypothesis means that there is no rule to be applied, but only interests to be weighed. In advance of a final adjudication by the highest court a given speaker has no standard by which he can measure whether his interest in speaking will be held of greater or lesser weight than the competing interest which opposes his speech. Without pretending that there can ever be complete certainty as to how a given rule will be applied in a new situation, if there is no rule at all then there is no certainty at all. The absence of certainty in the law is always unfortunate, but it is particularly pernicious where speech is concerned because it tends to deter all but the most courageous (not necessarily the most rational) from entering the market place of ideas. From this we all suffer through being cut off from exposure to ideas which could be valuable or even vital to our national well-being.

The second objection to ad hoc balancing in speech cases relates to the results likely to be reached. I think it is more than mere coincidence

[13]360 U.S. 109, 126 (1959).

[14]For other examples of ad hoc balancing see NAACP v. Alabama, 357 U.S. 449, 463-64 (1958) and Konigsberg v. State Bar, 366 U.S. 36, 51 (1961). It should be noted that the Court has recently indicated its rejection of the balancing approach. *See* United States v. Robel, 389 U.S. 258, 268 n.20 (1967).

[15]See the persuasive argument for ad hoc balancing on a constitutional level in Karst, *Legislative Facts in Constitutional Litigation*, 1960 SUPREME COURT REV. 75.

that in the overwhelming majority of the major free speech cases in which the ad hoc balancing approach has been applied, the weighing of interests has come out on the side which opposes freedom of speech.[16] It can be conceded that such an outcome is not a necessary result of ad hoc balancing, but it is the result that is likely to occur. This is because the free speech issue will never be tested in court unless a law has in some way been violated, and unless further the authorities determine to prosecute. Given the assumption inherent in our national heritage that most speech is to be tolerated, it is only those who espouse the most unpopular ideas, those against whom feelings run the highest, that are likely to be the subject of repressive laws, and only they are likely to be prosecuted. It is too much to expect that our judges will be entirely untouched, consciously or otherwise, by such strong popular feelings—feelings that have more than once reached the point of national hysteria—when they come to engage in the "delicate and difficult task"[17] of weighing competing interests. Thus at the very time when the right of freedom of speech becomes crucial, the scales may become unbalanced. Yet the fact that passionate national feelings oppose a given speaker's right to be hcard does not properly go to the question of whether the interest which opposes the speech rationally outweighs the interest which supports the speech. Otherwise, the mere fact that a popularly elected legislature passed a law repressing speech and a popularly elected executive brought the prosecution would automatically condemn the speech, and no constitutional issue would remain.

The third major objection to ad hoc balancing also relates to the likely results. In weighing the particular interests involved in a given case, the court must balance the interest in speech against the compelling force of a particular legislative judgment as molded in the law which has been violated. This might present no special problem if the law in question were enacted some time in the 19th century. But if, as is usually the case, most of the legislators that enacted the law still hold office, the court is likely to be swayed by their judgment in the weighing of interests. Certainly on a nonconstitutional level this is as it should be, and even in

[16]*See* Communist Party v. Subversive Activities Control Bd., 367 U.S. 1 (1961); Konigsberg v. State Bar, 366 U.S. 36 (1961); Barenblatt v. United States, 360 U.S. 109 (1959); Dennis v. United States, 341 U.S. 494 (1951); American Communications Ass'n v. Douds, 339 U.S. 382 (1950). The "speech" side prevailed in NAACP v. Alabama, 357 U.S. 449 (1958), but the precise interest protected was the right of association as derived from the right of free speech, and not speech itself. *See also* Sweezy v. New Hampshire, 354 U.S. 234 (1957), where, although the balancing approach was not employed by the majority, Justices Frankfurter and Harlan in a concurring opinion balanced in favor of the interest in speech.

[17]American Communications Ass'n v. Douds, 339 U.S. 382, 400 (1950), quoting Schnieder v. State (Town of Irvington), 308 U.S. 147, 161 (1939).

constitutional adjudication the legislative view is not entirely irrelevant. But the ingrained judicial deference to the legislative branch can and has in ad hoc balancing tended toward judicial abdication in the weighing process. This is evident in Mr. Justice Frankfurter's opinion in *Dennis*:

> [H]ow are competing interests to be assessed? Since they are not subject to quantitative ascertainment, the issue necessarily resolves itself into asking, who is to make the adjustment?—who is to balance the relevant factors and ascertain which interest is in the circumstances to prevail? Full responsibility for the choice cannot be given to the courts. Courts are not representative bodies. They are not designed to be a good reflex of a democratic society. Their judgment is best informed, and therefore most dependable, within narrow limits. Their essential quality is detachment, founded on independence. History teaches that the independence of the judiciary is jeopardized when courts become embroiled in the passions of the day and assume primary responsibility in choosing between competing political, economic and social pressures.
>
> Primary responsibility for adjusting the interests which compete in the situation before us of necessity belongs to the Congress. . . . We are to set aside the judgment of those whose duty it is to legislate only if there is no reasonable basis for it.[18]

Judge Learned Hand went even further, apparently not even requiring reasonableness upon the part of the legislature, but only good faith. "The standard set should prevail," he wrote, "unless the court is satisfied that it was not the product of an effort impartially to balance the conflicting values."[19] I do not know how to avoid the logical conclusion from this that there is no constitutional guarantee of freedom of expression. If the legislative judgment is to prevail absent a showing of bad faith, or possibly in the absence of any reasonable ground upon which the enactment could have been predicated, then in the real world no legislative abridgment of speech will ever be violative of the first amendment, and for all practical purposes it becomes a dead letter.[20]

Are we, then, left with a dilemma? The absolutist interpretation of the first amendment whereby literally all speech is protected is both unrealistic and undesirable for reasons indicated above. But if anything less than all speech is to be protected, then some selection must be made between that speech which is protected and that which is not. If such selection is to turn on rational rather than arbitrary considerations, it is obvious that the selection process requires a balancing of competing

[18] 341 U.S. 494, 525 (1951) (concurring opinion). It should be noted that a majority of the Court has never adopted this rather extreme position.

[19] L. HAND, THE BILL OF RIGHTS 61 (1962).

[20] There might be some residual significance in that such judicial restraint would not necesarily apply as to encroachments by the executive branch.

interests, and this returns us to the equally unacceptable alternative of ad hoc balancing.[21]

Or does it? The Supreme Court decision in *New York Times Company* v. *Sullivan*[22] indicates a third approach which avoids the all or nothing implications of absolutism versus ad hoc balancing. *Times* points the way to the employment of the balancing process on the definitional rather than the litigation or ad hoc level. That is, the Court employs balancing not for the purpose of determining which litigant deserves to prevail in the particular case, but only for the purpose of defining which forms of speech are to be regarded as "speech" within the meaning of the first amendment.[23] This at first blush may appear to be only a verbal distinction. Analysis suggests, however, that a good deal more is involved.[24]

In *Times* the Court for the first time ruled on the question of whether libel laws constitute an abridgment of speech in violation of the first amendment.[25] The New York Times had published an advertisement on behalf of the Committee to Defend Martin Luther King and the Struggle for Freedom in the South.[26] The advertisement admittedly contained some false statements.[27] In a subsequent libel action brought by L. B. Sullivan,[28] a Montgomery city commissioner,

[21]Until recent years civil libertarians put much reliance in the so-called clear and present danger test, first suggested by Mr. Justice Holmes in Schenck v. United States, 249 U.S. 47 (1919), and fully articulated by Mr. Justice Brandeis in a concurring opinion in Whitney v. California, 274 U.S. 357, 372 (1927). But, as became clear in Dennis v. United States, 341 U.S. 494 (1951), the test represents only a particular form of ad hoc balancing, and is subject to all of the infirmities described above.

[22]376 U.S. 255 (1964).

[23]*See* Mr. Justice Harlan's reference to "the 'real problem' of defining or delimiting the right" of free speecb. Curtis Pub. Co. v. Butts, 388 U.S. 130, 149 (1967).

[24]For various pre-*Times* formulations of the doctrine of definitional balancing see C. BLACK, *Mr. Justice Black, the Supreme Court, and the Bill of Rights*, in THE OCCASIONS OF JUSTICE 89 (1963); Emerson, *Toward a General Theory of the First Amendment*, 72 YALE L.J. 877, 916-18 (1963); Frantz, *The First Amendment in the Balance*, 71 YALE L.J. 1424 (1962).

[25]But in Beaubarnais v. Illinois, 343 U.S. 250 (1952), the Court upheld a so-called group libel law and in that case, as well as in a number of others, indicated in dicta that libel is outside the protection of tbe first amendment. *See* Konigsberg v. State Bar, 366 U.S. 36, 49 (1961); Times Film Corp. v. City of Chicago, 365 U.S. 43, 48 (1961); Roth v. United States, 354 U.S. 476, 486-87 (1957); Pennekamp v. Florida, 328 U.S. 331, 348-49 (1946); Cbaplinsky v. New Hampshire, 315 U.S. 568, 572 (1942); Near v. Minnesota, 283 U.S. 697, 715 (1931); Robertson v. Baldwin, 165 U.S. 275, 281 (1897).

[26]N.Y. Times, March 29, 1960, at 25.

[27]376 U.S. at 258.

[28]The advertisement did not refer to the plaintiff Sullivan by name, but the jury coneluded that tbe defamatory referenee to "police" in fact referred to him since he was the Montogomery commissioner who supervised the police department. This raised an impotant additional issue in the Times case, though not one under scrutiny in this article. The Court held that "an otherwise

against the Times and certain other defendants, an Alabama jury had awarded one-half million dollars in damages.[29] In reversing the judgement and holding for the defendants, the Court in effect defined the kind of defamatory speech which is protected by the first amendment. The Court held that, at least where the defamatory speech is directed against a "public official," such speech is protected by the first amendment unless the speech is made "with knowledge that it was false or with reckless disregard of whether it was false or not."[30]

Before considering whether the particular balance struck by the Court was correct, it should be made clear that there *was* balancing in *Times*,[31] but that it was not ad hoc balancing. There was balancing in the sense that not all defamatory speech was held to be protected by the first amendment. The Court could not determine which segment of defamatory speech lies outside the umbrella of the first amendment purely on logical grounds, and no pretense of logical inexorability was made. By in effect holding that knowingly and recklessly false speech was not "speech" within the meaning of the first amendment, the Court must have implicitly (since no explicit explanation was offered) referred to certain competing policy considerations.[32] This is surely a kind of balancing, but it is just as surely not ad hoc balancing.

If the Court had followed the ad hoc approach, it would have inquired whether "under the particular circumstances presented"[33] the interest of the defendants in publishing their particular advertisement outweighed the interest of the plaintiff in the protection of his reputation. This in turn would have led to such imponderable issues as: How important was it to the defendants (or possibly to the public at large) that this particular advertisement be published? How "serious" was the injury to the plaintiff's reputation caused by the advertisement? Apart from the difficulty of weighing these imponderables in the particular case, such an approach carries with it some of the previously discussed

impersonal attack on governmental operations" could not constitutionally be regarded as a libel on an official responsible for those operations since this would in effect amount to a constitutionally forbidden action for seditious libel. 376 U.S. at 292.

[29]The jury did not differentiate between general and punitive damages. No special damages were awarded. *Id.* at 279-80.

[30]*Id.* at 279. The Court speaks of this formulation as (for these purposes) a definition of "actual malice." Hatred or ill will does not constitute malice as here used. *See* Garrison v. Louisiana, 379 U.S. 64, 73-74 (1964).

[31]The opinion in *Times* does not acknowledge that the rule there articulated is based upon balancing. But note that Chief Justice Warren, concurring in Curtis Pub. Co. v. Butts, 388 U.S. 130, 164 (1967), refers to "the New York Times standard" as one which "balances to a proper degree the legitimate interests traditionally protected by the law of defamation."

[32]What these may have been is explored in section 11 *infra*.

[33]American Communications Ass'n. v. Douds, 339 U.S. 382, 399 (1950).

difficulties inherent in the ad hoc approach. If *Times* had been decided on the ground that in the circumstances presented the importance of the publication of the particular advertisement outweighed the seriousness of the particular resulting injury to the plaintiff's reputation, what would that tell potential future advertisers and public officials as to their respective rights in connection with future advertisements? Not only would it tell them nothing; it might well serve as a serious deterrent to anyone who intends to criticize public officials, since it can hardly be predicted which way the scales will fall in the particular circumstances of a new case. The absence of a rule to which judges can turn could also result in decisions unduly influenced by prevailing public emotions. Suppose in the next case defamatory statements are made about a public official by reason of his conduct in connection with the Vietnam war. If the only referent available to the judges is the weight of the competing interests in speech and reputation, can anyone doubt that the speech is likely to have rough sledding, or at the very least, that a decision finding that speech outweighs reputation will require unusual judicial courage?

It has been argued that any objections which may be stated against ad hoc balancing are equally applicable to definitional balancing, since the same competing interests which are considered in the former will have to be considered in the latter.[34] I would disagree with this for several reasons. First, it is not necessarily true that the same considerations are weighed in both definitional and ad hoc balancing. In the latter it is the interests presented in the particular circumstances of the case before the court which are weighed. For example, in a defamation case the court would weigh not the interest in speech generally but rather the interest (and hence the importance) of the particular speech which is the subject of the litigation. On the other side it would weigh not the interest in reputation generally, but the extent of the particular injury to reputation in the case before it. It may be argued that this would permit a more precise weighing of issues in ad hoc balancing than is possible at the definitional stage, and that, therefore, justice would more likely be done by ad hoc balancing. I shall deal with that argument presently. For the moment I would simply make the point that the weighing of interests is not precisely the same regardless of whether it is done by definitional or ad hoc balancing.

A more profound difference between the ad hoc and definitional lies in the fact that a rule emerges from definitional balancing which can be employed in future cases without the occasion for further weighing of

[34] *See* A. BICKEL, THE LEAST DANGEROUS BRANCH 96 (1962); *cf.* C. BLACK, *supra* note 24, at 94-97.

interests. Moreover, such a rule should continue to be applicable notwithstanding the subsequent enactment of new legislation which in some different manner attempts to protect an interest inimical to speech. It is the first amendment which is being defined, not any particular legislation. Thus the *Times* rule which immunizes reputation—injuring speech other than that which is knowingly or recklessly false would presumably be equally applicable to new legislation which seeks to protect official reputations through novel means. The very existence of the rule makes it more likely that the balance originally struck will continue to be observed despite new and perhaps otherwise irresistible pressures. This in turn offers some measure of certainty, and minimizes speech deterrence.

Two concessions must be made, but neither constitutes a refutation of the thesis here offered. First, I would concede that neither definitional balancing nor any other technique can offer absolute assurance that a given court under sufficient internal or external pressure in some "hard" case will not depart from a definitional rule. Nevertheless, definitional balancing can insulate a judge from legally irrelevant pressures to a considerable degree if the judge wishes such insulation. How much easier it would be for a conscientious judge in a Southern community to explain to the members of the Lions Club that he found as he did because that was "the rule," rather than because upon a weighing of the interests involved he found weightier the side that public opinion opposed.

Second, I would make the concession that, *in vacuo*, ad hoc balancing is more likely to consider fine nuances and therefore produce a more just result. Like every line, the line drawn in definitional balancing has two edges, and speech which might be protected if the particular interests involved in a particular case were subject to the precision of the ad hoc scalpel might well lose protection by the cutting of the blunter definitional knife. But this likelihood may be offset by the fact that in ad hoc balancing weight is likely to be given only to the particular speech involved and not to "speech" generally, so that the speech side of the balance may be underweighed when compared with the immediate impact of a particular injury to a particular reputation. Equally, the ad hoc balance may be distorted by a failure to recognize the interest in reputations generally and not only in that immediately before the court. Furthermore, such a likelihood would be present only in an ideal world where ad hoc balancing would not be subject to distortion from public and legislative pressures. We deal here only with speech cases; they in particular are not a part of such an ideal world. And even if the ideal could be achieved, the lack of a predictable line would still result in speech deterrence.

The point here is perhaps best illustrated in a nonspeech context but where pressures analogous to those found in speech cases might exist. Consider the unhappy history of the mythical state of Autophobia. The inhabitants of that state regarded the hazards of modern automotive travel as far more dangerous than any threat that might be posed by domestic or foreign communism. In some quarters hysteria ran rampant so that any driver of an automobile was suspect as probably a reckless driver, and even automobile passengers were regarded as fellow travellers. The more stable citizens, while recognizing the danger of reckless driving, also acknowledged the "competing interest" in expeditious transportation. When it came time for the state legislature to enact a speed law the more fearful members of the legislature argued that it would be dangerous to specify any specific maximum speed since this would constitute a green light for insidious drivers to proceed recklessly at just under the specified maximum. Their argument carried the day, and a law was enacted outlawing "excessive speeding," leaving it to the courts to determine in each case whether the driver's speed was in fact excessive.

The courts were thus required to engage in ad hoc balancing, weighing in each case the interest in safe driving against the interest in expeditious travel. This meant that drivers who wished to be sure of avoiding a brush with the law were deterred from driving at speeds which anyone might arguably contend were excessive. The absence of a rule as to what constituted excessive speed resulted in a traffic flow far slower than the interests of safety required. Still the law might have been found acceptable but for the further fact that whenever the courts were called upon to decide a case in which the defendant was charged with violating the speed law, they invariably found the defendant guilty. The popular hysteria against speeding made it very difficult for a judge in any given case to find that the defendant's interest in expeditious travel outweighed the community's interest in safe driving. The dissatisfaction of the more enlightened citizenry finally resulted in the enactment of a new speed law which specified given maximum rates in various areas with an overall maximum of 65 miles per hour. This maximum rate was determined by a kind of balancing of the interest in safety against the interest in expeditious travel, but the balancing occurred not on the ad hoc litigational level, but rather on the definitional level. The law now defined excessive speed and the courts were no longer called upon to weigh competing interests as presented by the facts in a given case. This was not without its disadvantages since, at least in theory, it meant that a particular driver who was preceeding at 67 miles per hour would be precluded from proving that in the given circumstances his speed was not excessive. But it was soon found that this lost privilege was more than compensated for by the fact that drivers who previously would have been deterred from safely driving at 55 miles per hour now were able to do so without fear of prosecution. It further meant that in speed case trials the courts were immunized from the pressures of the more hysterical or dogmatic segments of the community, since the rule to be applied required no further balancing, and hence no exercise of discretion which might be regarded as an undue coddling of subversive speeders.

The argument that ad hoc balancing is preferable to definitional balancing because the former permits a more sensitive appreciation of the equities in each particular case may be more easily made in non-speech areas where public passions do not generally ride as high. But even this may prove too much. It may be that if there were no legal rules but only beneficent judges, justice would be done more often. But if the ideal of a system of laws rather than men is not wholly attainable, that does not mean we should be ready to trade it for a system of men rather than laws.

One further objection might be advanced against definitional balancing of the first amendment. There is obviously nothing improper about a legislature engaging in definitional balancing in writing a law, as in the Autophobia example. But for a court to do this in applying the first amendment may be criticized as a form of judicial lawmaking, and as such a usurpation of the legislative function. The short answer to this argument lies in Marshall's overquoted but nevertheless pregnant maxim: ". . . we must never forget that it is a *constitution* we are expounding."[35] Students of the Constitution, activists and passivists alike, agree that not all speech can be regarded as "speech" protected by the first amendement. It follows, then, that if the first amendment is not to be regarded as incapable of application, someone must differentiate between that speech which is to be given constitutional protection and that which is not. And who may that "someone" be? Notwithstanding the recent erosion of the "political question" doctrine,[36] it remains true that some questions of constitutional interpretation and application remain in the exclusive domain of the legislative and executive branches. But where the question itself is a limitation on congressional power, as in the case of the first amendment, to conclude that such a question is for Congress and not for the Court to determine is to convert freedom of speech, "the matrix, the indispensable condition, of nearly every other

[35]McCulloch v. Maryland, 17 U.S. (4 Wheat.) 316, 407 (1819).
[36]*See* Baker v. Carr, 369 U.S. 186 (1962), and its progeny.

form of freedom"[37] into a legally meaningless exhortation. Chief Justice Marshall made the point in his most famous opinion:

> The powers of the legislature are defined and limited; and that those limits may not be mistaken or forgotten, the constitution is written. To what purpose are powers limited, and to what purpose is that limitation committed to writing, if these limits may, at any time, be passed by those intended to be restrained? The distinction between a government with limited and unlimited powers is abolished, if those limits do not confine the persons on whom they are imposed, and if acts prohibited and acts allowed are of equal obligation.[38]

Who, then, *but* the Court can undertake the task of giving reasonable meaning to the first amendment prohibition against congressional abridgment of "the freedom of speech"? If the Court is bound to enforce the first amendment and if such enforcement is possible in a reasonable manner only if protected speech is differentiated from unprotected speech, then it is not only proper but necessary for the Court to formulate a rule which accomplishes such differentiation. Moreover, ad hoc balancing by the Court (at least if there is not an uncritical deference to the legislative judgment) involves no less judicial legislation than does definitional balancing. It is true that the first amendment does not explicitly provide that defamatory statements are not to be protected if knowingly false or recklessly made. But neither does the first amendment by its terms exclude from protection that speech which upon balancing is found to weigh less than the demands of competing interests.

II

APPLICATION OF THE THEORY TO LIBEL

Even if definitional balancing is an approach which commends itself, it carries no assurance that the balance reached in connection with any particular aspect of speech will be properly drawn.[39] This brings into focus the precise balance drawn by the Court in *Times*. The Court might have gone along with the Black and Douglas concurrence, holding that all defamatory statements are protected by the first amendment. This is the absolutist position, and while I have argued above that no one can or should take the position that all speech under all circumstances is

[37] Palko v. Connecticut, 302 U.S. 319, 327 (1937).

[38] Marbury v. Madison, 5 U.S. (1 Cranch) 137, 176 (1803).

[39] The Court's decision in Roth v. United States, 354 U.S. 476 (1957), was in effect an exercise in definitional balancing. One may agree with the method and still believe that the Court was wrong in drawing that definitional line in such manner as to completely exclude the "obscene" from first amendment protection. *See* Nimmer, *The Constitutionality of Official Censorship of Motion Pictures*, 25 U. CHI. L. REV. 625, 652-55 (1958).

immunized, it is certainly tenable to take the absolutist position with respect to abridgments based on the defamatory content of speech. At the other extreme, the Court might have taken the position, suggested in the dicta of earlier cases,[40] that defamation is entirely outside the protection of the first amendment. Instead the Court held that all defamatory speech directed at public officials is within the orbit of first amendment protection except that speech which is knowingly false or which is made with reckless disregard of its truth or falsity. Why did the Court strike this particular balance? Since the *Times* decision was not explicitly based upon a balancing of interests, the Court's opinion is not very helpful in articulating the precise basis for the balance reached. But from portions of the opinion in *Times*, as well as the opinions in later cases applying the doctrine,[41] enough can be gleaned to permit an extrapolation of the Court's rationale. Such a rationale does, I submit, justify the definitional balance adopted by the Court.

In weighing the competing interests of speech and reputation, it is well to recall first some of the reasons why freedom of speech is important. Mr. Justice Brandeis in his concurring opinion in *Whitney* v. *California*[42] suggested three separate reasons: First, free speech is a necessary concomitant of a democratic society. We cannot intelligently make the decisions required of a self-governing people unless we are permitted to hear all possible views bearing upon such decisions.[43] Second, quite apart from its utility in the democratic process, freedom of expression is an end in itself. Self-expression is a part of self-fulfillment, or as Justice Brandeis suggested, liberty is "the secret of happiness."[44] Third, freedom of speech is a necessary safety valve. Those who are not permitted to express themselves in words are more likely to seek expression in violent deeds.[45] There may be other justifications for freedom of expression, but these are sufficient for our purposes.

Competing with these speech values is society's interest in protecting reputations from injury by false statements. Though it is intangible, this injury can be no less real than the injury from physical attack. The evil of defamation is self-evident, and tort protection here requires no greater theoretical justification than does tort protection against assault and battery, and other attacks upon the person.[46]

[40] *See* cases cited note 25 *supra*.

[41] Garrison v. Louisiana, 379 U.S. 64 (1964); Rosenblatt v. Baer, 383 U.S. 75 (1966); Curtis Pub. Co. v. Butts, 388 U.S. 130 (1967).

[42] 274 U.S. 357, 372-80 (1927).

[43] *See id.* at 375-76.

[44] *See id.* at 375.

[45] *See id.*

[46] "The right of a man to the protection of his own reputation from unjustified invasion and

With these two competing interests in view, the threshold question must be whether the speech values justify the Court in sweeping away most of the law of defamation where the statement is made against a public figure. The injury to reputation which results from defamation is no less by reason of the speaker's belief in the truth of the false statements uttered. Yet, *Times* holds that defamatory statements are protected speech notwithstanding the resulting injury. I submit that the Court was correct in according greater weight to the interest in protecting good faith but erroneous speech than it did to the interest in protecting reputations.

The particular balancing can be defended on several grounds: First, the content of the public dialogue on issues vital to the democratic process should not be limited by what a jury decides is true. Ordinarily we are content to rely upon a jury's findings of fact for the purpose of determining rights as between immediate litigants. But when the "fact" to be determined relates to the truth or falsity of speech, it is not only the immediate litigants that are concerned. All of society has an interest in hearing and evaluating the speech. What twelve men believe to be false, millions of others may believe to be true, and they should not be precluded by the twelve from making their own independent evaluation of truth. Second, speech which society may vitally need to hear may be deterred by the fear that a jury will find it to be false even though in fact the fear may be ungrounded and the jury, if given the opportunity, would find it to be true. Third, assuming that the statement is objectively false, if the speaker in good faith believes it to be true, then at least two of the three speech values suggested above nevertheless remain applicable. These are the interest in self-expression and the safety valve factor. Fourth, the cure for good faith reputation injury, like the cure for other evils arising from erroneous speech, should be found not in repressing the speech, but in answering it. As Mr. Justice Brandeis concluded in *Whitney*: "[T]he remedy to be applied is more speech, not enforced silence."[47] It is true that the refutation of infamy at times may not have the same impact as the charge of infamy, but isn't that merely a special application of the general risk we are willing to assume when we put our faith in the free and unfettered exchange of ideas? Is it less true here than elsewhere that "the best test of truth is the power of the thought to get itself accepted in the competition of the market?"[48] This is

wrongful hurt reflects no more than our basic concept of the essential dignity and worth of every human being—a concept at the root of any decent system of ordered liberty." Mr. Justice Stewart, concurring in Rosenblatt v. Baer, 383 U.S. 75, 92 (1966).

[47] Whitney v. California, 274 U.S. 357, 377 (1927) (concurring opinion).

[48] Abrams v. United States, 250 U.S. 616, 630 (1919) (dissenting opinion of Holmes, J.).

not to say that a real injury to reputation may not occur, but only that the evil, serious as it may be, is less than the injury to society generally from the suppression of good faith speech.

But if this reasoning is acceptable, it may be argued that no defamatory utterance should be held outside the protection of the first amendment. The Court in *Times* did not go this far. It found the balance of interests to weigh in favor of reputation and against speech when the speech is knowingly false, or made with reckless disregard of truth. Can this further balancing in the opposite direction also be defended? I believe that it can. In striking this new balance consider first the evil of injury to reputation. That evil at least remains constant; it is no less serious when balanced against speech which is held to be knowingly false than it is when balanced against speech held to have been made in good faith. But does the other side of the balance, the interest in free speech, continue to have a greater weight? It seems clear that the speech values suggested above are inapplicable to speech which the speaker knows to be false. A knowing lie hardly contributes to the democratic dialogue.[49] Quite the contrary, it distorts the collective search for truth. It is also hard to regard it as a necessary function of self-fulfillment. When I express ideas which I do not believe to be true, I am not in any real sense expressing my *self*, and abridgment of such expression is not an abridgment of self-fulfillment. Finally, the safety valve which is necessary for honestly believed, even though erroneous doctrine, is hardly necessary for that which is not truly believed. Men are not likely to resort to violence because they cannot express that which they do not believe.

But this does not answer the crucial objection made by the dissenters to the Court's exclusion of first amendment protection for the knowing and recklessly false. Their fear is that even if one speaks with a good faith belief in the truth of his speech, a jury may find that the statement was made with knowledge of its falsity or with reckless disregard of its truth or falsity, and more importantly, that many persons will be deterred from expressing themselves in good faith from the fear that a jury *might* make such a finding.

These are cogent objections which certainly bear weight, but, I would suggest, considerably lesser weight than the same concerns in connection with our original ad hoc balancing of speech against reputation. It is certainly possible that a jury will incorrectly find that a

[49]"For the use of the known lie as a tool is at once at odds with the premises of democratic government and with the orderly manner in which economic, social, or political change is to be effected." Garrison v. Louisiana, 379 U.S. 64, 75 (1964). *But see* New York Times Co. v. Sullivan,

statement was made without belief in its truth, or in reckless disregard of truth when in fact the speaker acted in a good faith belief. But the issue before the jury will not be the broad question of the truth or falsity of the defamatory statement, but rather the narrow question of the speaker's good faith. A jury will probably not go wrong on this narrow question of fact in view of the Court's statement in *Times* that the Constitution demands a standard of "convincing clarity"[50] in the proof of knowing or reckless falsity. Moreover, the burden of proof on this narrow issue makes it increasingly likely that an appellate court will reverse jury determinations against the speaker when the standard of convincing clarity has not been met. Such appellate reversal will be far easier to obtain than if the only question were whether there was evidence by which the jury might have reasonably concluded that the statement itself was false. Finally, the deterrent effect of the risk that a jury might find that the speaker acted without an honest belief in what he said is probably not great. Remember that the issue is not whether the speaker had a reasonable belief, but only whether he had an honest, good faith belief. It seems likely that most people who do in good faith believe what they say would be willing to risk the possibility of an adverse court determination on the narrow issue of their good faith even if they would not be willing to risk a legal determination of the truth of their statement. Confirmation of this may be found in other related fields. In copyright, for example, it is my experience that one who believes that another has infringed his copyright does not hesitate to openly accuse the other of infringement even though there is some risk of liability for slander of title or disparagement if the court finds both that there was no infringement *and* that the accusation of infringement was made in bad faith.[51]

The foregoing considerations suggest that the injury to the interest in freedom of speech is measurably reduced when there is abridgment only of defamatory speech which is knowingly false or recklessly made rather than abridgment of all defamatory speech.

For me the conclusive demonstration that in this more limited context the interest in reputation outweighs the interest in speech is the weakness of the alternative. It is true that some impairment of speech values remains even if we abridge only knowingly false or reckless

376 U.S. 254, 279 n.19 (1964), where the Court quotes John Stuart Mill: "Even a false statement may be deemed to make a valuable contribution to public debate, since it brings about 'the clearer perception and livelier impression of truth, produced by its collision with error,'" J. MILL, ON LIBERTY 15 (Oxford ed. 1947).

[50] 376 U.S. at 285-86.

[51] *See* M. NIMMER, COPYRIGHT § 110.6 (1968).

defamation. But consider the consequences of adopting the Black-Douglas view[52] that all defamation is protected under the first amendment. Under such a rule it is obvious that the interest in reputation would suffer greatly, if not be completely obliterated. But would we at least have a concomitant increase in the protection of speech values? Is it not clear that the contrary would be the case? Not only would the interest in reputation suffer, but the interest in speech itself would also suffer grave impairment. Remember that one of the chief reasons we value free speech is because of its central position in maintaining a democratic dialogue so necessary to an enlightened electorate.[53] Under a rule which immunized *all* defamation, reputation assassins could make with impunity and with utter disregard of the consequences completely irresponsible and monstrous accusations against anyone unfortunate enough to cross their path. Apart from the havoc this would wreak to reputations, what would it do to the democratic dialogue, one of the prime reasons for maintaining free speech? If there were no limits as to what might be said against a candidate for office, if accusations no matter how reckless and unfounded could be made with impunity, could we hope to preserve any rationality in our electoral processes? We might still hope that speech would answer speech; but if the basic values of free speech are inapplicable at this point, as indicated above, was not the Court wise to draw the line to save us from a blood bath of character assassination?

A final aspect of the Court's balancing in *Times* that must be considered is the limitation of first amendment immunity to defamatory statements concerning "public officials." Recently, in *Curtis Publishing Company v. Butts*,[54] the Court has gone further and extended such immunity to statements concerning "public figures" regardless of whether such persons are governmental officals.[55] Although admittedly something of a departure from the rationale relied upon the Court in *Times*,[56] the *Curtis* extension to persons who are public figures but not public of-

[52]*See* New York Times Co. v. Sullivan, 376 U.S. 254, 293 (1964) (concurring opinion).

[53]For general discussion of the purpose of the first amendment see A. MEIKELJOHN, POLITICAL FREEDOM: THE CONSTITUTIONAL POWERS OF THE PEOPLE (1960); Emerson, *Toward a General Theory of the First Amendment*, 72 YALE L.J. 877, 878-86 (1963); Kalven, *The New York Times Case: A Note on "The Central Meaning of the First Amendment,"* 1964 SUPREME COURT REV. 191 (1964).

[54]388 U.S. 130 (1967). This opinion combined the decisions in *Curtis* and in *Associated Press v. Walker*.

[55]Four members of the Court (Justices Harlan, Clark, Stewart, and Fortas) would have applied a different rule as to a public figure who is not a public official, under which such persons could recover in a libel action only upon a showing that the defendant had engaged in "highly unreasonable conduct constituting an extreme departure from the standards of investigation and

ficials is certainly consonant with the fundamental objectives of the first amendment. Those objectives require full and free discussion of public issues. Since discussion of public issues cannot be meaningful without reference to the men involved on both sides of such issues, and since such men will not necessarily be public officials,[57] one cannot but agree that the Court was right in *Curtis* to extend the *Times* rule to all public figures. Here again the Court has engaged in implicit balancing.

It may be argued that the Court did not go far enough in that apparently it would not invoke the first amendment to immunize defamatory statements concerning nonpublic figures in the context of a discussion of issues of legitimate public interest.[58] If the touchstone of first amendment rights is the promotion of uninhibited discussion of public issues, then shouldn't such discussion be protected even if the persons involved are in no sense public figures?[59] I would suggest that the Court was correct in implying that at this point the reputation interest

reporting ordinarily adhered to by responsible publishers." *Id.* at 155. Chief Justice Warren in a concurring opinion applied the *Times* standard without modification to public figures who are not public officials, expressing doubt that the standard suggested by Justice Harlan, "based on such an unusual and uncertain formulation could either guide a jury of laymen or afford protection for speech and debate . . . ."*Id.* at 163. Justices Brennan and White joined in this portion of the Warren opinion, and Justices Black and Douglas concurred in the "grounds and reason stated" in this portion of the Chief's opinion, but only "in order for the Court to be able at this time to agree on [an opinion]. . . ." Id. at 170. This appears to mean that five of the Justices would, insofar as they would apply the *Times* standard at all, apply it without distinction between public officials and public figures who are not public officials.

[56]The *Times* opinion rested at least in part upon an analogy to the doctrine in Barr v. Matteo, 360 U.S. 564, 575 (1959), where statements of a federal official were found to be absolutely priviledged if made "within the outer perimeter of his duties." *See* New York Times Co. v. Sullivan, 376 U.S. at 282 (1964). This rationale was also used in Washington Post Co. v. Keogh, 365 F.2d 965, 968 (D.C. Cir. 1966).

[57]*See* Curtis Pub. Co. v. Butts, 388 U.S. 130, 164 (1967) (concurring opinion of Warren, C.J.): ". . . many who do not hold public office at the moment are nevertheless intimately involved in the resolution of important public questions or, by reason of their fame, shape events in areas of concern to society at large."

[58]As to the converse situation, i.e., a defamatory statement directed against the private conduct of a public official, Mr. Justice Douglas would apparently part company from Mr. Justice Black, and hold the first amendment does not prohibit liability in a libel action in such circumstances. *See* the concurring opinion of Mr. Justice Goldberg joined by Mr. Justice Douglas in *Times*, 376 U.S. at 301. The *Times* decision has been so understood by lower courts. *See, e.g.*, People v. Mager, 25 App. Div. 2d 363, 269 N.Y.S.2d 848 (1966). It is possible that the Supreme Court might not go this far in limiting first amendment protection since it was deemed appropriate in Garrison v. Louisiana, 379 U.S. 64, 72 n.8 (1964) to state that as to "purely private libels" involving presumably both private issues and nonpublic figures, "nothing we say today is to be taken as intimating any views as to the impact of the constitutional guarantees . . . ." *But see* authority cited note 56 *infra*.

[59]"Yet if free discussion of public issues is the guide, I see no way to draw lines that exclude . . . anyone on the public payroll. . . . And [how about] industrialists who raise the price of a basic commodity? . . . And the labor leader who combines trade unionism with bribery and racketeering? . . . The question is whether a public *issue*, not a public official is involved." Rosenblatt v. Baer, 383 U.S. 89, 91 (1966) (concurring opinion of Douglas, J.).

outweighs the speech interest. To take a rigidly libertarian position and fault the Court for not extending defamation immunity to all discussion of public issues would be to overlook a fundamental ingredient of first amendment theory. The Brandeis prescription for meeting error with "more speech," and Justice Holmes "best test of truth" are grounded upon the presupposition of a free market place of ideas. If and to the extent speech cannot be answered with speech, the theory breaks down. Because " ' public figures' have as ready access as 'public officials' to mass media of communication, both to influence policy and to counter criticism of their views and activities"[60] the Court was justified in extending first amendment immunity to all public figures. But persons who have not achieved the celebrity of a public figure may not have access to the mass media to answer defamatory statements made against them. For this reason the speech interest at this point bears a lesser weight and may properly be subordinated to the reputation interest.[61]

It is important, however, not to use this reasoning to prove too much. Some would argue that in the present semimonopolistic posture of the news and information media, the presupposition of a free market place of ideas has become totally obsolete. One can agree that only if the monopolistic controls presently extant in newspapers and broadcasting are countered by devices for insuring the dissemination of minority views will the full values which underlie the first amendment be realized,[62] but this does not justify the withdrawal of first amendment immunity from public discussion because such devices are absent. Nevertheless, where the absence of the ability to mount an effective reply coincides with a strong antispeech interest, such as the interest in reputation, the resulting balance of interests may properly be weighed against the right to speak. It is to be hoped that the *Curtis* extension of *Times* will not be followed by a further extension of first amendment immunity to defamatory statements concerning "private" persons involved in public issues.

[60]Curtis Pub. Co. v. Butts, 388 U.S. 130, 164 (1967) (concurring opinion of Warren, C.J.).

[61]In Rosenblatt v. Baer, 383 U.S. 75, 86 n.13 (1966), the Court denied that the *Times* rule would be applicable to a night watchman accused of stealing state secrets since this "would virtually disregard society's interest in protecting reputation. The employee's position must be one which would invite public scrutiny and discussion of the person holding it, entirely apart from the scrutiny and discussion occasioned by the particular charges in controversy." Can this statement be reconciled with the immediately preceding footnote where the Court stated: "We intimate no view whatever whether there are other bases for applying the *New York Times* standards—for example, that in a particular case the interests in reputation are relatively insubstantial, because the subject of discussion has thrust himself into the vortex of the discussion of a question of pressing public concern?" *Id.* at 86 n.12. Did the hypothetical night watchman "thrust himself into the vortex" by being present at a time when state secrets were stolen?

[62]*See* Barron, *Access to the Press—A New First Amendment Right*, 80 HARV. L. REV. 1641 (1967).

III

MISAPPLICATION OF THE THEORY TO PRIVACY

In *Time, Incorporated v. Hill*[63] the Supreme Court for the first time explored the conflicting demands of the first amendment and the right of privacy. James Hill and his family had been held captive in their own home by escaped convicts. Subsequently one Joseph Hayes wrote a novel based upon such a situation. He later adapted the novel to play and motion picture form. Neither the novel, the play, nor the motion picture identified the Hill family as the participants in the harrowing incident. Dependant Time's *Life* magazine did, however, identify the Hill family as the real life counterparts of the Hayes characters. Hill sued for invasion of his right of privacy under New York statute.[64] He alleged *inter alia* that some of the facts contained in the Hayes play were untrue. The jury awarded Hill $50,000 compensatory and $25,000 punitive damages.[65] The appellate division of the New York supreme court sustained the jury verdict of liability but ordered a new trial as to damages.[66] In the second trial Hill was awarded $30,000 compensatory damages without punitive damages. The New York Court of Appeals affirmed,[67] and the U. S. Supreme Court noted probable jurisdiction[68] "to consider the important constitutional questions of freedom of speech and press involved."[69] The Supreme Court ultimately reversed and remanded on the ground that the jury instructions were erroneous in that they did not require that liability be predicated on a finding that the statements at issue were made with knowledge of their falsity or in reckless disregard of the truth.[70] Thus to resolve the first confrontation between privacy and free speech the Court chose to apply what is essentially[71] the *New York Times* doctrine to invasions of privacy.[72]

Was the Court right in drawing the definitional balance line for privacy in approximately the same place that it drew the line for

[63]385 U.S. 374 (1967).

[64]N.Y. CIV. RIGHTS §§ 50-51 (McKinney 1948).

[65]385 U.S. at 379.

[66]Hill v. Hayes, 18 App. Div. 2d 485, 240 N.Y.S.2d 286 (1963).

[67]Hill v. Hayes, 15 N.Y.2d 986, 207 N.E.2d 604, 260 N.Y.S.2d 7 (1965).

[68]Time, Inc. v. Hill, 382 U.S. 936 (1965).

[69]385 U.S. at 380.

[70]*Id.* at 395-96.

[71]But first amendment immunity for privacy-invading statements under *Time* is more extensive than such immunity for defamatory statements under *Times* since the former applies regardless of whether the subject of such statements is a public figure. See note 50 *supra* and accompanying text.

[72]The Court in *Time* carefully explained that it there applied "the standard of knowing or reckless falsehood not through blind application of *New York Times Co. v. Sullivan*, relating solely to libel actions by public officials, but only upon consideration of the factors which arise in the

defamation? I think the Court was in error, and that the error derives from the superficial similarity between defamation and the particular form of privacy invasion presented by the *Time* case.

It is necessary to recall first Dean Prosser's recent but already classic categorization of the four types of privacy cases. He lists these as:

> 1. Intrusion upon the plaintiff's seclusion or solitude, or into his private affairs.
> 2. Public disclosure of embarrasing private facts about the plaintiff.
> 3. Publicity which places the plaintiff in a false light in the public eye.
> 4. Appropriation, for the defendant's advantage, of the plaintiff's name or likeness.[73]

We may put to one side those forms of privacy invasion which Dean Prosser labels as "intrusion" and "appropriation." Intrusion does not raise first amendment difficulties since its perpetration does not involve speech or other expression. It occurs by virtue of the physical or mechanical observation of the private affairs of another,[74] and not by the publication[75] of such observations. The appropriation form of privacy invasion probably also does not raise first amendment problems, although here speech and other expression is involved. This right, sometimes called the right of publicity,[76] involves the commercial appropriation of values which, whether or not labeled as "property,"[77]

particular context of the application of the New York statute in cases involving private individuals . . . . [A]lthough the First Amendment principles pronounced in *New York Times* guide our conclusion, we reach that conclusion only by applying these principles in this discrete context." 385 U.S. at 390-91.

[73] Prosser, *Privacy*, 48 CALIF. L. REV. 383, 389 (1960). Essentially the same categorization is to be found in W. PROSSER, HANDBOOK OF THE LAW OF TORTS § 112, at 832-44 (3d ed. 1964), and in RESTATEMENT (SECOND) OF TORTS § 652A (Tent. Draft No. 13, 1967), for which Dean Prosser was the Reporter. The considerable number of cases which have adopted the Prosser categorization are collected in Bloustein, *Privacy as An Aspect of Human Dignity: An Answer to Dean Prosser*, 39 N.Y.U.L. REV. 962, 964 n.10 (1964), and in Wade, *Defamation and the Right of Privacy*, 15 VAND. L. REV. 1093, 1095 n.13 (1962).

This is not the place to explore the substantive differences between the right of privacy as developed at common law and under the New York statute. Such differences, however, are not as great as is sometimes assumed. *See* Spahn v. Julian Messner, Inc., 43 Misc. 2d 219, 250 N.Y.S.2d 529 (Sup. Ct. 1964), *aff'd*, 23 App. Div. 2d 216, 260 N.Y.S.2d 451 (1965), *aff'd*, 18 N.Y.2d 234, 221 N.E.2d 543, 274 N.Y.S.2d 877 (1966), *vacated and remanded*, 387 U.S. 239 (1967). For the purpose of delineating the line between the interest in privacy and that in free speech it is not necessary to dwell upon such substantive differences as exist.

[74] *See* RESTATEMENT (SECOND) OF TORTS, § 652B, comment *b* at 103 (Tent. Draft No. 13, 1967).

[75] *Id.* comment *a*.

[76] *See* Nimmer, *The Right of Publicity*, 19 LAW & CONTEMP. PROB. 203 (1954). The Restatement refers to this form of invasion of privacy as a right of publicity when claimed by a third party assignee of the person depicted. *See* RESTATEMENT (SECOND) OF TORTS 652C, comment *a* at 108 (Tent. Draft No. 13, 1967).

[77] *See* Nimmer, *supra* note 69, at 216; RESTATEMENT (SECOND) OF TORTS, § 652C, comment *a* at 108 (Tent. Draft No. 13, 1967).

may not be freely plundered under the banner of the first amendment.[78] The difficult first amendment questions in the privacy area are found only when a publication comes under either the "public disclosure of embarrassing private facts" or "false light" labels.

The Court in *Time* emphasized that it was dealing only with a false light type case, and that it was not deciding the question of constitutional sanction for truthful publication of matters " 'so intimate and so unwarranted in view of the victim's position as to outrage the community's notions of decency.' "[79] But the first amendment implications of the false light privacy cases cannot be understood standing alone. There must first be an understanding of the proper weight to be accorded the right of free speech as applied to the type of privacy case with which the Court said it was not dealing, that which involves questions of the public disclosure of embarrassing private facts. It is necessary to understand the manner in which the interest to be protected in such cases differs from the interest to be protected by the defamation torts.

The crucial distinction between privacy and defamation when private facts are disclosed relates to the markedly different interests that are to be protected by the right of privacy on the one hand, and defamation on the other. No defamation action would lie by reason of the publication of embarrassing private facts in view of the defense of truth. Defamation protects a man's interest in his reputation. Reputation is by definition a matter of public knowledge. Injury in a defamation action arises not by the act of bringing an alleged fact to public knowledge, but by the effect on a person's reputation which results from the disclosure of such fact. The right of privacy protects not reputation, but the interest in maintaining the privacy of certain facts. Public disclosure of such facts can create injury regardless of whether such disclosure affects the subject's reputation. The injury is to man's interest in maintaining a haven from society's searching eye.[80] Professor

[78] *See* Valentine v. Chrestensen, 316 U.S. 52 (1942), and the Court's statements distinguishing *Valentine* in New York Times Co. v. Sullivan, 376 U.S. 254, 265 (1964) and in Time, Inc. v. Hill, 385 U.S. 374, 405 (1967). *See also* RESTATEMENT (SECOND) OF TORTS, § 652F, comments *a* and *k* at 127, 134 (Tent. Draft No. 13, 1967).

[79] 385 U.S. at 383 n.7 *quoting* Sidis v. F-R Pub. Corp., 113 F.2d 806, 809 (2d Cir. 1940), *cert. denied*, 311 U.S. 711 (1940).

[80] This concept has been a recurring one. Judge Cooley spoke of the right "to be left alone," T. COOLEY, A TREATISE ON THE LAW OF TORTS 29 (2d ed. 1888). Consider, however, the explication of the Cooley phrase in Konvitz, *Privacy and the Law: A Philosophical Prelude*, 31 LAW & CONTEMP. PROB. 272, 279 (1966). Warren and Brandeis in their seminal article found that a necessary concomitant of the interest in an "inviolate personality" was the right of an individual to determine "to what extent his thoughts, sentiments, and emotions shall be communicated to others." Warren & Brandeis, *The Right to Privacy*, 4 HARV. L. REV. 193, 198 (1890). Some years later Mr. Justice Brandeis in his dissent to Olmstead v. United States, 277 U.S. 438, 478 (1928) returned to the same

Bloustein in a thoughtful article has stated the distinction well: "The gravamen of a defamation action is engendering a false opinion about a person, whether in the mind of one other person or many people. The gravamen in the public disclosure [privacy] cases is degrading a person by laying his life open to public view."[81]

Granting this distinction, how does it bear upon whether the first amendment definitional balance applied in defamation actions should be found applicable in privacy actions?[82] Prima facie it might be argued that greater first amendment protection should be afforded to privacy-invading publications than to defamatory publications, since the right of privacy (at least when dealing with the public disclosure of private facts) deals with matters admittedly true while defamation involves matters found to be false. Truth, it may be argued, deserves greater freedom than falsity. But this overly facile approach will not bear analysis. For the reasons set forth below, I would suggest that the privacy definitional balance should give a lesser scope to the first amendment privilege than is recognized under the *Times* definitional balance for defamation.

theme: "The makers of our Constitution undertook to secure conditions favorable to the pursuit of happiness. They recognized the significance of man's spiritual nature, of his feeling and of his intellect. . . . They sought to protect Americans in their beliefs, their thoughts, their emotions and their sensations. They conferred as against the Government, the right to be let alone—the most comprehensive of rights and the right most valued by civilized men." A variation of the theme recently reached fruition in Griswold v. Connecticut, 381 U.S. 479 (1965), although in the context of a constitutional shield essentially unrelated to the tort action sword here under scrutiny.

[81]Bloustein, *supra* note 67, at 981. *See also* Warren and Brandeis, *supra* note 73, at 197: "The principle on which the law of defamation rests, covers, however, a radically different class of effects from those for which attention is now asked. It deals only with damage to reputation, with the injury done to the individual in his external relations to the community, by lowering him in the estimation of his fellows. The matter published . . . must, in order to be actionable, have a direct tendency to injure him in his intercourse with others . . . the effect of the publication upon his estimate of himself and upon his own feelings not forming an essential element in the cause of action."

A number of cases have recognized the distinction between the interests to be protected by the right of privacy and the tort of defamation. *See, e.g.*, Themo v. New England Newspaper Pub. Co., 306 Mass. 54, 57, 27 N.E.2d 753, 755 (1940): "The fundamental difference between a right of privacy and a right to freedom from defamation is that the former directly concerns one's own peace of mind, while the latter concerns primarily one's reputation . . . ." *Accord*, Reed v. Real Detective Pub. Co., 63 Ariz. 294, 306, 162 P.2d 133, 139 (1945); Kelly v. Johnson Pub. Co., 160 Cal. App. 2d 718, 721, 325 P.2d 659, 661 (1958); Fairfield v. American Photocopy Equip. Co., 138 Cal. App. 2d 82, 86, 291 P.2d 194, 197 (1955); Continental Optical Co. v. Reed, 119 Ind. App. 643, 647-48, 86 N.E.2d 306, 308 (1949); Brink v. Griffith, 65 Wash. 2d 253, 255, 396 P.2d 793, 796 (1964).

[82]For reasons previously stated, see text following note 15 *supra*, it is desirable that some form of definitional balance be applied in privacy actions rather than the ad hoc balancing approach suggested in some privacy cases, *e.g.*, Barber v. Time, Inc., 348 Mo. 1199, 1206-07, 159 S.W.2d 291, 295 (1942): "Thus, establishing conditions of liability for invasion of the right of privacy is a matter of harmonizing individual rights with community and social interest. . . . It is for the court to say first whether the occasion or incident is one of proper public interest."

Indeed, with some diffidence, and subject to qualifications set forth below, I would go so far as to deny completely the application of the first amendment privilege to the public disclosure of embarrassing private facts.

I make two important qualifications to the foregoing thesis. First, I intend to deal here only with the public disclosure of embarrassing *private* facts, that is, with facts which but for the defendant's disclosure would not have been known to members of the public. Some privacy cases go beyond this limitation in that the defendant incurs liability by disclosing to a larger segment of the public that which was already known to some smaller public segment.[83] For our present purposes it is irrelevant whether as a matter of tort law this is or is not a desirable extension of the tort right of privacy. The point here is that the suggested exclusion of the first amendment from privacy cases goes only to those cases in which truly private matters are revealed. If a particular speech does not deal with private matters, then however one might characterize the interest which competes with the right of free speech, it seems obvious that it is not an interest in privacy.[84]

The second important qualification I make is that the public disclosure of an *embarrassing* private fact should be without first amendment protection only if the disclosure is embarrassing but not defamatory. If a disclosure adversely affects the subject's reputation, then the policy reasons which support the right of speech when reputations are attacked[85] outweigh the privacy considerations.

Notwithstanding these qualifications, there remains a significant privacy area having to do with truly private facts,[86] the disclosure of which, although noninjurious to the subject's reputation, is nevertheless

[83] *E.g.*, Strickler v. National Broadcasting Co., 167 F. Supp. 68 (S.D. Cal. 1958); Daily Times Democrat v. Graham, 276 Ala. 380, 162 So. 2d 474 (1964); Cason v. Baskin, 159 Fla. 31, 30 So. 2d 635 (1947); Gautier v. Pro-Football, Inc., 304 N.Y. 354, 360, 107 N.E.2d 485, 489 (1952): "So, one attending a public event such as a professional football game. . . . may be [televised] as part of the general audience, but may not be picked out of a crowd alone, thrust upon the screen and unduly featured for public view." But Prosser states that a privacy action will not lie unless the facts disclosed to the public are private, not theretofore publicly known nor matters of public record. W. PROSSER, HANDBOOK OF THE LAW OF TORTS § 112, at 836 (3d ed. 1964). *See also* Kalven, *Privacy in Tort Law—Were Warren and Brandeis Wrong?*, 31 LAW & CONTEMP. PROB. 326, 333 (1966).

[84] One may speak of a protectible interest in personality, or in human dignity, or in individuality, but though such phrases may have some utility in shaping tort law, they are not capable of constituting well-defined interests which can usefully counter the interest in free speech in striking a definitional balance.

[85] See Section II *supra* and text accompanying notes 90-92 *infra*.

[86] "Private facts" are not necessarily facts known only to the subject himself. They are facts which, though known to the immediate participants, are unknown to any substantial number of casual observers, *i.e.*, to the "public."

highly embarrassing or otherwise offensive to the subject.[87] The thesis here suggested is that there are greater speech values in a reputation-injuring statement than in a nondefamatory (or "pure") privacy-invading statement; consequently the definitional balance should more severely restrict speech in the case of the pure privacy-invading statement than in the case of defamation.

Where the injury is to reputation, the important consideration is the underlying rationale that the cure for injury due to speech should not be abridgment of that speech but rather "more speech."[88] Reputations which can be injured by false statements can be rehabilitated by further speech which establishes the truth.[89] But this rationale does not apply to invasions of privacy; when publication invades privacy the injury arises from the mere fact of publication, and further speech cannot remedy the injury. Suppose that a nude photograph of a young lady is surreptitiously obtained and published in a newspaper or magazine.[90] Assume further that the publication in no way imputes the cooperation of the young lady in making or publishing the photograph, so that no element of defamation exists. The young lady's privacy injury arises from the mere fact of publication. No amount of further speech can cure the injury—the indignity and humiliation which arose from the initial publication. The fact is that unlike injury arising from defamation, "more speech" is irrelevant in mitigating the injury due to an invasion of privacy.

Moreover, while it has been argued above that the basic rationale for speech justifies first amendment immunity for defamatory

[87]Plaintiff recovered, or the cause of action was recognized, in the following privacy cases: *Mau v. Rio Grande Oil, Inc.*, 28 F. Supp. 845 (N.D. Cal. 1939) (plaintiff, an innocent victim of robbery and shooting, depicted on a radio program which reenacted the events); *Bazemore v. Savannah Hospital*, 171 Ga. 257, 155 S.E. 194 (1930) (publication of nude photographs of plaintiff's malformed child taken in defendant's hospital); *McAndrews v. Roy*, 131 So.2d 256 (La. Ct. App. 1961) (plaintiff undertook treatment at defendant's health studio, and defendant thereafter published "before and after" photographs of plaintiff); *Barber v. Time, Inc.*, 348 Mo. 1199, 159 S.W.2d 291 (1942) (publication of photograph of plaintiff in bed while under hospital treatment for a rare noncontagious ailment, together with an accompanying article identifying plaintiff by name); *Griffin v. Medical Soc.*, 11 N.Y.S.2d 109 (Sup. Ct. 1939) (publication of plaintiff's photographs made by his physicians before and after treatment); *see Feeney v. Young*, 191 App. Div. 510, 181 N.Y.S. 481 (1920) (plaintiff permitted motion picture film to be made of her giving birth under a cesarean section operation, but only for the purpose of exhibiting the film to medical societies. Upon public exhibition of the film, held that testimony as to the content of the film should have been admissible, contrary to the ruling below.)

[88]See note 47 *supra* and accompanying text.

[89]See, however, text at notes 54-57 *supra*.

[90]For similar but not identical facts, see Meyers v. U.S. Camera Pub. Corp., 9 Misc. 2d 765, 167 N.Y.S.2d 771 (City Ct. 1957); Myers v. Afro-American Pub. Co., 168 Misc. 429, 5 N.Y.S.2d 223 (Sup. Ct. 1938), *aff'd mem.*, 225 App. Div. 838, 7 N.Y.S.2d 662 (1938) (libel action). The two nude plaintiffs Myers were not the same person.

statements,[91] this same rationale does not justify immunizing privacy-invading speech. First, speech necessary for an effective and meaningful democratic dialogue by and large does not require references to the intimate activities of named individuals.[92] This is to be contrasted with defamation where a fruitful dialogue may often require references to named individuals that reflect adversely upon the reputations of such individuals. Second, to a society that values privacy, it is difficult to conclude that the right to invade another man's privacy is a necessary function of self-expression or fulfillment. Again this is to be contrasted with defamation where the right to attack another man's reputation may properly be thought of as a valid exercise of self-expression. Finally, the "safety-valve" function does not operate here as it does in the realm of defamation. To permit an attack on a man's reputation may forestall the resort to physical violence. It is to be doubted, however, that the ability to publicly expose intimate activities serves as a sublimation for physical force. This is admittedly a rough-hewn guess as to the psychological forces at work, but I think most readers will agree with the conclusion.

Now return to the *Time* decision in which the Court limited its holding to the false light privacy cases. Since these, like defamation and unlike the private facts disclosures, deal with false statements, was the Court justified in this context in reaching a definitional balance which approximates the defamation balance? The Court fell into error by reason of its failure to pierce the superficial similarity between false light invasion of privacy and defamation, and by its failure to formulate a doctrine which rationally relates the false light cases to the underlying interest in privacy. The heart of the problem of finding a conceptual base for the false light privacy cases lies in the erroneous assumption that the untrue representations in a false light case are necessarily defamatory (or reputation-injuring) in nature.

It is true that this assertion can be supported by some of the authorities. Dean Prosser has expressed the view that in the false light cases "[t]he interest protected is clearly that of reputation, with the same overtones of mental distress as in defamation,"[93] and Professor Kalven, in denying any rational conceptual base for the false light cases, has

[91]See section II *supra*.

[92]Remember that we do not here speak of reputation-injuring speech.

[93]Prosser, *Privacy*, 48 CALIF. L. REV. 383, 400 (1960). Dean Prosser does state earlier that the false light "need not necessarily be a defamatory one," *id.*, but in view of the statement quoted in the text, this must be understood as meaning that the false statement may be actionable although it does not meet all of the technical requirements for liability under the law of defamation. He later enlarges upon this point in expressing concern that the false light cases may be "capable of swallowing up and engulfing the whole law of public defamation . . . . If that turns out to be the case, it may well be asked, what of the numerous restrictions and limitations which have hedged defamation about

rhetorically asked: "If the statement is not offensive enough to the reasonable man to be defamatory, how does it become offensive enough to the reasonable man to be an invasion of privacy?"[94] If Dean Prosser and Professor Kalven are correct in concluding that the untrue statements in false light privacy cases are necessarily reputation injuring, then the *Time* decision was correct in finding the definitional balance for false light privacy actions to be essentially the same as that for defamation. If a false statement will not constitute a cause of action for libel, why should a plaintiff be able to circumvent the limitations built into the law of defamation by labeling his action one for invasion of privacy?[95]

But the underlying premise is wrong. An untrue statement may in the same way as a public disclosure of embarrassing private facts constitute an invasion of privacy without in any manner constituting an injury to the subject's reputation. Once the false light cases are understood as a logical, even a necessary, extension of the private facts cases, the fallacy of equating the false light cases to defamation actions becomes apparent. The injury to the plaintiff's peace of mind which results from the public disclosure of private facts may be just as real where that which is disclosed is not true. It would be absurd to hold that the publication of an intimate fact creates liability, but that the defendant is immunized from liability (though the injury to plaintiff's peace of mind is no less) if the intimate "fact" publicly disclosed turns out not to be true, thus putting a premium on falsehood. The sensibilities of the young lady whose nude photo is published would be no less offended if it turned out that her face were superimposed upon someone else's nude body. The resulting humiliation would have nothing to do with truth or falsity. The unwarranted disclosure of intimate "facts" is no less offensive and hence no less deserving of protection merely because such "facts" are not true.

It should follow, then, that those false light cases which if true would fall into the public disclosure of embarrassing private facts branch of privacy should be regarded as conceptually indistinguishable from the latter category. If, as argued above, first amendment immunity is not properly applicable to the latter, it likewise should not be applied to the

for many years, in the interest of freedom of the press and discouragement of trivial and extortionate claims? Are they of so little consequence that they may be circumvented in so casual and cavalier a fashion?" *Id.* at 401. *See also* RESTATEMENT (SECOND) OF TORTS § 652E, special note at 122 (Tent. Draft No. 13, 1967).

[94] Kalven, *Privacy in Tort Law—Were Warren and Brandeis Wrong?*, 31 LAW AND CONTEMP. PROB. 326, 340 (1966).

[95] See note 85 *supra*.

former. This conclusion must be subject to qualifications similar to those expressed with reference to the public disclosure of embarrassing private facts. If the untrue statements in a false light case are not as to matters which *if true* would be private, then the interest in privacy is by hypothesis nonexistent and therefore cannot counterbalance any opposing interest in free speech. Such a publication may nevertheless be offensive, and tortious under the law of privacy,[96] but the tort defense of newsworthiness may carry with it the force of first amendment privilege without being met by the countervailing force of the interest in privacy.[97]

Moreover, if a particular statement not only constitutes an invasion of privacy but also injures the subject's reputation and is therefore prima facie defamatory (subject to the defense of truth), then the *Times* definitional balance for defamation should be applicable. If the first amendment protects such defamatory statements, the right to make them may not be abridged under state law even if the state law gives a "privacy" rather than a "defamation" label to such abridgment. As

[96] *E.g.*, Strickler v. National Broadcasting Co., 167 F. Supp 68 (S.D. Cal. 1958) (plaintiff alleging false depiction on a television program of his conduct on a commercial airliner in praying, wearing a Hawaiian shirt rather than his Naval uniform, smoking, and failing to assist in an emergency landing, held to state a cause of action); Fairfield v. American Photocopy Equip. Co., 138 Cal. App. 2d 82, 291 P.2d 194 (1955) (plaintiff's name listed among "thousands of leading law firms" that use defendant's machines, when in fact the plaintiff had found the machine unsatisfactory and had returned it); Battaglia v. Adams, 164 So. 2d 195 (Fla. 1964) (Richard Nixon held to have a right to privacy to prevent unauthorized use of his name on the Florida presidential primary ballot); Spahn v. Julian Messner, Inc., 43 Misc. 2d 219, 250 N.Y.S.2d 529 (Sup. Ct. 1964), *aff'd*, 23 App. Div. 2d 216, 260 N.Y.S.2d 451 (1965), *aff'd*, 18 N.Y.2d 234, 221 N.E.2d 543, 274 N.Y.S.2d 877 (1966), *vacated and remanded*, 387 U.S. 239 (1967) ("embarrassing distortion" of the plaintiff's war record so as to make him out to be a wartime hero); Goldberg v. Ideal Pub. Corp., 210 N.Y.S.2d 938 (Sup. Ct. 1960) (views on sexual freedom falsely ascribed to the plaintiff, a rabbi).

[97] It is possible to argue that false light cases which do not deal with matters which if true would be private should have the same exemption from the first amendment as should false light cases where the statement if true would relate to private areas of conduct. If a nude photograph which is false in the sense that the plaintiff's face has been superimposed upon the nude body of another will constitute an invasion of privacy not subject to a first amendment privilege if the setting purports to be the privacy of the plaintiff's bedroom, should the defendant's liability be any less if the setting is falsely depicted as a busy downtown thoroughfare? Despite this seemingly arbitrary distinction, I would submit that the definitional balance should shift when that which is depicted purports to deal in matters open to the public, and that in such circumstances the rule adopted in *Times* as restated in *Time* may properly be applied. As with any definitional balance, this rule will produce certain fringe absurdities, such as that suggested above, but it is nevertheless necessary in order to preserve the necessary breathing space for press and speech. If a publication purports to relate to a private aspect of conduct, then regardless of whether it is true or false, the publisher is on notice that he is invading the privacy of another. But if the conduct allegedly occurred in public, then to make the publisher's liability under the law of *privacy* turn absolutely on whether the statement is true or false would be to inhibit publication of that which the publisher may in good faith believe to be both true and nonprivate, and thus to stifle much that may be of legitimate public interest. At this point, on balance it seems preferable to adopt the rule which vitiates the first amendment privilege only in the event of knowing falsity or reckless conduct.

"libel can claim no talismanic immunity from constitutional limitations,"[98] neither can the talisman of "privacy" vitiate the constitutional protection for speech values contained in defamatory speech, even if that same speech also invades privacy.[99] This may seem to lead to an odd result. That is, one may obtain judicial redress if a statement merely invades one's privacy, but if it goes farther and both invades privacy and is detrimental to reputation, then (at least if one is a public figure) he may be precluded by the first amendement from a judicial remedy. But such a result is not so odd as might at first appear. If a reputation-injuring statement contains speech values not to be found in a privacy-invading statement, those values remain even if the statement combines reputation injuring and privacy-invading elements. The defense of such values justifies weighing the definitional balance so as to afford first amendment protection where the speech combines both such elements.

The foregoing qualifications would not require first amendment protection for all false light privacy cases. Dean Prosser and Professor Kalven to the contrary, there are many false light cases in which there is no reputation interest to be protected, but only the interest in protecting against embarrassment and humiliation which results from the public disclosure of factually untrue, but purportedly private facts.[100] Indeed, *Time, Inc. v. Hill* is itself a case in point. The defendant falsely reported that in a private setting—within their own home—the son of the Hill family was " 'roughed up' by one of the convicts . . . the daughter [bit] the hand of a convict to make him drop a gun . . . and . . . the father [threw] his gun through the door after a 'brave try' to save his family [and was] foiled."[101] In fact the convicts had treated the Hill family courteously, had not molested them, and there had been no violence. The Hill family was indeed depicted in a false light, and in such a manner

[98]New York Times Co. v. Sullivan, 376 U.S. 254, 269 (1964).

[99]This is roughly analogous to the decisions in Sears, Roebuck & Co. v. Stiffel Co., 376 U.S. 225 (1964) and Compco Corp. v. Day-Brite Lighting, Inc., 376 U.S. 234 (1964) wherein the Court held that if a design may be freely appropriated under the federal patent and copyright laws, such appropriation may not be rendered actionable under the state law of unfair competition. *See generally* M. NIMMER, COPYRIGHT § 35 (1968).

[100]For example, in Spahn v. Julian Messner, Inc., 43 Misc. 2d 219, 250 N.Y.S.2d 529 (Sup. Ct. 1964), *aff'd*, 23 App. Div. 2d 216, 260 N.Y.S.2d 451 (1965), *aff'd*, 18 N.Y.2d 234, 221 N.E.2d 543, 274 N.Y.S.2d 877 (1966), *vacated and remanded*, 387 U.S. 239 (1967), the plaintiff complained *inter alia* of the false depiction of the following: An alleged conversation between the plaintiff and his father's physician in which the latter tries to persuade the plaintiff that he bears no guilt for his father's illness; a fictitious scene depicting plaintiff's reunion with his fiancee upon his surprise return from Europe; other scenes depicting the plaintiff's deeply personal relationship with members of his immediate family and his introspective thoughts. *See* cases cited note 88 *supra* for other instances of false light cases in which the offensively false statements do not disparage reputation.

[101]385 U.S. at 377-78.

that a trier of fact might well find it to be offensive to persons of "ordinary sensibilities."[102] But, surely, nothing in such depiction was injurious to the reputation of any of the Hill family. A report of brutal treatment at the hand of criminals and a brave attempt to resist the criminals is hardly calculated to hold the victims up to public contempt, ridicule, and obloquy. It is submitted, then, that the Court in *Time* was wrong in applying to false light privacy cases in general, and to the particular case before it, a rule which can be justified only when the particular false light case contains defamatory elements, or does not purport to relate to public matters.

The fact that what allegedly happened to the Hill family was news should not in the name of the first amendment justify an obliteration of society's commitment to the values of privacy.[103] The reporting of intimate private matters, whether or not they are true, may pander to the public curiosity, but if the report does not reflect on the subject's reputation it cannot be said that the public interest, or that the factors which form the underlying rationale for freedom of speech, requires reporting the name or other identification of the subject of such private matters.[104] In such circumstances the public's interest in news reporting

[102]RESTATEMENT OF TORTS § 867, comment *d* at 400-01 (1939) provides that "liability exists only if the defendant's conduct was such that he should have realized that it would be offensive to persons of ordinary sensibilities." The tentative draft of the second Restatement uses the phrase "unreasonable publicity, of a kind highly offensive to the ordinary reasonable man." RESTATEMENT (SECOND) OF TORTS § 652D, comment *d* at 115-16 (Tent. Draft No. 13, 1967).

[103]The earlier newspaper reports should not detract from the private nature of the matters reported unless such newspaper accounts were made with the plaintiff's cooperation. A related and overlapping defense in privacy cases is based upon the plaintiff's status as a "public figure." *See* RESTATEMENT (SECOND) OF TORTS § 652F, comments *c* and *d* at 128-29 (Tent. Draft No. 13, 1967), which suggests that "to some reasonable extent" the privilege to report activities of public figures extends even as to "facts about the individual which would otherwise be purely private." Some decisions have seemed to regard this as an absolute privilege to report the private aspects of a celebrated figure's private life. *See* Sidis v. F-R Pub. Corp., 113 F.2d 806 (2d Cir. 1940); Peay v. Curtis Pub. Co., 78 F. Supp. 305 (D.D.C. 1948); Reed v. Real Detective Pub. Co., 61 Ariz. 511, 162 P.2d 133 (1945). Note that Warren and Brandeis qualified the right of privacy, so that "to whatever degree and in whatever connection a man's life has ceased to be private . . . to that extent the protection is to be withdrawn." Warren and Brandeis, *supra* note 73, at 215. If the thesis of this article is accepted then the plaintiff's status as a public figure should not affect his claim of a right of privacy as to nondefamatory matters which are truly private. The justification for the "public figure" limitation under the *Times* rule in limiting his right of action for defamation—*i.e.*, the fact that a public figure is in a position to invoke the self-help of "more speech," see text accompanying note 55 *supra*, is not applicable to privacy where more speech is irrelevant.

[104]This may be subject to a further qualification. If a news story is reputation-injuring (and therefore privileged) as to one individual, such privilege should not be negated by the fact that recounting the reputation-injuring events (whether true or false, but subject to the *Times* doctrine if false) will necessarily identify an innocent participant in the events reported. Thus, reporting that a named individual raped his sister will, if he has only one sister, necessarily identify and therefore

is sufficiently served by an account of the event itself without identification of persons innocently involved.[105]

CONCLUSION

Definitional balancing of interests is defensible as a judicial function. More than that, it is essential that the judiciary exercise this function in the interpretation and application of the first amendment if freedom of speech is to be meaningful as constitutional doctrine. The Supreme Court's decision in *New York Times v. Sullivan* implicitly recognized the need for definitional balancing and drew a definitional line which on the whole establishes a felicitous equilibrium between antithetical interests in speech and reputation. The Court's subsequent decision in *Time, Inc. v. Hill* is unfortunate in that it assumes that the definitional balance appropriate to the speech and reputation context is equally applicable in balancing competing interests in speech and privacy. A recognition of the manner in which the privacy interest differs from the reputation interest requires a markedly different definitional balance in determining the constitutional limits of the right of privacy.

invade the privacy of the sister. *See* Hubbard v. Journal Pub. Co., 69 N.M. 473, 368 P.2d 147 (1962); Franklin, *A Constitutional Problem in Privacy Protection: Legal Inhibitions on Reporting of Fact*, 16 STAN. L. REV. 107, 117, 134 (1963).

[105]This principle has received limited recognition on a statutory level in those states which by law prohibit the naming of a female victim of a sexual offense. *See* FLA. STAT. § 794.03 (1965); GA. CODE ANN. § 26-2105 (1953); S.C. CODE ANN. § 16-81 (1962); WIS. STAT. ANN. § 942.02 (1958); Franklin, *supra* note 95, at 121-28. *See also* Barber v. Time, Inc., 348 Mo. 1199, 1206, 159 S.W.2d 291, 295 (1942): "It was not necessary to state plaintiff's name in order to give medical information to the public as to the symptoms, nature, causes or results of her ailment."

[12]

Privacy and the Press

ERIC BARENDT*

William Prosser once wrote about privacy that 'no other tort has received such an outpouring of comment in advocacy of its existence'.[1] Similarly, a wealth of recent departmental and other committee reports has been devoted to the possible introduction of a privacy right into English law.[2] The Lord Chancellor's Consultation Paper has recommended the institution of a civil remedy to protect the right.[3] At times during the course of the last two years, the Government apparently has been on the point of issuing a White Paper with such a proposal, but a nervous administration, fearful of the power of the press, has (at the time of writing) hesitated to take the step. In the meantime press organizations have published *Media Freedom and Media Regulation*, described as an alternative White Paper, making the case against the introduction of a privacy right.[4]

As this account suggests, the rival arguments can easily be characterized as political. On the one side are ranged prominent public figures, mostly politicians and perhaps members of the Royal Family, anxious to protect their lives and activities from media scrutiny, while on the other the press fights to retain its liberty of publication. Nevertheless, both sides sometimes deploy intellectual arguments which should be taken seriously. For the balancing of the (moral) right to privacy against freedom of speech and of the media is a complex process, requiring sensitivity to both interests.

This chapter examines the principal arguments pertinent to this

* Goodman Professor of Media Law, UCL. I am grateful to Professor David Anderson, University of Texas, and Patrick Moloney, 1 Brick Court, for their helpful comments on a draft of this chapter.

[1] *Law of Torts* (1st edn., West Publishing, 1941), 1051.

[2] See in particular the *Report of the Calcutt Committee on Privacy and Related Matters* (1990), Cm. 1102, the Calcutt *Review of Press Self-Regulation* (1993), Cm. 2135, *Report of the National Heritage Committee on Privacy and Media Intrusion*, 1992–3 HC 294, and Lord Chancellor's Department Consultation Paper, *Infringement of Privacy* (July 1993).

[3] Ibid., para. 3.13.

[4] Published by the Association of British Editors, Guild of Editors, and the International Press Institute, Feb. 1994.

debate. I should make my position clear at the outset. My view is that privacy is a fundamental human right, which any civilized legal system should protect from infringement, whether by government, business, individuals, or the media. But it is rarely an absolute right. Against it should be balanced legitimate public policies, such as the investigation of crime and the maintenance of order, as well as the freedom of the press and broadcasting media to report matters of public interest. Moreover, it is for the courts (or some other tribunal, wholly independent of both the government and the media) to balance these interests.

This chapter covers only some of the questions relevant to privacy rights. It touches on some, but not all, of the justifications for a right of privacy, and is for the most part concerned with only one of the four torts identified by Prosser in his classic article on the subject:[5] the public disclosure of embarrassing private facts. A few of the arguments may also be pertinent to the 'false light' tort, where the plaintiff is given false, but non-defamatory, publicity, for example, in a broadcast drama–documentary. On the other hand, I am not concerned at all in this article with invasion of the plaintiff's physical seclusion[6] or with appropriation of his image or likeness; both these heads of privacy infringement may involve the press, but they may equally be committed by other categories of defendant and raise considerations outside the scope of this article. It also barely touches on the complex issues concerning privacy rights to the unimpeded use of contraceptive devices, an abortion, or to engage in homosexual activity, the so-called 'constitutional privacy rights', much litigated in the United States.[7] These rights implicate the state, and not the media. In contrast the media would usually be the defendants in actions for the public disclosure tort.

Part II briefly sets out the current English legal position, with some comparative law observations. Part III addresses the question how a right to privacy might be defined in the context of a public disclosure tort. Sometimes the media contend that this is an impossible enterprise, so that the right would necessarily be extremely vague and pose unacceptable risks to their freedom of reporting. Part IV deals with the more significant argument that the institution of the right would inappropriately deter the publication of *true* and *accurate* information, while Part V examines the proposition that it should be for the

[5] 'Privacy', 48 *Calif. LRev.* 383, reprinted in R. Wacks (ed.), *Privacy* (International Library of Essays in Law & Legal Theory, Dartmouth, 1993), ii.

[6] Some of the recommendations in the Calcutt Report are concerned to protect privacy in this sense of physical seclusion, as well as to inhibit the acquisition of private information or photographs: see n. 2 above, ch. 6.

[7] Art. 8 of the European Convention on Human Rights (ECHR) is as concerned with this type of privacy right, as it is with the right to keep information, such as correspondence, private: see *Dudgeon* v. *UK* (1982) 4 EHRR 149.

press, on behalf of the public, to decide what information is of public interest and should therefore be freely publishable. Neither of these propositions can, it seems to me, be accepted, if we regard privacy as an interest worthy of legal protection. In effect, both arguments deny that the interest in keeping some activity or information private is an important one, which, in *some situations* at least, should prevail over freedom of the press. Put this way, the conclusion is unattractive, yet, it seems to me, it is what the media are urging. Part VI offers a few concluding reflections.

II

It is trite law that there is no right to privacy as such in England.[8] The interests in keeping private certain behaviour or personal information may, of course, be protected through other civil actions in, for example, trespass and breach of confidence. Indeed, in many circumstances, it is possible to develop (or, some would say, manipulate) the torts of defamation or breach of confidence to bring what in substance is really a privacy action in all but name.[9] Perhaps one day the House of Lords, in a breach of confidence action (such as that brought by Princess Diana after the publication of photographs of her working out in a London gymnasium), will hold that English law does, after all, protect privacy. Such a course has been advocated by the distinguished advocate and writer, Lord Lester, QC.[10]

The law of defamation can be manipulated in two ways. First, the concept of 'defamatory meaning' may be applied to allegations which invade a plaintiff's privacy as much as they damage his reputation. What exactly constitutes 'reputation' is notoriously hard to define; one well-known attempt refers to the 'right to have the estimation in which [the plaintiff] stands in the opinion of others unaffected by false statements to his discredit'.[11] It has even been said that a loss of reputation can only occur when the public, or a section of it, has some knowledge of the particular attribute or conduct of the person concerned.[12] Or it reasonably assumes that the plaintiff has this attribute

[8] If authority is needed, see *Malone* v. *Metropolitan Police Commissioner* [1979] Ch. 344, and *Kaye* v. *Robertson* [1991] FSR 62 (CA).

[9] Something like this occurred, for example, in *Shelley Films Ltd* v. *Rex Features Ltd* [1994] 3 *Entertainment LR* 45, where Michael Mann QC granted an injunction to restrain the publication of photographs of a film set, probably obtained as a result of trespass. The interlocutory injunction was granted for breach of confidence, but there was no interference with any confidential relationship or contract.

[10] 'English Judges as Law Makers' [1993] *Pub. Law* 269, 284–6.

[11] Cave J in *Scott* v. *Sampson* (1882) 8 QBD 491, 503, cited with approval by Scrutton LJ in *Youssoupoff* v. *MGM Pictures Ltd* (1934) 50 TLR 581, 587.

[12] See the classic article by M. B. Nimmer. 'The Right to Speak from *Times* to *Time*: First Amendment Theory Applied to Libel and Misapplied to Privacy' (1968) 56 *Calif. LR* 935, 956–8.

or behaves in a particular way: e.g. we may all be assumed to be fundamentally honest. But in practice the law has been developed, and is applied by juries, to protect aspects of individuals' private life: their sexuality and sexual practices, family relationships, eating disorders, and so on. Indeed, it may be conjectured that the boundaries between an attack on reputation and an invasion of privacy have become blurred in English law, precisely because the tort of defamation has to do some of the work which might be done by an independent privacy tort.[13] Secondly, the huge damages awards sometimes made in libel cases may reflect the jury's hostility to newspaper disclosure of essentially private information.[14]

Of course, there is a fundamental distinction between defamation and the privacy tort of public disclosure of embarrassing private facts. Truth is an (absolute) defence to the former action, but not to the latter. Indeed, the gravamen of the public disclosure wrong is that essentially private facts or information have been disclosed; this is hurtful and wrong because they are true. (The 'false light' head of privacy protects plaintiffs against the publication of distorted, though non-defamatory, impressions.) This difference is crucial. For opponents of the disclosure tort argue, among other things, that it would be wrong for a privacy law to deter the publication of accurate information. In Part IV of the chapter I will contend that this argument misses the point, and that it is right in some circumstances for the law to intervene when truthful private information (for example, the contents of letters or a diary, or photographs) is published.

English law is unusual, though not unique, in its refusal (hitherto) to recognize a right of privacy. There is no such right in Australia or in Ireland. But it is recognized in most American states and in France and Germany.[15] Some Canadian Provinces have introduced statutory rights in the last twenty-five years or so. The Saskatchewan Privacy Act 1979, for example, provides a non-exhaustive list of examples of privacy violation, including 'the use of letters, diaries, or other personal documents'. None of the Canadian statutes is specifically aimed at the press, which moreover may rely on broad public-interest defences. It would perhaps be wrong to criticize English law, merely because it is out of step with the general trend in other jurisdictions. Nor is it clear that the United Kingdom is required to introduce the public disclosure tort under the European Human Rights Convention.

[13] This has apparently happened in Australia, where there is no tort of privacy: see R. Watterson, 'What is defamatory today?' (1993) 67 *ALJ* 811.

[14] See L. Blom-Cooper, 'The Right to be Let Alone' [1989] 10 *Jo. of Media Law and Practice* 53, 55.

[15] There are comparative law summaries in the Calcutt Report, n. 2 above, ch. 5 and in the Lord Chancellor Consultation Paper, n. 2 above, Annex B. Both summaries are rather quaintly given the title of the law or position 'overseas'!

Article 8 of the Convention guarantees the right to respect for private and family life, home, and correspondence, but only, it would seem, against interference by public authority.[16] Certainly, no reported case suggests that the Convention right affects the media.

What is odd, however, is that in the United Kingdom broadcasters are subject to redress for invasions of privacy, while the press and other media, for example, book publishers, are not. The Broadcasting Complaints Commission (BCC) exercises jurisdiction over complaints of 'unwarranted infringement of privacy in, or in connection with the obtaining of material included in' radio and television programmes.[17] There are very few complaints under this head, compared with the complaints of 'unjust or unfair treatment', but the Commission does annually adjudicate on a handful of privacy cases. Its findings have developed some sort of jurisprudence in the area. For example, it has held recently that Granada invaded the complainants' privacy by showing, without warning them in advance, film shots of their children, who had died in very distressing circumstances. On an application for judicial review, the courts held it was immaterial whether the complainant had actually taken part in the programme or had even seen it; nor was it material that the matter had only two or three years before been extensively covered by the media and so been in the public domain.[18] But no reference was made to the BCC's 'case law' by Sir David Calcutt in his first report on privacy and the press.[19] Nor did he consider the question of principle why the print and broadcasting media should be treated so differently in this respect.

Various reasons have been given for subjecting branches of the media to radically divergent regulation (or lack of it).[20] Whatever their general persuasiveness, they carry little conviction in the context of the protection of privacy. The question is not really whether there is a case for subjecting the broadcasting (and cable and electronic) media to somewhat tighter standards than those applied to books, magazines, and newspapers. There may well be such a case in the context of matters like pornography and violent material. Moreover, as an important German Constitutional Court decision indicates, the right to privacy should in some circumstances be given more weight when it is invaded by a television documentary than when it is balanced against

[16] Art. 8(2) provides that '[t]here shall be no interference by a public authority', except on prescribed grounds. It is possible to interpret the Art. as guaranteeing a privacy right against interference by anyone, while allowing interference by a public authority in certain circumstances. But the interpretation in the text seems preferable.

[17] Broadcasting Act 1990, s. 143(1)(b).

[18] *R.* v. *Broadcasting Complaints Commission, ex parte Granada*, *The Times*, 31 May 1994 (DC), and *The Times*, 16 Dec. 1994 (CA).

[19] N. 2 above.

[20] For a brief discussion of the unsatisfactory rationales for the regulation of broadcasting, see E. M. Barendt, *Broadcasting Law* (OUP, 1993), 3–10.

the freedom of the press (or other media) to report facts of contemporary public importance.[21] But the differences in privacy protection in English law are not merely matters of degree. There is no redress of any kind if a book reveals private information,[22] while there is an opportunity to complain to the Press Complaints Commission (an extra-legal remedy) if a newspaper or magazine makes a similar disclosure; but the BCC provides a legal remedy if a broadcaster does the same thing. (Although the BCC cannot award damages, it is able to direct the broadcaster to transmit its findings, a requirement which may be enforced by the Independent Television Commission.[23]) Surely little can be said in defence of this position? It is as absurd as if there were a legal complaints procedure for defamatory attacks on radio and television, but no such remedy for similar attacks in newspapers or in books.

III

One common objection to the introduction of a legal right of privacy is that it is very difficult, perhaps impossible, to define.[24] It must be conceded that the enterprise has baffled many, mostly American, legal commentators and philosophers.[25] The task is especially confusing in the United States, since critics there feel obliged to justify rulings, some of them of the Supreme Court, upholding rights to privacy in an extraordinary variety of contexts. Thus, there are the four torts identified by Prosser (see Part I above), statutory and other rights not to have confidential information disclosed, and the constitutional rights to the use of contraceptives and (within limits) to an abortion. The right to privacy has to be defined in the United States to encompass all these particular rights.

Attempts to introduce a public disclosure tort should not be defeated by abstract arguments of this character. One obvious point is that the legal definitions of all fundamental human rights are necessarily open-ended, requiring subsequent interpretation and development by the courts. That would be true, for example, of virtually all the rights set out in the European Human Rights Convention, which, many argue, should be incorporated into English law. 'Freedom of speech' is itself an extraordinarily imprecise concept, raising im-

[21] See the *Lebach* case, 35 BVerfGE 202, 227–30 (1973), discussed by B. S. Markesinis, 'The Right to be Let Alone versus Freedom of Speech' [1986] *Pub. Law* 67, 77–8.

[22] This is illustrated by *Re X (A Minor)* [1975] Fam. 47, where the Court of Appeal declined to grant an injunction in the exercise of its wardship jurisdiction to restrain the publication of a book which revealed details of the ward's father's private life.

[23] Broadcasting Act 1990, s. 146.

[24] See the *Report of the Younger Committee* (1972), Cmnd. 5012, ch. 4, especially para. 58.

[25] See the essays reprinted in R. Wacks (ed.), n. 5 above, i, especially in Pt. 1.

mensely difficult questions about its application to pornography, commercial advertising, sit-ins and other protest activity, and so on. Yet the journalists and editors who protest at the uncertainty of the concept of 'privacy' would be unlikely to make the same objection if it were proposed to introduce some (constitutional) right to freedom of speech. Moreover, the objection to privacy applies with as much, or with even more, force to the concept of 'reputation', which the courts have found baffling for centuries.[26] Yet the law works tolerably well, in this respect at least, although I argued earlier (see Part II) that the uncertainty of the notion of 'reputation' probably enables some privacy interests to be protected in libel actions.

Nevertheless, a privacy law, whether confined to the public disclosure tort or not, should attempt a definition of privacy, to provide some guidance for journalists, editors, and, of course, the courts. (That this is not absolutely necessary is shown by the broadcasting legislation, which has left the concept to be interpreted by the Broadcasting Complaints Commission, subject only to judicial review.) Three general points can be made about such definitions before a formulation is suggested. First, any definition should reflect the reasons why the right is valued, and (not necessarily the same thing) *ought to be* valued in our society. If we think, for example, that privacy is valuable, because it protects the freedom of the individual to do whatever he likes unless it causes some demonstrable harm to another person (or perhaps the community), then the law should devise a very broad right of privacy—perhaps the right to be let alone.[27] On that footing, the legislation compelling the wearing of safety-belts and crash helmets would violate privacy rights, though it is hard to see what implications a right formulated in these terms would have when details of an individual's private life were revealed by the media.

A second introductory point really concerns the drafting of the legislation. It might make sense, as in the Canadian statutes, to state a general principle, and then provide a non-exhaustive list of circumstances in which, subject to defences, the courts would be required to find a violation; for example, the publication of extracts from a personal diary or of intimate letters. The third point is more important. A broad right to privacy will inevitably conflict in many circumstances with the interests of the media and the public respectively to impart and receive information of real public interest. That is the major

[26] There is no significant English literature on the meaning of reputation, why it is valued and is thought worthy of rather a high degree of protection. For an American discussion, see R. C. Post, 'The Social Foundations of Defamation Law: Reputation and the Constitution' (1986) 74 *Calif. LR* 691.

[27] The 'right to be let alone', formulated by Judge Cooley, *Cooley on Torts* (2nd edn., 1888) 29, though much cited in American case law, is far too broad, and really collapses a right to privacy into the general liberty principle associated with John Stuart Mill.

reason the media finds its institution objectionable. To some extent the courts can be helped to balance the competing rights sensitively by the drafting of the 'public interest' defence, a topic further considered in Part V of this article. But a relatively precise and narrow formulation of the privacy right will also meet the media's point to some extent. Many contentious privacy claims would simply be excluded from the scope of the right to privacy.[28] One example would be publication of minutes of a Cabinet committee meeting; while it is very likely that in some circumstances this could be prevented on grounds of breach of confidence,[29] a new privacy right against disclosure should be so defined as clearly to exclude such minutes and the information contained in them.

As already indicated, there is an enormous literature, legal and philosophical, on the meaning of privacy and why the right (or interest) is valued. It has been variously defined broadly as 'the right to be let alone' or more narrowly as a right to control the use of personal information.[30] Privacy claims are related to claims of individual autonomy, but as the seat-belt case shows, they must surely be much narrower than the latter. Otherwise a privacy claim would be indistinguishable from Mill's general right to liberty, philosophically controversial, and much too broad to incorporate in a bill of rights or a privacy statute. Even the notion of 'personal information' needs clarification. Correspondence between a prospective employer and job applicant is in a sense personal, at least to the latter, and its disclosure might be stopped by an action for breach of confidence. It is doubtful, however, whether the disclosure of such material should be remedied by a privacy action, if one were instituted as part of English law.

Privacy claims, it has been argued, are essentially claims to a measure of control (or autonomy) over certain particularly intimate areas of an individual's life.[31] These areas concern to a considerable extent, but by no means exclusively, an individual's sexual life: the right (subject to some limits) to choose sexual partners and practices, to enjoy sexual relations in private, and not to have them divulged to the public to satisfy its taste for gossip. But they also include a right to keep personal correspondence, diaries, and other notes private; indi-

[28] See T. I. Emerson, 'The Right of Privacy and Freedom of the Press' (1979) 14 *Harvard Civil Rights-Civil Liberties LR* 329, 343.

[29] *A.G.* v. *Jonathan Cape Ltd* (The Crossman Diaries case) [1976] QB 752.

[30] R. Wacks, 'The Poverty of "Privacy"' (1980) 96 *LQR* 73, and *Personal Information* (OUP, 1989).

[31] Among the advocates of this general perspective are J. Inness, *Privacy, Intimacy and Isolation* (New York, OUP, 1992); C. Fried, 'Privacy' (1968) 77 *Yale LJ* 475; and T. Gerety (1977) 12 *Harvard Civil Rights–Civil Liberties LR* 199. Although the link with *intimacy* is not explicitly made, much of the argument in the classic article by S. D. Warren and L. D. Brandeis, 'The Right to Privacy' (1890) 4 *Harv. LR* 193 shares the perspective.

viduals also have a right to keep some facts about themselves private, for example, concerning their medical history and family relationships. We also surely have a right to choose the persons to whom we appear in a state of (relative) undress—persons such as doctors, nurses, and other people working out in a gym. And it would follow that we have a right not to be photographed without consent in that condition, and a right that the media does not publish such a photograph. These rights are valuable, simply because a degree of privacy is necessary for the formation and development of intimate relationships and friendships and for the moral and spiritual development of individuals.[32] It is a reasonable assumption that most people do value privacy on grounds such as these. Sadly, this is not incompatible with an insatiable curiosity about other people's private, particularly sexual, lives.

This perspective on the value of privacy highlights a number of its features. First, the right is essentially that of an individual human being. Corporations and associations should not be able to sue.[33] Interestingly, privacy in this respect differs from the right to reputation, which may be asserted by corporations, although not now by public authorities.[34] Secondly, privacy, and private information, can be relatively clearly distinguished from secrecy and confidential information. Cabinet papers, tax and other financial documents, and information about membership of churches or political parties are covered by official secrecy laws or the right to protect confidential information, but are probably inappropriate for protection under this definition of privacy. It was, therefore, misconceived to claim, as Sir Norman Fowler MP did in his evidence to the Home Affairs Committee of the House of Commons, that donors have a (moral or constitutional) privacy right not to disclose their contributions to political parties. (Corporations, of course, may protect their secrets by legal action, but have no right to privacy.)

The distinction between privacy and secrecy is further revealed by another aspect of the law, which at first sight is very baffling. The assertion of a privacy right in a public court hearing appears bizarre; the hearing ensures that it is given wider currency than it would otherwise have obtained.[35] But this phenomenon is explicable. The purpose of a privacy action for damages is not to

[32] It is unnecessary here to discuss whether a privacy right is based primarily or entirely on a more fundamental right to human dignity, stated to be inviolable by Art. 1 of the German Basic Law, or whether it is also grounded on social utility.

[33] This view is also expressed in the Lord Chancellor's Consultation Paper, n. 2 above, para. 5.36.

[34] *Derbyshire CC* v. *Times Newspapers Ltd* [1993] AC 534.

[35] Trade secret and official secrets cases may be heard *in camera* and subject to significant reporting restrictions.

keep the information away from the public gaze; indeed, it has *ex hypothesi* already received some publicity, for that is a precondition of the action.[36] Instead, the object is to vindicate the plaintiff's right to society's respect for his privacy. As Robert Post, a prominent American commentator, has argued, members of a community (and the media) should respect each individual's 'information preserves', an entitlement to share intimate information with people of his choice and not the public.[37] That can be vindicated by a court action, even if the secrecy of the particular information is thereby further infringed. This perspective perhaps is more easily appreciated if the privacy action is seen as essentially asserting a personality right.[38]

Post's argument also shows why the inappropriateness of a disclosure, and hence its actionability, may depend as much on its form and timing as on the contents of the publication. Thus, it is possible for a disclosure about a person's past life to become inappropriate, even though a publication of the same story, contemporary with the events described, would not be actionable. That is why the California Supreme Court upheld a privacy claim brought by a reformed prostitute (also a defendant in a murder trial) in respect of a film exhibited seven years after the events.[39] Further, disclosure to the general public, or a broad cross-section of it, obviously violates the plaintiff's self-respect and right to social respect, while the same disclosure to a small group of family or close friends usually does not.[40] This point in its turn explains why the media are particularly vulnerable to this type of privacy action.

A definition of 'privacy' in terms of individuals' right to control aspects of their intimate personal lives would cover claims which fall wholly outside the subject of this article: in particular, claims to a degree of autonomy in the conduct of sexual relations. Equally, it does not exhaust the circumstances in which a privacy claim might be considered appropriate. A privacy right defined in these terms would not, for instance, have helped the multi-million pound national lottery winner, whose identity was revealed by some newspapers towards the

[36] Injunction claims raise other issues; the free speech argument, then, is much stronger, and there is a powerful case for denying, as in libel actions under the rule in *Bonnard* v. *Perryman* [1891] 2 Ch. 269 (CA), all judicial prior restraints, at any rate when the defendant pleads a public interest defence.

[37] R. C. Post, 'The Social Foundations of Privacy: Community and Self in the Common Law Tort' (1989) 77 *Calif. LR* 957, 985–7.

[38] In Germany privacy has been largely derived from the constitutional right to the free development of personality, guaranteed by Art. 2 of the Basic Law.

[39] *Melvin* v. *Reid*, 297 P. 91 (1931). Recently the English CA has held that the fact that an incident has been in the public domain does not necessarily preclude its subsequent resurrection from being considered an infringement of privacy: *R.* v. *Broadcasting Complaints Commission*, *The Times*, 16 Dec. 1994.

[40] Post, n. 37 above, 987–95.

end of 1994.[41] Nor would it cover the disclosure of personal financial information, for example, concerning an individual's tax returns or his debts (except in so far as this information is contained in private correspondence or diaries). In many circumstances, of course, the disclosure of this type of information could be prevented by an action for breach of confidence, but it would not be covered by a privacy right based on the control of intimate personal life. In this respect the suggested definition is narrower than those given in the Private Members' Bills introduced in 1987 and 1989 by William Cash MP and John Browne MP respectively.[42]

The important point is that this definition, exemplified by reference to material such as diaries, personal letters, and intimate photographs, is relatively precise and covers most of the relevant ground. It is much more likely to command general acceptance than a broadly drafted right, which covered, say, office correspondence or telephone calls relating to tax payments or stock exchange transactions. The definition is also flexible enough to be applied in the light of contemporary mores. For it is clear that what is regarded as essentially 'private' varies from one generation to another. That does not amount to an argument against privacy rights. After all, the meaning of 'speech' under the First Amendment and equivalent constitutional provisions alters with changing social perceptions about the value, say, of sexually explicit literature and commercial advertising. So what was intimate, and therefore private, in one generation may not be so regarded in another. Fifty years ago, publication of a photograph of a person in beach-wear might have been regarded as an invasion of privacy; that is unlikely now. It also goes without saying that what is regarded as 'private' in one society may not be so regarded in another. The disclosure by *Paris Match* in the autumn of 1994 that President Mitterrand had an adult illegitimate daughter was regarded as a shocking invasion of privacy in France, by the rest of the press as well as by the public. It would not have been regarded in this way in either England or the United States.[43]

However, the point about cultural and temporal relativism should not be exaggerated. In all western European societies, and in all recent generations, the publication of some particular types

[41] It is doubtful whether a privacy right should cover this case, for there seems nothing essentially 'private' about the gaining of large sums of money in a national lottery, itself organized in a blaze of publicity. Moreover, arguably the identity of the winner of such an enormous sum is a matter of legitimate public interest, for it might be relevant to the question whether the jackpot is too large.

[42] These Bills are reprinted as Appendices J and K to the Calcutt Committee Report, n. 2 above.

[43] The argument here is not that publication would have been regarded in England as in the public interest (though it may have been that); rather, it would not have been considered to involve the disclosure of an essentially private fact.

of material would be regarded as violations of an individual's privacy, unless made with that person's consent: personal diaries and letters, photographs of a couple love-making or a woman giving birth, are obvious examples. It is quite feasible for a law to be framed to cover this sort of highly intimate material, and for it to be drafted in such a way as to cover other pieces of private information which under prevailing community mores should not be released.

IV

As already discussed, the truth of a disclosure is an absolute defence to a libel action; in contrast the privacy action for the public disclosure of embarrassing facts assumes that they are in essential respects correct. Opponents of the introduction of this tort into English law fasten on this point. They argue that the privacy action would deter the publication of truth and that it is wrong (save in very rare circumstances) for a liberal society to countenance such suppression. If truth is a defence in libel, why should the law countenance an action for the disclosure of accurate private facts?

The United States Supreme Court seems to have accepted this argument. First, in 1967 it applied the principles it had developed to limit the libel actions of public officials (later extended to public figures) to the 'false light' category of privacy tort.[44] In its landmark libel decision in *New York Times* v. *Sullivan*, three years earlier, the Court had ruled that a public official plaintiff must prove that the statements were made with actual malice, that is, that the defendant knew they were false or was indifferent to their truth.[45] The action in *Time, Inc.* v. *Hill* was brought with regard to an article which in certain respects inaccurately depicted the plaintiff's family involvement in a past, but still notorious, incident. The Court appeared to consider that free speech principles applied to this sort of privacy suit in the same way that they had done to libel. Consequently no action for 'false light' privacy could succeed without proof of malice. A more recent decision indicates there are also constitutional limits on actions for the publication of truthful embarrassing private facts; the Court reversed a holding that a newspaper was civilly liable under a Florida statute for disclosing the name of a rape victim.[46] This development was hardly surprising. The major reason for the formulation of the *New*

[44] *Time, Inc* v. *Hill*, 385 US 374 (1967).

[45] 376 US 254 (1964).

[46] *Florida Star* v. *B.J.F.*, 491 US 524 (1989). The action in this case was not brought in privacy, but the Court's judgment would seem to preclude such an action, save in exceptional circumstances.

York Times rule, and presumably its application to 'false light' privacy, was that otherwise some valuable true speech would be 'chilled'. On that basis it would be odd for the Supreme Court to allow privacy actions (at least those launched by public officials and figures) in respect of accurate disclosures.

Nevertheless, there is an important flaw in the argument. It assumes that the libel of a public official (or figure) and the invasion of a person's privacy right have the same free speech value. That assumption can be challenged. The reason the law should afford a generous immunity from libel actions is that it is important for matters relevant to the *reputation* of politicians, and perhaps other public figures, to be freely discussed. In the first place, it is difficult to disentangle defamatory attacks on such persons from the hostile criticism of government which lies at the core of free political speech.[47] If the crime of sedition is incompatible with freedom of political speech, so are libel actions by public authorities and politicians. Moreover, if true statements are not disseminated, we might have false beliefs about the competence of politicians and candidates or about the public life of other prominent figures.

The danger of false beliefs is central to two arguments frequently made for freedom of speech, whether as a political principle or as a constitutional right. John Stuart Mill made the case for a full liberty of discussion of political, moral, and social affairs, on the ground that otherwise society could not discover for itself truths and weed out erroneous beliefs.[48] (The discovery of truth may be regarded as self-evidently good, or as an essential means to social and individual improvement—a utilitarian argument.) Informed political discourse is also crucial to the conduct of elections and representative democracy. This second argument has proved particularly influential in the development of United States free speech jurisprudence,[49] and now recently to the implication of a freedom of speech on political matters in the Australian Constitution.[50] These arguments justify the imposition of significant constraints on the law of libel. The media should be free to publish the truth about the public conduct of individual politicians, as otherwise incompetence or dishonesty may go unchecked. We might accept the false beliefs induced by the (deceitful) claims of these politicians.

But these arguments do not apply so evidently to the case of privacy. For in this context the opposite of an awareness of the truth is not necessarily that the public entertains false beliefs, but that it has

[47] See the speech of Lord Keith in *Derbyshire CC* v. *Times Newspapers Ltd*, n. 34 above.

[48] *On Liberty* (Everyman edn., 1972), ch. II.

[49] For a brief discussion, see E. M. Barendt, *Freedom of Speech* (OUP, 1987), 20–3.

[50] *Nationwide News Pty Ltd* v. *Wills* (1992) 177 CLR 1, and *Australian Capital Television Pty Ltd* v. *The Commonwealth* (1992) 177 CLR 106. For the application of the principle to libel law in Australia, see p. **290** below.

no beliefs at all.[51] Thus, it may entertain no beliefs about, say, the sexuality of a politician or trade union leader or about that person's personal and family life. Ignorance may here be bliss. It enables the public, it is argued, to concentrate its attention on a politician's public conduct and political programme, matters on which it does, and should, form a true or false belief. Neither Mill's argument from truth nor the argument from democracy really justifies protection for speech when it invades someone's privacy. Revelations about a politician's private life do not obviously contribute to the discovery of social truths or the effective working of representative democracy.[52]

But suppose revelations are published about a politician who has made a speech in praise of the values of family life or who has put his family's picture on his election manifesto? In these eventualities, perhaps the invasion of privacy may correct a false belief that he is rigorously honest, that he is not a hypocrite and lives by the values he proclaims. If privacy is protected in these circumstances, it is because 'it enables us to be hypocritical—to pretend to be something we are not'.[53] The point probably must be met by drawing a distinction between active and passive misrepresentation. If someone wrongly claims in public to be heterosexual (an active or explicit misrepresentation), exposure of his homosexual orientation or practices corrects a false belief and may contribute to, perhaps valuable, public knowledge. In some circumstances such disclosure is justified in the public interest (see Part V below). The Press Complaints Commission Code, for instance, provides that an invasion of privacy may be justified on this ground, when, *inter alia*, it prevents the public being misled by a statement or conduct.[54] Or an action brought in respect of such 'outing' could often be interpreted as in substance a defamation claim: that the plaintiff has misrepresented his sexuality (and is therefore unworthy of electoral support), rather than to protect the privacy of his sexuality as such.

A distinction between active and passive misrepresentations is said to be troubling in principle and hard to draw in practice. Arguably, for example, a politician campaigning for votes with a woman at his side can be taken to represent that he is heterosexual, so rendering an 'outing' by a newspaper in the public interest. The point must be dismissed. To accept it would in practice be to compel public figures virtually to surrender their privacy rights. Some distinction between

[51] This argument has been put most persuasively by F. Schauer, 'Reflections on the Value of Truth' (1991) 41 *Case Western LR* 699, 704–9.

[52] See M. B. Nimmer, n. 12 above, 956–66.

[53] D. A. Anderson, 'Fundamental Issues in Privacy Law', Lecture given at Leiden University, Institute of Anglo-American Law, 27 Nov. 1992. This section owes much to the lecture and to correspondence with Professor Anderson.

[54] PCC Code, Cl. 18.

positive misstatement and silence must be maintained, and its drawing is itself dependent on the interpretation of social practices. When a male politician appears in public with a woman, or puts a family photograph in his election manifesto, how much is he really claiming about his private life or are these only acts in a complex political ritual? Perhaps, for instance, an impressionable young gay candidate is prevailed on by his agent to engage in such minor pretences, because he, the agent, believes (rightly or wrongly) this is politically useful. It would certainly be going much too far to conclude that the candidate is thereby consenting to invasion of his privacy.

The media's case with respect to the disclosure of truth is therefore inconclusive. It ignores the significant differences between libel and privacy and it assumes without argument that the public disclosure of intimate information is 'speech' for the purpose of the free speech principle. While the exposure of significant hypocrisy is certainly justifiable, that does not excuse the publication of all private information on the pretext that the public will otherwise hold false beliefs. Acceptance of that excuse would destroy the right of privacy.

V

The press, however, argues most vigorously that the introduction of a privacy tort would inhibit the investigation and publication of stories of real public interest. It is implicit in this case that the stories are (at any rate largely) true, but the more important point is that the public should have unimpeded access to them. The public has a right to know everything it considers relevant to the assessment of a politician's life, at least if it is true. Further, it is not for the courts to assess whether the publication is in the public interest. Ultimately that is a matter for the public itself to judge. The public, moreover, can only do that if the press and other media are allowed a wide defence of 'newsworthiness' to privacy actions. For example, the public might consider that a politician's extra-marital affairs, or even conceivably his sexual escapades as a student thirty years ago, are relevant to his fitness for office. It would be wrong for a newspaper editor to deny it access to that information, and even more wrong for the court to intervene after the editor has chosen to publish.

This argument has, it seems, largely been accepted by American state courts, which have all but eviscerated the public disclosure tort. The media enjoy a defence of 'newsworthiness', the paramount test for which is whether the matter is of legitimate public interest, in its turn determined according to community mores. The greater the public curiosity, the more it is entitled to know. Publishers should be free to satisfy the public's curiosity about its heroes, villains, and the victims of crime and disasters.[55] Thus, the press may publish detailed articles about the personal peculiarities and illiteracy of an intrepid body surfer,[56] and disclose the homosexual orientation of a man who had intervened to stop an assassination attempt on President Ford.[57]

This approach is unacceptable, for it appears to discard the concept of privacy as a normative constraint.[58] What is private is only what the public is not interested in and which, therefore, cannot be regarded under contemporary standards as newsworthy. But the law must set standards, and not just follow them. That is what the English law of libel and breach of confidence does when it distinguishes between a disclosure which is in the public interest and one which the public finds interesting.[59] The Press Complaints Commission (PCC) Code takes the same approach when it instances the detection and exposure of crime or serious misdemeanour, and the protection of public health and safety, as among the grounds for regarding an invasion of privacy as in the public interest.[60] A new public disclosure tort should provide a broad public interest defence, but it should not allow the publication of material just because it is interesting to the public.

The press in fact appears to have accepted much of the argument in the preceding paragraphs when it agreed to abide by the PCC Code.[61] It cannot coherently argue that it is impossible to draft a 'public interest' defence or that in practice it could not be applied properly, since that would make nonsense of the efforts of the PCC to do precisely that.[62] What it does argue is that courts or other tribunals should not adjudicate on privacy (or other) claims against the press with the ability to award damages and to enjoin further publication of the offending material.[63] Privacy issues should be left to self-regulation.

It is hard to know what to make of this, if the media argument is not taken as mere rhetoric. If the American 'newsworthiness' approach

[55] Second Restatement of Torts, S. 625D, Comment f.

[56] *Virgil* v. *Sports Illustrated*, 424 F.Supp. 1286 (1976).

[57] *Sipple* v. *Chronicle Publishing Co*, 201 Cal. Rptr. 665 (1984). The case was also decided on the ground that, as the plaintiff had disclosed his orientation in gay magazines and on gay marches, the information was already public. But that does not mean that disclosure in the San Francisco daily paper was appropriate (see Pt. III above).

[58] Anderson, n. 53 above, 8–10.

[59] See Lord Denning MR in *London Artists* v. *Littler* [1969] 2 QB 375, 391; Stephenson LJ in *Lion Laboratories Ltd* v. *Evans* [1984] 2 All ER 417, 423.

[60] Cl. 18. Another ground is preventing the public being misled by statements or conduct, referred to in Pt. IV above. These grounds do not, as Calcutt had recommended, provide an exhaustive formulation of the public-interest defence to privacy invasion.

[61] But the alternative White Paper, *Media Freedom and Media Regulation*, paras. 4.16–4.18, takes the view that 'gossip' material should be freely publishable.

[62] Whether the efforts of the PCC have been successful is another matter. For a very critical article, see Sir L. Blom-Cooper QC and L. R. Pruitt, 'Privacy Jurisprudence of the Press Complaints Commission' [1994] *Anglo-American LR* 133.

[63] For interlocutory injunctions to restrain initial publication, see n. 36 above.

were favoured, then of course it is better simply to leave things to editors and publishers. But once it is accepted that privacy and its defences should be treated as setting standards which are capable of impartial application, the courts (or some other independent tribunal) should be the final arbiters.[64] Otherwise the press would be claiming to be judge in its own cause. It would in effect be asserting that it should be apart from, or above, the law, the caricature of the position of the American press under the First Amendment once described by Lord Ackner.[65] It is no more attractive for the media to claim this freedom than it is for trade unions, the City, or other institutions which on occasion have asserted an entitlement to self-regulation even when their activities impinge on the general public.

Some of the points in this chapter can be well illustrated by a short discussion of a typical American case, as diverting to describe as it must have been painful for the plaintiff. Hilda Bridges was kidnapped from her place of employment by her husband and taken to an apartment at gunpoint. She was forced to undress to prevent her escape. Finally, the police stormed the apartment and rushed her out, covered only with a small cloth. The episode was photographed, and the local newspaper published a picture of the near-naked Hilda Bridges. Her claim for privacy succeeded at first instance, where she was awarded $10,000, but the Florida Court of Appeal allowed the paper's appeal.[66] The court held that the photograph did not appeal to sensual appetites, but revealed grief and fright; further, it showed little more than would be seen had the plaintiff been wearing a bikini on a beach. The newspaper did not lose its right to publish a newsworthy photograph merely because publication was embarrassing and distressing to the plaintiff.

In effect, the court abandoned its judgement on the balance between privacy and press freedom to the newspaper editor. The comparison of the photograph with her appearance in a bikini on the beach was wholly irrelevant; in the latter circumstance, she herself would have chosen her clothes, or lack of them, and would have chosen to appear in the bikini to her companions and other people on the beach. If, as I have argued in Part III of this chapter, we have a privacy right *to choose* when we appear in a state of (more or less) total nakedness, that right was surely violated by the publication of the photograph in this case. It is also quite beside the point that it revealed fright and emotional strain, rather than appealed to the public's sexual prurience. Privacy is a right to keep intimate facts

[64] See R. Gavison, 'Too Early for a Requiem: Warren and Brandeis were Right on Privacy *Vs.* Free Speech' (1992) 43 *S Carolina LR* 437.

[65] *A.G.* v. *Guardian Newspapers Ltd* [1987] 1 WLR 1248, 1306.

[66] *Cape Publications Inc* v. *Bridges*, 423 So.2d. 426, cert. denied by the Supreme Court, 464 US 893 (1983).

and images away from the public, irrespective of whether disclosure will reflect badly on its victim or not. It is clearly an invasion of privacy, for example, if an unwanted spectator intrudes into a hospital to witness the birth of a child,[67] or photographs of a woman in labour are published without her consent. The publication in Hilda Bridges' case was not far removed from the last (mercifully hypothetical) example.

Finally, it is surely clear that politicians and other public figures are entitled to the protection which may be afforded by a privacy right against embarrassing public disclosures. Granted that a 'public interest' defence would be more readily available when they sue, there is no reason why they should not rely on the right where, say, intimate personal correspondence or photographs have been published. It will not do for the press to argue that the public likes to look at this material and that its disclosure tells us more about the politician than we already know. For the defence to be available, the private information should have some bearing on a matter of genuine public interest, because, for example, it enables readers to evaluate the plaintiff's ability for office or public life.

VI

The arguments deployed by the media, generally the press, against a legally enforceable privacy right are, therefore, unconvincing. They exaggerate the damage which recognition of the right might do to freedom of speech and of the media. The press ignores the distinction which must be drawn between political and public discourse on the one hand, and the revelation of personal and private information on the other. More seriously, the media's arguments fail to do any sort of justice to the serious case for a right of privacy, a right which protects the free development of intimate relationships and of the individual's personality.[68]

The current debate prompts one or two further reflections. The obsession of the tabloid press with gossip and human-interest stories not only invades individual privacy rights, but also gives this material a prominence it does not deserve. As Warren and Brandeis put it in their classic article: 'When personal gossip attains the dignity of print, and crowds the space available for matters of real interest to the community, what wonder that the ignorant and thoughtless mistake its real importance'.[69] The manufacture of these stories requires an enormous amount of energy and ingenuity, which could more profit-

[67] *De May* v. *Roberts*, 9 NW 146 (1881).

[68] For a powerful recent statement of this case, see Gavison, n. 64 above, 459–62.

[69] N. 31 above, 196.

ably be devoted to the investigation of genuine political scandal or the coverage of foreign affairs. One incidental consequence of a privacy right is, then, that it might encourage the press to discharge its responsibility to inform and enlighten its readers.

The press, however, is certainly right on one matter. Too often recent privacy debate has seemed to single out newspapers for special treatment. The terms of reference of the Calcutt Committee were simply misconceived, for it was invited solely to investigate intrusions by the press. As I argued in Part II, it is in principle wrong in this context to treat the branches of the media in radically different ways. The right to privacy should be guaranteed against every potential defendant. So the debate got off to a very bad start, and it can be no surprise, therefore, that it has now become primarily a battle between the political establishment and the newspaper industry. It is unlikely that there will be privacy legislation in the next few years, not because, after serious reflection, it is thought wrong in principle, but because the present Conservative Government lacks the will to introduce it. (Nor is it likely that it will be a priority for any new administration.) For this reason there is a powerful argument for the House of Lords to formulate a privacy right if an appropriate case comes to it. Conflicts between fundamental rights should be resolved by the courts, when the government and legislature ignore them.

[13]

PRIVACY AND THE REASONABLE PARANOID: THE PROTECTION OF PRIVACY IN PUBLIC PLACES

Elizabeth Paton-Simpson*

The essence of civilized life is sharing space with others without intruding or being intruded upon.[1]

I *Introduction*

I want to introduce you to a person we shall call Prudence. In most respects Prudence is a very ordinary person; she has always been careful not to do anything that might attract public attention. However, Prudence goes to extraordinary lengths to protect her privacy. Living within sight of an apartment block, she keeps her curtains drawn and her shutters closed both day and night.[2] She refuses to chat with friends over the telephone,[3] much less in cafés or restaurants,[4] in case someone is listening in. She conscientiously puts the contents of her waste paper basket through a shredder before disposal.[5] She develops all her photographs herself, to keep them from the prying eyes of people who operate developing machines.[6] She never uses public restrooms, lest she be spied upon by security staff.[7] If she ever ventures out on a date, she behaves

* Lecturer in Law, The University of Auckland, New Zealand.

1 B.B. Greenbie, *Spaces: Dimensions of the Human Landscape* (Westford, Mass.: Saybrook Press, 1981) at 9.

2 *DiGirolamo* v. *D.P. Anderson & Associates, Inc.*, [1999] Mass. Super. LEXIS 190, online: LEXIS (States, MACTS) [hereinafter *DiGirolamo*].

3 *Malone* v. *Metropolitan Police Commissioner (No. 2)*, [1979] 1 Ch. 344 at 375–6 (all telephones), distinguished in *Francome* v. *Mirror Group Newspapers Ltd*, [1984] 1 W.L.R. 892; *Edwards* v. *State Farm Insurance Co.*, 833 F.2d 535 (5th Cir. 1987) [hereinafter *Edwards*] (mobile telephones); *Tyler* v. *Berodt*, 877 F.2d 705 (8th Cir. 1989) (cordless telephones).

4 *Wilkins* v. *National Broadcasting Co.*, 71 Cal. App. 4th 1066 (1999), *Dempsey* v. *National Enquirer*, 702 F. Supp. 927 (D.Me. 1988).

5 Unreported judgment of Wayne C.C. (9 November 1993), rev'd in part *Doe* v. *Mills*, 536 N.W.2d 824 (Mich.App. 1995). In the search and seizure context, even shredding does not create a reasonable expectation of privacy in trash; *United States* v. *Scott*, 975 F.2d 927 (1st Cir. 1992).

6 *Milton* v. *Savinkoff* (1993), 18 C.C.L.T. (2d) 288 (B.C.S.C.).

7 *Elmore* v. *Atlantic Zayre, Inc.*, 341 S.E.2d 905 (Ga.App. 1986); *Hougum* v. *Valley Memorial Homes*, 574 N.W.2d 812 (N.D. 1998) (judge believed intrusion was inadvertent). See also *Turner* v. *General Motors Corp.*, 750 S.W.2d 76 (Mo.App. 1988).

with great circumspection, conscious that anything she does may be permanently recorded and exhibited to the nation.[8] She never wears dresses out in public, in case someone aims a camera up her skirts.[9] She avoids shops and buys all personal items, such as lingerie and pharmaceuticals, by mail order in unmarked packaging, using a pseudonym and a post office box.[10] She would certainly never be seen attending counselling premises,[11] specialist health clinics,[12] or controversial meetings.[13]

To be blunt, Prudence could be accused of being paranoid. Although her perspective is 'reasonable' in the sense of perceiving risks to privacy that are not imaginary, it is paranoid inasmuch as it greatly exaggerates the significance of certain risks to privacy. It displays 'an abnormal tendency to suspect and mistrust others.'[14] However, according to a widespread view of the right to privacy in Anglo-American law, Prudence's behaviour is entirely reasonable. She is merely doing what many judges and commentators imagine a reasonable person does to protect her privacy. If she did not consistently take these and a host of other precautions, she could be judged to have given implied consent to surveillance and even media coverage of the matters in question, regardless of whether they were of any legitimate concern to anyone else. People who fail to take such precautions, who expose their affairs to the public eye, are commonly said to have no reasonable expectation of privacy. Thus the viewpoint is well established that anyone who does not behave as a 'reasonable paranoid' has waived any right to privacy.

This view is influential both in countries where there is no general legal protection for privacy and in countries where privacy is protected by statute or common law. In the former situation, as in the United Kingdom and Australia, the primary way for individuals to defend their privacy is through self-censorship and seclusion. The main incidental

8 *Gill* v. *Hearst Publishing Co.*, 253 P.2d 441 (Cal. 1953); *De Gregorio* v. *CBS, Inc.*, 473 N.Y.S.2d 922 (Sup. 1984); *Fayard* v. *Guardsmark, Inc.*, [1989] U.S. Dist. LEXIS 14211, online: LEXIS (Genfed, DIST).

9 *C'Debaca* v. *Virginia*, [1999] Va.App. LEXIS 72, online: LEXIS (States, VACTS).

10 *Jacova* v. *Southern Radio and Television Co.*, 83 So.2d 34 (Fla. 1955); *Nader* v. *General Motors Corp.*, 255 N.E.2d 765 at 771 (N.Y.App. 1970); *Batts* v. *Baton Rouge (City of)*, 501 So.2d 302 (La.App. 1 Cir. 1986); and *Batts* v. *Capital City Press, Inc.*, 479 So.2d 534 (La.App. 1 Cir. 1985), review denied 502 So.2d 482 (La. 1987).

11 *Crosten* v. *Kamauf*, 932 F.Supp. 676 (D.Md. 1996).

12 Unreported judgment of Wayne C.C. (9 November 1993), rev'd in part *Doe* v. *Mills*, supra note 5.

13 *International Union* v. *Garner*, 601 F.Supp. 187 (M.D.Tenn. 1985).

14 Definition of 'paranoia' from J. Pearsall & B. Trumble, eds., *The Oxford English Reference Dictionary*, 2d ed. (Oxford: Oxford University Press, 1996) at 1055.

protection for privacy is provided by the law of trespass.[15] The right of privacy, such as there is, largely hinges on the ownership and control of private space. Thus the Younger Committee in Britain, which advised against the creation of a legal right to privacy, advocated 'guarded speech about one's personal affairs, care of personal papers, caution in disclosing information on request, confining private conduct to secluded places, and the use of curtains, shutters and frosted glass.'[16]

In the United States, Canada, and New Zealand, where direct forms of privacy protection exist, such protection tends to apply only after certain sorts of precautions have been taken. The right to privacy is generally said to be forfeited as soon as a person ventures out in public; 'there is no liability for giving further publicity to what the plaintiff himself leaves open to the public eye.'[17] Thus the situation is not so different from the former type of jurisdiction; the primary protection for privacy is still to 'stay inside your house with the blinds closed.'[18] In many cases, especially in the United States, the exclusion of privacy protection in public places has been so broad as to require measures as extreme as Prudence's before privacy is seen to deserve protection. Every one of Prudence's precautions is based not only on general pronouncements in Anglo-American courts excluding privacy in public places but also on specific cases.

However, the dominant view is not the only view of privacy in public places to be found in Anglo-American law. There are signs that Canadian and New Zealand courts may be more open to developing a degree of protection for privacy in public places than their American counterparts. Even in the United States, there are numerous instances in which some right to privacy in public places has been recognized, and a couple of the cases on which Prudence's precautions are based were reversed on appeal.[19] Some commentators have left open the possibility of unspecified exceptions to a general exclusion; thus Raymond Wacks has stated that 'there may occasionally be circumstances in which, despite the public venue, a plaintiff may be regarded as having a complaint for public disclosure.'[20] The revisers of Prosser's classic textbook on torts have cast doubt on the validity of a general exclusion, contending that merely because a fact occurred in a public place, this does not mean it should

15 See R. Wacks, *Privacy and Press Freedom* (London: Blackstone Press, 1995) at 128–9, 144–8.

16 U.K., 'Report of the Committee on Privacy' Cmnd 5012 (1972) (Chair: K. Younger) at 25.

17 *Restatement (Second) of Torts* § 652D, comment b (1977) [hereinafter *Restatement*].

18 A.J. McClurg, 'Bringing Privacy Law Out of the Closet: A Tort Theory of Liability for Intrusions in Public Places' (1995) 73 N.C.L. Rev. 989 at 990.

19 As indicated in the relevant footnotes.

20 R. Wacks, *The Protection of Privacy* (London: Sweet & Maxwell, 1980) at 103.

receive widespread publicity if it does not involve a matter of public concern.[21] Andrew McClurg has argued strongly for a concept of 'public privacy' and for a re-definition of the American tort of intrusion to cover highly offensive intrusions in public places.[22]

This article examines and critiques the 'reasonable paranoid' approach to the assessment of reasonable expectations of privacy.[23] It explains how this approach has distorted thinking about privacy in public places and how it has also been applied in analogous situations where individuals take risks with their privacy, such as by using the telephone, giving a blood sample, or having a film developed. The first part of this article describes the reasonable paranoid standard in American privacy law and examines to what extent this approach has been influential in Canada and New Zealand. The second part addresses the empirical and normative assumptions underlying the reasonable paranoid standard. It attempts a realistic, non-paranoid assessment of the risks to privacy in public places, affirming that reasonable people do, in fact, enjoy and rely upon a significant degree of public privacy. It disputes the notion that failure to take precautions such as Prudence's signifies a waiver of any rights to privacy. Finally, it argues that public privacy is an important and valuable component of the overall level of privacy for an individual or society and should be afforded a degree of legal protection, while maintaining a balance with competing interests.

This article adopts the concept of privacy as a condition of limited accessibility. A number of theorists have developed and defended definitions along these lines, including Ruth Gavison[24] and Anita Allen.[25] They generally conceive of privacy as relating to limitations on 'accessibility in the form of being known or observed,'[26] although there are some

21 See W.P. Keeton *et al.*, *Prosser & Keeton on Torts*, 5th ed. (St Paul: West, 1984) at 859.

22 McClurg, supra note 18. The term 'public privacy' was earlier used by Alan Westin in *Privacy and Freedom* (New York: Atheneum, 1967) at 32.

23 This article makes two preliminary assumptions that are themselves hotly debated in the literature: that privacy is, or can be, valuable and worthy of legal protection; and that privacy should not automatically be sacrificed in every case where it conflicts with freedom of expression. I have defended these propositions in an earlier article; see Elizabeth Paton-Simpson, 'Human Interests: Privacy and Free Speech in the Balance' (1995) 16 N.Z.U.L.R. 225 [hereinafter 'Human Interests']. In contrast with the American position, the Supreme Court of Canada has affirmed that privacy and free expression are of equal constitutional importance; see *Hill* v. *Church of Scientology of Toronto*, [1995] 2 S.C.R. 1130 at 1179, 126 D.L.R. (4th) 129 at 163–4.

24 'Privacy and the Limits of Law' (1980) 89 Yale L.J. 421 [hereinafter 'Limits of Law'].

25 A.L. Allen, *Uneasy Access: Privacy for Women in a Free Society* (New Jersey: Rowman & Littlefield, 1988).

26 R. Gavison, 'Feminism and the Public/Private Distinction' (1992) 45 Stan. L. Rev. 1 at 6.

differences in detail. It is not necessary to resolve these differences here, since the main alternatives are all quite broad enough to capture the aspects of privacy central to this article.[27] One simple example is Jeffrey Reiman's definition of privacy as 'the condition in which other people are deprived of access to either some information about you or some experience of you.'[28]

The discussion in this article is directed at various forms of privacy protection found in Anglo-American law. Most American jurisdictions recognize a common law tort of invasion of privacy,[29] as do New Zealand[30] and, arguably, Canada.[31] Some of the Canadian provinces have statutory tort actions.[32] In some countries, privacy issues in broadcasting are handled

27 An article that discusses various 'limited access' definitions, as well as proposing a further one, is M. Powers, 'A Cognitive Access Definition of Privacy' (1996) 15 Law and Phil. 369. Of the definitions Powers discusses, only one is too narrow for the purposes of this article, namely that of W. Parent; see 'A New Definition of Privacy for the Law' (1983) 2 Law & Phil. 305 at 307. As Powers acknowledges (note 27), Parent himself did not see his account as a limited access definition. Reasons for rejecting Parent's narrow account are given in Powers at 377–9 and in E. Paton-Simpson, 'Private Circles and Public Squares: Invasion of Privacy by the Publication of "Private Facts"' (1998) 61 M.L.R. 318 [hereinafter 'Private Circles'].

28 J.H. Reiman, 'Driving to the Panopticon: A Philosophical Exploration of the Risks to Privacy Posed by the Highway Technology of the Future' (1995) 11 Computer & High Tech. L.J. 27 at 30.

29 *Restatement*, § 652A, comment a; *Prosser & Keeton on Torts*, supra note 21 at 851.

30 The tort is in its formative stages in New Zealand. See *Tucker* v. *News Media Ownership Ltd.*, [1986] 2 N.Z.L.R. 716 at 731–3 (H.C.); *Bradley* v. *Wingnut Films Ltd.*, [1993] 1 N.Z.L.R. 415 at 423–5 (H.C.); *X* v. *A.G.*, [1994] N.Z.F.L.R. 433 at 439 (H.C.); *Hobson* v. *Harding* (1995), 1 H.R.N.Z. 342 at 353–5 (H.C.); *P.* v. *D.* (25 February 2000), Auckland, C.P.126-SW99 (H.C.); J. Katz, 'Sex, Lies, Videotapes and Telephone Conversations: The Common Law of Privacy from a New Zealand Perspective' [1995] 1 E.I.P.R. 6.

31 A common law tort has been recognized in *Saccone* v. *Orr* (1981), 34 O.R. (2d) 317, 19 C.C.L.T. 37 (Co.Ct.); *Roth* v. *Roth* (1991), 4 O.R. (3d) 740, 9 C.C.L.T. (2d) 141 (C.J. (Gen. Div.)); *McKay* v. *Buelow* (1995), 11 R.F.L. (4th) 403, 24 C.C.L.T. (2d) 184 (Ont. Gen. Div.); *Lipiec* v. *Borsa* (1996), 31 C.C.L.T. (2d) 294 (Ont. Gen. Div.); and, seemingly, in *Harder* v. *Brown* (1989), 50 C.C.L.T. 85 (B.C.S.C.). See also *Capan* v. *Capan* (1980), 14 C.C.L.T. 191 (Ont. H.C.); *Dyne Holdings Ltd.* v. *Royal Insurance Co. of Canada* (1996), 135 D.L.R. (4th) 142 (P.E.I. App. Div.). However, no such tort was recognized in 1986 in *Bingo Enterprises Ltd.* v. *Plaxton* (1986), 26 D.L.R. (4th) 604 (Man. C.A.); and in *Ontario (A.G.)* v. *Dieleman* (1994), 117 D.L.R. (4th) 449 at 680 (Ont. Gen. Div.), Adams J. concluded, after a review of the case law prior to 1994, that one could not speak with confidence of a Canadian tort of invasion of privacy. See also J.D.R. Craig, 'Invasion of Privacy and *Charter* Values: The Common-Law Tort Awakens' (1997) 42 McGill L.J. 355.

32 See *Privacy Act*, R.S.B.C. 1979, c. 336; *The Privacy Act*, R.S.S. 1978, c. P-24; *Privacy Act*, R.S.M. 1987, c. P-125; *Privacy Act*, R.S.N. 1990, c. P-22; art. 3, C.C.Q.; and *Charter of Human Rights and Freedoms*, R.S.Q. c. C-12, art. 5.

through statutory complaints procedures.[33] There are also various forms of self-regulation, such as the consideration of privacy complaints by the Press Complaints Commission in Britain.[34] Some aspects of the discussion will also be relevant in the context of data protection legislation.[35]

II *The reasonable paranoid standard in Anglo-American law*

A. UNITED STATES

American courts recognize four separate privacy torts: intrusion, publication of private facts, 'false light' invasion of privacy, and appropriation of personality. The present discussion relates primarily to the two first mentioned.[36] As to intrusion, the intrusion must be into a private place or 'a private seclusion that the plaintiff has thrown about his person or affairs.'[37] There is generally no liability for observing, following, or photographing someone in a public place.[38] Similarly, the American tort of invasion of privacy by publication of private facts applies only to 'private' facts; and 'whatever the public may see from a public place cannot be private.'[39] Plaintiffs have been denied any right to privacy not only on the

33 For example, the Broadcasting Standards Commission considers complaints concerning privacy under the *Broadcasting Act 1996* (U.K.), 1996, c. 55, s. 110(1). The only legal sanction available to the Commission is to require the publication of an adverse finding, under s. 119. By contrast, New Zealand's Broadcasting Standards Authority may direct the payment of up to $5,000 compensation and may direct the broadcaster to refrain from broadcasting, or to refrain from broadcasting advertisements, for up to twenty-four hours; see *Broadcasting Act 1989* (N.Z.), 1989, No. 25, s. 13(1).

34 Since the Commission comes within the definition of 'public authority' in s. 6 of the *Human Rights Act 1998* (U.K.), 1998, c. 42, it will be prohibited from acting in a way that is incompatible with the European Convention on Human Rights, including the right to respect for private life under art. 8. See R. Singh, 'Privacy and the Media after the Human Rights Act' [1998] E.H.R.L.R. 712 at 728.

35 *E.g. Privacy Act 1993* (N.Z.), 1993, No. 28; *Data Protection Act 1998* (U.K.), 1998, c. 29; and Bill C-6, *An Act to support and promote electronic commerce by protecting personal information that is collected, used or disclosed in certain circumstances, by providing for the use of electronic means to communicate or record information or transactions and by amending the Canada Evidence Act, the Statutory Instruments Act and the Statute Revision Act*, 2d Sess., 36th Parl., 1999 (assented to 26 October 1999).

36 It is debatable whether 'false light' invasion of privacy and appropriation of personality are properly considered as 'privacy' torts at all; see R. Wacks, *Personal Information: Privacy and the Law* (Oxford: Clarendon Press, 1989) at 38.

37 *Restatement* § 652B, comment c.

38 Ibid.; *Prosser & Keeton on Torts*, supra note 21 at 855–6.

39 *N.O.C., Inc.* v. *Schaefer*, 484 A.2d 729 at 732 (N.J.Super. L. 1984).

street[40] but also in shops,[41] laundromats,[42] restaurants,[43] health spas,[44] parking lots,[45] airports,[46] common areas of cruise ships,[47] and school buildings.[48]

Certainly there are some exceptional cases where privacy suits have been successful. The *Restatement (Second) of Torts* declares, 'Even in a public place, however, there may be some matters about the plaintiff, such as his underwear or lack of it, that are not exhibited to the public gaze; and there may still be invasion of privacy when there is intrusion upon these matters.'[49] As many as four different types of cases in which American courts have, on occasion, recognized a right to privacy in a public place will be identified over the course of this article.[50] However, the only widely acknowledged exception is for persistent hounding and harassment; any other possible exceptions are ill-defined and not yet firmly established.

The usual rationale for the lack of protection in public is the assertion that someone in a public place has no reasonable expectation of privacy and has impliedly waived any right to privacy.[51] Thus a person could not complain of being photographed in an unemployment queue because 'appearance in a public place necessarily involves doffing the cloak of privacy.'[52] In *Gill* v. *Hearst Publishing Co.*,[53] a husband and wife were photographed without consent in an affectionate pose at their confectionery and ice cream stand in a public marketplace. The Supreme Court of California ruled that the publication of the photograph did not in itself[54] constitute an actionable invasion of privacy, stating as follows:

40 *United States* v. *Vazquez*, 31 F.Supp. 2d 85 (1998); *De Gregorio* v. *CBS, Inc.*, supra note 8; *Forster* v. *Manchester*, 189 A.2d 147 (Pa.Sup.Ct. 1963).

41 *Jacova* v. *Southern Radio and Television Co*, supra note 10; *Mark* v. *Seattle Times*, 635 P.2d 1081 (Wash. 1981).

42 *Batts* v. *Capital City Press, Inc.*, supra note 10; *Batts* v. *Baton Rouge (City of)*, supra note 10.

43 *Dempsey* v. *National Enquirer*, supra note 4; *Wilkins* v. *National Broadcasting Company*, supra note 4.

44 *Foster* v. *Livingwell Midwest, Inc.*, 865 F.2d 257 (6th Cir. 1988).

45 *Turner* v. *General Motors Corp.*, supra note 7; *Figured* v. *Paralegal Technical Services*, 555 A.2d 663 (N.J.Super. A.D. 1989) [hereinafter *Figured*].

46 *Fogel* v. *Forbes, Inc.*, 500 F.Supp. 1081 (1980).

47 *Muratore* v. *M/S Scotia Prince*, 656 F.Supp. 471 (D.Me. 1987).

48 *Jarrell* v. *Butts*, 379 S.E.2d 583 (Ga.App. 1989).

49 *Restatement* § 652B, comment c.

50 See text accompanying notes 124–34, 168–75, 192–8, and 215–21.

51 In addition to cases cited throughout this article, see, *e.g.*, *Dora* v. *Frontline Video, Inc.*, 15 Cal.App. 4th 536 at 544 (1993); *Machleder* v. *Diaz*, 538 F.Supp. 1364 at 1374 (1982); *Frazier* v. *Southeastern Pennsylvania Transportation Authority*, 907 F.Supp. 116 at 122 (E.D.Pa. 1995).

52 *Cefalu* v. *Globe Newspaper Co.*, 391 N.E.2d 935 at 939 (Mass.App. 1979), cert. den. 444 U.S. 1060 (1980).

53 Supra note 8.

54 The couple did have a cause of action against a magazine that used the photograph to illustrate the 'wrong kind of love' (see *Gill* v. *Curtis Publishing Co.*, 239 P.2d 630 (Cal.

> Here plaintiffs ... had voluntarily exposed themselves to public gaze in a pose open to the view of any persons who might then be at or near their place of business. By their own voluntary action plaintiffs waived their right of privacy.... In short, the photograph did not disclose anything which until then had been private, but rather only extended knowledge of the particular incident to a somewhat larger public....[55]

The wealth of American case law on privacy affords plenty of striking examples of the results of following this approach to its logical conclusion. In *International Union* v. *Garner*,[56] the mayor, chief of police, and various police officers had engaged in surveillance outside union meetings. They recorded the licence plate numbers of cars parked outside the meetings, traced these to automobile registrations, and informed the employer corporation of the identities of persons attending the meetings. The Court dismissed the plaintiffs' claim for invasion of privacy, stating that

> the Court finds that if the plaintiffs truly wanted their participation in the meeting to be private, they would not have left their cars in front of the meeting hall.... In sum, the Court finds that a person does not have a legitimate expectation of privacy, solitude, or seclusion in being free from the dissemination of inferences drawn from observations readily perceivable in public view.[57]

Similarly, in *Fayard* v. *Guardsmark, Inc.*,[58] the Court granted summary judgment on a woman's claim that her employer had watched outside her house and run licence checks on cars that came and went, to check for off-duty fraternization.

In *Batts* v. *Baton Rouge (City of)*[59] and *Batts* v. *Capital City Press, Inc.*,[60] the victim of a violent attack in a laundromat sued the municipality for disclosing her name and address to a newspaper, and the newspaper for publishing this information. The Court of Appeal of Louisiana held in both cases that there was no invasion of the victim's privacy, on the grounds that 'Anyone was free to be present at the laundromat and if present could have witnessed the occurrence and identified the participants.'[61]

1952)), and they were permitted to amend their complaint against Hearst Publishing Co. to allege that Hearst had consented to the use of the photograph in this connection.

55 *Gill* v. *Hearst Publishing Co.*, supra note 8 at 444–5.

56 Supra note 13.

57 Ibid. at 191.

58 Supra note 8.

59 Supra note 10.

60 Supra note 10.

61 501 So.2d 302 at 304; 479 So.2d 534 at 536. Quite apart from anything else, the Court seems to have been oblivious to the risk that the assailant, who was never identified or

The 'traditional' stance that there is no expectation of privacy in walking down a public street was applied in *United States* v. *Vazquez*[62] to women entering an abortion clinic. The Court stated:

> [A]ny images filmed by the video camera could also be viewed by members of the general public who were standing or walking in the vicinity of the clinic. Moreover, the videos were made out in the open and during broad daylight. Neither party argues that any ruse or subterfuge was employed to capture the subjects on film. Furthermore, the vicinity of [the clinic] is an area where persons on both sides of the abortion issue exercise their First Amendment rights on a consistent basis. Given these factors, a common law right to privacy does not exist because no one walking in this area could have a legitimate expectation of privacy.[63]

An especially egregious case was *Turner* v. *General Motors Corp.*[64] Late one night, a young man was waiting in the General Motors parking lot to give his father a ride home. A surveillance camera videotaped him in an act of masturbation. The tape was exhibited to numerous employees at the General Motors Plant, and the father was ridiculed and humiliated for months afterwards. In an unsuccessful action by the father for negligent infliction of emotional distress, the Missouri Court of Appeals held that General Motors had no legal duty not to publish the contents of the videotape and that the son would have no cause of action for invasion of privacy. Although the actions of General Motors' supervisors in allowing its security officers to show the videotape were 'reprehensible,' the son had no reasonable expectation of privacy for acts committed on another's private property.[65]

The message of these cases is, once reasonable people venture outside the safety of their own homes, they must expect that they may be followed, filmed, investigated and spied upon, by any person for any purpose. They must also expect that their families, co-workers, employers, acquaintances – indeed, the whole world – may be informed of every detail of their life beyond the four walls of their private abode. The onus is on individuals to take precautions against being intruded upon – those with whom they share space have no corresponding obligation not to intrude. Prudence and paranoia reign.

apprehended, could have learned the plaintiff's identity and address from the news accounts and used this information to victimize her further, as happened to a rape victim in *Florida Star* v. *B.J.F.*, 105 L.Ed.2d 443 (1989).

62 Supra note 40.

63 Ibid. at 91; compare *Doe* v. *Mills*, supra note 5.

64 Supra note 7.

65 Ibid. at 79. The Court observed in a footnote that a sign 'visible to all who entered the GM premises' stated that the grounds, including the parking lot, were subject to surveillance.

B. CANADA

It is not yet clear to what extent the Canadian common law courts will recognize a right to privacy in public places. Certainly the American approach has been influential in some Canadian cases. In *Silber* v. *B.C.T.V.*,[66] the owner of a furniture store sued under British Columbia's Privacy Act for the filming and broadcast of his tussle with a news crew in the store's parking lot. Lysyk J. found *Gill* v. *Hearst Publishing Co.*[67] instructive, and held in respect of the filming that the plaintiff had no reasonable expectation of privacy in the parking lot, since 'what transpired there was observable by anyone in the vicinity.'[68] However, Lysyk J. emphasized the high degree of visibility of events in the parking lot: '[The events] occurred in the middle of the day, on a site open to unobstructed view from an adjoining heavily travelled thoroughfare, in a busy commercial neighbourhood.'[69] His reasoning might not apply to a less exposed location. As to the subsequent broadcast, he declined to decide whether the reasoning in *Gill* v. *Hearst Publishing Co.* would apply under the Privacy Act, preferring to base his decision on public interest.[70]

The *Silber* decision was recently followed by the Newfoundland Supreme Court in *Druken* v. *R.G. Fewer & Associates, Inc.*[71] A private investigation firm used video surveillance to investigate the plaintiff's personal injury claims. Dunn J. dismissed the plaintiff's action for invasion of privacy under Newfoundland's Privacy Act, stating as follows:

> The plaintiff herein cannot have reasonably expected any degree of privacy pertaining to her actions in public. Likewise, any actions out and around her home in full view of the passing public would not give rise to an expectation of privacy as one might expect in relation to counselling records; private telephone conversations; conversations generally not in the vicinity of other individuals or surveillance of actions in the privacy and domain of one's dwellinghouse. Where the action occurs becomes relevant to the nature and degree of privacy to which an individual is entitled and which is reasonable in the circumstance. Arguably overt actions and behaviours occurring in public are not really 'private' in nature at all. Observation, where authorized, in my view, can hardly be seen to be offensive.[72]

66 [1986] 2 W.W.R. 609 (B.C.S.C.).
67 Supra note 8.
68 Supra note 66 at 616–7.
69 Ibid. at 615.
70 Ibid. at 617–8.
71 [1998] N.J. No. 312 (Nfld.S.C.), online: QL (NJ).
72 Ibid. at para. 43.

Although parts of this passage echo the American exclusion of privacy protection in public places, the qualification 'where authorized' in the last sentence suggests that there must be a legitimate purpose for the surveillance. Earlier in the judgment, Dunn J. discussed the need to balance the relevant Charter values in such a case and observed, 'Surveillance without purpose would engage different considerations.'[73] In *Davis* v. *McArthur*, the British Columbia Court of Appeal appears to have accepted that surveillance in public places could potentially breach the Privacy Act even where there is a legitimate interest in the plaintiff's conduct, although it concluded that the shadowing and observation in the instant case were 'not so close and continuous as to go beyond reasonable bounds.'[74]

In *Ontario (A.G.)* v. *Dieleman*,[75] the Ontario Court considered an argument that picketers who drew attention to women entering abortion clinics were invading their privacy. Adams J. looked to the American cases and to Professor Prosser's observations about the lack of privacy protection in public places and noted that, factually, the picketing was on public sidewalks, so the defendants were able to assert that there was nothing 'private' about these locations.[76] However, the Court did not reach a conclusion on the privacy issues, instead granting an interlocutory injunction based on public and private nuisance.

One case demonstrating that Canadian courts are as capable as American courts of descending into paranoia is *Milton* v. *Savinkoff*.[77] The plaintiff stopped in Vancouver on her way home from Hawaii, and the defendant, a friend, lent her his jacket while he gave her a ride to the airport. The plaintiff inadvertently left some photographs from her trip in a pocket of the jacket. She had shown him some of these photographs, but there was also one taken by a female friend at their hotel in Hawaii that showed the plaintiff topless. The defendant circulated this photograph to others, and the plaintiff sued for invasion of privacy. One of the factors that influenced Cooper J. in dismissing the action was that the plaintiff had apparently not minded the photograph being seen by an unknown film developer in Hawaii. Professor P.H. Osborne comments,

73 Ibid. at para. 21.

74 (1970) 17 D.L.R. (3d) 760 at 765. Although Tysoe J., delivering the judgment of the Court, said he had not found any Canadian, English, or American cases of assistance in construing the Act, in alluding to unreasonably close surveillance he probably had in mind such cases as *Nader* v. *General Motors Corp.*, supra note 10, which had been mentioned in the trial judgment.

75 Supra note 31.

76 Ibid. at 679.

77 Supra note 6.

Given the huge number of films processed in Hawaii it is unlikely that the processors have the time, let alone the inclination, to look at individual photographs. Even if they did the plaintiff would be unknown to them and there would not be the same embarrassment nor distress engendered by publication to friends.'[78]

Osborne observes that if people waive their right to privacy merely by having a film developed, then only those with their own dark rooms can have any privacy in personal photographs.

On the other hand, American law is not the only potential influence on the Canadian common law courts regarding privacy in public places. In Quebec, under civil law, quite a different approach has been taken. In *Aubry* v. *Éditions Vice-Versa Inc.*,[79] the Supreme Court of Canada upheld a decision of the Quebec courts awarding $2 000 damages to a young woman whose photograph was published in an artistic magazine. The photograph was taken without her consent as she sat on a step outside a building on a Montreal street. The Court held that the publication constituted a fault under Quebec law, as a fault is committed as soon as an identifiable image of a person is published without consent, unless justified by the public interest.[80] The majority also believed there was sufficient proof of damage. The majority judgment discussed situations in which the right to privacy in a public place would be outweighed by the public interest, such as where the person appears in only an incidental manner and is not the principal subject of the photograph.[81] However, such situations were seen as the exception rather than the rule, and the view that there was an unlimited right to publish photographs taken in a public place was expressly rejected.[82]

It remains to be seen how much impact the *Aubry* decision will have in the common law jurisdictions. It has been observed that there is 'little substantive difference' between the privacy law of Quebec and the statutory privacy torts.[83] The decision does give some indication of the Supreme Court's view regarding the appropriate balance of the relevant Charter values. Arguably, the Court placed a little too much weight on a

78 P.H. Osborne, 'Case Comment on *Milton* v. *Savinkoff*' (1994) 18 C.C.L.T. (2d) 292 at 296.

79 [1998] 1 S.C.R. 591, 157 D.L.R. (4th) 577 [hereinafter *Aubry* cited to S.C.R.].

80 Ibid. at 615, *per* L'Heureux-Dubé and Bastarache JJ., Gonthier, Cory, and Iacobucci JJ. concurring; ibid., 605, *per* Lamer C.J.C. dissenting.

81 Ibid. at 616–7, *per* L'Heureux-Dubé and Bastarache JJ. See also ibid. at 607, *per* Lamer C.J.C. dissenting.

82 Ibid. at 619–20.

83 J. Craig & N. Nolte, 'Privacy and Free Speech in Germany and Canada: Lessons for an English Privacy Tort' [1998] E.H.R.L.R. 162 at 166.

relatively minor breach of privacy, which was not proven to have caused any harm beyond the annoyance of being treated as a spectacle for others.[84] However, the merits of the case will be discussed more fully later in this article.[85]

There are other indications that Canadian law may be more receptive than American law to the notion of public privacy. In *Dagg* v. *Canada (Minister of Finance)*, the Supreme Court of Canada held that time entries in sign-in logs, recording when employees entered and left the workplace on weekends, constituted 'personal information' for the purposes of s. 3 of the federal Privacy Act.[86] La Forest J. stated, 'In my view, a reasonable person would not expect strangers to have access to detailed, systematic knowledge of an individual's location during non-working hours, even if that location is his or her workplace.'[87] He noted that even in the search and seizure context, in which 'the countervailing state interest in surveillance may be very strong,' there has been some recognition of a privacy interest in a person's physical movements.[88] *Dagg* is especially significant because a person's movements are perhaps the most basic information revealed when appearing in a public place.

The British Columbia Information and Privacy Commissioner has recognized the vulnerability to privacy invasion of people filmed in interactions with the police in public places.[89] In *KF Media Inc.* v. *Vancouver (Police Department)*,[90] the Commissioner investigated a complaint from the producers of *To Serve and Protect*, a 'reality television' show about day-to-day police work. The complaint concerned a decision of the Vancouver Police Department that the show could no longer reveal the identities of persons videotaped in public during 'ride-alongs.' The Commissioner affirmed the Department's policy and recommended that any police department that allows a film crew to accompany its officers on duty should require the production company to obscure the identities of members of the public before broadcast. He also commented that persons in contact with the police cannot give voluntary and informed

84 *Aubry*, supra note 79 at 620–1. Lamer C.J.C. and Major J. dissented on the grounds that there was no evidence of damage.

85 See text accompanying notes 260–2.

86 [1997] 2 S.C.R. 403, 148 D.L.R. (4th) 385 [hereinafter *Dagg* cited to S.C.R.]. However, the majority held that the information fell under s. 3(j) and so was subject to disclosure under the Access to Information Act.

87 Ibid. at 437–8. La Forest J. dissented on the application of s. 3(j).

88 Ibid. at 439, citing *R.* v. *Wise*, [1992] 1 S.C.R. 527, 70 C.C.C. (3d) 193.

89 Similarly, in England, Rose L.J. has deplored any general police practice of inviting media presence during investigative procedures; see *R.* v. *Marylebone Magistrates' Court, ex parte Amdrell Ltd.*, *The Times*, 17 September 1998, 148 N.L.J. 1230.

90 Investigation P95-004, [1995] B.C.I.P.C.D. No. 6, online: QL (BCIPCD).

consent to the disclosure of their identities when they are under great stress and may be incapacitated or intoxicated.

In summary, the reaction of Canadian decision makers faced with claims to privacy in public places has varied widely. Although American privacy cases have been influential, and a distinctly paranoid view has been adopted in at least one Canadian decision, nevertheless there are signs that Canadian courts may be more open to the notion of public privacy.

C. NEW ZEALAND

The New Zealand courts have invoked American case law in recognizing their own emerging tort of invasion of privacy and, in particular, have referred to the American private facts tort. However, McGechan J. commented in *Tucker* v. *News Media Ownership Ltd.* that if the tort is accepted as established, 'its boundaries and exceptions will need much working out on a case by case basis so as to suit the conditions of this country.'[91] In the *Tucker* case itself, the fact that the plaintiff's convictions were originally in the public domain did not prevent recognition of a tenable claim for invasion of privacy.[92] In *Bradley* v. *Wingnut Films Ltd.*,[93] Gallen J. refused to extend the emerging tort to the filming of the plaintiff's tombstone in the background of a splatter movie. He emphasized the very public nature of a tombstone in a public cemetery, and noted the comment in *Prosser and Keeton on the Law of Torts* that there is no right to be let alone in a public place. 'However,' he added, echoing the statement cited above[94] from the revised edition, 'I also accept that it is conceivable that in certain circumstances the fact that something occurred or exists in a public place does not necessarily mean that it should receive widespread publicity if it does not involve a matter of public concern. Had the defendant chosen to involve the plaintiff's tombstone directly in the action of the film as if for example the clergyman had been impaled upon it ... the situation might have been different.'[95]

New Zealand's Broadcasting Standards Authority has adopted a more rigid approach, despite having initially observed, in light of comments in the *Tucker* case, that public facts might receive greater protection in New Zealand than in the United States.[96] The Authority has been guided by

91 [1986] 2 N.Z.L.R. 716 at 733 (H.C.).

92 This was pointed out by Eichelbaum J. in *TV3 Network Services Ltd.* v. *Broadcasting Standards Authority* [1995] 2 N.Z.L.R. 720 at 728 (H.C.) [hereinafter *TV3* v. *B.S.A.*].

93 [1993] 1 N.Z.L.R. 415 (H.C.).

94 See text accompanying note 21.

95 Supra note 93 at 424.

96 See *McAllister* v. *Television New Zealand Ltd.* (B.S.A. 5/90, 3 May 1990); also *TV3* v. *B.S.A.*, supra note 92.

American tort law in formulating the principles it applies to complaints under the *Broadcasting Act 1989*, s. 4(1)(c), which requires broadcasters to maintain standards consistent with the privacy of the individual.[97] The first principle, modelled on the American publication tort, protects against the public disclosure of 'private facts.' Events occurring in a public place are classed as public facts, and their disclosure does not breach the first principle.[98] In a couple of oddly reasoned cases, the Authority has treated the name or identity of a person observed in a public place as a private fact and its disclosure as a breach of principle (i).[99] Now such cases are covered by principle (v), a strange new principle invented to fill in gaps left by the 'private facts' formulation. Principle (v) protects against non-consensual broadcast of the name, address, or telephone number of an identifiable person. This principle does not apply to details that are public information, or to news and current affairs reporting,[100] and is subject to a public interest defence.[101]

The second principle allows for protection against the highly offensive public disclosure of some kinds of public facts. However, it states that '[t]he "public" facts contemplated concern events (such as criminal behaviour) which have, in effect, become private again, for example through the passage of time.' Complaints have been upheld under this principle only where a significant lapse of time or a suppression order have intervened to make the facts private again.[102]

The third principle, modelled on the American intrusion tort, explicitly states that 'an individual's interest in solitude or seclusion does not provide the basis for a privacy action for an individual to complain about being observed or followed or photographed in a public place.' Complaints regarding filming in public places, including the sites of road crashes and other tragedies,[103] are rejected summarily by reference to this

97 See M. Stace, Privacy: Interpreting the Broadcasting Standards Authority's Decisions January 1990 to June 1998 (Palmerston North: Dunmore Press, 1998) at 27–8.

98 *Clements* v. *Radio New Zealand Ltd.* (B.S.A. 19/92, 14 May 1992) [hereinafter *Clements*].

99 Ibid; *M.B.* v. *Radio New Zealand Ltd.* (B.S.A. 100/95, 21 September 1995). For discussion of *Clements*, see 'Private Circles,' supra note 27 at 331–2.

100 In practice, the Authority has ignored this qualification and has instead focused on whether the person's identity is of legitimate public concern. For example, the principle has been applied to the naming of a woman filmed outside a courthouse, in a television news item on the sentencing of her partner; see *Bancroft* v. *Television New Zealand Ltd.* (B.S.A. 1996-087, 15 August 1996).

101 On its face, principle (v) would prohibit naming a person without consent even if a reasonable person would not object and no real harm is done, for example, where a radio station invites listeners to call in and nominate people for a 'good neighbour' award.

102 See *S.* v. *TV3* (B.S.A. 1/94, 19 January 1994), appeal dismissed *TV3* v. *B.S.A.*, supra note 92; *P.* v. *TV3* (B.S.A. 21/94, 28 April 1994); *Drury* v. *TV3* [1997] N.Z.A.R. 57 (B.S.A.).

103 See *Conway* v. *TV3* (B.S.A. 1996-115/116, 12 September 1996); *Halliwell* v. *Television New*

exception. Unlike the American courts, the Authority has generally neglected to consider whether the subsequent decision to broadcast such footage might raise separate issues under principles (i) or (ii).[104] The distinction between intrusion and publication could be important where, for example, a broadcaster captures an embarrassing public moment on film unintentionally but then chooses to televise it,[105] or where a disclosure is gratuitous or misleading.[106] On the other hand, the Authority has stated that 'filming from a camera hidden in a public place but directed towards a private place or the use of a telephoto lens while sited in a public place could be considered to amount to prying in some circumstances.'[107] Thus filming a woman in her own back yard from a neighbouring landfill was held to violate her privacy.[108] The Authority has also upheld one complaint under principle (iii) where a radio host eavesdropped on a couple's private conversation as they walked down the street and reported what he overheard.[109]

In summary, the courts in New Zealand appear open to the possibility of protecting public privacy in some circumstances, whereas the statutory Broadcasting Standards Authority has adopted fairly rigid rules excluding privacy protection in public places.

III *Beyond paranoia – the reality and importance of public privacy*

As mentioned above,[110] the courts generally justify the exclusion of public places from privacy protection on the grounds that since there is no reasonable expectation of privacy in a public place, a person venturing out in public waives the right to privacy. The concept of a 'reasonable' expectation of privacy is an amalgam of descriptive and normative

Zealand Ltd. (B.S.A. 1998-076/077, 23 July 1998); *Barton* v. *TV3* (B.S.A. 1998-032/033, 26 March 1998).

104 See, *e.g.*, *Conway* v. *TV3*, supra note 103. Confusion regarding the relationship between the two relevant American torts is apparent in *TV3* v. *B.S.A.*, supra note 92 at 729. Discussing principle (iii), Eichelbaum C.J. incorrectly lists the criteria for the private facts tort as limitations on the intrusion tort.

105 See, *e.g.*, *Taylor* v. *K.T.V.B., Inc.*, 525 P.2d 984 (1974). The plaintiff was filmed being arrested and taken from his home in the nude. The court held that a jury could award damages for invasion of privacy if the film clip was aired to embarrass the plaintiff or with reckless disregard for the plaintiff's humiliation.

106 See, *e.g.*, *Leverton* v. *Curtis Publishing Co.*, 192 F.2d 974 (3d Cir. 1951), which held that it was an invasion of the plaintiff's privacy to use her picture, taken after she was struck by a car, to illustrate a totally unrelated article.

107 *Smedley* v. *Television New Zealand Ltd.* (B.S.A. 29–30/94, 9 May 1994).

108 *S* v. *TV3*, supra note 102; compare *Barton* v. *TV3*, supra note 103.

109 *Black* v. *T.R.N. Ltd.* (B.S.A. 1999-003, 21 January 1999).

110 See text accompanying note 51.

notions. Descriptively, it is assumed that reasonable people do not anticipate having any significant degree of privacy in public, so they take precautions not to reveal anything in a public place that they would prefer to keep private. It is also assumed that people are free to choose whether to expose their affairs in public and that the failure to take effective precautions to safeguard one's privacy signifies a waiver of the right to privacy. Normatively, the position is taken that, to the extent public privacy exists, it is not worthy of legal protection. Each of these assumptions will be addressed in turn.

A. THE REALITY OF PUBLIC PRIVACY

Location is undoubtedly a relevant factor in determining how much privacy can reasonably be expected. Broadly speaking, people do not usually expect the same degree of privacy in public places as in their own homes:

> When we go into a public place we know that we are likely to be seen by others, strangers and acquaintances. We generally control ourselves according to that expectation, particularly in the way we dress and act. We know we are, *to some extent*, objects of public scrutiny. In a private place we may react quite differently, knowing or believing that we will only be seen by specific people, usually family or intimate friends. We relax our guard.[111]

However, the difference is a matter of degree rather than an all-or-nothing distinction. Most people spend a great deal of their everyday lives in public places without imagining that they are being observed any more than casually and by a limited number of people. A number of factors provide varying degrees of privacy in public places. These factors include varying degrees of exposure or seclusion in different places and at different times, anonymity and the limitation of attention paid, various social rules, the dispersion of information over space and time, and the ephemeral nature of our use of public space. A rogue factor that not only disrupts normal expectations of public privacy but also undermines the distinction between public and private places is the use of privacy-invasive technologies. All of these factors will now be examined in more detail.

1. Location, location, location

The term 'public place' covers a wide range of locations, from bustling thoroughfares to remote getaways. As used in privacy law, the term generally includes any place, whether publicly or privately owned, to

111 Australian Law Reform Commission, Report No. 11, *Unfair Publication: Defamation and Privacy* (Canberra: Australian Government Printing Service, 1978) at 125 [emphasis added].

which the public has access.[112] In American law, it also includes anywhere that is visible from a publicly accessible vantage point, such as parts of a house or garden that are visible from the street.[113] It may even include parts of the interior of one's home that can be seen with the naked eye from a neighbouring apartment.[114]

A potential problem of equivocation arises here, since a place that is 'public' in the sense of being publicly accessible can also be very 'private' in the sense of being secluded; public access is only loosely connected with public exposure. The blanket exclusion of all public places from privacy law allows for no distinction between the expectation of privacy when browsing in a quiet bookstore and the expectation of privacy when taking part in a street parade. In regard to expectations of privacy, there is not a sharp distinction between public and private places but a difference of degree. Reasonable people assess roughly just how 'public' a situation is and adjust their behaviour accordingly. Only the paranoid confuse remote risks with likelihoods and behave in all public places as if the eyes of the world were upon them.

The bifurcation between public and private places in privacy law is based on a fallacious view of privacy as an all-or-nothing concept.[115] Exposure to a limited number of people, or even to just one person, is equated with a complete loss of privacy. In reality, the small loss of privacy someone suffers if a nosy stranger observes which books she peruses in a bookstore is quite a different thing from having her browsing habits reported to her employer or publicized to the world. As one American legal scholar has pointed out, the courts' approach to public places is inconsistent with the standard they apply to determine whether a private fact has been wrongfully 'publicized':

> The 'fading' of a privacy interest attendant to a fact's prior public appearance should ... raise only a question of degree. The courts' analytical flaw here is most notable given that, in this context, 'public' only means the condition of being 'in

112 See, *e.g.*, *Batts* v. *Baton Rouge (City of)*, supra note 10 at 304 ('anyone was free to be present' in laundromat). See also the list of public places in text accompanying notes 40–8.

113 Places which are thus 'open to the public eye' may or may not themselves be labelled 'public,' but in any case the American law excludes from the scope of privacy protection anything that can be seen *from* a public place. See *Mark* v. *Seattle Times*, supra note 41 (no actionable claim for invasion of privacy where a pharmacist was filmed inside his pharmacy after opening hours from an adjoining driveway); *Aisenson* v. *American Broadcasting Co. Inc.*, 220 Cal.App.3d 146 (1990) [hereinafter *Aisenson*]; *Figured*, supra note 45 at 666–7.

114 *DiGirolamo*, supra note 2 at 9.

115 See 'Private Circles,' supra note 27 at 324–6; McClurg, supra note 18 at note 276.

public,' not the numerical standard courts require in the publicity element. Thus, defendants may disclose a private fact about a plaintiff to two persons without invading that plaintiff's privacy at all, but plaintiffs who expose the same fact to the same two persons 'in public' have destroyed their privacy interest in that fact entirely.[116]

It can even be meaningful to speak of privacy despite exposure to a large number of people in a public place, if they are all from a particular sub-group in society, such as others of the same sex or people attending a particular church.[117]

Of course, being in a public place does not necessarily entail exposure to anyone. There may be nobody else in sight at the time, or no one who is paying any attention. To quote Prosser, 'Suppose that a citizen responds to a call of nature in the bushes in a public park?'[118] Surely the mere risk of an unseen observer is not enough to transform this into a 'public' act?

2. Dispersion of information

Jeffrey Reiman has commented that 'privacy results not only from locked doors and closed curtains, but also from the way our publicly observable activities are dispersed over space and time.'[119] The belief that one is being persistently followed and observed is, in ordinary circumstances, a likely sign of paranoia.[120] It does not feature in the expectations of a reasonable person:

Even when engaged in a public act, such as driving, it is reasonable for the average, law-abiding citizen to expect that his/her actions will attract no more than casual observation by others. Anything more than casual observation has

116 J.B. Mintz, 'The Remains of Privacy's Disclosure Tort: An Exploration of the Private Domain' (1996) 55 Md.L.Rev. 425 at 441.

117 See *Huskey* v. *National Broadcasting Co.*, 632 F.Supp. 1282 at 1287–8 (N.D.Ill. 1986) (prison personnel and other inmates); and *Y.G.* v. *Jewish Hospital of St. Louis*, 795 S.W.2d 488 (Mo.App. 1990) [hereinafter *Y.G.*] (couples who had undergone *in vitro* fertilization), although public access was limited in both cases. See also *Doe* v. *Mills*, supra note 5, discussed below (see text accompanying notes 194–8).

118 W.L. Prosser, 'Privacy' (1960) 48 Cal.L.Rev. 383 at 395 note 104. Of course, if that someone happens to be royal, there is a good chance someone else will be hiding in the bushes with a camera; see E. Reguly, 'Trashy Newspapers Have Strong Appeal' *The [Toronto] Financial Post* (1 November 1991) s. 1, p. 11, re front-page picture of Prince William urinating in a park. However, even highly predictable intrusions may violate normatively reasonable expectations.

119 Supra note 28 at 29.

120 In *Pinkerton National Detective Agency, Inc.* v. *Stevens*, 132 S.E.2d 119 (Ga.App. 1963), the plaintiff said that she and others, including her doctor, initially assumed she was hallucinating.

the potential to profoundly affect personal freedom, and in the case of driving, this would include the freedom to travel where and when one pleases and to associate with whom one pleases.[121]

Systematic observation and accumulation of information about a person can have a very severe impact on privacy, producing a fairly detailed picture of a person's life and allowing inferences to be drawn beyond the facts observed.[122] Ordinary precautions may not be effective against this type of threat to privacy:

> If we direct our privacy-protection efforts at reinforcing our doors and curtains, we may miss the way in which modern means of information collection threaten our privacy by gathering up the pieces of our public lives and making them visible from a single point.[123]

The difference between casual observation and systematic surveillance has been recognized to some extent in American privacy law. The most widely acknowledged exception to the public place exemption is for 'conduct that amounts to a persistent course of hounding, harassment and unreasonable surveillance, even if conducted in a public or semi-public place.'[124] In *Gallela* v. *Onassis*,[125] the court granted injunctive relief against a paparazzo who 'insinuated himself into the very fabric' of Jacqueline Onassis's life, even endangering her children's safety in his 'frenzied' attempts to get pictures.[126] He invaded the children's private schools, bribed doormen, and romanced a family servant to keep him advised of the family's movements. The court held that his actions

> went far beyond the reasonable bounds of news gathering. When weighed against the *de minimis* public importance of the daily activities of the defendant, Gallela's constant surveillance, his obtrusive and intruding presence, was unwarranted and unreasonable.[127]

121 United States Department of Transportation, *National Program Plan for Intelligent Transportation Systems* (Final Draft, November 1994) at 2, as cited in S.A. Alpert, 'Privacy and Intelligent Highways: Finding the Right of Way' (1995) 11 Computer & High Tech. L.J. 97 at 115.

122 Reiman, supra note 28 at 29.

123 Ibid.

124 *Wolfson* v. *Lewis*, 924 F.Supp. 1413 at 1420 (E.D.Pa. 1996) and cases cited therein; also *Kramer* v. *Downey*, 680 S.W.2d 524 (Tex.App. 5 Dist. 1984).

125 487 F.2d 986 (2d Cir. 1973).

126 Ibid. at 994.

127 Ibid. at 995.

In *Pinkerton National Detective Agency, Inc.* v. *Stevens*,[128] a detective agency shadowed a personal injury claimant constantly over several months. The court said that the agency's actions were not limited to 'that reasonable and unobtrusive observation which would ordinarily be used to catch one in normal activities unaware'[129] and were sufficient to amount to a violation of privacy. The exception has also been applied in cases of stalking.[130] A common element in most cases applying the exception is that the victims have been frightened by the harassment.[131]

The New York Court of Appeals in *Nader* v. *General Motors Corp.* made comments going a step further than other cases in discussing a claim that General Motors had conducted a campaign of intimidation against an outspoken author and lecturer on automobile safety.[132] Fuld C.J. noted that 'overzealous' surveillance could be actionable and stated that

> [a] person does not automatically make public everything he does merely by being in a public place, and the mere fact that Nader was in a bank did not give anyone the right to try to discover the amount of money he was withdrawing. On the other hand, if the plaintiff acted in such a way as to reveal that fact to any casual observer, then, it may not be said that the appellant intruded into his private sphere.[133]

Of course, most shops are laid out in such a way that a casual observer could see quite easily what someone takes from the shelf to the counter, so this comment is of limited comfort to Prudence.

Breitel J. suggested that the courts may take into account the cumulative impact of surveillance:

> Although acts performed in 'public,' especially if taken singly or in small numbers, may not be confidential, at least arguably a right to privacy may nevertheless be invaded through extensive or exhaustive monitoring and cataloguing of acts normally disconnected and anonymous.[134]

3. Anonymity

A further factor providing a degree of privacy in public places is anonymity. Often the people with whom we share public space, especially in the city or away from our usual stamping grounds, do not know us from

128 Supra note 120.
129 Ibid. at 125.
130 *Kramer* v. *Downey*, supra note 124; *Summers* v. *Bailey*, 55 F.3d 1564 (11th Cir. 1995).
131 *Summers* v. *Bailey*, ibid. at 1566, states that surveillance is an unreasonable intrusion where it 'aims to frighten or torment a person.'
132 Supra note 10 at 771.
133 Ibid., Scileppi, Bergan, and Gibson JJ. concurring.
134 Ibid. at 772, concurring in result, in an opinion in which Burke and Jasen JJ. concurred.

the proverbial bar of soap. Any snippets of information strangers may learn from observing us are unconnected with our identities and are likely to be quickly forgotten. Alan Westin has noted that the ability to move about anonymously from time to time is a major aspect of privacy, which is lost by celebrities.[135] He describes how anonymity enables people to 'merge into the situational landscape'[136] and points out that anonymous relations give rise to the 'phenomenon of the stranger,' where people feel free to confide to a stranger matters that they would withhold from acquaintances.[137] Westin explains that 'the individual can express himself freely because he knows the stranger will not continue in his life and that, although the stranger may give an objective response to the questions put to him, he is able to exert no authority or restraint over the individual.'[138] This phenomenon is vital to survey research, since honest responses depend on the guarantee of anonymity and on people's willingness to give personal information to an interviewer who is a stranger to them.[139]

4. Social rules

A myriad of complex social rules and practices serve to minimize the risks of appearing in public. Most of these rules are unspoken, and we may not be conscious of them until they are broken. Nevertheless, their violation can attract opprobrium and more serious social sanctions, and learning the nuances of these rules in one's own culture is a major task of growing up. Some examples that have been documented by sociologist Erving Goffman are rules concerning territory and personal space in public places, civil inattention, and limitations on staring.[140] The interaction of these rules provides a balance among practicality, curiosity, and privacy. For instance, when people are in close proximity, the opportunity for 'inoffensive staring'[141] is limited. Goffman elaborates:

For example, urinals in public toilets in America bring men very close to each other under circumstances where, for a period of time, they must expose themselves. In such places considerable care is taken in regard to eyes lest privacy be violated more than necessary. When two men are urinating next to

135 Supra note 22 at 69.

136 Ibid. at 31.

137 Ibid., citing *The Sociology of George Simmel*, trans. and ed. K. Wolff (New York, 1950) at 402–8.

138 Supra note 22 at 31–2.

139 Ibid. at 53.

140 See E. Goffman, *Relations in Public: Microstudies of the Public Order* (New York: Basic Books, 1971), especially c. 2, 'Territories of the Self.'

141 Ibid. at 60.

each other, their eyes will have a very narrow surface territory that will be safe. Similarly, when an individual enters a new region, he may find few places available that are sufficiently far removed from other persons present to allow their being stared at with impunity....[142]

Another social rule, the 'greeting rule between acquainteds,' functions as a signal that one is no longer in an anonymous situation:

[U]pon newly coming into sight of someone with whom one is acquainted, there is an obligation to make one's presence felt by extending a greeting. An incidental effect of this rule is that it ensures a subject protection from being observed or overheard unbeknownst to himself by an acquaintance.[143]

The potential for social norms to provide a high degree of privacy even in a very public place is well illustrated by the legend of Lady Godiva and Peeping Tom of Coventry.[144]

The point is not that the law should directly enforce subtle cultural norms but rather that, empirically, these social factors are relevant in shaping people's expectations of privacy. For example, a person writing in her private diary while sitting under a tree in an un-crowded park would be surprised and offended if a stranger crept up behind her and read over her shoulder. If a reporter photographed the diary using a telephoto lens and published its contents in the human interest pages, it would be nonsense to defend this behaviour on the basis that the diarist lacked a reasonable expectation of privacy.

5. Impermanence

A dichotomy between public and private locations also overlooks the relevance of time and the transience of much of what appears in public. There is a world of difference between the long-term public exposure of a house[145] or a tombstone,[146] for example, and the fleeting revelation of one's purchases as they are taken to the pharmacy counter. Reasonable expectations can be violated by making a permanent record of what is revealed in public only briefly. However, American courts have been

142 Ibid. at 59.

143 Ibid. at 299–300.

144 The Lord of Coventry promised to remove certain taxes if Lady Godiva rode naked through the town. She did so, but the townsfolk all stayed indoors to preserve her privacy. Only a tailor named Peeping Tom peeped through his window, and he was struck blind for his disloyalty. See I.H. Evans, ed., *Brewer's Dictionary of Phrase and Fable*, rev. ed. (London: Carswell, 1981) at 489–90.

145 See, *e.g.*, *Jaubert* v. *Crowley Post-Signal, Inc.*, 375 So.2d 1386 (La. 1979) [hereinafter *Jaubert*].

146 See, *e.g.*, *Bradley* v. *Wingnut Films Ltd.*, supra note 93.

largely oblivious to this distinction. In fact, it is explicitly reasoned that it cannot be an intrusion to take a person's photograph without consent in public, since 'this amounts to nothing more than making a record, not differing essentially from a full written description, of a public sight which anyone would be free to see.'[147]

This reasoning has been challenged by McClurg, who points out three important ways in which a photograph or videotape intensifies invasion of privacy. First, 'the temporal limitations that are otherwise inherent in public intrusions are eliminated,' allowing intrusive scrutiny to be extended indefinitely.[148] Memories fade; photographs last longer. This is why some sexual offenders photograph or videotape their victims, and why a victim may feel that the assault continues while such records remain in the offender's possession.[149] Second, 'because of this permanent record, information may be revealed that would not be noticed by transitory observation with the naked eye.'[150] The potential for photography to freeze-frame an embarrassing moment is well illustrated by the facts of *McNamara* v. *Freedom Newspapers, Inc.*[151] The case concerned the publication in a local newspaper of a photograph taken during a high school soccer game. The photograph showed the plaintiff and another student running full stride after a soccer ball, and the plaintiff's genitalia could be seen, having been exposed at the exact moment the picture was taken. The court dismissed an action for invasion of privacy, reasoning that the plaintiff had been voluntarily participating in a spectator sport in a public place.

McClurg's third point is that a photograph permits dissemination of an image to a much larger audience, and also to different audiences than the subject intended. He comments that

> [c]onduct which would be appropriate for one environment may be inappropriate and embarrassing in another. For example, although many persons are willing to expose their flesh at the beach or poolside, most would not willingly expose the same image to other audiences or in other contexts.[152]

147 *Prosser & Keeton on Torts*, supra note 21 at 856.

148 McClurg, supra note 18 at 1041–2.

149 See, *e.g.*, *Harder* v. *Brown*, supra note 31. The plaintiff sought a mandatory injunction ordering the return of photographs taken during sexual assaults when she was a minor, claiming a continuing invasion of privacy. The injunction was granted without discussion of the legal basis for the remedy, whether at common law or under British Columbia's Privacy Act.

150 McClurg, supra note 18 at 1042.

151 802 S.W.2d 901 (Tex.App.–Corpus Christi 1991).

152 McClurg, supra note 18 at 1043.

The difference between a mere description and a permanent record is well recognized in the area of search and seizure. In *R.* v. *Duarte*, the Supreme Court of Canada said 'the law recognizes that we inherently have to bear the risk of the "tattle-tale" but draws the line at concluding that we must also bear, as the price of choosing to speak to another human being, the risk of having a permanent recording made of our words.'[153] Similarly, the United States Supreme Court has stated, in relation to participant monitoring, that

> words would be measured a good deal more carefully and communication inhibited if one suspected his conversations were being transmitted and transcribed. Were third-party bugging a prevalent practice, it might well smother that spontaneity – reflected in frivolous, impetuous, sacrilegious, and defiant discourse – that liberates daily life. Much off-hand exchange is easily forgotten and one may count on the obscurity of his remarks, protected by the very fact of a limited audience, and the likelihood that the listener will either overlook or forget what is said, as well as the listener's inability to reformulate a conversation without having to contend with a documented record.[154]

In regard to visual images, the difference between a description and a permanent recording is even greater. As observed in *Commonwealth* v. *Kean*, a videotaped image 'is likely to contain a richness of detail which could not be successfully communicated by even the most articulate of observers. One does not need a law degree in order to understand that a picture is worth a thousand words.'[155]

6. Technology and the public/private divide

A final factor undermining a dichotomy between public and private places is the impact of technology. Technological advances have contributed to a blurring of the boundaries between public and private places in modern society. As sociologist Gary T. Marx points out, 'Many of our most basic social assumptions have involved a physical rather than an electronic world.'[156] The boundary between the home and the workplace

153 [1990] 1 S.C.R. 30 at 48, 53 C.C.C. (3d) 1 at 14.

154 *United States* v. *White*, 401 U.S. 745 at 787–8 (1971) [citations omitted].

155 556 A.2d 374 at 382 (Pa.Super. 1989); compare *Anderson* v. *Fisher Broadcasting Co.*, 712 P.2d 803 at 810–1 (Or. 1986). Ironically, New Zealand's Broadcasting Standards Authority has decided, in effect, that one name is worth a thousand pictures. As discussed above (see text accompanying notes 99–104), a broadcaster has complete licence to publish images of identifiable people in public places, so long as no name is mentioned.

156 'The Declining Significance of Traditional Borders (and the Appearance of New Borders) in an Age of High Technology,' in P. Drogue, *Intelligent Environments* (Elsevier Science, 1997) at 484–94, online: http://socsci.colorado.edu/~marxg/ascbord.html (accessed 10 July 1999).

has become blurred,[157] and the home itself is set to become a site of electronic control and monitoring.[158] It is increasingly feasible to conduct unauthorized surveillance in private places without physical trespass; already a vast array of surveillance devices are available, including detectors that can scan underneath clothing and through walls[159] and microphones and transmitters that can hear through walls and at great distances.[160] It makes no sense to ignore such risks to privacy in private places, while taking an overly paranoid view of similar risks in public places.

By transcending the limits of sensory perception,[161] technology has almost limitless potential to contravene normal expectations of privacy in both public and private places. For example, in the ordinary course of things, a person expects to be observed only from certain angles and distances and does not expect to be scrutinized in close-up without realizing and being able to react.[162] These expectations were violated in a bizarre recent case, *C'Debaca* v. *Virginia*.[163] The appellant had been convicted of an offence for videotaping up a woman's skirt, using a camera concealed in a bag on the ground. (He might not have been caught had his technology been less primitive.) His conviction was reversed and dismissed, largely for valid reasons of statutory interpretation, but the court saw fit to add, 'Moreover, although appellant aimed his camera so that the lens pointed up the victim's dress, the victim had no reasonable expectation of privacy while standing on the public fairgrounds.'[164]

Technology can also contravene reasonable expectations by permitting surveillance to be covert rather than open. If people are aware that they are being observed in an intrusive manner, they can respond by applying social sanctions and can take evasive action to protect their privacy. For example, our diarist in the park is likely to notice someone

157 Ibid.

158 See F. Allon, 'The Electronic Home – Bill Gates' House' (Paper presented to *Cultural Crossroads: Ownership, Access, Identity Conference*, Sydney, Australia, 24–26 November 1997) [unpublished]. Abstract online: Abstracts Cultural Crossroads Conference http://www.gu.edu.au/centre/cmp/Abstracts_97_Conf.html#Allon.

159 See B. Phillips, 'Privacy in a "Surveillance Society"' (1997) 46 U.N.B.L.J. 127 at 129.

160 See McClurg, supra note 18 at 1018–9.

161 See Marx, supra note 156.

162 The use of street surveillance cameras to zoom in on women's cleavage violates these expectations. See J. Delvecchio, 'Australia: Big Brother's Eyes See All' *Sydney Morning Herald* (8 July 1994) 9; cited in Q. Burrows, 'Scowl Because You're on Candid Camera: Privacy and Video Surveillance' (1997) 31 Val.U.L.Rev. 1079 at note 174.

163 Supra note 9. There is apparently a thriving trade in the kind of videotape featured in this case; see 'Up-skirt Spy Trades Undiecover Videos on Internet' *NZ Herald* (14 November 1997) A1.

164 *C'Debaca* v. *Virginia* at 7–8.

creeping up behind her, and can then confront the intruder or simply close the diary and walk away. As Goffman has said, 'to use our naked senses is to use them nakedly and to be made naked by their use.'[165] Surveillance technology minimizes the social costs of spying on others and can uncover information that would otherwise not be revealed by consciously exploiting the subject's expectations of privacy. In the words of Stanley Benn, 'Covert observation – spying – is objectionable because it deliberately deceives a person about his world, thwarting, for reasons that *cannot* be his reasons, his attempts to make a rational choice.'[166] A recent decision in the English Court of Appeal has confirmed that clandestine filming in a public place can be an infringement of privacy under the Broadcasting Act 1996 even though the events filmed are not inherently private in any respect. The Court reasoned that secret filming deprives the persons filmed of the possibility of refusing consent or of taking action to prevent what they are doing being filmed.[167]

This brings us to a second group of exceptional cases in American law. There has been some, very limited, recognition of an expectation that surveillance in public places will not be technologically enhanced. A conversation can be deemed 'private,' despite its public location, if it could not have been overheard by unaided ears.[168] For example, in *Dickerson* v. *Raphael*,[169] a television talk show recorded a conversation in a public park between the plaintiff and her adult children, one of whom was fitted with a hidden microphone. The conversation concerned the plaintiff's income, the stability of her marriage, and her religious beliefs. The plaintiff sued for damages under the Michigan eavesdropping statutes. The Court of Appeals rejected the defendants' arguments that the conversation was not 'private,' noting that although the conversation occurred at a picnic table in a public park and an occasional passer-by may have walked near the table, no one had lingered to overhear the conversation. 'Moreover, many minutes of discussion of an intensely personal nature passed without the slightest intrusion.'[170]

165 E. Goffman, *Behaviour in Public Places: Notes on the Social Organization of Gatherings* (New York: The Free Press, 1963) at 16.

166 S.I. Benn, 'Privacy, Freedom, and Respect for Persons' (1971) in J.R. Pennock & J.W. Chapman, eds., NOMOS XIII, *Privacy* (New York: Atherton Press, 1971) (Yearbook of the American Society for Political and Legal Philosophy) at 10.

167 *R.* v. *Broadcasting Standards Commission ex parte British Broadcasting Corp.* (6 April 2000), London QBCOF 1999/0779/C (C.A.).

168 See *Shulman* v. *Group W*, 955 P.2d 469 at 491 (Cal. 1998).

169 564 N.W.2d 85 (Mich.App. 1997).

170 Ibid. at 90. On appeal, the Supreme Court held that reasonable minds could differ on the question whether the conversation was 'private'; 601 N.W.2d 108 (Mich. 1999).

However, this kind of reasoning has not been extended to visual recording. In *Dickerson*, the Court of Appeals noted that the video portion of the tape was not in issue. Although the plaintiff had gone to the public park specifically to find a private place to talk,[171] the Court stated, 'Because the meeting occurred in a public park, plaintiff's video image was open to the public.'[172] The use of telescopic lenses has been held to invade privacy only where directed at the interior of someone's home.[173] In *DiGirolamo* v. *D.P. Anderson & Associates, Inc.*, the court held that the use of enhanced vision to observe the plaintiff inside her apartment impaired a legitimate expectation of privacy because it is difficult for someone to gauge what can be seen through a telescopic lens.[174] However, it was not an invasion of privacy to watch the plaintiff inside her home with the naked eye, or to use telescopic lenses to observe her on her balcony, since 'while standing on her balcony, she enjoyed no greater right to be free of enhanced viewing than she did while standing on the street.'[175] With respect to visual technologies, then, the American courts have disapproved their use in opening the home to surveillance, but have thus far condoned their use in conducting covert surveillance in public places.

B. IMPLIED CONSENT OR WAIVER

Although we have seen that reasonable people do expect some degree of privacy in public places, it is nevertheless true that the risks to privacy are generally greater outside the home, and that people are aware of this difference. The courts have deduced from this awareness that the failure to stay indoors or take other effective precautions impliedly signifies a waiver of the right to privacy and consent to any intrusions or publicity, however unlikely. One writer has labelled this the 'knowledge equals consent' approach and has pointed out that knowledge and consent are in fact two very different things.[176] To explain why knowledge cannot be equated with consent, it will be helpful to examine more closely the defences of consent and waiver. Although these concepts are somewhat different, the terms seem to be used interchangeably in privacy cases, and the two can be considered in tandem for the purposes of this discussion.

171 Supra note 169 at 87.

172 Ibid. at 90, note 4.

173 See *Saldana* v. *Kelsey-Hayes Co.*, 443 N.W.2d 382 at 384 (Mich.App. 1989); *Aisenson*, supra note 113; *Salazar* v. *Golden State Warriors*, [2000] U.S.Dist. LEXIS 2366, online: LEXIS (Genfed, DIST).

174 Supra note 2 at 9–10.

175 Ibid. at 16.

176 Craig, supra note 31 at 396.

1. Scope of consent

As a defence to intentional torts, consent applies only 'when the plaintiff agreed to the very conduct which constituted the tort.'[177] If, while driving in a storm, I foresee that my car could be hit by a falling tree, I have not thereby consented to someone intentionally bashing my car with a branch. Similarly, it is not sufficient that the plaintiff foresaw a risk that some loss of privacy could occur, or that someone might intrude; he or she must have agreed to the particular conduct that constituted the invasion. For example, if, in *Fayard* v. *Guardsmark, Inc.*,[178] the plaintiff had foreseen a risk of someone informing her employer about her off-duty fraternization, this would not mean she had consented to her employer staking out her house. As McClurg has pointed out, the court in *Gill* v. *Hearst Publishing Co.*[179] failed 'to distinguish between merely voluntarily appearing in a public place and voluntarily consenting to be stared at, photographed, and publicized.'[180]

The implications of leaping from awareness of risk to waiver of privacy are apparent in the following passage from *Malone* v. *Metropolitan Police Commissioner (No. 2)*,[181] an English case concerning telephone tapping by the police, holding that there was no general right of confidentiality in telephone conversations:

> It seems to me that a person who utters confidential information must accept the risk of any unknown overhearing that is inherent in the circumstances of communication. Those who exchange confidences on a bus or a train run the risk of a nearby passenger with acute hearing or a more distant passenger who is adept at lip-reading. Those who speak over garden walls run the risk of the unseen neighbour in a toolshed nearby. Office cleaners who discuss secrets in the office when they think everyone else has gone run the risk of speaking within earshot of an unseen member of the staff who is working late. Those who give confidential information over an office intercommunication system run the risk of some third party being connected to the conversation. I do not see why someone who has overheard some secret in such a way should be exposed to legal proceedings if he uses or divulges what he has heard.[182]

David Feldman comments:

177 L.N. Klar, *Tort Law*, 2d ed. (Toronto: Carswell, 1996) at 382, note 111; also *Restatement* § 892A, comment c.
178 Supra note 8.
179 Supra note 8.
180 Supra note 18 at 1039–40.
181 Supra note 3.
182 Ibid. at 376.

To hold that one loses privacy rights when using a telephone is analogous to saying that one loses rights of property in respect of one's baggage when one takes it on an aeroplane, because we all know that bags are sometimes lost or stolen in transit.[183]

The *Malone* case was distinguished in *Francome* v. *Mirror Group Newspapers Ltd.*,[184] in which an interlocutory injunction was granted against publication of tapes obtained by private persons tapping the plaintiffs' telephone. Sir John Donaldson M.R. stated that

[a]lthough users of the telephone take the risk of crossed lines and of official telephone tapping, they are entitled to regard their conversations as confidential and anyone overhearing those conversations knows that that is the position. It is therefore idle for an eavesdropper, and particularly a deliberate eavesdropper, to contend that he did not know that the conversations were confidential.[185]

A point that is sometimes overlooked is that consent may be conditional or restricted in its scope.[186] For example, Osborne has commented that in *Milton* v. *Savinkoff*,[187] any waiver of privacy should have been construed as a very narrow one relating only to the film developing process.[188] In *Doe* v. *Dyer-Goode*,[189] a patient consented to a pre-marital blood test by his doctor, but the doctor also performed an unauthorized test for the AIDS virus.[190] The court held that there was no invasion of privacy, on the grounds that once the patient had relinquished his blood sample, it was no longer held in 'private seclusion.' This reasoning surely cannot be correct, and the decision was not followed in a subsequent case.[191]

Limitations on the scope of consent underlie a third group of exceptional cases in American privacy law. In *Y.G.* v. *Jewish Hospital of St. Louis*,[192] for example, a hospital held a social function for couples who had taken part in its *in vitro* fertilization program. The plaintiffs attended at the hospital's invitation, having been assured that there would be no publicity nor any public exposure of persons attending the function. In

183 'Secrecy, Dignity, or Autonomy? Views of Privacy As a Civil Liberty' (1994) 47 Current Leg.Probs. 41 at 67.

184 Supra note 3.

185 Ibid. at 895.

186 *Restatement* § 892A, comments c, f, and g.

187 Supra note 6.

188 Supra note 78 at 296.

189 566 A.2d 889 (Pa.Super. 1989).

190 She informed him that he had tested positive, although he subsequently re-tested negative.

191 *Doe* v. *High-Tech Institute, Inc.*, 972 P.2d 1060 (Colo.App. 1998).

192 Supra note 117. The case was treated as a motion for summary judgment (ibid. at 494), so was based on the version of the facts most favourable to the plaintiffs.

fact, a news crew was present, and the plaintiffs were twice requested to give an interview on camera. They refused and made every reasonable effort to avoid being filmed or interviewed. Nevertheless, a newscast that evening showed them at the function and, although not mentioning their names, reported that they were expecting triplets by reason of their participation in the *in vitro* program. The plaintiffs, who had told no one other than Y.G.'s mother about their attempt to procreate, received numerous calls and embarrassing questions after the broadcast; they were chastised at church and ridiculed at work. They sued both the hospital and the television company. Reversing a motion for summary judgment against the plaintiffs, the court said,

> [T]he allegations of the petition show that appellants were assured that the persons invited would include only other persons involved in the IVF program, and would not be open to the public or the media. By attending such a function, appellants clearly chose to disclose their participation to only the other *in vitro* couples. By so attending this limited gathering, they did not waive their right to keep their condition and the process of *in vitro* private in respect to the general public.[193]

This reasoning was taken a step further in *Doe* v. *Mills*.[194] The defendants had held up large signs outside an abortion clinic publicizing the names of two women about to undergo abortions. The information had been supplied by a third party, who had found it on a piece of paper in a refuse dumpster in the clinic's parking lot. The trial court, relying on constitutional search and seizure cases, held that because the information had been discarded into the trash, the plaintiffs had lost their right of privacy in the information. However, the Michigan Court of Appeals denied that the facts of the case established any waiver. The Court noted that waiver of the right of privacy requires knowledge and consent of the person entitled to waive, and that an implied waiver requires a 'clear, unequivocal, and decisive act of the party showing such a purpose.'[195] Even if the plaintiffs themselves had discarded the document, 'such an act does not demonstrate consent to having information in that document publicly disclosed.'

The Court then considered the argument that the plaintiffs' 'comings and goings to the clinic were acts exposed to the public eye.'[196] Noting that abortions took place within the private confines of the clinic, the Court reasoned that 'merely because the plaintiffs' "comings and goings"

193 Ibid. at 502. See similarly *Huskey* v. *National Broadcasting Co.*, supra note 117.

194 Supra note 5.

195 Ibid. at 831.

196 Ibid. at 832.

may have been visible to members of the public does not mean that the public was aware of the precise purpose of those "comings and goings."'[197] If the Court's ruling had rested on this basis alone, it would have done little to protect privacy in the future. Protesters and the media would be free to publicly identify women entering abortion clinics, so long as they left it to the public to infer the purpose of the women's attendance. However, the Court also based its decision on the ruling in *Y.G.*,[198] that attendance at a limited gathering does not constitute waiver of the right to privacy in respect to the general public. By applying this reasoning to appearance on a public street, the Court apparently accepted that exposure to just a few members of the general public, although not limited to any selected class of persons, does not deprive information of its private character. Thus the (only semi-voluntary) appearance of the plaintiffs in front of a handful of protesters and the odd passer-by did not constitute consent to publication.

Simply by appearing in public, people impliedly consent to no more than casual observation by those in the vicinity.[199] To find that the scope of implied consent goes any further requires careful examination of all the circumstances. The dissenting judge in *Gill* v. *Hearst Publishing Co.*[200] distinguished between merely venturing outside one's home, on the one hand, and people who voluntarily engage in events that are of news value, or intentionally place themselves on public display such as by taking part in a parade, on the other. Regarding the couple seated in an affectionate pose at their concession stand, he commented, 'By plaintiffs doing what they did in view of a tiny fraction of the public, does not mean that they consented to observation by the millions of readers of the defendant's magazine.'[201] Osborne suggests that consent to general publicity might be implied if a person 'has sought attention by placing himself or herself in a position likely to create a good deal of interest, such as appearing in public in scanty clothing, or appearing in association with famous people,' or when someone 'attends an event at which he or she knows there will be press or television coverage.'[202] Even in the latter situation,

197 Ibid. at 832.

198 Supra note 117.

199 See H.P. Glenn, 'Civil Responsibility – Right to Privacy in Quebec – Recent Cases' [1974] 52 Can.Bar Rev. 297 at 302.

200 Supra note 8 at 446–7.

201 Carter J., dissenting, supra note 8 at 446.

202 P.H. Osborne, 'The Privacy Acts of British Columbia, Manitoba and Saskatchewan' [hereinafter 'Privacy Acts'] in D. Gibson, ed., *Aspects of Privacy Law: Essays in Honour of John M. Sharp* (Toronto: Butterworths, 1980) 73 at 92; citing *Field* v. *United Amusement Corp.*, [1971] C.S. 283 (Que.Sup.Ct.) as an example of someone who impliedly consented to publicity when he frolicked in the nude in public at the Woodstock Music Festival.

the scope of consent to publication may be limited.[203] A distinction can be drawn between actual participants in public events and mere spectators:

> [O]ne attending a public event such as a professional football game may expect to be televised in the status in which he attends. If a mere spectator, he may be taken as part of the general audience, but may not be picked out of the crowd alone, thrust upon the screen and unduly featured for public view.[204]

In establishing the scope of implied consent, it may be helpful to imagine the likely response if express permission had been sought. It is meaningless to say that someone has impliedly consented when one knows that he or she would refuse permission if asked. In an analagous context, concerning the implied licence to enter private land to knock on the front door of the house, the New Zealand High Court has stated, 'Purposes for which it is known or understood that the occupier would not give consent will be outside the ambit of implication.'[205] Where people have expressly refused to be interviewed on a particular topic, we should be wary of finding that they impliedly consented to publicity on the matter merely by virtue of their physical location.[206] *A fortiori*, implied consent should be able to be explicitly revoked in normal circumstances.[207]

2. Voluntariness

The 'knowledge equals consent' approach assumes empirically that individuals have free choice in whether to expose their affairs in public.

203 Of course, consent is not the only potential defence in such situations; in many cases unwelcome publicity will be justified in the public interest.

204 *Gautier* v. *Pro-Football, Inc.*, 107 N.E.2d 485 at 489 (N.Y.App. 1952). This distinction applies in appropriation of personality cases, but it has not been applied to the American tort of publication of private facts because of the extremely broad newsworthiness exception in American law. See also *Aubry*, supra note 79 at 596 (*per* L'Heureux-Dubé and Bastarache JJ., Gonthier, Cory, and Iacobucci JJ. concurring).

205 *TV3* v. *B.S.A.*, supra note 92 at 732. A reporter entered onto private property to seek an interview, but also with the purpose of filming from a secret location whatever encounter ensued. Since the occupier would not have consented to entry for that purpose, and TV3 must have understood that, the entry was viewed as a trespass from the outset.

206 See *Green* v. *Chicago Tribune Co.*, 675 N.E.2d 249 at 253 (Ill.App. 1 Dist. 1996); *Y.G.*, supra note 117 at 502.

207 See 'Privacy Acts,' supra note 202 at 92–4, for discussion of the revocability of consent. In *De Gregorio* v. *CBS, Inc.*, supra note 8, the court held that the plaintiff could have no expectation of privacy in a public place, even though he expressly asked that film footage of him holding hands with a co-worker not be broadcast. Again the decision turned on the extremely broad newsworthiness exception in American law – romance was held to be newsworthy, so the plaintiff could not stop publication of the 'news.'

In tort law, consent is based on 'a presumption of individual autonomy and free will. It is presumed that the individual has freedom to consent or not to consent.'[208] Similarly, waiver has been defined as 'the voluntary relinquishment or abandonment of a legal right or advantage.'[209]

However, the 'choice' to appear in a public place is often far from voluntary. The extremity of Prudence's precautions serves to illustrate the lack of practical alternatives most people face in conducting their everyday activities. Often people are faced with a choice between taking a minor risk of public exposure or forgoing an activity or association altogether. For example, consider the court's declaration in *International Union* v. *Garner* that if the plaintiffs truly wanted their participation in the union meeting to be private, they would not have left their cars in front of the meeting hall.[210] It is difficult to imagine what alternative the plaintiffs had. Walking or catching a taxi would still carry the risk of being identified as they entered the hall, perhaps via video surveillance. Face recognition technology can identify individuals from a distance, even in a large crowd.[211] The only sure way to avoid being detected arriving at a controversial gathering is not to attend.

In other situations, there is not even the choice of forgoing the activity. As McClurg notes, 'Merely to survive in society requires that people spend a considerable amount of their time in places accessible to the public.'[212] For example, people may have to queue in a government building in order to collect social security payments that they need to survive.[213] It is ridiculous to find implied consent to publicity in such circumstances, and yet the media have even tried 'vigorously' to assert that calling paramedics to one's home constitutes implied consent to the entry of a television camera crew.[214]

Voluntariness is also an issue when an individual is in a 'distressed, ill or injured condition'[215] in a public place. A few such instances comprise a small fourth group of exceptional cases in American law. The dissenting judge in *Gill* v. *Hearst Publishing Co.* pointed out that if plaintiffs waive their rights to privacy by leaving their homes, then 'the blameless exposure of a portion of the naked body of a man or woman in a public place as the result of inefficient buttons, hooks or other clothes-holding

208 *Norberg* v. *Wynrib*, [1992] 2 S.C.R. 226 at 247 (*per* La Forest J.), 92 D.L.R. (4th) 449.

209 B.A. Garner, *A Dictionary of Modern Legal Usage*, 2d ed. (New York: Oxford University Press, 1995) at 923.

210 See text accompanying notes 56–7.

211 See Phillips, supra note 159 at 129.

212 Supra note 18 at 1040.

213 See *Cefalu* v. *Globe Newspaper Co.*, supra note 52.

214 *Miller* v. *National Broadcasting Co.*, 187 Cal.App. 3d 1463 at 1489 (1986). This argument received short shrift from the Court.

215 Australian Law Reform Commission, supra note 111 at 125–7.

devices could be freely photographed and widely published with complete immunity.'[216] However, faced with that kind of situation a few years later in *Daily Times Democrat* v. *Graham*, the court drew a distinction on the basis of voluntariness. The plaintiff had been at a county fair with her children; as she left the fun house, her dress was blown up by jets of air from a device under the platform, exposing her underwear. The local newspaper published a photograph taken at that moment, and the plaintiff sued for invasion of privacy. The Supreme Court of Alabama affirmed judgment for the plaintiff, stating that

> [t]o hold that one who is involuntarily and instantaneously enmeshed in an embarrassing pose forfeits her right of privacy merely because she happened at the moment to be part of a public scene would be illogical, wrong, and unjust.
>
> One who is part of a public scene may be lawfully photographed as an incidental part of that scene in his ordinary status. Where the status he expects to occupy is changed without his volition to a status embarrassing to an ordinary person of reasonable sensitivity, then he should not be deemed to have forfeited his right to be protected from an indecent and vulgar intrusion of his right of privacy merely because misfortune overtakes him in a public place.[217]

Similar reasoning was applied in *Leverton* v. *Curtis Publishing Co.*[218] regarding photographs of an accident victim. In *Taylor* v. *K.T.V.B., Inc.*,[219] the Supreme Court of Idaho ruled that a television station could be liable for maliciously broadcasting footage of the plaintiff being arrested and escorted from his home in the nude. Unlike the dissenting judge,[220] the majority appears to have seen the plaintiff's exposure as involuntary. However, no clear exception has been established by such cases, and the public places exemption has been strictly applied in some cases involving distressed, ill, or injured plaintiffs.[221]

C. THE IMPORTANCE OF PUBLIC PRIVACY

Any right to privacy would be on very shaky ground if it rested solely on expectations of privacy in the descriptive sense, since technological advances and social trends such as the advent of reality television could progressively diminish these expectations.[222] Neither are community

216 Supra note 8 at 446–7; compare *Neff* v. *Time Inc.*, 406 F.Supp. 858 (W.D.Pa. 1976).

217 162 So.2d 474 at 478 (Ala. 1964).

218 Supra note 106.

219 Supra note 105.

220 Ibid. at 989.

221 *E.g.*, *Shulman* v. *Group W*, supra note 168 (accident victim); *Neff* v. *Time Inc.*, supra note 216 (man with zipper open); *Reeves* v. *Fox Television Network*, 983 F.Supp. 703 (N.D.Ohio 1997) (arrestee).

222 See Note, 'Privacy, Technology, and the California "Anti-Paparazzi" Statute' (1999) 112 Harv.L.Rev. 1367 at 1374–6; Craig, supra note 31 at 396.

norms an adequate basis for privacy protection, since, as David Anderson points out, 'public expectations as to what is public and private are shaped by what is in fact made public.'[223] Anderson argues that privacy law should play a role in defining the appropriate relationship between society and the individual and that, if the law surrenders entirely to the mores of the moment, it 'fails to protect either the individual or the society from the brutalising effects of subjugating individual autonomy to the appetites of the group.'[224] Thus reasonable expectations of privacy should be assessed from a normative perspective,[225] bearing in mind the need to strike a balance between privacy and competing interests. Along these lines, John Craig has written that

> implied consent should be approached from the point of view of a reasonable person, entitled to the full respect of his dignity and autonomy, and thereby entitled to enjoy the maximum privacy compatible with life in Canadian society. If, in the plaintiff's circumstances, a reasonable person should be entitled to expect to be secure against an invasion of privacy, then the plaintiff's consent to the invasion cannot be implied.[226]

Although normatively reasonable expectations of privacy must be determined in the context of the particular case, it may be helpful to make some general observations concerning the value of privacy in public places and the need to give appropriate weight to competing interests.

1. Public privacy as a value

Underlying the 'reasonable paranoid' approach to privacy is the belief that public privacy is of little value to society and that individuals should bear the responsibility for taking precautions to protect their privacy. However, as may already be apparent from the discussion and examples given thus far, public privacy is actually an important component of the overall level of privacy in society, and it is valuable not only for the same reasons that privacy is valuable generally,[227] but also for its distinctive connection with freedom of association and for its role in facilitating more equitable access to the benefits of privacy.

The first thing to note is that a great deal of the information we regard as private is revealed, either directly or indirectly, in a public place at

223 D.A. Anderson, 'Fundamental Issues in Privacy Law,' in B.S. Markesinis, ed., *The Clifford Chance Lectures*, vol. 1, *Bridging the Channel* (Oxford: Oxford University Press, 1996) 123 at 129.

224 Ibid.

225 Craig, supra note 31 at 396.

226 Ibid. at 397.

227 For general discussion of the value of privacy, see 'Limits of Law,' supra note 24 at 440–56.

some point. Every time a person takes out a video,[228] borrows a public library book, goes shopping, or goes out on a date, he or she has revealed personal information in public and, according to the 'reasonable paranoid' approach, abandoned any expectation of privacy in that information. Reiman notes that a fairly detailed picture of a person's private life can be constructed just by accumulating a lot of disparate pieces of public information and drawing inferences therefrom.[229] To neglect the protection of public privacy is to leave many of the most sensitive details of people's lives vulnerable to unwarranted scrutiny.

The facts of *Crosten* v. *Kamauf*[230] are illustrative. The plaintiff had resigned from her job at a hospital because of alleged sexual harassment by her supervisor. She started seeing a counsellor at the hospital's pastoral counselling centre, which offered its services both to employees and to the general public. However, her counselling was discontinued after sixteen sessions at the instruction of the hospital, allegedly in retaliation after the plaintiff filed a sexual harassment complaint. The plaintiff brought an action against her former employer on a number of grounds, including invasion of privacy. She reasoned that the hospital administration must have informed the counselling centre of her sexual harassment claim, and that the counselling centre must have informed the hospital administration that she was receiving psychotherapy. The hospital moved to dismiss the privacy claim, arguing that the fact that the plaintiff was seeing a counsellor was not a private matter, since anyone could have seen her going to or coming from her counselling appointments and anything visible in a public place can be given publicity. The Court did not query the hospital's reasoning, but declined to dismiss the claim 'at this time' because it was not yet clear whether the plaintiff's conduct would have revealed to the public that she was engaged in therapy.[231]

The implications of *Crosten* are troubling, since many health services that carry a stigma are situated in separate premises. Clients of fertility clinics, abortion and sexual health clinics, and drug rehabilitation centres can theoretically be seen entering and exiting these premises in full public view. If the mere inference that a fact was ever discernible in a public place is enough to deprive it of the character of being 'private,' without even the need to point to any actual observers, then attendance at a specialist health centre, be it ever so discreet, can always be publicized with impunity. Recognition of the concept of public privacy, on the

228 The use of video lending records in an attempt to discredit a nominee for the United States Supreme Court led to passage of the Video Privacy Act 1988 (U.S.). It was discovered that such records were in demand for use in litigation, for example, to show that a spouse was an unfit parent. See M. Paterson, 'Privacy Protection in Australia: The Need for an Effective Private Sector Regime' (1998) 26 Fed.L.Rev. 371 at 374.

229 Supra note 28 at 29.

230 Supra note 11.

231 Ibid. at 684–5.

other hand, would allow people the freedom to seek treatment without fear of gratuitous publicity.

Public privacy has its own special role to play in furthering the values connected with privacy generally, such as freedom, individual self-fulfilment, autonomy, independent thought, and human dignity.[232] In particular, there is a close connection between freedom of association and privacy in one's public movements; this connection is well illustrated by the facts of *International Union* v. *Garner*.[233] As outlined above,[234] the mayor and police department had recorded and traced licence plate numbers in order to identify individuals attending union meetings and report them to the employer corporation. The context was an attempt to unionize a plant, and the employees and union officials, in suing for invasion of privacy, were clearly trying to defend their freedom of association. The refusal of the Court to acknowledge any concept of public privacy left union members potentially vulnerable to intimidation or victimization. In *Gibson* v. *Florida Legislative Investigation Committee*, the United States Supreme Court recognized '[t]he strong associational interest in maintaining the privacy of membership lists of groups engaged in the constitutionally protected free trade in ideas and beliefs.'[235] It warned that threats to the privacy of members of unpopular groups have a substantial 'deterrent and "chilling" effect on the free exercise of constitutionally enshrined rights of free speech, expression, and association.'[236] However, the District Court in *International Union* v. *Garner* failed to appreciate that surveillance in public places poses no less a threat to free association than compelling publication of membership lists. Technological developments such as face recognition technology have amplified this threat.[237] An impoverished concept of privacy that applies only when a person is in seclusion is completely inadequate to protect freedom of association. There seems to be little point in protecting the freedom to have one's name on a group membership list if one is not also free to meet personally with fellow members.

By way of contrast, the less rigid European approach to public privacy[238] is likely to be far more effective in protecting free association. For

232 See 'Limits of Law,' supra note 24 at 440–56; E. J. Bloustein, 'Privacy as an Aspect of Human Dignity: An Answer to Dean Prosser' (1964) 39 N.Y.U.L.R. 962.

233 Supra note 13.

234 See text accompanying notes 36–7.

235 372 U.S. 539 at 555 (1963).

236 Ibid. at 556–7.

237 See text accompanying note 211. Apparently the manufacturers of one such system claimed that by the end of 1997 their product would be able to scan a database of 50 million faces in less than a minute; see Phillips, supra note 159 at 129.

238 See B.S. Markesinis & N. Nolte, 'Some Comparative Reflections on the Right of Privacy of Public Figures in Public Places' in P. Birks, ed., *Privacy and Loyalty* (Oxford: Clarendon Press, 1997) at 113.

example, the Austrian Data Protection Commission has ruled that it was plainly illegal for the Department for Domestic Security, gathering information on an applicant's political activities, to record her number plate outside a convention on women's rights. The Commission held that the constitutional right to data protection included parts of a citizen's private life that take place in public, including participation in cultural and political events.[239]

Public privacy also has an important contribution to make in enabling more equitable access to the benefits of privacy. If privacy is confined to private spaces, it becomes a right enjoyed only by the affluent.[240] Many people cannot afford large private houses and gardens, private transportation, and the like. Westin has observed that 'people in crowded living quarters find privacy outdoors – in the streets of cities, in the corners of bars, in motion-picture houses, and in a host of "public" places where the necessary solitude, intimacy, anonymity and reserve can be found.'[241] Furthermore, given the role of privacy in promoting liberty and autonomy, the ability to find privacy outside the home may be especially important for those holding subordinate positions within the household, who, in a patriarchal society, are most likely to be women and children.[242]

An additional reason to provide a degree of legal protection for public privacy is that there is a cost to individual precautions to maintain privacy. It is a mistake to place too much onus on individuals to engage in defensive strategies to protect their own privacy because efforts such as Prudence's are socially wasteful.[243] For example, it would be inefficient for friends to have to arrange to meet in a private location every time they wished to chat about personal matters, rather than being able to make use of the telephone or of public space. Furthermore, the social and financial costs of trying to maintain secrecy would be borne disproportionately by stigmatized minority groups. It has been suggested that a degree of protection for privacy in public places would allow some 'breathing room' for homosexual people to live a normal life, without worrying about being publicly 'outed' if they visit gay bars or are seen in the company of other homosexuals.[244]

Having briefly explored the special role of public privacy in a democratic, efficient, and just society, we must nevertheless acknowledge that the normative claim to privacy in public places is somewhat more limited

239 Data Protection Commission, 13 June 1991, 120.285, noted [1997] 4 C.T.L.R. T-84.

240 See McClurg, supra note 18 at 1040.

241 Supra note 22 at 41.

242 See Allen, supra note 25, c. 3, for discussion of the difficulties women face in finding meaningful privacy in the home.

243 See R.S. Murphy, 'Property Rights in Personal Information: An Economic Defense of Privacy' (1996) 84 Georgetown L.J. 2381 at 2397.

244 See R. F. Wick, 'Out of the Closet and into the Headlines: "Outing" and the Private Facts Tort' (1991) 80 Georgetown L.J. 413 at 428.

than in private places, since 'we cannot normally claim to control who shares the public space with us, and we acknowledge that we owe duties to fellow-users not to behave in ways which are gratuitously offensive to them.'[245]

2. Competing interests

A final notion underlying the 'reasonable paranoid' approach is that protection for privacy in public places could jeopardize the legitimate activities of investigative reporters, private detectives, and others.[246] However, it is quite possible to accommodate competing interests without resorting to a blanket exemption for public places. The assessment of reasonable expectations of privacy must take place within the context of the case, weighing the value of privacy in the relevant circumstances against the value of any competing interests.[247] Three of the Canadian provincial privacy statutes expressly provide that 'the nature and degree of privacy to which a person is entitled ... is that which is reasonable in the circumstances, due regard being given to the lawful interests of others.'[248] Similarly, in American privacy law,

> [g]enerally, an actionable invasion of privacy exists only when the defendant's conduct is unreasonable and seriously interferes with the plaintiff's privacy interest. The reasonableness of the defendant's conduct is assessed by balancing his interest in pursuing his course of conduct against the plaintiff's interest in protecting his privacy. Where a defendant's action is properly authorized or justified by circumstance, it may be found reasonable and nonactionable even though it amounts to a slight invasion of the plaintiff's privacy.[249]

Location is a relevant consideration in assessing the nature and degree of an intrusion. While surveillance in public places should be justifiable where the defendant has a sufficient countervailing interest, electronic surveillance of people inside their homes should generally be actionable regardless of the defendant's purpose.[250]

It is important to distinguish between the assessment of reasonable expectations in the context of tort law and the notion of a 'reasonable

245 See Feldman, supra note 183 at 59.

246 See, *e.g., International Union* v. *Garner*, supra note 13 at 191.

247 For detailed discussion of the need for contextual balancing of privacy and free speech interests, see 'Human Interests,' supra note 23.

248 *Privacy Act*, R.S.B.C. 1979, c. 336, s. 1(2); *The Privacy Act*, R.S.S. 1978, c. P-24, s. 6(1); *Privacy Act*, R.S.N. 1990, c. P-22, s. 3(2).

249 *Parish National Bank* v. *Lane*, 397 So.2d 1282 at 1286 (La.Ct. 1981) [citations omitted]. See also *Jaubert*, supra note 145.

250 See *Prosser & Keeton on Torts*, supra note 21 at 856.

expectation of privacy' in search and seizure jurisprudence.[251] On occasion the constitutional standard has been directly applied in a tort case.[252] However, built into the requirement of reasonableness in search and seizure law is the need to balance privacy interests against governmental interests, and, as La Forest J. said in *Dagg*, 'It must be remembered ... that in the criminal law context, the countervailing state interest in surveillance may be very strong.'[253]

By contrast, in the context of tortious invasion of privacy, there is sometimes little or no legitimate countervailing interest: the defendant may be motivated by revenge,[254] voyeurism,[255] an attempt to intimidate an outspoken opponent,[256] or mere curiosity. The weight of a competing interest may be lessened if it is really a cover for an illegitimate purpose, as in a case where insurance investigators allegedly engaged in racially motivated harassment.[257]

A contextual analysis would have produced a more satisfactory outcome in *International Union* v. *Garner*.[258] In refusing to protect the privacy of workers attending a union meeting, the court referred to the potential chilling effect on investigative reporting if such cases were found to state a cause of action for invasion of privacy.[259] However, in the context of the case, freedom of the press was not at issue. Rather, the apparent purpose of the mayor and the police was to help the employer corporation resist an attempt to unionize its factory. Freedom of expression and association was much more likely to be chilled by condoning the defendants' actions in these circumstances, so the result failed to optimize the values at stake.

It would be a much closer call as to whether privacy or free expression ought to be accorded more weight on the facts of *Aubry*,[260] imagining that the case were heard in a common law jurisdiction. It would not be appropriate for the court to try to evaluate the artistic merit of the photograph, 'which was alleged to have served to illustrate contemporary urban

251 See *Aubry*, supra note 79 at 582–3, *per* Lamer C.J.C., dissenting.

252 See *Edwards*, supra note 3 at 541; also *Doe* v. *Mills*, supra note 5 at 831, stating that 'the trial court erred in relying on cases construing the Fourth Amendment as a basis for concluding that plaintiffs had somehow lost their common-law rights.'

253 Supra note 86 at 407.

254 See, *e.g.*, *Pemberton* v. *Bethlehem Steel Corp.*, 502 A.2d 1101 at 1106 (Md.App. 1986).

255 See, *e.g.*, *Yoeckel* v. *Samonig*, 75 N.W.2d 925 (Wis. 1956). See also Burrows, supra note 162 at 1100–11, regarding voyeuristic use of footage from video surveillance cameras.

256 See, *e.g.*, *Nader* v. *General Motors Corp.*, supra note 10.

257 *Ellis* v. *Safety Insurance Co.*, 672 N.E.2d 979 (Mass.App.Ct. 1996).

258 Supra note 13.

259 Ibid. at 191.

260 Supra note 79.

life.'[261] Instead, the artist's freedom to publish a person's image as a form of artistic expression must be balanced against the subject's freedom to withhold consent to the publication of her photograph. The question is complicated by the fact that the photograph represented the combined expression of two people – the young woman sitting on a step thinking her own thoughts and the photographer who captured the scene. In the context of the case, any harm to the plaintiff by way of 'moral damage' was minor. However, the defendant testified that he usually had to pay $30 to $40 per hour for the services of a model.[262] It seems that the defendant's artistic objective could have been achieved without infringing the plaintiff's rights, either by obtaining the plaintiff's consent to publication, with or without payment, or by paying a model and using the plaintiff's photograph as an aid in setting up the new picture. In all the circumstances, the interests at stake seem relatively minor on both sides, but the plaintiff's claim is probably stronger.

IV *Conclusion*

Contrary to a widely held assumption in privacy law, reasonable people do not intend to waive all rights to privacy by appearing in public places. Although aware of the risks involved in exposing their affairs in public, they also know that many of these risks are quite remote. To the extent that they have any choice in the matter, they generally refuse to be governed by suspicion and paranoia, preferring to trust that their privacy will be respected. They leave the relative security of their homes in order to survive and participate in society, and their experience and expectation is that public places do afford varying degrees of privacy. Such factors as the privateness of many 'public' places, dispersion of information over space and time, anonymity, social rules, and the transience of much of what appears in public all contribute to expectations of public privacy.

In other words, reasonable people are less paranoid and more trusting than the law often imagines them to be. This trust is essential to the efficient functioning of society, as well as providing a foundation for such fundamental values as individual autonomy and freedom of association. As such, it is vital that it be supported by a degree of legal protection, rather than being undermined by unchecked media excesses and advances in surveillance technology. There is a need to re-conceptualize public space as shared space, with mutual rights and responsibilities, rather than as a realm where human dignity and individual rights are subject to the whims of others.

261 Ibid. at 597.
262 Ibid. at 601.

[14]

PRIVACY AND SPEECH

PAUL GEWIRTZ

We often disclose ourselves to the world at large, or at least we act as if indifferent to the world's eyes. But at other times, most of us try to control the disclosure of certain matters about ourselves. Sometimes we share thoughts, feelings, information, personality, or bodily appearance with no one at all. More commonly, we share these things with a limited number of other people. Privacy in this sense—the ability to control and to avoid the disclosure of certain matters about oneself—is a widely recognized value, an important precondition for human flourishing.

Freedom of speech and freedom of the press are also deeply cherished values. The right to generally say and publish what one wants is a bedrock element of human freedom and democratic self-governance, and this encompasses saying and publishing things about other people, including things they would prefer not be said or published about them. The tension between free speech and privacy is not so much a conflict among camps of adherents as it is a tension within ourselves. Both privacy and speech are values of great importance, and people typically embrace both of them. Louis Brandeis, the co-author of the most famous article on privacy ever written,[1] was also the author of some of the greatest prose ever written about free speech.[2]

Although the tension between speech and privacy is hardly a

Paul Gewirtz is Potter Stewart Professor of Constitutional Law, Yale Law School.

AUTHOR'S NOTE: I am grateful to Zoë Baird, Jack Balkin, Philip Chen, Jacob Katz Cogan, Owen Fiss, Linda Greenhouse, and Spiros Simitis for their very helpful comments on an earlier draft, and to Daniel Marx for his excellent research assistance.

[1] Samuel D. Warren and Louis D. Brandeis, *The Right to Privacy*, 4 Harv L Rev 193 (1890).

[2] *Whitney v California*, 274 US 357, 372 (1927) (Brandeis concurring).

new one, it has expanding significance. New technologies have opened up wonderful new possibilities for communication and expression, but also have created ominous new possibilities for diminution of privacy. Any breach in privacy, of course, can be greatly magnified if the media discloses it to the public—and the public's appetite for information about other people's private matters, and the media's willingness to satisfy that appetite, have never been greater. These and other developments have underscored the vulnerability of privacy and have created new concerns about the balance between free speech and privacy.

The Supreme Court has considered this tension in a number of cases over the past decades, and there is a clear pattern. Speech almost always wins. In rejecting privacy claims, the Court's broadly stated First Amendment rationales leave little room for privacy protection in cases of a speech-privacy conflict. In this article, I argue that the Supreme Court should give more weight to privacy protection than it has. My goal is to define a constitutional position that gives strong weight to speech, recognizing its central and indispensable role, but that also gives sufficient weight to privacy, recognizing its crucial role as well.

My starting point is last term's decision in *Bartnicki v Vopper.*[3] *Bartnicki* continues the Court's basic pattern of ruling for the media in cases of speech-privacy conflict. In *Bartnicki*, the Court held, by a vote of 6–3, that the media has a First Amendment right to broadcast certain information that had been illegally intercepted from a cell phone conversation. The "opinion of the Court" written by Justice Stevens makes some bows in the direction of protecting privacy, but ends up giving privacy little weight.

But the case may well represent a turn on the Court toward greater protection of privacy and greater restrictions on the media and speech. It is misleading to think of Justice Stevens's opinion as a true "opinion of the Court." Justice Breyer, joined by Justice O'Connor, wrote an important and unusually interesting concurring opinion analyzing the speech-privacy conflict in a way far more protective of privacy than Justice Stevens's opinion. Although Justices Breyer and O'Connor joined the Stevens opinion, their votes were needed to make up the six-member majority.

---

[3] 121 S Ct 1753 (2001).

When read alongside the opinion of the three dissenters, who thought the media should lose this case, the Breyer opinion makes clear that a majority of the Court is prepared to uphold significant restrictions on the media in order to protect privacy.

The time is now ripe to establish a new framework for considering speech-privacy cases that gives enhanced protection to privacy. Justice Breyer's opinion is a start in that direction, as well as a significant installment in his little observed but important ongoing effort to develop a new approach to the First Amendment generally. As Justice Breyer's opinion suggests, it will be difficult to enhance privacy protection without, to some extent, modifying First Amendment doctrine as it currently exists. The challenge is to find greater room for protecting privacy within our constitutional law without undermining the media's freedom to perform its crucial roles. In this article, I seek to advance that effort.

I

At issue in *Bartnicki* was the constitutionality of a provision in Title III of the Omnibus Crime Control and Safe Streets Act that sought to prevent invasions of privacy that occur through the interception and disclosure of wire, oral, or electronic communications. The statute provides sanctions against "any person who . . . intentionally discloses, or endeavors to disclose, to any other person the contents of any wire, oral, or electronic communication, knowing or having reason to know that the information was obtained through the interception of" such a communication.[4]

The case involved the unlawful interception of a cell phone conversation between two union officials during a period of collective bargaining negotiations involving the teachers' union and a local Pennsylvania school board. The conversation concerned various matters related to the status and handling of the negotiations and a possible strike. At one point, one union official said to the other, "If they're not gonna move for three percent, we're gonna have to go to their, their homes . . . To blow off their front porches, we'll have to do some work on some of those guys."[5] The telephone call was covertly and unlawfully intercepted and taped by

[4] 18 USC § 2511(1)(c).

[5] 121 S Ct at 1757.

an unidentified person who gave the tape to a prominent union opponent, who then gave it to a radio station broadcaster. The broadcaster played the tape on his talk show. The union officials whose conversation had been intercepted filed suit for damages under Title III. The case reached the Supreme Court after a divided U.S. Court of Appeals for the Third Circuit ordered entry of summary judgment for the broadcaster.[6]

Justice Stevens's opinion for the Court affirmed, declaring the Act unconstitutional as applied because it restricted media freedom to publish the illegally intercepted material. Two factors were critical for Justice Stevens. First, the media was not itself involved in the illegal interception of the conversation. Second, the information disclosed involved a matter of "public concern"; the intercepted conversation was between two union officials discussing negotiations over the proper level of compensation for teachers in the union.

Justice Stevens starts his opinion by stating that "these cases present a conflict between interests of the highest order—on the one hand, the interest in the full and free dissemination of information concerning public issues, and, on the other hand, the interest in individual privacy and, more specifically, in fostering private speech."[7] But there is very little in what follows that treats these interests as if they were of equivalent importance and both of the "highest order."

Justice Stevens's legal analysis begins with notable elusiveness in discussing the governing legal standard. Both the majority and dissent in the Court of Appeals had concluded that an "intermediate scrutiny" test should be used, not "strict scrutiny," because Title III is a "content neutral" law.[8] The Solicitor General, urging reversal, agreed that "intermediate scrutiny" was appropriate.[9] These conclusions were not surprising in light of prevailing First-

---

[6] 200 F3d 109 (3d Cir 2000).

[7] 121 S Ct at 1756.

[8] 200 F3d 109, 121, 131 (3d Cir 1999). The other two Courts of Appeals that had considered the issue before the case came to the Supreme Court also applied intermediate scrutiny. *Boehner v McDermott*, 191 F3d 463, 467 (DC Cir 1999), vacated and remanded, 121 S Ct 2190 (2001); *Peavy v WFAA-TV*, 221 F3d 158 (5th Cir 2000), cert denied, 121 S Ct 2191 (2001). Both courts found Title III constitutional as applied to the facts of those cases.

[9] Reply Brief for the United States at 11–13, 16–33, *Bartnicki v Vopper*, 121 S Ct 1753 (2001) (Nos 99-1687, 99-1728) (available at 1999 US LEXIS Briefs 1687).

Amendment doctrine. "Strict scrutiny," the Supreme Court has said, is applied "to regulations that suppress, disadvantage, or impose differential burdens upon speech because of its content," but content-neutral laws of general applicability are subject to "an intermediate level of scrutiny" because they "pose a less substantial risk of excising certain ideas or viewpoints from the public dialogue."[10]

Title III is a content-neutral law of general applicability. It protects all private communications from unlawful intrusions and prohibits the use and disclosure of all illegally intercepted communications, without regard to the content of what is intercepted. The prohibition on disclosure is triggered by the source of the communication—an illegal interception—not the substance of an interception. Indeed, exactly the same content can be published if its source is not an unlawful interception.[11] Moreover, Title III applies generally to all "uses" of the unlawfully intercepted communication—speech uses and non-speech uses (say, using the information in buying securities or developing a product), and expressive uses by all media. Title III's purpose is not to suppress disfavored ideas, but to protect the privacy of communications, without regard to the content of what is privately communicated. In doing so, Title III not only protects privacy but also promotes free speech itself by encouraging uninhibited expression and reducing the fear that uninhibited discussions might be intercepted, used, and disseminated. As such, Title III's use and disclosure restrictions meet all the criteria for "intermediate scrutiny."

But Justice Stevens does not apply intermediate scrutiny—indeed he does not mention it, except in his summary of the Court

---

[10] *Turner Broadcasting System v Federal Communications Commission*, 512 US 622, 641–43, 661 (1994). See also *Cohen v Cowles Media Co.*, 501 US 663, 669 (1991); *San Francisco Arts & Athletics, Inc. v United States Olympic Comm.*, 483 US 522, 536–37 (1987). A content-neutral law of general applicability will be sustained under "intermediate scrutiny," the Court has said, "if it furthers an important or substantial governmental interest; if the governmental interest is unrelated to the suppression of free expression; and if the incidental restriction on alleged First Amendment freedoms is no greater than is essential to the furtherance of that interest." *Turner Broadcasting System v Federal Communications Commission*, 512 US at 662 (quoting *United States v O'Brien*, 391 US 367, 377 (1968)).

[11] Cf. *Seattle Times Co. v Rhinehart*, 467 US 20, 34 (1984) (media defendant may be placed under protective order not to disclose information that had come from the defendant in the discovery process, although it could publish identical infonnation that came from a different source).

of Appeals' opinion below.[12] Indeed, nowhere in the opinion does Justice Stevens say that he is applying either strict scrutiny or intermediate scrutiny. The closest he comes to articulating a governing legal standard is to say that the restriction here must be justified by "a need . . . of the highest order" (quoting *Smith v Daily Mail Publishing Co.)*.[13] The dissent calls this "strict scrutiny,"[14] and perhaps it is—although Justice Breyer, who joins the Stevens opinion, says in his concurrence that "strict scrutiny" is "out of place" in this kind of case.[15]

Justice Stevens takes this "need . . . of the highest order" standard from a series of four cases that do not seem applicable: *Florida Star v B.J.F.*,[16] *Smith v Daily Mail Publishing Co.*,[17] *Landmark Communications, Inc. v Virginia*,[18] and *Cox Broadcasting Corp. v Cohn*.[19]

---

[12] Justice Stevens begins his legal analysis of the case (Part V of the opinion) by saying that "we agree with petitioners" that Title III is "a content-neutral law of general applicability," and explaining why:

> [T]he basic purpose of the statute at issue is to "protec[t] the privacy of wire[, electronic], and oral communications. . . ." The statute does not distinguish based on the content of the intercepted conversations, nor is it justified by reference to the content of those conversations. Rather, the communications at issue are singled out by virtue of the fact that they were illegally intercepted—by virtue of the source, rather than the subject matter.

121 S Ct at 1760. Characterizing Title III as a "content-neutral law of general applicability" was exactly what led the Court of Appeals below and the Solicitor General before the Supreme Court to argue that the intermediate scrutiny test was appropriate here. Yet instead of taking the seemingly next step of saying that therefore this case is governed by intermediate scrutiny, Justice Stevens simply moves on. "[O]n the other hand," he says, "the naked prohibition against disclosures is fairly characterized as a regulation of pure speech, . . . not a regulation of conduct. . . . [A]s such, it is the kind of 'speech' that the First Amendment protects." Id at 1761. Leaving to one side the revealing characterization of the regulation here as a "naked" prohibition (of "pure" speech no less), this "on the other hand" discussion seems beside the point. It is true that intermediate scrutiny, in addition to being used for "content-neutral laws of general applicability," is sometimes also used for laws that regulate "conduct" and have only an incidental effect on "speech." Justice Stevens sensibly appears to be rejecting this alternative basis for using intermediate scrutiny. But rejecting a second possible ground for using intermediate scrutiny is not an "on the other hand" counterargument to the first ground. Having made this "on the other hand" point, though, Justice Stevens simply moves on, drawing no conclusion here at all about the appropriate legal standard to be used. All of Part V of the opinion reads like a false start.

[13] Id at 1761 (citing the *Daily Mail* case at 443 US 97, 102 (1979)).

[14] Id at 1770 (Rehnquist dissenting).

[15] Id at 1766 (Breyer concurring).

[16] 491 US 524 (1989).

[17] 443 US 97 (1979).

[18] 435 US 829 (1978).

[19] 420 US 469 (1975).

In all of these cases, the Court sided with the media in concluding that the First Amendment prohibited the government from punishing the publication of information claimed to invade people's privacy. Although superficially similar to *Bartnicki*, these cases were very different in fundamental respects relevant to both the choice of legal standard and the outcomes.

Most significantly, these cases all involved the publication of information that was "lawfully obtained." This was the explicit and crucial predicate for the legal standard used. As the Court in *Florida Star* summarized the rule governing these cases (referred to commonly as "the *Daily Mail* principle"), when "a newspaper lawfully obtains truthful information about a matter of public significance then state officials may not constitutionally punish publication of the information, absent a need to further a state interest of the highest order."[20] In each of these cases, the information published by the media was not unlawfully obtained by the media or by anyone else. In *Cox Broadcasting*, a television station broadcast a rape victim's name that had been in "official court records open to public inspection."[21] In *Landmark Communications*, a newspaper printed information about proceedings pending before a judicial inquiry commission, information that the Supreme Court emphasized had not been "secure[d] . . . by illegal means."[22] In *Daily Mail*, a newspaper published the name and photograph of a fourteen-year-old boy arrested for murder after getting the information by "routine newspaper reporting techniques."[23] In *Florida Star*, a newspaper published the name of a victim of a sexual assault after learning the name from a police report placed in the police department's pressroom.[24] Some of these cases are critiqued below for giving insufficient weight to privacy interests, but at least the published information in these cases was not illegally secured, as it was in *Bartnicki*.

The fact that published information has been lawfully obtained properly structures First Amendment analysis. More directly relevant here, the fact that information is *unlawfully* obtained properly

[20] 491 US at 533 (quoting *Smith v Daily Mail Publishing Co.*).

[21] 420 US 469, 495 (1975).

[22] 435 US at 837.

[23] 443 US at 103.

[24] 491 US at 527.

structures First Amendment analysis, and justifies a very different legal standard. This is because, where information has been obtained unlawfully, very different values are predictably involved—most obviously, there are likely to be distinctively strong privacy (or confidentiality) interests as well as an understandable desire to arrange incentives (including the incentives of the media) to reduce the incidence of unlawfulness.[25] In *Florida Star*, the Court not only repeated the formulation of the *Daily Mail* standard that is limited to "lawfully obtained" information, but specifically stated that a case would fall "outside the *Daily Mail* principle" if the information were in private hands and obtained "nonconsensual[ly]."[26]

Because the information broadcast in *Bartnicki* was unlawfully intercepted,[27] the case involves a range of concerns outside the *Daily Mail* principle. Justice Stevens makes much of the fact that the initial unlawful obtaining of the information was done by a third party rather than the broadcaster. But it is hard to see why this should make any difference. Title III limits the media only where it knows or has reason to know that the information comes from an illegal interception.[28] Surely the knowing exploitation of an illegality is not an innocent state of mind. More fundamentally, the illegal interception is what makes the broadcast a distinctive invasion of privacy, which properly prompts a constitutional analysis different from that in the *Daily Mail* line of cases.

The particular laws challenged in the *Daily Mail* line of cases and the circumstances of their application involved other features that further demonstrate why *Bartnicki* should have triggered a different analysis under current First Amendment doctrine. First, in all four cases, the challenged law was content-specific—and, as

---

[25] Doctrinal rules are rules of thumb that take account of the predictably competing values at stake in applying legal provisions in particular types of circumstances. It would defeat the purpose of doctrinal rules not to use different tests when predictably very different values are involved.

[26] 491 US at 534. At another point in the *Florida Star* opinion, the Court adds that "the *Daily Mail* principle does not settle the issue whether, in cases where information has been acquired unlawfully by a newspaper or by a source, government may ever punish not only the unlawful acquisition, but the ensuing publication as well." 491 US at 535 n 8.

[27] In addition, the information came to the radio station through a series of "disclosures" that were themselves illegal.

[28] The statute also limits liability to those disclosures that are "intentional." 18 USC § 2511(1)(c). Negligent disclosure of the contents of an illegally intercepted conversation is not sanctioned.

noted above, content-specific laws generally trigger strict scrutiny. In *Cox Broadcasting*, *Florida Star*, and *Daily Mail*, the challenged statutes prohibited disclosures of certain specific types of information in criminal cases (the names of rape victims in the first two, and the names of juvenile offenders in the latter). In *Landmark Communications*, the statute prohibited disclosures of the content of judicial commission proceedings only. Indeed, in at least *Landmark Communications*, the state law had the earmarks of the government trying to censor unpleasant information about government officials and limiting criticism of the government (allegations that might harm a "judge's reputation" or public "confidence in the judicial system"). In *Bartnicki*, by contrast, the law is content-neutral and has none of the earmarks of government censorship of particular information or ideas.

Second, in all of the cases except *Landmark Communications*, the challenged law applied only to disclosures by the media or by some media. Thus, these were arguably not laws of general applicability.[29] The limited scope of the laws in these cases raised questions not only about evenhandedness but also about whether the state was effectively furthering its claimed interests. In *Bartnicki*, by contrast, Title III is a law of general applicability, prohibiting all use and disclosure of illegally intercepted communications.

Third, in all four cases, the government itself was the source of the information. As the Court noted in each case, this means that the government (at least in theory) could have taken steps to control the information rather than creating causes of action against media entities that learn of the information.[30] In *Bartnicki*, by contrast, the communication involved private parties rather than the government—and private parties who were victims of a deliberate illegal interception, not their own casualness with the information.

In spite of these differences, Justice Stevens applies the *Daily*

[29] In *Cox Broadcasting*, the statute prohibited only the disclosure of rape victims' names by print, broadcast, television, or radio media. In *Daily Mail*, the statute probibited only newspapers from publishing the names of juvenile offenders. In *Florida Star*, the statute prohibited publishing rape victims' names only "in any instrument of mass communication." In *Landmark Communications*, the statute was not focused on particular media, but made it unlawful to "divulge" information about the proceedings.

[30] Arguably, the government should be allowed the additional tool of punishing further disclosures following a leak of its information that it failed to prevent. See text accompanying note 127. But the balance of interests in such a case is somewhat different from the balance in a case where information has been intercepted from private parties.

Mail standard in *Bartnicki.* He concludes that Title III does not advance a "need of the highest order" that would justify restrictions on the media's disclosures. The fact that the information broadcast was unlawfully obtained neither affects his choice of legal standard nor furnishes a justification to satisfy the standard.

The government identified two "interests" related to protecting privacy from illegal interceptions, but neither satisfies the Court. First, the government argued that punishing disclosures helps to "dry up the market" for illegally intercepted private conversations, and thus reduces the incentives to intercept in the first place. It is especially important to punish disclosures, including those by people who lawfully obtained the illegally intercepted material, because the original act of interception is often hard to detect and punish.[31] Justice Stevens states that "[t]he normal method of deterring unlawful conduct is to impose an appropriate punishment on the person who engages in it."[32] But in fact the law commonly tries to deter unlawful conduct by restricting those who try to piggyback on the illegality. Most obviously, the exclusionary rule in criminal cases rests precisely on the belief that police misconduct can be deterred by barring prosecutors and others from using the unlawfully seized evidence.[33] Moreover, the law regularly punishes the knowing receipt and sale of stolen property as a way of deterring thefts.[34]

Justice Stevens argues that it would be "quite remarkable" to "hold that speech by a law-abiding possessor of information can be suppressed in order to deter conduct by a non-law-abiding third party."[35] But there is nothing remarkable or novel about restricting speech that is the fruit of unlawful action as a means of deterring the unlawful action. For example, the First Amendment permits a ban on the distribution of erotic material portraying children, even though not legally obscene, as a means of controlling the illegal exploitation of children in the production of the material. As the

[31] 121 S Ct at 1773–75.

[32] Id at 1762.

[33] E.g., *Oregon v Elstad,* 470 US 298, 306 (1985); *Elkins v United States,* 364 US 206, 217 (1960). Indeed, Title III itself has an exclusionary rule barring the use of illegally seized communications as evidence, in order to deter illegal interceptions. 18 USC § 2515.

[34] 121 S Ct at 1773–74 (Rehnquist dissenting) (citing W. R. LaFave and A. W. Scott, Jr., 2 *Substantive Criminal Law* § 8.10(a) at 422 (1986)).

[35] Id at 1762.

Court said in *New York v Ferber*, "[t]he most expeditious if not the only practical method of law enforcement may be to dry up the market for this material by imposing severe criminal penalties on persons selling, advertising, or otherwise promoting the product."[36]

Illegal conduct that yields stolen information can be every bit as wrongful and offensive as illegal conduct that yields stolen goods, and there is no reason why deterrence of the former should be disfavored any more than deterrence of the latter. The fact that the fruit of an illegality is speech acts does not make it wrong to try to discourage the illegality, does not make distributing the fruits of the illegality praiseworthy, and does not make it improper to try to discourage the illegality by drying up the market for the illegally obtained material. To say otherwise is inescapably to say that we care less about deterring the illegal stealing of information than the illegal stealing of other things, and that is unjustified. Justice Stevens asserts that in most instances the identity of the person illegally intercepting the communication will be learned. Thus, he argues, there are few instances where prohibiting third party disclosures will help deter unlawful interceptions, and therefore no government interest of the "highest order" is involved. But Congress concluded that "[a]ll too often the invasion of privacy itself will go unknown. Only by striking at all aspects of the problem can privacy be adequately protected."[37] Especially since there is such plausibility to Congress's assumption that illegal acts will be deterred if wrongdoers are prevented from enjoying the fruits of their wrongdoing, the Court should not have substituted its own judgment.

---

[36] 458 US 747, 760 (1982). See also *Osborne v Ohio*, 495 US 103, 109–10 (1990) (it is "surely reasonable for the State to conclude that it will decrease the production of child pornography if it penalizes those who possess and view the product, thereby decreasing demand"). To be sure, the speech involved in *Ferber* and *Osborne*, although not legally obscene, is widely understood to have very limited value. It might be argued that suppressing speech that is related to public issues in order to deter the illegal conduct of others is a different matter (just as some object to an exclusionary rule that suppresses valuable probative evidence as a means to deter unlawful police searches). There is indeed a difference, which is one reason I would rest more on the government's second "interest" in limiting the media disclosures—protecting privacy by limiting the harm that the illegal conduct produces. See text accompanying notes 38–40. But *Ferber* and *Osborne* demonstrate that whether the fruit of illegal activity is property or speech, the Supreme Court has concluded that closing off outlets deters the illegal conduct.

[37] S Rep No 1097, 90th Cong, 2d Sess 69 (1968) (quoted in 121 S Ct at 1773 (Rehnquist, joined by Scalia and Thomas, dissenting)).

In any event, quite apart from deterring illegal interception, punishing the disclosure of illegally intercepted communications promotes a second and even clearer interest: protecting privacy by limiting the harm that the illegal conduct produces. Preventing media disclosure is more than a means to deter someone else's illegality (the government's first interest);. it also directly protects privacy. As the Court has recognized in other contexts, disclosing illegally intercepted communications "compounds the statutorily proscribed invasion of . . . privacy."[38] Such disclosures also deepen the chill on private communication. It is as much an invasion of privacy to disclose an illegally intercepted communication as to make the illegal interception in the first place. Indeed, the intrusion on conversational privacy from the disclosure is often the more serious intrusion, for it allows a far wider audience to "overhear" the private communication. If a legislature has a weighty interest in protecting privacy from unwarranted interceptions of private communications, surely it has the same interest in protecting that privacy from disclosures that many times over "compound[ ] the statutorily proscribed invasion."[39]

Nor is it at all remarkable, as Justice Stevens suggests, to limit publication where publication is what produces the harm. If someone breaks into my home and steals my diary or personal letters, of course that person can be sanctioned for publishing the diary's or letter's contents. This is usually a rule of government-created intellectual property law, and nothing in the First Amendment prohibits it.[40] Similarly, nothing in the First Amendment should

[38] *Gelbard v United States*, 408 US 41, 52 (1972).

[39] There appears to be an inconsistency in how Justice Stevens characterizes the weight of the interest in protecting privacy. At the outset of his opinion, Justice Stevens states that "the interest in individual privacy" is an interest "of the highest order." 121 S Ct at 1756. But once he announces that the governing legal standard is the *Daily Mail* standard requiring the government to show a "need of the highest order" to justify regulating the media, he stops characterizing the government's interest in protecting privacy as having that rank. Instead, at the point where he assesses the government's argument that punishing media disclosures prevents compounding the harm from the illegal interception (the government's strongest argument), Justice Stevens starts calling the protection of privacy of communication only "an important interest," id at 1764, obviously something less than "an interest . . . of the highest order." He nowhere reconciles the inconsistency.

[40] Copyright law, as well as the common law, have long protected private letters from unauthorized publication. See *Salinger v Random House, Inc.*, 811 F2d 90, 94 (2d Cir 1987); *Birnbaum v United States*, 436 F Supp 967, 978–82 (EDNY 1977); David Nimmer, *Nimmer on Copyright* § 5.04 at 5–57 (1999). Far from being barred by First Amendment principles of free expression, copyright law is understood as itself "an engine of free expression." *Harper & Row, Publishers, Inc. v Nation Enterprises*, 471 US 539, 558 (1985). Moreover,

prohibit the government from creating an analogous rule of privacy law in Title III.

It is significant that Title III limits its sanctions for disclosures to those "knowing or having reason to know that the information was obtained through [an illegal] interception." First Amendment law properly reflects a concern about "timidity and self-censorship" by the press in the performance of its valued roles.[41] But legitimate press activities will not be chilled by a rule that prohibits disclosures of material that reporters know was illegally obtained. And to the extent that the press becomes "timid and self-censoring" about publishing illegally intercepted material that invades people's privacy, that is a good thing.

Title III's prohibition on disclosures by those "having reason to know" that the information was illegally obtained is potentially more troublesome. This standard might leave reporters uncertain whether, after the fact, a trier of fact will conclude that they "had reason to know" even though they did not in fact know. This could chill the reporting of legally secured information out of fear that its origins will be misjudged. On the other hand, a "reason to know" standard, unlike a "should have known" standard, "imposes no duty of inquiry; it merely requires that a person draw reasonable inferences from information already known to him."[42] Significantly, in his briefs in the Supreme Court, the Solicitor General took pains to dispel any chill by strictly construing the "reason to know" provision.[43] Nevertheless, had the Court pointed to distinc-

---

copyright protection may not be ignored simply because the work "contains material of possible public importance" or there is "social value in dissemination," id at 558, 559 (internal citations omitted). The fact that an author's words "may of themselves be 'newsworthy' is not an independent justification for unauthorized copying of the author's expression. . . ." Id at 557.

[41] *Florida Star*, 491 US at 535; see *Bartnicki*, 121 S Ct at 1765 n 22; *New York Times Co. v Sullivan*, 376 US 254, 271–72 (1964).

[42] *Novivki v Cook*, 946 F2d 938, 941 (DC Cir 1991).

[43] "Title III's prohibition applies only to those who either have actual knowledge of the nature of the interception or actual knowledge of facts that make those origins 'so highly probable that' one should assume such to be true. Restatement (Second) of Torts, § 12, cmt. a (1965). Indeed, the facts surrounding the interception must be apparent, because Title III imposes no duty of inquiry. Ibid.; U.S. Br. 45–46. Consequently, Title III does not deter (and for the past three decades has not deterred) the press from reporting the news. Far from requiring reporters to research sources for fear of illegality, it merely requires them to refrain from use if they know or all but know that the source was an unlawful interception." Reply Brief for the United States at 20, *Bartnicki v Vopper*, 121 S Ct 1753 (2001) (Nos 99-1687, 99-1728) (available at 1999 US Briefs LEXIS 1687).

tive First Amendment concerns with the "reason to know" standard, it would have highlighted a legitimate concern about chilling reporting that relies only on *legally secured* information; it would have rooted the decision in the right to report legally secured information, rather than extending the mantle of First Amendment protection over reporting information that the press knows to have been illegally secured. And of course it would not have invalidated the application of Title III in cases where the press actual knows that the information was illegally intercepted.

In the end, for Justice Stevens nothing turns on the fact that the information here was stolen. *New York Times Co. v Sullivan* put the mantle of First Amendment protection around the publication of factually false information, but not the publication of information the media knows to be false.[44] Neither should *Bartnicki* have protected the publication of information known to be illegally secured.

A case that hangs over *Bartnicki*, and may help to explain why Justice Stevens gives so little weight to the fact that the published information was illegally obtained, is *New York Times Co. v United States*,[45] the *Pentagon Papers* case. Justice Stevens invokes it at the very outset of his discussion of why it is irrelevant that the conversation was illegally intercepted.[46] Decided in 1971 when public debate about the ongoing Vietnam War was intense, the *Pentagon Papers* case was a suit by the U.S. government against *The New York Times* and *The Washington Post* to enjoin their publication of materials from a classified Defense Department study of the war. It was apparently undisputed that the newspapers were publishing classified material that they knew had been stolen and given to them by Daniel Ellsberg.[47] The *Pentagon Papers* case is a free press icon. How could the Court now rule that the press had no right to disclose illegally secured information?

But *Pentagon Papers* is easily distinguishable from *Bartnicki*. First, *Pentagon Papers* was a prior restraint case. The only issue before the Court was whether the publication of the papers could be en-

[44] 376 US 254, 279–80 (1964).

[45] 403 US 713 (1971).

[46] 121 S Ct at 1761.

[47] Although this fact was not discussed in the majority opinions, Justice Harlan emphasized it in his dissent. See 403 US at 754.

joined. Prior restraints are distinctively disfavored in First Amendment law, and the Court's per curiam opinion concluded only that the government had not met the "heavy burden" of justifying a prior restraint. Post-publication criminal prosecution of the newspapers was not foreclosed, as Justices White and Stewart explicitly noted in their concurrence[48]—and, by implication, post-publication civil liability was also not foreclosed. *Bartnicki* was a post-broadcasting suit for damages, not a prior restraint case. Second, *Pentagon Papers* involved the publication of information held by the government. As noted above, in such a situation it can always be said that the government should take better steps to prevent the leak rather than allow actions against the press. Third, and most importantly, as Solicitor General Waxman put it in his oral argument in *Bartnicki*, in *Pentagon Papers* there was reason to think that the government had a "censorial motive" and was seeking "to take certain facts off the table."[49] In *Barnicki*, nothing like a censorial motive underlies the content-neutral privacy-protection provisions of Title III.

In the end, the crucial factor for Justice Stevens in *Bartnicki* is that the content of the illegally intercepted conversation involves a matter of "public concern." The presence of content of "public concern," he argues, "implicates the core purposes of the First Amendment" and outweighs people's interest in the privacy of their communications even in a case where that privacy is violated by an illegal intrusion.

There are several interrelated problems with the "public concern" concept in this context[50] and, taken together, they leave private matters very vulnerable to disclosure. First, the phrase "public concern" is undefined. "Public concern" might include anything that the public becomes concerned about. This might involve a threat to public security or an issue being debated in the legislature; but it might also include the way an actor treats his girlfriend, what government officials say to their children, or what ordinary

---

[48] Id at 735–40 (White, joined by Stewart, concurring).

[49] 2000 US Trans LEXIS 77, *17.

[50] The pbrase has been used in other contexts such as cases involving the scope of public employee speech, where it raises somewhat similar issues. See, e.g., *Connick v Myers*, 461 US 138 (1983); *Pickering v Board of Education*, 391 US 563 (1968); *Rankin v McPherson*, 483 US 378 (1987); *Waters v Churchill*, 511 US 661 (1994).

citizens buy from online sellers of videos—indeed, anything that becomes a matter of public curiosity.[51]

Even if "public concern" excludes mere public curiosity and includes only matters relevant to the public's understanding of issues or officials, private matters can all too easily come within the concept. For one thing, there is a self-fulfilling and ever-expanding quality to "public concern." Private matters can become subjects of "public concern" simply by being labeled so in the media. If a newspaper discloses how a government official treats his children, it will become a matter of public attention, public debate, and, at least for some voters, an element in political assessments. More generally, private matters can readily be deemed relevant to public concerns. Disclosure of private facts about virtually anyone can be said to enhance public understanding about some wider public phenomenon or public issue. If the relevance of a private fact to some public concern is sufficient to justify media publication, a justification will not be hard to give. An important cultural fact fuels this dynamic: we live in a prurient culture, with great public interest in other people's private lives, and certainly not only the private lives of "public figures." In these circumstances, "public concern" becomes an especially wide category, and, as a First Amendment justification, one that greatly endangers privacy.

But there is a more basic problem with Justice Stevens's approach: He looks to the content of the broadcast communication to decide whether the Constitution protects it, rather than to the circumstances under which the conversation took place. For Justice Stevens, if the content of the communication involves a matter of public concern, it is within First Amendment protection. But a different approach is possible: One could look to whether the original communication takes place within a protected zone. If a zone is deemed a protected private zone—which can be either a place or a kind of situation[52]—then the content of what is communicated

[51] See Edward J. Bloustein, *The First Amendment and Privacy: The Supreme Court Justice and the Philosopher*, 28 Rutgers L Rev 41, 54–57 (1974) ("[The] weight to be given 'the public interest in obtaining information' should depend on whether the information is relevant to the public's governing purposes. 'Publie interest,' taken to mean curiosity, must he distinguished from 'public interest' taken to mean value to the public of receiving information of governing importance. There is [no First Amendment right] to satisfy public curiosity and publish lurid gossip about private lives.").

[52] See Lloyd Weinreb, *Your Place or Mine? Privacy of Presence Under the Fourth Amendment*, 1999 Supreme Court Review 253 (contrasting what he calls "privacy of place" and "privacy of presence"); Robert C. Post, *The Social Foundations of Privacy: Community and Self in the*

within that zone would be irrelevant in deciding whether the First Amendment protects the media in reporting on it. The press could be sanctioned for publishing information about conversations within that zone, regardless of content.[53] In Title III, Congress sought to protect privacy by creating such a protected zone, and made intrusions on that zone illegal. The fact that a conversation involves a matter of "public concern" is not inconsistent with it also warranting the label "private" because it takes place within a private zone.

Put another way, speech acts must be understood in terms of audiences as well as content.[54] In our daily narrative transactions, we are always negotiating our relationship to an audience. Privacy is ultimately about our power to choose our audience. When privacy is invaded, we are compelled to have an audience we do not want. The Court in *Bartnicki* says that publishing the intercepted conversation contributed to public debate—but the two people speaking on their cell phones did not wish to contribute to a public debate before a public audience. Their words were taken from them by stealth and put into public debate against their will. If every private statement on a public subject may be forcibly disclosed because it contributes to public debate, then privacy is a dead letter. We cannot have it both ways.

Justice Stevens's approach, which analyzes "public" and "private" as a matter of content, is far less privacy-protective in this context than an approach that analyzes "public" and "private" as

---

Common Law Tort, in *Constitutional Domains: Democracy, Community, Management* 54–55, 72–73 (1995) (discussing Erving Goffman's concept of "information preserves").

[53] This approach is somewhat analogous to the approach under Fourth Amendment law. The existence of a zone of reasonably expected privacy generates more demanding requirements before tbat zone may be searched. The existence within that zone of particular "content" (evidence of criminal behavior) does not generally eliminate tbe need to observe the Fourtb Amendment requirements. In the end, of course, "content" is certainly relevant under the Fourtb Amendment, however. The requirements can be met, warrants will issue, and searches be allowed if law enforcement officers demonstrate that there is probable cause to believe that particular "content" (evidence of criminal behavior) actually does exist within the zone. But the existence of the zone generates the heightened requirements.

Similarly, one can view copyright law as creating a zone that is protected without regard to content. As noted above, the fact that an author's words "may of tbemselves be 'newsworthy' is not an independent justification for unauthorized copying of the author's expression . . . ." *Harper & Row, Publishers, Inc. v Nation Enterprises*, 471 US 539, 557 (1985); id at 558, 559; note 40 above. See also *Seattle Times Co. v Rhinehart*, 467 US 20 (1984).

[54] See, e.g., Roman Jakobson, *Closing Statement: Linguistics and Poetics*, in Thomas Sebeok, ed, *Style in Language* 353–58 (1960); Peter Brooks and Paul Gewirtz, eds, *Law's Stories: Narrative and Rhetoric in the Law* (1996).

a matter of zones and audiences.[55] It also makes the First Amendment standard itself content based—an ironic result given the fact that content-based rules are generally most vulnerable to First Amendment invalidation. The end result of Justice Stevens's approach is that it matters not at all that the communication here took place with the expectation that it would be private. Because of its content, the press is free to disclose it (so long as the press itself did not participate in the unlawful interception). The press is as unlimited in reporting the private conversation as it would be if the speakers were talking at an open public meeting.

Although Justice Stevens labels his decision "narrow,"[56] his opinion gives no indication about what legislative efforts to protect privacy against media intrusion would be constitutional. The media wins this case because a matter of "public concern" was involved, but Justice Stevens refuses to say that the media would have lost if a private matter was involved:

> We need not decide whether [the privacy interest] is strong enough to justify the application of [Title III] to disclosures of trade secrets or domestic gossip or other information of purely private concern. Cf. *Time, Inc. v. Hill*, 385 U.S. 374, 387–88 (1967) (reserving the question whether truthful publication of private matters unrelated to public affairs can be constitutionally proscribed).[57]

Elsewhere in his opinion, Justice Stevens emphasizes "this Court's repeated refusal to answer categorically whether truthful publication may *ever* be punished consistent with the First Amendment."[58] These "do not decides" and "refusals to answer" mean that Justice Stevens is leaving open everything that is distinctive about protecting privacy, because protecting a person's privacy is not limited to preventing publication of false statements (traditionally the realm of defamation law), but involves preventing the publication of true material that is justifiably private. If it is uncertain "whether truthful publication may ever be punished consistent with the First

[55] In other contexts, however, it might end up being more privacy protective. A "zone" approach might grant the press protection to publish photographs of any person in the public space. But see text accompanying note 149. A content approach might withhold protection if the photograph did not have content of public concern.

[56] 121 S Ct at 1756.

[57] Id at 1764.

[58] Id at 1762 (emphasis added).

Amendment," it is uncertain whether media disclosures infringing on privacy can ever be limited consistent with the First Amendment. In other words, the Court's opinion does not mark out any area in which privacy trumps media prerogatives.[59]

II

At the outset, though, I said that *Bartnicki* takes steps forward in privacy protection, and that is because Justice Stevens's opinion is "for the Court" only in name. Justice Breyer, joined by Justice O'Connor, wrote a concurring opinion. Although Justices Breyer and O'Connor also joined Justice Stevens's opinion to make up a six-member majority, in fact their separate opinion is much less speech protective, and much more privacy protective, than the Stevens opinion. Because Chief Justice Rehnquist, Justice Scalia, and Justice Thomas dissented in an opinion that would have upheld the limitations on the media here and is broadly protective of privacy, the Breyer opinion is determinative. The controlling law is Breyer's law.

Justice Breyer's opinion sets forth an analysis that is different from Justice Stevens's on almost all of the key matters except for the result, that points to a quite narrow constitutional immunity for the media in privacy cases, and that further develops his evolving and innovative general approach to the First Amendment. As Breyer analyzes the press versus privacy issue in *Bartnicki*, there are constitutional interests "on both sides of the equation."[60] On

---

[59] These statements by Justice Stevens are inexplicable for other reasons. In a variety of other circumstances, the Court has upheld sanctions on the press for publishing truthful information. See, e.g., *Cohen v Cowles Broadcasting Co.*, 501 US 663 (1991) (First Amendment does not bar a promissory estoppel action against a newspaper for publishing truthful information about the source of a political news story in breach of its promise to keep the source's identity confidential); *Harper & Row, Publishers, Inc., v Nation Enterprises*, 471 US 539 (1985) (First Amendment does not bar an action against a magazine for publishing truthful copyrighted material); *Zacchini v Scripps-Howard Broadcasting Co.*, 433 US 562 (1977) (First Amendment does not "immunize the media [from damage liability] when they broadcast a performer's entire act without his consent"); *Seattle Times Co. v Rhinehart*, 467 US 20 (1984) (First Amendment does not bar an action against a newspaper for publishing truthful information learned during discovery in a civil suit that was covered by a protective order).

[60] 121 S Ct at 1766 (quoting his earlier separate opinions in *Turner Broadcasting System, Inc. v Federal Communications Commission*, 520 US 180, 227 (1997) (Breyer concurring in part), and *Nixon v Shrink Missouri Government PAC*, 528 US 377, 402 (2000) (Breyer concurring)).

one side is the media's constitutionally rooted interest in publishing what it wishes. On the other side is a privacy interest "that includes not only 'the right to be let alone' . . . but also 'the interest . . . in fostering private speech.'"[61] "The assurance of privacy," Breyer emphasizes, "helps to overcome our natural reluctance to discuss private matters when we fear that our private conversations may become public. And the statutory restrictions [in this case] consequently encourage conversations that otherwise might not take place."[62]

This interest in fostering private speech, Breyer says, is itself a "constitutional interest" related to the system of free expression guaranteed by the First Amendment. Breyer cites his own previous separate opinions in which he characterizes the First Amendment's purposes in affirmative terms, such as "encouraging . . . open discussion," rather than simply as a prohibition on state action restricting speech.[63] Thus, Breyer says, there are "competing constitutional interests"[64] in *Bartnicki*, and competing constitutional interests related to free expression itself. Justice Stevens, by contrast, avoids saying that the interest on the privacy side is itself of "constitutional" dimension. Rather, he says only that "there are important interests to be considered on both sides of the constitutional calculus."[65] Justice Breyer himself hedges in one significant respect: Although he recognizes that the privacy interest includes both the "the right to be let alone" and "the interest . . . in fostering private speech," he labels only the speech-related aspect of privacy a constitutional interest and focuses his analysis on this speech-related aspect—leaving unclear how he would evaluate a case where only the nonspeech aspects of privacy were on the "other side of the equation."[66]

---

[61] Id (citations omitted).

[62] Id.

[63] *Nixon v Shrink Missouri Government PAC*, 528 US at 402; *Turner Broadcasting System, Inc. v Federal Communications Commission*, 520 US at 227. The relationship between Breyer's general conception of the First Amendment and the traditional conception is discussed further in Part IV.

[64] 121 S Ct at 1766.

[65] Id at 1764.

[66] There are suggestions in his opinion that Justice Breyer is in fact giving weight to those nonspeech aspects of privacy. "As a general matter," Justice Breyer says, "the Federal Constitution must tolerate laws of this kind because of the importance of these *privacy and speech-related objectives*." And the basic standard that Justice Breyer uses in deciding this case is to ask whether the "restrictions on speech . . . are disproportionate when measured

Because Justice Breyer sees "competing constitutional interests" on both sides, he concludes that the Court should not apply "strict scrutiny." Rather, he would use a much more flexible and multifactored approach that gives greater leeway for protecting privacy:

> I would ask whether the statutes strike a reasonable balance between their speech-restricting and speech-enhancing consequences. Or do they instead impose restrictions on speech that are disproportionate when measured against their corresponding privacy and speech-related benefits, taking into account the kind, the importance, and the extent of these benefits, as well as the need for the restrictions in order to secure those benefits?[67]

Breyer then explains why the statute here "enhances private speech,"[68] prevents "serious harm" to privacy,[69] and "resemble[s] laws that would award damages caused through publication of information obtained by theft from a private bedroom."[70] In light of this, Breyer concludes, "As a general matter, despite the statutes' direct restrictions on speech, the Federal Constitution must tolerate laws of this kind because of the importance of these privacy and speech related objectives."[71] The phrasing of this conclusion is in direct, and presumably intended, contrast to Justice Stevens's statement that "As a general matter, 'state action to punish the publication of truthful information seldom can satisfy constitutional standards.'"[72]

In the end, however, Justices Breyer and O'Connor decide for the media, but only on the narrowest of grounds, and only with a clear endorsement of the power of legislators to take significant

against the corresponding *privacy and speech-related benefits*." Id at 1766, 1767 (emphasis added). Thus, "privacy" benefits that are not "speech-related" appear to have some independent weight in the constitutional balance. Presumably, Justice Breyer is leaving open the possibility that he would uphold government action to protect privacy from media infringement where only the nonspeech aspects of privacy are involved, even though they are not themselves a "constitutional interest," just as in other cases he has concluded that nonspeech (and nonconstitutional) interests can sometimes justify a restriction on speech. See text accompanying notes 176–78.

[67] 121 S Ct at 1766.

[68] Id at 1766–67.

[69] "Media dissemination of an intimate conversation to an entire community will often cause the speakers serious harm over and above the harm caused by an initial disclosure to the person who intercepted the phone call." Id at 1766.

[70] Id at 1767.

[71] Id.

[72] Id at 1761 (citation omitted).

steps to protect privacy from media incursions. For Justice Breyer, there are two reasons why the media win this case. First, as Justice Stevens also had emphasized, the broadcaster was not involved in the illegal interception. Breyer suggests a further narrowing of the Stevens approach, however, by implying that Congress might have been able to reach the media in *Bartnicki* if it had made "receipt" of the illegally intercepted tape unlawful.[73]

Second, Justice Breyer says, "the information publicized involved a matter of *unusual* public concern, *namely a threat of potential physical harm to others*."[74] This formulation is much narrower than the one used by Justice Stevens. Far from relying on a general "public concern" rationale to outweigh the privacy interests here, as Stevens does, Breyer emphasizes that the public concern in this case was an "unusual" and "special" one involving "threats to public safety," since one of the overheard speakers suggested "blow[ing] off . . . front porches" and "doing some work on some of these guys."[75] One might question whether these remarks should be interpreted as a true and continuing threat.[76] But the

[73] The meaning of the relevant passage on "receipt" is somewhat uncertain. In the context of explaining that the media "engaged in no unlawful activity other than the ultimate publication," id at 1767, Breyer says: "[A]s the Court points out, the statutes do not forbid the receipt of the tape itself. *Ante*, at 9. The Court adds that its holding 'does not apply to punishing parties for obtaining the relevant information *unlawfully*.' *Ante*, at 17 n.19 (emphasis added)." Id. The implication seems to be, although this is not certain, that punishing the receipt in these circumstances might be constitutional even if punishing "the ultimate publication" is not. Justice Breyer quite clearly seems to consider "obtaining" to include "receipt." However, the full text of Justice Stevens's footnote 19 suggests that he is probably using "obtaining" to mean no more than directly stealing or intercepting the information. Footnote 19 seems simply to make explicit that "of course" it would be "frivolous" to assert that the First Amendment protects such direct intrusions even by the press.

In any event, it is hard to see why this case should be decided differently if Congress had made the "receipt" of illegally intercepted information itself unlawful. Congress has made unlawful both the "interception" of certain electronic communications and the "disclosure" of that intercepted information. Why should the constitutionality of these provisions depend on whether an interim step between the unlawful interception and the unlawful disclosure is also explicitly made unlawful?

[74] Id at 1766 (emphasis added).

[75] Id at 1766, 1767, 1768.

[76] Perhaps anticipating such a question, particularly when that characterization is key to resolving a motion for summary judgment, Justice Breyer adds: "Nor should editors, who must make a publication decision quickly, have to determine present or continued danger before publishing this kind of threat." Id at 1768.

It is also reasonable to ask whether it would be more appropriate to report the threat, if there was believed to be one, to law enforcement authorities. It is not settled, however, that Title III would permit this "disclosure" any more than it permits media publication. Several lower court cases have construed Title III to prohibit certain disclosures of illegally intercepted material to law enforcement entities. *In re Grand Jury*, 111 F3d 1066, 1077–

crucial point for present purposes is that Justice Stevens nowhere mentions this "unusual" and "special" public safety rationale at all.[77] Instead he focuses exclusively on the fact that the intercepted phone call involved a "public issue"—"the months of negotiations over the proper level of compensation for teachers . . . were unquestionably a matter of public concern, and respondents were clearly engaged in debate about that concern."[78] Again and again, Justice Stevens uses the unadorned phrase "public concern," never suggesting that he would limit First Amendment protection in cases of unlawful interception to disclosures involving "unusual" or "special" types of public concern. By contrast, Justice Breyer explicitly disclaims "a 'public interest' exception that swallows up the statutes' privacy-protecting general rule."[79] "Here," Breyer says, "the speakers' legitimate privacy expectations are unusually low, and the public interest in defeating those expectations unusually high. . . . I emphasize the particular circumstances before us because, in my view, the Constitution permits legislatures to respond flexibly to the challenges future technology may pose to the individual's interest in basic personal privacy."[80]

The privacy-protective nature of Justice Breyer's approach is also reflected in how he treats the fact that the speakers, officials in a public employees' union, were actively involved in public life. Considering this an additional, although not necessarily independent, factor in his analysis, Breyer characterizes the speakers as "limited public figures, for they voluntarily engaged in a public

79 (3d Cir 1997); *Berry v Funk*, 146 F3d 1003, 1011–13 (DC Cir 1998); *Chandler v United States Army*, 125 F3d 1296, 1298–1302 (9th Cir 1997). Indeed, when Justice O'Connor was a state judge in Arizona, she had such a case. *State v Dwyer*, 585 P2d 900 (Ariz App 1978) (affirming Judge O'Connor's suppression, in a homicide case, of a privately intercepted telephone conversation that had been given to law enforcement authorities). In his Reply Brief in *Bartnicki*, the Solicitor General, addressing disclosures to the police, stated that "the traditional defense of 'necessity' privileges conduct that is necessary to protect lives where (as here) the defense is not foreclosed by statute." Reply Brief for the United States at 19, *Bartnicki v Vopper*, 121 S Ct 1753 (2001) (Nos 99-1687, 99-1728) (available at 1999 US Briefs LEXIS 187). Justice Breyer himself suggests that there is a broader "privilege allowing the reporting of threats to public safety," not limited to reporting those threats to law enforcement officials. 121 S Ct at 1768.

[77] He does quote this part of the intercepted conversation in his opinion's statement of facts, id at 1757, but makes nothing of it in the remainder of his opinion.

[78] Id at 1765.

[79] Id at 1768.

[80] Id.

controversy."[81] But whereas Justice Stevens flatly states that "one of the costs of participation in public affairs is an attendant loss of privacy,"[82] Justice Breyer states that public involvement may produce only "*somewhat* greater public scrutiny and . . . a *lesser* interest in privacy."[83]

Justice Breyer then explicitly rejects the idea that "the Constitution requires anyone, including public figures, to give up entirely the right to private communication."[84] And he goes on to cite a number of lower court cases and authorities advocating privacy protection for public figures—emphasizing, in pointed parentheticals following each case or authority, that even where someone "famous" is involved or there is "interest of [the] public," publication of certain private matters does not involve a "*legitimate* public concern."[85] This distinction between "public concern" (Stevens's phrase) and "legitimate public concern" (Breyer's phrase[86]) significantly narrows the media's leeway. It makes clear that simply because there is a public interest in something does not justify its disclosure to the public. A normative judgment must be made, one that limits the potential breadth of the "public concern" concept. A public concern is not "legitimate" if it intrudes too far into other people's privacy.

Justice Breyer's short opinion does not set forth criteria for determining whether a matter involves a "legitimate" and "unusual" public concern. The threat to public security in this case, he says, comes within those categories, and he distinguishes this from the "truly private matters" in two lower court cases involving a "videotape recording of sexual relations" and certain personal informa-

---

[81] Id. The concept of "public figures" and "private figures" has been especially important in cases assessing the place of the First Amendment in defamation actions after *New York Times Co. v Sullivan*, 376 US 254 (1964). See, e.g., *Philadelphia Newspaper, Inc. v Hepps*, 475 US 767 (1986); *Wolston v Reader's Digest Assn, Inc.*, 443 US 157 (1979); *Time, Inc. v Firestone*, 424 US 448 (1976); *Gertz v Robert Welch, Inc.*, 418 US 323 (1974).

[82] 121 S Ct at 1765.

[83] Id at 1768 (emphasis added).

[84] Id.

[85] Id (emphasis added).

[86] Breyer takes the phrase from Warren and Brandeis's famous article on privacy, 4 Harv L Rev at 214 (cited in note 1), and it appears in Section 652D of the Restatement (Second) of Torts (1977), which establishes liability for those who "give[ ] publicity to a matter concerning the private life of another . . . if the matter publicized is of a kind that (a) would be highly offensive to a reasonable person, and (b) *is not of legitimate concern to the public.*" (Emphasis added.)

tion about a divorce. But his category of "truly private matters" appears to be at a polar extreme from matters of "unusual" public concern, so Breyer's boundary and the criteria for drawing it remain uncertain. Nevertheless, Breyer's requirement that there be both "legitimate" and "unusual" public concern to establish the media's First Amendment right in this context promises substantial protection for privacy.

Justice Breyer's opinion, therefore, leaves us very far from Justice Stevens's refusal to say "whether the truthful publication of private matters unrelated to public affairs can be constitutionally proscribed,"[87] and "refusal to answer categorically whether truthful publication may ever be punished consistent with the First Amendment."[88] Justice Breyer is clear that truthful publication can be punished in order to protect privacy.[89]

Justices Breyer and O'Connor do not go as far as the dissenters. The dissenters, using "intermediate scrutiny," treat the unlawfulness of the original interception as dispositive.[90] The dissenters would give no weight in this context to the fact that the intercepted information might involve information of "public concern," whether the public concern is ordinary or "unusual." They call "public concern" "an amorphous concept that the Court does not even attempt to define."[91] In the most important passage in their opinion, the dissenters embrace a privacy-protection approach that

[87] 121 S Ct at 1764.

[88] Id at 1762.

[89] Justice Breyer gives an interesting gloss on his own *Bartnicki* opinion in his recent Madison Lecture. Stephen Breyer, *Our Democratic Constitution*, the Fall 2001 James Madison Lecture, delivered at NYU Law School on Octoher 22, 2001 (copy on file with the author). He characterizes the *Bartnicki* decision as a "narrow" one and argues that the narrowness was appropriate because privacy questions are now "unusually complex." "]T]he complex nature of these problems calls for resolution through a form of participatory democracy," with "law revision that bubbles up from below." This, in turn, "suggests a need for . . . judicial caution or modesty" that does not "pre-empt" the democratic process. Id at 14–17. This is not just a general defense of narrow decisions in this area, however. It is pointedly an argument for narrowness in decisions in a particular direction—decisions that protect the media and limit the scope of privacy protection. The point is that the Court should "leav[e] open broadcaster liability in other . . . circumstances," id at 16, and allow the participatory democratic process to take privacy-protective steps.

[90] They do distinguish the *Pentagon Papers* case, however, saying that that case involved government information and was also a "prior restraint" case, rather than concluding that it was wrongly decided simply because Daniel Ellsberg had stolen the papers. 121 S Ct at 1776.

[91] Id at 1769.

is undoubtedly broader than the multifactored complexity of the Breyer approach:

> The Constitution should not protect the involuntary broadcast of personal conversations. Even where the communications involve public figures or concern public matters, the conversations are nonetheless private and worthy of protection. Although public persons may have forgone the right to live their lives screened from public scrutiny in some areas, it does not and should not follow that they also have abandoned their right to have a private conversation without fear of it being intentionally intercepted and knowingly disclosed.[92]

The Stevens and Breyer opinions, taken together, extend First Amendment immunity beyond prior cases in some respects, covering situations where the information was unlawfully obtained. But the Breyer and Rehnquist opinions, taken together, contract and limit First Amendment protections in several other respects, most obviously in sharply limiting the media's "public concern" rationale for invading privacy. Overall, the combined weight of the concurrence and the dissent establishes that five Justices seem quite receptive to restrictions on speech to protect privacy.

III

This broader receptivity to privacy protection is as it should be, in my judgment. The Court should give more weight to privacy protection in cases involving privacy-speech conflicts. This conclusion reflects not only a view of the importance of privacy, but also concerns about new technological threats to privacy and about contemporary social circumstances that have made privacy more vulnerable than speech. Ultimately, it also reflects a conception of freedom of the press as largely a freedom concerned with the public sphere.

1) The values served by privacy (understood here as the ability to control and to avoid disclosure of certain matters about oneself) are many and can be variously described: the need to be let alone; promoting development of the personality; developing trusting relationships of love and friendship; avoiding pressures for conformity; encouraging creativity; maintaining the rules of civility;

[92] Id at 1776.

allowing noncompliance with ambivalently supported laws; reducing unfair, out-of-context judgments of people; letting people bury their past; protecting human dignity; sustaining individualism; and developing a liberal and pluralistic society, to mention just some that have been discussed in the literature.[93] Privacy also promotes a system of free expression, for people are more likely to express themselves fully, openly, and robustly when they have confidence that what they say will be heard only by a known group of listeners. Fear of being overheard, fear of public exposure, fear of one's words becoming the subject of gossip, fear of intimacies being publicly scrutinized, fear of being sanctioned or disapproved of because of what one says—all of these have a profound inhibiting effect on expression, and make it crucially important for the law to protect a realm of privacy for communications. Far from threatening speech, protecting private communication is itself a central part of constructing a vibrant system of free expression.

Given the special status of free speech in the American constitutional firmament, it is easiest to argue for readjustments in the speech/privacy balance by emphasizing the ways in which protecting privacy itself promotes free expression. By doing so, one identifies speech interests "on both sides of the equation," and restricting speech to protect privacy can be justified as a speech-enhancing rather than a speech-restricting approach.[94] But not all concerns about privacy are related to expressive freedom. The other values that privacy serves may themselves at times be strong enough to justify some restriction on what the media may publish.

We need to see privacy in the same systemic way that we have come to see speech. Suppressing speech, we recognize, is not only a loss to the individual in question. It also deprives public debate and deliberation of the benefits of wide-open and robust discussion; it harms democratic self-government. Similarly, lost privacy is not only a diminishment to the individual directly concerned. It also reduces a sphere of life that is crucial for a particular kind

[93] See, e.g., Warren and Brandeis, 4 Harv L Rev 193 (cited in note 1); Ruth Gavison, *Privacy and the Limits of Law*, 89 Yale L J 421 (1980); Jeffrey Rosen, *The Unwanted Gaze: The Destruction of Privacy in America* (2000); Post, *The Social Foundations of Privacy* (cited in note 52); Charles Fried, *An Anatomy of Values* (1970); Amitai Etzioni, *The Limits of Privacy* (1999); Richard C. Turkington and Anita L. Allen, *Privacy Law: Cases and Materials* (1999); Spiros Simitis, *Reviewing Privacy in an Information Society*, 135 U Pa L Rev 707 (1987).

[94] 121 S Ct at 1766 (Breyer concurring).

of human functioning that sustains a pluralistic society. Moreover, when the media puts private matters into the public sphere, it has systemic consequences for the public sphere itself.

Those who do not participate in the public square at all can make the strongest claims to privacy protection. People only tangentially or episodically in the public eye—or those who have been forced into the public square because they are victims of crime or some other misfortune—also have strong claims. Cases involving public figures are the hardest privacy cases, since public figures seem to want it both ways, to embrace the public and yet evade it, and because the accountability of public officials and political candidates is a central element of democratic self-governance. But protecting some aspect of privacy for public figures is crucial for their own human functioning. Moreover, as discussed more fully below, protecting their privacy can further the values of democratic self-governance.[95]

But while privacy serves public values, at bottom privacy is anti-public. This is part of what makes it such a challenging concept for contemporary constitutional and political theory, and why many are reluctant to say that privacy should outweigh the public functions of a free press. Owen Fiss has written about a number of recent circumstances in which traditional supporters of free speech have supported restrictions on speech.[96] He discusses, for example, feminist support for restricting pornography in spite of liberalism's traditional support for freedom of sexual expression, support for hate speech laws among many in the civil rights movement in spite of their traditional opposition to censorship, and support of some civil liberties groups for campaign finance restrictions and regulations of the media to assure wider access and enhance the diversity of views available to the public. Some of these examples pit different conceptions of free speech against each other. Others, such as hate speech and pornography, can be seen as a conflict between free speech and equality, although Fiss sees them as a conflict within the First Amendment itself. But in each case, the argnment in favor of restricting speech rests at bottom on a conception of the "public"—a revised sense of public debate, or

[95] See text accompanying notes 120, 135–36.

[96] Owen M. Fiss, *Liberalism Divided: Freedom of Speech and the Many Uses of State Power* (1996). See also Owen M. Fiss, *The Irony of Free Speech* (1996).

collective self-determination, or social roles, or social status. As Fiss puts it, these arguments in favor of restricting speech rest on an understanding of freedom "in more social terms."[97]

But the arguments in favor of restricting speech to protect privacy are largely anti-"social"—or at least they seek to preserve a realm of the social and personal that often refuses to contribute to a wider "public." "Private speech" might be related to public issues or might be preparation for an ultimately more "public" formulation, but its value does not depend only on that, and that is not the primary reason we protect it from disclosure. We protect its privateness. We protect the right to choose a narrow audience, or no audience except oneself—to be what William Carlos Williams called "lonely, lonely," and as such to be "the happy genius of my household."[98] So too for the elements of privacy having nothing to do with speech—we protect them from disclosure largely because we know that humans are constituted in part by refusing to be public. One can and should identify public purposes served by protecting the private, as I have done above, but privacy's effort to subvert the public's knowledge and control is at the core of what it is—and, I believe, the core of its unique value.

2) In assessing the importance of enhancing privacy protection, we also need to take account of technological developments that create greater society-wide threats to privacy. It is appropriate and common for legal rules to adapt to the development of new technologies.[99] This is because legal rules are typically premised on often unarticulated background assumptions about what the world is like. When reality changes, and the background assumptions no longer hold true, existing law may not achieve its original purposes. If we adhere to existing rules in the face of new technologies, the existing balance between liberty and order may be transformed. Concerning privacy, for example, the law may not protect certain private activities or zones because there are few perceived threats to those activities or zones. The law allows access, but since access in practice is rare, the law does not occasion significant inva-

---

[97] Fiss, *Liberalism Divided* at 5.

[98] William Carlos Williams, *Danse Russe*, in A. Walton Litz and Christopher MacGowan, eds, *The Collected Poems of William Carlos Williams 1909–1939* at 86–87 (1986).

[99] See Paul Gewirtz, *Constitutional Law and New Technology*, 64 Social Research 1191 (1997).

sions of privacy. Our technological crudity protects us from wider invasions of privacy. But if new technologies create new capabilities that facilitate access and therefore open up new threats to privacy, we may have to change the rules if we wish to preserve the old rules' purposes.

Another privacy case decided last term, *Kyllo v United States*,[100] nicely illustrates one way that legal rules adapt to new technologies—specifically, adapt to what the Court described as the "power of technology to shrink the realm of guaranteed privacy."[101] *Kyllo* involved the police use of a "thermal-imaging" device in the course of a drug investigation. When aimed at a building from outside, such a device can pick up relative amounts of heat emanating from the building. In *Kyllo*, a thermal-imaging device was aimed at a private home from the street and was able to pick up hot zones suggesting that halide lights were being used inside to grow marijuana. The constitutional question was whether use of the device was a "search" within the meaning of the Fourth Amendment.

The Court acknowledged that visual observation traditionally has not been deemed a "search," but also underscored that individuals traditionally have had a reasonable expectation of privacy in "the interior of their homes." With "old" technologies, the two concepts are not in conflict. But with the "technological enhancement of ordinary perception" permitted by the "advance of technology," a conflict can emerge. The Court in *Kyllo* concluded that the use of thermal imaging on a house constitutes a "search," even though observation from the same spot without "technological enhancement" would not have been a "search."

> To withdraw protection of this minimum expectation [of privacy] would be to permit police technology to erode the privacy guaranteed by the Fourth Amendment. We think that obtaining by sense-enhancing technology any information regarding the interior of the home that could not otherwise have been obtained without physical "intrusion into a constitutionally protected area" constitutes a search—at least where (as here) the technology in question is not in general public use. This assures preservation of that degree of privacy against gov-

[100] 121 S Ct 2038 (2001).

[101] Id at 2043.

ernment that existed when the Fourth Amendment was adopted.[102]

Technological changes creating new threats to privacy should also affect legal rules in a broader way, encouraging reexamination of the rules governing the speech/privacy balance. As new technologies make outsiders' access to private matters easier (allowing ready interceptions of phone calls or eavesdropping on bedroom conversations or hacking into electronically stored information, for example), and as new technologies facilitate the creation of permanent electronic records and footprints and simplify the ability to gather personal information from dispersed sources, laws protecting privacy become more important. At the same time, the media has a greater potential to produce more extensive harms by broadly disseminating private material, and new media technologies such as the internet and e-mailing make possible new threats to privacy.[103] A continuing reluctance to limit the media in the face of new technologies, in short, may result in a major diminishment of privacy.[104] It may well be that in the years ahead further techno-

[102] Id (citation omitted). The Court in *Kyllo* relies on an earlier case in which technological change fostered a change in Fourth Amendment doctrine, *Katz v United States*, 389 US 347 (1967). In *Katz*, the Court discarded a constitutional rule that the Fourth Amendment was triggered only by a physical trespass, in significant part because new electronic technologies were allowing widespread intrusions on areas where there was a reasonable expectation of privacy even without any physical intrusion.

[103] See A. Michael Froomkin, *The Death of Privacy?* 52 Stan L Rev 1461 (2000); Rosen, *The Unwanted Gaze* at 57–58, 159–95 (cited in note 93); Lawrence Lessig, *Code and Other Laws of Cyberspace* 142–64 (1999); Turkington and Allen, *Privacy Law* at 311–25 (cited in note 93).

[104] Cf. Geoffrey R. Stone, *The Scope of the Fourth Amendment: Privacy and the Police Use of Spies, Secret Agents, and Informers*, 1966 Am Bar Found Res J 1193, 1216 (suggesting a "principle of conservation of privacy," which seeks "to maintain a cumulative level of privacy comparable to that existing at the time the fourth amendment was drafted"). This point is a general one, and has often been lost in discussions about the tension between liberty and security after the events of September 11, 2001. Many of our civil liberties doctrines and rules rest on background assumptions about the risks to security that will follow from civil liberties of a certain scope. For example, when we say it is better that ten guilty people go free than that one innocent person be convicted, we are implicitly assuming that the risk to society of setting ten guilty people free is a tolerable risk. But if technologies and access to technologies develop so that the ten guilty people have access to footlocker-sized nuclear weapons and the will to detonate them, then we may want to adjust our epigram (and at least some of our rules in some circumstances). Not to do so is to end up with a real-world balance between liberty and security that is very different from the one we started with. The point is just as applicable in the other direction. If we do not adjust existing rules when new investigative technologies give law enforcement officials much greater capacity to reduce liberty, then we will end up with a much different liberty/security balance than we thought we had. Liberty-oriented rules of wider scope will be necessary just to keep pace.

logical developments will themselves create better ways of advancing communication while also protecting privacy—for example, by strengthening encryption methods—but for now privacy protections will be significantly shaped by where the law draws the line between permissible and impermissible invasions.

3) Giving more weight to privacy in constitutional disputes is also warranted because of the contemporary social and cultural context within which these issues arise. Just as legal rules are typically premised on background assumptions about technologies, so too are such rules usually premised on assumptions about social conditions, behaviors, and attitudes. As these change, legal rules may require reexamination. Often in partnership with new technologies, social and cultural factors have made privacy more vulnerable than before—and, I would argue, more vulnerable than the press today—suggesting that legal efforts to strengthen privacy deserve added weight when balanced against press prerogatives. The events of September 11, 2001, and ongoing fears of terrorism will continue to augment the government's already great powers to collect information and monitor behavior. Employers have become expansive data gatherers and monitors. Legally, as well as culturally, there is a wider sense of a "right to know." The greater role of litigation in our society over past decades has created a new and extremely powerful engine to compel the disclosure of hitherto private information. A wider "politics of scandal" and "criminalization of politics" has unleashed powerful investigative machinery and increased mainstream attention to the private misdeeds of public figures and to the lives of private figures caught up in the investigative onslaught. I have elsewhere referred to an "Oprahfication" of American culture.[105] By this I mean that Americans have become ready and unashamed voyeurs, stimulated and allowed to peer into and judge the private lives of others, even as we typically try to hold on to our own privacy and support laws to protect it. Cultural boundaries between the public and private have become blurred, with private intimacies more casually the subject of public discourse, and new expectations created about what we may know about others.

The press itself has been changed by the more mainstreamed

---

[105] Paul Gewirtz, *Victims and Voyeurs: Two Narrative Problems at the Criminal Trial*, in *Law's Stories* at 135, 152 (cited in note 54).

prurience of the American people, and in turn has become a greater cultural force in diminishing privacy.[106] It has often been noted that "entertainment values" drive news coverage these days,[107] and a large part of what this means is that news coverage has increasingly broken down distinctions between what is public and what is private. The mainstream media devote more attention to personalities, gossip, and reporting on private lives of both the famous and the ordinary. Although we may seek to hold on to our own privacy and support laws to protect it, these broader cultural forces, along with new technologies, present new and serious threats to privacy.

On the other hand, the press today is not seriously endangered by government restrictions, and individual speakers are not seriously threatened by government-imposed conformity of viewpoint. Debate about public issues and public figures is extremely vigorous. The boundaries of the permissible have been extended very far out. In earlier times, this was not the case: the press and other speakers were subject to government legal action that directly sought to restrict criticism of the government and sought to limit a broad range of ideas from being expressed and heard. Understandably, free speech law sought to push back on these restrictions. But the press today has great leeway and boldness. It is true that the terrorist attacks of September 11, 2001, and the resulting war in Afghanistan have led the current administration to criticize the media—for example (and disturbingly), the Attorney General has criticized the media and others for giving "aid" to terrorists by their "fearmongering" objections to administration policies on civil liberties grounds.[108] But the government has taken no legal steps to restrict media criticism, and the media remains bold (although this popular war is also generally popular in the media). The system of free expression still needs to be strengthened—es-

---

[106] The point here is one of degree. Concerns about the press invading privacy and pushing boundaries in that direction are hardly new, of course. In a different social context where there were different cultural boundaries, Warren and Brandeis's famous article on privacy expressed analogous sorts of concerns about press behavior.

[107] See, e.g., James Fallows, *Breaking the News* (1996); Neil Postman, *Amusing Ourselves to Death* (1985).

[108] *DOJ Oversight: Preserving Our Freedoms While Defending Against Terrorism*, hearing before Senate Judiciary Committee, 107th Cong 1 (2001) (testimony of Attorney General John Ashcroft, Dec 6, 2001), available at <http://www.usdoj.gov/ag/testimony/2001/1206transcriptsenatejudiciarycommittee.htm>.

pecially by counteracting the dominance of media giants and further diversifying the voices that can be heard (without thereby diluting the power of strong press entities to be a true check on government[109])—but not by strengthening the press in its freedom to interfere with privacy. It is the latter value that is now often seriously threatened, and at times threatened by the press. In deciding how to strike the press/privacy balance, it is essential to take account of where the greater vulnerabilities and dangers are.

These various factors help to justify strengthening privacy protections. But freedom of the press from government abridgment is explicitly protected by the Constitution, and freedom from nongovernmental interference with privacy is not.[110] There are only two conceptual ways for privacy concerns to prevail in the face of the press' claim of First Amendment protection: (1) to conclude that the First Amendment right does not apply, or does not apply at full strength, when the press infringes on certain private matters; or (2) to conclude that privacy is a strong enough competing interest in particular circumstances to outweigh the First Amendment interest. Each conception is plausible, and indeed they are related.

The freedom of the press protected by the First Amendment must be seen as primarily about the press' contribution to democratic self-governance, to public debate, and to checking the power of the state.[111] This core freedom is a broad one, and it includes

---

[109] Vincent Blasi, *The Checking Value in First Amendment Theory*, 1977 Am Bar Found Res J 521 (1977).

[110] A right to privacy as the freedom to keep the government from having unwanted access to personal information is protected through the Fourth Amendment and also as an aspect of substantive due process under the Fifth and Fourteenth Amendments. *Whalen v Roe*, 429 US 589 (1977). The Fourth Amendment is phrased as a "right of the people to be secure . . . against unreasonable searches and seizure," and, as literally phrased, does not have a state action requirement. But the Fourth Amendment has not been interpreted as providing protections against nongovernmental interference, and I do not rest my argument on a claim that media interference with "privacy" violates a constitutional right of privacy.

[111] The idea that the First Amendment as a whole has this core meaning has its contemporary roots in the writings of Alexander Meiklejohn, e.g., *Free Speech and Its Relation to Self-Government* (1948), and has heen developed in recent years by Owen Fiss, e.g., *Liberalism Divided* (cited in note 96); *The Irony of Free Speech* (cited in note 96), and Cass Sunstein, *Democracy and the Problem of Free Speech* (1993). These writers do not distinguish between freedom of speech and freedom of the press. However, this understanding of the First Amendment seems to have distinctive force in understanding freedom of the press in particular, both because the institutional nature of media entities makes less relevant another standard rationale for free speech—promoting self-fulfillment—and, more importantly (as

not only explicitly "political" speech but also a broad range of "cultural" expression, since cultural expression contributes to our public life[112] and since experience teaches us that cultural censorship so often has a political motivation.[113] This understanding of freedom of the press as primarily about the puhlic sphere reflects both an affirmative concept about the press' role and also, I would argue, a recognition that a wider concept of press freedom would conflict with other values that a society properly cherishes, such as privacy. Thus concern about privacy is built into a proper conception of press freedom itself. Freedom of the press is not fundamentally about the freedom to disclose private matters or to invade the private sphere.[114] The freedom to publish the truth strikes many as the core of what freedom of the press is about; but truthful information about oneself is also at the core of what privacy protects. A plausible way to harmonize these ideas is to understand the press' freedom as focused primarily on the public sphere.

The alternative way to bring privacy protection into the constitutional analysis is to see privacy as a value that competes with the value of a free press. This is a plausible way of proceeding as long as we accept that interests not explicitly protected by the Constitution (here, the interest in protecting privacy from nongovernmental interference) can in certain circumstances outweigh interests that are.[115] In fact, almost all doctrinal "tests" in constitutional law

I note below), because a wider concept of freedom of the press would distinctively threaten privacy values.

[112] This was Alexander Meiklejohn's rationale, *The First Amendment Is an Absolute*, 1961 Supreme Court Review 245, 255–57. For a criticism of Meiklejohn's inclusion of culture, see Robert Bork, *Neutral Principles and Some First Amendment Problems*, 47 Ind L J 1, 26–28 (1971).

[113] See Sunstein, *Democracy and the Problem of Free Speech* at 135–36, 164–65 (cited in note 111). For a criticism of Sunstein's view—indeed, a broader criticism of approaches that see the First Amendment's primary purpose as promoting deliberation about public issues—see J. M. Balkin, *Populism and Progressivism as Constitutional Categories*, 104 Yale L J 1935 (1995).

[114] What differentiates freedom of the press from freedom of speech is that the former typically involves an institution of production and distribution. Since wide distribution of information is usually the main threat to privacy protection, arguably "freedom of the press" poses a greater danger to privacy than "freedom of speech" *simpliciter*—and therefore particular care should be taken in defining what comes within the constitutional concept of freedom of the press or particular receptivity shown when privacy values are balanced against it.

[115] There are countries in which both free press and privacy are explicitly protected by the Constitution—indeed, privacy is protected from both governmental and nongovernmental infringement. See text accompanying notes 140–55. In such countries it may not matter greatly which analytic route is followed and, in particular, whether a core conception of

reflect this, with, for example, "substantial" or "compelling" (but nonconstitutional) interests justifying restrictions on constitutional ones in certain circumstances. At bottom, under either approach, the task must be to reconcile protection for both a free press and for privacy, to reconcile protecting the need of the public to know with the competing need of individuals to keep things private. These are each things that we rightly cherish, and that the Constitution must be read as recognizing that we rightly cherish. Of course, "the right to be let alone [can] develop into an impediment to the transparency necessary for a democratic decisionmaking process."[116] But we must impose some limits on the transparency of the private, even where transparency might marginally enhance public deliberation, if we want to preserve a private sphere of meaningful scope.

In light of this, the concept of "public concern" is insufficient to mediate the press-privacy conflict. Superficially, this concept might appear to preserve the public/private distinction, but it does not. In fact, the notion that content of "public concern" justifies media attention protected by the First Amendment is an engine for destroying privacy. It is always possible to construct an argument that public knowledge about a "private" matter is relevant in some way to public understanding of public issues or public roles. It can always be said that some private fact is an exemplification of a wider public phenomenon and that informing the public about it will enhance public understanding.[117] If identifying "relevance" to

free press is defined. Even a very broad conception of free press will bave to be reconciled with or "balanced" against the privacy values protected elsewhere in the constitution itself. But in our Constitution, the stakes in understanding the rationale for protecting a free press may be higher, for in our press-privacy cases freedom of the press is the only explicit constitutional right in the picture.

[116] Simitis, 135 U Pa L Rev at 731 (cited in note 93).

[117] There are endless varieties of these kinds of weak and privacy-destroying nexus arguments. To give just one example from a well-known case, Judge Richard Posner upheld on First Amendment grounds the reporting about private facts about an ordinary citizen (as summarized by Posner, "his heavy drinking, his unstable unemployment, his adultery, his irresponsible and neglectful behavior toward his wife and children") using the following argument in part: "Reporting the true facts about real people is necessary to 'obviate any impression that the [general social] problems raised in the [reporting] are remote or hypothetical.'" *Haynes v Alfred A. Knopf, Inc.*, 8 F3d 1222, 1233 (7th Cir 1993). Obviously, if personal and embarrassing private facts (here, from thirty years previously) can be published simply because they establish that some general social problem is not remote or hypothetical, no one with "problems" has any protection from media disclosure. See also text accompanying note 128, discussing the way that the Restatement (Second) of Torts limits the privacy protections for "involuntary public figures."

a "public concern" is sufficient to justify media publication, some relevance can always be found or created, and privacy will be only a matter of media grace and forbearance. To preserve some realm of the private from public disclosure, we need to develop more nuanced criteria, which inevitably will turn on matters of degree: how private, what degree of public significance, how much relevance between private fact and public concern, and so forth. Justice Breyer's concept of "legitimate public concern" in *Bartnicki* is a recognition that a limiting normative judgment is required. The need for limiting criteria is even clearer once we appreciate that in this context the usual nostrum that the remedy for problematic speech is more speech has no applicability. More speech following disclosure of a private matter would only deepen the loss of privacy, not protect it.[118] To permit the media to invoke "public concern" to justify publicizing private information means either that no one will fight back or that the fighting back will further undermine privacy.[119]

I would also argue that limiting invasion of the "private" actually enhances public debate. Information about the private lives of public officials easily distracts us from their official actions. The public has great curiosity about these private matters, and the media has financial incentives to satisfy that curiosity. The public and the press each push along these tendencies in the other, but the fundamental element here is an aspect of human nature, the weakness for voyeurism that we all have, a weakness that drives out (or at least diminishes) public attention to official actions and policies when offered more prurient alternatives. It is no accident—and only slightly hyperbolic to point out—that while the media were endlessly reporting and re-reporting details about Representative Gary Condit's sex life, they barely noted the Rudman-Hart Commission's Report on Terrorism and offered virtually no criticism of our ineffectual antiterrorism policies or our utter unpreparedness for terrorist attacks. Enhanced media prerogatives do not necessarily mean improvement in public discourse or enhance-

[118] See Geoffrey R. Stone, Louis M. Seidman, Cass R. Sunstein, and Mark V. Tushnet, *Constitutional Law* 1075 (4th ed 2001).

[119] Litigation of a privacy claim, of course, presents a similar problem. See Harry J. Kalven, Jr., *Privacy in Tort Law—Were Warren and Brandeis Wrong?* 31 L & Contemp Probs 326, 328 (1966). However, establishing a privacy right would presumably deter publication to some extent.

ment of the press' role in society. To the contrary, augmented leeway to publicize private matters almost surely means less coverage of more public matters and a diminishment of political discourse. What may be even worse, it can transform what we consider to be "public and political discourse"—with private matters coming to play a comparatively greater role both in what passes for "public and political discourse" and also in the ultimate public judgments of public figures. At times, enhanced media prerogatives not only can damage the competing value of privacy, but can distort public debate itself. Strengthening privacy protection will help reclaim both the "private" and the "public."[120]

For all these reasons, then, the Court should be more receptive to rules that protect privacy even when the media's desire to publish certain truthful information is restricted. The Supreme Court has allowed the speech/privacy balance to shift too far against privacy interests. And the problem is not only the rules the Court has adopted and the Court's repeated "refusal to answer whether truthful information may ever be punished consistent with the First Amendment."[121] The problem includes the fact that, in virtually every case that the Supreme Court decides involving a press/privacy conflict, the privacy claim loses. The Court sends signals by its patterns, not only by its rules.

What privacy protections will be, of course, is initially in the hands of state and federal lawmakers, and there have long been different views about the appropriate scope of privacy protection "simply" as a matter of statutory or common law.[122] It is clear, however, that for some time statutory and common law tort rules have developed in the shadow of perceived First Amendment re-

[120] Cf. Lee Bollinger, *Images of a Free Press* 133–45 (1991) (arguing that members of a democratic society, aware of their own "deficiencies," may use public regulation to improve "the quality of public discussion"); Geoffrey R. Stone, *Imagining a Free Press*, 90 Mich L Rev 1246, 1262–63 (1992) (arguing for "some limit" on what the press reports about political candidates, "designed not only to respect [their] legitimate privacy interests . . . , but also to reflect our right, as a society, to decide that some matters simply should not play a significant role in our political process" because "the information has a greater potential to distract and distort than to inform our better judgment"); Rosen, *The Unwanted Gaze* at 143 (cited in note 93) ("knowing everything about someone's private life inevitably distracts us from making reliable judgments about his or her character and public achievements").

[121] 121 S Ct at 1764, and text accompany notes 57–59.

[122] See, e.g., Marc A. Franklin and Robert L. Rabin, *Tort Law and Alternatives: Cases and Materials* 1098–1215 (2001); Turkington and Allen, *Privacy Law* (cited in note 93).

strictions resulting from Supreme Court decisions. The Restatement (Second) of Torts is explicit that its "model" privacy tort rules take the shape they do because of the drafters' efforts to fit those rules within the constraints of existing First Amendment doctrine.[123] If the Court placed fewer First Amendment restrictions on state and federal flexibility to strengthen privacy protections, not only would statutes like Title III have wider force in protecting privacy, but other federal and state protections of privacy could well expand.

In my judgment, where information has been obtained *unlawfully*, and the law prohibits further disclosures, the First Amendment should not be interpreted to stand in the way of damage actions for media disclosures, except where there is an extraordinary justification for the publication. Justice Breyer may be right that the situation in *Bartnicki* presented the kind of public security threat that counts as an extraordinary justification. If so, however, it is important to be clear that, generally speaking, the publication of unlawfully intercepted conversations, even conversations about matters being publicly debated, is not protected by the First Amendment. Even when they have a public content, they come from a private zone that the state may protect from media intrusion. Although Justice Breyer emphasizes that *Bartnicki* involves an "unusual" public concern, and that he would "not create a 'public interest' exception that swallows up the statutes' privacy protecting general rule," his examples of information that the government may protect from disclosure are all from a polar extreme—"situations where the media publicizes *truly private matters*,"[124] by which he appears to mean "truly private" content (his examples concern sexual relations and divorce). Where information has been secured unlawfully, however, and a private zone has been unlawfully invaded, privacy law should be permitted to limit the media more substantially, restricting it from disclosing conversations from that zone which concern public issues as well as personal matters.

Where information is obtained *lawfully*, but the law seeks to prevent publicity and protect privacy, the First Amendment analysis is rightly more complex. The goal is to strike a balance that pro-

[123] Restatement (Second) of Torts, § 652D (1977) ("Special Note on Relation of § 652D to the First Amendment of the Constitution").

[124] 121 S Ct at 1768 (Breyer concurring) (emphasis added).

tects privacy but does not unduly restrict the press. A variety of factors should be relevant, similar to those identified in Justice Breyer's *Bartnicki* opinion.[125] One element of the analysis is the substantiality of the public concerns—put another way, the substantiality of free press concerns in light of the purposes of the First Amendment. This turns in part on the identity of the figure receiving public attention. A fuller range of a public figure's life is properly a subject of public scrutiny, and the media must have a wider "breathing space" in its coverage of such figures in order effectively to contribute to political deliberation and democratic self-governance. The nature of the information involved is also relevant. Information about "truly private matters," even concerning public figures, should generally be protectable. A second element of the analysis is the interrelated question of the extent and degree of the privacy invasion. This turns in part on content, whether intimate private characteristics or behavior is concerned. It also turns on the circumstances involved, whether the information comes from a zone of reasonably expected privacy.[126] Final elements in the constitutional analysis concern what might be called the "need" for the particular restriction involved. Are there reasonable and practical alternatives to restricting publication that would protect privacy? Does the law operate with undue selectivity, suggesting either a censorial motive concerning certain ideas or singling out of particular media unrelated to the privacy-protection rationale?

This approach would recalibrate the press/privacy balance and lead to different outcomes in some familiar cases. One example is

---

[125] See text accompanying note 67.

[126] As an element of the tort of "Publicity Given to Private Life," § 652D of the Restatement (Second) of Torts requires that the disclosure of a private fact be "highly offensive." See note 86. This is an incomplete measure. Even where a disclosure about intimate details of someone's life is not "highly offensive," protection may be justified. Consider a touching and tasteful story and photograph about a terminally ill teenager, published without his family's consent, or simply the publishing of ordinary personal details about a child. These may not be "highly offensive," but that should not end the inquiry. See also Rosen, *The Unwanted Gaze* at 50 (cited in note 93) ("In an age that is beyond embarrassment, it's rarely clear what a 'reasonable person' would find highly offensive.").

The Restatement also states that the tort cannot be established if the matter publicized is of "legitimate concern to the public." The word "legitimate" is in effect a placeholder, for it operates here essentially as a conclusion that the public concern is appropriate—a judgment that, as I indicate in the text, reflects a range of factors and normative trade-offs, including not only the substantiality of the public concern but also the degree to which privacy is invaded.

Florida Star v B.J.F.[127] A Florida statute made it unlawful to "print, publish, or broadcast . . . in any instrument of mass communication" the name of a victim of a sexual offense. The *Florida Star* violated the statute and its own internal policy of not publishing such names, and was sued by a rape victim for damages. The Court held that the First Amendment barred recovery, emphasizing that the information was "truthful" and "lawfully obtained." But why should that count for almost everything? Publicizing a rape victim's name is a cruel invasion of privacy concerning a matter of great sensitivity to the victim. Furthermore, in most cases, why is the name of a rape victim a matter of legitimate public concern? The fact of the rape or even the name of the alleged perpetrator is one thing, but the victim's name is ordinarily not something the public profits from knowing. If the rape victim is a public figure or limited public figure, it is only because she has been dragged into the public square against her will as a victim of crime. It is hard to see that publicizing her name contributes to the crucial role the press plays in promoting democratic self-governance. The balance in these circumstances seems very much on the side of privacy. In addition, the Florida law in question was clear and specific. It is hard to see how enforcing this law would "chill" any valuable reporting.

The Court, invoking the *Daily Mail* test requiring the state to show a "need of the highest order" to justify limiting publication of lawfully acquired and truthful information, points to two main factors to explain its holding. First, the *Florida Star* obtained the rape victim's name from a police incident report that had inadvertently included her name. Although the Sheriff Department could in theory have prevented the name from becoming public, the department's error cannot be seen as evidence that the state lacked a commitment to protecting rape victims' privacy. The privacy interests belonged to the victim. An error by the Sheriff's Department should not put her at the mercy of the newspaper, which knew full well that it had a legal obligation not to disclose the victim's name and itself had an internal policy against doing so. Protecting privacy should not be a game of gotcha. Second, the Court said that the Florida statute was underinclusive in that it

[127] 491 US 524 (1989).

prohibited publication only by "an instrument of mass communication," not by other means. But since Florida's primary concern was to prevent the widespread dissemination of rape victims' names, the statute's focus is understandable. This is not a case where the state has singled out one segment of the news media for adverse treatment in a manner suggesting that there are favored and disfavored media entities. It is hard to see how the interest in press freedom and free expression is harmed by this "underinclusiveness."

The flavor of the Court's opinion in *Florida Star* is that the Court will find any conceivable escape hatch for media liability. The Court gives only token recognition to the value of implementing legal protections of privacy. This extreme solicitude for the one and sharply limited solicitude for the other is what should be reversed.

Florida Star involved a private figure victimized by crime. Unfortunately, other types of "involuntary public figures" also receive too little privacy protection under current law. The official comments to Section 652D of the Restatement (Second) of Torts ("Publicity Given to Private Life"),[128] clearly influenced by existing First Amendment law, state:

> There are other individuals who have not sought publicity or consented to it, but through their own conduct or otherwise have become a legitimate subject of public interest. They have, in other words, become "news." . . . These persons are regarded as properly subject to the public interest, and publishers are permitted to satisfy the curiosity of the public . . . . As in the case of the voluntary public figure, the authorized publicity is not limited to the event that itself arouses the public interest, and to some reasonable extent includes publicity given to facts about the individual that would otherwise be purely private. (Comment f.)

I would not interpret the First Amendment to prohibit protections against disclosures of "purely private" and tangential matters. Consider the case of Oliver Sipple, who, while standing in a crowd of onlookers, blocked Sara Jane Moore's arm as she was about to shoot at President Gerald Ford. The *San Francisco Chronicle* thereafter disclosed that Sipple was gay. When Sipple sued the newspa-

[128] See note 86.

per for invasion of privacy, his case was dismissed on First Amendment grounds. The California appellate court noted that Sipple had not completely concealed his sexual identity (although the court did not dispute that Sipple had kept the information from his family and that, as a result of the publicity, Sipple's family abandoned him). But the court's main argument was that "the publications were not motivated by a morbid and sensational prying into appellant's private life but rather were prompted by legitimate political considerations, i.e., to dispel the false public opinion that gays were timid, weak and unheroic figures. . . ."[129] Given the intensely personal nature of Sipple's sexual identity and the care many homosexuals take to limit general knowledge about that identity, and given that Sipple did not seek notoriety, this asserted connection between the private fact and "political considerations" was simply too weak to warrant the *Chronicle*'s disclosure.[130]

The privacy protections permitted to a true public figure—a political official, an entertainment personality—must be more limited. Most obviously, the media must have a very broad right to cover the actions of political figures because of the presumptive connection between such coverage and the process of democratic self-governance and because the media must be given "breathing space . . . to ensure the robust debate of public issues."[131] Voters assess public officials on a wide variety of grounds, and the scope of press coverage properly reflects this. But this rationale should not make every aspect of a public figure's life fair game for media attention.

Public officials have some legitimate expectations of privacy because they are human beings as well as "public officials." They magnify and reconfigure, but do not abandon, our own complex and ambivalent relations to the public as we assume multiple roles in day-to-day life. Indeed, since public figures are typically our

---

[129] *Sipple v Chronicle Publishing Co.*, 201 Cal Rptr 665, 670 (Cal App 1st 1984).

[130] For a different view, see Rosen, *The Unwanted Gaze* at 48 (cited in note 93). Rosen describes "the brutal outing of Oliver Sipple" and recognizes the "psychological distress" it caused (Sipple eventually committed suicide), but concludes: "[D]espite the tragic personal consequences that often result from the disclosure of true but embarrassing private facts, it's appropriate, in a country that takes the First Amendment seriously, that invasion of privacy suits against the press rarely succeed."

[131] *Dun and Bradstreet, Inc. v Greenmoss Builders*, 472 US 749, 776 (1985); *New York Times Co. v Sullivan*, 376 US at 271–72.

proxies and representatives in the public space and perform so many public functions for us—letting us preserve more of the private than we otherwise could—we arguably owe them space for at least some reciprocal measure of our own ambivalence and our own needs for privacy. When Justice Stevens says in *Bartnicki* that "[o]ne of the costs of participation in public affairs is an attendant loss of privacy,"[132] he is making a descriptively true statement. But he seems to be using this inevitable descriptive truth as a justification for allowing the law itself to undermine privacies that can be preserved. Some people, of course, will enter public life even if they know that their lives will be lived on the front pages of newspapers; and there always will be some public figures complicitous in destroying their own potential privacy. Nevertheless, our legal regime should not compel those interested in public affairs to pay such a price against their will.

Reporting on sexual habits or on intimate family matters of public figures should generally be outside First Amendment protection, particularly when the information comes from circumstances of reasonably expected privacy. To be sure, media disclosures concerning these private matters can always be said to promote the greater accountability of public officials because there will always be some citizens who view those private matters as relevant to the official's suitability for office.[133] But that, by itself, cannot justify First Amendment protection for such disclosures. Accountability in this expansive sense should not trump all other values. It is a very important value, but not our democratic society's only value. If public figures should have some zone of protected privacy, then some limits on the media's leeway to invade privacy will have to be accepted, even if this also means some limit on accountability. I am prepared to accept this, although many will disagree and al-

---

[132] 121 S Ct at 1765.

[133] See Post, *The Social Foundations of Privacy* at 74–85 (cited in note 52); Geoffrey R. Stone, 90 Mich L Rev at 1262–63 (cited in note 120); Owen M. Fiss, *Do Public Officials Have a Right to Privacy?* in Dieter Simon and Manfred Weiss, eds, *Zur Autonmie des Individuums: Liber Amicorum Spiros Simitis* 91–98 (2001). For example, Professor Post writes: "The claims of public officials to a 'private' information preserve are simply overridden by the more general demands of the public for political accountability. . . . Because American law views the public, in its role as the electorate, as ultimately responsible for political decisions, the public is presumptively entitled to all information that is necessary for informed governance." Id at 76, 78.

though I recognize, and would seek to minimize, the risks of chilling more legitimate press coverage. The law already recognizes some of these limits on the media. As Justice Stevens himself notes in *Bartnicki*, we forbid reporters from stealing documents and from wiretapping, even if these activities would provide newsworthy information.[134] A prohibition on publishing certain lawfully obtained information involves different concerns, of course. But where a democratically elected legislature seeks to give limited additional protection to the privacy of public officials, neither First Amendment principles nor a commitment to democratic self-government should necessarily bar this.

Indeed, as I argued above, information about the private lives of public officials so readily distracts us from their official actions that limiting press coverage of these private matters would likely enhance public discourse and public debate that is at the heart of the First Amendment's purposes. Such limitations could also strengthen the process of democratic self-government in other respects. In the name of improving the quality of official actions by enhancing public scrutiny, media coverage that intrudes on private matters can distort the personalities of public officials and damage their performance. In addition, it is widely believed that many talented people are being deterred from running for office or assuming senior political appointments because of a concern about the extreme loss of privacy that now must be expected for oneself and one's family. If there were greater protections for privacy, the political system as a whole could be strengthened by drawing greater numbers of talented people into public service.[135] As Justice Breyer has argued in a recent speech,[136] we should see the Constitution as a whole and read the First Amendment as a part of that whole—a document seeking to advance a system of effective democratic self-governance. Certain media restrictions to protect privacy, even though limiting the press' leeway, may in overall effect contribute positively to advancing public debate and democratic self-governance.

[134] 121 S Ct at 1764 n 19. See also *Wilson v Layne*, 526 US 603 (1999) (Fourth Amendment violated by media "ride-along" to accompany police during attempted execution of arrest warrant in a person's home).

[135] See, e.g., Fiss, *Do Public Officials Have a Right to Privacy?* at 94 (cited in note 133).

[136] Breyer, *Our Democratic Constitution* (cited in note 89).

There are too many special circumstances related to President Clinton's relationship with Monica Lewinsky to make that a prime example here (the presidency is arguably a special case; the information about President Clinton's relationship with Monica Lewinsky developed out of the Paula Jones legal proceeding and then became relevant to a possible perjury prosecution and impeachment, raising distinctive questions regarding the proper scope of discovery, sexual harassment law, and "high crimes and misdemeanors"; and adulterous sexual relationships had already become an issue in President Clinton's political campaigns and in political judgments about him). But whatever one thinks about that episode (I consider it to have been a distraction from the public's business), I would not interpret the First Amendment as categorically barring efforts to prevent media disclosures about the private sexual behavior of public officials. Nor should it bar restrictions on the publication of other intimate personal matters, such as information about their children or private photographs. Once again, relevance to matters of public concern could undoubtedly be drawn in most cases—sexual behavior may suggest something about a person's character or general willingness to take risks, family details may reveal something relevant to the public policies the official has articulated, etc. At times the relevance to public matters may indeed be substantial, and therefore publication addresses a legitimate public concern. But if we allow any articulated relevance to a public concern to justify publication, however weak that relevance is, we have eliminated privacy protection for public figures, and that is too extreme.[137]

The constitutional law of other countries reinforces the reasonableness of the approach suggested here, or at least makes clear that our own Supreme Court's approach has judicial competitors. Other countries often take a significantly more privacy-protective and media-restrictive approach than we do. These countries, of

[137] "Public figures" from the entertainment world present somewhat different issues because such figures are typically less connected than public officials to the process of public deliberation and democratic self-government. Matters of public significance that might justify media publicity may therefore be less clearly involved. On the other hand, entertainment figures ofren utilize publicity about their private lives (including their sexual partners) to enhance their public image, so the interest in the privacy of personal facts may sometimes be less apparent. Nevertheless, in my judgment, there should still be protectable zones of privacy that the media may not invade—for example, publishing intrusively (if lawfully) secured photographs of entertainment figures with their children.

course, have somewhat different constitutional provisions, and I do not suggest that comparisons can be made in any simple fashion. But a few examples will illustrate that our Court has struck the speech/privacy balance quite differently from many other democratic countries with highly developed constitutional systems and a vibrant free press.

In Great Britain, for example, a well-known case quite analogous to *Bartnicki* was decided against the media, with more weight given to the fact that the published material had been unlawfully obtained. In *Francome v Mirror Group Newspapers Ltd.*,[138] an unknown person illegally bugged telephone conversations made to and from the home of a champion jockey—a criminal offense under British law. The *Daily Mirror*, a newspaper that had nothing to do with the bugging, obtained tapes of the telephone conversations and wanted to publish material based on them. Publication, the *Daily Mirror* said, was justified because the tapes revealed actions contrary to the public interest and possible criminal conduct by the jockey. The jockey sought to enjoin the *Daily Mirror*'s publication of the material. The Court of Appeal upheld the trial judge's granting of an injunction pending full trial. Sir John Donaldson wrote, "I regard [the *Daily Mirror*'s] assertion as arrogant and wholly unacceptable. . . . If . . . the *Daily Mirror* can assert this right to act on the basis that the public interest, as [it] sees it, justifies breaches of the criminal law, so can any other citizen."[139]

The Supreme Court of Germany and the German Constitutional Court, the most influential constitutional court in Europe, have developed a rich speech/privacy jurisprudence that is very different from ours conceptually, and that yields quite different results in particular cases, including one quite similar to *Bartnicki*. What we in the United States call the right to privacy is protected in Germany by the constitutional right to "the free development

[138] 2 All ER 408 (CA 1984).

[139] Sir John Donaldson added: "The media . . . are an essential foundation of any democracy. In exposing crime, anti-social behavior and hypocrisy and in campaigning for reform and propagating the views of minorities, they perform an invaluable function. However, they are peculiarly vulnerable to the error of confusing the public interest with their own interest. . . . In the present case, pending a trial, it is impossible to see what public interest would be served by publishing the contents of the tapes which would not equally be served by giving them to the police or to the Jockey Club. Any wider publication could only serve the interests of the *Daily Mirror*." Id at 413.

of one's personality"[140] in conjunction with the right to "human dignity."[141] The personality right "comprises the authority of the individual to decide for himself—based on the idea of self-determination—when and within what limits facts about one's personal life should be disclosed."[142] The right is conceptualized as a right to "informational self-determination."[143] The individual, however, "has to accept limitations on his right to informational self-determination for reasons of a predominant public interest." "In formulating enactments," the Constitutional Court has said, the legislature "has to observe the principle of proportionality"[144]—"proportionality" being the widely invoked concept of balancing in many constitutional courts and supreme courts around the world.[145]

The German courts have decided several cases addressing the balance between the right to "informational self-determination" and "freedom of the press." The courts' analysis, of course, depends upon a constitutional context quite different from ours: the privacy right is expressly protected by the German Constitution and applies to relationships among citizens, not simply between the citizen and the state. But the comparison is instructive. The *Bartnicki*-type case involved a suit against the magazine *Stern* for publishing the transcript of an illegally taped telephone call between two senior political party officials about political matters in Germany.[146] *Stern* knew that the information had been obtained unlawfully but had not participated in the intrusion. The German Supreme Court concluded that the plaintiffs' "personality" right was violated and that the defendant's "free press" right was not.

---

[140] Grundgesetz (Basic Law), Art 2. The English translations of the German materials discussed here are taken from Paul Gewirtz and Jacob Katz Cogan, *Global Constitutionalism: Privacy, Proportionality, The Political Case* (2001) (hereafter cited as *Global Constitutionalism*). Grundgesetz (Basic Law), Art 2, appears in *Global Constitutionalism* at II-27.

[141] Grundgesetz (Basic Law), Art 1, in *Global Constitutionalism* at II-27.

[142] *Census Act Case*, BVerfGE, 1 (1983), in *Global Constitutionalism* at I-3.

[143] Id at I-4. The right is understood as not only contributing to an individual's personal development but as also contributing to "the common good" because informational self-determination fosters important elements of a "free democratic community" such as "communication" and "participation." Id.

[144] Id.

[145] See Part IV (discussing proportionality).

[146] *On the Limits Placed on the Press by the Personality Right*, BGHZ 73, 120 (1978), in *Global Constitutionalism* at II-25.

"[B]alancing the conflicting interests,"[147] the Court concluded that "[o]nly a very grave public need to be informed could possibly justify" publishing the transcript of the phone call, which exposed the "personal sphere . . . in an unusually intrusive form."[148] That "grave public need" did not exist in this case, even though public officials were involved and the conversation concerned their public functions.

In another important decision, the German Constitutional Court ruled that Princess Caroline of Monaco's "personality" rights were violated by magazines that published photographs of her and her boyfriend in a garden cafe which had "the characteristics of . . . a sphere of seclusion" even though members of the public were present, as well as photographs of Princess Caroline with her children on a street and in a canoe.[149] The publication of other photographs showing Princess Caroline in "the public sphere" was held not to violate her personality rights.

In a well-known Indian speech/privacy case, the Supreme Court of India stated that "[t]he sweep of the First Amendment to the United States Constitution and the freedom of speech and expression under our Constitution is not identical though similar in their major premises."[150] Among these differences, the Indian Court concluded that a "proper balancing of the freedom of press" and the "right to privacy" means that "the victim of a sexual assault, kidnap, abduction or alike offense should not further be subjected to the indignity of her name and the incident being publicised in press/media."[151]

Lastly, the Supreme Court of Canada, which is generally strongly press-protective, has upheld a damages action for the un-

---

[147] Id at II-30. As a general matter, the Court observed, "[t]he more the information is private in character and the more it involves personal interests in keeping it secret and the more it involves personal harm, the greater the 'public value' will have to be if the press wants to disregard the person's wish in keeping it [private[." Id at II-31. Note the similarity to Justice Breyer's balancing approach in *Bartnicki* and his conclusion tbere that "tbe speakers' legitimate privacy expectations are unusually low, and the public interest in defeating those expectations unusually higb." 121 S Ct at 1768.

[148] *Global Constitutionalism* at II-27. The Court, in a crucial conceptualization, observed that the taped conversation "addressed very *personal* concerns, even though these were still related to their *public* occupations." Id at II-26 (emphasis added).

[149] *Princess Caroline of Monaco Case*, BVerfGE 101, 361 (1999), in *Global Constitutionalism* at II-33.

[150] See *Rajagopal v State of Tamil Nadu*, 6 S C C 632, 648 (1994).

[151] Id at 648, 650.

authorized publication of a photograph that a magazine photographer had taken of the plaintiff in a public place and published without that person's consent.[152] In doing so, the Canadian Court specifically disagreed with American constitutional law. The Court held that "the right to one's image is included in the right to respect for one's private life" protected by the Quebec Charter, that the "freedom of expression" was also involved here, and that it was necessary "to balance these two rights."[153] The Supreme Court of Canada rejected the approach of the Court of Appeal that "the public's right to information will prevail where the expression at issue concerns information that is 'socially useful.'"[154] The Court stated:

> This notion seems to have been borrowed from American law . . . . A photograph of a single person can be "socially useful" because it serves to illustrate a theme. That does not make its publication acceptable, however, if it infringes the right to privacy. We do not consider it appropriate to adopt the notion of "socially useful" for the purposes of legal analysis. . . . Only one question arises, namely the balancing of the rights at issue. It must, therefore, be decided whether the public's right to information can justify dissemination of a photograph taken without authorization. . . . In our view, the artistic expression of the photograph, which was alleged to have served to illustrate contemporary urban life, cannot justify the infringement of the right to privacy it entails. It has not been shown that the public's interest in seeing this work is predominant. . . . [F]reedom of expression must be defined in light of the other values concerned.[155]

No other democratic country forbids restrictions on expressive conduct as completely as the United States. Supreme courts and constitutional courts in most other democracies give greater weight to values of privacy and human dignity when they conflict with free speech claims, and they therefore are more inclined to permit legal actions against privacy invasions, libel, and hate speech. They also permit the state to play a much greater role in assuring wider public access to the media even though some restriction on the speech of others is involved. Although the consti-

---

[152] *Aubry v Editions Vice-Versa Inc.*, 1 S C R 591 (1998).

[153] Id at 615, 616.

[154] Id at 617.

[155] Id at 617–18.

tutional rules in these countries are somewhat different, the press is vibrant and robust. The glories of the American free speech tradition have had great and greatly beneficial influence worldwide. But to other countries, our current free speech doctrines seem to have become quite extreme, and our current law indeed is at the far end of the spectrum. Thus, far from being aberrational, giving more weight to privacy in speech/privacy cases would move American free speech law closer to the global democratic mainstream.

IV

Justice Breyer's concurring opinion in *Bartnicki*, while directly relevant for its treatment of the speech/privacy tension, deserves further comment because of its wider implications for First Amendment analysis generally. Many of Justice Breyer's key moves in *Bartnicki*—his conceptualization of speech on both sides of the constitutional analysis, his receptivity to some restrictions on speech where doing so would produce important "privacy and speech-related benefits," his utilization of flexible proportionality analysis—are part and parcel of an important new approach to First Amendment analysis that Justice Breyer has been developing in various separate opinions over the last several years.[156] He has recently developed these views further in his ambitious Madison Lecture,[157] placing his First Amendment views in the context of a wider constitutional theory that emphasizes "participatory self-governance" as a central theme in constitutional law generally.

Breyer's First Amendment approach has several key elements:

1) The First Amendment's protection of "the freedom of speech" seeks not only to prevent government restrictions on speech, but also to "enhanc[e]" speech,"[158] "to facilitate . . . public discussion and informed deliberation,"[159] and to help advance "the

---

[156] See *Turner Broadcasting System, Inc. v Federal Communications Commission*, 520 US 180, 225–29 (1997) (Breyer concurring in part); *Nixon v Shrink Missouri Government PAC*, 528 US 377, 399–405 (2000) (Breyer concurring); *United States v Playboy Entertainment Group, Inc.*, 529 US 803, 835–47 (2000) (Breyer dissenting); *Bartnicki v Vopper*, 121 S Ct 1753, 1766 (2001) (Breyer concurring); *United States v United Foods, Inc.*, 533 US 405, 450–59 (2001) (Breyer dissenting).

[157] Breyer, *Our Democratic Constitution* (cited in note 89).

[158] *Bartnicki v Vopper*, 121 S Ct at 1766.

[159] *Turner Broadcasting System, Inc. v Federal Communications Commission*, 520 US at 227.

Constitution's general participatory self-government objective."[160] In others words, the freedom of speech is not only a negative liberty but also an "active liberty,"[161] concerned with "encouraging the exchange of ideas,"[162] "encouraging . . . public participation and open discussion,"[163] "'assuring that the public has access to a multiplicity of information sources,'"[164] "facilitat[ing] . . . informed deliberation,"[165] and "prevent[ing]" the speech of "a few from drowning out the many."[166]

2) Current First Amendment cases tend to see the restriction of speech as the only free speech interest in the picture. However, many challenged laws enhance the speech of some people while restricting the speech of others. The "speech-enhancing"[167] dimensions of such laws promote First Amendment interests even though other aspects of these laws restrict First Amendment interests. Thus, in one of Breyer's central ideas, reiterated in *Bartnicki*, "[C]onstitutionally protected interests lie on both sides of the legal equation."[168]

3) Once one accepts that "constitutionally protected interests lie on both sides of the legal equation," conventional First Amendment doctrine becomes less useful and less appropriate. Under the conventional doctrines, laws that directly restrict speech typically trigger "strict scrutiny"—a strong presumption against a law's constitutionality, which almost always condemns the law to invalidation. But where laws have speech-enhancing elements as well as speech-restricting ones, Justice Breyer says, the proper constitutional analysis must involve balancing of these interests. The key question should be one of "proportionality"—whether the "laws impose restrictions on speech that are disproportionate

[160] Breyer, *Our Democratic Constitution* at 6 (cited in note 89).

[161] Id.

[162] Id.

[163] *Nixon v Shrink Missouri Government PAC*, 528 US at 401.

[164] *Turner Broadcasting System, Inc. v Federal Communications Commission*, 520 US at 227 (citation omitted).

[165] Id.

[166] *Nixon v Shrink Missouri Government PAC*, 528 US at 402.

[167] *Bartnicki v Vopper*, 121 S Ct at 1766.

[168] Id at 400.

when measured against their corresponding . . . speech-related benefits."[169]

4) Because the First Amendment seeks to advance "the Constitution's general participatory self-government objective" and not simply to "protect[ ] the individual's 'negative' freedom from governmental restraint,"[170] First Amendment doctrine must "distinguish among areas, contexts, and forms of speech."[171] Nearly every human action involves speech, and strict scrutiny is inappropriate in evaluating restrictions on commercial speech, government speech, or the speech of government employees. If the First Amendment is interpreted more expansively, it would impose "a serious obstacle to the operation of well-established, legislatively created, regulatory programs, thereby seriously hindering the operation of that democratic self-government that the Constitution seeks to create and to protect."[172]

Using these new building blocks of First Amendment analysis, Justice Breyer's separate opinions over the past few years take a more tolerant approach to laws limiting the speech of some in order to enhance the overall system of free expression.[173] He has shown greater tolerance for campaign finance laws that limit campaign contributions and spending so that the speech of "a few" does not "drown[ ] out the many."[174] He has embraced a more tolerant approach to telecommunications laws that open communications pathways such as cable to more diverse voices, even though the speech interests of the cable owners are somewhat restricted.[175] And, in *Bartnicki,* he showed a more tolerant approach to legislation that restricts the media in order to promote the privacy of communications and thereby "foster[ ] private speech."

---

[169] 121 S Ct at 1766.

[170] Id.

[171] Breyer, *Our Democratic Constitution* at 10 (cited in note 89).

[172] *United States v United Foods, Inc.*, 121 S Ct at 2346 (2001).

[173] As Jeffrey Rosen has noted in a recent article, Justice Breyer "is certainly the first Supreme Court justice to embrace this view of the First Amendment wholeheartedly, and to apply it consistently across a variety of cases." Jeffrey Rosen, *Modest Proposal: Stephen Breyer Restrains Himself,* The New Republic (Jan 14, 2002), 21, 24. Academic writing that has explored somewhat similar ideas in recent years include Fiss, *Liberalism Divided* (cited in note 96); Fiss, *The Irony of Free Speech* (cited in note 96); Sunstein, *Democracy and the Problem of Free Speech* (cited in note 111); and Post, *Constitutional Domains* (cited in note 52).

[174] *Nixon v Shrink Missouri Government PAC,* 528 US at 400.

[175] *Turner Broadcasting System, Inc. v Federal Communications Commission,* 520 US at 225.

Justice Breyer also seems willing to look at the constitutional equation in speech cases with greater receptivity for values on the "other side" that are not themselves "speech-enhancing." In *Bartnicki*, Breyer balanced the speech restrictions of the challenged law against both the "privacy and speech-related benefits" of the law,[176] not just the speech-related ones. In another First Amendment decision last term, Justice Breyer would have allowed the government to burden commercial speech in order to further rather ordinary economic regulation.[177] And in a case decided the prior year, Breyer wrote a dissenting opinion stating that he would uphold a statutory limit on the programming leeway of cable operators where the value on the "other side" was protecting children from indecent programming.[178]

These decisions represent an important new approach to the First Amendment on the Supreme Court. Breyer's core substantive idea is that in our constitutional system of participatory self-government, the First Amendment's role is not simply to protect individuals from direct government restraints on speech. "Freedom of speech" means a system of free expression that provides speakers wide opportunities for public and private expression, provides listeners diverse sources of information, encourages meaningful interactions between speakers and listeners, and fosters greater public participation. This sometimes requires restrictions on speech, but these can be justifiable where they enhance the overall system of free expression.

Breyer's opinions also indicate that he would modestly recalibrate the balance between speech and other interests to take account of contemporary threats to free speech as well as to other social interests. He clearly believes that current First Amendment law has tilted somewhat too decisively in the direction of protecting speech interests and does not give enough weight in certain contexts to other important interests such as privacy, human dignity, protecting children, and equality. Suggesting modifications in our free speech law undoubtedly causes concern in some quarters. But to preserve free speech, Justice Breyer suggests, the Court

[176] 121 S Ct at 1766–67.

[177] *United States v United Foods, Inc.*, 121 S Ct at 2346.

[178] *United States v Playboy Entertainment Group, Inc.*, 529 US at 835.

must be attentive to serious new threats that imperil free speech; and where there are serious new threats to other values, and laws can address them without significantly weakening free speech, the Constitution should not be interpreted to stand in the way.

Breyer's conception of constitutional rights as protecting "active liberty" has another interrelated effect—one with potentially general implications for constitutional law. Under conventional constitutional analysis, burdens on speech or privacy imposed by nongovernmental entities do not violate the First Amendment because of the state action doctrine. Therefore, in a case like *Bartnicki*, Title III's governmental interference with the media would come under First Amendment scrutiny, but the private broadcaster's interference with speech by publishing illegally intercepted conversations does not. Conceptualizing freedom of speech as an "active liberty," however, enables Justice Breyer to characterize the interests on both sides of the dispute as "constitutional interests." I do not understand Breyer to be saying that there is an independently enforceable constitutional right of free speech against nongovernmental interference, or to be saying that the state has a judicially enforceable constitutional obligation to protect speech from private interference (at least not yet). But his view does lead to a different understanding of the permissible roles of the state. In understanding free speech as an "active liberty," and the First Amendment as having positive goals of fostering an overall system of free expression, Justice Breyer sees state action that protects speech from private interference as furthering the same democracy-enhancing objective as the First Amendment and thereby furthering a "constitutional interest."[179] This allows him to give the privacy side of the equation in *Bartnicki* heightened stature (and greater weight) in the constitutional analysis, and in other contexts to uphold state actions that "strike a reasonable balance between their . . . speech-restricting and speech-enhancing consequences."[180]

The basic questions raised are not only whether this recalibrated balance is called for but also whether courts can be trusted to im-

---

[179] Breyer, *Our Democratic Constitution* at 6–7 (cited in note 89).

[180] Id at 7.

plement it. Justice Breyer's analysis requires judges to determine not only whether the government has imposed a substantial burden on someone's speech, but whether the overall balance of speech-restricting and speech-enhancing benefits of a law is reasonable. In at least some areas, such as laws governing election campaigns, this invites courts to assess the overall fairness and balance of public debate—is the voice of a few "drowning out the voice of the many"?—and creates a risk that courts will consciously or unconsciously favor certain points of view in making their assessment. But the question is which risk is greater: the risks of an unregnlated speech market (which risks a bias in favor of certain interests and viewpoints) or the risks of some regulatory efforts to foster more open and balanced debate (which risks smuggling in certain biases in the drafting of such legislation and in the judicial assessment of its fairness).

The balancing may be even more difficult where values other than speech are weighed against speech. In his separate opinions, Justice Breyer has indicated several values other than speech (or clear and present danger) that might justify certain restrictions on speech: protecting children from sexually explicit speech, protecting privacy (in its nonspeech dimensions), and economic regulation (where the restriction was on commercial speech). It is unclear how far Justice Breyer is prepared to go in this direction, what values are sufficiently important to justify speech restrictions, or how such balances will be made. Where speech is "on the other side of the equation," the justification for restricting speech is the same constitutionally rooted speech value, and at least in theory there is a common metric (e.g., enhancement of diversity of viewpoints). But where nonspeech values are on the other side, the justification for restricting speech will typically not itself be a constitutional value and, in addition, there will be no common metric. For those who consider free speech to be highly vulnerable in our society, and who greatly distrust whether legislatures and judges will adequately protect it, allowing nonspeech values to trump speech values will always be a very risky business (and especially so in times of national stress). In short, questions and concerns are understandable. But based on the evidence thus far, Justice Breyer has applied his approach in a finely tuned way that is taking more open and fuller account of the complex contending interests genuinely at stake, yet also remaining strongly speech-protective.

Justice Breyer's approach is also significant in its method. His opinions reveal a growing skepticism about the complex array of doctrinal formulas that now make up First Amendment law, a concern that they invite "mechanical"[181] applications and do not keep in view the purposes of the First Amendment or take open account of the full complexities and likely consequences of decisions or readily accommodate new social realities. Justice Breyer favors a more explicit and multifactored balancing of interests. In *Bartnicki*, for example, he rejects strict scrutiny, but does not embrace any other existing "test." Rather, he says:

> I would ask whether the statutes strike a reasonable balance between their speech-restricting and speech-enhancing consequences. Or do they instead impose restrictions on speech that are disproportionate when measured against their corresponding privacy and speech-related benefits, taking into account the kind, the importance, and the extent of these benefits, as well as the need for the restrictions in order to secure those benefits?[182]

As the word "disproportionate" in this passage indicates, one of the most striking things about Breyer's approach is that he has begun to embrace a formulation of balancing widely used by supreme courts and constitutional courts in other leading democracies: "proportionality." "Proportionality" is a general element of constitutional analysis used by these courts in diverse areas of constitutional law,[183] but it has not in so many words entered American

---

[181] *Nixon v Shrink Missouri Government PAC*, 528 US at 400; *United States v Playboy Entertainment Group, Inc.*, 529 US at 841.

[182] 121 S Ct at 1766.

[183] An analysis of the concept of "proportionality" as used by other countries' supreme courts and constitutional courts is beyond the scope of this article. For a fuller discussion, see Paul Gewirtz and Jacob Katz Cogan, *Global Constitutionalism* at IV-1-98 (cited in note 140). Examples of cases from other jurisdictions discussing and applying the proportionality concept include: *Lebach Case*, BVerfGE 35, 202 (1975) (Constitutional Court of Germany); *Cannabis Case*, BVerfGE 90, 145 (1994) (Constitutional Court of Germany); *Reiten im Walde Case*, BVerfGE 80, 137 (1989) (Constitutional Court of Germany); *R. v Oakes*, 1 S C R 103 (1986) (Supreme Court of Canada); *Dagenais v CBC*, 3 S C R 835 (1994) (Supreme Court of Canada); *Thomson Newspaper v Canada* (A.G.), 1 S C R 877 (1998) (Supreme Court of Canada); *Decision Dated April 26, 1995 (K.11/94)* (Constitutional Court of Poland), in *Constitutional Tribunal, a Selection of the Polish Constitutional Tribunal's Jurisprudence from 1986 to 1999*, at 153–58 (1999); *United Mizrahi Bank Ltd. v Migdal Village*, 49 (4) P D 221 (1995) (Supreme Court of Israel). See also P. van Duk and G. J. H. van Hoof, *Theory and Practice of the European Convention on Human Rights* 80–82 (3d ed 1998); Walter van Gerven, *The Effect of Proportionality on the Actions of Member States of the European Community: National Viewpoints from Continental Europe*, in Evelyn Ellis, ed, *The Principle of Proportionality in the Laws of Europe: A Comparative Study* (1999).

constitutional law. Justice Breyer has been the boldest of the current U.S. Supreme Court Justices in drawing upon concepts and examples from the constitutional jurisprudence of other countries, including "proportionality."[184] His concurrence in *Nixon v Shrink Missouri Government PAC*, for example, explicitly cited "proportionality" cases from the European Court of Human Rights and the Supreme Court of Canada, with Breyer writing:

> [W]here a law significantly implicates competing constitutionally protected interests in complex ways[,] the Court has closely scrutinized the statute's impact on those interests, but refrained from employing a simple test that effectively presumes unconstitutionality. Rather, it has balanced interests. And in practice that has meant asking whether the statute burdens any one such interest in a manner out of proportion to the statute's salutary effects upon the others (perhaps, but not necessarily, because of the existence of a clearly superior, less restrictive alternative). . . . [This approach] is consistent with that of other constitutional courts facing similar complex constitutional problems.[185]

In his dissent in *United States v Playboy Entertainment Group, Inc.*, he counsels the Court "not to apply First Amendment rules mechanically, but to decide whether, in light of the benefits and potential alternatives, the statute works speech-related harm (here to adult speech) out of proportion to the benefits that the statute seeks to provide (here, child protection)."[186] His recent Madison

[184] In addition to the "proportionality" concept, Justice Breyer has referred to other countries' constitutional law in other respects. See, e.g., *Printz v United States*, 521 US 898, 976–77 (1997) (Breyer dissenting) (discussing other countries' approach to federalism); *Nixon v Shrink Missouri Government PAC*, 528 US 377, 403 (2000) (Breyer concurring) (discussing other countries' approach to campaign finance); Breyer, *Our Democratic Constitution* at 7 (cited in note 89) (referring to same); *Knight v Florida*, 528 US 990 (1999) (Breyer dissenting from denial of certiorari) (discussing other countries' treatment of delays in capital punishment executions). In speeches he has also spoken approvingly of the fact that "[j]udges who enforce the law as well as those who write it increasingly turn to the experience of other nations when deciding difficult open questions of substantive law, particularly human rights law. . . ." He notes that U.S. courts "less frequently refer to judicial opinions from abroad" than other courts do, and has called upon American lawyers and academics to "themselves become familiar with foreign material relevant to particular legal disciplines and facilitate the judicial use of that material." Stephen Breyer, Dinner Keynote Speech, International Symposium on Democracy and the Rule of Law in a Changing World Order, New York University Law School, March 9, 2000 (copy on file with author).

[185] 528 US at 402, 403 (citations omitted).

[186] 529 US at 841. Citing his own separate opinion in *Bartnicki*, Justice Breyer also invoked the idea of proportionality in last term's dissent in *United States v United Foods, Inc.*, a commercial speech case:

> Several features of the program indicate that its speech-related aspects, i.e., its compelled monetary contributions, are necessary and proportionate to the legiti-

Lecture is the most direct: "The basic question the Court should ask is one of proportionality."[187]

It is fair to ask whether this balancing or "proportionality" review invites too much subjectivity and arbitrariness from judges. The question, of course, is not whether we trust judges like Justice Breyer to engage in this kind of balancing, but whether we trust our adjudicative system as a whole. I remain of two minds about this. Concerns about subjectivity and arbitrariness in balancing are altogether legitimate. But the system of doctrinal rules that we have now itself invites subjectivity and arbitrariness, both in deciding what rule to apply in a particular circumstance and in applying the selected rules. The variety of different doctrinal rules in contemporary First Amendment law—"strict scrutiny," "intermediate scrutiny," the *Daily Mail* principle, "clear and present danger," the *New York Times Co. v Sullivan* test, content neutrality, prior restraint, "public forum" rules, rules for commercial speech and other "low-value" speech, etc.—reflects the complexities of the balances that need to made and continuing disagreements about the appropriate approach. As the invocation of both "intermediate scrutiny" and "the *Daily Mail* principle" in the *Bartnicki* litigation itself demonstrates, the current doctrinal cacophony creates remarkable leeway for choosing which doctrinal rule to apply as well as what result to reach. Interest balancing often occurs, but not in a fully open way.

In this rather chaotic doctrinal situation, and in circumstances of social and technological change that create new background conditions, an open recognition of the factors at stake and a more direct consideration and debate about the values in the balance have distinctive value. With more open balancing, a fuller range of factors can be made visible. Justice Breyer's use of balancing and proportionality analysis has a refreshing candor and lucidity, and his very openness about the factors at work for him is a constraint on subjectivity.[188] What he says in his Madison Lecture

---

> mate promotional goals that it seeks. . . . [At] the same time, those features of the program that led [dissenters in an earlier case] to find its program disproportionately restrictive are absent here. . . . In consequence, whatever harm the program may cause First Amendment interests is proportionate.

533 US at 457.

[187] Breyer, *Our Democratic Constitution* at 7 (cited in note 89).

[188] See Rosen, *Modest Proposal* at 25 (cited in note 173).

about his pragmatic attention to "consequences" is as applicable to his balancing approach generally: An approach that exclusively emphasizes "language, history, tradition, or prior rules," at least in the "borderline" cases, will "produce a decision which is no less subjective but which is far less transparent than a decision that directly addresses consequences in constitutional terms."[189] In addition, many of the existing rules would still have value as guidelines because they reflect and crystalize past experience about where the balance should lie. The balancing inquiry may eventually lead to new guidelines. The debate about rules versus balancing is a perennial one in law, of course, and such persistence is usually a sign that there are real advantages and disadvantages to the contending approaches.[190] But in this context, the case for more open balancing appears strong, at least when compared to the current doctrinal rules.

Justice Breyer is developing the most important new ideas about the First Amendment on the Supreme Court since Justices Brennan and Black. To say the least, it will be interesting to watch how his ideas evolve, and to see whether they will come to shape First Amendment doctrine on the Court as a whole.

Conclusion

In the particular area of privacy and speech, *Bartnicki* demonstrates that there is currently no single view that a majority of the Justices shares. But a majority does seem prepared to allow some new restrictions on speech to protect privacy. This is a development to be praised. But even in this area, working out the details of a new approach will be difficult, requiring elaboration of the complexities of privacy in its speech and nonspeech dimensions,

---

[189] Breyer, *Our Democratic Constitution* at 22 (cited in note 89).

[190] See, e.g., Richard H. Fallon, Jr., *The Supreme Court, 1996 Term–Foreword: Implementing the Constitution*, 111 Harv L Rev 54 (1997); Kathleen M. Sullivan, *The Supreme Court, 1991 Term–Foreword: The Justices of Rules and Standards*, 106 Harv L Rev 22 (1992); T. Alexander Aleinikoff, *Constitutional Law in the Age of Balancing*, 96 Yale L J 943 (1987); Stephen E. Gottlieb, *Compelling Governmental Interests: An Essential but Unanalyzed Term in Constitutional Adjudication*, 68 BU L Rev 917 (1988); Paul Kahn, *The Court, the Community and the Judicial Balance: The Jurisprudence of Justice Powell*, 97 Yale L J 1 (1987); Charles Fried, *Two Concepts of Interests: Some Reflections on the Supreme Court's Balancing Test*, 76 Harv L Rev 755 (1963).

the complexities of different understandings of the role of speech and press in society, and a finely tuned accommodation of the competing interests. Above all, it will require the most sensitive attention to the risks that always attend limitations of speech. The only justification for taking these risks is the judgment—which I have now reached—that the risks of not doing so are greater.

[15]

Is *Von Hannover v Germany* a Step Backward for the Substantive Analysis of Speech and Privacy Interests?

M.A. Sanderson
Pupil Barrister, 8 King's Bench Walk

Von Hannover v Germany *concerns the breach by the German State of its positive obligations under Art.8 ECHR to protect Princess Caroline of Monaco from intrusive media attention. Although the Court was almost certainly right to find that the German State had improperly balanced the demands of Arts 8 and 10 in the present case, the opinion which justifies this outcome is a deeply flawed one. There are essentially two levels of argument in the opinion of the Court. The macro-level relies on the* a priori *adoption by the Court of a highly restricted and counter-intuitive conception of "public", with the apparent effect of excluding the Princess from the necessity of public scrutiny, and the micro-level relies on this meaning as a premise in order to make a series of subsidiary points about the contribution made by such scrutiny to public discourse in a democratic society. While the first level of argument fails due to a lack of explanatory and prescriptive power, the second fails due to a basic logical circularity which infects the body of the Court's opinion.*

The position of Princess Caroline in the state hierarchy of Monaco

It is difficult to sympathise with a Princess. It does seem true, however, that Princess Caroline of Monaco, the second child of Prince Rainier III and Princess Grace of Monaco and second in line to the throne of Monaco,[1] has had, in many respects, a life of unusual pressures. Photographers commonly trail her whenever she leaves her home, and photograph her from a distance when she has reserved herself to more private spots. Married three times, most recently to Prince Ernst-August of Hannover following the death of her second husband in a 1990 racing accident,[2] if her life has perhaps not been touched by a greater degree of tragedy than most others of her age and position, one imagines that tragedy has been sharpened, and perhaps aggravated, by the intense nature of the media coverage which has surrounded it. Although the Princess currently holds no official position and exercises no official powers within the State of Monaco, she is the President of various charitable institutions in which the

[1] Art.10, *Constitution de la Principauté du Monaco*, December 17, 1962 (amended by Law No.1.249 of April, 2 2002) (*www.monaco.gouv.mc/Dataweb/GouvMc.nsf/(ListCh)/8EAC97F95 6A58C44C12569D1004E6ABF?OpenDocument*).

[2] For a more detailed profile of Princess Caroline's life written in irresistibly high-camp *Hello!* magazine prose, see *www.hellomagazine.com/profiles/princesscaroline*.

632 Is *Von Hannover v Germany* a Step Backward?

ruling family of Monaco maintains an interest, such as the Princess Grace Foundation[3] and AMADE Mondiale.[4]

The Princess lives for most of the year in the town of Saint-Rémy-de-Provence, in the south of France. The legal regime for the protection of privacy in France is very different from that in the United Kingdom or Germany. In almost all cases the written permission of a subject is required prior to the publication of photos taken of them in anything other than an official context.[5] The same is, of course, not true in most other European jurisdictions, with a substantially more permissive approach to personal privacy taken in Germany, whose tabloids provide a ready market for pictures of the Princess. As a result, the strict legal protections for one's own image provided by French law are of comparatively little value to the Princess, as the prospect of sales in other European jurisdictions continues to operate as an incentive for the paparazzi who trail after her, and the pictures which result continue to appear in European tabloids.

The proceedings in Germany

Since the early 1990s the Princess has pursued a series of court actions in a variety of European jurisdictions in what has been an often vain attempt to prevent the publication of pictures taken of her in various unofficial contexts.[6] The decision of the European Court of Human Rights ("ECtHR") in *Von Hannover* concerns photographs taken in 1993 and 1997 and published in the German magazines *Bunte*,[7] *Freizeit Revue*[8] and the *Neue Post*.[9] It originated in three separate sets of German proceedings, in 1993, 1997 and 1998, all seeking to prevent either the publication, or the republication, of pictures taken of the Princess at unguarded moments.

The first set of proceedings originated with an application in the Hamburg Regional Court for an injunction to prevent the publication of the first series of photos on the grounds that they violated the right of the Princess to the protection of her personality rights as guaranteed in ss.1(1)[10] and 2(1)[11] of the German Basic Law, and to the control

[3] *www.fondation-psse-grace.mc/foundation.html.*

[4] *www.monte-carlo.mc/amade.*

[5] *Von Hannover v Germany* (App. No.59320/00), judgment of June 24, 2004, para.44. For two good accounts of the legal regime for the protection of privacy in France see Catherine Dupré, "The Protection of Private Life Versus Freedom of Expression in French Law" in Madeleine Colvin, ed., *Developing Key Privacy Rights* (Hart Publishing, Oxford, 2002), p.45 and E. Picard, "The Right to Privacy in French Law" in B. Markesinis, ed., *Protecting Privacy* (Clarendon Press, Oxford, 1999), p.91. A very similar right to the protection of one's own image is recognised in Quebec, see *Aubry v Editions Vice-Versa Inc* [1998] 1 S.C.R. 591.

[6] *Von Hannover*, n.5 above, para.9.

[7] *www.bunte.de.*

[8] *www.freizeitrevue.de.*

[9] *Von Hannover*, n.5 above, para.10.

[10] "The dignity of man is inviolable. To respect and protect it is the duty of all state authority." Basic Law for the Federal Republic of Germany, May 23, 1949 (as amended by the Treaty of Unification, August 31, 1990 and the Federal Statute of September 23, 1990, Federal Law Gazette II, p.885) s.1(1). Translation provided by the German Law Archive of the Comparative Law Society (*www.iuscomp.org/gla/index.html*).

[11] "Everyone has the right to the free development of his personality insofar as he does not violate the rights of others or offend against the constitutional order or the moral code." Basic Law, s.2(1).

of her image as guaranteed by ss.22 and 23 of the German Copyright (Arts Domain) Act.[12] However, because Princess Caroline was what the Regional Court termed a public figure "par excellence",[13] the court found that she had only the most limited right to the protection of her private life. As aptly described in the subsequent opinion of the ECtHR, in the jurisprudence of the German court, for such figures " . . . the right to protection of private life stopped at their front door".[14]

The Princess appealed first to the Hamburg Court of Appeal, which in 1994 largely upheld the original judgment,[15] and then to the German Federal Court of Justice, which in 1995 granted an injunction against any further publication of the pictures showing the Princess and the French film actor, Vincent Lindon, at lunch. Although the Federal Court accepted that as a public figure "par excellence" the right of the Princess to the protection of her private life was extremely limited, in contrast with the judgments of the two lower courts it found that there was some scope for its protection outside of her own home.[16] The Federal Court devised what the ECtHR usefully terms a "spatial" test.[17] Although, for the most part, a public figure cannot rely on the protection of their privacy when they are in public, under this test if they were to retire to a secluded spot " . . . where it was objectively clear to everyone that they wanted to be alone",[18] then it would be a violation of their right to privacy to photograph them. As the Princess and M Lindon appear to have retired to just such a spot during their luncheon, the Federal Court was willing to grant an injunction in respect of those pictures.

The proceedings in Germany: the 1999 judgment of the Constitutional Court

The first set of domestic proceedings concluded in the German Constitutional Court which, in a 1999 judgment, largely upheld the judgment of the Federal Court, only referring back to the lower court for further consideration those photos of the Princess that also featured her children. Although the Princess pursued two further sets of litigation,[19] these judgments closely followed the 1999 judgment of the Constitutional Court. As before, given the position the Princess as a public figure "par excellence", the court was extremely hesitant to interfere with the publication of photographs which featured her, no matter how apparently personal or unguarded their circumstances.

The proceedings before the ECtHR: the submissions of the applicant

The limited nature of the protection offered by the "spatial" test formed the major strand of the submissions made by the Princess to the ECtHR. Arguing that the

[12] "Section 22(1) of the *Copyright (Arts Domain) Act* provides that images can only be disseminated with the express approval of the person concerned. Section 23(1) no.1 of that Act provides for exceptions to that rule, particularly where the images portray an aspect of contemporary society (*Bildnisse aus dem Bereich der Zeitgeschichte*) on condition that publication does not interfere with a legitimate interest (*berechtigtes Interesse*) of the person concerned (section 23(2))." *Von Hannover*, n.5 above, para.41.

[13] *"eine 'absolute' Person der Zeitgeschichte"*; *Von Hannover*, n.5 above, para.19.

[14] *Von Hannover*, n.5 above, para.19.

[15] *ibid.* para.21.

[16] *ibid.* para.23.

[17] *ibid.* para.54.

[18] *ibid.* para.23

[19] For a description of the second set of litigation see *ibid.* paras 27–32 and for a description of the third set see paras 33–38.

decisions of the German courts had infringed her right to private and family life as guaranteed by Art.8[20] ECHR,[21] the Princess stated that the present German law was insufficient to protect her from being " . . . constantly hounded . . . "[22] by the press. The "spatial" test had been interpreted far too narrowly by the domestic courts to allow the Princess a reasonable private life. Further, the protection offered by this test was itself essentially impractical as it placed the onus on the Princess, first, to establish that her chosen location was sufficiently "secluded" to qualify for protection and, secondly, to maintain a continuing record of her location so that this test might be used to prevent the improper publication of photos which had often been taken weeks, or even months, earlier. Although the Princess conceded the importance of a free press in a democratic society, it was her submission that this interest was not in conflict with her own as she sought only to restrict the actions of " . . . the entertainment press seeking to satisfy its readers' voyeuristic tendencies and make huge profits from generally anodyne photos showing her going about her daily business".[23]

The proceedings before the ECtHR: the submissions of the Government

In response, the Government of Germany argued that the domestic courts had struck a fair balance between the Art.10[24] rights of the press and the Art.8 rights of the Princess. Although freedom of the press was of fundamental importance in Germany, present German law contained enough safeguards to protect the private life of even public figures "par excellence". The Government argued, in response to criticism of the "spatial" test, that the " . . . public had a legitimate interest in knowing how the person behaved generally in public".[25]

The proceedings before the ECtHR: the submissions of the interveners

Somewhat more substantive arguments were put forward by the interveners, the Association of Editors of German Magazines, who, noting that the " . . . boundary

[20] Art.8: "(1) Everyone has the right to respect for his private and family life, his home and his correspondence. (2) There shall be no interference by a public authority with the exercise of this right except such as is in accordance with the law and is necessary in a democratic society in the interests of national security, public safety or the economic well-being of the country, for the prevention of disorder or crime, for the protection of health or morals, or for the protection of the rights and freedoms of others."

[21] Convention for the Protection of Human Rights and Fundamental Freedoms (as amended by Protocol No.11) November 4, 1950, ETS 5, 213 UNTS 222. The Convention, as well as the decisions and other materials produced by the European Court of Human Rights, are available on the Court's website (*www.echr.coe.int*).

[22] *Von Hannover*, n.5 above, para.44.

[23] *ibid.* para.44.

[24] Art.10: "(1) Everyone has the right to freedom of expression. This right shall include freedom to hold opinions and to receive and impart information and ideas without interference by public authority and regardless of frontiers. This article shall not prevent States from requiring the licensing of broadcasting, television or cinema enterprises. (2) The exercise of these freedoms, since it carries with it duties and responsibilities, may be subject to such formalities, conditions, restrictions or penalties as are prescribed by law and are necessary in a democratic society, in the interests of national security, territorial integrity or public safety, for the prevention of disorder or crime, for the protection of health or morals, for the protection of the reputation or rights of others, for preventing the disclosure of information received in confidence, or for maintaining the authority and impartiality of the judiciary."

[25] *Von Hannover*, n.5 above, para.45.

between political commentary and entertainment was becoming increasingly blurred",[26] argued that the public's legitimate interest in being informed should extend beyond politicians to public figures, such as the Princess, who were well known for other pursuits. Further, given the diverse European standards for the protection of privacy, the German State should properly be accorded an extremely wide margin of appreciation, with the position in French law being one extreme position, rather than an ideal European model.[27]

Separate submissions were made to the Court by *Burda* magazine. They argued that as Princess Caroline was presently, what they referred to as the "first lady" of the royal family of Monaco, she was an example to the public and, as a result, the media attention devoted to her was legitimate. Further, as the Grimaldi family had itself courted media attention in the past for its own purposes, they were themselves largely responsible for present media and public interest in the family.[28]

The judgment of the ECtHR: the "functional" and "spatial" tests

The ECtHR first considered the classification by the domestic courts of the Princess as a public figure "par excellence", pursuant to s.23(1) of the German Copyright (Arts Domain) Act, what the Court terms the "functional" test. The Court appears to have accepted the account of her role offered by the Princess as someone who does not exercise any official functions on behalf of the State, concluding that, as a result, the Princess was not properly considered a "public" figure. As the Court explains:

> "... although the public has a right to be informed, which is an essential right in a democratic society that, in certain special circumstances, can even extend to aspects of the private life of public figures ... this is not the case here."[29]

Although the Court found that the classification of a public figure "par excellence" may be appropriate for a politician exercising an official function, given that such a classification removes nearly all protection from one's private life, it could not be justified in the case of the Princess, the public interest in whom stems solely from her membership of the royal family.[30]

The Court then considered the one test which the German courts were willing to apply in protection of the private life of the Princess, what the ECtHR terms the "spatial" test. Accepting the submissions of the Princess on this point, the Court concluded that, although the test was superficially attractive, it was, "... in reality too vague and difficult for the person concerned to determine in advance".[31] This points to one of the most immediate effects of *Von Hannover* for the United Kingdom, the need to consider reform of the Code of Practice of the Press Complaints Commission,[32] as it

[26] *ibid.* para.46.
[27] *ibid.* para.46.
[28] *ibid.* para.47
[29] *ibid.* para.64.
[30] *ibid.* para.72.
[31] *ibid.* para.75.
[32] Jonathon Coad, "A Summer of Discontent for the Paparazzi Following Von Hannover v Germany", *The Lawyer*, August 2, 2004.

636 Is *Von Hannover v Germany* a Step Backward?

relies on very similar criteria to determine when the photography of individuals without their consent is inappropriate.[33]

The judgment of the ECtHR: balancing the demands of Arts 8 and 10

In its opinion the Court repeatedly emphasised the need to balance the protection of individual privacy against the right to free expression found in Art.10 ECHR, which it refers to as "... one of the essential foundations of a democratic society".[34] Indeed, the Court offers an extremely strong defence of the role of the press in democratic society, stating that "... its *duty* is nevertheless to impart‾in a manner consistent with its obligations and responsibilities‾information and ideas on all matters of public interest ... ".[35] However, the Court concluded that:

> "... the publication of the photos and articles in question, of which the sole purpose was to satisfy the curiosity of a particular readership regarding the details of the applicant's private life, cannot be deemed to contribute to any debate of general interest to society despite the applicant being known to the public."[36]

Taking into account the continuing climate of harassment in which the photographs of the Princess were taken,[37] the Court found that:

> "... the public does not have a legitimate interest in knowing where the applicant is and how she behaves generally in her private life even if she appears in places that cannot always be described as secluded and despite the fact that she is well known to the public."[38]

The ECtHR concluded that the German courts did not strike a fair balance between the competing rights at issue, concluding that "... the criteria on which the domestic courts based their decisions were not sufficient to protect the applicant's private life effectively".[39]

The need for an "intermediate" stage of privacy protection

Despite the repeated emphasis given by the Court in its opinion to balancing the demands of Arts 8 and 10, one is struck upon reading the opinion of the Court by how very little substantive argument is offered in support of its conclusions, either in relation to the merits of the speech acts at issue, or the degree of protection appropriate for the Art.8 rights of the Princess. The Court seems to assume that because the information in question is generally "personal" in nature that it necessarily follows from this that it falls outside the public interest. The Court appears to further assume (or is, at least, content to remain ambiguous on this point), that because the Princess

[33] "3(ii) It is unacceptable to photograph individuals in private places without their consent. Note: Private places are public or private property where there is a reasonable expectation of privacy." Press Complaints Commission Code of Practice (*www.pcc.org.uk/cop/cop.asp*).
[34] *Von Hannover*, n.5 above, para.58.
[35] *ibid*. para.58 (emphasis added).
[36] *ibid*. para.6.
[37] *ibid*. paras 59 and 68.
[38] *ibid*. para.77.
[39] *ibid*. para.74.

does not herself exercise any official functions on behalf of the State, her personal life should be accorded roughly the same degree of Art.8 protection as that of a wholly private person, that is to say, someone who is entirely unknown to the public.

Although the Court is critical of the use by the domestic courts of what it refers to as "functional" criteria to classify the Princess as a public figure "par excellence", this appears to be on the ground of the disproportionate effect of such categorisation, rather than any clearly articulated conviction as to the appropriate status, public or otherwise, of the Princess. As the Court explains:

> "Since that definition affords the person very limited protection of their private life or the right to control the use of their image, it could conceivably be appropriate for politicians exercising official functions. However, it cannot be justified for a 'private' individual, such as the applicant . . . "[40]

Although the Court does affirm that the classification of a public figure "par excellence" may be appropriately applied to some politicians, in the context of media coverage at least, politicians must be taken as a sort of special paradigmatic case. If we are concerned with two competing meanings of a "public" person, that is, public because they exercise public functions (*i.e.* functions on behalf of the state), and public because they are well-known to the general public, then it is only politicians that embody both meanings of this term. It is because of the manner in which they tend to embody both senses of the word "public" that there is very nearly universal agreement, as there was throughout all levels of the judiciary in this case, that the media is generally entitled to examine the private, as well as the public, lives of politicians.

So it remains unclear whether the Court would consider a modified form of this category, say one which accorded slightly greater protections to the public figure concerned, to be appropriate under the ECHR, or whether it is happy with the test as it stands, and dissatisfied only with its application to the Princess. That is to say, if a classification of the sort designed by the German courts "cannot be justified for a 'private' individual", what sort of classification can? Notably absent from the opinion of the Court is any substantive discussion on the appropriate degree of protection, regardless of how this is to be enforced, for the Art.8 rights of what might be termed "intermediate" figures. That is, those figures, like the Princess, who while they do not perform any formal state functions, enjoy a sufficiently high public profile to be of interest to the general public.

Keeping in mind the comparatively strict wording of Art.8, it is difficult to see how interferences with the private life of the Princess of the nature and extent licensed by the German courts could be truly " . . . necessary in a democratic society. . . for the protection of the rights and freedoms of others". However, when one takes into account the high public profile maintained by the Princess and her family, the manner in which the Grimaldi family has courted publicity in the past, the position of the Grimaldi family in the State of Monaco, and the cultural, social and economic power all of these circumstances lend to the Princess, it seems equally wrong to permit her the same degree of Art.8 protection that one might allow an ordinary citizen who does not enjoy a similar quality of influence. This would seem especially true should material about

[40] *ibid*. para.72.

the Princess become available which was of a less anodyne nature, say, pictures of her involved in criminal or flagrantly immoral activity.

Although the Court makes clear its willingness to distinguish between politicians and "private" citizens for the purpose of analysing their Art.8 rights, the Court never properly explains the reasons that justify this distinction. The closest the Court ever comes to explaining the reasoning behind this distinction is in its description of the different practical effects of reporting "facts capable of contributing to a debate in a democratic society relating to politicians in the exercise of their functions"[41] and "details of the private life of an individual". As the Court explains[42]:

> "While in the former case the press exercises its vital role of 'watchdog' in a democracy by contributing to 'impart[ing] information and ideas on matters of public interest' . . . it does not do so in the latter case."[43]

This seems very naturally to follow from the wording of Art.8(2), and its limitation of Art.8(1) in so far as it "is necessary in a democratic society . . . to protect the rights and freedoms of others". It seems entirely sensible to conclude that one of the primary obligations on a democratic society, in order to protect the rights and freedoms of others, is to establish conditions which assure, in so far as it is possible to do so, the vigorous scrutiny by a free press of the actions of state officials. But this is a distinctly unproblematic area of ECHR jurisprudence. Far more complicated an issue is how the concept of a "private life" is to be shaped. Will it, for example, allow for the concept of an "intermediate" figure as described above? If so, how, and to what degree, should the privacy of such intermediate figures be protected? Given her present proximity to the throne of Monaco, how much further will the Princess need to move toward exercising official state functions before losing her Art.8 protections in this respect? One might also ask that given a world economic order which is manifestly unequal in its effects, and despite a general consensus as to the equal moral worth of all human beings, how is it possible that pictures of a privileged European royal enjoying her many leisure pursuits fail to contribute to "matters of public interest"? It is clear that distinctions of effect, such as the one suggested above by the Court, do not in themselves contain a substantive ethical core. The application by the Court of such a distinction in the present case, without offering any further criteria as to what amounts to a "private life" and what does contribute to the "public interest", is merely to restate the intuition of the Court, adopted without reasoned argument as a wholly *a priori* proposition, that the concept of "public" applied in such cases should be an explicitly and formally political one, that is to say, concerned solely with the exercise of official state functions.[44]

The reliance by the Court on a changed conception of "public"

While the domestic courts and, indeed, the concurring opinions of Judges Cabral Barreto and Zupan I,[45] appear to have adopted a conception of "public" which they applied to the Princess by virtue of her celebrity, the ECtHR was concerned only to

[41] *ibid*. para.63.
[42] *ibid*. para.63.
[43] *ibid*. para.63 (citations omitted).
[44] *ibid*. paras 8 and 62–64.
[45] *ibid*. concurring opinions of Judge Cabral Barreto, para.2, and Judge Zupan I, para.1.

diagnose the official role that the Princess played in the State. Early on in its opinion the Court found that the Princess carried out no official functions on behalf on the State of Monaco. The Court's subsequent finding against the Government of Germany, in so far as it concerned the rejection of the classification of the Princess by the German courts as a public figure, appears to flow directly from this early finding. It is important to emphasise that the finding of the Court on this point does not rest on fresh information, a different understanding of the role of the Princess within the State, or a changed understanding of the jurisprudential test to be satisfied, but on the application to those same facts of a very different conception of "public", one which relates only to the exercise of official state functions. The substance of the present case could, therefore, be very accurately described as linguistic, rather than jurisprudential.

This appears to be why the Court felt it reasonable to reject the classification by the German courts of the Princess as a public figure without entering into a reasoned discussion of the underlying interests served by media scrutiny of intermediate figures such as the Princess. Although both the German Constitutional Court[46] and *Burda* magazine[47] argued that the Princess, as a well-known public figure and "first lady" of the Grimaldi family, was a role model to the public and, further, one who had made efforts to draw the attention of the media to herself in the past, these arguments went undiscussed by the ECtHR. The Court in the present case appeared content to disapply the category of "public" from the Princess purely on the basis of its changed, and highly restricted, conception of "public".

Although the Court found that the "decisive factor" in balancing the demands of Arts 8 and 10 is the " . . . contribution that the published photos and articles make to a debate of general interest",[48] the Court appears to use the words "general", "official" and "public" interchangeably throughout its opinion. As the Court began its opinion by excluding the Princess from the category of a "public" person,[49] in the understanding of the Court, one who did not carry out official functions on behalf of the State, the conclusion of the Court from the same paragraph of its opinion that "[i]t is clear in the instant case that [the photos] made no such contribution since the applicant exercises no official function and the photos and articles related exclusively to details of her private life'[50] is, therefore, a purely analytical one.[51]

Analytical statements are not, of course, necessarily logically circular. It is perfectly feasible to make what is a wholly definitional statement (for example, all unmarried men are bachelors or clean-shaven men do not have beards) without seeking to prove the second part of that statement by reference to a premise contained in the first part.

[46] See the discussion by the German Constitutional Court contained in the extended excerpt at *ibid.* para.25.

[47] *ibid.* para.47.

[48] *ibid.* para.76.

[49] *ibid.* paras 8 and 62–64.

[50] *ibid.* para.76.

[51] "In all judgments in which the relation of a subject to the predicate is thought (if I only consider affirmative judgments, since the application to negative ones is easy) this relation is possible in two different ways. Either the predicate *B* belongs to the subject *A* as something that **is** (covertly) contained in this concept *A*; or *B* lies entirely outside the concept *A*, though to be sure it stands in connection with it. In the first case, I call the judgment analytic, in the second synthetic." Immanuel Kant, *The Critique of Pure Reason* (Cambridge University Press, 1989), A:6–7.

640 Is *Von Hannover v Germany* a Step Backward?

However, the conclusions of the Court contained in this paragraph also illustrate the degree to which much of the Court's reasoning in the present case is infected with circularity. In the example of the paragraph under discussion the Court concludes that the photos concerned make no contribution to a "debate of general interest" (the Court here assuming a purely political conception of the "general interest" synonymous with its use of "public"), because "the applicant exercised no official function" (again using one of the three recurring synonyms for "public") and the photos related exclusively to "her private life" (the Court is here assuming what needs to be proved: the question is do they relate exclusively to her private life?) Although disguised by the Court's adoption of a variety of synonyms for "public", the conclusion of the Court in this example is achieved by assuming as a premise a specific and highly restrictive definition of "public", and then relying on it to prove that the photographs in question do not contribute to debates of general, or "public", interest.

In essence there are two different levels of argument co-existing in the opinion. At a micro-level there are numerous arguments as to the contribution such material makes to public discourse, such as the one just considered, which fail due to circularity, and at the macro-level there is a more logically respectable argument which fails due to its lack of explanatory power. One can perhaps better understand the macro-argument of the Court if one expresses it as a syllogism:

- A public figure exercises official state functions
- Princess Caroline does not exercise any official state functions
- Princess Caroline is not a public figure

The fatal misunderstanding of the Court appears to be the belief that in excluding the Princess from the category of "public", it has offered something that is prescriptively substantive about the nature and extent of the category of "private" when, in reality, it has left this area, and the standards which relate to it, wholly undefined.

The importance of considering the substantive merits of competing privacy and speech interests

The reticence of the Court on these points is especially confusing given its previous willingness to discuss substantively the merits of various and competing material elements of privacy. In *Z v Finland*,[52] for example, referred to in *Campbell v MGN*[53] by both Lord Hoffmann[54] and Baroness Hale,[55] the Court found that "the protection of medical data is of fundamental importance to a person's enjoyment of his or her right to respect for private life", while the Court has long held in cases such as *Dudgeon v United Kingdom*[56] and *Lustig Prean v United Kingdom*[57] that information relating to one's sexuality engages one of the most intimate aspects of our private lives. The Court has been similarly willing to discuss the substantive merits of various categories of speech,

[52] (1998) 25 E.H.R.R. 371.
[53] [2004] UKHL 22; [2004] 2 W.L.R. 1232.
[54] *ibid.* at [53].
[55] *ibid.* at [145].
[56] (1982) 4 E.H.R.R. 149.
[57] (2000) 29 E.H.R.R. 548.

extending the highest levels of protection to political speech[58] (including respectable journalism), with successively less protection extended to artistic[59] and commercial[60] speech.

As a result the ECtHR would seem ideally placed to conduct the sort of substantive evaluation of the privacy and speech interests at stake in *Von Hannover* necessary to balance appropriately the demands of each right. However, while it is a comparatively straightforward task to construct an argument around the low value of the speech acts concerned in *Von Hannover*, it is a far more difficult task to express the nature of the privacy right at stake. Indeed, it is because the speech acts at issue in *Von Hannover* concern only the most mundane aspects of Princess Caroline's life that it is difficult to balance them against any specific privacy value vested in the nature of the material itself. The Court in *Von Hannover* must, therefore, concern itself with the all-encompassing nature of the observation to which the Princess was subject, that is to say, the defence of the "private life" *per se*, rather than any individual element within it. Thus, the concern of the Court in the present case with the nature of the Princess's role, rather than with any substantive discussion of the material concerned, may seem an almost inevitable response to the classification of the Princess as a public figure "par excellence" by the German courts, and the disproportionate degree to which this effectively licensed media observation of her.

However, it seems especially problematic for the continuing development of privacy jurisprudence within the United Kingdom that the ECtHR should base its judgment on an analysis of the role of the central applicant, rather than an analysis of the degree or form of protection appropriate to that role. Perhaps ironically this judgment comes as the United Kingdom itself is beginning to move away from its traditional concern with the roles of tortfeasors, that is, whether they had entered into a confidential relationship[61] or were put on notice as to the confidential nature of the material concerned[62] and, under the influence of Art.8, towards an approach which is concerned with the substantive analysis of those interests most properly concerned in what we continue to refer to as "breach of confidence" cases. Indeed, it is the English courts which over the past two years have taken the lead in developing substantive criteria to determine what amounts to "private" material. This appears to be one of the most felicitous outcomes of the gradual evolution of the tort of breach of confidence itself from being concerned only to constrain the unconscionable conduct of those persons in receipt of information for which they had either actual or constructive knowledge of its confidential nature, to one concerned with the protection of individual privacy generally and, therefore, the nature of what should be considered objectively private material.[63]

[58] *Sunday Times v United Kingdom* (1980) 2 E.H.R.R. 245; *Observer and Guardian v United Kingdom* (1992) 14 E.H.R.R. 153; *Jersild v Denmark* (1995) 19 E.H.R.R. 1.

[59] *Muller v Switzerland* (1989) 13 E.H.R.R. 212; *Handyside v United Kingdom* (1979–80) 1 E.H.R.R. 737; *Otto-Preminger Institute v Austria* (1995) 19 E.H.R.R. 43; *Gay News v United Kingdom* (1983) 5 E.H.R.R. 123; *Wingrove v United Kingdom* (1997) 24 E.H.R.R. 1.

[60] *Casado Coca v Spain* (1994) 18 E.H.R.R. 1; *Stambuk v Germany* (2003) 37 E.H.R.R. 42.

[61] For the traditional position see *Prince Albert v Strange* (1849) 2 De G. & Sm. 293.

[62] *Creation Records Ltd v News Groups Newspapers Ltd* [1997] E.M.L.R. 444; *Shelley Films v Rex Features Limited* [1994] E.M.L.R. 134.

[63] For the detail of this evolution see Gavin Phillipson, "Transforming Breach of Confidence? Towards a Common Law Right of Privacy Under the Human Rights Act" (2003) 66 M.L.R. 726.

642 Is *Von Hannover v Germany* a Step Backward?

The beginning of this evolution is generally tracked to the speech of Lord Goff in *Attorney-General v Guardian Newspapers Ltd (No.2)*, where he found that a duty of confidence may arise where someone "has notice, or is held to have agreed, that the information is confidential".[64] This obligation was substantially expanded by Lord Woolf C.J. in the more recent case of *A v B plc*, where he found that:

> "A duty of confidence will arise whenever the party subject to the duty is in a situation where he either knows *or ought to know* that the other person can reasonably expect his privacy to be protected."[65]

This objective duty of confidence has, in turn, been expanded upon in two exceptionally bold judgments by Butler-Sloss P.,[66] and in a series of judgments concerning the domestic affairs[67] of celebrities, while the recent decision of the House of Lords in *Campbell* contained a specific acknowledgment of the private nature of medical treatment (in this case, group therapy conducted within the auspices of Narcotics Anonymous). Unfortunately, however, while the UK courts have begun to develop a much more substantive approach to the individual elements of one's private life, they have so far failed to engage with the parallel analysis of the ECtHR in regard to speech acts. They have continued to treat practically all forms of speech as essentially "monolithic, of unvarying weight . . . ".[68] And unless the UK courts begin to develop a calculus for determining the proper importance of speech interests in the same way that they have begun to do for privacy interests they will find themselves, in Gavin Phillipson's striking phrase, "with weights for one side of the scales only"[69] and, thus, debarred from undertaking the sort of balancing exercise necessary to recognise properly the equally fundamental nature of the privacy and speech rights at stake.

An example of just such lop-sided reasoning may be found in the recent case of *Theakston v MGN*,[70] where a well-known BBC presenter was surreptitiously photographed during a visit to a Mayfair brothel. Although he was successful in his application for an injunction to prevent publication of the photographs, he was unsuccessful in his injunction to prevent publication of the newspaper story detailing the events of his visit. The judge in this case was content to let the most prurient and trivial forms of speech outweigh the interest of Mr Theakston in protecting what the ECtHR has repeatedly recognised as one of the most intimate aspects of one's private life, information relating to one's sexuality. For many steeped in the Anglo-American tradition of preference for free speech rights, and the suspicion of both the prior restraint of publication and content-based speech restrictions, such restrictions may well be difficult to accept. However, to accord Art.8 and Art.10 rights anything less than equal weight is simply to ignore the structure of the ECHR itself and to reduce Art.8 to

[64] [1990] 1 A.C. 109 at 281.

[65] [2003] Q.B. 195 at [11(ix)].

[66] *Venables v News Group Newspapers Ltd* [2001] Fam. 430; *X (A woman formerly known as Mary Bell) v SO* [2003] EWHC 1101, [2003] E.M.L.R. 37.

[67] *A v B*, n.65 above; *Beckham v MGN*, June 28, 2001 unreported; *Blair v Associated Newspapers* 2000 WL 33116509.

[68] Phillipson, n.63 above, at 756.

[69] *ibid*. at 756.

[70] *Theakston v MGN* [2002] EWHC 137; [2002] E.M.L.R. 22.

the level of a subsidiary restriction.[71] Although s.12(4)[72] of the UK Human Rights Act does instruct the courts to have "particular regard" to the value of freedom of expression, as explained by Sedley L.J. in *Douglas v Hello! Ltd*:

> "The European Court has always recognised the high importance of free media of communication in a democracy, but its jurisprudence does not-and could not consistently with the Convention itself-give Article 10(1) the presumptive priority which is given, for example, to the First Amendment in they United States. Everything will ultimately depend on the proper balance between privacy and publicity in the situation facing the court."[73]

In its concern to exclude the Princess from the category of "public", rather than in providing a more substantive discussion of the nature of the "private" interests to be protected, the decision in *Von Hannover* has the potential to delay further the development of a substantive calculus in the United Kingdom for the effective balancing of both speech and privacy interests and to support those who would seek to constrain the law of confidence in the United Kingdom within its traditional concern for the equitable relationships between applicants and erstwhile tortfeasors. Although the concern of the Court in the present case with the nature of the role of the Princess might seem an inevitable response to the classification of the Princess as a public figure "par excellence" by the German courts, in reality it contains an unacknowledged demand for the articulation by the ECtHR of the privacy interests at stake in such cases and the substantive analysis by the Court of the degree of Art.8 protection appropriate for intermediate figures like the Princess.

Conclusion

Although the Court's chosen conception of "public" is a highly specific one and is, as a result, comparatively easy to apply, the opinion of the Court leaves the contours of the "private" wholly undefined. The ECtHR fails to make clear whether its opposition to the classification of the Princess as a public figure "par excellence" is based on the disproportionate effect of this classification or whether this is purely in response to the non-political role of the Princess. This is important because it continues to leave open the possibility of an "intermediate" stage of privacy protection which allows for the heightened public scrutiny of figures such as the Princess who, although not formally political figures, because of their public profile enjoy an unusual degree of social, economic and cultural, and possibly political, influence.

This possibility would seem especially compelling should material concerning the Princess of a less than anodyne nature become available. This possibility in itself suggests an interesting paradox. One of the central reasons for the finding of the Court in the present case was the very anodyne nature of the material involved. Because of

[71] Phillipson, n.63 above, at 750.

[72] "The court must have particular regard to the importance of the Convention right to freedom of expression and, where the proceedings relate to material which the respondent claims, or which appears to the court, to be journalistic, literary or artistic material (or to conduct connected with such material), to (a) the extent to which (i) the material has, or is about to, become available to the public; or (ii) it is, or would be, in the public interest for the material to be published; (b) any relevant privacy code."

[73] [2001] Q.B. 967 at 1004.

644 Is *Von Hannover v Germany* a Step Backward?

this it was easy for the Court to balance what were the comparatively weak demands of Art.10. The paradox of this judgment is that although it may prevent the publication of the most trivial and domestic material, the more potentially damaging the material at issue is, the less likely it is that the Court will act to prevent publication. Although the more intimate the information is, the stronger the protection it will initially attract from the applicant's Art.8 rights, once information crosses over into the realm of what is properly (if not necessarily respectably) "newsworthy", it will very quickly attract the traditionally heightened protection extended by the Court to political and journalistic speech.

This effect has been nicely predicted in *Campbell* where Naomi Campbell's privacy interest in the details of her treatment for drug addiction was quickly overwhelmed by the journalistic interest in establishing the fact of her addiction in the wake of her many public denials. As explained in Baroness Hale's clear-sighted account of the facts:

> "... all of the information about Miss Campbell's addiction and attendance at [Narcotics Anonymous] which was revealed in the *Daily Mirror* article was both private and confidential, because it related to an important aspect of Miss Campbell's physical and mental health and the treatment she was receiving for it ... That simple fact has been obscured by the concession properly made on her behalf that the newspaper's countervailing freedom of expression did serve to justify the publication of some of this information. But the starting point must be that it was all private and its publication required specific justification."[74]

While up until now the attention paid to the Princess has been mostly favourable, this judgment may well act as a spur for those most unscrupulous members of the paparazzi to focus on what are potentially more unsavoury aspects of the private conduct of public figures in order to guarantee that their stories will enjoy a defensible claim to "public interest". Until now many popular magazines in the United Kingdom have filled out their pages with trivial, if no doubt embarrassing, photos of celebrities sunbathing topless and having bad hair days. However, unless those same magazines are willing quietly to close up shop or rely entirely on pre-arranged *Hello!* magazine-style celebrity interviews and photo shoots, *Van Hannover* may well mark the point when the kid gloves of the gutter press begin to come off for real.

[74] *Campbell v MGN* [2004] UKHL 22; [2004] 2 W.L.R. 1232 at [147].

Name Index